THE JOURNALS AND
LETTERS OF
FANNY BURNEY

FANNY BURNEY

Engraved from a portrait by Edward Francesco Burney

THE JOURNALS AND LETTERS OF

FANNY BURNEY

(MADAME D'ARBLAY)

⟨∾⟩

VOLUME V

WEST HUMBLE AND PARIS 1801 – 1803

LETTERS 423–549

⟨∾⟩

Edited by

JOYCE HEMLOW

with

GEORGE G. FALLE, ALTHEA DOUGLAS

and

JILL A. BOURDAIS DE CHARBONNIÈRE

OXFORD

AT THE CLARENDON PRESS

1975

Oxford University Press, Ely House, London W. 1

GLASGOW NEW YORK TORONTO MELBOURNE WELLINGTON
CAPE TOWN IBADAN NAIROBI DAR ES SALAAM LUSAKA ADDIS ABABA
DELHI BOMBAY CALCUTTA MADRAS KARACHI LAHORE DACCA
KUALA LUMPUR SINGAPORE HONG KONG TOKYO

ISBN 0 19 812467 8

© *Oxford University Press 1975*

*Printed in Great Britain
at the University Press, Oxford
by Vivian Ridler
Printer to the University*

ACKNOWLEDGEMENTS

To the list (i, xi–xix) of those who helped in so many ways in the production of the new edition of Madame d'Arblay's Journals and Letters, the editors wish to add the names of those persons in Europe who went to great trouble in supplying information much needed for volumes v and vi. The editors are grateful to Colonel P. Bertiaux of Joigny, France, whose searches in parish registers and other documents there made it possible to construct the genealogical table of the Bazille and Piochard d'Arblay families (vi) and to elucidate the family crises touched on in the d'Arblay correspondence of 1804; and, to the same end, M. Jean Fromageot, Vice-Président de l'Association Bourguignonne des Sociétés Savantes, of the Société d'Archéologie et d'Histoire du Tonnerrois, and also M. Elie Thiré of that Society, who kindly traced the branch of the Bazille family settled in Tonnerre. For exact information about the families Tanquerey d'Hyenville and l'Heure de Cambernon, also relatives of M. d'Arblay, the editors are indebted to M. Yves Nedelec, Directeur des Services d'archives de la Manche, Archives Départementales de la Manche, Saint-Lô; and for information about the Greenwood-Solvyns family, that of General van Rijssel, and the comte de Ricci, acknowledgements go to Mr. J. Fox, Deputy Keeper of the third Department, Algemeen Rijksarchief (Archieven van Holland), at the Hague; and to M. C. Wyffles of the Archives Générales du Royaume, Bruxelles. For the names and dates of Swiss bankers, etc., the editors wish to thank Mlle Norah M. Lenoir of Geneva and the skilled archivists of Archives Cantonales Vaudoises, Lausanne.

In Paris, it was Mme Jill A. Bourdais de Charbonnière who trekked to Vincennes for the dossiers of d'Arblay's military acquaintances; and for the identities of obscure personages emerging in the Burney–d'Arblay papers from almost every walk of life, she searched archives throughout the city as well as records extant in relevant notarial offices. It was she to whom it occurred on these laborious rounds to found the skilled company of Paris Research Associates.

In Montreal research was facilitated by the Napoleonic Collection, the Rare Book Room of the McGill University Libraries,

Acknowledgements

and the editors are especially indebted to Mrs. Elizabeth Saunders, Curator of the Map Collection, for guided tours through priceless holdings in eighteenth-century French maps.

Professor Falle wishes to thank Vicomte Fleury and also M. Cailleux, the distinguished art dealer, of Paris, for their help in locating the David portraits of Madame David. He is grateful also to M. J. Pieters, Bibliothécaire-Archiviste, and to M. Cocheteux, Assistant Librarian, of the Dunkirk Municipal Library, for their courtesies and most generous assistance in the Dunkirk researches.

To H. Rocke Robertson, M.D., D.Sc., FRCS(E), sometime Surgeon-in-Chief of the Montreal General Hospital, who kindly consented to read Madame d'Arblay's account of the operation she underwent in Paris in 1811 (before the adoption of anaesthetics), the editors are happy to accord credit and thanks for comments and corrections that, needless to say, add greatly to the interest and value of the piece.

To be mentioned for active and rewarding searches is Dr. Susan Auty, late of the Polytechnic, Huddersfield; and among the county archivists ceaselessly importuned for information about persons, who, known to Madame d'Arblay, chanced to live or die in their counties, we wish to thank, among many others, Mr. E. J. Davis, County Archivist, Aylesbury, Bucks., who searched the Carrington Papers for clues to the identities of the ancient Catholic family of Whorwood-Greenwood.

For data and often for very interesting letters from the keepers of parish registers, whether retained still in vestries or deposited in county archives, the editors have to thank scores of clergymen and archivists alike whose reward must be in contributions, difficult to come by, and sometimes infinitesimal, to genealogical lore and local history.

For kind and careful proof-reading and many a useful query, readers are indebted to Mr. Warren Derry, editor of volume ix of the series. For deciphering passages obliterated by Madame d'Arblay in her husband's letters, the editors are wholly dependent on Miss Caroline Cronk, M.A. (Linguistics), of the Université de Montréal.

To be mentioned finally is Mr. Garry Bowers, who prepared the Appendix (vol. v) and who, with Mr. Paul Duchow and Althea Douglas, compiled the Index to volumes v and vi.

CONTENTS

LIST OF PLATES   ix

ABBREVIATIONS AND SHORT TITLES   xi

INTRODUCTION   xix

LETTERS AND JOURNALS OF FANNY BURNEY (MADAME
D'ARBLAY) AND M. D'ARBLAY
from 3 October 1801 to 14 May 1803, Numbers 423–
549   1

APPENDIX
General d'Arblay's military career   450

LIST OF PLATES

FANNY BURNEY

From a painting by EDWARD FRANCESCO BURNEY, *engraved for the 1st edition of* Diary and Letters of Madame d'Arblay

Frontispiece

I. THE PARIS DILIGENCE, 1803

Drawn by SIR JOHN CARR *as an illustration for his book* The Stranger in France, *published in 1803 by J. Johnson of St. Paul's Churchyard*

Facing page 217

II. RUE DE MIROMÉNIL and the HÔTEL DE BEAUVAU,

and

A VIEW OF PASSY

From a drawing by JEAN-JACQUES LE VEAU. *By permission of the Bibliothèque Nationale, Paris*

Facing page 393

ABBREVIATIONS

MEMBERS OF THE BURNEY FAMILY
AND SOME OF THEIR FRIENDS

AA	The Revd. Alexander Charles Louis Piochard d'Arblay, 1794–1837
CAB	Charlotte Ann Burney, 1761–1838
CBF	after 1786 Mrs. Francis
CBFB	after 1798 Mrs. Broome
CB	Charles Burney (Mus. Doc.), 1726–1814
CB Jr.	Charles Burney (D.D.), 1757–1817
CF	Clement Robert Francis, 1792–1829
CFBt	Charlotte (Francis) Barrett, 1786–1870
CPB	Charles Parr Burney (D.D.), 1785–1864
EBB	Esther (Burney) Burney, 1749–1832
FB	Frances Burney, 1752–1840
FBA	after 1793 Madame d'Arblay
GMAPW	Georgiana Mary Ann (Port) Waddington, 1771–1850
HLT	Hester Lynch (Salusbury) Thrale, 1741–1821
HLTP	after 1784 Mrs. Piozzi
JB	James Burney (Rear-Admiral), 1750–1821
JCBT	Julia Charlotte (Barrett) Thomas, 1808–64
JCBTM	after 1842 Mrs. Maitland
M. d'A	Alexandre-Jean-Baptiste Piochard d'Arblay, 1754–1818
MF	Marianne Francis, 1790–1832
SEB	Susanna Elizabeth Burney, 1755–1800
SBP	after 1782 Mrs. Phillips
SHB	Sarah Harriet Burney, 1772–1844
TT	The Revd. Thomas Twining, 1735–1804

SHORT TITLES

Standard encyclopaedias, biographical dictionaries (both national and professional), peerages, armorials, baronetages, knightages, school and university lists, medical registers, lists of clergy, town and city directories, road guides, almanacs, and ephemerides of all kinds have been used but will not be cited unless for a particular reason. Also consulted were annual Navy, Army, and Law Lists, *Royal Kalendar*, and the many editions of Edmund Lodge's *The Peerage of the British Empire as at Present Existing* and of Sir John

Abbreviations

Bernard Burke's *A Genealogical and Heraldic History of the Peerage and Baronetage* and *A Genealogical and Heraldic History of the Landed Gentry of Great Britain and Ireland*. In all such dated series, though the wording of titles varies somewhat, citation will be to the commonly used short title with the date of the volume or edition.

Add. MSS.	Additional Manuscripts, British Museum.
Admiral's Widow	Brig.-General Cecil Aspinall-Oglander, *Admiral's Widow: Being the Life and Letters of the Hon. Mrs. Edward Boscawen from 1761 to 1805*, 1943.
Admiral's Wife	Brig.-General Cecil Aspinall-Oglander, *Admiral's Wife: Being the Life and Letters of the Hon. Mrs. Edward Boscawen from 1719 to 1761*, 1940.
AR	*The Annual Register, or a View of the History, Politics, and Literature . . .*, 1758– .
Barrett	The Barrett Collection of Burney Papers, British Museum, 43 vols., Egerton 3690–3708.
Berg	The Henry W. and Albert A. Berg Collection, New York Public Library.
Berry	*Extracts from the Journals and Correspondence of Miss Berry from the year 1783 to 1852*, ed. Lady Theresa Lewis, 3 vols., 1866.
Boigne	Charlotte-Louise-Eléonore-Adélaïde, comtesse de, *Memoirs of . . . 1815–1819*, ed. and trans. Charles Nicoullaud, 3 vols., 1907.
Bouchary	Jean Bouchary, *Les Manieurs d'argent à Paris à la fin du XVIIIe siècle*, 3 vols., 1939–43.
Bunsen	*The Life and Letters of Frances Baroness Bunsen*, ed. Augustus J. C. Hare, 2 vols. in 1, New York, 1879. For an unabridged section of these memoirs, see Fraser.
Burke, *Corr.*	*The Correspondence of Edmund Burke*, ed. Thomas W. Copeland, 10 vols., Cambridge and Chicago, 1958–70.
Carr	Sir John Carr, *The Stranger in France, or a Tour from Devonshire to Paris, 1803*, 1803.
Catalogue	*A Catalogue of the Burney Family Correspondence 1749–1878*, compiled by Joyce Hemlow with Jeanne M. M. Burgess and Althea Douglas, New York, 1971.
Cazenove d'Arlens	Constance de Cazenove d'Arlens, *Deux mois à Paris et à Lyon sous le Consulat (février–avril, 1803)* 1903.

Abbreviations

CCR	The Court and City Register.
Clifford	James L. Clifford, *Hester Lynch Piozzi (Mrs. Thrale)*, Oxford, 1941.
Comyn	The John Comyn Collection of Burney Papers, The Cross House, Vowchurch, Turnastone, Herefordshire, England.
Constant	Louis Constant Wairy, *Mémoires de Constant, premier valet de chambre de l'Empereur, sur la vie privée de Napoléon, sa famille et sa cour*, 4 vols., 1894.
Corr. Geo. IV	*The Correspondence of George, Prince of Wales, 1770–1812*, ed. A. Aspinall, 6 vols., 1963– .
C.R.S.	Publications of the Catholic Record Society.
Dard	Émile Dard, *Un Confident de l'Empereur, le comte de Narbonne*, 1943.
Dean	Capt. G. G. T. Dean, *The Royal Hospital, Chelsea*, 1950.
DL (1842–6)	*Diary and Letters of Madame d'Arblay*, ed. Charlotte Barrett, 7 vols., 1842–6.
DL	*Diary and Letters of Madame d'Arblay (1778–1840)*, ed. Austin Dobson, 6 vols., 1904–5.
ED	*The Early Diary of Frances Burney, 1768–1778*, ed. Annie Raine Ellis, 2 vols., 1913.
[Edgeworth, Maria] *Life*	*The Life and Letters of Maria Edgeworth*, ed. Augustus J. C. Hare, 2 vols., 1895.
Eyre	Edmund John Eyre, *Observations made at Paris during the Peace and Remarks in a tour from London to Paris through Picardy and to England by the route of Normandy . . .*, Bath, 1803.
Farington	Joseph Farington, *The Farington Diary*, ed. James Grieg, 8 vols., 1922–8.
Fauche-Borel	*Mémoires de Fauche-Borel, dans lesquels on trouvera des détails et des éclaircissemens sur les principaux événemens de la Révolution*, ed. A. de Beauchamp, 4 vols., 1829.
FB & the Burneys	*Fanny Burney and the Burneys*, ed. R. Brimley Johnson, 1926.
Forbes	James Forbes, *Letters from France written in the Years 1803 and 1804*, 2 vols., 1806.
Forneron	H. Forneron, *Histoire générale des émigrés . . .*, 3 vols., 1884–90.
Fortescue	The Hon. J. W. Fortescue, *A History of the British Army*, 13 vols. in 20, 1899–1930.

Abbreviations

Fraser	Maxwell Fraser, 'The Waddingtons of Llanover, 1791–1805 . . .', *National Library of Wales Journal*, XI, Winter 1960, No. 4, pp. 285–329.
GEC	George Edward Cokayne, *The Complete Peerage* . . . revised by Vicary Gibbs *et al.*, 13 vols., 1910–59; *The Complete Baronetage*, 6 vols., Exeter, 1900–9.
GM	*The Gentleman's Magazine*, 1731–1880.
Godechot	Jacques Godechot, *Les Institutions de la France sous la Révolution et l'Empire*, 1951.
Gontaut	Marie-Louise-Joséphine, duchesse de Gontaut-Biron, *Mémoires de* . . . *1773–1836*, 1892; also trans. Mrs. J. W. Davis, 2 vols., 1894.
Greatheed	Bertie Greatheed, *An Englishman in Paris*, ed. J. T. Bury and J. C. Barry, 1953.
Harcourt Papers	*The Harcourt Papers*, ed. Edward W. Harcourt, 14 vols., Oxford, 1880–1905.
Hauterive	Ernest d'Hauterive, *La Police secrète du Premier Empire*, 3 vols. [1804–7], 1908–22; n.s. [1808–10] 1963–4.
Herold	J. Christopher Herold, *Mistress to an Age: A Life of Madame de Staël*, New York, 1958.
HFB	Joyce Hemlow, *The History of Fanny Burney*, Oxford, 1958.
Hillairet	Jacques Hillairet, *Dictionnaire historique des rues de Paris*, 2 vols., n.d.
Hyde	The Hyde Collection, Four Oaks Farm, Somerville, New Jersey.
JRL	The John Rylands Library, Manchester.
Judd	Gerrit P. Judd, IV, *Members of Parliament, 1734–1832*, New Haven, Conn., 1955.
Juniper Hall	Constance Hill, *Juniper Hall, a Rendezvous of Certain Illustrious Personages during the French Revolution Including Alexandre d'Arblay and Fanny Burney*, 1904.
Laquiante	*Un Hiver à Paris sous le Consulat* . . . *d'après les lettres de J.-F. Reichardt par A. Laquiante*, 1896.
Later Corr. Geo. III	*The Later Correspondence of George III*, ed. A. Aspinall, Cambridge, 7 vols., 1963– .
[La Tour du Pin, Mme] *Journal*	Henriette-Lucie, marchionesse de La Tour du Pin de Gouvernet, *Journal d'une femme de cinquante ans, 1778–1815*, ed. Colonel Comte Aymar de Liedekerke-Beaufort, 2 vols., 1916; ed. and

Abbreviations

	trans. Walter Green, 1920; ed. and trans. Felice Harcourt, 1970.
Lawrence	James Henry Lawrence, *A Picture of Verdun, or the English detained in France*, 2 vols., 1810.
Lefebvre	Georges Lefebvre, *Napoléon*, 6th ed., 1969.
Lewis	Michael Lewis, *Napoleon and his British Captives*, 1962.
Life	*Boswell's Life of Johnson* . . . ed. George Birkbeck Hill, revised by L. F. Powell, 6 vols., Oxford, 1934–64.
Locks of Norbury	The Duchess of Sermoneta [Vittoria (Calonne) Caetani], *The Locks of Norbury*, 1940.
Lonsdale	Roger Lonsdale, *Dr. Charles Burney*, Oxford, 1965.
Madelin	Louis Madelin, *Histoire du Consulat et de l'Empire*, 16 vols., 1937–54.
Manwaring	G. E. Manwaring, *My Friend the Admiral: the Life, Letters, and Journals of Rear-Admiral James Burney, F.R.S.*, 1931.
Maurois	André Maurois, *Adrienne, ou la vie de Mme de Lafayette*, 1960; trans. Gerard Hopkins, 1961.
Melvin	Frank Edgar Melvin, *Napoleon's Navigation System: a Study of Trade Control during the Continental Blockade*, New York, 1919.
Memoirs	*Memoirs of Doctor Burney, Arranged from His Own Manuscripts, from Family Papers, and from Personal Recollections*, by his daughter, Madame d'Arblay, 3 vols., 1832.
'Memoirs'	Autograph Manuscripts of Dr. Burney's Memoirs, fragments of which survive in Berg, Osborn, and BM.
M.I.	Memorial Inscription.
Morgan, Lady	Lady Morgan [Sydney *née* Owenson], *France*, 2 vols., 1818.
Namier	Sir Lewis Namier and John Brooke, *The House of Commons, 1754–1790*, 3 vols., 1964.
Nelson	R. R., *The Home Office, 1782–1801*, Durham, N.C., 1969.
NPG	The National Portrait Gallery, Trafalgar Square, London.
NYPL	The New York Public Library, Fifth Avenue and 42nd Street, New York.
Oman	Carola Oman, *Sir John Moore*, 1953.

Abbreviations

Osborn	The James Marshall and Marie-Louise Osborn Collection, Yale University Library, New Haven, Conn.
Paquet-Syphorien	M. Paquet-Syphorien, *Voyage historique et pittoresque fait dans les ci-devant Pays-Bas, et dans quelques Départemens voisins, pendant les années 1811, 1812, et 1813*, 2 vols., 1813.
Parl. Hist.	*The Parliamentary History of England from the Earliest Period to the year 1803*, ed. William Cobbett and John Wright, 36 vols., 1806–20; the first 12 vols. are entitled *Cobbett's Parliamentary History of England* . . .
P.C.C.	Prerogative Court of Canterbury.
PML	The Pierpont Morgan Library, 33 East 36th Street, New York.
Potocka	*Mémoires de la Comtesse Potocka, 1794–1820*, ed. Casimir Stryienski, 8th ed., 1902; trans. Lionel Strachey, New York, 1900.
PRO	Public Record Office, London.
Queeney Letters	*The Queeney Letters, being Letters addressed to Hester Maria Thrale by Dr. Johnson, Fanny Burney, and Mrs. Thrale-Piozzi*, ed. the Marquis of Lansdowne, 1934.
Rambuteau	Claude Philibert Barthelot, comte de, *Mémoires . . .*, 1905.
Révérend, *1ᵉʳ Emp.*	Vicomte Albert Révérend, *Armorial du premier empire; titres, majorats et armoiries concédés par Napoléon Iᵉʳ* . . ., 4 vols. in 2, 1894–7.
Révérend, *Restauration*	Vicomte Albert Révérend, . . . *Titres, anoblissements et pairies de la restauration, 1814–1830*, 6 vols., 1901–6.
Révérend, *Monarchie*	Vicomte Albert Révérend, *Titres et confirmations de titres; monarchie de juillet, 2ᵉ république, 2ᵉ empire, 3ᵉ république, 1830–1908*, 1909.
R.H.I., Windsor	Royal Household Index, the Queen's Archives, Windsor Castle.
Rose	J. Holland Rose, *The Life of Napoleon I*, 2 vols., 1901–2.
Rovigo	*Mémoires du Duc de Rovigo pour servir à l'histoire de l'empereur Napoléon*, ed. A. Bossange, 8 vols., 1828.
Scholes	Percy A. Scholes, *The Great Dr. Burney*, 2 vols., 1948.

Abbreviations

Six	Georges Six, *Dictionnaire biographique des généraux et amiraux français de la révolution et de l'empire* (*1792–1814*), 2 vols., 1934.
Solovieff	*Lettres de Madame de Staël à Narbonne*, ed. Georges Solovieff, 1960.
Stenger	Gilbert Stenger, *La Société française pendant le Consulat*, 6 vols., 1903–8.
Stuart, *Dtrs. Geo. III*	Dorothy Margaret Stuart, *The Daughters of George III*, 1939.
Thompson	J. M. Thompson, *Napoleon Bonaparte*, New York, 1952.
Vincennes	Archives du Service historique de l'armée, Château de Vincennes.
Vitrolles	Eugène-François-Auguste d'Arnaud, baron de, *Mémoires*, ed. Pierre Farel, 2 vols., 1950–1.
Walpole	*The Yale Edition of Horace Walpole's Correspondence*, ed. W. S. Lewis, 33 vols., New Haven, Conn., 1937– .
Warren	The Revd. Dawson Warren, *The Journal of a British Chaplain in Paris during the Peace Negotiations of 1801–2* . . ., ed. A. M. Broadley, 1913.
Welvert	Eugène Welvert, *Princesse d'Hénin, histoire d'une grande dame du temps passé*, Versailles, 1924.
Whitworth, *Despatches*	*England and Napoleon in 1803. Being the despatches of Lord Whitworth* . . ., ed. Oscar Browning, 1887.
Wilmot	*An Irish Peer on the Continent, 1801–1803: being a narrative of the tour of Stephen, 2nd Earl Mount Cashell* . . ., as related by Catherine Wilmot, ed. Thomas U. Sadleir, 1920.
Woelmont de Brumagne	Henri de Woelmont, Baron de Brumagne, *Notices généalogiques*, 8 vols., 1923–35.
'Worcester Journal'	A typescript of a family chronicle entitled 'Memoranda of the Burney Family, 1603–1845', once in the possession of Dr. Percy Scholes (as described in Scholes i, 1 n., and ii, 391). The location of the original manuscript is unknown, but in former times Dr. Scholes kindly allowed the general editor to take the copy that is still in her possession.
Young	John G. Gazley, *The Life of Arthur Young 1741–1820* (Philadelphia, 1973).

INTRODUCTION

THE years 1793 to 1801 were, with the exception of the death in 1800 of her favourite sister, Susannah, years of quiet, almost unclouded happiness in the lives of Fanny Burney and her husband, General Alexandre-Jean-Baptiste Piochard d'Arblay (1754–1818), whom she married in July 1793. The birth of their son, Alexander Charles Louis, in December 1794, the marriage in 1800 of her niece 'Marianne' to Lambert-*Antoine* Bourdois (like M. d'Arblay, a native of the town of Joigny in the *département* of Yonne), the large Burney family connection in England, the almost pastoral idyll they enjoyed in Camilla Cottage (West Humble, near Dorking, in Surrey) close to their devoted friends the Locke family of Norbury Park—all these contributed to a pleasant life of retirement: Mme d'Arblay happily occupied with her maternal responsibilities and, when time permitted, with her literary career; M. d'Arblay, after an active military career in France, content with the pleasures and pursuits of the simple country life, his books, and his 'spade and cabbages'. But soon after the autumn of 1801 the Arcadian landscape was shattered; and the events of the next ten years in the lives of the d'Arblays were, as the present volumes of letters record, marked by political and financial anxiety, illness, and the many frustrations occasioned by life in France at war with England, the France of the consulate and, after 1804, the imperial dynasty of Napoleon Bonaparte.

It is readily understandable that in the autumn of 1801 M. d'Arblay, an *émigré* in England for nearly ten years, was seriously considering a return to his native France. Many of his aristocratic friends who as *émigrés* had settled at the Juniper Colony and other refuges that England had provided for them had already returned home and were appealing, with varying success, to the consular government for the removal of their names from the proscription lists and for the restitution of their properties. M. d'Arblay knew that he had a rightful claim to a pension for his military services in France under the *ancien régime*, and moreover he hoped to recover at least some of his confiscated property in the neighbourhood of Joigny.[1] More personally, d'Arblay was anxious to visit his host of relations in his native town and, more particularly, his maternal uncle, Jean-Baptiste-*Gabriel* Bazille, a man now about seventy years of age, to whom he was attached by ties of the deepest filial devotion. In October 1801 passports were secured for the d'Arblay family, and it was originally intended that they should spend about a year or eighteen months in France; but the illness of young Alexander made it impossible for Fanny to travel, and M. d'Arblay set out alone. On 28 October, he wrote from Gravesend, but a series of perilous storms forced his small boat to take harbour at Margate, at Deal, and finally at Dover, before crossing to Calais, where a landing was made on 7 November. M. d'Arblay proceeded directly to Paris, where he stayed at the Hôtel Marengo, 1185, rue de Miroménil, in the faubourg Saint-Honoré.

To arrive at a clear and consistent character of General d'Arblay from the available materials presents a number of problems and seeming contradictions. When Bertie Greatheed first met him in late January 1803, he described him as a 'pleasant and a handsome man, very intelligent', and of a 'most excellent character'.[2] His military career would suggest a man of action, and yet he seemed to lack the energy and drive of his friend Lafayette. A man of honour, courage, and conscience, it is questionable whether, given the opportunity, he would have ingratiated himself with Bonaparte, been willing to compromise himself, as his former comrades-in-arms Lauriston and Berthier had done, in the interests of high position. While fortunately free of the soulless egotism and opportunism of Louis, comte de Narbonne-Lara, perhaps his most intimate friend and the godfather of his son, d'Arblay's unassuming and self-effacing character was deficient in the political *savoir faire* and social panache that ultimately won for Narbonne favour with Napoleon, as they had earlier won him the favours of Germaine de Staël. Certainly little favoured by

---

[1] It was at first customary, after the name of an *émigré* had been erased from the lists of proscription, to restore to him such parts of his property as remained in the hands of the government; d'Arblay was not aware, however, that an edict was 'passed within the last six months to stop all restitution'. See Warren, p. 54; cf. Lefebvre, pp. 148–9. M. d'Arblay never succeeded in recovering his property in Yonne.
[2] Greatheed, p. 38.

fortune (except in his domestic happiness), d'Arblay seemed to suffer from a political and social inertia; but such a condition may be more apparent than real, especially in the face of Fanny's vigorous opposition to his resumption of a military career, which was, after all, his proper *métier*. While many of his friends, the hard-headed realists, were soon to ride the crest of the Napoleonic wave, in 1805 d'Arblay was reduced, by financial necessity, to accepting what can only be considered a menial position in a sub-division of a department of the Ministry of the Interior. His erstwhile military associates in high position seldom appear in the correspondence, and d'Arblay found his modicum of personal happiness in the affectionate company of his wife and child, and in the associations of a few very loyal and devoted friends.

Upon his arrival in Paris in November 1801, M. d'Arblay was warmly welcomed by his many military associates of the past. General Lafayette, with whom he had served in the Army of the North and in the National Guard, had retired temporarily from public life after declining various official positions. His discreet opposition to the régime dismayed Bonaparte, who still hoped to win him over, and his influence remained appreciable. This he was willing to exert, where and when necessary, in d'Arblay's interest. General Lauriston and General Berthier, advantageously placed as Bonaparte's first aide-de-camp and minister of war respectively, were willing to serve him, and he had the pleasure of renewing his friendships with the comte de Narbonne, César de Latour-Maubourg, and a host of military personnel whom he had known during the *ancien régime* and the first years of the Revolution. Distinguished ladies were no less solicitous, and he was entertained by Mme de Tessé (an aunt of Mme de Lafayette), the ci-devant princesse d'Hénin, Mme de Laval, and the celebrated Mme de Staël, all of whom would play an important part in the social activities that followed upon Fanny's arrival in the spring of the following year. Perhaps most personally gratifying to M. d'Arblay was his reunion in Joigny in mid-December with the family of his beloved uncle M. Bazille.

Since d'Arblay's name had been removed from the proscription lists in the previous year, his most immediate business in Paris was to appeal, through Berthier, to the first consul for his military pension. The process was long and complicated and fraught with delays. In early January 1802, Bonaparte suggested that in return for his pension d'Arblay (with the rank of colonel) should join the expeditionary force in the French colony of San Domingo (the present island of Haiti), which had set out on 14 December with General Leclerc, Bonaparte's brother-in-law, as commander-in-chief. Leclerc's orders were to destroy the power of Toussaint-Louverture, who, supported by a substantial army of blacks, had rebelled against the French administration of the island and in May 1801 had drafted a new constitution that was to be effectively in his own control though nominally under French protection. For a time it appeared that d'Arblay was to accept the offer, subject to the condition that, upon the termination of his services there, he would resign from the army and receive his pension. Such a condition was unacceptable to the first consul and about 20 January d'Arblay set out for England. Disenchanted by the failure of his major business in France, he was none the less delighted to return to the warmth of Fanny's affection in their modest cottage in Surrey. About 10 February, however, he received a communication from Berthier to the effect that the French government were willing to accept his terms and that he should return to France to prepare for his departure for San Domingo. On the same date d'Arblay wrote directly to the first consul, expressing his thanks for the appointment but making it clear that he could accept it only upon the condition that he would never be required to bear arms against England, 'le pays qui pendant 9 ans nous a nourris'. Having secured a passport he set out a few days later for France and shortly after his arrival in Paris learned from Berthier that the order authorizing d'Arblay to set out for San Domingo had been cancelled. On 8 March he wrote disconsolately to Fanny: 'La cause qu'il assigne à cette disgrace, à la quelle je n'etais rien moins que preparé, est *ma declaration de ne point servir contre la patrie de ma femme, qui peut encore être armée contre la Republique.*'[1] Although his firmness of principle was admirable and his honour remained unsullied, the future seemed bleak indeed, especially since the validation of his passport was dependent upon his agreement to make no appeal to return to England

[1] See L. 488, pp. 168–9.

for at least a year. It was clear that Fanny and Alex must join him in Paris as soon as possible, and after the necessary preparations had been completed and the sad adieux made they set out on 15 April. Little did Fanny know on Good Friday, 1802, as she watched the cliffs of Dover recede into the distance, that she was looking upon England for the last time for more than ten years.

The journey from London to Paris held few pleasures for Mme d'Arblay, fully responsible as she was for Alex, an active and excitable boy of seven, and also for a little six-year-old girl, Adrienne de Chavagnac, who, upon her *émigré* parents' return to France when she was still an infant, had been entrusted to the care of the Lockes of Norbury Park. Fanny's journey to Paris seemed to present an admirable opportunity of restoring the child to her family. In addition to the two children, she had the care of passports, tickets, trunks, cases, and boxes, as well as the unpleasant task of coping with the bureaucratic procedures of immigration and customs officials. They had no sooner left Dover when a calm settled over the Channel, and that part of the journey, normally a matter of a few hours, took them twenty-four, during which Fanny, deathly ill, remained prostrate in her hammock. After a day's respite in Calais they boarded the Paris diligence at five o'clock on Easter Sunday morning, 18 April, and for two days and two nights rattled their way via Boulogne and Amiens to the French capital. While later Fanny was able to describe in vivid and graphic detail her fellow-passengers and some of the more arresting events and sights *en route*, the happiest moment arrived when the diligence drove in to the rue Notre-Dame-des-Victoires between ten and eleven o'clock on Tuesday morning and she fell into the arms of the faithful d'Arblay, who had been there since seven. A half-hour's drive in a fiacre and they were at the Hôtel Marengo, where the apartments that d'Arblay had rented ('up 3 pair of stairs' and with a fine view of the gardens of the ci-devant Hôtel Beauvau) were all that Fanny could wish, 'close to les Champs elisés' and 'entirely out of the bustle & close air of Paris'.

From 1802 to 1812, the years of the d'Arblays' residence in or near Paris, the French capital was a centre of cultural, political, and social activity. The splendour and magnificence of its public buildings (the Louvre, the Tuileries, the Invalides, the Palais-Royal, the great cathedral and churches, the sumptuous hôtels, once private residences but now, by confiscation, properties of the state), the glamour of its opera and theatre that provided a variety of entertainment to satisfy every taste, the riches of its museums and private *ateliers*, its beautiful parks and gardens, its distinction in the arts and the sciences—these were some of the attractions that appealed to visitors, who came from all parts of the civilized world and who revelled in the enjoyments offered by a great city where the social conventions were, to say the least, less rigorous than they were at home. Of equal (and indeed often of greater) importance to the traveller were the city's distinguished men and women, for Paris was no less the world of Lafayette and Talleyrand, Jean-Joseph Mounier and Chénier, of Mme de Staël, Benjamin Constant and Chateaubriand, Morellet, Ricard, and the marquis de Tracy, of Talma and Caroline Vanhove and Vestris, of the exquisite Mme Récamier and Pauline Bonaparte, of Mme Tallien and Laure Junot (later the duchesse d'Abrantès). Paris indeed provided an *embarras de richesses*, but, as Sir John Carr makes very clear,[1] the greatest of all attractions in the French capital was Napoleon Bonaparte, whose meteoric rise to the consular dignity had won him the confidence of almost all of France and, at the same time, the awe and, more often, the contempt of the rest of Europe.

Whatever one's views of the total career of Bonaparte, it may be plausibly argued that by 1803 he was well on his way to becoming what Greatheed called 'the very pinnacle & weathercock of greatness'. One would not call into question the heroism of his early military career nor the triumph of the battle of Marengo (June 1800). Those were among the influences preparing the way for an important constitutional change: the decision taken in May 1802, then ratified by an overwhelming plebiscitary majority and formally enacted by a *senatus consultum* of 2 August, to make Napoleon consul for life, an honour that James Forbes interpreted as 'the death-blow' to the French people's idea of liberty.[2] In March 1802, he had ratified the Peace of Amiens, the terms of which were most advantageous to the French Republic. At the time of the signing of the

---

[1] Carr, pp. 210–11; also Greatheed, pp. 11–12. [2] Forbes, i. 339.

preliminaries of the treaty (in early October 1801) Mme d'Arblay's plea that 'God avert mischief from this Peace' was indeed premonitory since it was in large part England's no less than France's unwillingness to keep the terms of the agreement that plunged the two nations into war once again in May 1803. On 8 April 1802, the Concordat (or what Catherine Wilmot chose to call 'the resurrection of the publick Faith which had slept with its holy fathers during the long period of the French Revolution') was made law, and officially proclaimed on Easter Sunday, 18 April, just a few hours after Mme d'Arblay had set out from Calais for Paris. In the account of that journey she makes frequent mention of the universal joy with which the people she met *en route* welcomed 'the restoration of the *Dimanche*, and abolition of *Decade*', although the republican calendar was not formally withdrawn until 1 January 1806. Miss Wilmot[1] witnessed the proclamation of the Concordat in Notre Dame on that Easter Sunday and provides a lively account of the 'godly fopperies' of a ceremony lasting seven hours: the 'aisles . . . all hung throughout with Gobelins' tapestry'; the 'two canopies of crimson and gold, towering with plumes of white feathers', beneath which stood Bonaparte with his 'host of Generals' and Cardinal Caprara, the papal legate, with his array of ecclesiastical dignitaries, and Mme Bonaparte, 'a blaze of diamonds'—a splendour that seemed to presage the panoply of ceremonial occasions after the establishment of the Napoleonic imperial dynasty about two years later.

To the French people Bonaparte was the hero of the hour, and in early 1802 Miss Wilmot wrote facetiously that 'His image (in Plaster of Paris) reigns the Monarch of even every Gingerbread Stall, and you can not buy a bit of Barley sugar to cure your cold, without having "le Premier Consul's" head, in all his heroic laurels, sent down your throat.'[2] Other visitors, more politically minded and more aware of the possible implications of Bonaparte's dictatorial tactics than was the charming but somewhat naïve Miss Wilmot, observed with alarm that France, now a republic in name only, was gravitating more and more towards the traditions of the former court of the Bourbons. The slogans of the Republic were still visible on the

[1] Wilmot, pp. 59–60.   [2] Ibid., p. 21.

façades of the great public buildings, but Mme Bonaparte had begun to appoint *dames d'honneur* and the chamberlains of the first consul were fitted out in uniforms covered with embroideries, ribbons, and lace.[1] Writing in February 1803, Bertie Greatheed was more articulate on the subject of his reservations and suspicions pertaining to the government and its indomitable leader. For him Paris had become the capital of

> a vast, active, compact, nation, without any virtue or morality, under the absolute and immediate sway of a soldier, intirely, incessantly, devoted to the spirit of ambition and of conquest: possessed of abilities to attain his object; of a mind inflexible, secret, laborious in the extreme, undaunted, sudden, observant, full of expedient and full of penetration. Yet is this hero full of littleness, not contented to be great, he must be gaudy; his apartments must be finer than Louis 14: that we should say what we please of him in England is what he cannot support, for the conqueror of Marengo is unable to bear the sarcasms of the *Courier* or a *Morning Chronicle.*[2]

And at about the same time James Forbes provided an eloquent and succinct account of his impressions:

> though letters of gold may boldly emblazon *Liberty, Fraternity,* and *Equality,* on every public portal, such privileges exist not in this republic: here is no confidence between man and man; venality and corruption operate powerfully among the great; envy and distrust pervade the middle classes; and, although the poor may be benefitted by the suppression of some evils which they formerly suffered, the conscription is now become an alloy to every enjoyment. The government, notwithstanding names and forms, is, in effect, a complete system of military despotism: France contains not those germs of virtue which, when they spring forth, may nourish a republic: the elements for such a system do not exist in this servile nation.[3]

There is something rueful in Greatheed's pithy comment (1 January 1803) that 'The old evils are returned or returning without the old elegance.'

In January 1803 Greatheed met M. d'Arblay, who in October of the previous year had installed his family in a little house in Passy ('the Richmond of Paris', according to Maria Edgeworth), 'very poor, & keeping but one maid'. Just a month later they

[1] Cf. Lefebvre, p. 149.   [2] Greatheed, pp. 61–2.   [3] Forbes, i, 338–9.

dined together in Paris with a group of friends including General Junot, and Greatheed's later observation in his journal that in the days of Lafayette d'Arblay, 'now existing on a couple of hundreds a year was Camp marshall . . . [and] Junot now Commandant of Paris was a common grenadier', is a reminder of the ironic turns of fortune that dogged the career of Fanny's estimable husband. By the beginning of May war between England and France seemed inevitable, and the departure of Lord Whitworth, the British ambassador, on the twelfth threw the English residents of Paris into a state of anxious despondency. On that very day Greatheed walked to Passy to see d'Arblay and found him 'in great uneasiness'. Fanny was so agitated that she was obliged to retire to her room. 'This approaching war', he wrote, 'seems quite to overset them, so linked are they to both countries that to separate from either is ruin and to hold to both impossible.' On 16 May Britain officially declared war,[1] and six days later Bonaparte issued an 'unjust and extraordinary decree, ordering all the English between the age of eighteen and sixty to be constituted prisoners of war . . ., on the pretence of being detained to answer for the citizens of the French republic, who were taken in some of their vessels, which were captured by the English before the declaration of war'.[2] Forbes recorded his sense of outrage in a vivid paragraph.

No intelligent liberal Frenchman endeavours to justify this act of the First Consul; but, on the contrary, all who have the courage to avow their sentiments, consider our detention as one of the most abominable violations of the law of nations ever committed in a civilized country. They ascribe this cruel breach of hospitality to

[1] Some months before that date the British fleet had taken up a position of war, and Napoleon had resorted to embargoes and the acts of aggression (mentioned in L. 542 n. 2) that made war inevitable.

[2] Forbes, i. 236. According to Rose (i. 426), the French ships were seized on 20 May, four days after the declaration of war on France. On 17 May an embargo had been placed on British ships in French ports, and three days before the declaration of war Bonaparte had instructed his envoy in Florence to lay an embargo on British ships in Tuscan ports.

French historians offer a rather different emphasis. Lefebvre writes (p. 166) that, before the official declaration of war, 'des navires de guerre capturèrent en mer, sans avis préalable, les bâtiments de commerce français, ce qui fut imputé à la "perfide Albion" comme un acte inqualifiable de piraterie'. And Madelin: 'Avant même que cette guerre eût été officiellement déclarée — le 16 mai 1803 — le gouvernement anglais mettait *l'embargo* sur tous les bâtiments français dans les ports de la Grande-Bretagne, et déchaînait la chasse contre ceux qui tenaient la mer.' See *Le Consulat et l'Empire* (2 vols., 1932), i. 177.

the hasty orders of capricious despotism, issued in a moment of passion; but to us the consequence of his capricious and irritable nature may be lasting and terrible.[1]

By 1 June, the English residents of Paris were no longer introduced at the consular court. Their social isolation was complete, and for people like the d'Arblays their only stay against confusion was a small circle of sympathetic and solicitous friends drawn mainly from the ranks of the *ancien régime*.

Declared emperor by the Senate in May 1804, Napoleon was 'crowned' on 2 December by Pope Pius VII amid the greatest pomp and circumstance that Paris could afford. To witness this great event the d'Arblays spent three nights in Paris with their niece and nephew, Marianne and Antoine Bourdois. Entries in Fanny's diary for 1804 provide an account of the imperial procession to Notre Dame, as seen from their perch in front of a house in the quai des Orfèvres on the Île de la Cité, and of 'the beautiful fairy illuminations of the Tuileries' in the evening. In the years that followed Napoleon pursued his policy of French aggrandizement in many parts of Europe, a policy that would ultimately lead to the disasters of the Russian campaign, to Elba, and finally to Waterloo and St. Helena. In the midst of this great national upheaval the d'Arblays lived a quiet and secluded life in Passy until M. d'Arblay's appointment as *rédacteur* in the Ministry of the Interior made it more expedient for them to take up residence again in Paris. With the sudden change from Republic to Empire it was natural that a similar transformation should take place in the intellectual and social life of the great French capital. The imperial family and their countless relatives, friends, and hangers-on had by 1806 established a new social élite that was contemptible in the eyes of most of the *ancienne noblesse*. The kings and queens, princes and dukes created by Napoleon were, to members of the previous generation, little more than upstart parvenus, and people like Mme de Laval mercilessly mocked their pretensions, while Lafayette saw, in the very conception of an imperial France, the collapse of all his hopes for a truly liberal state based on the ideals of a constitutional monarchy. And yet the brilliance and splendour of the capital continued to assert itself, if, as Lemaistre points out, with a difference.

[1] Forbes, i. 236–7

Introduction

Paris still remains a capital of vast importance: but the objects for which it deserves to be visited, are very different from those which induced strangers a few years ago to flock thither from every part of Europe. It is no longer the seat of refined and polished society; but it still offers all the pleasures and varieties of unbounded luxury, besides the finest specimens of ancient art, and the best-informed teachers of modern science. The statuary, the painter, and the man of letters, have each the happiest opportunities of cultivating their favorite pursuits. The elegancies and superior manners of the old court exist no longer; but the present government, created by the arts, the crimes, the talents, and the good-fortune of the extraordinary individual now at its head, points him out as an object of no common curiosity; while the various effects of the late revolution, now rapidly sinking into a new despotism and a new dynasty, excite the observation and astonishment of all persons used to meditate on political affairs. Paris, in short, though at present it presents a less pleasing form than formerly, is more than ever the spot to which all eyes are directed.[1]

During the ten years of the d'Arblays' residence in France Paris was less celebrated for its fashionable literary salons than it had been in the previous century. When she was not at Coppet, her home in Switzerland, and when Bonaparte permitted her to live in Paris, Mme de Staël's house in the city was frequented by intellectuals whose interests were, at that time, more political than exclusively literary. Visitors to the salon of the young Mme Récamier were doubtless more attracted by the aesthetic atmosphere created by their hostess than by the play and poetry readings they enjoyed there, although in later years Chateaubriand gave to her evenings a blended flavour of literature and politics. Still an important figure in education and literature, Mme de Genlis presided over a very select literary circle. During her visit to Paris in 1802–3 Maria Edgeworth paid her respects to this distinguished lady of letters but Mme d'Arblay seems not to have renewed her acquaintance.[2] Nor did she move in the social circle of Mme Récamier, and for political and personal reasons she chose not

---

[1] J.-G. Lemaistre, *Travels after the Peace of Amiens* (3 vols., 1806), ii. 454–5.
[2] The reasons are fairly clear if one recalls Mme d'Arblay's earlier comments upon Mme de Genlis. That lady, who in 1786 had, in the words of Fanny Burney, been 'the apparent pattern of female perfection, in manners, conversation, & delicacy', had by 1792, because of her political and moral intrigues, been reduced to an 'accomplished . . . hypocrite' (i. 158, 241).

to respond to the importunities of Mme de Staël, whom she had known and admired in England.

Mme d'Arblay was, however, not without literary friends and acquaintances in Paris. She was pleased to report to her father in 1805 that she had seen the abbé Morellet, whom she had met for the first time in Dr. Burney's house in London in 1772, and who, in 1807, at the age of eighty, was to touch her heart by singing for her a 'gay, touching, amusing & informing' ballad of his own composition. Academician and member of the Institut, this 'man of science and learning' won Fanny's admiration and affection as in October 1802 he had won Maria Edgeworth's.[1] Earlier she had dined in the company of Abbé Dominique Ricard, the celebrated translator of Plutarch and author of the poem *La Sphère*, whose manner was 'so gentle, so quiet, so modest, so reserved, that he appeared an almost *singular* character in these times'. Through her friendship with his wife, Mme d'Arblay met frequently one of the leading French philosophers of his day, Destutt de Tracy, and on 21 December 1808 she attended the meeting of the Institut when he delivered as his inaugural address a eulogy on the late Cabanis, to whose place he had been elected earlier in the month, and when the comte de Ségur, the husband of another close friend, made the official response.

Despite her friendly intentions, Mme de Souza, whose 'petit roman anglais', *Charles et Marie*, Sainte-Beuve considered 'un peu dans le goût de miss Burney',[2] received but a cool reception from Mme d'Arblay, who found it difficult (if not impossible) to reconcile her moral principles with Mme de Souza's rather questionable reputation.[3] She also had slight acquaintance with Mme Allart (Marie-Françoise Gay), who had translated Ann Radcliffe's novel *The Italian* under the title *Eléonore de Rosalba*, and with the celebrated Mme Campan, the formal closing of whose school in Saint-Germain-en-Laye she attended in the summer of 1802. It was on this occasion that she

---

[1] Life, i. 102–3.　　[2] *Nouvelle galerie de femmes célèbres* (1865), p. 511.
[3] It was generally accepted that the dashing young comte Charles de Flahaut was the illegitimate son of Mme de Souza (formerly Mme de Flahaut) and Talleyrand. Mme d'Arblay was, however, spared the ultimate irony of this illicit relationship when it transpired that Napoleon III and his minister, the duc de Morny, were half-brothers. They were both sons of Hortense de Beauharnais: the emperor, by virtue of her marriage to Louis Bonaparte, king of Holland; the duc de Morny, by virtue of her liaison with Charles de Flahaut.

Introduction

met a famous *alumna* of the school, Mme Murat (the first consul's sister Caroline, later Queen of Naples), 'extremely handsome in the Cleopatra style'; and there also was Mme Louis Bonaparte (Hortense de Beauharnais, the first consul's step-daughter and sister-in-law, later Queen of Holland), 'a perfectly good young woman without any species of art, coquetry, pride or love of dissipation', whose dashing (if neurotic) husband Fanny was later to find so amiable and exemplary of conduct when she met him in the autumn of 1802 in Joigny, where he was quartered with his regiment.

While the d'Arblays could count among their acquaintance a number of distinguished French intellectuals and writers, their precarious financial circumstances made it impossible for them to enjoy the tremendously varied musical and theatrical entertainment that Paris offered. Moreover, from the time of Fanny's arrival in mid-April of 1802 until September of 1805 they lived in Paris proper for only a month and a half. The summer of 1802 was spent in Monceau, in those days almost a suburb of the city and a considerable distance from the centre of its social activities; and, after a visit of six weeks in Joigny in the early autumn, they moved to the small house in Passy, where they remained for three years. Upon their return to Paris in 1805 they continued to live a very sequestered life on their small income, deriving their social pleasures from their little circle of similarly impoverished friends.

But to its residents and visitors with money to spend, Paris could be a city of perpetual entertainment and amusement. Of its three musical theatres the Opéra was celebrated not only for its productions of Haydn, Piccini, Mozart, and the more serious work of Paisiello, but also for its ballet, in which, much to M. d'Arblay's delight in January 1802 (before Fanny's arrival), the dancers were 'absolument nues'—or at least gave that impression, with the flesh-coloured, skin-tight, transparent gauzes that served as costumes. The théâtre Favart (better known as the Opéra bouffe or the Opéra Italien) provided lighter operatic fare—Cimarosa, Sarti, and the comic operas of Paisiello—in the Italian style and with a fine cast of Italian singers led by Mme Grassini. It was in this house in the box of the duc de Choiseul, borrowed for the occasion by Mme d'Hénin, that Fanny, shortly after her arrival, enjoyed the

xxxi

first act of Giuseppe Sarti's *Le Nozze di Dorina*, was 'lulled to a drowsiness' in the second, and was quietly removed before the opportunity presented itself of sleeping soundly through the third. The théâtre Feydeau (the Opéra Comique) was noted for its French repertoire (Méhul, Grétry, Sedaine, Dalayrac), and it was there that the d'Arblays heard Dalayrac's *La Maison à Vendre* in which the singing-actor Elleviou enjoyed 'un triomphe retentissant'.

Established since 1799, when the republican group of actors amalgamated with the royalist *comédiens*, the théâtre Français was the greatest of Paris's twenty-odd theatres, as today, under the name of the Comédie Française, it continues to bear that distinction. The home of Talma, the finest French actor of his time, of Dugazon, Molé, Fleury, Mlle de Raucourt, Mme Vestris, and Louise Contat, this theatre was, in the year of Mme d'Arblay's arrival in the French capital, most celebrated for its productions of a number of plays of Voltaire, Corneille's *Le Cid*, Racine's *Phèdre* and *Andromaque*, in addition to the usual repertoire of Molière. While at a performance of *Andromaque* in Brussels Maria Edgeworth's father, accustomed in England to the splendid performances of Garrick and Mrs. Siddons, found Mme Talma (Caroline Vanhove) incomparable in the title-role, the more conventional reaction of English visitors was expressed by Forbes,[1] who was willing to concede French superiority in comedy but not in tragedy, and by Maria Edgeworth, who found French tragedy marred by academic and excessively extravagant diction.[2] Mme d'Arblay and her friends were little interested in the parodies for which the théâtre de Vaudeville, a favourite resort of the Junots and of other members of the fashionable world, was famous, or in the farces and burlesques of the théâtre des Variétés, whose most distinguished patron was the second consul, Cambacérès, and whose main attraction was the comic actor Brunet. In 1805 d'Arblay's employment in the Ministry of the Interior and the family's subsequent move from Passy back to Paris made it possible for Fanny to introduce young Alex, now in his eleventh year, to the fine performances, especially of Molière, at the national theatre.

In the early years of the nineteenth century, Paris was, as it is

---

[1] Forbes, i. 426.   [2] *Life*, i. 91.

now, the European centre of feminine elegance and high fashion. Not a frequenter of Frascati in the boulevard des Italiens, where the elegant world assembled after the opera, nor of the consular and (later) imperial *assemblées*, Mme d'Arblay makes only occasional comment in her letters of the new *style grecque* or *classique*, a vogue first set by the notorious Mme Tallien and immediately assumed by ladies of the generation of the princess Borghese, Mme Récamier, and Mme Junot. That it was in marked contrast to the dress of English women was soon observed by Miss Wilmot, a young woman of twenty-eight, who wrote that she and the other ladies of Lord Mount Cashell's party were 'caparison'd so differently from other people, we look'd as if we took a traveller's prerogative, and providently carried all our goods and chattels upon our backs for safety', as compared with the French ladies, who were 'dress'd or rather Undress'd to the extent of the Parisian fashion'.[1] What she chose to designate their 'allegoric' appearance—'sleeveless arms, encircled by a diamond Bracelet, and a glittering crescent on their temples, bound by glossy braids of jet black hair. Others in Juno's bright Tiara and Leopard Mantle, assume the Goddess, and deck themselves with Cameo Joves'—offended the Revd. Dawson Warren one evening in late November 1801, when he dined at the home of the rich Paris banker Perregaux:

I sat next a lady who seemed to have nothing more on than a chemise and a gown and even these left the whole bust exposed. . . . The rooms are very warm from the stoves and the women wrap themselves well in shawls before they go out, or I should wonder how their health could stand such exposure to the cold. But the effect this fashion must have on the morals of the country it is fearful to reflect upon.[2]

On the other hand, when she attended the 'grande revue' in May 1802, Mme d'Arblay found that 'the light drapery' worn by the ladies was 'not by any means so notorious nor so common as has been represented', and in a letter to Miss Planta she gives an amusing account of the exclamations of her friends

---

[1] Wilmot, pp. 23–7. Or, more usual, 'in light (almost transparent) drapery', no sleeves to the gown but 'gold chain twisted round the upper parts of [the] Arm . . . and the neck entirely seen'.

[2] Warren, pp. 49–50.

as she goes about the business of 'refitting' her 'sumptuous wardrobe' and 'reorganizing' her 'poor exterior':

This wont do!—*That* you can never wear! *This* you can never be seen in! *That* would make you stared at as a curiosity!—*THREE* petticoats! No one wears more than one!—STAYS? every body has left off even corsets!—Shift sleeves? not a soul now wears even a chemise!' &c &c.—In short, I found all that I possessed seemed so hideously old fashioned, or so comically rustic, that as soon as it was decreed I must make my appearance in the *grand monde*, hopeless of success in exhibiting myself in the *costume français*, I gave over the attempt, & ventured to come forth as a Gothic *anglaise*, who had never heard of, or never heeded, the reigning metamorphoses.[1]

As the fashionable ladies seemed inclined to wear less and less, their military escorts tended to wear more and more; and the elaborate and flamboyant uniforms of Bonaparte's generals (particularly the outlandish get-ups of Murat) were as much the talk of the town as were the alluring *décolletages* of his sister Pauline, who was reputed to spend a number of hours each day in baths of tepid milk. Except on great ceremonial occasions, Bonaparte himself usually dressed very simply 'in plain regimentals' in striking contrast to the splendour of his aides, whose uniforms Mme d'Arblay considered 'too gorgeous to be noble'. Small of stature, he appeared, as Forbes observed, 'to the greatest advantage on horseback',[2] and in December 1802, when Miss Edgeworth attended the 'grande revue' of the troops, she was deeply impressed by the 'thin, sad' countenance of the first consul and by the quiet dignity with which he sat his horse, a beautiful white Spanish stallion, probably the 'cheval fougueux' of David's equestrian portrait of *Bonaparte au Mont Saint-Bernard*. At the 'grande revue' of the previous May, Mme d'Arblay had been similarly struck by the 'deeply impressive cast' of Bonaparte's face, 'pale even to sallowness, while not only in the Eye, but in every feature, Care, Thought, Melancholy & Meditation are strongly marked, with so much of character, nay, Genius, & so penetrating a seriousness—or rather sadness, as powerfully to sink into an observer's mind.' It was the face of 'a profoundly studious & contemplative Man'.[3]

---

[1] See L. 516, pp. 289–90.   [2] Forbes, i. 279.
[3] See L. 518, p. 313.

Writing many years later for her 'Son's Fire-Side Rectory' (a kind of metaphor she used for her hopes of Alex's future, which were never fulfilled), Mme d'Arblay made a succinct observation upon the kind of society she had enjoyed during the ten years of her residence in France: 'In select French Society there is a Life, a Spur, a spirit of pleasure, that give it a zest rarely indeed to be met with in England.'[1] While she has hastened to add that she had been fortunate enough to enjoy that English 'rarity' at Mrs. Thrale's in Streatham, at the Lockes', at Mrs. Delany's, at her father's house, and at Court, it is clear from the correspondence that she thoroughly delighted in the charm of French society and in the company of those ladies and gentlemen who made up her 'select' group. Despite her very English ways, her natural timidity, and her perennial difficulties with the language, it is similarly clear that she won the affection and the respect of a segment of society that ranged from ci-devant princes and princesses to the more modest families of her husband's native Joigny. Many of the people she met upon her arrival in Paris she had, of course, known during their years of emigration in England; but as many again were friends and associates of General d'Arblay whom she was meeting for the first time. During the first few weeks of her residence in the French capital she was inundated by visitors and well-wishers, including her niece and nephew, Marianne and Antoine Bourdois, now resident in Paris, and the wife and daughter of M. d'Arblay's beloved uncle, M. Bazille of Joigny, who 'had come to Paris to receive Me into their family, with the most affectionate, flattering, & cordial kindness'. Exhausted by her recent journey, deeply concerned about the health of her son, not altogether settled in her apartments and consequently inadequately prepared to receive guests, Mme d'Arblay was none the less touched by such kind and sympathetic attention, and, with the notable exception of two ladies closely associated with the comte de Narbonne-Lara, gave her callers as warm a reception as her domestic circumstances would allow.

Upon their respective arrivals in Paris the d'Arblays had not seen Louis de Narbonne since he had left for Switzerland in the summer of 1794, after almost two years in England. In 1782 he

[1] See L. 631.

had married Mlle de Montholon, a rich heiress from Rouen, who had borne him two daughters, but the marriage had not been a happy one, and the comtesse had lived for some years in Italy with his mother, the duchesse de Narbonne, who was *dame d'honneur* to Madame Adélaïde, a daughter of Louis XV. Removed from the proscription lists in 1800, the comte bought a house in Paris near the Hôtel Marengo in the rue de Miroménil, although at the time of Mme d'Arblay's arrival he was living with the vicomtesse de Laval. This liaison with the mother of Mathieu de Montmorency-Laval, one of Mme de Staël's current favourites, was the talk of Paris and so scandalized Narbonne's mother and wife that they firmly rejected his plea, after the death of Madame Adélaïde, to join him in France. Between 1800 and 1809 his 'friend' Talleyrand, though ostensibly trying to secure for Narbonne favour with Bonaparte, deliberately jeopardized his opportunities; but upon Talleyrand's disgrace in 1809 Narbonne joined the emperor's army in Vienna. Until his death in 1813 he occupied, with distinction, a number of significant diplomatic posts, and in May 1812 accompanied the emperor to Russia as aide-de-camp. Six months later he returned to Paris with Murat, king of Naples, and was promptly sent to Vienna as ambassador, and later to Prague.[1] Though one of d'Arblay's closest friends, Narbonne was not very much in evidence during Fanny's years in Paris. Until 1808 he visited them from time to time and always received a warm welcome, but after his successful entry into the imperial circle he seldom appeared. That his absences occasioned Mme d'Arblay grave disappointment would seem questionable, since, despite her admiration of Narbonne, his private life, according to her ethical principles, left much to be desired.

As a young man the handsome and gallant Louis de Narbonne was a great favourite with the ladies, although Marie Antoinette distrusted him, probably because of the prevalent rumour that he was the natural son of Louis XV's daughter. After 1809, when he had reached his mid-fifties, contemporary memoir-writers were less sympathetic to him than his earlier admirers had been. Indeed in 1811 Emperor Alexander I informed Napoleon that his intention to appoint Narbonne

[1] For a full account of the comte de Narbonne's career, see Dard.

Introduction

ambassador to the Russian Court was unacceptable, and a short time later Marie-Louise similarly declined her husband's suggestion that Narbonne be named master of the empress's household. In 1812, after he had been appointed ambassador to Wilna, Mme de Choiseul-Gouffier paid tribute to his 'esprit agréable, brillant, mais versatile' and to 'l'élégante facilité de son langage', but concluded that, as 'Homme de salon et de plaisirs', he was 'peu propre à remplir une mission diplomatique'.[1] Recalling her visit to Paris in 1810 the Countess Potocka made a shrewd comment that might have served as the epitaph of the former idol of French society when she wrote: 'Le comte de Narbonne était un de ces hommes richement doués, mais qui traversent l'histoire sans y laisser la place glorieuse que leurs talents auraient dû leur assigner.'[2]

Mme d'Arblay would appear to have been unaware of Narbonne's liaison with Mme de Staël until some time after it had been terminated. Driven to the verge of suicidal despair, Mme de Staël had pursued her faithless lover to England in late 1793, only to discover the truth of what for many months she had feared, that her irrepressible passion for Narbonne (so eloquently reflected in her letters)[3] was no longer reciprocated. Not insensitive to the rumours concerning Narbonne that were circulating freely before Mme de Staël's arrival in England, Fanny was comforted by d'Arblay's assurances that, whatever the degree of her intimacy with Narbonne in the past, 'en ce moment [March 1793] cette liaison n'est que de l'amitié la plus respectable'.[4] Whether the argument was merely a device to allay Fanny's moral concern or merely a piece of special pleading is not clear; but it would appear that d'Arblay knew the condition of Narbonne's heart's affections some time before Mme de Staël's worst fears were finally confirmed. In England Fanny was charmed by the distinguished French author, and delighted in her company; but when Mme de Staël called at the Hôtel Marengo in April 1802 with the clear intention of renewing friendship, Mme d'Arblay's sense of moral delicacy led her to employ a series of evasive tactics that bordered upon

[1] *Reminiscences sur l'Empereur Alexandre Ier et sur l'Empereur Napoléon Ier* (1862), pp. 42–3.
[2] Potocka, p. 190.
[3] Jasinski, *Lettres . . . à Louis de Narbonne* (1960). See i, p. lxiv.
[4] See ii. 32.

the absurd. In a letter of the following March she explained her position to Miss Planta:

How greatly is it to be lamented that such parts & talents [as Mme de Staël's] should be bestowed where there are no principles! & the more is it to be regretted, as she has qualities the most bewitching, of kindness, generosity, & zeal, joined to almost every intellectual attribute that can elevate a human being. Unrestrained passions, in short are her bane; for her heart is as good as her head; & she is so eminently agreeable & engaging, vivacious & clever, & possesses such a boundless fund of good humour, & such nearly matchless charms of conversation, that I can never cease regretting the ungrateful part I have seemed to act towards her, though I was impelled to it by a belief it was indispensably right.[1]

It was not, however, Mme de Staël's moral character alone that was responsible for this seeming ingratitude; her political character was equally suspect. When in 1797 she first met Bonaparte she found much to admire in his sincere republicanism, his moderate political views, and his indifference to public honours; but before long, as Mme de Rémusat observed, 'une sorte de défiance s'établit entre eux, et, comme ils étaient tous deux passionnés, cette défiance ne tarda point à se changer en haine'.[2] By 1798 her liaison (both adulterous and political) with Benjamin Constant seriously aggravated the situation. The first consul became more and more suspicious of what he considered the subversive political activities of those who frequented her salon in the faubourg Saint Germain; but when he learned that she was attracting to her 'foyer des mécontents' some of his own ministers, political and military colleagues, and even members of his own family (notably his brother Louis), he was infuriated and determined to rid himself of 'cette canaille de Constant' and 'cette coquine de Mme de Staël' by imposing upon them periodic terms of exile. For people like the d'Arblays, who, in their attempts to secure the general's military pension, were totally dependent upon the good will of the first consul, it was politically expedient as well as morally desirable to avoid any situation that would suggest friendly relations with the notorious Mme de Staël.

When the vicomtesse de Laval called at the Hôtel Marengo on the day of Mme d'Arblay's arrival, yet another moral

---

[1] See L. 541, p. 419. [2] *Mémoires* (3 vols., 1880), ii. 398.

problem presented itself; for, as Fanny was to write a few days later to Mrs. Locke, 'certain reports against this lady, with respect to her *amitié* for an old & admired friend of ours [Narbonne] had made me anxious to defer the acquaintance, till I should know better with what degree of intimacy or coldness to begin it'. While Mme d'Arblay discerned in her guest 'a look that, had I not been prejudiced against her, would have struck me as mingling benevolence of character with spirit of disposition',[1] Mme de Laval was better known to the frequenters of her salon for her personal charm, her piquant and mildly malicious wit, and her legion anecdotes of the 'grand petit homme' [Bonaparte]: his domestic life at the Tuileries and the bourgeois attempts there at courtly etiquette, his 'manières conjugales', and his constant concern for Madame Joséphine, 'dont le seul défaut est de mentir par habitude'. In 1803 Mme de Cazenove d'Arlens was enchanted by Mme de Laval and her somewhat eccentric appearance ('un grand chapeau de paille sur le nez, une petite canne à la main'),[2] and seven years later the Countess Potocka discovered in the exclusive society of her 'petit salon . . . un brevet d'amabilité et de bon goût'.[3] Others were less favourably disposed to Mme de Laval: the baron de Barante remembered her as a witty woman 'sans nulle bienveillance',[4] and Mme de Coigny described her as 'la plus piquante, la plus gaie, la plus absolue, la plus aimable et la moins bonne des femmes'.[5] Though always circumspect in her relations with Mme de Laval, Mme d'Arblay was grateful to her for her 'zealous exertions' in securing for M. d'Arblay in 1805 his appointment in the Ministry of the Interior. 'Quite charmed' by Mathieu de Montmorency-Laval, she is never free of prejudice in her judgements of his mother. She 'is a charming woman—O how much to be pitied for *les égaremens* into which the want of firm principles has suffered the love of pleasure to lead her! It is evident she wishes now to cultivate only higher & purer feelings.'[6]

The ci-devant princesse d'Hénin (1750–1824), whom Mme d'Arblay 'had known particularly in England' where she had spent the years of her exile, was one of her first visitors in the rue

[1] See L. 511, p. 249. [2] Cazenove d'Arlens, p. 106.
[3] Potocka, p. 226. [4] *Souvenirs* (8 vols., 1890–1901), i. 89.
[5] *Mémoires*, ed. Étienne Lamy (1902), pp. 198–9.
[6] See Notebooks, vi, '4 juillet 1805'.

de Miroménil.[1] During the first months of Fanny's residence in Paris and Monceau, Mme d'Hénin was the 'Dear kind Constant' friend who arranged drives in the parks, an excursion to Passy to meet the Latour-Maubourg family, dinner parties, an evening at the opera, and the midsummer visit to Mme Campan's school. In October 1804, after having spent two years in Bordeaux on a visit to her nephew the marquis de La Tour du Pin, she called at the d'Arblays' home in Passy, all 'friendly goodness, & confidential sensibility'. In the years that followed, and especially at the time of Mme d'Arblay's operation in 1811, Mme d'Hénin remained one of her closest and kindest friends. Her marriage, which had been ruined by her husband's liaison with Mlle Raucourt, one of the leading actresses at the théâtre Français, was terminated when the prince was guillotined in 1794, and after that time Mme d'Hénin found a degree of happiness in her friendship with the marquis de Lally-Tolendal, whom the d'Arblays had often met at Norbury Park, and who at one time, it was thought, might have escorted Mme d'Arblay and the children on the journey from London to Paris in the spring of 1802. A political follower of Jean-Joseph Mounier and the liberal republicans, Lally-Tolendal was much admired by all who knew him, particularly for the success of his dedicated efforts to rehabilitate the reputation of his father, who, as a result of false accusations against him for his part in the surrender of the French to English forces at Pondicherry in India, had been beheaded in 1766, 'a victim', as Mme d'Arblay was to record in her notebook for 1804, 'to party, prejudice & false judgement'. In a letter to Miss Planta she expressed her warm sentiment when she wrote of M. Lally, whom she had known 'long intimately' during his many years of emigration in England, that 'A man of more worth & honour & Patriotism I do not think exists.'[2]

Three other ladies related by marriage to Mme d'Hénin, the ci-devant princesse de Poix (1750–1833), the ci-devant princesse de Beauvau-Craon (1774–1854), and her sister Mlle de Mortemart (1776–1809), figured largely in Mme d'Arblay's social life during her first months in Paris. 'Cruelly lame' and a victim of

[1] For a biography of the princesse d'Hénin, see Welvert.
[2] See L. 529 p. 377.

perennial ill-health, Mme de Poix, the 'confidential and intimate friend' of Mme d'Hénin for thirty years, was a woman of great charm, wit, and even gaiety. Unable to emigrate with her 'booby husband' and children, she remained in Paris and, by the ruse of a divorce, had preserved life and possessions against the depredations of the Revolution and the Terror. Never enjoying with Mme de Poix the degree of intimacy she knew with Mme d'Hénin, Mme d'Arblay none the less admired her new friend for her courage and her irreproachable moral conduct. Much younger, Mme de Beauvau and her sister, daughters of the duc de Mortemart, were grand-daughters of the duc d'Harcourt, members of the English branch of whose family Fanny had known during her years at Court. *Émigrés* in England for nearly ten years, the Beauvau family and Mlle de Mortemart had enjoyed the hospitality and the security offered by their English relatives, and when Mme d'Arblay arrived in Paris she brought with her letters from Mrs. Harcourt and from one of her earlier charges, the Princess Elizabeth, second daughter of George III and Queen Charlotte. At first not favourably disposed to M. de Beauvau (whom d'Arblay had known intimately as a child), in whom she discerned 'the style of a common English young man of fashion, not of elegance', Mme d'Arblay was, however, later touched by his affection for his bewitchingly beautiful wife and for his lovely children. One of her most moving letters in the summer of 1802 provides an account of her visit, in the company of Mme d'Hénin, to the prince's step-mother, the very elderly maréchale de Beauvau, a member of the great Rohan-Chabot family, who, having renounced all society, lived in a 'small & insignificant house' at Saint-Germain-en-Laye, alone with the remembrance of things past. Though possessed of neither the grace nor the beauty of her sister, Mlle de Mortemart (who in 1804 was to marry the duc de Crussol) won Mme d'Arblay's affection for her 'Warm, energetic, enthusiastic' nature, no less than her gratitude for her ability to speak English. Again, while their connection with this distinguished family was never close, the d'Arblays were delighted when, some years later, shortly before Mme de Beauvau's return to Paris following a visit to the Austrian Court in the suite of the Empress Marie-Louise, whose *dame du palais* she had become in 1812, she gave to

M. d'Arblay for his mineral collection some fine specimens of tin ore, souvenirs from the mines of the Prince de Clary. Within a few years the Beauvau family were in political disgrace, but Mme d'Arblay never failed to defend their 'real worth & character'.[1]

Among M. d'Arblay's many French friends of long standing, the people whom Mme d'Arblay was perhaps most eager to meet were the marquis de Lafayette, his wife (*née* Adrienne de Noailles, daughter of the duc d'Ayen, later duc de Noailles), their three children, now young adults, and Mme de Lafayette's maternal aunt, the comtesse de Tessé. Shortly after her arrival and a few weeks before making the acquaintance of the great general, no less celebrated in American than in French history, Mme d'Arblay was visited by 'his virtuous & heroick Wife'. Totally unprepared to receive such a distinguished caller—'In a close Cap,—my feet, in their Native undrapered state, hidden by a large wrapping Morning gown . . ., reclined on a Bed'—she was none the less deeply moved by the sight of the devout and kindly woman who, despite her lameness (the result of blood-poisoning she had contracted when, with her two daughters, she had shared for nearly two years her husband's imprisonment in a miserable dungeon in Olmütz in Austria), had climbed the three 'pair of stairs' to pay her respects and 'to put in her claim for a long given promise of M. d'Arblay's that we should spend a few days at La Grange', a fine old château that was part of Mme de Lafayette's inheritance from her maternal grandmother. A few years after their release from Olmütz in 1797 the Lafayettes had settled permanently at La Grange, located about thirty miles from Paris, and in drastic need of repair after years of disuse. While Mme de Lafayette went about the exhausting business of having her husband's name and the names of his friends erased from the proscription lists, the former general set to work to make the château habitable for his family and to cultivate the extensive farmlands that were part of the property.

When the d'Arblays made their only recorded visit to La Grange about the second week of May 1802, they found 'only one room . . ., an octogone, . . . modernized'. Busy with his farm, M. de Lafayette, 'With all the various faults charged

[1] See ix, L. 1051.

against him in public', was, in his own home, according to Mme d'Arblay,

all that is reputable & amiable, fond, attentive, & instructive to his children, active & zealous for his friends, gentle & equal with his servants, & displaying, upon every occasion the tenderest gratitude to the wife, who followed him to captivity, & to whom, from that period, he became, by universal account, far more warmly & exclusively attached than he had ever been formerly: though her virtues & conduct had always been objects to him of respect & esteem.[1]

At La Grange the renowned Lafayette family lived 'with the utmost simplicity and economy . . ., keep no sort of equipage, dress in the plainest and cheapest style, & never come to Paris but upon business too important to be arranged by commission'. With them lived their children: Anastasie, who in 1798 had married Charles de Latour-Maubourg; George Washington Lafayette, preparations for whose forthcoming marriage (in June 1802) to Emilie Destutt de Tracy, daughter of the logician and philosopher, were, at the time of the d'Arblays' visit, under way; and Virginie, aged twenty, who in the following year was to marry the comte de Lasteyrie.[2] At the end of their visit Mme de Lafayette and Virginie returned with the d'Arblays to Paris. *En route*, they passed 'the Barriere', near the Place de la Nation, where in July 1794 Mme de Lafayette, herself in prison at the time, lost to the guillotine within an hour her paternal grandmother, her mother, and her favourite sister Louise, vicomtesse de Noailles; and at that moment 'Mme de Laf. sunk into profound silence, & the most melancholy rumination: . . . She soon after struggled to revive, but her spirits returned no more.' After 1802 the two families seldom met, but M. de Lafayette continued to pay the occasional call, and on 30 May 1805 the d'Arblays had the pleasure of meeting the Lafayettes at the home of their son, George Washington. Upon that occasion Mme d'Arblay observed in her notebook

[1] See L. 541, pp. 420–1.
[2] The present owner of La Grange, the comte de Chambrun, is a descendant of the comte and comtesse de Lasteyrie. Since his occupation of the château in 1955 an enormous treasury of Lafayette documents has been discovered in what was the general's library, located in the north-west tower. While the definitive biography of the marquis de Lafayette has yet to be written, André Maurois' *Adrienne . . .* (1960), based on such material there as has yet been catalogued, offers the most authoritative biography of this great woman.

Introduction

that '*He* was all friendship, warmth, zeal, openness & trust, *She*, all goodness and flattering kindness.' Though unrecorded in either correspondence or notebooks, Mme de Lafayette's death occurred on Christmas Eve, 1807; the marquis lived for another twenty-seven years. They are buried a few feet from the common ditch where the bodies of the beheaded Noailles women had been thrown in 1794, and on the site of which Mme de Lafayette had been instrumental in building a chapel and a convent to house the Sisters of Perpetual Adoration, who continuously to this day recite a prayer written by Adrienne shortly before she died.[1]

Upon her first meeting with Mme de Tessé at a 'select little assembly at M^e d'Hénin's', Mme d'Arblay was somewhat intimidated by the formidable appearance, the high air, and formal manners of that august lady. Greatly admired by M. d'Arblay for her 'high principles, elevated sentiments, & talents for conversation equal, though not of a similar nature, to those of Mad. de Staël', Mme de Tessé had demonstrated her remarkable spirit of enterprise and generosity when she prepared in various parts of Europe safe and comfortable refuges for the Lafayettes, Latour-Maubourg, and others, upon their release from Olmütz. Possessed of 'a very large fortune' before the Revolution, Mme de Tessé and her quiet, mild-mannered husband, whose father had been first equerry to Louis XV's queen Maria Leczinska, lived 'in modest comfort' if reduced circumstances in the rue d'Anjou, but a short distance from the various apartments occupied by the d'Arblays during their several periods of residence in Paris. Once settled they received from Mme de Tessé every mark of solicitude and esteem, and before long Mme d'Arblay came to share her husband's high opinion of the lady who, according to young Alex, could recount an anecdote 'just like one of Addison's Guardians', and who received from Fanny high praise for her 'enlightening & enlivening conversation', 'her goodness & kindness, as well as spirit & intelligence'. When they returned to Paris from Passy in the autumn of 1805, the d'Arblays frequently enjoyed her company, and as late as 1811, the critical year of Mme d'Arblay's operation for a breast growth,

---

[1] For some of these details the writer is grateful to the comte de Chambrun who kindly placed at his disposal a copy of his 'Address at Valley Forge'.

the seventy-year-old Mme de Tessé showed her customary sympathy and concern and 'insisted upon sending all that might be necessary, & of keeping me in ignorance' of the sinister preparations required by the surgeons. During the ten years that Mme d'Arblay spent in France few friends showed greater kindness and sympathy than Mme de Tessé.

Mme d'Arblay's acquaintance with the large Latour-Maubourg family began when in the autumn of 1802 the small d'Arblay establishment moved to Passy, the home of César, comte de Latour-Maubourg (1758–1831), and of his sister Mme de Maisonneuve, who two years earlier had divorced her husband. A younger brother Victor, M. d'Arblay's 'ami intime', had recently returned with Bonaparte's expeditionary force from Egypt, where he had suffered a serious head wound at the battle of Canope, and was probably in Passy with his brother César at the time the d'Arblays took up residence there. After his marriage in 1804 to Mlle Van Rijssel, daughter of a Dutch general well known to Lafayette, Victor de Latour-Maubourg was recalled to service in the imperial army leaving his wife in Passy. While he enjoyed a very distinguished military career in the Prussian, Spanish, and Russian campaigns (1806–12), he was strongly royalist in his political views and antipathetic to Napoleon, whom he served loyally but for whom he had neither sympathy nor affection. Upon the restoration of Louis XVIII he was in high favour and, at the request of the king's brother, the comte d'Artois (later Charles X), he served on the commission charged with the reorganization of the French army. From Louis he received many honours: in 1817, by royal letters patent he was created marquis de Latour-Maubourg, and in 1819 he was named minister of war. To Mme d'Arblay he was 'our excellent M. de Maubourg . . ., a Man of sound judgement, playful & comic humour, warm affections, & exalted honour—with cold manners & a stiff & severe demeanour'.[1] The third and youngest brother, Charles, who had married Anastasie de Lafayette and lived at La Grange, seems to have been little in the society of the d'Arblays. Their most intimate friends in Passy were the family of César, his sister Mme de Maisonneuve, and their elderly aunt, the former abbess of Saint-Paul-de-Beaurepaire.

[1] See Notebooks, vi, '15 mai 1805'.

Introduction

In early 1792, César de Latour-Maubourg commanded the avant-garde of the Armée des Ardennes, which was under the supreme command of Lafayette. Later that year Lafayette and his suite, consisting of César de Latour-Maubourg, Alexandre Lameth, and Bureaux de Pusy, crossed the (then) Netherlands frontier near Liège and were arrested by the Prussians and the Austrians, who imprisoned them first in the citadel of Luxembourg, later at Wesel and Magdeburg, and finally in the gloomy fortress of Olmütz, whence they were released in September 1797, a decision confirmed by the treaty of Campo Formio about a month later. Sheltered for a time by Mme de Tessé, César did not return to France until after Bonaparte's coup of 18 Brumaire (9 November 1799), and consequently he had not long been settled at Passy when the d'Arblays moved there in 1802. In partial retirement he devoted himself to his large family of seven children and to politics, and until named senator in 1806 he served as a member of the *Corps législatif* of the French government. Despite his strong royalist sympathies he served the imperial government in several official capacities. However, upon the restoration of the Bourbon monarchy following Napoleon's exile to Elba he accepted a military appointment in the royalist army, and in 1814 he was promoted to the rank of lieutenant-general and created peer of the realm. During the period of the Hundred Days, he returned to the service of the emperor, and received an imperial peerage in early June 1815. Upon the Second Restoration, he was excluded from the chamber of peers by the king's ordonnance, only to be reinstated in early 1819. In later years the d'Arblays, forever loyal to France's royalist cause, were understandably troubled by the seeming political opportunism of their old friend.

The home of the César de Latour-Maubourg family was located in the 'immediate vicinity' of the d'Arblays', in the rue Basse (now the rue Raynouard), but in the summer of 1805 César, probably in the interests of his sons' careers, accepted service under Napoleon as Governor of the fortress of Cherbourg, removing his family to Picardy, a loss that 'quite saddened' the d'Arblays. In August Mme d'Arblay declined the kind invitation of Mme de Latour-Maubourg that she and young Alex should spend the school vacation with her and her family

xlvi

at their country residence St. Nicolas since Fanny could not face the thought of separation from M. d'Arblay, who in the previous March had begun his work in the Ministry of the Interior; and in any case they had already decided to move back to Paris. While she makes no observations at the time upon the character of M. de Latour-Maubourg, Mme d'Arblay records in a letter to Mrs. Locke her admiration of his wife, whose 'highly dramatic face' recalled to her 'the style of M^{rs}. Siddons'. During the years of the Revolution and of her husband's imprisonment she had had the sole care of her children, and had succeeded in saving the greatest part of her considerable fortune. Mme d'Arblay was moved too by her 'unerring' moral judgement, her strong religious principles, and 'a never failing equanimity of temper'. A few years later when she came to know her more intimately, she described her with greater informality as 'always chearful, easy, well bred, & full of *bon sens*'.

During the years at Passy and, indeed, for years after her return to England in 1812, Mme d'Arblay's most intimate friend was Mme de Maisonneuve (1770–1850), who was for both Fanny and her husband 'a lady of the first eminence for every virtue'. Early in their acquaintance she is described with customary formality: 'modest even to timidity'; possessed of a 'perfect private character', a 'native dignity of person & manner', and a 'right & highly principled mind'; though in reduced circumstances, 'treated with universal respect, & never named but with admiration'. As acquaintance warmed into close friendship Mme d'Arblay came to discern in Mme de Maisonneuve 'one of the sweetest women I have ever known' (1804), one who 'grows more dear to me at every interview—'tis a *Sisterly* affection & confidence I feel with & for her, & that I have had the rare happiness to inspire on her part' (1806). Like Mme d'Arblay she undertook to give 'the rudiments of his education to an only little Son', Maxime, a lad of Alex's age and a special chum of his at M. Sencier's school in Passy. One of the very curious things in the intimate relationship between Mme d'Arblay and Mme de Maisonneuve is that Fanny seems not to have known of her friend's divorce from Gérard-Joseph Bidault de Maisonneuve, whom she had married in 1791. In two different letters of 1802 she wrote that she believed

M. de Maisonneuve was still 'in emigration', but there are no further references to him; and in the more than 200 letters Mme de Maisonneuve wrote to Mme d'Arblay in the course of their many years of close friendship, her husband is never once mentioned. 'I know not yet her history,' Fanny wrote in 1802, 'except that it is unfortunate, & submitted to with the most pious resignation.' Mme de Maisonneuve was the ever-faithful companion of Mme d'Arblay's ten years in Paris. When she called she was frequently accompanied by her aunt, the 'dear & revered Abbess', and as late as 1809, when the abbess was in very advanced years, Fanny was delighted to observe in her notebook that she still retained 'all her intelligence, her sweetness & acuteness unimpaired'.

Two other ladies whom Mme d'Arblay saw frequently in the company of her Passy friends were Mme de Ségur and Mme Destutt de Tracy. In a letter to her father in 1810 she described the 'charming Wife' of Louis-Philippe de Ségur as 'a lady who, though now a Grand Mother, retains the beauty of 25—& the grace & attraction of 18 years of Age'. During the reign of Louis XVI her husband had had a varied career as military man, diplomat, and author; although he had not emigrated, his properties were confiscated during the Revolution; but in 1804 he had sufficiently ingratiated himself with Napoleon to be appointed imperial *grand maître des cérémonies*. Member and (for a time) president of the Institut, he made the formal response to the marquis de Tracy's inaugural address at the assembly Mme d'Arblay attended in 1808. The (Louis-Philippe de) Ségurs' daughter-in-law, Mme Octave de Ségur, was also known to Fanny since her eldest boy was a pupil at M. Hix's school in Paris, which Alex d'Arblay attended after his parents moved back to the capital from Passy. Mme de Tracy, wife of the distinguished philosopher, was Mme d'Arblay's 'obliging & most pleasing & constant Friend'. Closely associated with the César de Latour-Maubourgs and the Lafayettes, and living at Auteuil, not far from Passy, the de Tracys were kindly and most helpful friends to the d'Arblays until Fanny's departure for England in 1812. Indeed in that year it was with the help of Mme de Tracy, who was indirectly related to the dreaded Savary, duc de Rovigo, *ministre de la Police* and successor to the equally dreaded Fouché, that they were able to secure passports.

Introduction

In addition to this array of French 'female Worthies' Mme
d'Arblay numbered among her acquaintance certain English
ladies whose French marriages had brought them to Paris. One
of these was the comtesse de Cadignan, formerly Catherine
Hunter, 'of English Parentage, though born in America', whose
husband, a former aide-de-camp to Lafayette, had been
arrested in 1791 but had managed to escape to England. There,
as a result of severe losses in financial speculation, he had
suffered 'a stroke of apoplexy', and the much-admired Mme de
Cadignan was required 'to act for him not merely as his housekeeper, & steward, but as his Lawyer'. They had returned to
France, where M. de Cadignan's condition became 'utterly
hopeless' and where his courageous wife won universal admiration; 'to hear her named & to hear her praised is always the
same thing', wrote Mme d'Arblay in 1802, but in later years she
found it necessary to modify that opinion. Another English
friend, the former Harriet Collins, had married Jean-Baptiste
Chastel de Boinville, who in 1789 had been sent on a diplomatic mission to England. He later joined the Napoleonic
forces and served in Russia, where he died early in 1813. Yet
a third English acquaintance was Mme Bartélemy Huber (*née*
Lydia Strutt), whose husband had acted in 1803 as intermediary between the French and English governments in their
unsuccessful attempts to avert war. Although these ladies did
not play a major part in Mme d'Arblay's social life in France,
she was always pleased to receive them since they usually
brought English news and, after the declaration of war in May
1803, occasionally provided an opportunity of sending letters
home.

Shortly after Fanny's arrival in Paris in 1802, the wife and
daughter (Mme Meignen) of M. d'Arblay's beloved maternal
uncle, M. Jean-Baptiste-Gabriel Bazille, made a special journey
to the capital from their native Joigny to greet and welcome her.
Mme d'Arblay was deeply touched by such kindness, and the
six-week visit of the family to Joigny in the early autumn was
the occasion for Fanny and young Alex to meet the general's
very large family connection in the provincial town that was
his birth-place. In 1802 Joigny was a small, secluded community, in the *département* of Yonne, of a few distinguished
families, almost all of whom were related by marriage and

xlix

descended from the *ligne seigneuriale* of Estienne Porcher, General Piochard d'Arblay's earliest known ancestor, whose fourteenth-century statue remains one of the treasures of the town's Église Saint-Thibault. Situated in gently rolling country on the banks of the river Yonne, Joigny could boast fine properties and estates notable for their flourishing vineyards no less than for their commanding view of a quiet pastoral landscape.

Built into the side of a very steep hill on the north bank of the river, Joigny was a town of narrow streets, family houses, and ancient churches. At the top of the hill was the old château, the residence of the governors, many of whom had been Piochards, and it seems likely that General d'Arblay was born in this mansion, precipitously located and commanding a panoramic view of the valley of the Yonne and of the southern terrain. In the small and congested area of the town the old families—Piochard de la Brûlerie, Bazille, Bourdois, Ragon, Gillet, Charié—had houses, although their properties lay beyond the town and across the river to the south, where M. d'Arblay had once owned land. Either directly or indirectly related to the Piochard d'Arblay family, all were well-known citizens of Joigny, and in many cases had served their country with honour and distinction. General d'Arblay's father, Sieur Pierre Piochard d'Arblay, had held a colonelcy in the royal artillery, and his uncle Bazille had, in the course of his life, served as king's counsellor and as deputy to the *Assemblée Constituante*.

It was into this society that Fanny and young Alex were introduced in the autumn of 1802, and her accounts of that visit in letters to England are filled with anecdotes that reflect her delight in the affection and sympathy she received from her many new friends in Joigny, especially from her husband's much-loved uncle Bazille and his wife. Although it became increasingly difficult for Mme d'Arblay to travel to Joigny, M. d'Arblay went more frequently, on sadly urgent family business: the death of Mme Bazille in October 1803, and of the eldest Bazille son in September 1804. Although M. Bazille was later to visit the d'Arblays in Paris, Mme d'Arblay was, in subsequent years, to see few of the Joigny connection apart from the Bourdois brothers who were resident in Paris: Edmé

1

Joachim, a distinguished doctor, and Antoine, Marianne Burney's husband, whose early death in 1806 was a grievous loss to the d'Arblays and, indeed, to the entire Burney family. During her ten years' residence in and about Paris, Mme d'Arblay visited only two provincial towns of France: Joigny, where she enjoyed the hospitality and affectionate regard of members of her husband's closest family (and, not to be forgotten, the gallant attentions of Louis Bonaparte); and Dunkirk, where in July and August of 1812 she spent, with her son, some five anxious and dreary weeks awaiting a ship that would reunite her with her family in England. With the help of Mme de Tracy the necessary passports had been secured, places in the Paris–Dunkirk diligence had been reserved, and arrangements to sail on an American vessel, the *Mary Ann*, from Dunkirk to Dover, completed. The small ship was officially bound for America, but unofficially it had been scheduled to dock briefly at Dover. Mme d'Arblay and Alex arrived at Dunkirk in early July, but only after weeks of mysterious delays did they actually set sail. Since the United States and Britain were at the time in a state of war, the *Mary Ann* was boarded and seized in the Dover Straits by a British 'sloop of war', but through the good offices of one of the sloop's lieutenants, who had heard of Mme d'Arblay, she and Alex were safely conveyed aboard the British ship to Deal. There the commander-in-chief of the Downs, Sir Thomas Foley, and his wife, a daughter of the Dowager Duchess of Leinster and, in former years, a visitor to the Lockes of Norbury Park and to the d'Arblays at Camilla Cottage, took the weary voyagers into their care. On 20 August, Mme d'Arblay and her seventeen-year-old son, accompanied by her brother Charles, arrived in Chelsea and, after a separation of more than ten years, were reunited with her beloved father, now in his eighty-seventh year.

GEORGE G. FALLE

Trinity College
Toronto, Ontario, Canada
1 March 1972

West Humble, 3 October 1801

To Doctor Burney

A.L. (Diary MSS. vi. 5258–[59], Berg), 3 Oct. 1801
Originally a double sheet 4to, of which FBA later discarded the second
leaf 2 pp.
Edited by FBA, p. 1, annotated and date 1801 retraced and underlined: ⋇ 1801.
(4) Peace, & projected visit to France.
Edited also by CFBt and the Press.

West Hamble, Octr 3^d 1801.

God avert mischief from this Peace,[1] my dearest Father!—for
in our Hermitage you may imagine, more readily than I can
express, the hopes & happiness it excites—M. d'Arblay now
feels paid for his long forbearance, his kind patience, & compliance with my earnest wishes not to re-visit his native Land
while we were at War with it. He can now go with honour as
well as propriety, for every body, even the highest personages,
will rather expect he should make the journey, as a thing of
course, than hear of it as a proposition for deliberation. He
will now have his heart's desire granted, in again seeing his
loved & respectable Uncle,[2]—& many Relations, & more
friends, & his own native Town, as well as soil: & he will have
the delight of presenting to that uncle, & those friends, his
little Pet Alex.

With all this gratification to one whose endurance of such
a length of suspence, & repetition of disappointment, I have
observed with gratitude, & felt with sympathy—must not I,
too, I find pleasure?—though, on my side, many are the drawbacks—but I ought not, & must not listen to them. We shall
arrange our affairs with all the speed in our power, after the

___

423. [1] Late in the afternoon of 1 October the foreign secretary Lord Hawkesbury (iv,
L. 293 n. 5) and the French envoy Ludwig Wilhelm Otto (L. 429 n. 1) had signed
the Preliminaries to the Treaty of Amiens, establishing peace between France and
Great Britain, Spain, and Holland. The treaty was officially signed by Joseph
Bonaparte and Lord Cornwallis on 25 Mar. 1802 (Madelin, iv. 160; Lefebvre,
p. 111).
[2] M. d'A's maternal uncle Jean-Baptiste-*Gabriel* Bazille (1731–1817) of Joigny,
Yonne. For his family, see Genealogical Table, vi, or iii, facing p. 1.

ratification is arrived,³ for saving the cold & windy weather—
but the approach of winter is unlucky, as it will lengthen our
stay, to avoid travelling, & voyaging, during its severity—
unless, indeed, any internal movement, or the menacing aspect
of any, should make frost & snow secondary fears, & induce us
to scamper off. But the present is a season less liable, in all
appearance, to storms, than the seasons that may follow.
Fêtes, joy, & pleasure, will, probably, for some months, occupy
the public in France, & it will not be till those rejoicings are
past, that they will set about weighing Causes of new commotion, the rights of their Governors, or the means, or desir-
ability of changing them. I would far rather go immediately,
than 6 months hence.

I hope, too, this so long wished view of friends & Country
gratified, my life's Partner will feel a tranquility without which,
even our little Hermitage, & Great Book Room cannot make
him completely happy.—

[*the second leaf is missing*]

424   [West Humble], 5 October 1801

To Esther (Burney) Burney

A.L. (Diary MSS. vi. 5260–[61], Berg), 5 Oct. 1801
Double sheet small 4to 2pp. *pmk* DARKING 6 ⟨1802⟩ wafer
Addressed: Mrs. Burney, / Beaumont Street, / Devonshire Place / London—
Endorsed by EBB *in pencil*: Received / Oct 5
Endorsed by EBB *in ink*: 1801
Edited by FBA, p. 1 (5260), *date retraced*: Octʳ 5—1801
Edited also by CFBt *and the* Press.

Octʳ 5—1801

We shall have your kindest & warmest wishes I well know,
my dearest Esther, upon this Peace—which, if ratified,¹ will

---

³ The preliminaries were ratified in Paris on 5 October and in London on the
10th (*London Gazette Extraordinary*, 10 Oct.; *The Times*, 12 Oct. 1801).
424. ¹ See L. 423 nn. 1, 3.

2

carry us to the Country that gave birth to one of the most deserving of human sojourners. I cannot bear you should hear this but from myself—our plans are not yet settled—but we are all in Air—& M. d'A. almost in Heaven, with so fair a hope & prospect of visiting his paternal soil. We shall surely see you before we go,—see you all—if go we can—but we have yet taken no Measures, except internally: & politics may prevent any other—but I hope not, for it will be my delight to ᛁ pay by my alacrity in promoting his happiness, his extreme patience & forbearance in not breaking into mine, by going over during the War. I have now time for no more—I am inexpressibly occupied in *MIND*, though not yet in hands. Heaven bless you, my dearest Esther—My best Love to Mr B[urney] & dear good aunt Beckey,[2] whom we *MUST* embrace before our departure— should it take place.

425   [London, 12 October 1801]

M. d'Arblay

To Madame d'Arblay

A.L.S. (rejected Diary MSS. 5266–[69], Berg), Lundy
Double sheet 4to 3pp. *pmk* 12 OC .801 wafer
Addressed: Madame Darblay / Westhumble / near Dorking / Surry
Edited by FBA, p. 1, *top margin, dated and annotated*: ᛭ 12. Oct^r ⌐1800¬
1801 19/2 on An Interview with M. de *Lauriston*, when he came to England as Minister of Peace, from Buonaparte.

Printed here also is a text ('Un mot seulement, . . . leur exemple.') appearing on the *recto* of a fragment (2·3 to 3·0 × 7·3″) that had been cut from a letter of an unknown date and pasted (probably by CFBt) over lines (4 to 9 of the 10 lines) that FBA had obliterated at the beginning of this letter. As it seems to have been written by M. d'A early in Oct. 1801, it is printed here.
Edited also by CFBt *and the* Press.

2 Dr. Burney's sister Rebecca (1724–1809).

3

Lundy à 3ʰ passées
mourrant de faim

ᴦMʳ Vansittart[1] is not en ville, il est à Oxford et l'on ne sait pas encore quand il arrivera, mais la lettre de Madᵉ Locke parviendra demain matin, ainsi qu'une 1ᵉʳᵉ. Je lui ai ecrit pour le prier d'adresser sa reponse (if any) to Mʳ Locke at Woodlands. J'ai vendu à 67[2] J'ai laissé à Mʳ Coutts[3] une lettre d'attorney pour vendre &c. Le 600 £ restant perdu, en notre absence, je lui ai remis 80 £ sterling dont j'ai le reçu. je lui ai laissé aussi ta recette.ᴨ

En revenant de chez James, j'ai rencontré au Pall-mall, Mʳ et Mᵈᵉ Angerstein.[4] ᴦ*Jamais je n'aurais reconnu cette derniere,*ᴨ elle m'a fait vingt signes avant que je pusse *deviner* d'où ils venoient, ᴦet cependant elle était tout près de moi;ᴨ | j'ai reconnu son mari et me suis approché du Phaëton qui était arreté. On n'est pas meilleurs et plus aimables que tous deux ne l'ont été. Ils voulaient absolument que j'allasse, fait comme j'etais, coucher à Woodlands. En les quittant j'avais le coeur serré et me suis senti les yeux mouillés. mon dieu que la santé de cette chere A — m'inquiete!

Avant tout cela j'avais passé chez Lauriston,[5] et j'y avais

425. [1] A friend of the Angersteins and the Lockes, Nicholas Vansittart (1766–1851), M.A. (Oxon. 1791), M.P. (1796–1823), P.C. (1805), F.R.S. (1822), cr. Baron Bexley (1823). He had recently returned from Denmark (Mar. 1801), where he had temporarily filled the post of Minister Plenipotentiary, replacing Lord Robert Fitzgerald (iv, L. 292 n. 47), Mrs. Charles Locke's half-brother, whose term had come to an end on 1 Aug. 1800. An eminent financier, he was in this year appointed Joint Secretary to the Treasury. For his career and character, abilities and benevolence, see *DNB* and his obituary, *AR* xciii (1851), 261.

[2] According to *AR* xliii (1801), 'Appendix to the Chronicle', 183, the 3 per cent consols ranged between 59¼ and 69½ during the month of October. For d'Arblay's investments in 3 per cents, see iv, p. 57.

[3] Thomas Coutts (1735–1822), banker.

[4] John Angerstein (c. 1773–1858) and his wife Amelia *née* Locke, who, since their marriage on 2 Oct. 1799 (iv, L. 262 n. 3; L. 332 n. 1) lived at Cumberland Place, Regent's Park, and at Woodlands, Blackheath. Occupied by the Angerstein family as a country villa from 1774 to 1870, Woodlands is still standing. See Cyril Fry, iv, L. 333 n. 2.

[5] Jacques-Alexandre-Bernard Law (1768–1828), comte de Lauriston (1808, 1815), pair de France (1815), marquis de Lauriston (1817), maréchal de France (1823). Like d'Arblay, he had begun his active military career as a lieutenant en 2ᵉ in the artillery regiment at Toul (1785) but, unlike d'Arblay, who in the difficult years 1788–9 had transferred to the Paris National Guard and in 1791, to the infantry, Lauriston remained with the artillery and with an apparent change of loyalties (explained by FBA, *Memoirs*, iii. 304–11) became in 1800 aide-de-camp to the First Consul in the reserve army in Italy. Sent on a diplomatic mission to Copenhagen in 1801, he was entrusted on 4 Oct. 1801, the month of this letter, with the signed ratification of the Preliminaries to the Peace, which he had just

laissé un billet dicté par l'intimité, resolu de n'être reçu que sur ce pied, et me disant: s'il ne me reçoit pas, il sera bien changé! Dès le premier mot j'ai vu à la mine bien differente d'une espece de Valet de chambre ou plutot *maître des ceremonies*, qu'il etoit le même. En effet | il s'est precipité dans mes bras, et nous nous sommes tenus assez longtems tellement serrés l'un contre l'autre que l'homme qui l'habilloit n'a pu s'empêcher de partager notre emotion. J'en ai été plus que content. Demain je dejeune avec lui à 9ʰ et demain aussi, je te conterai tout plus en detail.

Il se chargera de toutes les lettres que je voudrai lui donner. Eh bien ne commence-tu pas à avoir un peu de respect pour moi?

Adieu ma chere, chere amie, à demain.

Λ

J'embrasse toi et mon petit. que je suis faché d'avoir manqué mon ami Lally.⁶

[Fragment of a letter by M. d'A of about this time]

Un mot seulement,⁷ ma bonne amie, et cela pour te dire que la lettre que mon ami Boinville⁸ a jugé à propos de suprimer etait de la Fayette qui m'engageait à rentrer; et me mandait qu'il avait obtenu pour Siccard et la Colombe de rentrer dans leur grade avec un traitement qui serait aussi le mien: je me decidais à suivre leur exemple.⁹

brought to England (*London Gazette Extraordinary*, 10 Oct.; *The Times*, 12 Oct. 1801). FBA made much of this meeting in *Memoirs* (*supra*).
⁶ Trophime-Gérard, comte de Lally-Tolendal (i, L. 17 n. 21; Intro., ii, p. xvii; iv *passim*; Intro., p. xl).
⁷ See headnote, above.
⁸ Jean-Baptiste Chastel de Boinville (1756–1813), Charles Sicard (1763–1842), and Louis-Saint-Ange Morel de La Colombe (1755–*post* 1801), all members of Lafayette's *état-major*, had accompanied Lafayette in his flight from France in August 1792. Sicard went eventually to England (see ii, p. 13) and La Colombe to the United States, where he had formerly served with Lafayette. For the diplomatic mission of Chastel de Boinville to England in 1789, his residence there, his marriage to Harriet Collins (*c.* 1773–1847), their support of Lafayette, and her 'radical salon' at Bracknell, see Kenneth N. Cameron, *Shelley and his Circle, 1773–1822* (4 vols., 1961–70), iii. 275–8.
⁹ Mistakenly believing that Sicard and La Colombe had been reinstated in their army ranks and given discharges with pension, d'Arblay wrote to Louis-Alexandre Berthier (1753–1815), ministre de la Guerre (11 Nov. 1799–4 Apr. 1800; 8 Oct. 1800–9 Aug. 1807), requesting the same 'justice'. Two drafts of such a letter are extant in the Berg Collection (NYPL). The rougher draft, in which the names Sicard and La Colombe actually appear, makes a point of d'Arblay's 28 years of

To Charles Burney

A.L. (Osborn), *n.d.*
Double sheet 8vo 1 p. *pmks* DARKING 22 OC ⟨18⟩01 22 OCT
1801 wafer
Addressed: Dʳ Charles Burney, / Greenwich, / Kent.
Docketed in pencil, p. 1: 1801

Wednesday
afternoon.

My dearest Carlos,

Not at all knowing how to direct to M. d'A at this moment,
& knowing him very uneasy about our Pet[1]—I beseech you,
unless you have reason to think him, as I hope, returning, send
off this very scrawl after him, to let him know the little rogue
has ⟨just⟩ eat a wing of a fowl, & quarrelled with me for with
holding the Leg. I see he will recover as rapidly, the fever once
turned its crisis, as he grew ill.

I would I could hear as much of your poor Rosette—to whom
my kind Love, & to Charles—& kind Compᵗˢ to Mrs. Bicknell.[2]

Should M. d'A be returned—I know my kind Carlos will
still be glad of this intelligence

service and his plans to return to France with his family, and FBA, in docketing
the letter in later years, explains further that it was a faithful copy: "'Tis the original
sketch of a Letter of M. d'Arblay's to Berthier, taken to France by General Lauriston, and to be delivered by M. de Narbonne.' A shorter version, putting the case
in general terms, is dated 2 Oct. 1801. When General Lauriston left London on
14 October, he took with him, supposedly, some version of d'Arblay's petition,
which he was to deliver to the comte de Narbonne to take to Berthier.

426. [1] Alexander d'Arblay, now nearly seven years old.

[2] The story of the foundling named Sabrina Sidney (i, L. 7 n. 18), whom
Thomas Day resolved to educate for a wife (see *DNB*), a story related also by
Richard Lovell Edgeworth (*Memoirs*), FBA retold with considerable augmentation
of detail in her French Exercise Book I, pp. [57–79], Berg. 'Enfin, il [Day] se
disoit, que rien ne doit rendre un homme aussi heureux qu'une femme qu'il avoit
lui-même preparé pour être la compagne de sa vie, *qu'il avoit* lui même appris ses
propres idées sur les devoirs et les douceurs de l'état conjugale. As that time approached she simply disappeared ('tout d'un coup'), and what was his despair to
find that 'elle l'avait quitté pour épouser un autre'—namely, John Bicknell (?1746–
87), a barrister-at-law who, dying two years later and in debt, left her with two
infant sons to educate.

It was William Seward who, finding her placed 'comme une Bonne, dans une
petite école', recommended her to Charles Burney for his school and, the bargain
struck, Charles on his part found her 'une amie fidelle à tous ses interêts, Elle, de

427   [West Humble, *c.* 21 October 1801]

To Cassandra Cooke

A.L.S. (Osborn), *n.d.*
Single sheet 8vo   2 pp.   with a binding tape along right margin, p. 2
Docketed in unknown hand in ink, p. 1: *Madame D'Arblay* [*in pencil*:] Fanny
Burney [*in red ink*:] 31   Authoress of Evelina Cecilia &c &c

Nothing short of a nearly continual expectation of getting to Bookham, could have prevented my writing my situation to my ever kind Mrs. Cooke.¹ I *must* promise myself still I shall accomplish that point before my departure, should it take place this winter. But we are fixed not to risk, at such a season, a long Voyage for our little boy, &, as yet, we have found difficulties in the way of a passport by Dover that ┃ keeps our ultimate resolutions suspended. M. d'Arblay, for the 4ᵗʰ time, is absent upon this business. My poor Alex is just now ill,—but amending —from a severe attack of fever. I am much hurried, & much perplexed—but ever more truly, & with all my heart, m[y] dear Madam, your most obliged

      & affectionate F d'A.

    If we go, my good sister Broome will come hither, for a one night's journey, to see us first.

    My kindest Respects to Mr. Cooke, & comps to Miss Cooke & her Brothers.

coté, a trouvée dans celui . . . un ami qui l'estime, un bienfaiteur pour sa fortune, et un gardien et un tuteur pour ses Enfans . . . rien ne peut surpasser la douçeur ni l'utilité de leur liaison. Il peut tout confié à ses soins, à sa prevoyance, à sa fidelité, et elle, elle est toûjours bien sure d'être traitée par lui comme son egal, son amie, et une personne dont les virtues sont honorées autant que les talens sont utiles.'

427. ¹ For the Revd. Samuel Cooke, vicar of Great Bookham, and his family, see iii, L. 122 n. 8; and iv, L. 263 n. 7.

To M. d'Arblay

A.L. (rejected Diary MSS. 5264–[65], Berg), Oct.
Single sheet 4to 2 pp. Page 1 has 15 lines retraced by FBA *pmks*
DARKING OC⟨ ⟩1801 wafer
Addressed: Alex. d'Arblay, Esqr, / At Mr. Burney's, / Beaumont Street, /
Devonshire place
Edited by FBA, p. 1 (5264), *annotated and dated*: (20) 1801. Written imme-
diately after our First separation, for M. d'A. to revisit his own Country
Edited also by CFBt *and the* Press.

Oct.

Mr. Locke came just now to tempt me to an evening,—with
him & Augusta;[1]—but I am best—a little while—with only my
cher-cher Ami's own Representative—. His list Mr. Locke says
includes all the portraits he *possesses*—whatever else you can
procure, to add to it, will gratify him. I impatiently long for
to-morrow Morning—[*tear*] the next Morning—& the next, &
the next!—till I hear you are safe landed.[2]—Believe me, I will
then revive, & think only of the happiness of your excellent
Uncle, your Aunt—& affectionate Cousins, & many fond
friends, in again embracing you.[3]—The delight, too, you will
experience at the first sight of your own Coast—at the first
tread on its shores!—& the entrance into your natal town—
I feel all this—& I never think of it but with a pleasure that
makes me present at every meeting—This must be my solace
for your absence—THIS, & the recollection of your kindness—
Your tenderness—all the happiness I owe you—& the hope of
all you have in store for me. Heaven ever bless you. |

Mr. Lock was all tender goodness & sympathy, & could not
rest without making me this immediate & consolatory visit.
Poor Mrs. Lock has caught cold, but hopes quickly to nurse it

---

428. [1] William Locke (1732–1810) of Norbury Park, and his daughter Augusta
(1775–1845). For the Locke family, see further L. 472 n. 2; and *Locks of Norbury*.
[2] Between 21 and 26 October, M. d'Arblay, evidently assured of a passport to
France, had returned to West Humble, where it was decided that FBA must
remain to nurse Alexander through a child's illness, and that M. d'A must set out
alone. He was now on his way.
[3] See iv, L. 381 and *passim*; genealogical table, iii, facing p. 1.

off. Speak for me to what you see of my Friends. And don't carry off my Letters for my dear Father & sister to France— How I long to hear about your passport! what a joy to me should it be for Dover! our dear Boy has eaten his Egg with great delight at Noon, & broth at Dinner. He told me just now, that the reason why he chopt his hair in that manner, was that he thought he would make it look more like papa's wig!— once more Heaven ever bless

you, my Heart's best—& fondest Friend!

429 [London, 26 *or* 27 October 1801]

M. d'Arblay
To Madame d'Arblay

A.L. (Berg), *n.d.*
Single sheet 4to   1 p.   *pmks*   BEAUMONT / STREET   27 OC .801 wafer
Addressed: Madame Darblay / Westhumble / near Dorking / Surry
Edited by FBA, p. 1, *top margin, dated and annotated*: 27. oct⸢ ⸢1802⸣ 1801 ⸢N⸣ 1⸣ 21/2 THE QUEEN
A folder (double sheet 4to, N° 4*) at one time enclosing the letters of* 1801, FBA *annotated, probably in the* 1820s: Parts / of mutual / Letters / Between / Alexandre Jean Baptiste / Piochard d'Arblay / And Frances / in the year / 1801. / preserved to let our dear son / Alexander Charles Louis Piochard d'Arblay / (&, I hope, his progeny) / Learn something of our history / at that period, / The First of our anxious separation / between England & France.

De chez M⸢r⸣ Otto[1] en attendant qu'il vise mon passeport.

J'arrive de Chelsea où ton pere qui m'a parfaitement bien reçu m'a dit qu'à l'instant même où tu lui ecrivais en detail ce qu'il approuve sans restriction, il etait à preparer une lettre, dans la quelle il comptait te demander des nouvelles de Paris, où tu avais eu tout le tems d'arriver. [xxxxx 7 *lines*]

429. [1] Ludwig Wilhelm Otto (1754–1817), comte de Mosloy (1805), French Commissioner in London, who was entrusted by the First Consul with the negotiations for peace, resided at this time in Hereford Street near Portman Square. See Warren, pp. xxix, xxxvi–xxxvii.

Actuellement je cours chez dumergue² qui vient de dire à Bourdois³ qu'il sortait de chez La Reine où il avait beaucoup été question de nous en presence de Mᵉˡˡᵉ Planta⁴ qui s'etait mélée de la conversation.

La Reine a la premiere dit à Dumergue: 'Mʳ D'A. — va donc en france et emmene Mᵈᵉ D'A — ?' — 'Je demande pardon à S.M. Mʳ D'A — part seul — ' 'Non je sais que Mᵈᵉ D. part avec lui.' — 'J'ose assurer à S.M. qu'elle est mal informée. je suis sûr que Mʳ D'Ar — part seul.'

La Reine s'est informée de mille choses qui ont rapport à mon existence en France, et Dumergue, qui, par parenthes — n'a jamais entendu parler [de] moi que depuis deux ans environ — l'a *ASSURÉE* que tu avais fait un très bon mariage, et est entré dans des details dont il n'a pas la moindre connoissance, fesant de moi des miens &c. &c le plus grand eloge possible.!! La Reine lui a demandé s'il pensait que je retrouverais quelque chose en France; Il a repondu qu'il n'en doutait point; et S.M. à mis fin à la conversation en disant qu'elle en serait charmée.

Voilà ce que vient de me dire Bourdois, et je cours en attendant le diner savoir tout par moi même. Je t'embrasse. Ecris vite.

[xxxxx ½ *line*]
[xxxxx 4 *lines marginal writing*]

430   [London, 2⟨7⟩ October 1801]

M. d'Arblay
To Madame d'Arblay

A.L. (Berg), *n.d.*, probably posted with L. 429
Single sheet 4to   2 pp.
Edited by FBA, p. 1, *top margin, annotated and dated*: 27—octʳ ⌐1802⌐   1801
⌐No. 2⌐   22   The Queen [*encircled*]

² Charles Francis Dumergue (*c.* 1738–1814), dentist (1785–1814) to the Prince of Wales and in 1814 to the Duchess of York (R.H.I., Windsor) as well as to Queen Charlotte (*Later Corr. Geo. III*, iv. 286). Born in the province of Angoumois, France, but naturalized on 28 Mar. 1793, he lived in Hanover Square and, later, Piccadilly. See *List of Naturalization Acts*, Huguenot Society, Quarto Series, xxvii (1923), 198 and *GM* lxxxiv (1814), 702.

³ Lambert-*Antoine* Bourdois (iv *passim*), originally of Joigny, but now living at Sand Place, Dorking, and 1 Clarges Street, London.

⁴ Margaret Planta (i, L. 3 n. 2), English governess to the younger princesses.

M. Dumergue[1] etant occupé, je t'ecris de son sallon ce qu'il m'a été impossible de te mander hier. Tu sais le principal, c.à.d. que je pars. Voici les details. Nous n'arrivâmes hier qu'à 2 heures; et je craignais bien qu'il ne fût trop tard. Par un coup de fortune, comme j'allais à l'office de Lord Hauksbury[2] je rencontrai Mr F. Moore en grand deuil, ce qui dabord m'effraya. mais je sus bientôt que son Pere va beaucoup mieux, [xxxxx 2 *lines*]. Quant à mon affaire Mr F. Moore[3] quoiqu'occupé par dessus les yeux [xxxxx 1 *line*] n'a pas perdu un instant p[r] en parler. [xxxxx 1 *line*] Instruit de la resolution definitive que nous avions prise, et du besoin que j'avais de faire prolonger le tems porté sur mon passe-port, M[r] M[oore] me dit [:] je suis contraint d'entrer dans la maison que vous voyez. Si vous pouvez m'attendre cinq minutes, Je suis à vous et vous conduirai à l'Allien office. En effet bientôt il reparut, et me dit: Pardon mais j'ai une lettre indispensable à expedier, elle ne sera pas longue, et sur le champ nous ferons expedier votre affaire. Au moment d'entrer au Bureau des affaires etrangeres, je vis quelqu'un qui me saluait et m'aborda. C'etait un ch[ier] de Malthe, le Ch[ier] de la Bentynaie,[4] ami de Ste Croix,[5] et fort lié avec Lord Harvey,[6] qu'il attendoit . Mr Moore, me voyant arreté, dit aussitôt à un jeune Clerc. Vous amenerez M[r] dans ma chambre aussitôt qu'il sera libre, et me saluant d'un air tout à fait aimable il me quitta. Le Ch[r] de la B. me dit qu'aussitôt

430. [1] See L. 429 n. 2.

[2] Robert Banks Jenkinson (iv, L. 293 n. 5), *styled* Lord Hawkesbury (1796), at this time Foreign Secretary.

[3] Francis or 'Frank' Moore (1767–1854), 4th son of John Moore, M.D. (ii, L. 68 n. 41) and brother of Sir John Moore of Corunna fame, was at this time a senior clerk in the Foreign Office. As assistant secretary (Nov. 1801–Mar. 1802) to Lord Cornwallis, British plenipotentiary in the negotiations at Amiens, he carried the treaty that had been signed on 25 March to London (*The Times*, 30 Mar.; and *Later Corr. Geo. III*, iv. 20). It was in this capacity that up to this date he was able to carry letters to and from France. See also Oman *passim*.

[4] Agathon-Marie-René (1758–92), chevalier de La Bintinaye, and his brother François-Marie (1751–1816), the abbé, had come to England in 1791, when they visited Edmund Burke and others (i, L. 5 n. 20) in the interest of the princes. Agathon was drowned in the Thames in 1792. A third brother Jean-Baptiste-Simon-Marc (b. 13 Sept. 1761, at Rennes), chevalier de l'Ordre de Malte, a cavalry officer, was probably the 'Ch[ier] de Malthe' whom d'Arblay encountered at this time in London.

[5] Louis-Claude Bigot de Sainte-Croix (1744–1805), ministre des Affaires étrangères (1–10 Aug. 1792), had emigrated to London, where he lived until his death.

[6] Frederick William Hervey (1769–1859), *styled* Lord Hervey (1796), 5th Earl of Bristol (1803), at this time Under-Secretary of State (Foreign) in the Addington Ministry. See also iv, L. 269 n. 11.

qu'il aurait dit deux mots à Lord H. que le Groom attendait avec un cheval de main, il comptait aller voir Ste Croix, que si mon affaire etait promptement expediée, il serait charmé de faire cette course avec moi, parceque il etait bien aise de causer un instant sur ce qui l'interessait &c. &c. J'acceptai. Arrivé chez Mr M. je fus reçu dans un appartem^t vaste et très agreable, et, sa lettre finie, nous nous rendions à l'Allien-office. [xxxxx 3 *lines*] où après avoir encore tenté envain de faire substituer Douvre à Gravesend, fait effacer le terme des 10 jours ecoulés, et ecrire au dessus *twenty*. Je le remercie et nous partons, moi fort content comme bien tu penses. Tout en retournant, à son office j'eus le tems d'arranger *tout* p^r *NOTRE CORRESPONDANCE* aussitôt son arrivée en France; et lui donnai mon adresse à Paris c.à.d celle de Lajard.[7] C'est lui même qu'un

Je suis interrompu, ou p^r mieux dire j'ai été interrompu par Dumergue Voyons dabord vos dents — oh! vous n'en avez pas eu trop de soin — mais je les brosse tous les jours — oui avec une brosse de soie — je l'ai dans ma poche — à merveille cà n'vaut pas l'diable. — tenez en voici une, mettez la dans votre poche non — prenez ce miroir, trempez la brosse comme cà, seulement p^r l'humecter, et p^r que ce sel s'y attache frottez bien, ne craîgnez pas de faire saigner vos gencives, avant huit jours elles ne saigneront plus, et seront dures comme la corne d'un cheval — dans quelque tems vous prendrez une brosse encore plus forte

La reine disait à Melle Planta — Croyez vous que Mad^e Darblay soit encore à Londre? Elle doit être partie à present. — Madame. ai-je dit aussitôt, je puis assurer vôtre Majesté que M^e D'ar — n'est pas parti, il [|] m'a fait l'honneur de m'ecrire &c — — moi j'ai pris cette occasion de dire de vous tout ce que je pense — quoique vous n'en ayez pas besoin, j'ai dit enfin &c — &c. La Reine a dit que vous aviez bien raison de tenter de recouvrer quelque chose — qu'il serait coupable de ne pas le faire — qu'elle souhaitait de tout son coeur que vous puissiez reussir. &c. Elle a dit aussi que vous aviez un bien joli enfant qui annonçait beaucoup d'esprit. [xxxxx 4 *lines*]

---

[7] Pierre-Auguste Lajard (iv, L. 291 n. 5).

M. d'Arblay
To Madame d'Arblay

A.L. (Berg), *n.d.*
Originally a double sheet 4to, of which FBA later discarded the second
leaf   2 pp.
Edited by FBA, p. 1, *top margin, dated and annotated:* ⁑   2⟨6⟩. Oct. 1801
1801   20/1   de M. *d'Arnaudin*

Greenwiche Mardy soir entre 8 et 9.

Je te remercie, mon amie, des *demi* bonnes nouvelles que j'ai
reçues de toi *Ce* matin chez Ste Croix.[1] Tu remarqueras que je
venais d'ecrire hier dont j'ai fait le *ce* sous ligné. Cela seul te
prouvera combien le tems me parait long quand je ne suis pas
auprés de toi. Je suis charmé de savoir que notre petit est mieux,
mais fort inquiet d'apprendre que cette maudite fievre ne l'a
pas quitté. Hier en descendant de la voiture qui m'avait porté
en Charring-cross, je m'arretai un instant devant la boutique
d'un libraire pour regarder un *camilla* trés bien relié et j'allais
entrer p^r l'ouvrir et regarder si je m'appercevrois de quelques
changemens,[2] lorsque je m'entendis nommer par un *gentleman*
qui me dit: ne me reconnaissez vous pas? — pardon Monsieur,
dutout! — comment vous ne vous rappelez pas d'Arnaudin.[3] —
beaucoup mais — mais vous ne voulez pas que ce soit moi —

431. [1] This is L. 438, probably carried to 'chez Ste Croix' (L. 430 n. 5) by EBB.
[2] M. d'A was evidently looking for the second (and revised) edition of *Camilla*,
which was not to appear, however, until 1802 (see iv, L. 314 n. 5; and L. 316 n. 5).
[3] Henri-Étienne d'Arnaudin (b. 5 May 1749 at Versailles), ingénieur (1770),
lieutenant (1776), was enrolled (15 Sept. 1791) in the Vivarais Infantry Regiment as
an 'ingénieur géographe militaire', becoming capitaine de compagnie (15 Dec.
1791). Trained, like so many of d'Arblay's friends, at Metz, he was employed in
1792 as 'adjutant' in the Armée du centre, but transferred later with the rest of
the *état-major* to the Armée du nord. Appearing (*post* Mar. 1793) in a list of the
1st battalion of the 71st as capitaine in the 'Armée Dumouries', he was by his own
account (or that of M. d'A) promoted to the rank of colonel, and he was with
Dumouriez (ii, L. 67 n. 7), as he says, when that general, defeated by the Austrians
at Neerwinden in Belgium (18 Mar. 1793), deserted the Republican cause and
fled into the Austrian camp.
   Of his subsequent career we have only his own account (*supra*), but that eventually he was attached to the *état-major* of the Duke of York is borne out by his
work *Mémoires des Campagnes de 1793–4*, a manuscript copy of which is in the
Library of the War Office, London. See Alfred H. Burne, *The Noble Duke of York*
(1949), p. 337.

pardon j'entens fort bien à present votre voix: maîs actuellement même que vous vous êtes nommé, je dois en conscience
vous dire que je ne vous reconnais pas du tout: cette perruque
si en avant, et votre air tellement anglais — Bref c'est moi et
j'ai tant de plaisir à vous retrouver qu'il faut bien me permettre
de desirer vous le voir partager — quant à cela mon cher
d'Arnaudin vous auriez tort d'en douter; mais que faites vous
ici. (ce Mr Arnaudin etait un de mes adjoints à l'armée de L.F.)
Ce que je fais ici, ma foi — assez bien mes affaires — j'en suis
charmé; avez vous quelques projets en ce moment — aucun —
eh bien nous pourrions nous donner rendez vous pour diner
ensemble — trés volontiers — fort bien, j'ai quelques emplettes
à faire et sur les 4 heures — si vous n'avez que des emplettes et
pas d'autres affaires, moi qui n'en ai aucune je puis être avec
vous — nous causerons — de tout mon coeur. je vais en leicester
square — àllons; nous passons devant mon logement; Peu de
tems aprés votre départ, je fus fait Colonel et après la bataille
de Nerwinde je passai avec dumourier chez les Autrichiens, en
conservant mon grade et mes appointemens. Le Duc D'York
desira m'avoir avec lui, et depuis ce tems je ne l'ai pas quitté. je
jouis en ce moment de ma demi-paye mais je crains beaucoup
que ce traitement ne nous soit pas continuée à la paix definitive,
ce qui me ferait d'autant plus de tort que si j'étais resté au
service d'autriche, j'aurais encore mon traitement entier que
mes camarades conservent. (Tu sauras le reste quand nous
nous verrons)

�◃Mercredy matin, revenant de Woodlands

Rien de fini ma bonne amie, et je ne sais en verité quand tout
ceci finira. Mr Angerstein n'a point vu Mr King[4] hier comme il
me l'avait promis. Il croit que le tems de 10 jours est de
rigueur; et ce point si essentiel vu la mauvaise santé de mon
petit me console de ce nouveau retard. Au reste il m'a beaucoup
promis d'insister pour avoir 15 jours si cela n'est pas absolument impossible. C'est ce matin qu'il doit surement voir Mr
King et lui demander instament un passeport.▹

(Mercredy à midy) [xxxxx 2½ *lines*]

[4] John King (1759–1830), Under-Secretary of State in the Home Department
(*Later Corr. Geo. III*, iii. xxx).

[West Humble, 27 October 1801]

To M. d'Arblay

A.L. (Barrett, Eg. 3693, ff. 232–3b, with P-tab, f. 231), *n.d.*
Double sheet 4to   4 pp. *pmks* DARKING   28 OCT 1801   wafer
Addressed: A d'Arblay Esqr— / at Mr. Burney's, / Beaumont Street, /
Devonshire Place / London.
Edited by FBA, p.1, *dated obviously from the postmark and annotated*: ⁂   28
Oct. / West Humble—1801.   1 / 24
Edited also by CFBt(?)

The Trees for Mr. Angerstein & Mr. Thompson[1] of one—
two—or three years of age.
Those for Mr. Lock, of only one years, & the Peach Trees
worked upon *Almond* Stocks.
And a dozen Rose Trees for Mrs. Lock, of any recommended
varieties.

Dearly as I love Mr. Lock & his sweet wife—I most devoutly
hope my own Heart's beloved Friend will be set out, & not
receive this commission—it may easily follow. But every
moment's retard of going, is a retard of returning. It would be
cruel to tell you how I miss you already, & wish you back—&
yet, it seems ungenerous, if not unjust, to forbear—for *WHY*
do I miss—& so wish for you?—God Speed you, my most dear,
to our arms!
Your Boy gets better—but ¦ is so thin, & still pale, I every
minute see reason to rejoice in our final determination. Mr.
Cooke has been here this Morning, & I have now the certificate

432. [1] Frequent visitors to Norbury Park, John Thomson (d. Jan. 1839) and his
wife Charlotte *née* Jacob (d. 18 May 1824) of Salisbury are mentioned casually in
Mrs. Locke's Journals (Barrett, Eg. 3697, ff. 95–178b). A member of a firm that
traded extensively with Russia, Thomson had purchased Waverley Abbey in
1796 and according to CB (A.L.S. to Mrs. Crewe, Berg, 27 Sept. 1802) farmed
'very rationally & scientifically: a speculative & experimental cultivator of Soil'.
His daughter Harriet Poulett (*c.* 1783–1837) was to marry on 18 Apr. 1805 Mr.
Locke's third son, the Revd. George Locke (1771–1864), at this time curate at
Mickleham but later (1803) rector of Lee, Kent. On 22 July 1814 Thomson was to
take by Royal Licence the names 'Buncombe and Poulett'. His third son Charles
(1799–1841), M.P. (1826–39), P.C. (1830), G.C.B. (1841), and Governor-General of
Canada (1839–41), was created (1840) Baron Sydenham of Sydenham, Kent, and
of Toronto, Canada. See *GEC* and *AR* lxxxi (1839), 319.

of our Alex's baptism.² I shall keep it, unless you direct me to do otherwise, for I cannot risk it to the post in utter uncertainty if this may find you. *This* I hazard, because you [ma]y perhaps not leave Town till after the Post. Mr. Cooke sends you every good & kind wish. Mr. Locke came again today,— & I could not refuse to take an airing with him, because a visit would have made him lose that salutary exercise: though I am still but ill disposed for leaving Alex—& home. But Mr. Locke is irresistable. I had another Clerical visit this Morning—Mr. Andrews,³ who stayed here an Hour, & was very instructive & intelligent, & particularly ǀ amiable & pleasing. — — our little Rogue is at this minute entertaining himself with reciting *Qui se batte*⁴ with sword in hand, & the attitude of fencing—& when he adds *et s'enfuit*—he runs off, helter skelter, to the furthest end of the room, & there quietly stands, to say—*Du Moins a cette chance, que, s'il le veut,* — — and then he starts back to his supposed antagonist, & resuming his threatening posture, calls out '*il recommence!*—'

When Mrs. Noel⁵ said to him—'You'll be sadly at a loss in France, my dear, for you don't know french.' 'Yes, I do! he cried, I know four lines of Poetry!—And they are my Papa's own making!' — —

⌜Am I to mind Mathematics and fr⟨ench⟩ with her—he makes his demand?⌝

If you receive this—Speak for Me in the kindest manner to all our dear Friends—especially to my dearest sister—Heaven preserve you, my beloved! ǀ

'Tis impossible to tell you the delight the joy with which I read your intimation of our corresponding through Mr. Moore⁶ —how good, how kind he is! Mr. Lock was as much gratified, when I told it him, as if it had been an engagement for his own hearing from his Fredy.—

---

² The Revd. Samuel Cooke (iv, L. 263 n. 7), vicar of Great Bookham (1769–1820), had baptized Alexander Charles Louis Piochard d'Arblay (b. 18 Dec. 1794) on 11 Apr. 1795 (iii, L. 158 n. 1).
³ The Revd. Gerrard Andrewes (1750–1825), M.A. (1779), D.D. (1807), was rector of Mickleham (1800–13), of St. James's, Piccadilly (1802), Dean of Canterbury (1809–25), vicar of Great Bookham (1820–1). See M.I., parish church (St. Nicholas), Great Bookham.
⁴ From John Towneley's translation (1757) of *Hudibras*.
⁵ Unidentified, though the parish registers of Mickleham show members of a Neal (or Nowell) family.
⁶ Frank Moore (L. 430 n. 3).

433   Gravesend, 28 [October 1801]
M. d'Arblay
To Madame d'Arblay

A.L. (Berg), 28
Double sheet 4to   4 pp.   *pmk*   29 OCT 1801   wafer
Addressed: Madame Darblay / Westhumble / near Dorking / Surry
Edited by FBA, p. 1, *top margin, dated and annotated*: oct^r 28 [*retraced* 1801]
23/1   Mrs. C. Burney / The Locks—Alex
Docketed, p. 4: Octr 28.—1801—

Mercredy soir 28 à *Gravesend*
en descendant de voiture.

Ne m'ccris plus, ma bonne amie, parce que j'ai dejà retenu
une place sur un bâtiment qui j'espere partira après demain.
[xxxxx 6 *lines*]

Je compte sur une lettre de toi demain, et serais cruellement
dejoué si je n'en avais point. Celle que tu m'as ecrite hier
mardy,[1] m'est parvenue grace à cette chere Mad^e Burney qui
a eu la bonté de me l'apporter dans l'auberge même à Charring
Cross pendant que j'avalais un morceau à la hâte. Comment
crois tu que j'ai reconnu cette attention de veritable soeur? J'ai
continué à manger comme un affamé et ne l'ai pas même
reconduit à une voiture dans la quelle elle avait laissé je crois
Maria et Fanny,[2] pour venir elle même me donner ta lettre à la
table où j'etais et où je suis resté assis. En verité j'en suis en ce
moment | d'une honte qui me fait mal. C'est tout au plus je
crois si je lui ai fait la plus legere excuse. Certainement je n'en
peus trouver dans la faim qui me devorait, ni dans le peu de
minutes que j'avais pour essayer de l'appaiser. J'aime mieux
croire que j'avais un peu perdu la tête et veritablement outre
la peine que j'eprouve en fesant la moindre absence de notre
chere Trio, à plus forte raison en m'en eloignant pour cinq
semaines, j'avais en cet instant les yeux sur cette phrase de ta

433. [1] This is FBA's letter of Tuesday 27 Oct. (L. 432), which, as the London postmark and address show, would have been delivered at Beaumont Place on the
28th. EBB then took it to M. d'A at what must have been the Golden Cross Inn at
Charing Cross, from which coaches set out.
    [2] In all probability EBB's daughters Maria Bourdois and Fanny Burney (Intro.,
i, p. lxix).

lettre. *I every minute see reason to rejoice in our final determination, He is so thin & still pale* &c.

Bien heureusement les details qui suivent ont un peu diminué mon inquietude. God bless *him!* God bless *you,* my dear dear soul! God bless too my dearest kindest friend Mrs Locke! En un mot, God bless them *all!* Ce n'est pas de sang froid que je quitte cette Isle où j'ai trouvé ce que tant de personnes cherchent en vain, ce que si peu de gens savent conserver quand ils en jouissent. Puissè-je ne jamais le perdre et de plus en plus m'en rendre digne!

Amen!

[xxxxx 3 *lines* p. 2]
[xxxxx 2½ *lines* p. 3]
J'ai bien esperé que tu serais aussi contente que moi de l'obligeance de Mr F. Moore. [xxxxx 2½ *lines*]
[xxxxx 4 *broken lines, F.* Moore's *address*]
Je suis bien sur que quelque bonheur que j'aye lieu d'esperer dans mon voyage, le plus grand sera celui que me fera eprouver cette lettre, surtout si elle m'apporte de bonnes nouvelles de la santé de mon petit. Je te supplie de me dire la verité. Tout deguisement sur ta santé, sur la sienne, serait une veritable barbarie. C'est un appel que je fais à ta tendresse, et de ce moment, sûr que tu diras oui, je prens la resolution de croire avec / confiance / tout ce que tu me manderas.
[*On peut distinguer, à travers 8 lignes, oblitérées plus tard par Madame d'Arblay, quelques mots qui indiqueraient qu'il s'agit de préparatifs financiers pour le voyage de Monsieur d'Arblay.*] ¦ [xxxxx 4 *lines*] ne m'attens pas ma chere bonne amie avant le 10 ou 15 decembre; car je ne voudrais pas pour tout au monde te desappointer. Si je puis decement venir plutôt, Rapporte t'en à ton ami. [xxxxx 4 *or* 5 *words*] Dis à Mr Locke que je le remercie with heart & soul pour tous les airings qu'il t'a dejà fait, et qu'il te fera encore prendre, mais dis lui qu'il a beau être tous les jours plus *kind,* il ne faut pas qu'il compte que je puisse l'aimer jamais davantage. Et cette chere M^de Locke et William et sa femme³ et *tous,* oui tous. En verité je les porte dans mon coeur. [xxxxx 5 *lines*] ¦

Remember my dear Alex, you solemnly promised me to take care of Mama and not to stand in the damp. Kiss at least every

³ For the Locke family, see L. 472 n. 2.

18

morning & every night our best friend for me, besides what you intend to do for your self. Pray study your French heartily and go on in your writing. I hope you will send sometimes a specimen of your improved hand to your — —
[xxxxx 28 *lines, marginal and crosswriting*]

434   West Humble, 29 October 1801

To Mrs. Broome

A.L. (Berg), 29 Oct. 1801
Double sheet small 4to   4 pp.   *pmks* DARKING   3 NOV 1801   wafer
Addressed: Mrs. Broome, / Brighthelmstone, / Sussex.
Endorsed by CBFB: Sister d'arblay / Nov^r / 1801 / ans^d Novr 12th

West Hamble, Dorking.
29. oct. 1801

Your kind purpose, my ever kind Charlotte, of coming hither for a *chaste embrace* before my departure gave me infinite pleasure—& I caught at the offer with great eagerness—but our plan is now changed—& yours, therefore, I would wish altered for coming at a better season, unless convenience favours the present in any preferable manner. Our poor little Boy has had a violent fever & though it was short, & is now quite over, it has left him so much thinner than ever, & looks so much as if a Cold or Cough would demolish him, that we have relinquished letting him hazard such a voyage at this season, & I stay at home with him, to endeavour to nourish & strengthen him for a more favourable time. We do not, indeed, purpose going before June—& then we mean to remain 4 months. This is a far better project than our first—except for the separation it compels at present: M. d'Arblay could hardly outlive l a disappointment of seeing his Friends & Country immediately, & he has, also, some hopes of being able to rescue something from the wreck of his property. He has therefore set out alone: & mortified as we both are not to enter France, & see his Family together, my little Boy looks so unfit for a winter voyage, that I am hourly congratulating myself that we had

19

the fortitude to change our measures. In summer it will be delightful,—& such a new scene, with my satisfaction in making acquaintance with M. d'A.'s family & friends & Country, will be more beneficial to my spirits & happiness than any other event has any chance of being.

Miss Cooke[1] talks of going to Brighton, & if I can get this Letter to her I will.—Her worthy & respectable Father was here yesterday; & well; & always, as is Mrs. Cooke, sincere in enquiries & concern for your health & welfare. I am very sorry for the hints I have gathered of your alarms, & Mr. Br[oome]'s perplexities & provocations about a young person[2] who might have been a comfort to you all, if this perverse & disgraceful taste had not marred her own desire for any thing of a higher sort. I am sure Sophy[3] must have been a great pleasure to you— She is a very amiable Girl, & her gaiety has a Good humour & innocence that make her drollery & quaint fancies remarkably agreeable to me. She is very high in my Niece-favoritism.— And this brings me very naturally, & very heartily, to your dear Charlotte,[4] whom I love so sincerely & affectionately, & from whom I expect nothing but what is good & right, so fair & kind & proper is all I have either seen or heard of her. She will be, I hope, the model of her Sister. M. d'A. has seen your dear Clement,[5] who is well.

M. Bourdois & Maria charge me With Love & Compliments to you & Mr. Broome & Charlotte & Sophy, & still hope to see you all, notwithstanding the immediate course of the proposition no longer exists: but they will hold themselves

434. [1] Mary Cooke (iv, L. 263 n. 7).
[2] Probably Miriam Broome (*c.* 1781–*c.* 8 Sept. 1840), illegitimate daughter of Ralph Broome Sr. (1742–1805) by 'an Indian lady' (iv, L. 257 n. 11). Mentioned by Broome in his will (P.C.C. Nelson 251, pr. 10 Apr. 1805), on equal terms with his son Ralph and his daughter Miriam, is a third child, Amelia Margaret by name, perhaps his own child, perhaps Miriam's, then under the care of a nurse at Exmouth. In 1803 Broome arranged for Miriam to marry his nephew Ralph Broome (1781–1838), a lawyer whose somewhat motley career can be traced through the Law Lists (1809–23).
[3] EBB's daughter Sophia Elizabeth (1777–1856).
[4] Charlotte Francis (1786–1870).
[5] Clement Francis (1792–1829), at this time at CB Jr.'s school at Greenwich.

stationary, & their apartments disengaged, till you arrive. Should any thing therefore prevent you, You will let them know, that their disappointment may not be lengthened: if not you are sure of a cordial welcome; &, at all events, when ⎸ the Sophina's visit is finished, M. Bourdois will meet her half-way, & escort her to Sand place.[6] Mrs. G. Cambridge,[7] & my dear & excellent Friend, your Name-sake, agree that your little Ralph is a very pretty Babe.[8] I hope you often see my good & dear Miss Baker,[9] who is one of the worthiest Creatures breathing, & amongst my best & most prized friends. Pray give her my kindest love when you see her. Miss C[ambridge] gave me a good account of your looks, & of my dear Charlottina, whom I regard as an unappreciable consolation & delight to you. Well I know what a Child can be!—Take once more my best thanks for your very kind thought of giving me so great a pleasure as seeing you before I leave the Kingdom, though only for 4 Months—& let me hope you will certainly put it in execution, whether now or nearer the expedition. adieu, My dearest Charlotte ever

Most truly yours
Best Comp[ts] to Mr. Broome—& Love to Charlotte Sophy Marianne[10]—& ralph.—

435   Gravesend, 30 October 1801

M. d'Arblay
To Madame d'Arblay

A.L. (Berg), 30 Oct. 1801
Originally a double sheet 4to, of which FBA later discarded the second leaf 2 pp.
Edited by FBA, p.1, *top margin, annotated, the year date* 1801 *encircled*: 24/2 sweet *trait* of Character.

6 Sand or, historically, Sondes's Place (iv, L. 399 n. 1).
7 Cornelia (*née* Kuyck van Mierop), wife of the Revd. George O. Cambridge (iv, L. 311 n. 5), and his sister Charlotte (i, L. 1 n. 6).
8 Ralph Broome Jr., or 'Dolph', was born in Brighton *c.* 4 July 1801 and baptized on 5 Sept. 1801 (see certificate, Eg. 3708, f. 135).
9 Sarah Baker (i, L. 10 n. 6).
10 Marianne Francis (1790–1832).

21

Gravesend ce 30. Oct^re 1801

Quel excellent dejeuner je vais faire, ma bonne amie. Hier dans mon impatience je m'etais levé à six heures un quart, pour attendre la poste, qui ne m'apporta rien, qu'un cruel des-appointement; Aujourdhui, sachant qu'elle n'arrivait que sur les 9 heures, je n'ai quitté mon lit qu'à 8, et j'etais en bas à 8^h ½ precisement lorsque le messager a apporté quatre lettres, dont deux pour ton heureux ami. Voilà mon thé fait, je te quitte pour le prendre. God bless thee & him YOU VOUS [xxxxx 2 *lines*] ⌐de la plus grande importance pour moi. J'étais parti de Londre très fâché, comme je te l'ai mandé de n'avoir aucune nouvelle de Boinville.¹ ǀ Precisement il entrait par une porte tandis que moi je sortais par l'autre, et sur cela Bood² qui est fort mal en train me gronde (c'est sa manière) c'est à dire très obligeament mais enfin il me dit *'Une autrefois tu donneras un peu plus de tems à Boinville pour ecrire et faire sa course de Watford à Londre. Boinville est venu hier seulement (Mercredy) sur ta lettre où tu avais eu ⟨l'esprit⟩ de lui dire que tu partais MERCREDY SOIR. Il a passé à ⟨8⟩^h dans Beaumont Street &c.* [xxxxx 2 *lines*]

J'avais ecrit deux lettres à Boinville à part celle où je lui annonçais que je pars seul.

Cette demande ne pouvait partir plutôt, puisque ce n'est que le dimanche que nous avons decidement arrêté notre nouveau plan, dont l'execution ne pouvait être differée, et que ce même jour les lettres pour en prevenir mes ⟨amis⟩ etaient toutes parties.

Boinville a certainement reçu la sienne Lundy matin et il etait depuis longtems prevenu de mon depart et que je ne serais qu'un jour à Londre. Il m'avait repondu qu'il viendrait suivre et m'y voir et me remettrait probablement quelques lettres. Assurement ces lettres eussent du être prêtes.

Au lieu d'un jour que je devais être à Londre, j'y suis resté deux jours, et c'est même principalement pour donner à Boinville le tems de revenir de Watford que je ne suis parti que le Mercredy au lieu de Mardy, ce qui par parenthèse, est un peu different car je serais actuellement en France: car j'aurais certainement passé dans un Batiment qui a mis ce même jour Mercredy sur les 3^h après midy à la voile pour Boulogne.

435. ¹ Jean-Baptiste Chastel de Boinville (L. 425 n. 8).
² Antoine Bourdois (L. 429 n. 3).

Je ne me rappelle point d'avoir écrit à Boinville que je partirais de Londre *Mercredy matin,* | mais je me souviens parfaitement de lui avoir mandé que j'attendrais ses commissions dans Beaumont Street jusqu'à midi le mercredy et j'ai ajouté 'parceque je partirai LE SOIR pour *Gravesend'.* je ⟨me dis⟩ que j'aurais même droit de dire parceque une ou deux heures après je comptais partir dans le stage pour me rendre à Gravesend. Dans ma jeunesse j'avais comme l'ennemy d'avoir la mauvaise habitude de confondre souvent l'aprés midy et le soir, ce qui est pourtant fort different. Je disais aussi dans mon jeune tems *l'après-midy* ou *l'après-diner* indifferament, mais il y a bien à present quelque distinction à faire entre l'un et l'autre. A mon âge il est sans doute inexcusable d'avoir commis cette faute de grammaire, et serieusement j'en suis trés peiné puisqu'elle me prive de l'extrême plaisir que j'aurais eu à faire les commissions de mon ami Boinville[1] qui m'a envoyé une lettre scellée p[r] le Commissaire français à Calais mais n'a osé me faire passer de même celle qu'il avait compté me donner pour son propre compte.[Π]

J'ai été interrompu par une lettre qu'on m'apportait d'un *Mr Fiesinger*[3] que je ne connois point mais qui est ami de Boinville. Il se sert du nom de ce dernier pour me recommander une pauvre femme presque tout à fait stupide, la quelle est venue dans ce pays pour voir son fils qui precisement dans ce même tems a été envoyé en Allemagne. Je me suis chargé volontiers de cet être foible, qui me causera bien quelqu'embarras, mais comme dit souvent l'oncle que je vais voir, et dont je t'ai souvent parlé, qui n'est bon que pour soi n'est bon qu'à noyer. Sancho[4] n'eut pas rejetté ce proverbe, même lorsqu'il gouvernait son Isle.

[Π]Il m'a fallu repondre à Mr Fiesinger, et ecrire une longue lettre à Boinville. Je le prie de t'envoyer l'adresse de son fils et celle de son frère. tu voudras bien me les faire parvenir dans la 1ere lettre que tu m'ecriras après les avoir reçues. Je vais prendre l'air, n'ayant fait qu'ecrire depuis que je suis levé.

(à mon retour et avant mon diner qu'on prépare car ici on ne veut vous donner que ce que vous demandez exprès)

---

[3] Unidentified.
[4] The recollection of Gabriel Bazille's *dicta* reminds M. d'A of Sancho Panza's impressive repertory of proverbs, which he knew would be fresh also in FBA's mind.

J'ai fort bien fait d'aller me promener. Je reviens te dire que le bâtiment dans le quel je dois m'embarquer est arrivé ici, et qu'il pourrait en repartir dans trois heures par le meilleur vent et le plus beau tems possible, mais que j'ai grand peur qu'il n'en veuille rien faire.

En arrivant sur le port, on est venu suivant l'usage m'offrir d'aller voir ce bâtiment qui était arrivé et devait repartir pour Calais avec des passagers. J'ai demandé son nom et on n'a pu me le dire. Des lors, j'ai cru qu'on me fesait un conte et qu'on voulait seulement m'arracher quelques Shellings, comme cela m'est arrivé l'année dernière. J'ai donc refusé en disant que j'etais certain qu'il n'y avait point de bâtiment pour France et qu'à l'allien office on venait de me l'assurer. Deux matelots ont insisté et m'ont offert⁷ |

[*the second leaf is missing*]

436   West Humble, 30 October 1801

To M. d'Arblay

A.L. (Barrett, Eg. 3693, ff. 235–6b, with P-tab, f. 234), 30 Oct. 1801
Double sheet 4to   4 pp.   *French pmk*   S⟨A⟩ / A.4^E
Addressed: Mr. Darblay— / chez Mr Lajard, / N° 43. Fauxbourg St. Martin, / à Paris.
Edited by FBA, p. 1, *annotated*: ❖ (2/23)   Alex at West H⟨u⟩mble
Edited also by CFBt.

West Hamble Dorking
30. Octr 1801.

En fin, I am beginning, I trust, a Letter to mon meilleur ami which will follow him to his native land.[1] This is the thought that softens separation, & makes his absence even desirable— for what could be my heart if it did not feel every comfort of yours?—God be praised our Boy goes on well—Not that he is

---

436. [1] Because of delays, explained at length in L. 442, d'Arblay's ship did not put out for France until 6 November. FBA heard of his safe arrival only on the 12th (L. 443).

all I wish & hope to see him, but I shall not rest from studying & attending him till I bring him nearer that mark. As he is wholly free from fever, & has no actual complaint, I am beginning a new regimen: I shall drop all medicine whatever, except a little rhubarb occasionally, & only try red port wine, with a little salt dissolved in it, the first thing when he wakes, again at noon, & the last thing at night. I have consulted Mr. Norbury, our oracle in all,—& have his approbation for the plan. If he has worms—as I have every reason to believe, red wine & salt are especially good for him; if not, the red wine is bracing, & may help his re-establishment. But his symptoms are all of a *wormy* tendency! his sleep is uncertain, his appetite very capricious & irregular, | he is thin in extreme, & has a starting manner, & a degree o[f] unnatural impatience, that all announce his old enemies to be assailing him. The James's powders have happily removed all fever: but he is not in sufficient flesh for Ching;[2] I hope, therefore, you will approve my present scheme; which I communicate at full length, to shew you how religiously I shall comply with your demand of acquainting you with strict truth how he goes on in health.—For myself,—I do as well as I now can. I am unusually attentive to keep well, & obey your injunctions of air & exercise most literally. I spend two hours every morning *in our Grounds,*—&, hitherto, have regularly aired afterwards in Norbury's Phaeton.

How I lingered over every word of your precious long Letter this Morning! datcd 28ᵗʰ—ⁱ I will not fail to let my kind sister H[etty] know your feelings upon her errand & exertions—I am sorry to inform you Bood[3] called on you just after you were gone, with a Large pacquet of Letters, which he said might have been particularly useful to you, & he seemed excessively disappointed. This Maria has written to Richard, & Richard to me.[4] The Boods are expected today, at Dorking & have sent, by the same vehicle, an invitation to us to meet them, & keep their wedding Day.[5]

---

² 'Ching's Worm-Destroying Lozenges' (iv, L. 310 n. 1).
³ Lambert-*Antoine* Bourdois (iv *passim*).
⁴ Maria Bourdois and her brother the Revd. Richard Allen Burney (1773–1836).
⁵ Marianne Burney (now Maria) had married Antoine Bourdois on 30 Oct. 1800 (iv, pp. 455–7), and he had rented for a time Sand Place (iv, L. 399 n. 1) near Dorking.

I could not let my Alex go to a 5 o'clock dinner, & 9 o'clock bed, at present, for any consideration.—This, when I represent, will, I am sure, satisfy them. I have refused Norbury by the same notion, & good Mrs. Cooke has hopes to press us to Bookham, for a visit of a few days, which I have declined without hesitation. I shall devote myself wholly to my one beloved representative, till I see him reinstated & fatter & stouter, & I well know how dangerous to the progress of obtaining what so much I covet would be any irregularity. I fear you got unconsciable short scraps from me at Gravesend but my Letter relative to Dumerg had taken practically all my morning.[6] I hope it will prove satisfactory. I am truly vexed any report so *near* truth should have reached them before I described my situation. How very—very kind you have been to write so punctually! I am excessively earnest you should reach Paris for the Fête[7]—O that I could enjoy it at your side! What a fête for US! what a union to my dearest Friend of all he values! Speak for me to your excellent Uncle, your amiable aunt, & all your dear & deserving Cousins. I trust I shall claim their kindred kindness for myself & our Alex next summer. I shall spend all the 9th with you! I shall follow you all over Paris, & feel your Joy on so blessed a Festival. I could not read even the plan of it in the common⊓ | [n]ews papers, without tears of joy.—At Joigny I shall follow you again thro your meetings, partake in all your delight, & embrace your belo[ved] uncle with the most cordial affection. — — I must not, I know, omit certain domestic details: your friends the Pigs are perfectly well; the potatoe man has finished the Meadow, at last, & is now in the Garden, & Betty, & Nanny, & the Cat, & the Kitten, & the Rabbits, are all in good health—but!—Bully has again eloped! Nanny forgot his chain one morning, & off he marched, in search of some of his favorite fair females. A Dog of greater gallantry never existed. — — ⌐Amelia, &c. are all in Lincolnshire till xmas.—You will let me know how often I may write, &c. &c. & how direct, *at full length*. I know

---

[6] Evidently a letter (cf. pp. 29–30) to the Queen and the Princesses, correcting a report they had heard of FBA's intention to visit France at this time (see LI. 429, 430.

[7] The celebration of the *coup d'état* of 18 Brumaire (9 Nov. 1799). FBA could have noted incidental references to the coming fête in the *London Chronicle*, 20, 21, 24, 29 Oct. 1801; or *The Times*, 23 Oct. See also L. 446 n. 1.

nothing of the minutiae of foreign addresses (Bood & Edward just this moment enter in—) I consulted Bood where to direct & he thinks better only to send those that I have for you, lest I make any mistake. He has sent you an especial Letter & been extremely active & good to get it to you. I hope it will have arrived on time—heaven bless you my noblest ami. I have no doubt I will soon get Alex stout—He ran just now *Qui Sait* to Bood & Edward with great energy ⟨& sureness⟩

adieu—adieu—You will ask, I hope, for your Letters— Should I write? tell me, when, & where?⊓

437   West Humble, 2 November 1801

To Doctor Burney

A.L. (rejected Diary MSS. 5270–[73], Berg), 2 Nov. 1801
Double sheet 4to   4 pp.   *pmks*   DARKING   3 NOV 1801   3 NO 1801 wafer
Addressed: Dr. Burney, / Chelsea College, / Middlesex.
Edited by FBA, p.1, *annotated*: ⁙ (5)   M. d'Arblay detained by the Wind at Gravesend   Intercourse with the Gracious Queen.
Edited also by CFBt *and the* Press.

West Hamble,—Dorking.
2ᵈ Nov. 1801

I was sure my dearest Father could not blame our delay, & every day I have fresh reason to rejoice that we changed our measures, for my poor little Boy, though all spirit & gaiety in the day, has not recovered his sleep at Night, ⌜nor any regularity of appetite, & has, besides perspirations at nights that keep me in great anxiety, but⊓ he has no complaint, & never failing activity & liveliness. I now devote all my attentions to nourishing & fattening him & bracing him. I am sure I shall have my dearest Father's kind wishes for my success.

Poor M. d'Arblay is still at Gravesend — ⌜— — or was on Friday night, when he wrote to me last.[1] He had hopes of sailing yesterday, & was most⊓ excessively fatigued at such loss

437. ¹ On 30 October (L. 435).

of time: he has been disappointed two days following, after solemn promises of beginning the voyage without delay. The commander's of these little Vessels engage any thing that is demanded, to detain passengers, & fail, in the same extensive way, to wait for getting more.

Yet—had we but known he would be detained so long, in how much more pleasant & expeditious a manner he might have made his excursion! Lord Pelham[2] has granted ⌐ our petition, & accorded to M. d'Arblay's representation a passport for himself, me, Alexander & Adrienne,[3] by Dover. Had poor M. d'A. but received it!—⌐Yesterday, when I first knew of it, through Mr. Frank Moore,[4] there was no post—I have sent word of it, however, to Gravesend, in case the sailing is still delayed, that he may return hither to wait, & convert his passport for a shorter passage.⌐ *We* 2, at any rate, cannot go, my poor Alex being utterly unfit for such an expedition, at this season, after such an attack.

I have been made excessively happy this morning, & filled with gratitude, by a letter from Kew.[5] I wrote, at full length, for Her Majesty's perusal, our situation: that M. d'Arblay, though erased from the list of Emigrants these two years, had religiously adhered to his resolution of refusing to visit France while it was at war with This Country; & had only gone to Holland,[6] thence to send a procuration, in order to attempt the recovery of what little might yet remain unsold of his small patrimony: but that now there was PEACE, he meant immediately to visit his Relations & friends, & ⌐ take with him his wife & son for the winter:—our poor Boy's illness, had, however, changed our plan, M. d'Arblay was gone alone, & would return when he had satisfied his affections, & settled what was

---

[2] Lord Pelham (i, L. 24 n. 63), Home Secretary (1801–3) in Addington's ministry. The passport to France *via* Dover seems not to have been preserved.

[3] Adrienne-Adélaïde-Anne de Chavagnac (1795–1868), daughter of Louis-Vigile (1765–1819), comte de Chavagnac, and his wife Agathe-Françoise *née* de Montecler (1773–98). Adrienne, born in London *c*. 3 Dec. 1795, had been left in the care of the Lockes of Norbury Park when her mother, after the establishment of the Directory (26 Oct. 1795), returned to France in the hope of reclaiming property (iii, L. 201 n. 5; L. 215 n. 12). The child was now to rejoin her father in Paris and to travel under FBA's protection.

[4] See L. 430 n. 3.

[5] A letter of approval or permission from the Queen, through the medium of Margaret Planta. The original is missing, but FBA evidently hoped the paraphrase above might quiet CB's fears for the fate of her pension, should she go to France.

[6] For d'Arblay's voyage to Holland, see iv, pp. 458–84.

possible of his affairs, & that in June we should all go together, & remain till october. My answer of this morning I must, in part, Copy. Miss Planta begins by saying, ⌐that the indisposition of The Princess Augusta, confining her to Her Royal Highness's chamber, had prevented her showing my Letter to the Queen till that Day.¬—Her Majesty then ordered her to write to me immediately, in answer—'And Her Majesty has commanded me to acquaint you, that She quite approves of Monsr D'Arblay's visiting his native Country; that it is a duty he owes to his family,—& that you will be quite right in accompanying him thither in June.'

What comfort & satisfaction this has given me!—she adds also much condescending kindness from the Princesses, with their Royal Highnesses wishes that Monsr D'Arblay's visit to France may be attended with success, & their gracious & kind concern for the illness of my little Boy.—I am sure I need not add that I wrote instantly my warmest acknowledgements.

The present high winds make me scarcely know what to wish as to M. d'A.'s sailing.[7]—I know not if he had ever time to mention to you his meeting with General Lauriston?[8] | ⌐or that Lord Cornwallis' under secretary, Mr. F. Moore, has promised to aid our corresponding before the General Posts to France are open? — — I told Mr. Lock what you said of the Porcupine,[9] and he was much pleased; 'Good God, he said, can a man think it *Patriotism* to point out, in a public print, our weakness, if any there be, in making the peace? point it out to our Enemies, & *suggest* the possible evils they may bring upon us? What is honest, as well as natural, to be uttered from man to man, & friend to friend, in conversation, is danger, & ought to be treason from nation to nation.'¬

⸻

[7] For an account of d'Arblay's crossing and the high winds that beat his ship along the coast from Gravesend to Margate, see Ll. 438, 439, 442 *passim*, and L. 441 n. 1.

[8] The circumstances of the meeting (related by M. d'A, L. 425), FBA recounts in *Memoirs*, iii. 304–11.

[9] Dr. Burney's letter to FBA is missing but in a letter (Berg) of 7 November to Mrs. Crewe he inveighed against the criticisms of Lord Hawkesbury and of the recently negotiated treaty with France that had lately appeared in a series of nine letters (12 Oct.–4 Nov. 1801) in *The Porcupine*, edited by William Cobbett (1763–1835), commonly called 'Peter Porcupine'. However inexpedient it may be to make such a peace at present, CB observed, 'it *is* made, and will not be broken to oblige Mr Peter Porcupine, or even L^ds Spencer & Grenville, or Messrs T. Grenville & Windham—*à quoi bon* to put the nation out of humour with it—and expose our weakness & ill humour to the enemy—now to be regarded as friends?'

Should you ever, by chance, meet Lord Pelham,[10] I beg you, dearest Sir, to express our gratitude for his compliance with our request. It was a favour entirely personal, & has been refused to all around us here, *Sir John Coghill*,[11] &c. ⌐& Mr. King[12] & Mr. Flint[13] had rejected his petition.⌐ I once met Lord Pelham at Mrs. Crewe's. He is Brother in Law, by his first marriage, to our Lord Leslie—who, by the way, with his Lady, called upon us last Week. ⌐The Bourdois's are all well, & Richard is now quite domesticated there. I am glad of it for many reasons. He also seems better. Edward[14] is now there also. The good M. Bourdois is hospitality itself. I am extremely thankful for your kind mention of your abated cough & rheumatism. I beg my best love to dear Fanny, & am ever & ever dearest sir,

your most dutiful & affecte

F d'A⌐

438   Margate and Deal, 2–4 November 1801

M. d'Arblay
To Madame d'Arblay

A.L. (Berg), 2–4 Nov. 1801
Double sheet 4to   3 pp.   *pmks* DEAL   5 NOV 1801   wafer
Addressed, p. 3: Madame Darblay / Westhumble / near Dorking / Surry
A second address given but apparently not used, p. 4: for Mrs Darblay / at. Capt. James Burney's. / N° 9 Charles Street / Soho / London
Half a crown to be given to the *Bearer* / A. Darblay
to be forwarded / *as soon as possible.*
Edited by FBA, p. 1, *top margin, annotated and year date* 1801 *encircled*: (25)
Amusing Travelling Nuptials.

10 FB had met Lord Pelham at Mrs. Crewe's villa in Hampstead (i, p. 206). His younger sister Henrietta-Anne (1757–97) had married in 1789 George William Evelyn-Leslie, styled Lord Leslie (1773), which family the d'Arblays knew (see i, L. 23 n. 69). Lord Leslie had married secondly Charlotte Julia *née* Campbell (see iv, L. 292 n. 45).
11 Sir John Coghill (1766–1817), 2nd Baronet (1790), though refused a passport at this time, was to accompany Lally-Tolendal to Bordeaux in November 1803 (L. 509 n. 5).
12 John King (L. 431 n. 4), Under-Secretary of State, Home Department.
13 Sir Charles William Flint (1777–1834), Superintendent of the Alien Department (*GM* lxii (1802), 272; and *Corr. Geo. IV*, vi. 461).
14 Edward Francesco Burney (i, p. lxxv).

Devant. Margate à l'ancre
ce 2. 9bre 1801.

Je viens, ma chere bonne amie, de m'assurer que le Capitaine, qui est un tout à fait bon homme, pourra te poster cette lettre ⌐que j'espere que tu recevras bientôt. Il me parait entendre son etat à merveille. Je t'ai mandé, je crois, avoir embarqué p^r passer la nuit à l'ancre.⌐ Ce matin une heure avant le jour nous avons mis à la voile, après avoir passé bien tranquillement une nuit fort orageuse, et nous sommes arrivés ici, conduits par un vent excellent quoiqu'un peu fort. ⌐Demain matin nous leverons l'ancre une heure avant le jour, et trés probablement nous arriverons à Calais, d'où je ne pourrai t'ecrire, mais où tu seras sur que je serai rendu, si le Cap^{tne} qui m'y aura quitté te fait passer cette lettre. Je compte même l'engager à la porter lui même chez James,[1] et pour ccla je compte mettre sur l'adresse *half a crown to be paid to the bearer*. En ce cas tu auras l'attention d'en tenir compte à ton frère que j'embrasse.

En arrivant ici à 4^h du soir nous y avons trouvé deux batimens allant ainsi que nous à Calais, les quels sont partis l'un mardy dernier, l'autre mercredy. Je ne puis concevoir comment ils ne sont pas encore rendus à leur destination. Quoiqu'il en soit, me voilà tout à fait debarrassé du petit regret que j'avais de n'être pas parti de Londre un jour plutôt. J'ai tout lieu au contraire d'en être enchanté car il y a mille contre un à parier que nous serons à Calais avant ces deux batimens partis bien avant nous.

Ecoute ce qu'on vient de rencontrer.⌐ Au milieu de la niut j'ai été reveillé par les cris les plus dechirans, poussés par une jeune femme mariée hier matin, ⌐ à un français. Voici cette histoire, qui n'est pas tout à fait celle des unions comme on en voit tant. Les français envoyés en france sur le même batiment que moi, et aux frais du gouvernement, ont été logès à Gravesend dans une auberge qui, comme tu le penses bien, n'est pas la plus elegante de l'endroit. Ils etaient tous dans la même chambre au nombre de 22 ou 23, y compris les femmes et les enfans, et etaient servis par toute la maison, composée d'une vielle femme et deux servantes. Un des soldats, natif de provence, et gai comme tous les gens de cette province, paraissait

438 [1] At the address (see headnote) shared at this time by JB and his half-sister SHB. For their elopement, see iv, pp. 204–20.

regarder ces demoiselles avec un air qui remarqué par la Dame de la maison lui attira ces douces paroles, 'Est-ce que vous voudriez marier Betti?' — 'Betti? pourquoi non? Cependant je prefererais Suzanne' — 'oh Suzanne soit!' Et la vielle met les mains des jeunes gens l'une dans l'autre. Le provençal prend la chose au serieux, et dès le matin court toute la ville pour se defaire de deux guinées, et prendre en echange une licence, dont il a fait un si bon usage, que le matin de notre embarquement les deux enflammés ont été publiquement mariés. Le soir la femme a suivi son mari a bord, se conformant en cela au precepte de S^t paul, qui dit &c — mais les loix d'Angleterre, en contradiction avec l'Apôtre, ont fait parler tout autrement le commis de l'Alien office, qui a separé ce que le Ciel venait de joindre et cela malgré les cris de Melusine,[2] dont j'ai déjà fait mention. L'épousée a donc quitté notre vaisseau, et est retournée vers Gravesend, mais non pas à terre, car elle n'a fait que passer du bateau dans le quel etait le commis dans un autre, où se trouvait un ami du mari, le quel mari s'est arrangé de maniere qu'il est actuellement nanti de sa femme, qui arrivera avec lui à Calais | demain j'espere, et cela au très grand contentement de tous deux jusqu'à nouvel ordre; je puis même ajouter au grand contentement des passagers, que cette histoire a beaucoup amusé tout le jour.—

4. 8bre 1801 Mercredy matin a 11^h devant Deal.
    Sois sans inquietude depuis 2 jours nous sommes battus par les vents mais sommes ici sans danger. [xxxxx 1 *line*]

---

    [2] The forced separation and the despairing wails recalled to M. d'A the parting of the lovers Raymond and Mélusine in medieval French romance.

Deal to Dover, 5 [November 1801]

M. d'Arblay
To Madame d'Arblay

A.L. (Berg), 5
Originally a double sheet 4to, of which the second leaf has been discarded 2 pp.
Edited by FBA, p. 1, *top margin, annotated and year date* 1801 *encircled*: Novr N° 1 (26) written in a passage of 3 Days Hurricane from Gravesend to Dover! A few lines of unexampled consideration to a solicitude equally unexampled!
Edited also by CFBt.

Jeudy 5 sur la route de Deal à Dover

Assurement, ma bonne amie, si je vais ce train là, je ne suis pas encore pret à t'embrasser! Jamais je crois on n'a vu dans un si court passage une telle succession de contrarietés, occasionnées par un très gros tems, et des vents qui quelquefois de la plus grande violence sont toujours precisement le contraire de ce qu'ils devraient être eu egard aux marées. Je ne suis au reste inquiet que de ton inquietude, et c'est pour la dissiper que je te griffonne ceci mourant de froid et de faim. Notre batiment est excellent et presque neuf. Quant au Capitaine il est de bonne humeur, experimenté et trés prudent, peut être même un peu trop: mais ce n'est pas ce que tu aimeras le moins en lui j'en suis sûr.

┌Tu dois avoir deux lettres de moi dont 1 d'hier soir devant Deal. Je suis le seul des passagers *gentleman* qui n'ai point voulu aller à terre parceque une demie guinée que les hoteliers ont demandé par tête et autant au moins┐ qu'il en coutera pour le diner m'ont paru bons à epargner. A cela il faut ajouter le coucher et le dejeuner et diner d'aujourdhui, car la mer a été si haute qu'ils n'ont pu revenir à bord. Nous avons donc été contraints de partir sans eux pour Douvre après avoir deux fois hissé notre ┃ ┌pavillon.┐ [xxxxx 3 *lines*] Ceci ma chere bonne amie, te parviendra j'espere, tout aussi surement Je compte en charger le pilote que nous attendons de Douvre. Nous venons de hisser pour cela le pavillon, et je te quitte, ne pouvant plus tenir ma plume.

(à 2ʰ dans le port de Douvres moyennant 7 guinées! que nous avons été obligés de donner à un pilote!)

Tu vois ma bonne amie que tu peus être parfaitement tranquille. J'ai aidé à la manoeuvre et suis fatigué en diable.

ᴦmes tendres respects et complimens à Norbury & à Dorking.[1] je ferme cette lettre et vais chercher quelqu'un pʳ la faire mettre à la poste. ⟨De grâce⟩, ma bonne amie, aye soin de toi et de notre cher petit. Je vous embrasse comme je vous aime.

D'A.ᴨ

440   Dover, 5 November 1801

M. d'Arblay
To Madame d'Arblay

A.L. (rejected Diary MSS. 5274–[75], Berg), 5 Nov. 1801
Originally a double sheet 4to, of which FBA later discarded the second leaf   2 pp.
Edited by FBA, p. 1, *top margin, annotated and year date* 1801 *encircled:* (27) Duc de Duras. meeting at Dover.
Edited also by CFBt *and the* Press.

Douvre Jeudy 5, 9ᵇʳᵉ 1801

Je t'ecris, ma chere bonne amie, de Douvre où / sont arrivés / nos compagnons de passage debarqués à Deal [xxxxx 3 *lines*] Nous avons fait ici ᴦà la *Ship Inn*ᴨ[1] un excellent diner, dont j'avais grand besoin: car depuis 3 jours je n'avais rien mangé; mon vin ayant été renversé et mes provisions gatées par le mauvais tems qui avait tout mis sens dessus dessous dans le vaisseau: mais nous voici bien parfaitement en sureté. [xxxxx 1½ *lines*] Dejà la mer est moins haute, et probablement demain nous serons à Calais. Ce qu'il y a de très certain, ma chere bonne amie, c'est que nous ne partirons qu'avec un bon vent et que tu peus être parfaitement tranquille.

439. [1] That is, to the Locke and Bourdois families.
440. [1] One of the four principal inns of Dover. See *The Dover and Deal Directory and Guide* . . . [1800].

[*A travers 11 lignes, oblitérées plus tard par Madame d'Arblay, on peut distinguer des références à une lettre que Monsieur d'Arblay vient d'écrire à sa femme et au moyen qu'il a utilisé pour l'expédier:* 'j'etais encore sur le bateau quand je l'ai donnée avec un shilling à quelqu'un qui s'est chargé de la mettre à la poste'. *Il parle du contenu de la dite lettre et de l'argent qu'il a pu épargner en restant sur le bateau au lieu d'aller sur terre comme l'ont fait certains de ses compagnons de voyage.*] |

Comme nous allions nous mettre à table j'ai vu par la fenêtre deux Messieurs qui nous regardaient et reconnaissant Amedée Duras[2] je suis sorti et nous avons *shaked hand*. Il est ici à attendre son passage. Il m'a dit qu'il avait une lettre du prefet pour passer par Anvers, mais que craignant beaucoup la mer, il avait preferé passer par Douvre, et se proposait de dire au Com^re du Gouvernement. M^r j'imagine que dans un moment ou tout le monde a la gaîté dans le coeur, vous aurez l'humanité de ne pas faire une exception p^r moi, qui depuis onze ans n'ai vu ma mere,[3] et qui viens p^r l'embrasser. Gardez moi si vous voulez en prison, jusqu'à ce que j'aye des nouvelles de Paris, mais au moins permettez moi de les attendre! Nous avions tous les deux les larmes aux yeux en nous serrant la main, mais comme il y avait avec lui une autre personne que je ne connais point, j'etais sur mes gardes. La premiere chose qu'il m'avait dite etait d'ailleurs 'ne me faites pas connaître' — [xxxxx 4 *lines*]

---

[2] Here FBA added the superscript ·✕· and the explanation '·✕· The Duc de Duras'. Amédée-Bretagne-Malo de Durfort (1771–1838), 6th duc de Duras, capitaine de chasseurs à cheval (1789), who became after his emigration (1791) aide-major général des logis in the Army of the Princes. In 1793 he emigrated to Spain, in 1795 to England and, appointed premier gentilhomme de la chambre du roi, was to figure in the emergence of Louis XVIII from Hartwell in 1814 (see vii, L. 770 n. 24; L. 771 n. 19), becoming pair de France (4 June 1814) and maréchal de camp (24 Nov. 1814). Following, like d'Arblay, Louis XVIII to Ghent in 1815, he was created duc-pair héréditaire (31 Aug. 1817) and chevalier du Saint-Esprit (30 Sept. 1820).

FBA was to encounter the duc de Duras at a reception given by Louis XVIII at Grillon's Hotel on Albermarle Street on 22 Apr. 1814, when he presented her to the king.

[3] His mother Louise-Henriette-Charlotte-*Philippine née* de Noailles (1745–1822), a cousin of Mme de Lafayette, had married in 1760 Emmanuel-Céleste-Augustin de Durfort (1741–1800), marquis, later duc, de Duras, maréchal de camp (1780), premier gentilhomme de la chambre du roi, who had died in London. Imprisoned with her parents during the Terror, she wrote in 1804 *Journal des prisons de mon père, de ma mère et des miennes* (1888).

M. d'Arblay
To Madame d'Arblay

A.L. (Berg), 7 Nov. 1801
Double sheet 4to   3 pp.   *pmks* SHIP ⟨L⟩ETTER   11 NOV 1801   wafer
Addressed: To Madame Darblay / West humble. / near Dorking / *Surry*
Edited by FBA, p. 1, *top margin, dated and annotated*: / Nov^r / 1801   (28)
Dreadful Passage and Dangers!

Calais 16 Brumaire (7. 9bre Vieux Style) 1801

Je voudrais, ma bonne amie, pouvoir donner des ailes à cette lettre, car j'ai été si inquiet de ton inquietude que j'ai grand besoin de la faire cesser. Notre traversée qui a duré une semaine complette pourrait donner lieu à un nouvel Odyssée (pour le moins)![1] mais le desir de te donner plutôt connaissance de l'heureuse issue de mon voyage me fait remettre à un autre tems des details dans les quels je n'aurais pas le tems d'entrer. Combien dans ce passage orageux à l'excés, je me suis comme toi applaudi de nous être definitivement arreté au parti plus sage d'attendre la belle saison pour venir ici tous ensemble. Croirais tu que j'ai poussé cette resignation jusqu'à benir même le Ciel de la legere incommodité qu'il avait envoyé à notre cher petit pour nous decider à une separation qui, quelque courte qu'elle puisse être, sera bien longue encore. Que n'aurais-je pas donné cependant pour vous sentir près de moi ce matin, toi et notre cher Alex, au moment oû j'ai apperçu le rivage. Quel moment, mon amie! Si je n'avais pas été retenu par les regards de trente individus, qui avaient l'air de m'observer, certainement ⟨j'aur⟩ais obei avec delice au sentiment qui m'engageait à remercier à genoux l la providence qui m'a enfin permis de revoir cette patrie que j'ai toujours portée dans mon coeur. Notre Capitaine que nous avons comblé de presents

441. [1] Setting out from Gravesend on 1 November, d'Arblay's ship, driven along the coast, finally anchored at Margate (2–4 Nov.). Venturing on to Deal and to Dover (4–5 Nov.), the ship set sail on the 6th, arriving in Calais on the 7th. *The Times* of the week records 'the most heavy gales of wind ever remembered', ships dragging at anchor, and tremendous damage suffered on water and land. On the English coast there were thirty ships in distress, many of which foundered and sank; and on the French coast, 25 gunboats *en route* from Calais to Dunkirk were driven ashore, with the loss of all on board.

parceque reellement nous devons la vie à sa prudence, me
promet d'ajouter encore aux obligations que je lui ai, en te
faisant parvenir surement cette lettre. ⌐Je n'en doute point,
parce que c'est un honnête homme, et d'ailleurs comme je
viens de te le dire, nous l'avons recompensé magnifiquement.
Tout pauvre que je suis j'aurais cru, dans cette situation, mal
servir tes desirs en ne temoignant pas la même reconnaissance
que les autres.⌐ A present que nous sommes ici sans aucun
danger, je te dirai que nous en avons courru de tres grands, et
que sur les 8 jours que nous avons été sur mer, plus de 6 n'ont
été qu'une tempête continuelle. Je t'ai mandé que nous avions
trouvé devant Margate 2 galliotes parties de Gravesend pour
Calais le mercredy, c.à.d. 4 jours avant nous. Aucun de ces
deux batimens n'est encore arrivé; et malheureusement il y a
tout lieu de craindre que l'un des deux a peri, la nuit ou devant
Deal, les passagers de notre batiment etaient allés à terre, moi
excepté. La mer etait très haute et le vent terrible changeait
à tout moment. Tout à coup sur les 3^h $\frac{1}{2}$ c.à.d plus de trois
heures avant le jour, le matelot de garde crie que nous chassons
sur notre ancre. J'etais dans cet instant on ne peut pas plus
souffrant: mais pour la seconde fois j'ai eprouvé que le mal de
mer si terrible d'ailleurs, n'est rien à l'aspect imprevu d'un
danger imminent. | Moi qui depuis 24 heures ne pouvait être
un instant sur le tillac, que soutenu sous le bras, tant il etait
glissant, je sautai hors de l'espece de magasin qu'on avait
baptisé d'un plus beau nom p^r nous faire payer 2 guinées de
plus, et tout aussi à mon aise que le matelot le plus leste, je
me mis à l'ouvrage avec tout le zele qu'un pareil moment peut
inspirer. Il etait tems, et si nous n'eussions pas presque miracu-
leusement reussi dans nos efforts, nous aurions—*4 minutes!!!*
plus tard été mis en pieces, sans que 30 vaisseaux de guerre
au milieu des quels nous etions mouillés, pussent nous être
d'aucun secours. C'est cette même nuit, et à la même place,
que l'une des galiottes partie avant nous a ⟨aussi⟩ chassé sur
ses ancres, et a heureusement pris le large, mais ⟨sans qu'on⟩
en ait entendu parler depuis. La veille nous avions mouillé
devant Margate à l'endroit même où l'année derniere Melle La
Landelle,[2] 28 autres passagers, et tout l'equipage, commandé

[2] Sister of Pauline de Gouvello *née* de La Landelle. See L. 451 n. 1; also iii,
L. 215 n. 14.

par le frère même de notre *mate,* avaient peri, sans que personne put se sauver. Cette nuit là un des cordages de nos ancres quoique neuf et gros comme mon bras avait été fort endommagé. Un second n'etant en guere meilleur etat après la nuit devant Deal, nous fûmes forcés d'entrer dans le port de Douvre, d'óu, comme je te l'ai ecrit, nous partîmes hier matin.

[xxxxx *3 lines*]

442   West Humble, 11 November 1801

To Doctor Burney

A.L.S. (Diary MSS. vi. 5276–[79], Berg), 11 Nov. 1801
Double sheet 4to   4 pp.
Addressed: Dr. Burney, / Chelsea College, / Middlesex.
Edited by FBA, p. 1 (5276), *annotated & date retraced*: ⁙ ⁙ Novʳ 11ᵗʰ 1801.
(6)   M. d'Arblay set out for France   Tempest   Danger—M. le Duc de Duras
Edited also by CFBt *and the* Press.

West Hamble, Novʳ 11ᵗʰ 1801.

I did not purpose writing to my dearest Father till my suspense & inquietude were happily removed by a Letter from France[1]—but as I find he is already anxious himself, I will now relate all I yet know of my dearest Traveller's history. On Wednesday the 28ᵗʰ of October he set off for Gravesend. A Vessel, he was told, was ready for sailing; & would set off the following Day. He secured his passage, & took up his abode at an end, whence he wrote me a very long Letter,[2]—in full hope his next would be from his own Country. But Thursday came— & no sailing—though the wind was fair, & the weather, then calm; he amused his disappointment as well as he could, by visiting divers *Gardeners,* & taking sundry lessons for nursing & managing Asparagress,—┌of which he wrote me long details, to be ready for an unearthing on his return—┐ Friday, also, came—& still no sailing!—he was more & more vexed—but had recourse, then, to a *Chymist,* with whom he revived much of his

442. ¹ See L. 441 nn. 1, 2.
    ² Probably L. 435, one leaf of which is missing.

early knowledge ⌐& passed enough of the Day to make the rest of it less *ennuyant*.⌐ Saturday followed,—no sailing!—& he found the people waited on & on, in hopes of more passengers, though never avowing their purpose, ⌐but regularly promising, Hour by Hour, to go out of the Port.⌐ His patience was now nearly exhausted, & he went & made such *vif remonstrances*, that he almost startled the managers: ⌐the *Captain* himself had only the ship business to transact for, ∣ not the time of sailing.⌐ They pretended the ballast was all they stayed for: he offered to aid that himself—& actually went to work, & never rested till the Vessel was absolutely ready:—orderss *enfin*, were given for sailing next morning,—though he fears, with all his skill, & all his eloquence, & all his aiding, they were more owing to the arrival of 4 new passengers, than to himself. That Night, October the 31st he went on board,—& November the first, he set sail, at 5 o'clock in the morning.—

⌐The name of the vessel he has never ascertained nor of the Captain. This I much regret.⌐

You know how high a wind arose on Sunday the 1st—& how dreadful a storm succeeded, lasting all Night—all Monday,— & all Night again—How thankful—how grateful am I to have heard of his safety since so terrifying a period!—they got on, with infinite difficulty & danger, as far as Margate—they there took anchor,—& my kind voyager got a Letter for me sent on shore, '*moyennant un Schilling*.' To tell you my gratitude in knowing him safe after that Tempest—no! I cannot!—Your warm affections, my dearest Father, will easily paint to you my thankfulness.—

Next, they got on to Deal—& here anchored again—for the Winds, though they abated on shore, kept violent & dangerous near the Coast. Some of the Passengers went on shore—& put two Letters for me in the Post—assuring me all was safe. These two Passengers ∣ who merely meant to dine on shore, & see the town,—were left behind!—the Sea rose so high, no Boat could put off to bring them back, & though the Captain hoisted a flag, to announce he was sailing, there was no redress. They had not proceeded a league, before the sea grew yet more rough & perillous—& the Captain was forced to hoist a flag of distress!—every thing in the Vessel was overset—My poor M. d'Arblay's provision Basket flung down, & its contents demolished,—his Bottle of wine broke by another toss, &

violent fall—& he was nearly famished!—The Water now began to get into the Ship—all hands were at work that could work—& he—my poor Voyager, gave his whole noble strength to the pump, till he was so exhausted, so fatigued, so weakened, that with difficulty he could hold a Pen to repeat that still— I might be *tranquille*, for all danger was again over!—A Pilot came out to them from Dover, for 7 Guineas, which the higher of the Passengers subscribed for—(& here Poor M. d'A was reckoned of that Class!) & the Vessel was got into the Port at Dover, & the Pilot—*moyennant un autre schilling*, put me again a Letter, with all these particulars, into the Post.—

This was Thursday the 5th the sea still so boisterous, the Vessel was unable to cross the Water. The magistrates at Dover permitted the poor passengers all to land—& M. d'Arblay wrote to me again, from the Inn, after being regaled with an excellent dinner, of which he had been much in want. Here they ⌐ met again the two Passengers lost at Deal—who, in hopes of this circumstance, had travelled post from thence to Dover. Here, too, M. d'A. met the Duke de Duras—an hereditary officer of the Crown—but who told him, since Peace was made, & all hope seemed chaced of a proper return to his Country, he was going, *incognito*, to visit a beloved old Mother, whom he had not seen for 11 years. I have no passport, he said, for France —but I mean to avow myself to the Commissary at Calais; & tell him I know I am not *erazed*, nor do I demand to be so— I only solicit an interview with a venerable Parent,—send to Paris, to beg leave for it—you may put me in prison till the answer arrives—but, for Mercy, for humanity's sake, suffer me to wait in France till then!—Guarded as you please! — —This is his purposed address—which my M^r d'A says he heard *avec les larmes aux yeux*—I shall long to hear the event. On Friday, Nov. 6th He wrote me two lines—

'Nov. 6. 1801. Je pars! —the wind is excellent— *au revoir* —²

This is dated 10 o'clock in the morning.—

I have not had a word since!³ though he said he would write back by his Captain, who was to return immediately. I pray God to end this anxious suspense!—This is my full account, my

³ It was not until 12 November that FBA had news of M. d'A's arrival at Calais on the 7th (L. 443).

dearest Father. I thank you a thousand times for your most kind invite to Chelsea, but my Alex, though recovered from all danger, is still in want of all my attention, regular hours, regimen, & constant exercise in this pure air. Surely, the instant I hear, I will write again—Heaven bless & preserve my dearest Father!

prays his most dutiful & affec
F. d'Arblay.

A thousand thanks to my dearest Fanny for her kind Letter & kind ⟨words⟩ & news of Norbury Mr & Mrs. Charles Lock are just arrived, with their 3 children. They were in the last tremendous storm & barely saved![4]

443 West Humble
[26 October]—12 November 1801

Conjointly with Alexander d'Arblay

To M. d'Arblay

A.J.L. & PS. (rejected Diary MSS. 5288–[91], Berg), 12 Nov. 1801, relating events from 26 Oct. to 12 Nov. 1801
Double sheet large 4to   4 pp.   wafer
Addressed: Mr. Darblay— / chez M. Lajard, / N° 43. / Fauxbourg St Martin / Paris   [*added in another hand*:] Rue de Miromesnil / Hotel Maringo.
Edited by FBA p. 1 (5288), *annotated*: ⌗ ⌐39¬. N° 33 / 1   *date* Nov. *retraced*
Edited also by CFBt *and the* Press.

West Hamble, Nov 12—1801

Never shall I be able to tell you the Joy of this morning— never—never! for you could only understand it by knowing all the agony of inquietude preceding it. O mon ami!—how & which way can I thank you for all the exquisite kindness & consideration of writing to me so frequently! your Letters have

---

[4] In August 1801 Locke had resigned his post as British Consul at Naples (iv, L. 292 n. 47), where his third child Lucy had been born on 26 June 1801. For the situation at Naples, the ascendancy of Lady Hamilton, and Cecilia's discomfitures, see *Locks of Norbury*, pp. 142–209.

been my support rather than my consolation —— & to indulge me so often, without the Spur of one word of answer—indeed I can never express to you the gratitude I feel.—What a voyage —What a dreadful voyage you have had!—all your late Letters, all since the storm of Monday, I have opened upon my knees, in thankfulness at every fresh sight of your hand. ⌐I have longed to write to you—& I hoped for your address more fully. I can wait no longer, now I know you safe in France—I send on chance—will he¹ know to give this to you. I sent him one immediately before he left London.⌐ I must now begin you a little Journal of our goings on since we lost you; if I allow myself to enter more fully upon your Letters. I have so much in heart & soul to say to you of them all, I shall give you no intelligence, & have my whole Paper filled with comments & acknowledgements.

———

The 26 [October]. after you were gone I won't tell you what first ensued—but what secondly happenned you will like to hear: our dear Mr. Norbury² came—& was too considerate to ask me even to take an airing—he mounted into the Book Room, & made me a long & most solacing visit, talking the whole time of your renovated life & happiness in again seeing your loved Country, & earliest Friends.—I won't say dear*EST*, dear as I know them to your inmost Heart—for you have two left behind you, whose whole happiness hangs on the belief of standing, now, first. The rest of the Day, I settled accounts. You know when I am unhappy, that is one of my first resources for employment.

27ᵗʰ I cheared a little, always satisfied we had done well to part for the present, by the much yet remaing to be done for re-establishing our beloved Boy. He had no complaint, but was so pale, so thin! I then began the *Red Wine* system, I have mentioned in my former Letters: & I took an Airing with dearest Mr. Norbury; his sweet Wife was confined with a cold, but Augusta accompanied him. Guess, again, our theme. |

28. 29. again airings with Mr. N[orbury] & Augusta, & dear Breakfast Letters.

443. ¹ Pierre-Auguste Lajard (iv, L. 291 n. 5), at his Paris address (*supra*).
² William Locke, Sr. (L. 428 n. 1).

30. Arrived Bood, Maria, & Edward, from London. They did not stay. I was but sad, & had no spirit to press them, & they could not urge my *wedding visit*[3] to them, which I hope we shall keep doubly next year,—to make l'amende honorable for your magnificent dinner on the occasion at Gravesend.[4] your histories there, both of Gardening & chymistry & *Ballasting*, amused me much, vexed as I was, every way, for your detention. ⌐However you will not stop *dining first*!

31 Again Mr. Norbury & airing &, as he was alone,—Alex had the happiness of making our third.

Nov. 1 Began the storm which has proved so dreadful & which, nevertheless, I must never call to mind without thankfulness for your escape—

2d There was one storm all day & I passed it in making Flags attached to a walking stick—a walking stick which I held out of the window nearly every five minutes to watch the course of the wind. Most fortunately for my peace, I then believed you arriving in France—for your last Gravesend Letter did not reach me till Five Days afterwards, & I therefore believed you had sailed on Friday night.—This was an omission in your letter, most providential, for my poor heart & *head* too!—

When the *3d* & *4th* days without a Letter, I had not a doubt but you were safe in France—

On the *5th* came a Letter from Gravesend—then, indeed, my courage failed—Mr. & *Mrs.* Norbury called—& I could not refuse to take an airing—*She*, as usual, strove all in her power to give me thoughts like her own, *couleur de roses*—& I caught all I could from them of hope—but my heart sank, & my spirits could not rally. Mr. Norbury was very silent,—& very thoughtful.—Bood came, *certain* all was well, a day or two before, on his way to Town, & Edward accompanied him. He, Edward, could stay from Town no longer. He just saw our Hermitage, liked your retreat, quarrelled with mine, & took leave. I hope he will renew his visit, when you can receive him.

6 A dear precious letter from Deal gave me new life.[5] I pray that you were safe & well after Monday's terrific storm & Rain—we had not even any *wind* with it! How ill we can judge,

---

[3] The first wedding anniversary (30 Oct.) of Lambert-*Antoine* Bourdois and Marianne *née* Burney (see iv, pp. 455-7). Edward Francesco Burney (i, p. lxxv), the artist, was Maria's uncle.

[4] See L. 435, pp. 21-4.   [5] L. 438, pp. 30-2.

by land, of the dangers at sea!—I was quite, therefore, relieved, & only disturbed for your loss of time, & the idea of your not arriving for the Fête at Paris.⁋ Dearest Kindest more than ever dear Mr. *Norbury* came again in the midst of Rain & sleet— alone, & *not* he said, to take *me* an airing in such bad Weather! but he could not rest without knowing if I had heard from you after the ˡ Monday's storm—& he would not *send*, lest that, had I *not* heard, might alarm me! He then said he had been *dreadfully uneasy* for you—& rejoiced in my Letter from Deal till he brought Tears twenty times into my Eyes, of gratitude & sympathy. Nothing else, he said, could have brought him out on so wet & bad a Day!—Do you think he went unthanked?—

⁋7ᵗʰ Dover Letter⁶—& here let me tell you what I ought to have mentioned in the beginning. Lord Pelham granted the *Passport by Dover*. Unfortunately, it arrived here on *Saturday*, when there is no post—I wrote you word of it on Sunday, but that Letter was returned me from Gravesend. Had we been aware of that, how long & terrible a voyage might have been spared you. The passport was for us all Four, Adrienne included.⁷ I hardly know if you will be most pleased at hearing of a request acceded at once, or most provoked not to hear it in Time.

8ᵗʰ again your dear Dover Letter⁶—'Tis, indeed, the *Friday* 5 *Oᵇʳᵉ 'Je passe'* be[gan to] make my heart palpitate! it never beat regularly till to Day—& *not yet*, I may more truly say, for I cannot conquer the trepidation with which I have read of your dangers as the Joy is as yet too turbulent to be without pain—yet I would not exchange it, Heaven knows, for any other feeling, that any earthly event could produce or offer. This morning, after church, Mr. William called upon me, purposely to make enquiries after you. I read him several select passages from your Letter—& loved him when his ⟨interest⟩ was signalized so affectionately. Indeed he is most deserving your utmost friendship. He talked even *fluently* for *William*, talked fluently of the idea of your happiness, which he had conceived upon your first sight of your native soil, after so long an absence—upon your meeting with your Heart's earliest Friends. I have never known him so eloquent, & so *loquacious*.

---

⁶ L. 439, of which, however, the second leaf has been torn away.
⁷ See also L. 437, p. 28.

Mr. & Mrs. Norbury came afterwards—& so rejoiced you were set sail—

9. I believe that our best Friend has heard the event, with joy, on the *10.* when I had again a visit from William, who acquainted me, his Brother had arrived the preceeding Day.[8] He had been in dangers similar to yours, in the tremendous storm, with the additional charge & apprehension of wife & 3 babies. How do I love my best ami! thankfulness on the subject of a journey! God knows it would have been a trial difficult to sustain to have been in the inside of such a Tempest with the dear child! myself, too, by nature so cowardly!—William was full of anecdotes of his Brother—all interesting—but not very pleasant!

11. Bood's birthday[9]—& he meant to have spent it here—but his cold prevented him. I went out with our dear Friends who had been, the Day before, to see Cecilia & her children, at her mother's, the Duch⁵ Leinster.[10] Cecilia is naturally fatigued & harassed by her many voyages ⌐ but otherwise well. The Children, they say, are very lovely.⌐

12ᵗʰ This Day I have had the blessing of the news of your safe arrival. Alex is now very considerably stronger & better: the red wine did not agree with him,—it heated him—I have left it off, & all medicine whatever, giving him only Eggs slightly warmed, chocolate, & Broth in abundance, & this method is very successful at present. He looks far better, & is certainly rather less thin. All our family are quite well. The most essential News I can send you, is that, in answer to my Letter to Miss Planta,[11] I received the most gracious approbation of your Journey, & approbation also of my own intended one next June. This has been great comfort to me indeed! Heaven—Heaven bless you!—

⌐Truly we are very well⌐

[*By Alexander d'Arblay*]

My dear Papa

I desire my love to my Cousins in France.[12] And I hope they are very well. BETTY has just made me a pair of Spatterdashes

---

[8] See L. 442 n. 4.   [9] Bourdois was born on 11 Nov. 1761.
[10] For the Duchess of Leinster, mother of Cecilia Margaret Locke *née* Ogilvie, see iii, L. 171 n. 11.
[11] See L. 437, pp. 28–9.   [12] See Genealogical Table, vi.

for the Garden, which I think will suprize you very much. I
have also got a Great Coat and a pair of Socks for the garden.
my Spatterdashes make my legs look like yours Good by dear
dear Papa

[*Madame d'Arblay here added interlinearly six lines of writing, now obliterated,
apparently a report on Alex's progress in mathematics and French, etc. She closed her
letter on the right fold and margins in some eight lines, also obliterated.*]

444   [West Humble],
                                          12 November 1801
To Doctor Burney

A.L. (Berg), 12 Nov. 1801
Single sheet 4to   1 p.   *pmks*   DARKING 13 NO 1801 ⟨1801⟩ wafer
Addressed: Dr. Burney / Chelsea College / Middlesex
Endorsed by CB: d'A—'s arrival at / Calais
Edited by FBA, p. 1, *annotated and date retraced* ⁝⁝· Novr 12—1801. (7)
M. d'Arblay's arrival at Paris after a dreadful storm

                                            Novr 12—1801.
   With what joy—my dearest Father, do I tell You I have just
now received a Letter from M. d'Arblay, dated *Calais*, Nov.
⌐9th⌐ 7^thɪ—He has had a terrific voyage—in so much as to
bless Heaven for the illness of the Child, since it was the cause
that he & I were not in similar danger! He was 3 Days without
food—the fury of the Storm overturned his Basket [of] provisions—which, I suppose, were trod under foot, [for] he says
he could get none to eat—& his bottle of wine was broken—
He was called up in the middle of the night, with cries that the
Ship was driving over the anchor—he was then sick to death—
but *instantly cured*, & sprung up, & worked harder than any
sailor—till the ship got into Port—6 days & a half out of 8 were
spent in storm! Thank God, he is now safe! as I had written all
the enclosed Yesterday, though too late for the post I think
you would rather have it than let me burn it for 4d.—Heaven
bless you, dearest Sir—I am still agitated—though with joy—

444. ¹ This is L. 441.

46

445

To Charles Burney

A.L. (Hyde Collection), 12
Single sheet 4to   2 pp.   *pmks*   DARKING   13 NOV 1801   ⟨ ⟩ 1801
wafer
Addressed: Dr. Charles Burney, / Greenwich, / Kent
Docketed in pencil, p. 1: 474

12th.

My dearest Charles—

Thank Heaven my Letter—destined for an *apology*, that
M d'A could not get to you—has been deferred till it can be
a porter of good news—I have a Letter this Morning from Calais
—where my poor M d'A arrived the 6th—after a very frightful
& dangerous passage from Gravesend—round the Coast, to
Dover—where they were obliged to make a signal of distress
for a new pilot—& then to be landed for refitting—

He is now safe—& in his own Country—& soon—I hope,
will again be in ours.

I hope, too, poor Rosette is much better—I am harrassed
with much agitation but shall now refit, also.

Heaven bless you,
my dearest Charles—

What is this story of ⟨Kemble⟩?[1]

Mr. Angerstein[2] says he shall be certainly glad to know
Dr. Charles Burney but only *personally*, as he is fatigued out of
all health for any new business of any sort. He is now in
Lincolnshire at Mr. Boucherett's.

445. [1] 'Mr. John Kemble has quitted Drury-Lane Theatre in consequence of
a dispute between him and Mr. Sheridan' was an item in *The Times* (30 Oct. 1801)
that FBA may well have read. The actor and manager did not part company,
however, until the end of the season (1802). See Herschel Baker, *John Philip
Kemble* . . . (1942), pp. 246–7.
[2] See L. 425 n. 4. One of the magistrates for the county of Kent, M.P. for Camel-
ford (1796–1802), and for Greenwich (1835–7), Angerstein was at this time visiting
Ayscoghe Boucherett, M.P. for Great Grimsby (1796–1803), and his wife Emilia
née Crokatt, a connection of the Angerstein family (iii, L. 150 n. 14).

M. d'Arblay
To Madame d'Arblay

A.L. (Diary MSS. vi. 5280–3, Berg),   *n.d.*
Double sheet 4to   green   4 pp.   pp. 1 & 4 crosswritten   *pmk*   2 〈   〉
NO .801   wafer
Addressed: Madame Darblay / Westhumble / near *Darking* / *Surry* / Eng¹
Edited by FBA, p. 1 (5280), *annotated and dated*: ⨥ Novʳ—12:   1801   (29)
Lettre charmante — Fete pour la Paix   M. de Narbonne   M. de La
Fayette — Buonaparte. ⌣, PARIS. ⌣,

Il m'est impossible ma chere Fanny, d'entrer dans beaucoup
de details vu que je n'ai qu'un instant dont je puisse profiter
pʳ t'envoyer ceci par une occasion sure. La fete du 18 Brumaire¹
a dû surpasser tout ce qu'on pouvait s'être flatté d'y voir, et
quoique je sois bien malheureusement arrivé trop tard pour en
jouir, c'est avec l'interest le plus vif que j'ai examiné depuis
tout ce qui en reste. Il est impossible de se faire une idée du
gout qui a presidé à l'ensemble et de l'agrement de tous les
details. Je ne sais point encore positivement quand il me sera
possible d'aller voir mon oncle. L'affaire de mon traitement de
reforme n'est rien moins qu'avancée et il est faux que Sicard et
la Colombe l'ayent obtenu.² Tout ce qu'il y a de positif c'est
que le 1ᵉʳ Consul a dit au Gᵃˡ L.F. que la demande etait juste,³
qu'il y aurait egard, mais que pour le moment cela etait
impossible. Il y a de cela environ deux mois, et La Fayette fera
une nouvelle tentative. Je ne puis t'exprimer combien je suis
faché d'avoir été ainsi trompé, non pas tant pour le retard d'une

---

446. ¹ Although d'Arblay had missed the activities of the day itself (18 Brumaire,
9 Nov.), the cannonades, the proclamations, the illuminations, the massing of
superbly dressed troops, and the thronging multitudes in happy holiday clothes,
he could still have seen the triumphal arches on the Pont-Neuf and, over the
theatre at the Place de la Concorde, the Temple of Peace. He would have seen the
inscriptions and the graffiti in praise of Bonaparte, 'vainqueur et pacificateur'.
'Il a, par ses hauts faits, surpassé les mortels;/ On eût pour lui jadis élevé des autels'
(*Journal des Débats*, 11 Nov.).
    ² See L. 425 nn. 8, 9.
    ³ Lafayette would have by no means been a wise choice as an intermediary. For
the uneasiness he inspired in Bonaparte, see Paul Chanson, *Lafayette et Napoléon*
(Lyons, 1958), pp. 133–45.

grace que sur la parole de Bonaparte je crois certaine, que pour la fausse demarche que mon erreur m'a fait faire, en citant comme faite une chose à faire. Je suis passé ce matin chez Lauriston[4] que je n'ai point trouvé. De là je suis allé chez L.F.[5] à qui j'avais demandé hier un rendez vous pour une heure. Il n'en etait que dix et dejà il avait envoyé chez le Gen[al] Narbonne[6] p[r] savoir mon adresse, grondant beaucoup la portiere l de ce qu'elle ne me l'avait point fait laisser. Il loge chez M[de] Tessé qui est à la campagne.[5] Un moment après il est rentré et nous nous sommes embrassés avec toute la cordialité que tu peux supposer. Il devait aller diner à la campagne chez M[de] de Tessé, et donnait l'ordre au domestique de partir seul, parce qu'il voulait t'aller voir sur le champ, et te presser de venir absolument t'etablir à la Grange[5] — mais M[de] Darblay n'est point ici   Ta femme n'est pas ici? (et jamais desappointement ne s'est peint sur un visage d'une maniere plus prononcée.) Alors je l'ai engagé à rappeller le Domestique de M[de] Tessé, ce qu'il a fait, en lui donnant l'ordre d'attendre, et nous avons causé: mais il a fallu que je l'assurasse premierement que trés certainement je t'amenerais cet été, et que très certainement aussi nous irions le voir à la Grange. Entr'autres choses voici ce qu'il m'a dit

'Je t'assure que dans ma prison et au moment où le traitement que j'ai eprouvé etait le plus rigoureux, deux Auteurs seulement m'ont transporté comme dans un monde nouveau, où la politique, mes malheurs, mes souffrances avaient disparu. et ces Auteurs sont Richardson et M[de] Darblay. J'avais lu ses ouvrages, mais comme peut les lire quelqu'un au milieu du tourbillon des affaires, et des projets qu'elles font naitre et suivre. Imagine mon ravissement lorsqu'au milieu du double bonheur qu'ils me faisaient eprouver, j'apprens ton mariage avec cette enchanteresse, lorsque je reçois la nouvelle que mon ami vient,

---

[4] In 1804 General Lauriston (L. 425 n. 5) was living in the cour du manège at the Tuileries.

[5] Lafayette, when in Paris, stayed at 24, rue d'Anjou, the house of his wife's aunt, Mme de Tessé (iii, L. 242 n. 12; v, Intro. p. xliv). Her country house was at Aulnay. His, La Grange-Bléneau, in Brie, about 30 miles from Paris, was a fifteenth-century castle that in 1799 Mme de Lafayette had managed to salvage from the Noailles possessions. For illustrations of the château, see André Maurois, *Adrienne, the Life of the Marquise de la Fayette*, translated by Gerard Hopkins (1961).

[6] The comte de Narbonne, last heard of in Germany (iv, pp. 69 and 308), had returned to Paris in mid-June 1800 and was now established at 1205, rue de Miroménil.

selon moi, de faire la plus haute fortune au quel un mortel puisse aspirer.'

Eh bien, Fanny! — j'espere que voilà du bon anglais— Demain matin j'ai rendez vous avec Du Taillis,[7] aide de camp de Berthier.[8] En sortant de chez lui, j'espere voir Talleyrand:[9] mais ce que je desire infiniment c'est de ne pas partir avant d'avoir au moins entrevu le 1ᵉʳ Consul, cet homme si justement celebre. La fête a donné lieu a beaucoup d'inscriptions en vers, | faits à sa louange: mais en general, ils m'ont paru fort au dessous du sujet. Relativement à l'obligation que nous, cy devant, portés sur la liste des Emigrés lui avons, Narbonne me disait aujourdhui 'Il a mis toutes nos têtes sur ses epaules.' J'aime cette expression, et tu vois qu'en cela, comme en tant d'autres choses il est parfaitement d'accord avec nous, et qu'il croit que notre interêst est parfaitement d'accord avec notre reconnoissance.[10]

[xxxxx 19 *lines*] |

Je vais demain avec le Gᵃˡ la Fayette à Passy[11] demander à Diner à Maubourg.[12] J'y verrai Pusy[13] qui vient d'être nommé

---

[7] On 1 Sept. 1789, the date on which Adrien-Jean-Baptiste-Amable Ramond du Bosc (1760–1851), comte Dutaillis, was made capitaine-aide-major of the 3rd battalion of the 6th division of the Paris National Guard, d'Arblay became major of the 2nd division. After serving in the Armée du nord (1792–3), Dutaillis became (Mar. 1795) aide-de-camp to Berthier; and after distinguished service at Marengo (14 June 1800) he was attached (9 Aug. 1801) to the ministère de la Guerre. M. d'A obviously hoped that in this latter capacity, he might, as an associate and friend of long standing, present his claims to Berthier. He was to encounter him later in connection with the expedition to San Domingo (see L. 465, p. 110).

[8] Louis-Alexandre Berthier, ministre de la Guerre. See L. 425 n. 9.

[9] See Intro., ii, p. xviii.

[10] With the aid of Talleyrand and Fouché, the comte de Narbonne had arranged to have his name erased from the proscription lists on 15 Oct. 1800, and on 8 Mar. 1801 he had obtained a pension (half-pay). Thus favoured, he could encourage d'Arblay to hope for similar favours. In later years, however, FBA annotated the words of praise: 'N.B. This compliment was requisite to make the Letter safe.'

[11] A village with a population of some 1,700 situated near the Bois de Boulogne on the outskirts of Paris, Passy was incorporated with the city only in 1860, by which time it had become fashionable as a residential district for literati and artists. It had something of this character when in October 1802 FBA and M. d'A took a house there.

[12] Marie-Charles-*César*-Florimond de Fay (1758–1831), comte de Latour-Maubourg (1803), a former constitutional monarchist and one of Lafayette's most devoted followers (ii, Intro., p. xvii; and Appendix I, pp. 186–7). In 1778 he had married Marie-Charlotte-Hippolyte Pinault de Thenelles (d. 1837) and had eight children (L. 456 n. 10). The family lived in Passy, where the d'Arblays were to remove in 1802.

[13] Jean-Xavier Bureaux de Pusy (1750–1805), a former deputy to the National Assembly, who, like César de Latour-Maubourg, had been imprisoned with Lafayette at Olmütz (ii, p. 187). Pusy was named prefect of Allier (2 Nov. 1801)

Prefet je ne sais où. Le pauvre Jaucourt,[14] qui s'est cassé le bras, est mieux. Je n'ai pu voir encore ni M. Moore,[15] ni Riccé,[16] ni Lajard,[17] à qui j'ai ecrit. A revoir ma tendre amie. Combien ma bonne amie j'ai parlé à fond sur un sujet que je n'ose entamer! Quelles larmes j'ai vu couler. Tu peus juger si j'y ai melé les miennes, et elles n'ont pas été les seules. M[de] de Laval[18] elle même en a versé d'ameres sur le sort *of that departed Angel.*[19] Je l'ai trouvée au fait de tout ce qui entoure et a entouré notre petit hermitage. Elle ne cesse de me demander si effectivement cette famille L[ocke] est la pureté celeste elle même, si Norbury est le paradis terrestre, ou si tout simplement M[r] de N[arbonne] n'est qu'un enthousiaste. Devine si tu peus ma reponse. J'embrasse Alex, et toi comme helas! je puis vous embrasser — ce n'en est pas moins de toute mon ame

D [

Mr de N. et les Lameth[20] sont les seuls qui ayent obtenu un traitement. Ces derniers, imprudens et imprevoyans à leur ordinaire, ont excité la jalousie de l'armée ce qui nuit beaucoup au succès de ma demande. Il semble que je sois toujours

and later, prefect of Rhône (30 July 1802). At this time both Latour-Maubourg and Pusy, associates of Lafayette, were closely watched by the police.
  [14] Arnail-François de Jaucourt (1757–1852), formerly a deputy to the National Assembly, who, emigrating in 1792, joined the constitutional monarchists at Juniper Hall, Mickleham, Surrey (Intro., ii, pp. xvi–xvii, and Six).
  [15] Frank Moore (L. 430 n. 3).
  [16] Gabriel-Marie (1758–1832), comte de Riccé, who, abandoning service under Lafayette on 16 Aug. 1792 and emigrating to Holland, had established himself as a banker in Hamburg before emigrating to England (Six; and iv, pp. 178–9).
  [17] Pierre-Auguste Lajard (iv, L. 291 n. 5).
  [18] Catherine-Jeanne Tavernier de Boullongne (c. 1748–1838), who had married in 1765 Mathieu-Paul-Louis de Montmorency-Laval (1748–1809), vicomte de Laval, comte de l'Empire (1808). For Mme de Laval, see further L. 469 n. 6; and L. 511 n. 6; and Intro., pp. xxxviii–xxxix.
  [19] An allusion to FBA's sister Susanna (Burney) Phillips, her domestic sorrows, exile, and untimely death at Parkgate on 6 Jan. 1800 (iv, pp. 380–6). Mme de Laval, who, unlike some of her friends, had emigrated to Switzerland rather than to England, knew SBP and the Lockes only by report.
  [20] The three comtes de Lameth, Alexandre-*Théodore*-Victor (1756–1854), *Charles*-Malo-François (1757–1832), and *Alexandre*-Théodore-Victor (1760–1829), had been erased from the lists of *émigrés* on 29 May, 21 and 28 April 1800, respectively. It was their good fortune to have fought in America, as had Berthier, now ministre de la Guerre, who, 'contemporain et frère d'armes des Lameth', acceded readily to the requests of the brothers for their *traitement de réforme*. Lebrun (L. 465 n. 4) also agreed, but Bonaparte, suspicious of their political activities, delayed the favour until 8 Mar. 1801. See Théodore Lameth, *Mémoires*, ed. Eugène Welvert (1913), pp. xiv–xv; and M. J. Sydenham, *The French Revolution* (1966), p. 80. A quarrel between the brothers and Lafayette (described op. cit., p. xii) may account for the bias of d'Arblay's remarks.

destiné à les trouver dans mon chemin d'une manière facheuse, car tu sais combien, dans le cours de la revolution nos opinions ont peu été en mesure. apres avoir obtenu leur traitement de reforme, ils ont voulu être presentés à Bonaparte et ont cru se faire valoir en lui vantant la part qu'ils avaient prise à la revolution. Le Consul après les avoir ecoutés patiement leur a dit du ton le plus glacial. Je vous crois honnetes et d'après tout ce que je viens d'entendre vous devez être profondement malheureux et il les a quittés. Tu peux compter sur cette anecdote telle que je te la rapporte; et tu vois que Bonaparte est le même en tout. N. de qui je la tiens, dit que sa capacité en ⟨ce⟩ genre est au dela de tout ce qu'on peut se figurer dans les limites du possible.

Mathieu Montmorency²¹ me prie de le mettre aux pieds de la Sainte famille. c'est l'expression recue ici. Il est à la tête des hopitaux et de l'etablissement des sourds et muets. J'ai vu aussi avec grand plaisir Adrien Montmorency.²² Mes tendres respects à ton Pere. Amitiès à toute ta famille. |

Tout va bien lentement excepté mon argent qui court ⟨à sa perte⟩. Ce n'est pas la faute de mes amis. Mᵈᵉ d'Henin²³ et Mᵈᵉ de Laval se disputent à qui m'aura le plus souvent à dejeuner et à diner; et ne veulent pas que je mange ailleurs mais mes affaires ne me permettent pas de faire sur cela ce que j'aimerais le mieux. |

[xxxxx 6 *lines*]

²¹ Mathieu-Jean-Félicité de Montmorency-Laval (1767–1826), vicomte de Laval (1809), had in 1792 joined the Juniper Colony in Surrey for a short time only. His personal history (the arranged marriage of his youth, his liaison with the baronne [de Staël], the loss of his brother, and his religious melancholy) is detailed by FBA in her French Exercise Book III, pp. 10–23, Berg. See also Lefebvre, pp. 129, 425.

²² Anne-*Adrien*-Pierre de Montmorency-Laval (1768–1837), prince de, *later*, duc de Laval, duc de San-Fernando-Luis and grand d'Espagne de 1ᵉ classe, maréchal de camp (1814), minister of state at various times to Spain, Rome, Vienna, and London, pair de France (1820), chevalier-commandeur de l'Ordre du Saint-Esprit (1820), chevalier de la Toison d'or. He was a cousin of Mathieu-Jean-Félicité (*supra*).

²³ Adélaïde-Félicité-*Étiennette* Guinot de Monconseil (1750–1824), who was married on 29 September 1766 to Charles-Alexandre-Marc-Marcellin d'Alsace-Hénin-Liétard (1744–94), prince d'Hénin, a brother of the prince de Chimay. The years of her exile she had spent in London and Richmond (see ii *passim*; and Intro., v, pp. xxxix–xl), and FBA, who had often met her there, was to make her earlier life, the unhappiness caused by the flagrant unfaithfulness of her husband, his seizure at Bagatelle during the Terror, and his death by the guillotine, the subject of 'une petite historiette' in French Exercise Book IV, pp. [121–31], Berg. Mentioned often in the *Journal* of Mme de Latour du Pin, the princesse is the subject of a biography by Eugène Welvert (see p. xvii).

M. d'Arblay
To Madame d'Arblay

A.L. (Berg), 16 Nov. 1801
Double sheet 4to   4 pp.
Addressed: Madame Darblay / Westhumble / near *Dorking*, / *Surry*
Edited by FBA, p. 1, *top margin, annotated and year date* 1801 *encircled*: ✠ /
Novr. / ⌐41⌐ 30 Acc^t of Masiquet Valet de Chambre fidele—et M
Tapponier

Ce 25 Brumaire 1801 (16 9bre vieux style.)

[xxxxx 16 *lines*]

J'ai eu aujourdhui un bien grand plaisir en embrassant cet excellent Massiquet,[1] lequel au reste est devenu riche à force de porter les depèches des Generaux. Je crois en verité qu'il n'y a plus que l'Angleterre qui puisse lui offrir quelque chose de nouveau. Son attachement pour moi, les risques que cet attachement lui a fait courrir, sans l'empêcher de le manifester en toute occasion, m'ont extremement touché. Je suis sûr que tu aurais été tentée toi même de l'embrasser | en lui entendant dire 'Quelque puissans qu'ils fussent, pas un d'eux n'osait dire du mal de vous en ma presence. Je ne l'aurais point souffert. Mais il faut être juste, bien peu vous voulaient du mal, et beaucoup au contraire m'ont souvent dit de vous tout le bien possible, et vous ont sincerement regretté.'

N'est ce pas là, suivant ton expression, du *bon Anglais*?

Ce Massiquet est un excellent garçon, qui avec son titre de '*mon ancien valet de chambre*' (c'est son expression) s'est si bien faufilé dans toute ma famille, et parmi les plus honnêtes gens de mon pays, que dernierement il a été invité à aller passer les vendanges à Joigny, où tout le monde se l'est disputé. Il me dit, dans sa très precieuse simplicité, que partout les plus grands egards étaient pour Massiquet, et que pour cela il n'avait qu'à parler beaucoup de moi, et un peu de tout ce qu'il a vu pendant

447. [1] M. d'A's valet of former days. Lucratively employed as a messenger with 'Prince Charles' of Austria, i.e., the Archduke Charles (1771–1847), he is to reappear in Paris in 1817, offering devoted services to d'Arblay in his illness (ix *passim*).

la Guerre, tant à la suitte des Armées, que dans les Courts etrangeres où il a été envoyé, près du Prince Charles, par exemple, &c — &c — &c. (Cela n'est pas d'un bien mauvais augure pour moi; qu'en dis tu?) Ce brave homme au reste a, comme je te l'ai dejà dit, amassé une petite fortune qui serait bien plus considerable s'il en eut su tirer parti. Mais suivant sa coutume, il n'avait pas plutôt cent louïs qu'il s'empressait de les offrir à ceux près de qui il etait; et je meurs de peur qu'il ne les trouve pas aussi exacts que moi. La manière dont mes amis le traitent, ne lui a point au reste tourné la tête, et son premier soin a été, après m'avoir grondé du derangement de mes hardes, de les mettre en ordre, de brosser l'habit que j'allais mettre, et de courrir en bas, c-à-d de descendre plus de cent marches de l'escalier m'allumer une bougie pour cacheter quelques paquets. Il est bien vrai que tout au travers de ses recits, et des marques de son attachement, il me frappe quelquefois sur l'epaule; mais pour tout au monde je ne voudrais point lui voir reprimer cet excès, et devoir plus de *decorum* à une contrainte qui nuirait à l'epanchement de son coeur.

Tu ne peus te faire une idée de ma vie ici. Tu sais qu'en arrivant ici j'avais été près de 11 jours sans me deshabiller, et presque sans fermer l'oeil; Eh bien depuis que je suis ici, je ne me suis pas encore couché avant 3 heures, et je suis levé tous les jours à 7. Cependant je n'ai vu aucun spectacle, je ne suis entré dans aucun Caffé, je n'ai été voir ni tableaux ni statues, je n'ai diné qu'une fois avec Narbonne,[2] qui est parfait pour moi, je n'ai vu Lajard[2] qu'une demie heure; et n'ai été chez M^de d'Henin[3] que deux fois; et c'est à peine si j'ai eu le tems d'embrasser mon Cousin Bazille celui qui etait Com^re des Guerres en Hollande.[4] Que faites vous donc, diras tu? Rien.

Malgré tous mes soins je ne suis guere plus avancé que le premier jour. De tous les gens *en place* que j'ai été à portée de voir, Lauriston[5] est dans le fait le seul qui soit pour moi en mesure, au moins avec ce que j'en attendais. Ah, que je serais bien ici, si je n'avais rien à demander à personne: mais en ce

---

[2] See L. 446 nn. 6, 17.

[3] The princesse d'Hénin was living at this time at the corner of the rue de Miroménil and the rue Verte (today the rue de Penthièvre). See L. 513, p. 265 and n. 15.

[4] Jean-Baptiste Bazille (1768–1808), called 'Précourt'. See Genealogical Table, vi; and L. 586 n. 1.

[5] See L. 425 n. 4.

cas combien encore j'aimerais mieux être auprès de mon amie et de notre cher petit! La perfection serait en y joignant Norbury Dorking Chelsea Greenwich Beaumont et James Street,[6] de vous reunir tous à quelques lieues d'ici, dans un beau site, et il n'en manque pas. [xxxxx 2 *lines*] |

[xxxxx 10 *lines*]

Hier en passant sur le pont neuf je remarquai un *Gentleman* en surtout bleu qui paraissait me reconnaitre, et que j'etais sûr d'avoir vu sans pouvoir me rappeller où, 3 fois j'avais retourné la tête et rencontré ses yeux. Je m'arrête, il en fait autant et nous nous joignons en faisant chacun la moitié du chemin. Pardon Monsieur je m'appelle Darblay — et moi Monsieur, je me nomme Taponnier[7] Capitaine de votre Regt. (Ce capitaine est comme tu l'as pu voir par ce qu'en ont dit les gazettes, un des bons generaux français) — ma foi mon cher general, je suis d'autant plus heureux de vous voir, que je crois pouvoir me flatter que vous m'avez conservé quelque amitié (un serrement de main de sa part tres expressif) D'ailleurs vous me devez quelques remercimens pour ma profession et moi je m'applaudis beaucoup d'avoir reussi à vous empêcher de vous retirer en vous annonçant des succès que vos talens m'avaient fait prevoir — Tu juges que cette rencontre m'a fait un plaisir sensible. Mille et mille tendres complimens à nos excellens amis.

---

[6] The addresses respectively of the Lockes, Antoine Bourdois, Dr. Burney, Charles Burney, Esther, and James.

[7] Alexandre-Camille Taponier (1749–1831) was a captain in the 103rd infantry in August 1791, at which time M. d'A was colonel of the regiment. With the usual promotions, général de division (7 Nov. 1793), commandant of various divisions, 1795, 1796 (see Six), he had been 'admis au traitement de réforme' on 29 Mar. 1801.

M. d'Arblay
To Madame d'Arblay

A.L.S. (Diary MSS. vi. 5292–[95], Berg), 16 Nov. 1801
Double sheet 4to, greenish, with a strip (2·3 × 7·6″) cut from the bottom
of the second leaf, but now replaced. It had been reversed to form the end
of a paste-up on p. 4 [5295]. 3 pp. *pmks* P. 61. P. / CALAIS   1 DEC
1801   wafer
    Addressed: England / Madame Darblay / Westhumble — / near Dorking /
England
    Edited by FBA, p. 1 (5292), *annotated and dated*: ⁑· ⁑· / Nov^r / 1801   No. 2
(31 / 1) des traits de Buonaparte —   *annotated*, p. 2: from *Le Chevalier d'Arblay
to Madame d'Arblay, and re-dated*: Paris Novr 16. 1801.
    Edited also by CFBt *and the* Press.

Paris 25 Brumaire an. 10.
(16. 9bre 1801 vieux style)

⌐Ce matin, ma bonne amie, j'ai donné à un monsieur qui
part pour Londre[1] une lettre qu'il te fera passer surement. Je
sors de chez le Médecin qu'on m'avait tant recommandé de
consulter pour sa manière et pour sa repute de bon homme. Il
pense comme toi que ce sont des ⟨cures⟩ qui commencent ces
⟨douleurs⟩ et il approuve le regime qu'on m'a conseillé de
suivre. Je t'ecrirai une autre fois dans plus de détail. aujourdhui
cela me serait impossible parce que nous avons été interrompus
au milieu de notre conversation à ce sujet. Quant à ma niece[2] il
m'assure qu'elle ne doit pas avoir la plus petite inquietude, et
c'est très mal à propos qu'elle s'était allarmée. Qu'elle continue
à prendre de l'exercice afin que preparée au voyage qu'elle
doit faire incessament, elle ne soit point incommodée. à revoir
ma chere amie. je t'embrasse comme je t'aime.

    Il est arrivé à la pauvre petite M^de d'Haussé[3] dont tu m'as

---

448. [1] Unidentified.
    [2] Maria Bourdois (L. 436 n. 5), FBA's niece, who was shortly to accompany
her husband to Paris.
    [3] Perhaps an abbreviation for Haussonville (cf. D'hausse^e, p. 127), and thus,
conjecturally, Jeanne-Marie-Thérèse Falcoz de la Blache (d. 1854), who on 10
Oct. 1801 had married Charles-Louis-Bernard de Cléron (1770–1846), comte
d'Haussonville, who, serving with the Army of the Princes, had emigrated in 1791
to Germany and later to England. Related on his mother's side to the Harcourts

quelquefois entendu parler, un grand un trés grand malheur. J'ai été la voir et l'ai trouvée dans la désolation. Neanmoins elle m'a reçu avec tous les témoignages d'une extrême satisfaction. J'y ai trouvé un homme avec qui jadis je m'etais brouillé pour elle. Depuis ce tems, il etait du petit nombre de ceux qui pouvaient se dire mes ennemis quoique je n'eusse aucun désir de les traiter comme tels. Non seulement nous nous sommes raccomodés mais comme nous avons à force de prieres et d'excellentes raisons gagné sur M^{de} ⟨d'h⟩ de prendre quelqu' exercice et de permettre à ses amis de tenter de la distraire, aprés l'avoir décidé à accepter un diner très peu nombreux j'en ai moi même été prié, et moi seul j'ai fixé le jour afin que La pr.[4] m'aide avec mes affaires. Demain 26 je presente ma petition p^r avoir ma carte de sureté,[5] qui dit on me sera bientôt expediée. Quant à mon autre affaire, elle est au même point et je ne sais pas comment elle peut prendre une meilleure tournure: car je ne puis présenter demain que les mêmes ⎮ raisons et les mêmes raisonnemens dejà vieux sous les yeux des autorités. J'ai reçu aujourdhui de mon cher oncle une lettre que je n'entends pas bien, en ce qu'il me parle de difficultés qu'on veut me faire relativement à la bagatelle qu'on m'a sauvée.[6] Il ne serait pas gai de n'avoir reussi à rien, et de se trouver en dernier resultat uniquement avec des dettes qui sans être considerables seraient néanmoins fort genantes. Parlons de choses plus gaies.¶

(L. 513 n. 1), he was given refuge with other members of the French Harcourt families at Staines but was often in London, returning to France via Hamburg at the beginning of 1800. Created comte de l'Empire in 1810, he accepted an appointment as *chambellan* at the Imperial court, but a royalist and a Constitutionalist at heart, he welcomed the return of Louis XVIII, who admitted him to the rank of lieutenant-général de la garde nationale.

Mlle de la Blache, who had also emigrated to England in the 1790s, there sustained the tragic loss of her fiancé Charles Virot (1770–95), vicomtede Sombreuil, who, noted for his bravery, was placed in command of the second embarkation to Quiberon on what was to have been his wedding day.

The stories of these emigrations, as well as recollections of the Empire, the First and Second Restorations, and the crowning of Charles X, are related by her son Louis-Charles-Othenin-Bernard de Cléron (1809–84), comte d'Haussonville, membre de l'Académie française, in *Ma jeunesse, 1814–1830* (1885). M. d'A may have known the elder *émigrés* in London, and the story of the blighted wedding was apparently well known (see Larousse).

4 The princesse d'Hénin (L. 446 n. 23).
5 *Cartes de sureté* were identification cards by which, as the Revd. Dawson Warren explains (p. 33), 'we may go any where without fear of being molested'. His was apparently signed by Talleyrand. See also Greatheed, p. 168.
6 Jean-Baptiste-*Gabriel* Bazille (L. 423 n. 2) of Joigny, in spite of whose efforts most of d'Arblay's property in Joigny had been sold. See further L. 461 and vii, Appendix I.

Dernierement il était question de savoir au Senat si les membres qui le composent seraient ou non armés ou parés d'un sabre. Tous les militaires pensaient que rien n'etait moins en mesure avec les fonctions des senateurs. Cette reflexion etait vivement combattue par Volney. Le G ᵃˡ Lefevre dans la chaleur de la discussion lui dit *Si vous avez un sabre, il faut donc que j'en porte deux moi.*[7]

Bonaparte a nommé Pusy[8] Prefet, et lorsqu'il lui est venu faire ses remerciemens, il lui a dit. 'C'est bien peu, mais il faut bien commencer par quelquechose qui vous mette à même de deployer de nouveau cet excellent esprit, que vous avez montré dans l'assemblée Constituante. Voici un autre trait de lui plus aimable encore.

La Tour Maubourg l'un des compagnons du General L. F. voulait marier sa fille à un Emigré non rayé.[9] Il avait obtenu du 1ᵉʳ consul un rendez vous dans le quel il etait entré dans beaucoup de details sans lui cacher les raisons qu'on pouvait objecter contre la radiation demandée. Bonaparte l'interrompt et lui dit. 'Ce jeune homme convient il à Mademᵉˡˡᵉ votre fille? — oui General — vous convient il à vous Mʳ de Maubourg? — beaucoup General. — eh bien l'homme que vous jugez digne d'entrer dans une famille comme la vôtre, est surement digne aussi d'être citoyen francais.

A revoir, mon amie, je te quitte pour aller solliciter ma carte de sureté, muni d'une excellente apostille à mon memoire. Cette apostille est de mon ami Lajacqueminiere[10] | membre du Tribunat lequel me sert avec beaucoup de chaleur. Je n'en puis dire autant de plusieurs autres personnes sur les quelles j'avais

---

[7] The debate took place, d'Arblay says, between Volney and Lefebvre, that is, between Constantin-François de Chasseboeuf (or Boisjirais) (1757–1820), comte de Volney (1808), linguist, historian, author, and savant, a man of independent mind, whose opinions would demand respect; and François-Joseph Lefebvre (1755–1820), duc de Danzig (1808), maréchal de l'Empire (1804), pair de France (1814), who thought that swords were the prerogative of soldiers, not civilians. Volney, however, carried the day. See *Journal des Débats* (12 June 1800): 'L'esprit militaire a pénétré dans le Sénat conservateur. Il a décidé, dans sa séance du 18, que chacun de ses membres ajouterait le sabre antique à sa costume; et l'on assure que le Corps législatif et le Tribunat pourraient bien suivre cet exemple.' Swords were to make part of the formal dress of the Empire.   [8] See L. 446 n. 13.

[9] César de Latour-Maubourg (L. 446 n. 12), whose daughter Adèle de Fay (1782–1811) had married on 20 Sept. 1801 François-Timoléon Stellaye de Baigneux de Courcival (1772–1850), *styled* marquis de Courcival.

[10] Louis-Charles Gillet de la Jacqueminière (1752–1836), a cousin of M. d'A from Saint-Julien-du-Sault (Yonne). Director of the post since 1777, he became 'procureur syndic' for Joigny to the provincial assembly of Île-de-France and was

bien davantage lieu de compter — ainsi va le monde. je te repete que si je n'avais besoin de personne, tout le monde à ce qu'il me parait serait infiniment empressé à me servir.

ᵀObligé de couvrir cet espace seulement parceque deja ⟨rencontrerais je près⟩ le peril de fermer ma lettre bien faché de ne t'envoyer que du papier blanc Je t'embrasse de tout mon coeur, de toutes mes forces. Ecris moi donc. il me semble que j'aurais du moins une lettre de toi. Voici une voie qui te sert dans le cas où tu ne voudrais point abuser de celle que tu as déjà. Tu peus mettre ta lettre sous une enveloppe et l'adresser à *Madame Grandsire Hotel* [*Kingston*] *à Cal*[*ais*][11] Comme nous ne traitons que de nos affaires tes lettres sont sures de me parvenir. Je n'ai point encore ma carte de sureté. Mon oncle m'ecrit: ta tante,[12] ta voisine et cousine sont toutes folles de plaisir de te revoir.

Mes tendres respects à Norbury et mille amitiés à Dorking.[13] Ma niece doit bientôt avoir de mes nouvelles, si elle lit les presentes envoyées. Mande moi si elle a fini mon affaire. Dis moi aussi si la bonne volonté de Mʳ Angerstein nous vaut quelque chose;[14] c.à.d. si on ⟨le verra⟩ même ⟨de loin⟩. Ces deux choses sont pour moi du plus haut interêt.

Surtout soigne bien ta santé et celle d'Alexandre; et donne m'en souvent des nouvelles. Tu m'adresseras toujours tes lettres chez Lajard Nᵒ 43 fʳᵍ St Martin. S'il n'est pas à portée de ⟨moi⟩ chez ⟨lui même⟩, il me les fera passer.

T'ai je mandé que Mᵈᵉ de Tessé m'a écrit un billet charmant pour m'inviter à l'aller voir à la campagne. il m'a jusqu'à présent été impossible d'en profiter. Le père d'Adrienne[15] a fait la conoissance.ᵀ [xxxx 2 *words*]

Songe qu'il faut que tu sois en bien bonne santé ainsi qu'Alex

---

elected député du Tiers aux États généraux (18 Mar. 1789), acting as secretary to the Constituante. Deputy to the Conseil des cinq cents, he favoured the *coup d'état* of 18 Brumaire, was nominated to the Tribunat (26 Dec. 1799), becoming chief adviser in the Court of Accounts and was created chevalier de l'Empire on 3 June 1808.

[11] A hotel well known to the English from Hogarth's *A Gate of Calais or O! the Roast Beef of Old England*.

[12] For the wife of Gabriel (*supra*), Marie-Edmée-Euphémie *née* de la Mare (1745–1803), and the other members of the family, see the Genealogical Table, vi.

[13] To the Lockes, and to Maria and Antoine Bourdois at Sand Place.

[14] John Angerstein (L. 425 n. 4).

[15] Louis-Vigile, comte de Chavagnac (L. 437 n. 3).

pour que nous venions tous ensemble dans la belle saison. Embrasse pour moi le cher M^r L[ocke] au revoir ma chere et unique amie

ton heureux epoux

A. Darblay

[xxxxx 3 *lines*]

449   [Paris, 21 November 1801]

M. d'Arblay *conjointly with* Louis, Comte de Narbonne To Madame d'Arblay

A.L. mutilated. Originally a double sheet 4to, of which there remain the three cuttings that were pasted to L. 448.

The top segment of the first leaf, bearing the date and the opening of the letter, is cut away and missing. The remainder of the first leaf was cut into two segments (7·4 × 7·6 and 1·4 × 7·6″), extant in the paste-overs (above). Extant also is a sliver (0·3–0·5 × 7·6″), bearing the line of text (demande . . . est arrivé.), which was used to complete the paste-up (above). See Textual Notes. The remainder of the second leaf is missing. 2 pp. plus one line

Edited by FBA, p. 1 *annotated*: Buonapartes Guards—et M. de Narbonne p. 2 *annotated*: NB—the 5 following lines written by M. de Narbonne.

[*the top of the page is missing*]

[xxxxx 2½ *lines*]

Je me sens tellement bien ce soir que j'aurais bien pu sortir: mais ne pouvant rien faire pour hâter mon affaire, à quoi puis-je mieux employer mon tems qu'à causer avec mon a[mie] auprès d'un bon feu, et sans aucune distraction. Depuis que j'ai commencé ceci, il s'est fait q[uelque] changement dans mes plans. Je dois toujours quitter Paris après demain 2 frimaire (23 — 9bre) ⟨mais⟩ je partirai seul, et il est presumable que j'irai droit à Joigny, remettant à un autre tems [ma] course à [*blank*] chez Jaucourt,^{1} et à la Grange,^{2} chez Mr de Lafayette, 3 lieues plus loin. Ce dernier qui d'après notre premier plan,

449. ^{1} Probably the Château de Combreux in Brie. ^{2} See L. 446 n. 6.

est parti pour sa campagne, où il nous attendait, Narbonne et moi, est obligé de revenir après demain. D'un autre côté, j'ai decouvert que Narbonne avait payé à la diligence sa place pour lui et son domestique, et conséquement qu'en m'attendant, il perdrait cette avance. A la verité je me porte assez bien p^r partir demain, mais outre qu'un jour de plus de repos ne peut me faire que du bien, je ne puis me faire à l'idée de manquer l'occasion d'être probablement de quelqu'utilité à mon cousin.[3] Je suis enfin parvenu à decider Mr de N. à partir demain, mais auparavant je lui ai fait ecrire un joli petit billet, dont je serai porteur, et qui j'espère ne contribuera pas peu au succés de ma tentative auprés de Mr Gau,[4] qu'il est extremement difficile de voir. Si je n'allais point à son diner, au quel il ne m'aurait peut être pas invité s'il avait su que j'avais à lui parler d'affaires. Ce ne fut qu'à la fin de ma visite que je lui dis: 'Bazille[3] est ici, et sans emploi pour le moment. C'est le seul parent que j'aye placé, et sa conduite fait que j'en suis fier. Il est comme votre enfant — Il a été accusé d'un peu de legereté — ce peut être à tort. Il est d'ailleurs franc, honnête, et capable — oui — vous ne tarderez point à le remplacer? — Je l'espere

Ce *je l'espere* de la part de quelqu'un de qui, d'aprés ce que me dit tout le monde, ce remplacement depend uniquement, m'inquiete beaucoup, et certainement demain, je ne negligerai rien pour le faire expliquer d'une maniere tout à fait claire. J'ai sur lui des droits qui sont de vielle datte. Il s'est dit mon ami depuis longtems, il l'est du pere de Bazille, et son pere l'etait du mien. En outre je suis ainsi que je te l'ai dit muni d'un joli billet de Narbonne, qu'il aime beaucoup, et avec qui il a passé en Allemagne le tems de sa deportation. On est bien fort quand on ne demande que ce qui est de toute justice. D'un autre coté quand je pense à la foule de sujets que la paix fait trouver sans places, je ne puis m'empêcher d'être très inquiet. Lui ne l'est gueres et pourrait bien avoir tort. je souhaite |

[*the top of the page is missing*]

[3] Apparently Jean-Baptiste Bazille de Précourt (L. 447 n. 4).
[4] Almost certainly Jean-François Gau des Voves (1748–1825), commissaire des Guerres. In 1795 he was elected deputy for Yonne to the Conseil des cinq cents. As the brother-in-law of an *émigré* he was excluded from all legislative functions and, in September 1797, deported. Recalled by the Consuls in 1801 and established in the ministère de la Guerre, he was to become in 1802 a conseiller d'État. It was, doubtless, in view of these advantageous positions that d'Arblay hoped for interest in placing young Bazille (*supra*).

[By the comte de Narbonne]

Arblay s'ennuye de vous ecrire, et c'est moi qui en souffre, car il veut que je vous ecrive, et qu'ai-je à vous dire — si non, que j'ai, et que j'aurai jusqu'à mon dernier soupir, l'honneur de vous aimer de toute mon ame, c'est a dire tout autant que vos voisins et [vos] voisines. Est il vrai que nous les verrons bientot — j'ai, je vous assure, bien besoin de [me] ⟨reposer⟩ et vous croirez sans peine que c'est l'idée a la quelle j'attache le plus de bonheur.

[M. d'Arblay resumes]

Je reprens la plume pour *m'ennuyer* encore. Ce vilain homme, dont sans doute tu reconnoitras l'ecriture, ne s'est il pas avisé de revenir *du bout* non *du monde* mais de Paris, pour passer une heure avec moi indigne? il vient de me quitter, pour aller passer le reste de la soirée chez Talyrand — Je suis sûr qu'il trouvera l'occasion de parler de mon affaire, et tout aussi sûr qu'aprés l'avoir fait naître, il ne manquera pas d'en profiter.

Je vais partir de Paris sans avoir pu voir le premier Consul. quelques uns de mes amis voulaient que par le moyen de Lauriston,[5] je tentasse d'avoir de lui une audience, dans la quelle, après l'avoir remercié de ma radiation,[6] j'aurais peut être eu occasion d'entrer dans quelques details sur ma position, mais après y avoir murement reflechi, je m'y suis decidement refusé, malgré mon extrême desir de juger par moi même le quel des mille et un portraits que je vois de lui est ressemblant, afin de te le porter. Au reste, j'espere être de retour pour le 15 frimaire, jour de grande Parade,[7] et comme Lauriston m'a promis un billet, je compte pouvoir l'examiner tout à mon aise. Ce ne sera pas la même chose que si j'avais eu une audience de lui; mais j'ai craint, probablement avec raison, d'être accusé de presomption; et j'avoue que pour peu qu'on me l'eut fait entrevoir, je m'en serais senti très mortifié. La Garde consulaire est en honneur tout ce que l'on peut se figurer de plus remar-

5 Now aide-de-camp to Bonaparte (L. 425 n. 5).
6 M. d'A's name had been erased on 21 Apr. 1800. Thanking Napoleon for this would merely serve to introduce the subject of the pension.
7 This was the Parade and Audience set for the 15th of each month of the Republican calendar, in this case, 6 Dec. 1801. FBA was to attend such a parade on 5 May 1802 (L. 517, pp. 303-7).

quablement beau; à l'exception des off[ers] generaux qui sont tout chamarés d'or. Rien n'est plus simple et plus veritablement noble. Les simples gardes ont d'ailleurs des preuves bien autrement difficiles à faire que celles exigées des cy devant gardes du Corps dont ils font le service. Maubourg[8] m'a assuré que pour être admis dans ce Corps, il fallait avoir reçu trois blessures, où prouver quelqu'action d'eclat. Aussi quiconque parmi ces gardes est coupable d'un duel, est sur le champ chassé, ordonnance par laquelle Bonaparte donnera probablement le dementi à ceux qui ont pretendu qu'il etait impossible d'abolir parmi les français cette coutume barbare. De mon tems la crainte du deshonneur etait bien plus forte que la crainte de la mort, dont les loix punissent le duel. Mais ici quel deshonneur pretendu peut atteindre de tels braves? Depuis ma conversation à ce sujet, je n'en vois pas passer un sans être tenté d'aller shake hand avec lui.

Demain matin je dejeune avec M[de] d'Henin. t'ai-je dit que j'avois vu chez elle Mr de Poix,[9] qui m'a beaucoup | demande de tes nouvelles. Son neveu[10] que je t'ai mandé avoir vu à Douvre, est arrivé.

[the remainder of the leaf is missing]

450   [Paris], 26–27 November 1801

M. d'Arblay
To Madame d'Arblay

A.L. (Berg),   5 Frimaire an 10
Double sheet 4to   4 pp.   *pmk*   3 DEC 1801   wafer
Addressed: Madame Darblay / Westhumble. / near Dorking / *Surry*
Edited by FBA, p. 1, *top margin, dated incorrectly and annotated*: ⁝✻⁝ ⌐25. Novr 1802⌐ 12 Decr 1801   (37)   Reforme   La Fayette   Lajard

[8] Probably César de Latour-Maubourg (L. 446 n. 12).
[9] Philippe-Louis-Marc-Antoine de Noailles (1752–1819), prince de Poix (ii, L. 112 n. 1).
[10] Here FBA supplied the superscript 'X' and the footnote: 'X Duc de Duras'. See L. 440 n. 2.

Hotel Marengo rue Miromenil N° 1185

Ce 5 Frimaire an 10

Quand j'ai t'ecrit (le 20) Je devais partir le surlendemain
pour Joigny après avoir diné chez Mr Gau:[1] mais depuis ce
tems mes amis s'accordent à me dire que j'avais tort de
quitter la partie si vite, et que mon absence m'exposerait à la
presque certitude de perdre le fruit de toutes mes demarches, je
me suis decidé à attendre encore quelque tems icy. ⌐Une autre
raison qui a beaucoup contribué à cette resolution, c'est que
bien réellement ma presence peut être fort utile à mon cousin
le Commissaire des Guerres.[2] Son affaire eut été tout à fait
manquée sans moi, ainsi que je te le conterai quand nous nous
verrons. Elle est actuellement en bon train, mais d'un moment
à l'autre cela peut changer.⌐ Le très grand mal de cette varia-
tion dans mes plans est qu'une lettre de toi, que j'attendais
avec l'impatience la plus vive, est actuellement sur la route de
Joigny, parceque j'avais ecrit à notre ami [Frank Moore] de
m'y adresser ce qui me viendrait de toi.[3] Un contr'avis est arrivé
trop tard, ainsi que je l'ai appris hier, après m'y être presenté
quatre fois en vain, à la cinquieme je l'ai trouvé; et quoique je
sois très vexé de savoir que mon bonheur ait ainsi été retardé,
il m'est impossible de t'exprimer à quel point je suis content de
savoir que je pourrai bientot revoir et baiser ce qu'aura tracé
ta main cherie.[3] Ma tendre amie! Je n'avais pas besoin d'être
separè de toi pour savoir que je t'aimais par dessus tout au
monde, et sans comparaison aucune; mais il me fallait cette
absence pour le sentir comme je le fais. ⌐Ecris moi toujours par
notre ami aussi souvent que tu le pourras, mais en outre ne ∣
manque pas de m'ecrire deux fois par semaine directement
à l'Hôtel Marengo Rüe Miromesnil N° 1185. Il suffira que ton
frère ait eu soin d'affranchir ta lettre jusqu'à Douvre. Quelqu'
impatience que j'aye de te rejoindre, et il est impossible qu'elle
soit plus grande, je ne vois aucune apparence de pouvoir partir
avant un mois, ce qui montre mon extrême surprise à perdre
[xxxxx ½ *line*]. J'espere repondre et encore le gagner, mais je
ne veus pas jetter mon argent par la fenêtre.

A propos d'argent. J'ai été obligé de faire chez Mr Gau une

---

450. ¹ See L. 449 n. 4.   ² 'Précourt' Bazille (L. 447 n. 4).
    ³ FBA's letter of 12 November (L. 443), which is also referred to in L. 453, p. 75
and n. 2.

partie où j'ai gagné 15^{ff}. Il m'est venu à l'idee d'en donner 12 à M^{de} ⟨de Lavallance⟩ dont je t'ai parlé, la quelle tient un bureau de lotterie.[4] J'ai voulu qu'elle ⟨prête⟩ sur même les numeros tous impairs. Eh bien, j'ai gagné du ⟨nombre⟩ de 108^{ff} sur les quels j'ai donné 3^{ff} à sa domestique, et sur le champ je lui ai donné 24^{ff} pour remettre au tirage suivant. Si je gagne, tant mieux. Si je pers, Je te jure de ne pas mettre un sol de plus. Les 12^{ff} que j'avais hazardés n'etaient qu'une espece d'honneté que je voulais faire à la pauvre Buraliste.

Dis à ma niece[5] de ne point manquer de passer chez Monsieur otto qui lui donnera tout ce qui lui sera necessaire pour son voyage.

Au revoir, je vais m'habiller pour diner avec la soeur de mon medecin chez son frere, chef de division aux relations exterieures.[6]

N'oublie pas que si tu veus que je me porte bien, il faut que tu m'ecrives très souvent. J'ai mis deux personnes en mouvement pour la commission de ⟨N'bury⟩, mais je n'en suis pas jusqu'a présent plus avancé.⊓ |

(Vendredy 6)

⊓Veus tu bien ma bonne amie ⟨demander à Bood⟩ d'acheter pour Gillet[7] deux livres du meilleur quinquina qu'il pourra se procurer.

---

4 In Paris at this time there were about 150 'bureaux de loterie', each of which, licensed under the Loterie Nationale established by the government in 1797 and subjected to inspection, was required to exhibit its number without. In addition there were about 60 authorized pedlars hawking lottery tickets all over Paris between the hours 7 a.m. and 7 p.m. Mme de Lavallance, not otherwise identified, was probably the owner of such a bureau or perhaps the owner of a tobacco shop, for after 29 Dec. 1810 when tobacco also became a state monopoly, the 'buraliste' or owner of a licensed 'bureau de tabac', often handled lottery tickets as well—which franchises were often distributed by the government by way of recompense to the widows or orphans of public servants. See René Renault de la Vigne, *La Loterie à travers les âges* (1934).

5 Maria Bourdois (L. 436 n. 5) and Ludwig Wilhelm Otto (L. 429 n. 1), French Commissioner in London, Hereford Street, near Portman Square.

6 This family included Mme Vermond (iv, L. 381 n. 1), her brother, the eminent physician Edmé-Joachim Bourdois de la Motte (1754–1837), his wife Marie-Geneviève *née* d'Hermand de Cléry (*c.* 1757–1838), and her brother Louis-Joseph d'Hermand de Cléry (1757–1817), a diplomat. Having served in various consular capacities in Spain and Portugal (1776–98), he was attached in 1799 to the Département de relations commerciales as Chef du Bureau des Consulats. It was his name and 'direction' ('au Citoyen D'Hermand Chef des relations commerciales') that d'Arblay was to use (see L. 538) as a safe address to which packets destined for England might be sent.

7 Undoubtedly Bourdois's friend the notary Antoine-Louis Gillet (*fl.* 1801–51), who in 1805 was to take over an 'étude' or practice at 331, rue Saint-Honoré.

Je me suis levé ce matin un peu plus tard que je n'en avais le projet. j'ai rendez vous avec notre [xxxxx ½ *line*] ma lettre dans le cas où il aurait une occasion prompte. Cela m'oblige de laisser ce papier blanc. Pardon.⁊

(à 9ʰ)

J'arrive de chez M. de Lafayette, qui est pour moi non seulement excellent, mais fort au dela de ce que j'avais lieu d'attendre.⁸ Le premier Consul part, dit on, le 20 pour Lyon (11 Decembre) Je voudrais bien que mon affaire fut finie avant son depart. ⌐ Elle prend au reste une très bonne tournure.⁊ Je t'ai mandé, je crois, que je n'aurais point la reforme de marechal de camp, mais simplement de Colonel, parcequ'il faut avoir été deux ans dans le dernier grade.⁹ Cela rendra ma reforme bien moins considerable, et la reduira à 12 ou 1500ᶠᶠ, je ne sais point exactement le quel, mais 50 louis de plus ne laisseront pas que de nous aider. J'attens M. de L. F. qui doit venir me prendre pour me mener chez Dumas,¹⁰ qui se conduit à merveille dans cette affaire. ⌐Donc j'irai comme j'en avais le projet chez

⁸ Preceded by Talleyrand, who left Paris on 4 Jan. 1802, Bonaparte was to set out for Lyons on the 9th. Arriving on the night of the 11th, he was welcomed rapturously and, in contravention of the Treaty of Lunéville (9 Feb. 1801), accepted for a term of ten years the presidency of the Cisalpine Republic (*AR* xliv. 77–82). His triumphal return to Paris (30 Jan.) was to be marked by cannonades and salvoes exceeding any marks of distinction accorded in previous times, it was said, to the kings themselves.

⁹ M. d'Arblay had been promoted to the rank of colonel du 103ᵉ regiment d'infanterie on 3 Aug. 1791. He had been named maréchal de camp on 22 July 1792, but having deserted with Lafayette on 19 Aug. 1792 and having resigned on 1 September, he had never received that commission. With respect to rank, therefore, his claim had to be based on the rank of colonel, with about a year's service in that rank.

His official records can be seen in the 'Dossier du Général de division Piochard d'Arblay' (Vincennes), which contains among other documents three reports: the first, dated '12 frimaire, an x' [3 Dec. 1801], was sent from the 'Bureau des Etats Majors 3ᵉ Division' to the ministère de la Guerre. A second, dated only 'an 10' [*pre* 18 Dec. 1801], was sent from the ministère de la Guerre to the Consuls. And the third, dated 'le 27 frimaire an dix' [18 Dec. 1801], was forwarded from the ministère de la Guerre to the First Consul.

All three relate the same facts with respect to d'Arblay's army service from 1768 to 1792. See Appendix.

¹⁰ Mathieu Dumas (1753–1837), comte (14 Feb. 1810), formerly colonel and aide-de-camp to Lafayette (10 Oct. 1789), had after 10 Aug. 1792 hidden but managed to escape to Switzerland in disguise (1793). Returning after 9 Thermidor (27 July 1794), he became a member of the club de Clichy during the Thermidorian period and under the Directory (Godechot, p. 422). Attached to the ministère de la Guerre (1795), he was proscribed in 1797 for suspected complicity in the unsuccessful royalist plot of 18 Fructidor (4 Sept.) of that year, but escaped to Hamburg. When he returned to France after 18 Brumaire (9 Nov. 1799), he resumed an active military and, later, a diplomatic career, having been appointed conseiller d'État on 27 June 1801.

notre ami pour savoir [les meilleures] conditions p^r faire partir ma Lettre, ⟨sinon⟩ je te l'enverrai par Melle Grandsire.$^{⫿11}$ Tout le monde m'assure que mon affaire ne peut souffrir aucune difficulté et le premi[er Consul] qui a trouvé la reclamation juste demande seulement qu'on ne lui presente que peu [d'autres] en même tems. En ce moment les proposés sont Laumoy,^{12} M^{al} de Camp, Maubourg^{13} Je ne suis pas, comme tu vois, en mauvaise compagnie. Je suis seulement faché que Lajard^{14} ne soit pas du nombre, et qu'il soit remis à une autre fois, ce qui prouve au reste que je ne suis pas mal servi, car il est l'ami intime de Dumas, et de Berthier,^{15} l'un ministre, l'autre conseiller d'etat, chargé de la partie de la Guerre. Heureusement, il me semble que notre digne ami Lajard est moins pressé que moi, et qu'il fait assez bien ses affaires. $^{⫿}$Je le crois interessé dans une entreprise considerable qu'a faite son frère,^{14} cy devant Grandsire, et actuellement à la tête d'une manufacture de poterie. Je dois diner aujourdhui chez lui mais compte me degager de cet engagement si la chose est possible, et cela parceque | Mad. d'hénin^{16} vient de m'envoyer prier à diner avec M^{de} de Tesse qui arrive d'Aulnay et repart ce soir même. Malouet^{17} sera de la partie. Je serais très fâché de n'en être pas.$^{⫿}$

[*Dans 4 lignes partialement oblitérées par Madame d'Arblay, M. d'A explique pourquoi il préfère dîner chez M^{de} d'Hénin et voir M. Lajard à un autre moment. Il termine sa lettre avec des salutations pour ses connaissances à Norbury Park et aux environs.*]

^{11} Later Mme Toulière. Her death (4 Feb. 1807) in lodgings in Canterbury is recorded in *GM* lxxvii (1807), 377.

^{12} Jean-Baptiste de Laumoy (1750–1832), 'général du génie', formerly maréchal de camp at Metz (1791) and chef d'état-major of the Armée du centre under Lafayette (1792). Fleeing on 19 Aug. 1792, he was admitted to the 'traitement de réforme' on 8 July 1803 (Six).

^{13} See Intro., v, pp. xlv–xlvii.

^{14} For the Lajard brothers, see iv, L. 291 n. 5; and L. 292 n. 8.

^{15} See L. 446 n. 8.

^{16} The princesse d'Hénin (L. 446 n. 23) and Mme de Tessé (L. 446 n. 5).

^{17} Pierre-Victor Malouet (1740–1814), who, though an *émigré* in England in 1792, had offered to defend Louis XVI (ii, L. 40 n. 2). Arrested on his return to France in 1801, he was freed by order of Bonaparte, who, removing him from the proscription lists was shortly to send him to Antwerp as commissioner-general and maritime prefect (he had been an intendant of the navy at Toulon before the Revolution, and in the years 1789–91, a deputy to the National Assembly). See his *Mémoires* (2 vols., 1874).

To Esther (Burney) Burney

A.L.S. (Berg), [*misdated*] 27 Oct. 1801
Double sheet large 4to 4 pp. *pmks* DARKING ⟨ ⟩ N⟨ ⟩ 1801
wafer
Addressed: Mrs. Burney, / Beaumont Street, / Devonshire Place, / London.
Endorsed by EBB: Answered / 1801

West Hamble, 27. Oct^r ⟨180⟩1.

I know how kindly you would partake in my relief from unspeakable anxiety, my dearest Esther, had you known its excess; but I never, on those occasions, unless compelled, write to those I love. I am now as happy as I now can be, while separated from my Hermit, though I have no spirit to be other than a Recluse in his absence. My dearest Father has kindly invited me to Chelsea; but my alex is in a state of health that demands all my time & thoughts, & if I stopped now his cold bathing, early hours of Dinner & of rest, & perpetual air & exercise, I should see before me a return of the Fever which prevented our accompanying our beloved Traveller. I am now satisfied it was a *Worm Fever*,—a disorder which brought me to death's door when very nearly at his Age: & to watch what will agree with him, & change his regulations by what I observe, occupies me continually. Upon the *result*, our joint happiness wholly hangs—his Father's & mine. I refuse even to go to Norbury Park, where they promise I shall spend my life as *maternally* as at home: but that I know is impossible, with all their indulgence: here, therefore, I had best rest, till I see | the little soul somewhat less thin, & freed from his stomach complaints. Stronger, gayer, more alive & active, I can never wish him. These odious worms are the only enemies to his health; those apart, no Child could give less uneasiness on that score.

Your Letter—as all your Letters on that subject do,— touched me deeply for poor Me Gouvelle[1]—in whom I always

451. [1] The de La Landelle family, *émigrés* of 1790, SBP had known in the winter of 1795–6 (see iii, L. 215 n. 14; and *FB & the Burneys*, pp. 218, 231–2, 242–3). A son

recollect one who has personal reason to know what we have lost. You may be sure nothing was left undone I had power to do, of adding weight or pleasure to the kindness from Sand place. Nor could I forbear relating all you wrote to me to Mrs. Locke—who instantly told me her little remaining hoard, now much diminished, for the poor Emigrants, should be at your disposal—either for those worthy unfortunate persons, or any others you judged yet more in distress. The sum is £1: 18: 6.— she has given it into my hands; & I shall send it you the next time I know of M. Bourdois visiting you. This is a very great pleasure to me, for small as that is, it is much in hard cases, & I know the joy with which you will be its dispenser. I had hoped the return of so many to France, since the Peace, would have enabled the Committee to have been more bountiful: but perhaps their resources are lessened.

M. d'Arblay writes me word that M. de Narbonne,[2] in talking of our departed Angel, burst into an agony of Tears— If he, indeed, who knew her so well, who was so able to appreciate her rare merit, & ¦ who could not but see what a Pearl was thrown away, had not mourned her irreparable loss, I should have thought his heart was stone. But that is far from being its composition—the account has been soothing to me,—the least bitter tears I shed are those drawn forth by any sympathy, & I am always gratified & softened in my sorrow when I find any one who seems to understand its cause—O my dear Esther!— —its *effects* I shall feel to my dying day!—*on* that Day may it help my own passage! — —[3]

My dear—loved—invaluable neighbours on high come to me daily at this widowish period: & they are now working for *your Son*—They wish to procure him the curacy of Dorking, now

had died at Quiberon in July 1795, and of the sisters mentioned by SBP, one had drowned in a shipwreck off Margate in 1800 (L. 441 n. 2).

In 1798 Pauline de La Landelle (1767–*post* 1818) had married Paul de Gouvello (1748–*c.* 1803), an army man who, having emigrated to England, had taken part in the royalist attack on Quiberon. Pauline's troubles were by no means at an end. In 1802 the Gouvellos went to the French legation in London to take an oath of allegiance to the Consulate, explaining that they could not return to France immediately because of their child's illness. They were amnestied, and Gouvello returned to France, probably in 1803, but died shortly thereafter. In 1818 Mme de Gouvello was to apply for a pension for her daughter on the basis of her husband's services to the princes during his emigration, and those of her brother at Quiberon (Archives Nationales).

[2] See L. 446.

[3] FBA was in fact to die on the same day (6 Jan.), though not until 1840.

suddenly vacant:[4] & Richard[5] seems really desirous to obtain it: but alas, I heard such an account, yesterday, from Lord Leslie,[6] of its hard duty, that I fear it will be impossible to him to acquit himself with the Parish, but at a risk of health that may be fatal. This has much damped my first pleasure in the proposal, & the energy of the dear & honoured Friends, who made it. Lord Leslie[6] says, the Clergyman must be ready, in all weathers, & almost at all hours, to give the Sacrament to the sick, & to baptize Infants, *four miles* round!—This—with such roads, & Richard's inability to ride, makes me deem the office really impracticable. However, I have written him these particulars, which we knew not yesterday morning, when Mr. & Mrs. Lock took me with them to Sand place. He looks *considerably* better, & has just sent for the Parish Clerk, Maria writes me word, to consult with him whether there may not be some other clergyman who could occasionally I assist him, when ill, or fatigued, &c. I wish heartily this may succeed. I hope you get to Chelsea sometimes; I hear our dearest Father looks well. Charlotte Francis is still at Sand Place—She is a dear affectionate little Girl. What a history is Miss Broome's![7] Sophy will have given it you at full length. I think it well such a Girl should be separated from poor Charlotte's Children. Poor M. Bourdois[8] has been grievously disappointed of the expected happiness of seeing his Brother, who has just written him an excuse, begging that Paris, not London, may be the place of interview. M. d'Arblay has repeatedly seen La Princesse d'Henin—who joins in sincere lamentations for our heavy misfortune.[9] I hope dear Mr. Burney is well? my love to him, & to

---

[4] The curacy at Dorking had apparently been vacant since November 1800 (or perhaps from the beginning of 1801), when the Revd. Thomas Ash (*c.* 1766–1812) left for Mullion, Cornwall, to which living he had been presented in 1799. That he was not replaced immediately is indicated by the fact that the vicar himself, the Revd. George Feacham (1766–1837), officiated at the Dorking weddings from January to November of 1801. The vacancy that the Lockes had in mind for Richard was filled on 4 Dec. 1801, for a short time only, by the Revd. Joseph Blake Ogle (*c.* 1770–1849).

[5] EBB's son the Revd. Richard Allen Burney (1773–1836), B.A. Oxon. (1799). For his ill health and the various attempts of Bishop North and his family to find him a living, see iii, L. 229 n. 7; and iv *passim*.

[6] George William Evelyn-Leslie, *styled* Lord Leslie (i, L. 13 n. 8; and iv, L. 292 n. 45).

[7] Presumably the birth of an illegitimate child to Miriam Broome (L. 434 n. 2).

[8] The physician Edmé-Joachim Bourdois (L. 450 n. 6).

[9] The princesse d'Hénin (L. 446 n. 23) had got to know SBP in their mutual efforts for *émigrés* in the winter of 1795–6.

Amelia. I earnestly hope your vile *old Complaint* is removed? I suppose it your teeth—I don't mean I hope *them* all removed —you make me love Miss Sayer[10]—do you see her in town? & do you keep up with the friendly Ellerkers?[11] My love when you see her, to my dear Fanny Phillips—adieu, my dearest Esther— yours ever & ever— F. d'A. [1]

Pray thank James for a kind little congratulatory note[12] when you see him.

M. d'A. has not been able yet to arrange his affairs at Paris, or get on to his Uncle, at Joigny.—

452   West Humble, 29 November 1801

To M. d'Arblay

A.L. (rejected Diary MSS. 5284–[87], Berg), 29 Nov. 1801
Double sheet 4to   4 pp.   wafer
Addressed: Darblay—
Edited by FBA, p. 1 (5284), *numbered & dated*: West Hamble, Novr 29th 1801 34/2
Edited also by CFBt *and the* Press.

West Hamble Nov. 29th 1801.

I sent you a few hurried lines, by a sudden information of an opportunity, the day I received the first intelligence of your being in Paris.[1] From your Letter of the 7th at Calais,[2] I had

---

[10] Frances Julia Sayer (1756–1850), the daughter of James Sayer (*c.* 1719–99) of the Manor House, Marsh Gate, Richmond, 'Deputy High Steward of Westminster, and Steward of the Manor of Richmond' (*The Record of Old Westminsters* . . . ed. G. F. Russell Barker and Alan H. Stenning, 2 vols., 1928, ii. 824). He had married on 18 July 1755 as his second wife (see his will, P.C.C. Howe 312, pr. 18 Apr. 1799) Julia Margaret Evelyn (d. 1777), a cousin of the Hon. Mrs. Boscawen (iii *passim*). As godchild and the companion of Mrs. Boscawen's old age, it was Julia who, valuing quite rightly her godmother's letters (among the most elegant and entertaining of the age), had them bound and saved for posterity. See Brig.-General Cecil Aspinall-Oglander, *Admiral's Wife* (1940) and *Admiral's Widow* (1943).

[11] Elizabeth (1751–1831) and Harriet (1759–1842), daughters of the late Eaton Mainwaring Ellerker (d. 9 July 1771) of Risby Park, Yorks. The sisters (see iii, L. 126 n. 7; and iv *passim*) lived at Richmond.

[12] This note is missing.

452. [1] Many letters sent by FBA to M. d'A in France at this time have been lost.
[2] L. 441.

heard nothing, till our friend of Dorking[3] sent me word of one of his Correspondents had answered a Letter which you had delivered in Person—O mon ami! I hardly know if you would have been most gratified or frightened to have seen me as I read that account, after above a fortnight's suspence the most anxious, & total incertitude if you had left Calais, or waited there for Letters, &c. I bless God my terror was groundless—but I had apprehended the fatigues of your Journey, & your horrible voyage, had overpowered even your strength, & that illness caused your silence. I now find it was only want of conveyance, or that some Letter has miscarried. The following day, I received Two from you;[4] ⌐only with *no date* but I make it out, by conjecture, to have been of the 14th & the other is the 16th & was delivered to me by Mr. L[ock] I have unsealed⌐ O what a regale!—I spent the whole morning in reading them, dwelling on every line & sentence, & translating & arranging the whole for our alex, who begs a Letter of Papa's instead of a story, for his reward after being good at his lessons. | ⌐How interesting these Letters are, 'tis impossible for me to say. How good of you to make them so long, & satisfactory I ⟨confess⟩ that I feel disturbed not to know your address—which I have particularly begged. Have you received my *second* Letter, directed like the first, to Rue St. Martin?⌐5 'Tis grievous you should be kept so long from your Uncle. I hope you write to him. What exquisite kindness in his wish & intention to come hither! No, no,—we will all go to *him*. Arrange the time with him, & all your friends—but O no more winter voyages! & no more separations! May this be the last of either! Alas, mon Ami, *ma pauvre tête*, autant que mon Coeur, suffers too much. When the wind blows, while I think you at Sea—when the post fails, while I believe you at land,—I cannot keep from conjectures of mischief, & terrors of misfortunes, that really affect my faculties. You know too well the deadly blow they have received! — — God be praised, I can assure you our Boy is *perfectly well* at this moment: but I will go no where, that I may continue his present

<hr>

[3] Antoine Bourdois (see A.L., Berg, *pmk* ⟨24 NO⟩).

[4] One of these letters, probably that referred to in L. 451, is almost certainly L. 446, *pmk* G.P.O. inland post, evening duty, 2 [5 or 6] NO .801 A second undated letter, which FBA conjectures to be of 16 November is missing. There are extant, however, two other letters, clearly dated '16 9bre' (Nos. 447, 448). The latter, bearing a London *pmk* 1 DEC 1801, she could not yet have received.

[5] This is L. 443, addressed c/o M. Lajard, Faubourg St. Martin.

regîme, & shew to his fond Padre such as he is to day—bright, clear, glowing with rosy health, & bounding with vigourous joy. His sole enemies, the worms, I have now, once more, conquered, & my management has succeeded beyond my expectations;—He goes into the Tub as soon as he rises, in defiance of snow, frost, ice—& then, before his *drapery* is thrown over | him, he drinks a Glass of *red wine* & *bark*: then he is well wrapt up, in warm cloaths, & takes his exercise, of running, with a whip in his hand, to imitate (what he most admires) a Postillion. Then we take 3 lessons while I am dressing; & at Breakfast have our rewards;—sometimes what dear ones to us both! then he goes into the Garden, where he runs about, or builds his *fortifications*, & where he is preparing a *room underground*, to surprise Papa. The idea of it, he says, he took from Papa's account of the subterraneous passage under the Thames. Then he comes in, to his *lunch*, which is now chocolate & Milk, or an Egg, or broth: but the former generally, as it is his favourite. Then some more lessoning,—& at dinner, 3 times a week, a few grains of Rhubarb: & for his desert, 2 or 3 roast apples. This, alltogether, agrees with him so well, that I can make no change in it, till I see him quite robust. I hope you will approve my proceeding.

When I saw him climbing, the other day, & charged him not to run such risks, he gravely answered 'But, Mama, I *must* be a *little riskful*, you know!' 'And why?'—'Because—can't you guess, mama?—' 'No.' 'Why—Papa himself is one of the *risky* sort!—' He is sure, he says, you will come home for his Birth day (the 18ᵗʰ) because you did last year, | '& I know, he says, Papa is too kind to give me a disappointment just on my happiest day—because Papa is so kind, he would not give me one on my *dis*happiest day.' He wants much to know if The ladies rule you, now you are in France; Bood having told him the Ladies govern there entirely. He says, he dares say you don't let them, only when you like it!—but he laughed violently to himself, afterwards, & when I enquired why, said 'I suppose, Mama, if the ladies rule everybody in France, even if there is a man of quality, that meets with a *lady*, that happens to be a beggar, he must let her govern him?' Shall I ask your pardon for all this *bavardage*?—Have you seen or heard of Adrienne's

73

papa?[6] I have much to say in answer to your truly interesting Letters, but my paper is full. I shall write again to Rue St Martin, as before, very soon. Let me hear ALWAYS when you can, *short* Letters, where you have not time for such treats as your long ones prove to me—& remember me to all I know as you judge I would like—adio!—

Heaven preserve you, my dearest Friend—all we love are well. Pray date your Letters.

453   [Paris], 30 November 1801

M. d'Arblay
To Madame d'Arblay

A.L. (Berg), 30 Nov. 1801
Originally a double sheet 4to, of which FBA later discarded the second leaf 2 pp.
Edited by FBA, p. 1, *top margin, dated and annotated*: ⌜30 Nov^r⌝ (33 / 2) 30 Novr Domestic Letter des plus tendres.

Hotel Marengo rüe Miromenil
ce 9. Frimaire an 10 (30 9bre 1801)

Ecoute bien ma chere amie, et ne manque point de me repondre le plutôt que tu le pourras à ce que je vais te dire.

Riccé[1] que tu aimes et qui m'a beaucoup parlé de toi *en très bon anglais* te prie instament de t'informer de la santé de sa femme et de son petit enfant[1] qu'elle a fait inoculer. Il ne peut concevoir qu'elle soit restée si longtems sans lui en donner des nouvelles, et te supplie d'avoir la bonté de me mander ce que tu pourras en savoir par le moyen de Boud.

---

[6] The comte de Chavagnac (L. 437 n. 3).

453. [1] The comte de Riccé (iv, L. 292 n. 11; v, L. 446 n. 16), who had married secondly (1797) Henriette-Louise-Wilhelmine *née* von Hompesch (1774–1809). Their daughter Charlotte-Jacqueline was baptised (July 1798) at Carshalton, Surrey, Antoine Bourdois standing as godfather. See *CRS* xxv (1926), 257. A second daughter, Josephine-Françoise-Charlotte, born at Hampton Court on 4 Aug. 1802, died at Walburg Castle, the Netherlands, on 1 Feb. 1875.

J'ai commencé par cette commission parceque, bien que je l'eusse fort à coeur, j'ai eu peur de l'oublier si une fois je commençais à te parler du trésor qu'on vient de me renvoyer de Joigny où il etait allé me chercher ainsi que je te l'ai mandé.[2] Je la tiens enfin cette lettre où ton ame se peint si bien, où la mienne aime tant à trouver tous les sentimens dont elle est remplie! Je ne t'ai encore lue que cinq fois. Oui ma chere Fanny tu es, NOW, the FIRST the *best* the *all*! plus mille et mille fois que je ne pourrai jamais te l'exprimer. Il est tard, et je ne t'ecrirai pas aujourdhui une bien longue lettre. je compte m'en dedomager bientôt. ⌐Notre ami est parti ce matin pour ⟨turin⟩.[3] je suis arrivé chez lui au moment où il venait de monter en voiture. Cela m'a infiniment contrarié. Je ne savais point qu'il dut quitter sitôt la Capitale. Je ne l'ai appris que par hazard. J'avais mille choses à lui dire, et aulieu de cela, il faut que je lui ecrive. Le bon Augustin qui me sert avec autant de zele qu'il sert son maître, et qui me prie en grace de te presenter son respect doit se lever demain ou pour parler plus correctement aujourdhui deux heures avant le jour pʳ porter mes lettres au cocher de Mʳ. N. le quel ǀ doit partir avant 7 heures. C'est comme tu vois un vrai service d'ami qu'il me rend. Sans cela j'irais certainement moi même vieil harassé que je suis. J'ai profité d'un jour de repos pour lire deux vol in 8° de nouveaux ⟨mélanges⟩ par Mᵈᵉ N. J'en ai fait un assez long extrait que tu recevras en même tems que ceci si notre ami ne trouve point le papier trop gros. S'il est au contraire trop considerable, je lui mande de garder cet extrait que je prendrais en passant, et que je te posterais moi même.⌐

Je suis pret à devenir fou quand je pense qu'il y a plus d'un mois que je suis eloigné de toi, et que tout ce que j'ai gagné jusqu'à present est beaucoup de fatigue, sans savoir si definitivement je serai plus avancé en restant un plus longtems. Je meurs d'envie d'embrasser mon oncle, et n'ose quitter. Le 1ᵉʳ consul devant aller à Lyon[4] à peu près vers le 20 de ce mois, (le 11 decembre) Il est pour moi de la plus haute importance d'obtenir avant cette epoque ce que je demande de sa justice. ⌐Malheureusement à la suitte d'une si longue ⟨guerre⟩, il y a tant de

---

[2] This is FBA's letter of 12 Nov. 1801 (L. 443), which had been sent on to Joigny.
[3] This is the comte de Narbonne.　　　　　　　　　[4] See L. 450 n. 8.

demandes. La mienne assurement n'est rien moins que deplacée mais tant d'autres sont appuyées de tîtres si respectables.⁷ᵀ Tout cela me tourmente beaucoup; d'autant que dans la même journée je suis plein d'esperances, puis decouragé, puis esperant de nouveau. Je serais cent fois moins à plaindre s'il me fallait prendre tout de suite le parti de n'y plus compter, et pourtant, il faut convenir que ce serait pour moi un coup terrible; d'autant qu'il me faudrait renoncer à venir m'etablir ici avant d'avoir amassé les moyens d'y vivre. [xxxxx 1 *line*] ¹

[*the second leaf is missing*]

454 West Humble, 4 December 1801

To M. d'Arblay

A.L. (rejected Diary MSS. 5296–[99], Berg), 4 Dec. 1801
Double sheet 4to   4 pp.   wafer
Addressed: Mr. Darblay, / chez M. Lajard / NO [43] Fauxbourg St Martin / à Paris—
Edited by FBA, p. 1 (5296), *annotated*: ⌗ 36 / 1
Edited also by CFBt *and the* Press.

West Hamble, 4. Dec. 1801

Ah, my dearest Friend, this indeed is a terrible disappointment! another Month from *5. Frimaire*!¹—& I thought you almost here—almost in our very Book Room!—my disappointment, however, is quite unmixt with any murmur; if business requires your stay, it is better make it, than return with any regret or self-blame: & if you can be of any use to your Cousin,² all other considerations must give way to a pleasure & duty so combined.

—How, or where to begin thanking you for your Letters, indeed I know not, but the blessing they prove to me is unspeak-

---

454. ¹ M. d'A's announcement of a change in his plans is not to be seen in any letter that we know of, but cf. L. 450.
² For M. d'A's efforts on behalf of 'Précourt' Bazille, see L. 449 nn. 3, 4.

able. At first sight of your hand, I feel almost as if you were returned—& all the time I am reading I have the same sort of illusion, & my heart is lightened in proportion—but when I have finished,— ce n'est pas tout à fait si gai! — ⌐I am grieved I cannot write oftener, & by all the means you indicate, but I have none except our original & your niece. What you say of directing to you at your hotel, & par Me Grandsire,³ Mr. Norbury tells me is premature, for *this* country, & that Many Letters will be kept back, at the post office, till the posts are positively opened. I may *receive your Letters*, but not answer them; to *answer* makes the *correspondence*, & the *correspondence*—incurs the penalty. I did not oppose his opinion, & therefore ¹ must continue to trouble Mr. Moore.⁴ But⌐ how good you are — how infinitely kind, to write on thus constantly, without the encouragement of even knowing I receive—or how I bless your Letters!—but that *last* you cannot doubt!—Those who, in my late deep—&ever-irreparable loss, have known what I suffered, may have supposed it was *all I could suffer*, & that to see HER no more was the heaviest evil I could endure: but I knew even then—even in my almost frantic grief, it was not so!—Judge, then, whether, when we are separated, it is essential to me to know you are safe & well? — — Your kind words of our Hermitage—our Boy—his Mother—how balsamic they are!— how doubly so, coming from you in such a moment—in your own loved *païs* — & surrounded by friends so exquisitely valued—& on the point of embracing him you love as a Father, & his honoured Wife, & amiable family!—I cannot tell you how I feel your expressions at such a period. They double my attention to my health, & my spirits & powers of exertion. You will not suppose by this I have ever doubted your kindness— no indeed—I have never been so miserable for a single moment: yet what internal confidence can weigh with the soft satisfaction of your voluntary—almost *in*voluntary assurances? I could not have been surprised had the feelings of enjoyment awaiting your first return absorbed you wholly, &, for a time, sufficed for your happiness. But you knew too well the pleasure with which I should have ¹ partaken of your joy, not to want me at

³ At Grandsire's Hotel, Calais, or the Hôtel Kingston, as it was called at that time.
⁴ Frank Moore (L. 430 n. 3).

77

your side.—Alex, God be praised, is going on perfectly well. ⌐I shall continue his *regime*, according to my last account to you, till when it is perfectly restored.⌐ He gets all I translate to him of your Letters by heart, & flies to Mr. Norbury, when he calls in his Phaeton, before I can join him, to tell all the particulars he has learnt: I heard him calling out, with great energy, t'other day 'Do you know, Mr L[ocke]—Papa has had a very bad Cold, & kept his room two days, & it was MY Godpapa⁵ that nursed him & made him well! My own God-papa, that was so kind, for all I've never seen him! —' — Having seen, also, in a Letter of Bood's, the words 'Le Gen¹ Alexandre Darblay' he concludes you have been made a General upon returning to France, & t'other day, said, very gravely 'I suppose, Mama, now papa's made a General, when he comes home, he'll be in his armoury.' ⌐He studies his French with more pleasure than any other of his lessons, & he makes much progress. His writing lessons are now all suspended by copies from ideas of Letters for *you* & he gives you daily accounts of the Pigs & Rabbits, Maids, Norbury & Dorking.⌐

His spirits are always the same, more gay, violent, noisy, & wild than any thing I ever saw or heard of *EXCEPT* — — — you know what I have told you of his OWN opinion why he ought I to be a little *RISKFUL*: to be a little *turbulent in gaiety*. keep the same plan, ⌐*else who better*—I rejoice at your resolution not to answer your part of the letter just yet—I am *sure* it is best acted upon when it's probable solidity has hung on to the dear offer of Amelia, nothing can be serious at all when nothing being settled,—but⌐ Mr. Norbury will remember *you* as soon as he can remember *himself*.⁶ We can *build* only upon our own little possession—with that happier—together—than with all that all others covet, asunder! *I* build upon Nothing in this world, save your return!—& philosophy to endure your *own* disappointment, should it try you as *I* shall endure ALL when with you!—

⁵ The comte de Narbonne.
⁶ The relevant letter is lost, but Amelia Angerstein had obviously made some offer of help, possibly that of her husband or father with respect to investments.

M. d'Arblay
To Madame d' Arblay

A.L. (Diary MSS. vi. 5300–[03], Berg),   6 Dec. 1801
Double sheet small 4to   4 pp.   *pmk*   14 DEC 1801   red seal
Addressed: Angleterre / Madame Darblay / West Humble / near Dorking /
Surry
Edited by FBA, p. 1 (5300), *annotated and dated*: ⊞ 1801   Nº 1   (34/1)
Edited also by CFBt *and the* Press.

Hotel Marengo Rue Miromenil Nº 1185
Ce 15 Frimaire an. 10. (6. decembre) 1801

Suivant toute apparence, ma chère amie, je n'obtiendrai
point le traitement que je demande. *tout* le monde dit que rien
n'est plus juste, mais tant de personnes qui ont fait toute la
guerre se trouvent à present reformés, que je meurs de peur
qu'il n'en soit de mes services passés comme des proprietés de
toute ma famille, et cela par la même raison, par l'impossibilité
de faire droit aux demandes, toutes fondées qu'elles sont.
Cependant, ma bonne amie, il est impossible de nous dissimuler
que depuis plusieurs années nous n'avons vecu, malgré toute
notre economie, que par le moyen de ressources qui sont ou
epuisées ou bien prêtes à l'être.[1] La plus grande partie de notre
revenu n'est rien moins qu'assurée,[2] et cependant que ferions
nous si elle venait à nous manquer? La morale de ce sermon,
est que tandis que je suis propre à quelque chose, il est de mon
devoir, comme epoux et comme pere, de tacher de tirer parti des
circonstances pour nous menager, s'il est possible, une viellesse
totalement independante; et à notre petit un bien être qui ne
nous fasse pas renoncer au nôtre. Ne vas pas t'effrayer de ce
preambule: car tu dois savoir que rien au monde ne me | fera
devier de la ligne que j'ai constament suivie depuis que
j'existe. Je n'ai pas plus d'ambition que lorsque je suis entré

---

455. [1] A reference to the £2,000, the proceeds of *Camilla* (1796), which by a recent
computation came to the equivalent of $40,000. See Michael E. Adelstein, *Fanny
Burney* (1968), pp. 95–6.
  [2] FBA's pension of £100 per annum.

avec toi dans Phoenix farm[3] et certes je ne porte envie au sort de qui que ce soit. Le mien, ma bonne amie, n'est il pas mille et mille fois au dessus?. mais nous serions coupables de ne pas profiter des lumières de l'experience. L'espoir de nous partager entre ton pays et le mien, tant que nous ne serons pas plus aisés, est une chimere, à la quelle il ne m'est plus permis de songer, et comme certainement je suis loin de vouloir renoncer à un pays qui m'a donné ma Fanny, et qui renferme d'autres êtres qui me sont bien chers, voici l'idée qui m'est venue pour me procurer cette aisance si necessaire.

On n'a point encore nommé les commissaires des relations commerciales en Angleterre. Cette place à Londre sera très bonne, et peut être, quoique elle soit trés demandée, ne me serait il pas impossible de l'obtenir. Il est au moins probable que j'en pourrais avoir une dans un des ports. mais je ne m'en soucierais pas infiniment, parce que le traitement serait beaucoup moindre, et tout au plus suffisant. D'ailleurs Quoique la place de Londre fut en chef, je crois, sans trop me flatter que je serais fort en etat de la remplir, aprés m'être consulté avec le chef dans cette partie, homme aimable qui a été longtems consul | general en Espagne.[4] Il y a vingt ans que nous sommes liés ensemble et le Ministre d'ailleurs appuyerait volontiers ma demande.

Repons moi sur le champ je t'en conjure. Vois si cela ne contrarie aucun de tes gouts: car tu sais qu'il n'est pour moi qu'un seul bonheur possible. ai-je besoin d'en dire davantage?

⌐Les places de Dublin et de Corck seront aussi trés bonnes, mais ne nous conviennent reellement.¬

Il y a quelques jours que me trouvant dans une société, la conversation tomba sur mon ancien metier, et sur les droits que je pouvais faire valoir pour obtenir le traitement que je demandais. Le surlendemain le maître de la maison / me dit: / Savez vous devant qui vous parliez avant hier? — non! — C'etait le G^{al} ⟨N⟩ —[5] En verité! — Quand vous fûtes parti, il demanda vôtre nom, et dès qu'on vous eut nommé — Quoi, dit il, celui du comité central? — oui — Eh bien je dois être commandant

---

[3] Phenice Farm, at the summit of Blagden Hill, near Great Bookham, where the d'Arblays lived for several months after their marriage (28 July 1793).

[4] Louis-Joseph d'Hermand (L. 450 n. 6).

[5] An unidentified general, but d'Arblay seems here to be preparing his wife for the possibility that, to qualify for a pension, he might have to re-enter the army.

gen^{al} de — — . S'il veut s'embarquer avec moi, je me fais fort de le faire employer dans son grade d'off^{er} general, et de le pr⟨endre⟩ pour mon second &c. &c. &c. — Il est très possible qu'il se soit un peu avancé; quoique, son etat major laissé à sa nomination, il est probable qu'il reussirait. Dans tous les cas je lui devais une reponse polie, et ce devoir je m'en suis acquité tout en refusant.

⌐Dis ⟨bien⟩ à ton neveu[6] qu'il est indispensable qu'il aille sur le champ chez M^r otto qui le fait chercher partout pour lui remettre ce qu'il a pour lui. Il a mandé ⟨ici⟩ qu'il ne pouvait le trouver, et l'attendait avec impatience. Pour Dieu il est aussi trop attentif.⌐ |

Je te quitte pour aller à la fameuse revue que le 1er Consul ne fait plus que les 15 de chaque mois. J'ai la plus vive impatience de voir tout à mon aise cet être qui remplit l'univers entier de son nom. à revoir mon amie, mes tendres respects à Norbury. Consulte l'ange des anges et embrasse le pour moi, ainsi que sa trés digne better half.

[*Dans 8 lignes oblitérées plus tard par Mme d'Arblay, on distingue des références à des commissions que M. d'Arblay veut bien faire pour des membres de la famille de sa femme*: Dis à ton Pere que je ne ⟨cesse⟩ de sa commission qui n'est pas très facile à faire. Charles ne veut il pas m'en donner quelques unes.]

J'embrasse de toute mon ame et de toutes mes forces Alex et sa mere. j'ai pleuré de joie en lisant la lettre de ce cher petit

⌐J'ai vu hier le spectacle le plus rationel et le plus excitant, Le Temple de Mars.[7] Imagine toi plus de deux mille drapeaux

---

[6] Antoine Bourdois and the French Commissioner (L. 429 n. 1).

[7] This was the church of the Invalides, converted in revolutionary times to a Temple of Mars and developed by Napoleon as a focus and resting place of military glory.

What d'Arblay apparently saw were the spoils of battle that had been deposited with ceremonious oratory at the Invalides on 14 July. After an elaborate speech on revolution, liberty, and war, by Lucien Bonaparte, général Lannes presented the flags taken at the battle of Marengo, and an aide-de-camp, acting for général Masséna, those seized by the armée d'Italie. A spokesman for général Lecourbe, commandant en chef de l'armée du Rhin, mentioned not only flags, but the capture of '50 pieces de canon, 18,000 prisonniers de guerre, des trésors pour payer les troupes, de riches magasins pour les nourrir . . . tels sont les autres trophées . . . à la gloire immortelle du nom français'. 'Les cris de *vive la republique*! *vive Bonaparte*! retenti de toutes parts' (*Le Moniteur*, 16, 17 July 1800).

On 3 Aug. 1800 Bonaparte had had the remains of Turenne (1611–75) removed to the church of the Invalides, which was to become a necropolis of heroes (including Napoleon himself). Often in the cour d'honneur he was to review the Guard, and the Invalides was to become 'en quelque sorte, sa maison'.

suspendus ou reunis en trophées arrangés avec un gout au quel mon emotion ne m'a pas dabord permis de prendre garde. [xxxx 2 *lines*].⊓

[Part of an earlier letter by M. d'A (unfinished) appears upside down on p. 1]

⊓Prompte reponse je t'en supplie: adresse la moi
au Citoyen Darblay chez le Cⁿ Bazille
rüe de l'Etape à Joigny
departⁿᵗ d'Yonne

tu mettras ensuite une enveloppe que tu adresseras à Madame Grandsire

Hotel Kingston *à Calais*

Ecris moi *par Duplicata* par Mʳ Moore à la même adresse *à Joigny*. Je te demande des lettres courtes mais frequentes. Entens ta⊓

456   [Hotel Marengo, Paris]
                                  10 December [1801]

M. d'Arblay
To Madame d'Arblay

A.L. (Berg), 10 Dec.
Double sheet and a single sheet 4to   linked by numbers 4 and 5   6 pp.
red seal
Addressed: Madame Darblay / Westhumble / near Dorking / *Surry*
Edited by FBA, p. 1, top margin, annotated and dated: ⋕ 1801—(35) Nº 1
sweetly kind—& sur les de Maubourgs—Le Marqˢ *Victor* de la Tour Maubourg—
   p. 5, *annotated*: ⋇ 1801. 35/2 (No. 2) Decᵇʳᵉ 10 *continuation.*
grievement [*repeated to link this ss. to the ds. or p. 5 to p. 4*]

Ce 20 Frimaire. (10 Decembre)
à une heure du matin

Oh dear! dear! dearest soul! What a wife! What a friend! Those words, I have just repeated twenty times in reading your letter of the 4th december.[1] What a treat! Ma chere et chere adorable amie! Que ne donnerais-je point pour voler à tes pieds te remercier du bonheur que je viens d'eprouver, et jouir de tout celui que je ne puis connaître qu'auprès de toi! — Que me parles tu ma chere Fanny, de plaisirs qui loin de toi peuvent assez m'occuper pour me distraire un moment; pour eloigner même la seule idée à la quelle toute mon existence tient! Ne sais tu pas que mon amour est telle qu'en t'adorant, je n'en aime pas moins mes amis mais que toi seule peus me tenir lieu de tout. Qu'elle est aisée cette philosophie que j'aurai très surement près de toi, quelque soient les desappointemens qui peut être m'attendent! C'est bien veritablement que je ne crains aucune des combinaisons de ce genre que le sort pourrait mettre en usage pour me rendre malheureux. Jamais il n'y reussira tant que je pourrai vivre avec toi, mon fils, les amis qui entourent notre hermitage, et de tems en tems ceux que je voudrais bien pouvoir visiter avec toi ici. Au ǀ nom d'un interêst aussi cher, ma bonne et excellente amie, occupe toi et surtout soigne bien ta santé. Je te prêcherai d'exemple. Je puis bien, mon amie, te dire que quoique nous soyons separés je n'ai pas encore été un instant sans toi. Toujours ton idée se colle pour ainsi dire à tout ce qui me frappe, et j'aime à te mettre de part dans tout ce qui m'arrive. On me rit au nez ici toutes les fois que je montre de l'impatience et de l'etonnement concernant le retard qu'eprouve mon affaire. J'aime au reste à te dire qu'elle prend une assez bonne tournure. Il me revient de toutes parts que le Ministre y prend un interêst reel. D'un autre côté, j'ai su que plusieurs Generaux, même parmi ceux dont je suis à peine connu, trouvent que rien n'est plus juste. Aujourdhui j'ai été voir dans la loge de la Jacqueminiere,[2] aux Français,[3] une jeune debutante[4] elève de Melle Clairon — Elle a joué Zaire de manière à donner de trés grandes esperances. Le reste m'a paru au dessous du mediocre, et au total je me suis peu amusé. Si tu eusses été avec moi, c'eût été bien

456. [1] L. 454.
   [2] M. d'A's cousin Louis-Charles Gillet de la Jacqueminière (L. 448 n. 10).
   [3] For Paris theatres of the time, see Intro., v, pp. xxxi–xxxii.
   [4] Marie-Thérèse-Étiennette Bourgoin (1785–1833), an actress who had made her début in *Zaïre* on 5 Dec. 1801. Mlle Étiennette was a pupil of Marie-Françoise Dumesnil (1711–1803), however, not of Claire-Joseph-Hippolyte Legris de Latude (1723–1803), *dite* Clairon, a *tragédienne* whose success in performances of Voltaire apparently made d'Arblay infer that she must have been the tutor concerned.

different! Lorsque de retour ici, j'ai trouvé ta lettre,[5] juge si j'ai regreté de n'être pas rentré plutôt. Mais en verité, je n'en ai pas été le maître. La Jacqueminiere s'est si bien et si cordialement conduit avec moi, que je ne puis pas quelquefois | refuser de paraitre prendre grand plaisir à ce qu'il imagine devoir m'en faire beaucoup. Le fait est cependant que j'aurais bien mieux aimé rentrer de bonne heure, pour aller passer ma soirée chez M[de] de Laval,[6] qui est on ne peut pas plus aimable. Tu sens bien qu'en disant cela je te peins seulement mes idées anterieurement à la connoissance que j'avais une lettre de toi. Que de richesses! Quatre lettres depuis hier matin! [xxxxx 4 *lines*] Je ne sais ce que je deviendrais sans ⟨lui⟩. car je ne suis pas aussi philosophe que tu le crois quand je suis longtems sans recevoir de tes nouvelles. Puisque tu ne peus ecrire que par cet ami.[7] Ne manque je te prie aucune occasion. [xxxxx 1 *line*] Dis à nos amis de Norbury que je n'avais pas besoin d'être eloigné d'eux pour sentir combien je leur suis tendrement attaché, et cependant il est certain que j'eprouve chaque jour davantage combien leur bonne et | indulgente amitié m'est necessaire. Je te remercie du nouveau Regime. Il n'y a qu'un seul point que je puis approuver, et que même je condamne. C'est ta *sauvagerie*, qui en est la suitte Je n'aime point que tu vives autant dans la retraite; et si, comme je le crois, le tems des visiteurs de Norbury est un peu passé, je te supplie de reprendre le jour par semaine. [xxxxx 2 *lines*] Cher petit Alex! comme tout ce que tu me dis de lui me fait bonheur! Je voudrais bien qu'il m'ecrivit encore une fois dans une de tes lettres. Cependant, si tu crois que cela retarde trop ses progrès et te donne plus de peine, je n'insiste point. Embrasse le bien tendrement pour moi, bien entendu qu'ensuite, lui à son tours te rendra en mon nom un baiser bien tendre. Chers — Chers amis — rapportez vous en à moi sur le moment de nous rapprocher, et croyez que si je reste plus longtems absent que nous ne l'avions compté, c'est pour moi un vrai sacrifice à notre bonheur futur. Aujourdhui pendant que j'etais à diner chez La jacque-

---

[5] Apparently FBA's letter of 29 November (L. 452).

[6] Mme de Laval, having by this time returned from Glaris, Switzerland, where she had spent the years of her emigration (see Dard, pp. 140–1), had obtained a house in the rue Roquépine, which is in the general area of Place Beauvau and the rue de Miroménil and may be described as the Faubourg Saint-Honoré.

[7] Frank Moore (L. 430 n. 3). See FBA's editorial interpolation, Textual Notes.

miniere, on m'a apporté un billet de Maubourg:[8] le voici tout entier

'as tu reçu mon billet où je t'engage à venir diner avec Victor?[9] Si le chemin ou les eaux te font peur, reponds moi à l'autre partie relativement à mon fils.[10] tout à toi

Latour Maubourg.'

Ce Victor dont il parle est son frère, revenu d'Egypte, où il a été très grievement [1] blessé en chargeant dans la mer à la tete de la Cavalerie lors du debarquement. C'est mon ami intime. Il avait la modestie et la figure d'une très jolie femme: mais sa blessure, qui est à la tête, lui donne dit-on, l'air d'un vieux hussard. Une chose plus fâcheuse c'est qu'elle a affecté sa memoire. Mais j'imagine que les grandes chaleurs ont beaucoup contribué au retard qu'eprouve son retablissement. J'espere qu'ici, il va bien vite se retablir. Quelle charmante et delicieuse famille! Croirais tu que je ne l'ai pas revue depuis ma rencontre aux tableaux? Les distances sont si grandes en ce pays, que l'on est arrivé à la fin du jour, sans avoir fait autre chose que courrir le plus souvent pour rien. Demain matin je courrirai à Passy, (car Maubourg n'a ici qu'un pied à terre où il est rarement) et tacherai de savoir à quoi je puis lui être bon relativement à son fils.[10] J'imagine que cela a rapport à la demande [que j'ai] déjà faite à Lauriston. Je crois t'avoir mandé que le jour [de son] arrivée, je m'etais trouvé avec Saintignon[11] à la prefecture. Depuis ce tems, j'ai beaucoup desiré le voir sans en trouver le tems, et ce n'est qu'il y a deux jours qu'enfin nous

---

[8] César de Latour-Maubourg (L. 446 n. 12).

[9] César's brother Marie-*Victor*-Nicolas de Fay de Latour-Maubourg (1768–1850). Colonel de 3ᵉ chasseurs à cheval (5 Feb. 1792) and Lafayette's commandant de l'avant-garde, he emigrated with Lafayette and his brother César on 19 Aug. 1792, was taken prisoner by the Austrians, and, when liberated, retired to Holland. Returning to Paris, however, in 1799, and sent to Egypt on 12 Jan. 1800, he was named on 27 July 1800 'commandant provisoirement des 22ᵉ chasseurs à cheval'. Wounded in the head at Alexandria on 13 Mar. 1801 (see Six) and in favour with Napoleon, he was made baron de Latour-Maubourg (1808). At the Restoration he was made comte (1814), marquis (1817), and, as FBA adds in a footnote: 'Apres Ambassadeur à Londres pour Louis 18 en 1818 [*error for* 1819]'.

[10] Of César's four surviving sons, d'Arblay may have been interceding for Just-Pons-Florimond, aged 20; Alfred-Marie-Florimond, aged 17; or Rodolphe, aged 14.

[11] Possibly Nicolas-Auguste-Marie Rousseau (1770–1858), comte de Saint-Aignan, artillery officer, chef de bataillon and chef d'escadron (1804), and probably a former friend of M. d'A. He became écuyer de l'Empereur (1809), and was in 1820–4, and again in 1829–34, député de la Loire-Inférieure.

nous sommes rencontrés. Sa soeur[12] est morte, heureusement pour elle et pour les autres. Je remets les details sur ce qui la concerne au tems ǀ où nous pourrons causer les pieds sur les chenets. Je fais demander mon passe-port pour Joigny, et j'espere après l'avoir obtenu pouvoir m'y rendre d'ici à quatre ou cinq jours. j'en resterai dix avec mon oncle, trois pour revenir, environ 8 ici (et moins si je puis, mais cela n'est pas probable) ensuite 4 pour aller à Calais, pareeque je m'arreterai un jour à Amiens. Tu vois, ma bonne amie que sans compter un jour que j'irai à la Grange chez M. de L.F. où je n'ai pu aller tout cela me retiendra encore bien longtems! C'est bien mal finir ma lettre. je le sens bien. Au nom de notre bonheur, ma chere Fanny, ne neglige aucun des moyens de passer ce tems là le moins desagreablement possible, et songe que cette separation sera j'espere la derniere, et que le bonheur de ma vie depend uniquement du soin que tu prends de me conserver tout ce que j'aime. A revoir. Je vous embrasse de toute mon ame et de toutes mes forces.

457   [West Humble, 10 December 1801]

To Doctor Burney

A.L. (rejected Diary MSS. 5304–[05], Berg), *n.d.*
Originally a double sheet 4to, of which FBA later discarded the second leaf   2 pp.
Edited by FBA, p. 1 (5304), *annotated and dated* (*probably from pmk on the discarded address page*): ⌐⟨2ᵈ Septʳ⟩¬ 11 Decʳ 1801   (8)   M. d Arblay in Paris.
Edited also by CFBt *and the* Press.

Why, my dearest Orkbornerie[1] Pappy — I really begin to think you hold the meaning of '*a few pleasing words*'[2] to be that a FEW words must needs be pleasing!—I never now get a page from you—& I am so disappointed at such *ALWAYS* Scraps *you've no notion.*[3]

12 The passage is somewhat ambiguous and the sister, unidentified.

457. 1 Dr. Orkborne is the pedant in *Camilla* (1796).

2 A tag often used by FBA and CB, the origin of which is obscure.

3 'You've no notion' is part of the repetitive vocabulary of Miss Larolles in *Cecilia* (1782).

Terribly indeed have I been alarmed & distressed, in various ways, about my Traveller—& now at this moment I am severely mortified, to find he cannot hope to return for a Month from the date of his last Letter,[4] which was the end of November. He had flattered me—& therefore himself—he should be able to regain his Hermitage for his Boy's Birth Day, the 18th of this Month: but the business he has in hand, of endeavouring to obtain something from his many lost rights, cannot so soon be determined. What business, in which Money has any part, is ever executed as speedily as hoped?—I am the less philosophic in this delay, as I have myself, no expectations of ultimate success. But I am truly happy in the happiness with which he has seen again his poor Country, & met, & been met by his many & deserving friends. ⟙ Your commissions will, I hope, now be received. Though out of the 6 Letters I have written & sent, he ⏐ has received but two. However, any thing you have told him he will not, I am sure, forget. in almost every letter he says mes tendre respects à vôtre père—& it will be a delight to him to execute any commission for you in his power. You will easily believe how much he amazed me in one of his late Letters by saying he had been just told that Col. Ph[illips] was in Paris. A Gentleman whom M. d'A met with had actually dined with him at some Banker's, and named him to M. d'A as an *english man*, without suspicion of any connexion. He, Col. Ph. had said, at table, to the gentleman & the company, he had just sold his estate in Ireland for £25,000.—Can that be?⟙[5]

But let me put by all else, to mention that the good & generous & worthy M. Bourdois is safe in his own Country. Maria had a Letter from him yesterday, dated Calais. How very expeditious has been his journey & passage! & how I rejoice he had set out before the high & frightful Winds of Tuesday & Wednesday, that is last Night. M. d'Arblay will now remain till the Dover passage is open without favour; or else I should try to move Heaven & Earth to procure him a passport from Calais, & even prefer his staying a month for it, to his

---

[4] L. 453.
[5] Molesworth Phillips (Intro. i, pp. lxx–lxxi; and iii and iv *passim*), husband of the late SBP. Far from having £25,000 in pocket, he had been for many years deeply in debt with his Irish estates heavily mortgaged. The hero, however, of Cook's last expedition, he enjoyed the favour of Sir Joseph Banks (1743–1820).

risking again such another voyage as his last by Gravesend.—
ᴦsince I applied for Dover lately, I thinkᴫ

[the second leaf is missing]

458   [Hotel Marengo, Paris],
                               11 December [1801]

M. d'Arblay
To Madame d'Arblay

A.L. (Berg), 11 Dec.
Originally a single sheet large folio, from which a section has been cut
away from the bottom of the leaf 2 pp. (9×8″)
Addressed: [Madame] Darblay / [Westhumble] / Dorking / *Surry.*
Edited by FBA, p. 1, *top margin, dated and annotated*: ⁙ ᴦ1802ᴫ 1801 36/2
Le Genl Hedouville—&c [*and directions, partly lost on the missing lower segment
recopied at top of* p. 1]: Adresse ᴦmoi toute de suitte une lettreᴫ à Joigny
Depⁿᵗ d'Yonne

Ce 11 Decembre

Que de tresors mon adorable amie, la journée d'hier m'a
valu! J'avais passé une mauvaise nuit parceque la veille en
allant diner chez Lajard,[1] après avoir su de lui qu'il y avait
chez son frere | une lettre pour moi, j'avais appris ensuite que
cette lettre avait été, par megarde, emportée par un monsieur
qui venait de sortir. [xxxxx 1 *line*] à peine hors de table j'avais
couru à son auberge, mais en vain: j'y avais passé une seconde
fois à minuit sans plus de succés, et j'y retournais hier matin,
lorsque le valet de chambre de T[aleyrand], que je rencontrai
sur les boulevards me dit que mon neveu[2] etait arrivé. La
lettre après la quelle j'avais tant couru sans être sur, sans
même osé croire qu'elle fût de toi, n'était autre que celle que
tu as ecrite a la hâte par je ne sais quelle occasion. Comment
t'exprimer, ma bonne Fanny, mon emotion en reconnaissant

458. [1] Pierre-Auguste Lajard (iv, L. 291 n. 5) and his brother, either Daniel-
Barthélemy (1752–1838), or, more probably, Pierre Esprit-*César* (iv, L. 292 n. 8),
both of Montpellier.
[2] Antoine Bourdois and his brother Edmé-Joachim, the physician (L. 450 n. 6).

ton ecriture?—L'adresse qu'un autre avait mise ne m'y avait point du tout preparé. Accouru chez le frere de mon neveu,[2] j'appris qu'il avait une lettre pour moi, et qu'il etait allé me la porter à mon logement — tu peux juger si je volai. Bientot elle[3] fut dans mes mains, et tout ce qu'elle contenait ne tarda point à être gravé devine où — N'importe, cela n'empeche pas que la derniere lettre de toi, ne soit constament lue chaque jour en me levant et en me couchant. Outre ces deux lettres reçues hier j'ai ici une troisième écrite à mon neveu, et dans la quelle tu lui dis *I am quite in Heaven by your news my dear Bood.*[4]—Comme j'ai baisé ces mots, comme ils me sont chers! O mon amie! plus de separation! — tu as bien raison: il faut desormais que nous soyons de moitié en tout; et c'est pour rendre l'execution de ce plan possible que je travaille ici sans relâche. Je suis faché de t'avoir peut être donné un moment d'*uneasiness*, en te demandant conseil sur une chose à la quelle j'ai entierement renoncé, comme à tout ce qui pourrait y ressembler.

[*the bottom of the leaf is missing*]

[Le General] I de Division Hedouville,[5] m'a fait ⌐aussi¬ beaucoup d'avances et m'a fort engagé à l'aller voir, et sur ce que je lui ai demandé, vu ses immenses occupations en ce moment, à quelle heure je pourrais le rencontrer, le priant de me faire ecrire chez son portier il m'a repondu très obligeament et tout haut que jamais sa porte ne serait fermée à *un homme tel que moi.*—&.—&.—Cela se passait dans les appartemens le jour de la revue. Malheureusement je ne puis découvrir où est la rüe Cisalpine, dans la quelle il m'a dit loger.

⌐Dis a notre cher et excellent ami que j'ai remis sa commission à quelqu'un qui la fera bien mieux que moi. C'est Mr

---

3 This was FBA's letter of 29 November (L. 452).
4 This was a letter of *c.* 26 November, thanking Bourdois for news of M. d'A's arrival in Paris, thus ending a 'fortnight's suspence' (L. 452, p. 72).
5 Gabriel-Marie-Théodore-Joseph (1755–1825), comte d'Hédouville, general and diplomat. In 1792 he had served in the Armée du nord under Lafayette, and though subsequently suspended from service and imprisoned (3 Dec. 1793) in the abbey of Kaiserslautern, he was released (12 Aug. 1794) and allowed to retire. Reinstated as général de brigade (19 Apr. 1795), he achieved the rank of général de division (26 Nov.), and with varied commands and responsibilities, including that of 'agent civil et militaire à Saint-Domingue' (1797–8), he was at this time 'inspecteur d'infanterie dans les 12e, 13e, et 22e divisions militaires'. In 1803–4 he was to be sent as ambassador to Russia (see Six).

11 December 1801

de N[arbonne] qui en charge le jardinier des Tuilleries[6] qui l'etait jadis à Bellevue. [xxxxx 3 *lines*] |

Ah! plains moi de ne pouvoir passer le 18 de ce mois avec mon cher petit et sa mère adorée! Tout ce que je puis faire, et je le ferai sûrement, c'est d'aller celebrer ce cher anniversaire avec mon cher oncle. Unissez vous donc tous deux d'intention avec moi mes chers — chers et meilleurs amis! |

[*the bottom of the leaf is missing*]

[*Marginal writing*]

Je te prie de me faire ecrire un mot par Alex! [*part of leaf missing*] lettre à Joigny Dep^nt d'Yonne

[*On the mutilated address fold, parts of 4 lines of a PS. to Alexander d'Arblay can be read.*]

Try, my dearest Alex,
dear Papa who cares
your so much beloved
your health with your |

---

[6] The commission (described by FBA, L. 432) to purchase peach, almond, and rose trees for Poulett-Thomson of Waverley Abbey, the Lockes of Norbury Park, and the Angersteins of Woodlands, had evidently reached d'Arblay, who had passed on the request to his friend the comte de Narbonne, who in turn proposed to consult an eminent gardener, evidently Jean-Georges Le Sage (d. 1806). Le Sage had been the chief gardener at Bellevue from 1786 to 1791 (at which year the relevant archival record ends) and he had been appointed in 1800 (at the latest) as 'jardinier-terrassier' for the Tuileries at the enormous salary of 16,000 francs.

Members of the royal family residing in pre-revolutionary times at Bellevue (built *c.* 1750 by Mme de Pompadour) include Marie-Adélaïde de France (1732–1800), to whom the comte de Narbonne's mother Françoise *née* de Chalus (iv, L. 323 n. 10) had served as dame d'honneur for forty years. The comte, therefore, would have had ample opportunity to know the gardener and the beautiful garden at Bellevue, which, situated on a wooded bank overhanging the Seine between Sèvres and Meudon, was, it was said, 'a dream of beauty, terraces, bosquets, avenues of Judas trees, lilacs and poplars, leading to cascades and statues'. For descriptions and coloured illustrations of Bellevue, see Nancy Mitford, *Madame de Pompadour* (1968).

West Humble, 15 December 1801

Conjointly with Alexander d'Arblay
To. M. d'Arblay

A.L. & A.L. (Diary MSS. vi. 5310–[13], Berg), 15 Dec. 1801
Double sheet 4to   4 pp.
Addressed: Au / Citoyen Darblay / Chez le Cᵗ Bazille, / rue de l'Etape /
À Joigny, / Departᵗ d'Yonne
Edited by FBA, p. 1 (5310), *annotated*: 34 / 3
Edited also by CFBt *and the* Press.

West Humble, Decʳ 15ᵗʰ 1801

The relief, the consolation of your frequent Letters I can
never express—nor my grateful sense of your finding time for
them situated as you now are—& yet—that I have this moment
read, of the *15. Frimaire*[1] has made my heart-ache heavily.
Our Hermitage is so dear to me — our Book-Room so precious,
& in its retirement, it's beauty of prospect, form, convenience
& comforts, so impossible to re-place—that I sigh—& deeply,
in thinking of relinquishing it.—Your happiness, however, is
now ALL mine; if, deliberately, therefore, & from your own
persuasion it will be better, you wish to try a new system, I will
surely try it with you, be it what it may. I will try ANY thing
but what I try NOW — — absence! Think, however, well, mon
tres cher ami, before you decide upon any occupation that
robs you of being master of your now *Time, leisure, Hours,
Gardening, scribbling, & reading!*—

In the happiness you are now enjoying, while it is so new to
you, you are perhaps unable to appreciate your own value of
those six articles, which, except in the moments of your bitter
regret at the privation of your first friends & beloved Country,
have made your life so desireable. Weigh, weigh it well, in the
detail I cannot write.

Should you find the Sum total preponderate in favour of
your new scheme, I will say no more. ALL schemes will to ME |
be preferable to seeing you again *here* without the same fondness

459. ¹ L. 455.

for the place, & way of life, that have made it to me what it has been.

With regard to the necessity, or urgency, of the measure, I could *Say* much that I cannot write. You know *how* I can live, with YOU — — & you know I am not without views, as well as hopes, of ameliorating our condition.[2]

I will fully discuss the subject with our Oracle, if I see him today, but the weather has an aspect not promising for his arrival. Yet he has not, I am sure, missed five days since you have been gone,—& his kindness, his affection for you—but Yesterday, when I produced your Letter of the [*blank*] & the extracts from Me Neckar,[3] & was going to read some, he said, in that voice that is so penetratingly sweet when he speaks from his heart, 'I had rather hear ONE LINE of D'Arblay's, tha[n] a Volume of Me Necker's' — — yet, at the same time, begging to peruse the MS when I could spare it. I wish you could have heard the *TONE* in which he pronounced those words! it vibrated in my Ears all day.

I trust, by this time, you have seen your nephew, who, I hope, will find more pleasure from his return than the dragging reluctance with which he at last set out indicated his expecting.

Pray, give my best *wishes* to him, & tell him his fair wife looked extremely well, when I saw her walking over with Charlotte & Sophy,[4] on Saturday, & she was animated with great delight by a Letter from Mr. Otto,[5] offering to forward all she might write. The three good & pretty Girls all dined & spent the day with Alex & me last week, previous to Charlotte's return to Brighthelmstone. Poor Richard was not well enough for the double walk, as the weather was rainy. They have promised to come & ¦ keep our Alex's Birthday on Friday. —Here comes Mr. Norbury.

---

[2] This was probably the period in which FBA wrote her most successful comedy, 'A Busy Day', described by Adelstein (op. cit., p. 112) as 'An Unpublished Masterpiece'.

[3] After the death of Suzanne Necker *née* Curchod (ii, L. 96 n. 4) in 1794, her husband edited her papers: *Mélanges extraits des manuscrits de Mme Necker* (1798), *Nouveaux mélanges extraits des manuscrits de Mme Necker* (1801).

[4] CBFB's daughter Charlotte Francis (1786–1870), EBB's daughter Sophia Elizabeth (1777–1856), and the Revd. Richard Allen Burney (i, p. lxix) were evidently visiting Maria Bourdois at Sand Place.

[5] The French Commissioner in London (L. 429 n. 1).

I have spent near two Hours upon this Theme with our dearest oracle & his other Half—He is much affected by the idea of any change that may remove us from his daily sight, but, with his unvarying disinterestedness, says he thinks such a place would be fully acquitted by you. If it is of consul *here*,[6] in London, he would rejoice for you, & me,—if at last, something must be done, & This Hermitage no more be our sole home, he would not, he says, then hesitate to accept it, & he is sure you would fill up all its functions even admirably.—In any other Post, he thinks, with me, there must be great inducement, indeed, to charm you from a retirement where you are completely master of your own predilections & actions. Indeed for *me*, any country town, any residence, but in the real country, such as ours, or in London or Paris, would be irksome & beyond all means. I put, however, the whole consideration into your own hands; what, upon mature deliberation, *YOU* judge to be best, *I* will abide by. Heaven guide—& speed your determination! — —

My dear Father is very anxious about his Books[7]—all the family are well in all its rounds. I am delighted to direct, at length, to Joigny & entreat your beloved uncle & Aunt to accept my sincere & most respectful devoirs, & all your dear cousins to ⎪ prepare themselves to give me a little portion of the love they bear you. Alex is perfectly well & at the moment brandishing a carnation green stick for a spear, while his sword which he has broke, he has fixed in front for a Dagger.

---

[6] See L. 455, p. 80.

[7] Cut off from Paris for ten years and more, English booksellers and savants were greedily anxious to know what had been published in the years of revolution and war. Dr. Burney, engaged in writing articles on music and musicians for Rees's *Cyclopaedia*, had a pressing interest in the volumes on music that were to form part of the comprehensive *Encyclopédie méthodique* (192 vols., 1782–1832), the first editors of which were, as he knew, Diderot and d'Alembert. According to Scholes (ii. 188), CB had been making use of the articles prepared by Messrs. Framery and Ginguené for the volume *Musique*, published by Panckoucke in 1791, a volume that went alphabetically from *A* to *G*. The next volume (*H* to *Z*), which CB so urgently desired, was not to appear until 1818. 'Aucune des parties de l'Encyclopédie méthodique n'a éprouvé peut-être autant d'obstacles & de retards dans son exécution que celle-ci', explained M. Framery in the 1818 Preface. 'La rédaction générale en fut d'abord confiée à MM. Suard & l'abbé Arnaud. La mort arrêta ce dernier au milieu des ses recherches . . . [et] les occupations de M. Suard, étrangères à cet ouvrage, en se multipliant de plus en plus, l'empêchoient d'y donner une attention suivie.'

It was with respect to these matters that CB was to belabour every member of his family travelling to Paris with requests to procure information. See his A.L.S. (Osborn) to FBA, 20 May 1802; also L. 460, p. 96; L. 475 n. 2, L. 521 n. 8.

15 December 1801

He begs a few lines left for his own writing. I shall write next post day a duplicate as you desire. The two dear souls I have consulted send you their truest love &c, & warmest wishes. This subject has swallowed up all others. Finally make your decision with confidence. I will abide by it to the best of my power, your bon amie. And Bood will tell of mes amis —

[*By Alexander d'Arblay*]

My dear Papa

I hope you are well   I have read the Cuning Man[8] Love is just like April Weather   Never the same an hour together that is the reason I write it because I like it best
Pray come home as soon as you can

460   [West Humble], 17 December 1801

To. M. d'Arblay

A.L. (rejected Diary MSS. 5314–[17], Berg), 17 Dec. 1801
Double sheet 4to   4 pp.   *pmks* DARKING   FOR[EIGN] OF[FICE] red wafer
Addressed: Au / Citoyen Darblay, / Chez le Citoyen Bazille, / à Joigny, Depart^nt d'Yonne— / France
Edited by FBA, p. 1 (5314) *dated* 1801, *and date* Decr 17th 1801 [*framed*]
Edited also by CFBt *and the* Press.

17 Dec. 1801

I wrote instantly upon receiving your's of the 6th by notre ami, in hopes some dispatch may forward my answer before the regular Post; but as you desire a duplicate, I will now prepare one by your other addre$s.—I hardly know how to write again all I put down instantly on my first impulse— relative to my fears you would yourself be disappointed, once in office, at the consequences, namely, the loss of the *independance of Time & action* to which you have so long been accustommed.

---

[8] *The Cunning Man, A Musical Entertainment* (1766) was CB's adaptation of Rousseau's *Le Devin du Village* (see both Lonsdale and Scholes, *passim*). AA's quotation, substantially correct continues: 'Forward, fickle, wanton, wild, / Nothing, nothing but a child.'

94

My conversation, after I had written what struck me as obstacles, with our dear Oracle, has softened my objections in some measure, for he did not hesitate to pronounce he thought you fully qualified for the undertaking in every way.[1] Yet he, too, apprehends you may regret your *chosen leisure: ALL*, however, is not to be obtained at once,—& the more I reflect, the more I feel *I* can know no *happiness* but *yours!—misery* I may taste in many shapes; but *Happiness* & *you* are linked, for *me*, inseparably. I will begin, therefore, here, in my duplicate, where in the first sketch, I ended, by saying DELIBERATE very well, & *ALONE*—I mean unbiassed; & then, RESOLVE, & *ACT*. assured I will abide by your decision, & *endeavour to make it as chearful as possible* to us both. |

I have been think that, perhaps, the renewed public sort of life you are leading, has lessened your taste for retirement,— though I am well convinced it will not lessen your tenderness for Her to whom you have so long made it happy;—this must be taken into solemn consideration, for your return hither, *without* that taste for your retreat, would make me far more wretched than relinquishing it myself. That indeed shall *not* make me wretched, if it be your *OWN*, & your *deliberate* opinion it will be better for us to change our system. But you must not be *biassed*, you must not let even the kindest of your Friends judge for you. Those who have not seen how happy you can be in retirement, may naturally conclude, by your gaiety in society, that our Hermitage is a mere residence of *triste* necessity. It has not been such yet—it has NEVER been *triste*, but by MY misery for my eternally lamented loss[2] or *your* occasional repinings & grief at your exile from your first friends & Country. ⸀This latter will exist no longer, the intercourse will be open, you may write & hear from them all, &, on any great occasion, be with them in a week. This will make a considerable change in your feelings. — — The kindness & goodness | of our oracle are truly affecting: I am sure he will feel our removal from his daily view with real sadness: but he never mentioned it — *You*, only, he said, could judge what you should do; he was completely convinced you could suit the part you talked of, &,

460. [1] For a post as commissioner of French commercial relations in England. See L. 455, p. 80.
[2] The death of SBP (6 Jan. 1800).

were it in *London,* he thought it far too desirable for a moment's hesitation.[1] *Elsewhere,* he believed we might buy its profits too dear. — — Of this, indeed, I am fully persuaded. I detest all residence but real Country, or real Metropolis. The claims upon Time, leisure, attentions, spirits, in all other places, are such as to render existence burthensome.—

Yet, *this,* even this, will be preferable to seeing you *here* with regret upon your Mind! M*rs* Norbury had Tears in her Eyes during the whole consultation—yet attempted no opposition. I represented the matter as impartially as I could, & there was nothing to wonder at in your projected exertion. Nor, indeed, knowing as I do the *possible* withdrawing from our income, could I myself forbear *forwarding* rather than shrinking from the attempt—but I have views & hopes of another sort,[3] & which would not break into our way of life,—*else,* believe me, your disappointment of the *reforme,*[4] & of your *patrimony,* would make me, also, think you ought not to sit longer quiet.— however, my views & hopes are precarious—& therefore, I must not urge them. The result is, & shall be, THIS:⌐

Do as you JUDGE best, & FEEL happiest, & I shall be best content. Yes, my dearest best loved Friend, your long forbearance—your waiting my wishes for the PEACE, call for my liveliest gratitude, & shall ever meet it, by an entire concurrence with your own decision for our future life. Did I not promise to carry your knapsack? — Shall I do less after so many years CONVICTION of your worth, than I promised upon its *faith?* ⌐I have much else to talk of but this subject swallows all my paper, & just now absorbs all my thoughts — for, however, I must not fail to thank you for the charming & entertaining accounts in the Notes, which makes me read it as if we sat together—not *quite!* I hope your nephew is with you!—& writing to Maria — Give my love to him; I hope that our Padre's commissions arrived too[5]—But you have still beads enough to decorate all the Prayer books for him.

My best respects & my duty to your dear & excellent uncle & A⟨unt & family⟩. & to your cousins. Alex is in ecstasy for his birth-Day to-morrow. Mrs. Lock has sent him a Horn—&

---

3 The hope of producing a lucrative comedy (cf. L. 459 n. 2).
4 Defined by M.d'A (L. 523, p. 332) as an 'espece de half-pay . . .'.
5 See L. 459 n. 7.

his Godpapa uncle a Turkey, a Tea pot, a plum-cake & a pound of Almonds & Raisins! Imagine his Joy ⟨to see⟩ the *Stage*, directed to himself M. Alexander d'Arblay! If you could bring Mrs. Norbury a couple of *Shuttle cases* she would be overjoyed. I can never find room to tell you the kindnesses every body send you—*Mr.* Norbury so expressively!—& his Freddie—so tenderly—I think they love you more & more—

461   Joigny, 18–22 December 1801

M. d'Arblay
To Madame d'Arblay

A.L. (Berg), 18–22 Dec. 1801
Double sheet 4to   4 pp.   *pmks*   SHIP LE[TT]ER   31 DEC 1801   red seal
Addressed: Madame Darblay / Westhumble *near Dorking* / Surry
Edited by FBA, p. 1, *top margin, annotated and date retraced*: ⁙ 18ᵐᵉ Decembre 1801   38   Noble ⟨conduct⟩ of our uncle Bazile—to be always preserved in the d'Arblay Family both for *security* & Gratitude.   Affaires
Edited also by CFBt.

Joigny, 18 Decembre 1801

Aujourdhuy, ma chere amie, nous avons celebré par un gouté fort joli donné aux petits Cousins et Cousines d'Alexandre,[1] sa fête[2] que je n'ai pu faire avec vous dans notre cher Hermitage. Il y a eu beaucoup de gaieté et surtout de bruit: mais tout s'est passé de manière qu'Alex et toi vous eussiez aimé egalement à en être temoins. Je te laisse à juger qui en eut été bien aise. je devrais dire *le plus aise*, car mon oncle, ma tante, leurs enfans,[1] et pour m'exprimer en moins de mots, toute la Ville me montre le plus grand regret de ne pas te voir ici avec moi. Assurement, ma bonne et bien chere, toujours plus chere Fanny, à la satisfaction generalement repandue sur les visages

---

461. [1] See Genealogical Table, vi.   [2] Alexander's seventh birthday.

de ceux que je rencontre, je puis me flatter que si, lorsqu'on a mis mon nom sur la fatale liste, on eut pris les voix de ceux qui avaient été le mieux à même de me juger, la presqu'unanimité s'y serait opposée. Quoiqu'il en soit cependant, on s'est tellement hâté de vendre mon bien[3] et celui de mon frere, et de ma soeur, que tout arrangement pour le racheter devient à peu près impossible. Tout a été vendu, et l'on n'a payé aucune dette, ni remboursé aucune rente. Celles qu'on m'avait mandé me rester ne suffiraient pas à beaucoup près à payer ce que je dois. Encore a t'il été decidé que les arrerages (le revenu annuel) de ces rentes ne m'appartenait qu'à dater du jour de ma radiation, ce qui assurement est en contradiction manifeste avec l'engagement de nous faire rentrer dans la portion de nos biens *non vendus*, ce qui me semblait vouloir dire, des biens dont nous restons les seuls possesseurs. J'ai eu beau dire: mais ces arrerages echus ne font ils pas partie de mon bien? D'ailleurs quel est l'esprit du decret rendu sur les Emigrés rentrans? La Nation ne leur dit elle pas. *nous reconnaissons que c'est à tort que vous avez été mis sur la liste d'où nous effaçons vos noms; cette radiation vous rend l'exercice de tous vos droits, mais une raison d'Etat, la crainte des troubles qu' occasionerait surement votre rentrée dans la portion de vos biens dont la nation a garanti la vente, nous force quoiqu'a regret à vous imposer la loi d'y renoncer?* MAIS *vous redevenez les legitimes possesseurs de tout ce dont vous pourrez jouir sans exposer à ces troubles votre patrie, fâchée d'être contrainte de mettre des bornes à la justice qu'elle aimerait à vous rendre?* L'article de l'arreté des Consuls est positif;[4] et dés qu'on m'en a eu donné communication, je n'ai plus rien eu a repondre. Il porte que 'Quant aux arrerages de rentes non payés, les Emigrés rentrans n'en percevront que la portion echue depuis leur rentrée, *à compter de l'epoque de leur radiation, l'autre portion* de ces arrerages dus avant cette epoque, devant être perçue par les Recevants de la Republique.' Tres certainement, je suis loin de murmurer, et tu sais si je suis heureux d'avoir pu revoir ma Patrie, quelques soient les conditions mises à mon retour dans mes foyers, mais il me semble que cette disposition est en opposition directe avec l'esprit de la loi dont ⏐ ⟨elle⟩ fait partie.

---

[3] For further details on M. d'A's property, see vii, Appendix I.

[4] M. d'A's present attempts to regain his property proved as futile as the efforts made by his uncle in 1800 (see iv, L. 396 n. 5).

(Decembre 22.)

Prepare toi, ma bonne amie, à ne me voir rien rapporter de mon voyage que quelques livres que j'ai retrouvés ici. Du reste j'avais bien raison de te dire que le sort avait probablement decidé que ton enfant et moi nous te devrions tout, absolument tout. Ce n'est assurement point la faute de mon oncle. Mon malheur a voulu que pendant le regne de la terreur il habitât Paris pour se soustraire à la persecution de quelques jaloux de ce pays. Il a été ainsi plus de deux ans, et il est impossible de se figurer à quel point l'obligation dans la quelle il s'est ainsi trouvé de faire double menage l'a constitué en depenses. S'il eut pu rester ici, il aurait racheté tout mon bien. Malheureusement il n'en a eu qu'une partie. Tu te rappelles surement mon inquietude relativement à ce que je lui devais. cette inquietude n'a été que trop fondée. Toutes les avances qu'il m'avait faites pendant vingt ans etaient bien mentionnées dans notre correspondance durant cette epoque. Mais lorsqu'il l'a produite pour se faire tenir compte de ce que je lui devais, on a pretendu en abuser pour lui faire rapporter les sommes qu'il y disait avoir reçues pour moi, de sorte qu'il a encore été trop heureux de retirer ces pieces dont on voulait abuser, bien loin de la faire servir au recouvrement des sommes qu'il reclamait. Le peu de bien qu'il a pu acheter est bien loin de le dedomager d'une perte aussi considerable, et pourtant lorsqu'il en a été question entre nous, non seulement il n'a point voulu que j'en parlasse: mais même il pretendait me rendre ce qu'il a acheté. C'est comme bien tu penses, ce que ni toi ni moi, ne pourrions jamais accepter. Quand je parle, au reste, des sommes qu'il m'avait avancées pendant 20 ans et plus, je n'entens parler que de ces sommes effectives et non des interests dont il n'a jamais voulu qu'il fût question. Quel homme! J'aime à penser que si Madᵉ et Mʳ L[ocke] le connaissaient, ils l'aimeraient beaucoup. Quant à toi, je suis sûr que lorsque tu le verras — ainsi que ma tante — tu partageras tous les sentimens de respect de veneration et de tendresse qu'ils m'inspirent. Et leur fille! Et leur fils! Ce dernier a acheté le petit bien de L'Epauche dont tu m'as entendu parler. La premiere chose qu'il m'a dite c'est qu'il n'avait fait cette emplette que pour moi; qu'en consequence j'en etais le maitre comme auparavant. Hier je fus m'y promener par un tems epouventable. Voici en quoi [|] consiste ce bien. Imagine toi une ferme avec un très petit pavillion que mon pere avait fait bâtir pour un pied à terre. La ferme consiste en l'habitation du fermier une ecurie assez petite et une grange capable de contenir 7 à 800 gerbes de bled, — greniers caves &c — : Le pavilon ne consiste qu'en deux chambres assez grandes, un grenier au dessus, et une cave au dessous. Ces bâtimens ont besoin de reparation. Leur situation est fort isolée, et à l'abri du Nord parcequ'ils sont au bas d'une montagne couronnée de vignes et de bois dont deux arpens seulement dependent de la ferme. Quant aux terres il y en a tout au tour de la ferme 92 arpens dont on pourrait faire un parc, n'y ayant que 1 arpent et $\frac{1}{4}$ qui appartiennent à un proprietaire du voisinage, encore est-ce sur la lisière, et croit on qu'on pourrait les echanger. Les terres sont assez bonnes, mais à cause de leur isolation, le fermier ne doit par son bail que 92 bichets de bled savoir 20 de froment et 72 de meteil. chaque bichet pese 66 livres et l'on estime 4^{tt} celui de meteil et 6^{tt} celui de froment: D'où il suit que cette ferme ne rapporte que 408^{tt}. Au prix actuel des fonds cela vaudrait au plus 6000^{tt}. Je sais très bien que pour quelqu'un qui l'habiterait, cela pourrait valoir beaucoup plus, mais, pour nous, cela ne peut nous convenir. D'ailleurs, quoique mon cousin y ait fait 1800^{tt} de reparation, il faut y mettre encore au moins 1200^{tt} pour que le[s] batimens soient en etat. Je crois donc que nous la laisserons à l'acquereur; au re[ste] je remets tout arrangement definitif au tems où tu seras ici avec moi. Mon on[cle] pretend que je lui ai dejà donné dix ans de vie, et il se promet bien d'en ajouter autant au moins qu'il attend du bonheur que tu lui feras surement eprouver quand nous serons reunis ici cet été. Je ne te parle point en detail de la manière dont il m'a reçu, mais il ne te sera peut être pas impossible de t'en faire une idée d'après tout ce que tu sais dejà du caractere de cet homme excellent. J'ai craint dabord que notre premiere entrevue ne lui eut fait mal. heureusement, il n'en eprouve que bonheur, et moi la satisfaction la plus douce et la plus complette. J'en excepte pourtant l'argent: car celui que nous retirerons d'ici se reduira probablement à zero, tout ce qui me reste devant être absorbé par les dettes ou rentes dont aucunes m'ont été remboursées, ni payées par la nation. Je ne te parle [|] [pas] encore de mon retour, parcequ'il m'est impossible encore d'en assigner l'epoque exacte mais crois que je meurs d'envie de retourner dans mon hermitage, embrasser et serrer contre mon coeur, ma Fanny, mon Alex, et nos amis. A revoir la plus aimable comme la plus aimée de toutes les femmes. L'heure de la poste qui me presse, m'empêche de remplir mon papier.

462   West Humble, 19–[21] December 1801

To Esther (Burney) Burney

A.L. (Diary MSS. vi. 5306–[09], Berg), 19 Dec. 1801
Double sheet large 4to   4 pp. *pmks* DARKING   22 DEC 1801 wafer
Addressed: Mrs. Burney, / Beaumont Street, / Devonshire Place, / London.
Edited by CFBt *and the* Press.

West Hamble, Dec. 19. 1801.

Tears of pleasure, my dearest Esther—rare Tears!—your kind Letter brought into my Eyes. The verification of my anxious hopes in your share—so PRINCIPAL to ME—of happiness in this connexion,[1] is indeed dear to my heart. I know how much more there is than you *can* say hanging upon the *collateral* circumstances; & the *straight line* is all we can wish. Maria is truly amongst the happiest of Wives, & her fond attachment for her husband is such as he merits to inspire.—The idea of *YOU*, laying your dear head down to rest with relieved solicitude, & cheared feelings & prospects, is indeed truly precious to me—& draws into my so often tardy hand my Pen, at the moment the Letter is scarcely finished. Particularly, too, I am pleased to see you write once more as if with a consciousness you write to me alone;—& here let me assure you, my dearest Etty, I *never* shew your Letters to Any human Being—but my other Soul—I read paragraphs, &c—but never produce them, two excepted, which appeared to me written so as to almost *belong* to M. Bourdois, relative to your visit at his house,

462. [1] The marriage between EBB's daughter Maria and Lambert-*Antoine* Bourdois, which was arranged by the d'Arblays (see iv, L. 381 and *passim*).

& to his kind donation to your *bequeathed protegée*![2] — ¦ I beg you, therefore, to use the same unrestrained language as formerly, in the certainty they never *dream* of seeing my Letters: even the most unimportant, I forbear putting out of my hands, that no ¦ curiosity or conjectures may be raised for others that are withheld. With respect to the grand subject of your Letter, Religious instruction for dear little Amelia,[3] I would I could help you better than I can!—Had my alex been a Girl, I could have had a far greater chance of hitting upon some thing that might serve for a hint; for then I should have turned my thoughts that way, & have been prepared with their result: but I have only weighed what might be most serviceable to a Boy. And this is by no means the same thing, though Religion for a *man* & a *woman* must be so precisely. Many would be my doubts as to the old Testament for a Girl, on account of the fault of the Translators, in not guarding it from terms & expressions impossible—at least utterly improper, to explain. With respect to Alex, as I know he must read it at school, I think it best to parry off the danger of his own conjectures, questions, or suggestions, by letting him read it completely with me, & giving such a turn to all I am sorry to let him read, as may satisfy his innocent & unsuspicious mind for the present, &, perhaps—'tis my hope!—deter him from future dangerous enquiries, by giving him an internal idea he is already well informed upon the subject. So much, however, I think *with you* that Religion should spring from the Heart, that my first aim is to instill into him that general veneration for ¦ THE CREATOR OF ALL THINGS, that cannot but operate—though perhaps slowly & silently, in opening his mind to pious feelings & ideas. His Nightly prayers I frequently vary; whatever is constantly repeated, becomes repeated mechanically: the Lord's prayer, therefore, is by no means our daily prayer; for as it is the first & most perfect composition in the Universe, I would not have it lose its effect by familiarity. When we repeat it, it is always with a commentary. In general, the prayer is a recapitulation of the errors & naughtiness, or forbearance & happiness of the Day; & this I find has more success in impressing him with delight in goodness, & shame in its reverse, than all the little—

---

[2] Mme de Gouvello (see L. 451, pp. 68–9).
[3] EBB's daughter Amelia Maria, now about ten years old.

or great Books upon the subject. Mrs. Trimmer[4] I should suppose admirable for a *Girl*; I have told you my motive for
taking the Scripture at large for a *Boy*: I would rather all risks
& dangers should be run *with* than *without* me. *We* are not yet
far enough advanced for such Books as you talk of for Amelia,
but I will enquire what these are, if possible, & let you know.
I think, however, *conversation* & *prayer* are the great means for
instruction on this subject; there is no knowing when they
read on what is so serious, *what* they understand, or *how* they
understand; & they should be *allured*, not *frightened* into a
religious tendency.—That the little soul loves you is the best of
all signs, & I doubt not but you will make her *good* & *acceptable*
while you keep her filial piety in its right state. May it be
ever! — |

I must take this side for other matters. I am very glad of
what you did about F[anny] P[hillips] how indiscreet a little
Soul![5] She *well knows* the danger & fascination of her encouragement—how I wish Richard's *health* & situation made that
affair less to be dreaded! he is *far* better—but *far* from *well* —
— My Traveller is so indulgent as to write to me twice a week—
& I almost live on his Letters—but you will be sorry to hear his
late ones are quite dejected as to all his hopes of his patrimony,[6]
or any consideration of his military services. *I* had entertained
so little idea he would regain any thing, that my personal
disappointment is next to nothing; but *he*—sanguine, & full of
consciousness of his rights & claims, is deeply mortified, &
depressed: & this afflicts me—but will, I hope, pass off. He
has bid me direct my future Letters to his Uncle—so that his
residence, as well as his hopes, at Paris, I conclude over.
Maria has never heard from Mr. Bourdois since her Calais
Letter—I have had no intelligence within the time he might
reasonably be supposed to have arrived there. But I will keep
a line open for to-morrow morning, in case any news arrives.
Maria, Sophy & Richard kept my Boy's Birth day yesterday
here, all well. the little rogue is perfectly well, too. So are all at

[4] Sarah Trimmer *née* Kirby (1741–1810), author of forty or more books for
children (i, L. 3 nn. 107, 108).
[5] SBP's daughter Frances Phillips (1782–1860), now living with her grandfather CB at Chelsea College. A vividly attractive girl in her teens, she was to
captivate her cousin (EBB's son), the Revd. Richard Allen Burney, but of this,
much more, e.g. L. 464 n. 6 and L. 483, p. 157.
[6] See L. 461 n. 3 and iv, L. 396 n. 5.

Norbury Park. I am very sorry for your Cold, my dear soul,—pray dismiss it. My Love to dear Mr. B[urney] & remember me at Chelsea when you go thither & at Charles Street.⁷ Heaven bless You!—
Monday. Joy, Joy, my dearest Esther! the excellent news is just come to me. Write to the *Bishop yourself!*⁸—pray! 'Tis for *you* 'tis done at last. I have also a Letter from my best of best, & M. Bourdois is safe & well in Paris, though Maria has not heard from him directly. What an exquisite business is this Clerical business at last! How I kiss you for joy in my heart!—Joy to dear Mʳ B[urney] —

463   [West Humble,
post 25 December 1801–January 1802]

To Doctor Burney

A.L. (Diary MSS. vi. 5238–[39], Berg), *n.d.*
Originally a double sheet 4to, of which FBA later discarded the second leaf. 2 pp.
Edited by FBA, p. 1 (5238), *dated incorrectly and annotated:* ⁜ 1800 13. Decʳ (8) M. d'Arblay at the Hague. Death of Mrs. Chapone & of Mr. Langhton.
Edited also by CFBt *and the* Press.

I have been quite enchanted at the sight—this Minute—of the Man who had had the sight but yesterday of my dearest Father.¹ Yet I am much alarmed at this sore throat,—for heaven's sake keep the *Thieve's Vinegar,*² & *camphor,* always

---

⁷ Perhaps the address at this time of JB and SHB.

⁸ Bishop of Worcester (1774) and of Winchester (1781), Brownlow North (1741–1820), a friend and patron of the Worcester Burneys (i, L. 3 n. 10), had now presented the Revd. Richard Allen Burney to a living (paying £350 per annum) at Rimpton, Somersetshire (see 'Worcester Journal' and L. 464, pp. 107–8). In a letter (Osborn) to CB on 24 Dec. 1801, the Bishop took pleasure in attesting to 'what Patrons can not always say, that I have very highly gratified myself, by making this arrangement in his [Richard's] favor. I remember old times; I have long had a great respect for the name & family, & I look upon Richard, as a happy specimen of Burnean worth, temper, & talents . . . I was aware of his tender health, but flatter myself he may measure strength with Duty at Rympton [where the previous incumbent] had rarely more than two Baptisms in a year'.

463. ¹ Possibly William Locke.

² Thieves' Vinegar, or *Acetum Aromaticum*, in use also at Mansfield Park (Chap. 7), is vinegar to which is added the liquor expressed from a mash of such herbs as

about you,—*never* out of your rooms,—poor Fanny[3] will I trust escape further attack by this small one—but I tremble for Molly[4] and if for *her* — —! — Dearest Sir, had not *you* better come to West Hamble, than ask *US* to Chelsea? Cold we are, however, & unable to accommodate you—but how many would delight to take the opportunity?—

Your commission is arrived just as I am going to write to my dear Chevalier, *I hope* for the last Letter upon this separation. But he is not certain yet of his return. What a dreadful fright the True Briton gave me one day last Week, of a new *movement* in Paris![5] God keep all quiet there—but *him*, & may he be *restless* till he quits it! — — I was going to begin a Letter to you the other day, in the fullness of my heart, to exult, with *YOU*, on a testimony of I respect & veneration which are so highly honourable paid to the wisdom & authority of our so dear & revered Dr. Johnson, by the Lord Chancellor,[6] in his reprimand

rosemary, sage, lavender, and cloves. According to Andrew Duncan, *The Edinburgh New Dispensatory* . . . (1789), this was 'an elegant improvement' over *Acetum Prophylacticum*, which contained the juices of wormwood, rue, garlic, cinnamon, etc. Duncan also supplies the anecdote that gave the remedy or disinfectant its name. 'It is said, that during the plague at Marseilles, four persons, by the use of the acetum prophylacticum as a preservative, attended unhurt, multitudes of those who were infected; that under colour of those services, they robbed both the sick and the dead; and that one of them being afterwards apprehended, saved himself from the gallows by discovering the remedy.'

[3] Frances Phillips (L. 462 n. 5).   [4] Mary More (ii, L. 68 n. 30).

[5] A copy of the *True Briton and Porcupine* for the relevant date the editors have not been able to find, but on the dates 7, 8 Jan. 1802 the newspaper found itself obliged to retract and modify some exaggerated statements recently made on the success of 'a powerful Confederacy' (see Madelin, iv. 139–45) that for some time past has 'been thwarting the present Administration of France'. 'The Jacobins, and the original Republican Party, better known under the name of Brisotines, have viewed, with a jealous and malignant eye, every measure of Imperial power which has marked the conduct of the First Consul, since his accession to supreme authority', including the steps leading to the Concordat. The newspaper could only condemn 'any attempt to invalidate and subvert the Government, which, at least, in the absence of the Ancient Monarchy, promises security to Europe, and repose to France'; and on the next day (8 Jan.) it expressed its relief from 'great anxiety'. 'No principles of illegitimate ambition have disturbed the authority of a Government, on whose efficiency the peace of Europe in a great measure depends.' See also the *Observer* of 3 Jan. 1802.

Such was the political thought of the hour, and to FBA and others what seemed worst at this time was the overset of government and the recurrence of revolutionary horrors.

[6] John Scott (1751–1838), M.A. (1773), Lord Chief Justice of the Common Pleas (1799), Lord Chancellor (1801–27), whose knowledge of Dr. Johnson had emerged in his Oxford days in a 'stilted' prize poem (*DNB*).

Now in the summing up (on 26 Dec. 1801) of the complicated case (brought before the Court of Chancery on 10 Nov.) respecting the mismanagement of Drury Lane Theatre, the Lord Chancellor had turned last of all to the responsibility of the manager in the theatrical debts and his self-confessed negligence.

to Mr. Sheridan. I hope you had the same words I read? I was really *lifted up* by them. The Chancellor gave in his language the rebuke he loved not to give to a M. P. & so powerful an antagonist, as Mr. Sheridan. But I have been much grieved for the loss of my faithful as well as honoured friend Mrs. Chapone[7] — very sorry for good Mr. Langton.[8] How is our Blue club cut up! But Sir William Pepys[9] told me it was dead while living, all such society as that he formerly belonged to, & enjoyed, being over.—┌I suppose now William[10] is gone for his holydays to Portsmouth.—Is his Father, then, returned from France? M. d'Arblay has never mentioned him since that first time, when he had been informed of his dining at a Banker's by a french man, who said he was of the party. Yes I hope Richard will follow your advice,[11] & go over┐

[*the second leaf is missing.*]

464   West Humble, 29 December 1801

To M. d'Arblay

A.L. (rejected Diary MSS. 5318–[19], Berg), 29 Dec. 1801
Originally a double sheet 4to, of which FBA later discarded the second leaf   2 pp.
Edited by FBA, p.1 (5318), *numbered*: 39
Edited also by CFBt *and the* Press.

Applicable to him, he thought, were the moral observations with which Johnson had concluded his *Life* of Savage: 'nothing will supply the want of prudence; and . . . negligence and irregularity, long continued, will make knowledge useless, wit ridiculous, and genius contemptible.' FBA could have seen this reproof in 'Law Report', *The Times* (28 Dec. 1801).

[7] Hester Chapone *née* Mulso (1727–1801) had died at Hadley on 25 December. Her friendship, unlike that of Mrs. Ord and others, had survived FB's marriage to an *émigré* (a Frenchman, a Roman Catholic, and a constitutionalist), and for this, and the introduction in earlier days (*DL*, ii. 167, 193–202) to Mrs. Delany, FBA had always been particularly grateful (iv *passim*).

[8] FBA is evidently commenting on an ominous report in a letter from CB, now missing. Bennet Langton had died at Southampton on 18 Dec. 1801.

[9] William Weller Pepys (1740/1–1825), cr. Baronet (1801).

[10] Second son of Molesworth Phillips and SBP, William Phillips (1791–1833), at this time a pupil at CB Jr.'s school at Greenwich. He was, supposedly, to spend the vacation, as his brother Norbury often did, at Portsmouth with his father's friend William Bayly (1737–1810), who, as an astronomer on Cook's second and third voyages, had been appointed (1785) headmaster of the Royal Academy at Portsmouth. It was probably under his influence, as well as his father's, that William determined as soon as possible to go to sea.

[11] If the Revd. Richard Allen Burney, probably for the improvement of his health.

106

West Hamble. 29 Dec. 1801

I hope & trust my most beloved Friend has now delighted his heart with fond embraces of his dear & honoured uncle,[1] & that now he will be returned to Paris. ⌐I wrote to Hotel Marengo by the post last week, & two Letters, two of Nov. to you at Joigny.[2] I shall get Bood, through Maria, to forward this, should raison *so douce* still there detain you.⌐ How I was enchanted with your last Letter, & renunciation of the *commerciale* plan[3]—at least till we have reviewed our affairs together! I shall never oppose, with either reluctance or entreaty, any scheme you deliberately form; but I know you must have been, of late, in a state somewhat unnatural, & such as to over-power your solid & permanent inclinations, by a renovation of scenes & persons & views dear to your heart, & rendered doubly precious by long privation: nevertheless, I am by no means convinced that your sober, unbiassed, ultimate happiness would agree with any occupation that robbed you of independant leisure. certainly no Man ever knew better how to fill up & enjoy it;—& therefore I rejoice we shall meet before any new system be adopted.—I cannot tell you half enough of the kindness expressed for you in your absence by *ALL*;— *chiefly*, as chiefly known to, Norbury Park—but my dear Father has sent & written sundry enquiries; & my dear sister Burney loves you quite tenderly, as well as *gratefully*.[4] Think of her happiness in this promotion of her Son! Richard wrote me word, yesterday, ⌐ the living[5] turns out to be beyond his hopes— £350 per annum, ⌐ if he moves instantly, it is in a delightful part of England, Somersetshire, on the border of Dorsetshire. —& the surroundings &c, picturesquely beautiful. The house belonging to it is in perfect repair. How he will get to it is all the difficulty—he means to walk to town the first dry day, when he is to see the Bishop. We are all in the dark as to his designs of housekeeping,—but he has begged Blue to come

---

464. [1] Jean-Baptiste-Gabriel Bazille (L. 423 n. 2).
    [2] The letter addressed to the Hôtel Marengo is missing, but Ll. 459 and 460 are those addressed to Joigny.
    [3] See L. 458, p. 89.
    [4] For arranging her daughter's marriage (L. 462 n. 1).
    [5] Richard's letter is missing, but for particulars about the living provided by Bishop North see L. 462 n. 8. It was now arranged that his maiden aunt Elizabeth Warren Burney (1755–1832) was to set out *c.* 15 Mar. 1802 to help settle him in his rectory at Rimpton (see 'Worcester Journal', p. 55).

from Worcester, & go with him to *Rympton*, his living, & settle him in his new establishment. This she kindly consents to: but will *that* persist long? I am very anxious about my dear Fanny—very, very uncertain, what to *wish* for her. But the last thing to surprise me will be his writing his proposals —or her accepting them.⁶ Mr. Norbury sent words of *such* love, & his tender, penetratingly tender, joy, the sum of his kindness. I have just been a long airing with him & Augusta. Mrs. N[orbury] has again a little cold, but nothing important. She had been quite well for some time. Alex is so well! Maria & Sophy came to me, for a short time, on his birth day, both well. Charlotte Francis is returned to Brighton,⁷ where Mr. Broome is much enraged with Buonaparte's spending your income!— she, I know, wishes to exact for my visit while you are away. Mrs. 'Ock is charmingly well again, & has her family, each in turn all at Norbury Park.—Mrs. William, Mrs. Charles,⁸ Greville Upton, & Capt. Upton (*Sophy* Upton's Brother from Hesse)⁹ were all brought to see a picture by William—& M˖ʳˢ Chˢ made me shew her M. de Narbonne's portrait,¹⁰ *because* he had been so kind to Charles when he was in Paris. *Wed* I write again to my dearest beloved anchor *No*ᵑ

[*the second leaf is missing.*]

⁶ FBA was, in part, right: Richard had sent a written proposal of marriage to his cousin Fanny Phillips (see L. 483, p. 157; L. 521, p. 325; and L. 527, pp. 355–6), which was rejected.

⁷ Charlotte Francis (L. 459, p. 92), having completed her visit to Maria Bourdois at Sand Place, had returned to her mother Charlotte Broome (see 'The Burney Family', i, pp. lxxii–lxxiii), who in the spring of 1800 had moved, with her family, to Brighton. The letter Charlotte Francis must have written to her aunt on her return is missing.

⁸ Mrs. Locke's daughters-in-law, Elizabeth Catherine *née* Jennings and Cecilia Margaret *née* Ogilvie. See L. 472 n. 2.

⁹ Frequent visitors at Norbury Park from their earliest years were the children of Mrs. Locke's life-long friend Lady Templetown (iii, L. 216 n. 16). There at that time were Fulke *Greville* Upton (1773–1846), *later* Howard; his sister Sophia (1780–1853); and Arthur Percy (1777–1855) of the Coldstream Guards (1794). Arthur had been educated at the Royal Military College, Berlin, and on 2 Dec. 1795 was gazetted Captain. He was A.D.C. to Sir Ralph Abercromby (1799), on the Quarter-Master General's staff in Wellington's army (1812–14) and eventually attained the rank of General (11 Nov. 1851).

¹⁰ Narbonne's portrait was offered for sale at Sotheby's on 19 Dec. 1960 (Lot 296). The present whereabouts of the portrait is unknown to the editors.

M. d'Arblay
To Madame d'Arblay

A.L. (rejected Diary MSS. 5322–[25], Berg), 1–3 Jan. 1802
Double sheet small 4to   4 pp.   cover missing
Edited by FBA, p. 1, *top margin, annotated and year date encircled*: 3/1   à Paris /
ce /
Edited also by CFBt *and the* Press.

á Paris
ce

ᴦ11 Nivose, an 10 — ᴨ Ce 1ᵉʳ Janvier 1802
[xxxxx ½ *line*]

ᴦJe viens, ma bonne chere amie, causer un moment avec toi;
je dis un moment car il faut à present que je les prenne comme
⟨cela vient⟩, n'osant plus t'ecrire trois ou quatre heures de la
nuit, comme je le fesais il y a quelquetems. Je me porte tout
aussi bien qu'alors mais le tems que j'ai passé à Joigny me fait
revenir à mon envie ⟨originale relativement à tout⟩ sommeil
dont je ne puis me passer sans en souffrir.ᴨ Quand reverrai-je
donc notre hermitage! Quand presserai-je dans mes bras celle
qui remplit tellement mon coeur, celle avec qui seule je puis
être heureux! Il serait assez simple de penser que cette reunion
tant desirée ne depend que de ma volonté Point du tout; mille
et mille contrarietés se succedent pour la retarder. ᴦAvant de
partir de Joigny j'ai cru, à tort, ⟨avec l'aide⟩ d'un passeport
de mon departement passer par dessus toutes les difficultés
qu'occasionnent les formes aux quelles on est obligé de se
plier ici. J'ai heureusement été detrompé à tems, et ce passe
port m'est trés insuffisant. J'aurais été obligé de revenir de
Calais en demander ici un autre.ᴨ Mes affaires ᴦet celles de
mon Consulᴨ ont d'ailleurs pris une tournure si singuliere qu'il
ne m'est pas même possible, à dix jours prés, de te mander
l'epoque de mon arrivée. Au nom de notre amour, occupe toi:
prends de l'exercice; et dis toi souvent, qu'il n'est pour moi de
bonheur que dans notre retraite, que je ne serai vraiment
heureux que lorsque j'y serai rendu, que jamais je n'ai tant
senti combien, la vie que nous y avons menée est douce et

remplie de jouissances que rien ne peut remplacer, et qu'enfin celle à qui je les dois fut—est—et sera toujours pour moi *tout l'Univers*. Oui ma bonne amie c'est là ce que me dicte mon coeur, c'est là ce que tu y lirais, si nous pouvions être à portée de nous entendre . Je lis et relis tes lettres, elles sont ma plus douce consolation: pourquoi en ai-je besoin? pourquoi n'es tu pas ici? ou pourquoi ne suis-je point près de toi. Je t'ai toujours aimée de toute mon ame, de toutes mes forces, et pourtant je ne t'ai jamais tant aimée qu'à present. C'est aujourdhui le premier jour de l'année. sera t'elle heureuse pour nous? Reviendrons nous ensemble en passer | en passer ici une partie? Viendrons nous y apprendre *ensemble* à priser, s'il est possible, encore plus que nous ne l'avons fait, le bonheur d'un genre de vie dont il est impossible que les autres se fassent une juste idée? Nous sera t'il possible de le continuer? ou serons nous forcés par raison, par devoir, de l'interrompre pour y revenir, être à même de toujours le suivre? Crois, mon amie, que jamais je ne l'ai mieux apprecié, mais qu'aussi jamais je n'ai fait de plus serieuses reflexions sur les evenemens qui pouvaient influer sur sa durée. Je crois t'avoir mandé qu'aussitôt qu'on m'eut fait faire la reflexion que le Gouvernment au lieu de la place flatteuse dont on m'avait parlé, m'en donnât une qui ne t'eut pas autant convenu je renonçai à une idée que mes amis seuls avaient fait naître. Il n'en a donc plus été question: mais ce que j'etais loin de prévoir, c'est la lettre suivante[1] que je trouvai hier matin en rentrant. Elle est de Mr de L. F. actuellement à La Grange.

Avant de te copier cette lettre, je dois te dire que j'étais passé le matin chez Du Tailly[2] Gal de Brigade et aide de Camp de Berthier pour qui je lui avais laissé ce billet.

'D'ar. prêt à partir prie le Ministre de la Guerre de lui accorder un rendez-vous le plutôt possible.

Salut et respect.'

A present voici la lettre de M. de La Fayette.

'Je ne sais où vous êtes, mon cher D — mais d'après votre dernier billet' (je lui avait ecrit en partant pour Joigny) 'je

---

465. [1] The original of this letter, dated 5 Nivôse [26 Dec. 1801], is in the Berg Collection.
[2] Dutaillis (L. 446 n. 7) was d'Arblay's 'contact' in the ministère de la Guerre.

vous attends ici. Ce sera pour moi un bonheur partagé par
toute la famille; nous voulons, avant notre depart, vous
montrer cette retraite, où j'espere que vous viendrez avec
M^de D'a— et votre bon petit garçon nous faire de longues
visites. Il faut que je vous parle *d'une conversation relative à
Laumoy'*[3] (M^al de Camp passé avec nous) *'et à vous*. Je l'ai sue
par le consul le Brun,[4] et le Ministre de la Guerre. Le resultat
est un ajournement de l'affaire de reforme, mais la possibilité
d'un emploi de chef de Brigade (Colonel) aux Colonies, ce
qui vous met dans le cas au bout de quelques mois de prendre
votre retraite. (Cette retraite serait de mille ecus *125^l
sterling*) Je ne vous dis cette proposition que parcequ'elle m'a
été faite par le Ministre. J'ai repondu vaguement, et de
maniere à ne point vous engager. Depuis ce tems, j'ai ecrit
au premier Consul un mot sur les droits et les interêts de mes
compagnons. N'allez pas au reste regarder le mode indiqué
par Berthier, *d'après ce qui s'est passé chez Bonaparte*, comme une
obligation pour vous. Votre situation est tout à fait à part, et
c'est elle qui doit regler vos calculs et votre choix. Je vous
embrasse mon cher D'ar. —

L. F. ¹

[*M. d'Arblay continues.*]

(Janvier 2. 18⟨0⟩2)

Mon amie, mon unique amie! je reviens à toi, à toi que
j'aime mille fois plus que moi même. Toi seule, tu peus avoir
une idée de l'impression que me fit eprouver la lettre que tu
viens de lire. Toi seule tu peus concevoir tous les combats aux
quels mon pauvre coeur s'est vu en proie, pendant plus de 4
heures qui s'ecoulerent jusqu'à l'instant où, après avoir relu tes
deux dernieres lettres, après m'être penetré de plus en plus du
danger certain au quel notre bonheur mutuel allait être exposé,
si je courrais le risque du moindre regret et du plus leger
mecontentement de moi même, je pris la plume pour faire cette
reponse.

³ Jean-Baptiste de Laumoy (L. 450 n. 12), whose application for a pension was
being investigated at the same time as d'Arblay's.
⁴ Charles-François Lebrun (1739–1824), 3ᵉ Consul de la République française
(25 Dec. 1799), duc de Plaisance (1808), pair de France (1814, 1819). He was at
this time charged with financial organization.

Copie de mon billet au Ministre de la Guerre[5]

le 11 Nivose an 10.

'Dar — ne reçoit qu'à l'instant même communication de l'offre du Ministre de la Guerre de le faire employer comme chef de Brigade.

Si c'est pour aller à St Domingue,[6] aider à faire rentrer cette Colonie dans l'ordre, il ne doit point hesiter, et accepte avec reconnaissance.

Partout ailleurs où il n'y aurait point de coups de fusil à essuyer il demande la permission de ne point accepter.

La course qu'il vient de faire dans son departement lui ayant demontré que de toutes les proprietés, et de deux heritages, il ne lui reste rien, et qu'on ne lui a laissé que quelques dettes qui vont diminuer encore les moyens de subsistance que la plus stricte economie rend à peine suffisans, il desire infiniment obtenir le plus promptement possible le rendez vous qu'il demanda hier au Ministre

Salut D'a — '

[*M. d'Arblay continues.*]

Apres avoir achevé ce billet je me sentis satisfait: mais que j'etais loin d'être content, et surtout tranquille! Cependant, ma bonne amie, daigne observer que notre separation, dans le cas où je reçoive l'ordre de rejoindre l'expedition, ne peut être bien longue; et qu'une fois cette expedition terminée, rien ne peut s'opposer à ce que j'obtienne la retraite que surement je demanderai, ne voulant très certainement point, quelque traitement qu'on m'offrit, servir ailleurs qu'au feu. Crois mon amie que je n'ai pas cessé un moment de penser ainsi que toi, que le premier de tous les | biens c'est l'independance, c'est à

---

[5] A draft of this letter to Berthier, in d'Arblay's hand, is preserved in the Berg Collection.

[6] San Domingo, where the liberator Pierre-Dominique Toussaint-Louverture (*c.* 1746–1803), supported by an efficient army of blacks, had drafted a constitution for an independent state. To quell the resistance, to regain control of the richly productive island, and secretly wishing to restore slavery on the plantations in spite of his earlier public affirmation of the emancipation decrees passed during the Revolution, Bonaparte had sent on 14 December the largest force that had ever sailed from France (20,000 veteran troops and five or six of his ablest officers) with, as commander-in-chief, his brother-in-law Victor-Emmanuel Leclerc (1772–1802). With repeated calls for reinforcements, 34,000 in all were sent, of whom by 14 Oct. 1802, 24,000 had died, 8,000 were in hospital, and only 2,000 fit for duty. Arriving at Le Cap on 2 February, Leclerc himself was to die of yellow fever on 2 November. See C. L. R. James, *The Black Jacobins* (1938); and Rose, i. 332–7.

dire l'emploi volontaire des courts momens de la vie. La notre, c.à.d. la mienne avec une compagne comme ma Fanny, est si douce! Mais conviens qu'un peu plus d'aisance nous serait necessaire. De mon coté j'ose avouer que si je le devais à quelqu'heureux fait d'armes, que les circonstances peuvent encore me fournir, et que j'espere bien ne pas laisser echapper, notre retraite si aimable, tant aimée, me serait encore plus chere. Je me livrerais d'autant plus volontiers à cette idée, mise en opposition avec tes craintes, et l'inquietude que ces craintes me donneraient, qu'assurement l'expedition de St Domingue est approuvée de ton Gouvernement,[7] qui doit s'interesser à son succès. Dans tous les cas, c'est sur mon cher Alex, que je m'en repose du courage et de la fermeté d'ame que sa mere trouverait sûrement. Je les embrasse tous deux comme je les aime. C'est l'expression la plus sincere comme la plus forte de ma tendresse pour eux.

(le 3 Janvier) à 1.⟨h⟩ après midy.

Je sors de chez le Ministre avec qui j'avais rendez vous. Voici en propres termes ce qu'il m'a dit, ou plutôt toute notre conversation en abregé

'J'ai parlé au premier Consul. '*Qu'il aille, a t'il dit 'à St Domingue, faire ce qu'a fait Maubourg en Egypte.*[8] *Qu'il revienne comme lui avec une blessure, il sera bien vu de l'armée et sera confirmé dans son grade de Chef de Brigade.* Je vous ferai donner;' a ajouté le Ministre, une lettre pour le General le Clerc,[9] qui vous employera dans votre grade.' Ma reponse a été que je ne pouvais partir qu'employé par le ⟨Gouvernement⟩ et non par un individu. Apres beaucoup de difficultés il a dit qu'il allait proposer au 1er Consul de me donner sur le champ mon traite-ment de reforme sous condition: c.à.d. ne devant avoir lieu

---

[7] Whatever the outcome of the French expedition, the English stood to gain. Having themselves lost 100,000 men in West Indian campaigns (Fortescue, pt. 1, 385, 565), they had no objection to corresponding losses of French soldiers. Nor, on the other hand, with the island of Jamaica in mind, were they much in favour of the liberator Toussaint and the possible contagion of his ideas.

What caused both surprise and alarm in England, however, was the departure of a huge fleet from Brest before the negotiations at Amiens had been concluded or the Peace signed. See *AR*, 'History of Europe', xliv (1802), 92, 209–42. Accord-ingly, reconnaissance fleets of five sail and later of thirty sail were sent out to observe the courses and the progress of the French transports.

[8] See L. 456 n. 9.

[9] See n. 6 (*supra*).

qu'à dater de mon arivée à St Domingue.[10] Forcé dans mes retranchemens, je ne vois rien à objecter, et il est possible que j'aye à peine le tems de recevoir ta benediction!!!

Du courage mon amie!

Pense à Alex et aime toujours

son pere — ! —

466 [Hotel Marengo], Paris,

5 January 1802

M. d'Arblay
To Madame d'Arblay
and Alexander d'Arblay

A.L. & A.L. (Berg), 15 Nivose an 10

Double sheet large 4to, of which the conjugate leaves have been separated, with the loss of some marginal writing on the inner spine 4 pp., the letter to AA being written on the lower fold of pp. 3 & 4. *pmks* 14 JA 1802 14 JA .802 T.P.P. PIMLICO wafer

Addressed: England / Madame Darblay / West humble / near Dorking / *Surry*

Edited by FBA, p. 1, *top margin, annotated, and dated*: 5. Jany 1802 4/1

p. 4, *address panel, annotated*: NB. NB. Keep this beautiful Letter my dear Alexander, for our successors — It paints the character, conduct, Disposition, situation, Bravery & Tenderness, of such a Husband & Father as il y en a peu, peu, peu!!

Paris ce 15 Nivose an 10.

Je me repens beaucoup d'avoir Hier trop precipitament et peut être *bien inutilement* plongé dans la douleur l'être pour le quel et par le quel seul j'existe. Aujourdhui mes amis c.à.d. ceux dans les quels j'ai le plus de confiance, s'accordent à dire que je'm'exagere les pretendus devoirs de ma position. Ils pretendent que la question se reduit à savoir *si les cent louis ou mille écus de retraite qui pourront me revenir valent le peine d'accepter ce qu' on me propose.* Ils persistent dans l'opinion que mon honneur

---

[10] For the delay in committing this verbal understanding to paper, see L. 468, p. 121.

et ma delicatesse ne doivent en aucune maniere être mis au rang des objections pour ou contre, ni l'un ni l'autre ne pouvant être compromis. Ils me representent en outre que si reellement je n'ai point l'intention de me rattacher au service pour y rester, il est très possible que je ne sois pas le maitre de me retirer après l'expedition finie; et sur ce que je repons que j'ai moi même prevenu le Ministre de ma ferme resolution de debuter par dire à ceux qu'on m'enverrait commander *'que très certainement mon intention n'est point de venir leur enlever des places qu'ils ont si bien gagnées: mais que je viens uniquement payer ma retraite le prix qu'on y a mis, très decidé si on ne me l'accordait point après l'expedition, à donner ma demission.* Ils repondent: que très probablement le Ministre ne se rappellera rien de notre conversation, que d'ailleurs le Ministre peut changer, que ma demission pourrait être mal vüe, et qu'en definitif, j'aurais fait une campagne ruineuse, et cela sans en tirer aucun fruit.

Il y a bien une autre raison bien plus forte contre le projet en question. C'est tout ce qui te concerne; C'est l'obligation peut être de le mettre à execution avant même d'avoir reçu ta benediction, avant de recevoir de toi la promesse solonnelle de ne rien negliger pour soutenir cette epreuve, pour conserver à notre cher et innocent Alex la plus tendre et la meilleure des meres, et pour laisser à son pere desolé la douce certitude qu'il obtiendra à son retour le prix le plus cher de ses sacrifices. Ah si j'avais cette assurance, si ton courage que je connais avait pu te la dicter, si ta tendresse maternelle, si les soins de tes amis, et la perspective d'un bien doux avenir te donnaient la force de tenir tout ce que cette assurance m'aurait promis, je l'avoue, je passerais par dessus toute autre consideration, et partirais, malheureux de te quitter, mais plein de l'espoir de te rejoindre, et content de devoir à un sacrifice qui ne peut être long, la satisfaction de n'avoir point à me faire en aucun tems le reproche d'avoir laissé echapper l'occasion d'ameliorer notre sort. La perte totale de mes proprietés, et le secours tres precaire, quoique si necessaire, que nous offre ta pension, ne me sortent point de l'esprit. Nous avons fait l'epreuve qu'avec toute l'economie possible notre revenu ne peut suffire à une existence tant soit peu comfortable, et il a fallu pour attraper la fin de l'année, que des circonstances qui ne peuvent guere renaître vinssent à notre secours, et secondassent tes soins si vigilans.

He bien, mon amie, que serait ce si ta pension venait à cesser d'être payée? Mais me dira t'on, n'est il pas possible que cette cessation de paiement soit une suitte de la demarche à la quelle vous vous resoudriez bien plus facilement, si vous pouviez la discuter avec l'être qu'elle interesse le plus, et dont l'assentiment vous est si necessaire? à cela je repons que la conduite qu'a tenue l'auguste personnage de qui seule depend la continuation de la pension, sur la quelle on voudrait exciter mes inquietudes, ne me permet pas même de m'arrêter un seul instant sur la possibilité d'un retranchement qui serait si peu en mesure avec tout ce que nous avons eprouvé jusqu'à ce jour, surtout quand cet auguste personnage serait prevenue que je n'ai pris du service pour une expedition qui, loin de contrarier ses interêts, les sert. D'un autre côté, mes esperances detruites entièrement relativement au peu qu'on disait me rester, nous privent des vingt cinq louis de revenu que par arrangement mon neveu[1] s'etait engagé à nous faire. Il est clair que deslors cet engagement est nul. Il est vrai que je dois aux soins de ce cher neveu le recouvrement des deux cent louis dont nous t'avons parlé, et c'est une surprise que je comptais te menager à mon retour. Nous ne perdrions consequement point 25^f mais seulement 15, les 200 dont je parle ayant dejà été placés à 5 pour 100. Reste à tenir compte de mon voyage.

Mais tous ces calcules d'interêt sont de bien peu d'importance opposés à l'inquietude au tourment continuel où je suis chaque fois que je me dis: tu peus partir sans avoir un mot d'elle, tu peus rester tous le tems que tu seras eloigné d'elle, sans savoir si elle a eu la force de suivre les plans que lui dicteront sa tendresse pour votre cher petit, tu peus ignorer à jamais si elle t'a rendu justice, si elle a connu tes combats, si elle a su que tu n'as ni provoqué ni prevû une offre d'autant plus singuliere qu'elle est faitte au moment ou l'on a reformé vingt cinq mille officiers, à ajouter à un nombre presqu'aussi considerable, dejà dans le même cas. En verité une pareille situation est trop dechirante. Plût à Dieu que je pensasse, comme le disent mes amis, que les mots *honneur*, *delicatesse*, sont tout à fait deplacés dans la discussion qui m'occupe! Je ne suis rien moins que convaincu sur cet article, et lorsque je me dis avec orgueuil, que toute ma vie j'ai fait en ce genre plutôt *plus* qu'*assez*, il m'est

466. [1] Jean-Baptiste Bazille *called* 'Précourt' (L. 447 n. 4).

possible d'être à calculer le point precis où je reste tout plate-
ment sur la ligne d'où si l'on ne s'est point elevé, on n'a du
moins pas tombé: *between rising & sinking* Malgré cela, le desir
de me rapprocher de toi pour ne plus m'en eloigner donne aux
representations ⏐ de mes amis un poids qui a tellement emporté
la balance, que je viens de charger l'un d'eux de voir le Ministre
à ce sujet, et d'agir entierement comme il le ferait pour lui
même. Je conviens avec lui, que bien que le tems du danger
existe peutêtre encore, celui de la gloire est tout à fait passé,
et qu'il serait fou de partir sans avoir au moins la certitude
d'être employé non pas simplement par le General commandant
l'expedition,[2] mais par le Gouvernement lui même. Si donc, il
en est encore tems, les arrangements definitifs n'etant point
irrevocablement pris, je renoncerai plutôt à ma demande, et
serai bientot pres de toi. Dans tous les cas tu recevras par la
premiere occasion une autre lettre. Ecris moi vîte, et par la
poste et par notre ami. Jamais un pareil soin ne fut plus necessaire. Je te prie même de m'envoyer un billet dans une lettre
de ta niece; son mari me la remettrait aussitôt.[3] Probablement
cette derniere voie serait la plus prompte, comme aussi la plus
sure. Que ne donnerais-je point pour causer avec toi ne fut-ce
qu'un instant! Il n'est pas un genre de tortures au quel depuis
trois jours je ne me sois vu en proie Ah si je puis ratraper mon
independance, si ta volonté seule a le droit d'influencer
l'[arrivée] des doux instans dont toi seule composerais ma vie,
ne crains pas que je me laisse jamais entrainer encore aux
hazards qui la pourraient compromettre. La leçon est forte,
et elle ne sera pas perdue.

[xxxxx 3½ *lines*] ⏐

Au nombre des livres que j'ai pour toi, de la part de mon
oncle, se trouvent, le Cours de Litterature de la Harpe très
bien relié,[4] et la nouvelle edition de l'abregé de l'Histoire
universelle par Anquetil.[5] Ce dernier ouvrage est broché parcequ'il ne fait que de paraitre. Il y a en outre une magnifique

---

[2] General Leclerc (L. 465 n. 6).
[3] Maria and Antoine Bourdois (L. 436 n. 5).
[4] Jean-François de La Harpe (1739–1803), *Cours de Littérature* . . . (16 vols.,
1799–1805), the last four volumes of which had not yet appeared but were to be
published posthumously.
[5] Louis-Pierre Anquetil (1723–1806), *Précis de l'histoire universelle, ou Tableau
historique présentant les vicissitudes des nations* . . . (evidently the 2nd edition, 12 vols.,
1801).

edition de la Jerusalem du Tasse. Je crois que M. Locke sera charmé de la voir. ⌐C'est en folio.⌐6 Il y a une in 4°. superbe que je comptais echanger à Londre ainsi que quelques manuscrits |

J'ai reellement beaucoup d'esperances de te rejoindre bientôt: mais dans le cas où je m'eloignerais davantage; songe au prix dont sera pour moi une lettre de toi. Ne perds pas une minute. Je ne demande qu'une ligne. Envoye la moi par Duplicata

Qu'en songeant à notre independence, je fais bien l'application des vers7 que tu aimes tant. J'en ai bien joui mais à present que je suis menacé de la perdre. Il me semble que je n'en ai pas assez su jouir. Ah comme ceci m'enseigne à l'appretier!

Si comme je l'espere, nous ne sommes point separés, combien je me repprocherai de t'avoir ainsi allarmée. Helas! je n'ai pu ⟨resister⟩ à l'idée de m'eloigner ainsi sans un mot de toi: [*spine torn*] ... [je ne] m'en suis pas senti la force me le pardonneras tu? J'etais si troublé et d'ailleurs si pressé chez le Ministre où l'on me disait: le courrier part et n'attend que votre lettre!! Pardon Pardon

[*To Alexander d'Arblay*]

I have my dearest Boy Many things for you, which I hope to carry and give myself to my Alex. If contrary to my warmest wishes I were obliged to send and not carry them to you, I depend upon you as to the comfort you may give to your dearest Mama, to the tenderest of your dear friends. Never live a day without telling her I shall never forget the exquisite

6 The folio of which M. d'A writes is most probably the magnificent two-volume Bodoni edition, *La Gerusalemme Liberata di Torquato Tasso* (Parma, Nel Regal Palazzo, MDCCXCIV), which includes a dedication page 'All' Augustissimo Cattolico Monarca Delle Spagne CARLO IV di Borbone Imperadore delle Indie. Giambatista Bodoni'. Since in her Notebook for 1806 FBA refers to 'Le Brun's Tasso. 2 vols.', the 'superb' quarto edition to which M. d'A refers is probably the French prose translation of 1774 by Charles-François Lebrun.

7 In the editorial capacity of her later years FBA here supplied the explanatory note: 'This alludes to Shenstone's [*A Pastoral Ballad* (1755)]

I pris'd every Hour that pass'd by
Beyond All that had pleas'd me before.'

She had Alex memorize the ballad, and this was one of the pieces he recited for the Princesses on 10 Apr. 1800. See iv, L. 374; and a copy of a letter (Berg) to Mrs. Locke, November 1824.

happiness I owe her, and that the last beating of my heart will be for you both, for YOU / both / the very soul of my life!— Be always good to be always happy. Be attentive and obedient when your dear dear Mama speaks, I entreat you my dear Boy, to send me, without any delay, some of your hair, tied with some of your Mama's. I wish to have them in a little paper written by you both, ⌐for our future meeting.⌐ Be sure I love you with all my heart and soul. Be sure you never were, you never will be a single moment without being the first, the tenderest of my thoughts. Don't loose a minute to send your answer to the present request. I send you the heartyest kiss, which you will share with the person you and I love the best.

Tell our dear friends I shall for ever love them, in whatsoever place and situation I may be. Your God-papa / M. de Narbonne / sends you his best love; give his tenderest respects & best wishes to your Mama and to our dear Norbury friends—

467   [Hotel Marengo, Paris,
                          7 January 1802]

M. d'Arblay
To Madame d'Arblay

A.L. (Berg), *n.d.*
A fragment (4·1 × 5·5″) cut from a 4to sheet 1 p.
Addressed: Madame Darblay / Westhumble near Dorking / Surry.
Edited by FBA, p. 1, *top margin, dated and annotated*: 7. Jany 1802 4/2

Je t'ai ecrit hier, ma chere amie, tout ce que je sais de l'affaire qui m'interesse uniquement. Aujourdhui je ne sais rien de nouveau, et j'en suis toujours à attendre la reponse ministerielle. Mon ami de Juniper[1] doit voir ce matin Berthier à ce sujet. J'ai remis mes interêts c.à.d les notres entre ses mains, et comme il est d'avis que ce qu'on m'offre ne doit être pour moi qu'un affaire de calcul dans [lequel] mon honneur n'est nullement compromis, tu ne peus pas douter que s'il y [a un]

467. ¹ The comte de Narbonne (L. 446 n. 6).

moyen honnête de m'empêcher de partir il ne l'employe. Mon dernier mot est que sans ma reforme je ne pars point. Or il n'est guere probable que cette condition ainsi dictée soit acceptée. Dans le cas contraire il faudra convenir que ce parti pris de m'employer quand on refuse une foule de demandans sera très singulière. Dès que l'affaire sera decidée je tâcherai de trouver le moyen de te faire parvenir une lettre un peu differente de celle-ci où retenu par l'idée que j'ecris dans le paquet d'un autre je ne puis me livrer à tout ce que j'eprouve en ce moment de crise. [xxxxx 3¼ *lines*] Je t'aime mille et mille fois plus que jamais on n'a aimé.

468 [Hotel Marengo, Paris]
10 January 1802

M. d'Arblay
To Madame d'Arblay

A.L. (rejected Diary MSS. 5342–[43], Berg), *n.d.*
Originally a double sheet 4to, of which FBA later discarded the second leaf   2 pp.
Edited by FBA, p. 1, *top margin, dated and annotated*: 10 Jany 1802   7 ⌐N⁰ 1 ¬
⌐Sacred, because Historical ¬

Voici comment mon affaire a fini. Tu as surement reçu les deux petits chiffons[1] que je t'ai envoyés dans une lettre de Bood? Sur l'un etait ou à peu près la copie d'un billet à M. de Narbonne. Dans ce billet j'insistais sur la resolution de ne servir que durant l'expedition contre St Domingue repetant[2] le priant de repeter de nouveau au Ministre que *mon intention etait uniquement de payer ma retraite le prix que le premier Consul y avait mis; mais que du reste, pour qu'on me rendit justice, j'avais commencé par me la faire, et qu'en consequence ne voulant occuper la place de personne, j'etais decidé, aussitôt après l'expédition, à donner ma demission si l'on me refusait ma retraite.*

468.   ¹ One of 'les deux petits chiffons' is probably L. 467.
   ² In making a syntactical change in his sentence, M. d'A neglected to delete the word *repetant*.

M. de N. expliquait tout cela au Ministre [Berthier], lors qu'un tiers qu'il avait jusques là pris pour un Commis prit la parole. 'Je ne puis, dit il, m'empêcher de repeter ici ce qu'hier je representais à Darblay lui même. Je crains beaucoup qu'il ne s'enferre sans le vouloir et qu'il ne soit dupe de l'esprit chevalresque qui l'a toujours guidé. Il croit pouvoir au retour de St Domingue obtenir sur le champ *sa retraite*. Pour cela, il faudrait qu'on lui tint compte du tems qu'il a été absent et moi j'ai de fortes raisons pour l'assurer du contraire.' &c &c 'ce qui l'obligerait à servir encore au moins cinq ans.'

C'etait le Gal Gassendy,[3] un de mes anciens camarades de l'Artillerie, et qui la veille m'avait donné à diner. Je passe ici sous silence toutes les choses flatteuses qu'il ajoute sur mon compte, surtout relativement aux precautions que le Ministre croyait devoir prendre quant à ma reforme, que le premier Consul, ne voulait absolument me donner qu'à dater du moment où je serais arrivé à St Domingue. De cette maniere, j'aurais très bien pu faire très inutilement les plus grands sacrifices. *Il n'est personne, disait Gassendi, sur la parole du quel le Ministre doive plus compter, toute autre precaution est superflue.* Mais revenons. M. de N. à ce doute sur la possibilité d'obtenir ma retraite, à la quelle il savait que je tenais, se recusa et dit qu'il ne pouvait passer outre avant de m'avoir fait part de ce nouvel incident | Instruit de cette conversation, pour moi très interessante, voici ce que j'ecrivis au Ministre.[4]

General

'*Jaloux de repondre à la bienveillance du 1er Consul, j'allais à St Domingue, sans crainte d'exciter la JALOUSIE de personne, puisque j'annonçais franchement ma resolution de prendre ma retraite aussitot cette expedition achevée.*

---

[3] Jean-Jacques-Basilien, comte de Gassendi (1748–1828), général d'artillerie who, commissioned (14 Sept. 1800) général de brigade, was to become (21 Jan. 1802) 'commandant à l'École d'artillerie d'Auxonne'. Comte de l'Empire (1809), he was named grand officier de la Légion d'honneur (1811), chevalier de Saint-Louis (1791, 1814), pair de France (1814, 1819). M. d'A had known him in the early years of their careers as artillery officers. See M. d'A to FBA (Berg), 31 May 1815: '... j'avais été attaché environ deux ans à ces forges avec Gassendy ...'

[4] The original of this letter is extant in a dossier in the Archives du Service historique de l'Armée, Vincennes. M. d'A's copy (above) is fair enough in essence, though purposely perhaps, out of consideration of FBA's feelings, he omitted the P.S.: 'Si le Ministre veut bien obtenir du premier Consul qu'il soit fait mention dans ma reforme de la non interruption de mes services, je pars sur la champ pour St. Domingue.'

Je pensais qu'ayant, à l'epoque de la proscription que j'ai fuie, 31 ans de services, dont 25 effectifs, sans même y comprendre les deux années accordées aux officiers d'Artillerie pour leurs etudes preliminaires, ma reforme effaçait la lacune que semble presenter une absence involontaire.

J'apprens, mon General, que votre opinion, tout à fait contraire, est que cette lacune doit toujours subsister.

Des lors, le même sentiment qui me portait à accepter du service pour le tems où je crois être sûr que j'y aurais mis toute l'activité necessaire, me fait refuser cet honneur quand j'ai la certitude, que ni ma santé, ni mes affaires, ne me permettraient la même activité pendant le tems qui me manquerait pour être susceptible d'une retraite.

J'espere, mon General, que vous rendrez justice à mes motifs que je vous prie de faire connaitre au premier Consul'

Salut &c

Le Ministre consentait à me donner ma *reforme conditionelle* avant de partir. La condition exigée etait mon arrivée à St Domingue pour y être employé à l'expedition. Du reste mes appointemens ne devaient dater que du jour où je serais employé et l'on ne me faisait aucune avance. A la verité on m'offrait une route jusqu'à Brest. ⌈Il m'eut fallu au moins trois douzaines de chemises, deux habits uniformes complets plusieurs gilets et pantalons brodés, au moins six paires de bottes des instrumens de Mathématique pinceaux couleurs — &c — de plus un domestique, et de l'argent pour acheter des chevaux en debarquant.⌉ Deux cent cinquante louis m'auraient à peine suffi / pour les preparatifs / ; et neanmoins si les vents ou quelqu'accident arrivé au bâtiment m'eussent empêché d'arriver à tems à St Domingue, toutes mes depenses eussent été en pure perte. En verité, mettant à part, le tourment inconcevable de m'eloigner de toi sans avoir pu nous consulter, je ne crois point que mon fils ait à se plaindre par la suite du parti au quel l'incertitude sur ma retraite m'a fait m'arreter.

M. d'Arblay
To Madame d'Arblay

A.L. (rejected Diary MSS. 5338–[41], Berg), 10 Jan. 1802
Double sheet 4to   4 pp.   wafer
Addressed: England / Madame Darblay / West humble / near Dorking *Surry*
Edited by FBA, p. 1, *top margin, dated and annotated*: ⌜1801⌝ 1802   6
Edited also by CFBt *and the* Press.

Paris 20 Nivose an 10 (10 Janvier ⌜1802)⌝

L'orage est detourné, ma bonne amie. Je n'irai decidement
point à St Domingue mais des raisons politiques m'empêchent
de te rejoindre aussi vîte que je le voudrais. Tu les approuveras
surement. Occupe toi neanmoins tout de suitte de mon passeport que je desire trouver à Douvre. Nous allons être bien
pauvres, plus pauvres que jamais. Qu'importe, nous savons
comment jouir même de nos privations. Je n'en connais qu'une
de veritable. c'est celle que j'éprouve loin de toi. Dans ta
lettre du 29[1] qui vient de m'être remise, tu m'accuses d'être
dans un etat peu naturel, parcequ' effrayé de la possibilité,
de la probabilité d'une diminution très considerable, et peut
être peu eloignée de notre revenu, j'ai desiré trouver quelque
moyen d'y remedier. En verité, mon amie, tu te trompes.
J'oserai même te dire que tu es tout à fait injuste. J'ai toujours
connu toute l'etendue du sacrifice qu'il me faudrait faire pour
embrasser même momentanement, un autre genre de vie que
celui qui nous a jusqu'à present si bien reussi. Mais, il n'est
pas difficile de sentir que le tems s'approche où nos besoins
augmenteront; et que peut être ce sera à l'epoque où nos
ressources seront de beaucoup diminuées. Dejà le jardinage n'a
plus pour moi le même attrait. Je suis tout effrayé des suittes
fâcheuses qu'il peut avoir. Ressaguier,[2] ancien capitaine de

469. 1 L. 464.
  2 Antoine-Nicolas de Resseguier (1755–1820) of Joigny, who had married in
1791 in the chapelle de l'Hôpital de Joigny Nicole-Catherine-Magdaleine Charié
(1753–1834), daughter of Jean-Baptiste-Nicolas Charié (see vi, L. 555 nn. 4, 6).
A cavalry officer, sous-lieutenant (1772), lieutenant (1779), capitaine réformé
(1783) in the Lorraine Dragoons, Resseguier transferred in 1784 to the Mont-
morency Dragoons, which became in 1788 the Chasseurs des Évêchés. On his

Dragons, mon ami intime, m'a encore plus frappé que la mort de ce pauvre M. Cook.[3] Il existe encore, mais quelle existence! plus jeune que moi, il est plus cassé que ne le paraissent dans la même ville des viellards de 84 ans. A peine y a t'il un jour dans la semaine où il puisse respirer un peu à l'aise. Je suis sûr que je me suis arreté à tems. j'etais dejà fort attaqué et il m'en reste, dès que je trouve une air humide, une petite toux seche qui m'est assez penible. Du reste, je me porte à merveille, et beaucoup mieux que je ne m'y attendais, et que ne devrait le faire croire l'etat ou j'ai été depuis quelques jours. Je ne crois pas que creature humaine puisse souffrir davantage. L'idée de me separer, peut être pour jamais de toi, d'Alex, de nos Amis sans peut être avoir le tems de recevoir de vos nouvelles, me rendait quelquefois l'existence tout à fait à charge. Eh bien! c'est alors—et alors seulement que je suis allé dans le grand monde. La solitude m'était devenue insupportable. Elle m'etait si douce quand je voyais dans une perspective très rapprochée notre reunion! Ce sentiment je le retrouve enfin au fond de mon coeur, et le danger que j'ai couru de voir toutes mes esperances s'evanouir, n'en rend l'impression que plus vive. A present je voudrais être ⌐ toujours vis-à-vis de moi même: mais ce serait un bien mauvais moyen de me retrouver bientôt avec toi. Aujourdhui, C'est *decade*,[4] et consequement je ne pourrais rien faire. Demain j'irai prendre les informations necessaires relativement à mon passeport. Je suis tenu à beaucoup de menagemens qu'il ne serait pas prudens de ne pas prendre. Aujourdhui je dine chez M^{de} d'Henin.[5] Il est impossible de t'exprimer à quel point elle

marriage in 1791 he retired from the army and changed his residence from Brion to the rue de la Mortellerie, Joigny, where he lived for the rest of his life.

3 Possibly the Revd. Samuel Cooke (1741–1820), formerly Fellow of Balliol and vicar of Great Bookham since 1769, who in the 1790s had suffered serious illnesses, a record of which survives in an entry, signed and dated in his own hand, in one of the parish account books (courtesy of the present incumbent), entitled 'Accounts of Sir George Shiers Charity to Great Bookham Parish': 'N:B: This Book thro' the inadvertency of myself, or some of the Family, in a fit of sickness, or rather very severe and long illness, was put away with Family Writings & Parchments, where it was lost for some years; . . . S. Cooke, 1793'. From 1800 on, as their correspondence shows, the vicar and his wife (see iii, L. 122 n. 8) spent a great part of each year in Bath or Brighton.

4 The French Republican Calendar (adopted 5 Oct. 1793) divided the year into 12 months of 30 days, with the five remaining days called *jours complémentaires*. Each month was divided into three equal parts of ten days each, called the 1st, 2nd and 3rd *décades*. The tenth or last day, referred to as *le décade*, was a day of rest.

5 For the princesse d'Hénin's dwelling, see L. 513 n. 15

a été bonne pour moi. Ce n'est pas de l'interêst qu'elle a pris à notre affaire. c'est mille et mille fois plus que cela. Et cependant, depuis deux mois que je loge dans la même rüe, et tout à fait vis à-vis d'elle, à peine l'ai-je vu en quatre fois une heure. Je t'ai mandé, je crois qu'elle m'a engagé à dejeuner et diner avec elle, sans façon, toutes les fois que je ne serais point engagé ailleurs. Mais elle ne dejeune point avant onze heures. Moi je sors assez regulierement avant 9 pour ne rentrer le plus souvent qu'à dix ou onze heures du soir; rarement plus tard. tout ce que je te dirais ici de M. de Narbonne et de M^{de} de Laval ne pourrait approcher de la verité.[6] Il n'y a pas d'attentions delicates, de soins empressés qu'ils ne m'ayent prodigués. M^{de} de Laval à 52 ans est encore belle. Elle a de l'esprit, un ton excellent, de la sensibilité, et un tact tres fin. Quand je t'ai parlé plus haut de ma dissipation, toute necessaire qu'elle me fut devenue, ne vas pas croire qu'elle ait été poussée bien loin. Je n'ai été que deux fois dans le grand monde, encore la seconde a t'elle été la suitte indispensable de la premiere qui en entrainera une troisieme. là se bornaient mes courses de ce genre. C'est le 3 de la decade passée[7] que j'ai debuté chez la cy devant Duchesse de Luynes[8] où il n'y avait qu' environ 300

[6] It is perhaps to Mme de Cazenove d'Arlens that one owes the most intimate glimpses of Mme de Laval and the Narbonne-Laval ménage on the rue Roquépine, of which 'M. de Narbonne est au premier avec Augustin; Mme de Laval avec Zoé et une autre au-dessus' (p. 15).
'Sa maison est petite, arrangée à l'anglaise; des tapis sur l'escalier; tout est propre et simple' (p. 15). 'C'est un ménage singulier, et leurs sociétés ne sont pas toutes les mêmes, ni leurs opinions ni leurs affections. C'est elle qui rend sa vie matérielle heureuse: il met dans leur commerce quelques soins, quelque complaisance; il est l'homme avec qui elle cause des bizarreries du régime actuel. Mais il n'a pas l'air heureux et cela ne peut pas être' (p. 114).
Still frequented by intellectuals and wits, including Talleyrand, Mme de Laval's salon was one of the brightest in Paris. 'Elle est fort engraissée et plus belle, plus malicieuse, plus drôle que jamais!', and the piquancy of her remarks made one 'mourir de rire'. One of her butts was 'du travail des etiquettes qui occupe très sérieusement le Consul'. 'D'abord, dit-elle, le Héros prend, le matin, l'uniforme de sa garde par galanterie; puis pour recevoir les ministres, les généraux, les ambassadeurs, il passe un grand habit de velours. La troisième pièce de l'habillement est toute militaire: de petites bottes, une épée de diamants, une cravate noire' (p. 26). The piquancy, wit, and beauty did not purify a character that, in much of contemporary opinion, was thoroughly 'bad'.
[7] On 13 Nivôse (3 Jan. 1802).
[8] Formerly dame de palais de Marie-Antoinette, Guyonne-Élisabeth-Joséphine *née* de Montmorency-Laval (1755–1830) had married in 1768 Louis-Charles-Joseph-Amable d'Albert (1747–1807), duc de Luynes et de Chevreuse (1771), in pre-revolutionary times, maréchal de camp et pair de France. Favouring ideas of reform and voting with the constitutional monarchists, he was imprisoned, but released in 1794, he retired to Dampierre, his beautiful seventeenth-century

personnes. J'y ai vu M^de de Stael[9] qui m'a fait beaucoup de reproches de ne m'être pas presenté chez elle, et m'a fait promettre d'aller le surlendemain à un thé où je me suis rendu, et où j'ai entendu Frederic[10] donner du Cor dans une perfection dont la possibilité n'était pas même soupçonnée. Il y avait aussi une harpe mais fort inferieur a M. Marin.[11] Ces deux virtuoses ont executé des Duos ravissans. Je compte retourner le 3 de la decade[12] où nous entrons, chez M^de de Luynes, et pour cause. Il est impossible d'être mieux accueilli que je ne l'ai été. mais ces grandes assemblées ne sont pas ce que j'aime le plus, surtout quand on n'en sort qu'à 2 heures du matin. C'est quand j'ai gagné cette heure en ecrivant à mon amie, que j'ai passé le tems sans m'en appercevoir. Je conviens neanmoins que l'assemblée de M^de de Luynes etait brillante sous tous les rapports. J'aurais desiré pourtant y voir plus de monde nou-

château (of which illustrations may be seen in Nancy Mitford, op. cit., pp. 50–3). Returning to Paris after 18 Brumaire, the couple occupied the hôtel de Luynes in, the Faubourg Saint-Germain, which mansion, built in 1650, and 'souvent agrandi, toujours embelli, resta dans sa famille jusqu'à sa démolition [1900 et] était le plus majestueux du quartier' (Hillairet, ii. 79). The duchesse remained solidly royalist in sympathies, and the 'court' at the hôtel de Luynes remained in opposition to that of Malmaison.

   Strongly masculine in intellect and in pursuits (such as gambling), the duchesse undertook to support the expenses of the establishment by making it a house of pleasure, where foreigners (like the Poles) could dance, where persons of the highest fashion could be met, and where in rooms remote there were gaming tables and high play. In 1803 Mme d'Arlens (pp. 21–4), ascending 'le grand escalier, éclairé, rempli de fleurs', espied Talleyrand in the distance, and besides, 'tous les ambassadeurs résidant à Paris, tous les princes, toutes les princesses, . . . les hommes en habits brodés, avec leurs ordres, les femmes en robes de velours, beaucoup de satin blanc et de robes de crêpe blanc; d'autres en robes de dentelles noires, beaucoup de diamants'. In 1810 the Countess Potocka had opportunity to see the fierce gambling of 'la vieille duchesse', who 'jouait avec rage, avait une voix de stentor, riait aux éclats, faisait de l'opposition avec une rare grossièreté; le tout passait pour de *l'originalité*' (p. 214).

   [9] Mme de Staël, having left Coppet for Paris in November 1801, had settled in the rue de Grenelle, Faubourg Saint-Germain (Herold, p. 228).

   [10] Author of *Méthode pour le cor* (c. 1802), Frédéric Duvernoy (c. 1765–1838) was a self-taught horn player and composer. In 1788 he was invited to join the orchestra of the Comédie Italienne and in 1797, that of the Paris Opéra, where he remained high on the list of 'attractions' until 1817. Professor of horn at the Conservatoire from its founding (1795), first horn to the Chapelle-musique, and much admired by Napoleon, he had now fallen into oblivion.

   [11] Marie-Martin Marcel (1769–1861), vicomte de Marin, harpist, violinist, and composer, who, having studied in Italy as well as in France, was made, at the age of 14, a member of the Académie des Arcades in Rome. After a few years at the École militaire, he withdrew in 1786 and, given leave to travel in Austria, Prussia, and Spain, he was absent at the outbreak of the Revolution. Proscribed, he took refuge in London, where, for his elegant person, courtly manners, and his harp sonatas, some of which were published in 1799–1800, he met with great success. It was doubtless in London that FBA and M. d'A would have heard him play.

   [12] On 23 Nivôse (13 Jan. 1802).

veau. On a dansé, mais d'une maniere reellement inconcevable. Les danseurs jusqu'à present cités ne paraitraient que des pantins. En verité je n'exagere point. Il y a quelque chose de ravissant, de presque celeste, dans les pas nouveaux, d'ailleurs trés decents, en societé j'entend: car à l'opera les Danseuses sont absolument nues. L'oeil du moins ne peut que les juger telles, puis qu'elles n'ont, sur un taffetas couleur de chair, exactement collé sur la peau, qu'une gaze tout à fait transparente, Au reste rien, à très peu d'exceptions près, n'est moins ¦ en mesure, avec l'intention de celles qu'une depravation sans bornes fait ainsi s'⟨approcher⟩, Quand je t'ai parlé, ma chere amie, de l'eloignement que je me sens pour le jardinage, peut être as tu craint que notre solitude m'en devint moins chere. Que tu me connoitrois peu! Non mon amie, et je puis même dire en toute verité que c'est precisement le contraire. Je n'ai jamais passé, je ne dis point un jour mais deux heures sans regretter notre hermitage, sans me porter en idée dans notre cher *Book-room* dont par parenthèse tu ne risques rien d'augmenter les etageres. Nos richesses en ce genre vont en effet être augmentées de beaucoup d'excellens articles, qui remplaceront passablement bien j'espere, et la danse et surtout le jeu enorme qu'on joue ici dans les grandes assemblées. Je n'ai pas besoin de te dire que je n'ai eu garde d'y prendre part. J'ai pourtant fait, en ce genre, une petite folie: mais il n'y avait pas moyen de s'en dispenser. C'etait chez M^de D'hauss^e,[13] où j'avais diné avec Bood et son frere. On a proposé une bouillote qu'on ne pouvait faire sans moi. j'y ai perdu 30^ff ce qui fait que depuis mon depart il m'a coute 9^ff. Cela te prouve que je n'ay joué que ce qu'on nomme ici trés petit jeu. Quant à l'heure à la quelle je suis sorti de chez M^de de Luynes: Pourquoi diras tu n'avoir pas quitté plutôt. Parceque n'ayant pas de voiture, j'ai attendu qu'on me ramenât, la distance etant d'au moins 6 miles. J'en ai eu l'obligation au *Commandeur de Chreptowich chambellan de Sa M. L'Emp^eur de toutes les Russies.*[14] C'est une connoisance fort aimable dont je n'ai l'obligation qu'à *Evelina Cecilia Camilla,*

[13] See L. 448 n. 2.
[14] Chamberlain Chreptovich, with his enthusiasm for English novels, was probably related to Michael Chreptovich (1809–91), the Russian diplomat, who, sent to London as 3rd Secretary in 1835, was to accompany Czar Nicholas I on his visit there in 1844 and who in 1856 was appointed Ambassador to the Court of St. James.

dont il est, comme de raison, trés enthousiaste. J'aurais bien pu revenir dans la voiture de M^de de Laval, qui m'avait proposé de me ramener, mais elle s'etait dejà chargée de M. de Narbonne et sa fille,[15] ce qui n'etait dejà pas mal pour un carrosse coupé. La petite de Narbonne aura je crois de l'esprit. Elle me parait parfaitement elevée. Elle est petite, trés petite, et même il y a dans sa physionomie fort interessante quelquechose de nain; Elle danse assez bien, ce qui est beaucoup dire en ce moment— Je reviens sur les 6 [milles] de distance de M^de de Luynes à mon logement. Je crains que tu t'imagines que j'exagere, [mais tout] bien pesé, je crois qu'il y en avait plutôt 8 que 6, à cause des tours et detours que l'inondation forçait de faire, ce qui ne diminua point le service que me rendit M. de Chreptowich. J'ai vu ce même soir tous les Ambassadeurs etrangers, et consequement le trop fameux *Lucchesini*.[16] Assurement je n'ai rien à lui reprocher, et pourtant il m'est impossible de le voir de bon oeil. Charle[s] [Locke?] j'espere me le pardonne. Dis à sa femme que lorsque je la verrai, je me flatte qu'elle n'aura pas tout à fait oublié les bons soins que j'ai eu d'elle sur le vaisseau qui la portait à Naples.[17] J'ai la plus grande envie de faire promptement connaissance avec la 3eme Grace dont elle devait être mère. Nous savons à present de qui c'est le tour. S'en occupe t'elle? Tu ne me dis rien d'Amelia à qui il a plu de⟨revenir⟩ par là Est-ce qu'elle n'est point à Norbury? Tu voudras bien reserver la reponse à ces questions pour le tems où j'en aurai bien quelques autres à te faire. C'est à dire que je te prie de ne plus m'ecrire ici. N'es tu pas bien fâchée de cette priere? Ne va pourtant point t'inquieter et te mettre martel en tête pour un passage de 3 ou 4 heures I puisque je m'embarquerai à Calais pour Douvre ou je te repete que j'espere que tu me feras trouver mon passeport à l'Alien office.[18]

---

15 Marie-Adélaïde-Charlotte de Narbonne (1790–1836), now eleven years old.

16 Girolamo Lucchesini (1751–1825), Prussian diplomat who, in Berlin in 1779, gained the favour of Frederick the Great. 'A little, lively, talkative, pleasant man' with an 'insinuating address' (Warren, p. 35), he was in 1800 sent by Frederick William III on a mission to Paris.)

17 Help offered at Norbury Park by M. d'A in October 1798, presumably, when Charles Locke and his wife Cecilia Margaret *née* Ogilvie were making preparations for their sailing to Naples (*Locks of Norbury*, chap. xiv; and iv, L. 292, p. 192).

18 As an *émigré*, M. d'A required a passport that would allow him to travel inland in England, in this case from Dover to London. FBA was not to receive his requests for this passport (see Ll. 470, 474, and 476) until March, when an accumulation of seven letters was delivered to Norbury Park (see L. 492, p. 184).

Je t'ecrirai surement encore d'ici plus d'une fois. Car c'est tout au plus si je pars le 22. Janvier. Ecris moi encore une fois sous l'enveloppe de Madame Grandsire,[19] en lui mandant de garder la lettre pour me la remettre à mon passage. J'en attens une de toi avec une impatience inexprimable. C'est celle en reponse au paquet que M. Otto[20] a du envoyer à Norbury. Combien actuellement je voudrais ne l'avoir point ecrit! Mais mon amie, je t'ai dit les raisons de cette precipitation, dont actuellement je te demande pardon. J'espere que tu en auras trouvé l'excuse dans ton coeur. J'ai reellement été prêt à perdre la tête à l'idée seule de me separer de toi, sans recevoir de tes nouvelles, sans savoir où et comment je pourrais jamais en recevoir. C'est alors que j'ai connu combien je t'aime, combien mon existence est absolument dependante de cet amour, combien la certitude de ta tendresse m'est necessaire. —Oui tu me pardonneras tout le mal que t'a fait eprouver ma precipitation toute barbare qu'elle ait été [xxxxx 4½ *lines*] J'embrasse de tout mon coeur Alex et sa mere, pres de la quelle je le prie d'être mon representant.

[xxxxx 5 *lines marginal writing*]

[19] The Hôtel Grandsire or the Lion d'Argent, the gate of which was depicted by Hogarth in *O! the Roast Beef of Old England* (1749), emerges in travels, letters, and memoirs of the century, including the *Mémoires* . . . (*1773–1836*) (1891) of Mme de Gontaut. An *émigrée*, she had ventured to return to France in 1797 via Calais as a seller of lace, but suspected, brought before a Committee of Public Safety and placed under guard at the hotel, she was rescued by Mme de Grandsire, who, disguising her in a peruke, chapeau, and redingote belonging to M. Grandsire (1703–74), brought her before Lord Malmesbury, the British diplomat, who, sent by his government to France (*c*. 23 July 1797) on a mission of peace (iii, L. 205 n. 5), had stopped, with his suite, at the hotel. Enlisting the help of her French friends, he secured her release. Returning to Calais in 1814, Mme de Gontaut sought her benefactress in vain. 'Ma pauvre amie n'existait plus.' In an obituary notice for a daughter of the house (Mme Toulière), who had died in Canterbury on 4 Feb. 1807 at the age of 62, memories were again evoked of 'the former postmaster and landlord of the Lion d'Argent at Calais' M. Grandsire and of the 'cheerfulness' of his hostel, 'well known to many English travellers' (*Kentish Gazette*, 6 Feb. 1807). See further, L. 508 n. 7.

[20] See L. 429 n. 1.

470   [Hotel Marengo], 11 January, 1802
M. d'Arblay
To Madame d'Arblay
and Alexander d'Arblay

A.L. (Berg), 11 Jan. 1802
Single sheet 4to   1 p.   wafer
Addressed: pour Madame Darblay
Edited by FBA, p. 1, top margin, annotated and year date 1802   encircled: 9

Paris ce 11 Janvier, 1802
Tu dois ma chere amie, recevoir par notre ami, une longue
lettre de moi, dans la quelle je te prie de ne pas perdre un
moment pour me faire adresser à *Douvre* à l'*allien office* un
passeport qui me permettra d'en partir sur le champ pour
Londre, où ta soeur[1] serait bien aimable de te recevoir une
couple de jours que je serai probablement obligé d'y passer.
J'aimerais bien mieux aller droit dans notre hermitage. . Oui
oui cela vaut mieux en effet, quitte à retourner à Londre pour
une couple de jours. C'est dans notre cher Westhumble qu'il
faut que nous nous revoyons, quand même pour cela je devrais
te voir 24^h plus tard. Ce calcul là, ce n'est certes point la
froideur qui le dicte. O mon amie combien je suis heureux
d'avance en pensant combien je dois l'être bientôt! Ne l'es tu
pas déjà un peu en lisant ceci? Que ne donnerais-je point pour
t'avoir epargné le chagrin que t'a sans doute fait eprouver mon
trop de precipitation! Quelle dure epreuve nous avons eue là!
Comme j'en vais aimer davantage ma Fanny son petit, et
cette chaumière qu'ils rendent tellement preferable à tous les
Palais! ᴦJe t'ecris près du feu de Bood qui se [xxx 2 *words*] veiller.
Il est ainsi que moi un peu surpris de toute cette societé,
n'étant sorti (de sa chambre) une bonne partie de la journée. En
cela il est plus heureux que moi, qui ai été obligé de courrir
comme poursuivi, chat maigre à peu près tout le tems qui j'ai
passé eloigné de tout ce que j'aime. J'emporte les ⟨restans] et
tous les portraits que j'ai pu rassembler. Nous avons été ⟨inter-

470. ¹ Esther Burney (EBB), who was living at this time at 43 Beaumont Street,
Portland Place, London.

130

rompu⟩ par un *gentleman* pere d'un joli petit enfant de onze ans qui me parait extremement spirituel. Bood a ⟨ajouté⟩ de trés bonnes raisons pour le trouver fort gentil. Moi qui n'y suis pas tout à fait du même interest, je le trouve charmant, et d'honneur il l'est reellement. J'imagine que tu le trouverais tel, et trés probablement tu le verras quelque ⟨jour⟩ chez [B]ood. A propos ⟨de ce⟩ [cher Bood il] te prie en grace de voir sa femme. Continueras tu, ⟨entêtée,⟩ d'être si sauvage? En es tu [*tear*] Je te demande comme une grace de ne point negliger cette recommandation. Tu ne me dis presque rien de cela et tu ne m'en diras pas davantage et je te prie de ne pas ecrire *ici* mais seulement et une seule fois à Calais chez M^de Grandsire Hotel Kingston. Bood est en ce moment en marché d'une maison charmante prés de Auteuil.[2] Il la trouve comme de raison infiniment preferable à un appartement, et comme son projet est d'avoir pour Maria une maison privée, ils ne s'appercevront point de l'eloignement où ils seront de quelques parties au reste les moins frequentées de cette grande ville qu'on embellit tous les jours. Aujourdhui chez jackson,[3] je me suis mis en regle pour mon passeport. Demain je vais à la Grange chez Mr de la Fayette,[4] de là chez M^de de Jaucourt[5] et peut être chez M^de de Tessé.[6] Je reviendrai ensuite ici, où je passerai au plus 4 jours à finir mes visites, après quoi j'irai à Amiens où je resterai un jour puis enfin à Calais où je m'embarquerai aussitôt que les vents me le permettront. J'imagine que ce sera vers la fin du mois, mais comme il est trés possible que je puisse gagner quelques jours, je te repete que je te serai vraiment obligé de me faire envoyer mon passeport le plus promptement possible à Douvre, où sans cela je serais forcé de rester plusieurs jours et d'où cela contribuant je compte pouvoir partir sur le champ [xxxxx ½ *line*].⁋

[To Alexander]

Dearest Alex, I am much obliged to you for your kind mention of me in y^r last letter to your Papa. You need not ask me

[2] Antoine Bourdois eventually acquired a house at 4, rue de Choiseul.
[3] Francis James Jackson (1770–1814), diplomat, ambassador to the Porte (1796), Minister Plenipotentiary to France (2 Dec. 1801), to Prussia (1802–6), and to the United States (1809–11).
[4] La Grange-Bléneau, in Brie (L. 446 n. 5).
[5] At the Château de Combreux, also in Brie. For Mme de Jaucourt, see ii, Intro., pp. xv–xvii.   [6] Probably at Aulnay (see L. 446 n. 5).

to *remember* you; I love you too well, ever to forget you, and not only I shall never forget how dear you are to me, but my attachment and my Friendship for you will go encreasing every day, as long as you study and behave well, and as long as your Papa and Mama shall be as satisfied with you as they now are. Pray give my best love to your Mama; when you see Maria Bood & Sophy give each of them a good kiss in my name and I will return it to you when I see you again.

471   [West Humble], 12 January 1802

Conjointly with Alexander d'Arblay

To M. d'Arblay

A.L.S. (rejected Diary MSS. 5326–[29], Berg), 12 Jan. 1802
Double sheet small 4to   4 pp.   wafer
Addressed: M. Darblay, / Chez M. Lejard, / Nº 43— / Fauxbourg St. / Martin— / à Paris—
Edited by FBA, p. 1 (5326), *annotated and redated*: 12ᵗʰ Janʸ 1802 ⌜5/3⌝ on the news of an accepted military command to Sᵗ Domingo.
p. 3 (5328), 8: ✳·
Edited also by CFBt *and the* Press.

12ᵗʰ Janʸ 1802
A poor little moment only is allowed me to say Heaven bless you! — — Guide—direct—prosper—& restore you!—¹
I will try to support myself—I will look at my Alex all day— I am too disturbed—too astonished to know what I say—but I will do the best I can—
This is a great surprise indeed—I thought you on the road! — — hither—to me—O mon ami!—Heaven's best blessings be upon you! & guard you from *RASHNESS*—recollect your

471. ¹ Before 2 Jan. 1802 d'Arblay had decided to accept Berthier's offer (see L. 478) and join the French expedition to San Domingo (L. 465 nn. 6, 7). This decision he had not yet broken to FBA directly, but on 2 January he wrote to William Locke requesting him to go to Camilla Cottage 'et faites que la foudre tombée sur notre hermitage n'écrase pas votre amie! Soutenez-la—Rendez la à toute son ⟨energie⟩ Je profite d'un courrier des affaires étrangères qui n'attend que ma lettre—Respect, amour, amitié, tendresse,—helas tout cela doit pour un moment céder au devoir.'

courage is known—you have nothing to fear from *Prudence*—&
is it not due to a wife who *lives* only in *your* life?—though she
will preserve her *existence* for your representative?—you ⏐ will
let me know your vessel—it's Captain—all intelligence
possible—

I hardly breathe yet for consternation—but take with you
all the comfort I can give in again saying never yet had any
man a more perfect right to judge for himself than you have!—
That *THIS* is your judgement you will be sure I grieve—but
I will not suffer myself to speak more while convinced your
decision is such as you deem necessary. O my friend! husband!
dearest loved on Earth!—& most covetted in Heaven! let no
rashness, at least, part us! — — I dread an over-strained effort
of courage, a *desire d'une blessure* more than words can say—ah,
remember, *une blessure* is most commonly ⏐ but a lingering
death!—I dare not say *avoid danger*—I am not so mad—but do
not *wantonly* rush into it!—O do not!—Come, my Alex, & sign
O do not! — —

[By Alexander d'Arblay]

O do not dear Papa be long before you come home Good by
my dear Papa pray come home soon

[Continued by Madame d'Arblay]

M^r & Mrs Lock have been with me till this minute—all
kindness & consolation—I have promised to go home with them
for two or 3 days to-morrow—I feel I must not stay here at
present—when more reconciled to this so unexpected disappointment, I will return—

Assure yourself I will exert every nerve to bear up—you
know what my *promises* are, how sacred I hold them;—be not
therefore ⏐ for *ME* uneasy—except to try every possible means
of getting me a line from you—if any occur—Heaven—Heaven
bless & preserve you!—

I wish to give you a thousand blessings—& not one *pain*!
—but the flutter of my spirits is inconceivable—& I cannot
command a word—yet fear inexpressibly you should miss this
poor adieu & the tender—tenderest prayers of a Creature
wholly yours—

F d'A

133

To M. d'Arblay

A.L. (rejected Diary MSS. 5336–[37], Berg), 15 Jan.
Single sheet 4to   2 pp.
Edited by FBA, p. 1 (5336), *annotated and dated*: ⁙ 1802 ⌐1802 (5)⌐ II
Edited also by CFBt *and the* Press.

2ᵈ Letʳ   Janʸ 15. Norbury Park
a 1ˢᵗ & 3ᵈ shall
go off immediately, by
the channels you direct.

I have just indulged my pen[1] with a little of the joy of my heart in the hope you have now permitted me once more to cherish, beloved of my soul!—I almost blame myself for venturing so soon to give such weight to it—but its power is irresistible.—Yet—how *déchirante* is the picture you draw of the state of your mind! your internal combats & sufferings! How well do I comprehend them! how fully feel my own sad share in their torture!—Were I sure the blow must be struck—I would forbear wholly to touch upon the Hope you have given —but that Hope will, now, preponderate, in defiance of every struggle that reason, & terror & prudence combine to make against it.—Yet do not repent to have awakened it, even if forced to crush it! for it has lightened *one* day in the terrible interval to ensue, & *THAT* Day is the anniversary of the Wedding of our so much loved Friends![2] a day you will be so rejoiced to have cheared by giving me the power to smile upon their

472. ¹ This is the reply to M. d'A's letter of 5 January (L. 466).
² The marriage of Frederica Augusta Schaub (1750–1832), a minor, of the parish of St. George, James's Square, to William Locke (1732–1810) of the parish of St. Marylebone took place in that parish on 15 Jan. 1767, with the consent of 'Lady Margaret Schaub widow the natural & lawful Mother of the said Minor'. Of the marriage there were four sons, William (1767–1847), who had married on 4 Aug. 1800 Elizabeth Jennings (c. 1781–1846); Charles (1769–1804), who had married on 9 July 1795 Cecilia Margaret Ogilvie (1775–1824); the Revd. George (1771–1864), who was to marry on 18 Apr. 1805 Harriet Poulett Thomson (c. 1783–1837); and the youngest son, Frederick Augustus (1785–1805), who died unmarried. The daughters were Mary Augusta (1775–1845), who was to marry on 29 May 1815 Sir George Martin (1764–1847); and Amelia (1776–1848), who had married on 2 Oct. 1799 John Angerstein (c. 1773–1858). Of grandchildren, there were born at this time Charles's daughters Emily Frederica (1796–1822), Georgina Cecilia (1798–1867), and Lucy (1801–93); and Amelia's eldest son John Julius (b. 9 Nov. 1800).

loved countenances. The whole Family is assembled—the
Four sons, two Daughters, two Daughters in Law, & 4 Grand
Children. It is a lovely group. Amelia is much recovered, in
health, &, at present, quite revived in spirits. ¹ her little Boy
is a very fine sturdy handsome creature, greatly improved.
The three little *Italian* Girls, of Mʳ Charles, are sweet little
loves, the 2ᵈ of them *spirituelle* & pretty in a high degree. *He* is
disappointed,³ mortified, & ill treated in a truly melancholy
manner. Every one charges me with kindest remembrances to
you—The *Oracle* with a softness of Voice & accent so touching!
He told me he had written whatever he thought would most
comfort you, in the supposition the step was inevitable—but
how few can rejoice more than *he* should it prove otherwise!—
Indeed you are dear to his very heart.—And your Letter to
him⁴—O What a Letter!—how is every word of it engraved
on my heart!—I must not talk of it—I will not—till I know my
doom—till another tells me—either that I shall be happier than
I have ever been, from the tremendous contrast—or, that I must
submit to a calamity which Duty only can make me bear—but
which Duty to my Boy, & Love to his Father SHALL make me
bear—though every particle of joy, peace, happiness & comfort will sail in that vessel which wafts you from me! — — Be
as happy—however, as the perfect assurance of my entire &
unfeigned conviction you will do what you think *right* can make
you—

How do I love & thank those good friends who see the transaction so much as I feel it—who honour your motives—yet
think them from exaggerated punctilio!—Heaven—Heaven
bless you!—

³ For Charles Locke's career as British Consul at Naples, see *Locks of Norbury*,
pp. 155–6, 209.
⁴ This is William Locke's reply (Berg) of 12 Jan. 1802 to M. d'A's letter (Berg)
of 2 January (L. 471 n. 1): '. . . I am this instant returned from our poor friend, who
bore the communication of the contents of your letter better than I had expected. . . .
In the midst of her distress I was glad to observe that what she most dwelt upon was
the pain which her last letter woud give you, written at a time when she expected
your return in a few days, & might, without danger of distressing you, communicate to you how much she had suffered, & the impossibility of visiting any longer.
—She trusts in Providence, to which she resigns herself, without doubting that all
is for the best. . . .
'*We* are disappointed too but approve of what you have done. Dieu vous conduis
& restore you to us soon! I represented to her the cheerful return of every morning
in future when you rose satisfied with what you had done as a military man, &
found yourself relieved from that severe economy which you had been labouring
under.'

To M. d'Arblay

A.L.S. (rejected Diary MSS. 5334–[35], Berg), 15 Jan. 1802
Single sheet 4to 2 pp.
Edited by FBA, p.1 (5334), annotated and dated: 1802 (5/2)
Edited also by CFBt and the Press.

Norbury Park, Jany. 15. 1802.

This is my third Letter of this morning[1]—this blessed morning, to my most loved Friend—This blessed morning!—the anniversary of the marriage of our dearest Friends—& opening of new life, in sweet Hope, to your own FdA—May I talk of that Hope?—or is it by this time all abolished?—ah, what a suspence!—How will it terminate? To day; I will at least indulge in sun-shine—All here are so thankful for a ray of chearfulness to their poor Guest on This Day—all so ready to fly to me with congratulation! — — yet I dare not receive it— I curb all I can—to avoid a 2ᵈ blow.—La *foudre tombée sur nôtre hermitage* — ah, oui! — — I will not speak of it—should you Yet be going—I must not distract you with the short joy of this interval.—I am wholly at a loss how to write so as to avoid giving you pain!—uncertain of your own actual position full of hope, yet trembling with fear—

Should this excursion prove—at last—certain—I conjure you by every tie of your tenderness—conjugal & paternal—to spare nothing that can render it safe—purchase whatever it is possible to procure of warmth & comfort—O remember, NO evil is irremdiable but loss of health—Consider yourself as clothing & gratifying Alex & me whenever you take care of your precious self—As to the *de quoi'*, whatever | you take up of kind Bood, I can repay Maria—I solicit I *supplicate* you to attend to this—& to your *Health*—beyond all other attentions. O yes! yes! I do justice—full justice to the combats of your kind Heart! to it's feelings & sorrows for so heavy a disappointment, if it is to be!—I have run away from my solitude—I could not endure it with safety to my intellects or constitution—

473. ¹ The first letter is missing, perhaps lost at Amiens or Calais. See L. 474, p. 137.

Ah—should you be returning hither!—
will not new faculties—a new existence be lent me, to pay
you with my joy?—do exert in every way to repair our hopes?
Heaven bless you!—

Most dear & dear!—

474   Calais, 22 January 1802

M. d'Arblay
To Madame d'Arblay

A.L.S. (Berg), 22 Jan. 1802
Originally a double sheet 4to, the second leaf (i.e. the address cover) is
torn away and missing   2 pp.
Edited by FBA, p. 1, *top margin, annotated and year date* 1802 *encircled*: 10

Calais ce 22 Janvier 1802.

Je m'etais bien promis, ma chere amie de t'eviter l'inquietude
que tu ne manqueras pas d'avoir relativement à mon passage
et je comptais ne te donner de mes nouvelles que rendu à
Douvre: mais la crainte de n'y[1] pas trouver mon passeport
m'oblige à renoncer à ce projet. ⌐Je profite donc de l'occasion
d'un courrier envoyé par Lord Cornwallis[2] pour te prier si tu ne
m'as pas encore fait expedier mon passeport, de ne pas perdre
une minute. J'écris au reste à James, pour qu'il ait la bonté
de passer à ce sujet à l'Alien office.[3] Peut être cette precaution
est elle suffisante. Peut être aussi ⟨l'emportera la seule puis-
sance⟩ de la demande que tu en feras, si elle n'a pas encore
été faite.⌐

Je suis dans la plus mortelle inquietude de n'avoir reçu rien
de toi depuis la fatale lettre où je te mandais la proposition (qui
avait tout l'air d'un ordre) faite par le 1er Consul. J'esperais

474. [1] That is, at Grandsire's Hotel (the Hôtel Kingston) at Calais (see L. 469,
p. 129).
[2] Charles Cornwallis (1738–1805), 2nd Earl (1762), 1st Marquess (1792),
appointed in October 1801 to negotiate peace, was to sign the Treaty of Amiens on
25 Mar. 1802 (L. 423 n. 1).
[3] The English passport enabling foreigners to travel inland (L. 469 n. 18).

trouver un mot de toi ou à | Amiens, où ici. Rien. Je suis dans un etat de souffrance et d'inquietude inexprimable. Probablement je ne serai pas longtems ici. Au nom du ciel, envoye moi mon passe port à Douvre ou à la Douanne ou à l'Alien office. [xxxxx ½ *line*] quand te sentirai-je près de moi!

A. d'A.

⌐P.S. Je descendrai à Douvre à l'Hotel ⟨*le*⟩ *York*⁴ chez Mʳ ⟨   ⟩.⌐

475

West Humble
[*pre* 24] January 1802

Conjointly with Alexander d'Arblay
To M. d'Arblay

A.L. (Berg), Jan. 1802, with 4 lines (p. 3) in hand of AA, aged 8
Double sheet 4to   3 pp.   wafer
Addressed: M. Darblay, / at M. Lajard's, / No. 42. / Fauxbourg Sᵗ Martin, / à Paris
Edited by FBA, p. 1, *annotated & dated and date retraced*: 1802   1802.   (1/1)

West Hamble,
January 1802

In the fervant hope you will be set out before this reaches Paris, I shall write only a few lines, to satisfy you of our healths, in case any untoward circumstance should interfere with your last purpose.—But let it not be so!—I grow sick, very sick, of so lengthened an absence—*3 Months* running on for what I had hoped would be *3 Weeks*.¹

⌐In a Letter this morning from my dear Father,² he says— 'beg M. d'A—or Mr. Bood, if possible, *one*, or *both*, to apply to

---

⁴ York House. See *The Dover and Deal Directory and Guide* . . . [1800].

475. ¹ M. d'A had left West Humble between 6 and 11 Oct. 1801.

² CB's missing letter evidently contained explicit and informed directions on the search for the second volume of *Musique*, which was then in preparation by Jean-Baptiste-Antoine Suard (1733–1817), Nicolas-Étienne Framery (1745–1810), and Pierre-Louis Ginguené (1748–1816) and which was to form part of the *Encyclopédie méthodique* (see L. 459 n. 7).

M. Suard, and Framery, or Guinguenés, or Pancoucke the Bookseller, to enquire of them whether any more vols. of the musical Encycl. will ever be published? & when?—'

our friends upon the hill are well, & send you a thousand kindnesses, & many thanks to you & M. de N[arbonne] about the Tasso[3]—I can never tell you half the kind enquiries continually made about you by them, Chelsea, Beaumont St.

I am sure you will have been charmed at Richard's Rectory £350[4] a year! his health, however, is terrible, he was from Tuesday to Sunday walking hence to Tea!⌐ |

My flattering *hope* makes you set out for our Cottage *to-morrow*!—⌐if so, this may perhaps meet you at Amiens—If not, Mr. Lajard[5] will keep it for any time or post it, or give it to Bood to guard for his return—*Bood* thought you would set out the 10 or 12ᵗʰ—⌐ ah, mon ami! I think of nothing else!—all round are well, The *Million de choses* you have to tell me scarcely awakes my curiosity, so entirely are all my thoughts occupied by the sole wish of your return! ⌐If you stay, however—endeavour again to give me a long & satisfactory Letter, such as before the last, for a few words when you *stay* is too cruel—⌐ I am sorry I remained here!—I am surely nearly exhausted, in spirits & faculties, since your stay has been so often prolonged, & so different to our calculations at your departure. ⌐Maria & Sophy have just been here ⟨to⟩ call—Bood has favoured me with his sympathizing wishes for your speedy return⌐ Yet—should this find you, by no means let it distress or hurry you, if indeed circumstances make it more fitting you should remain a little longer. I should vex too much to have any thing | essential left undone, after a sacrifice so considerable,—which nothing can reward but your returning completely satisfied with your visit. ⌐You say nothing of my Letters —but I have sent 4—2 to Joigny, one to Hotel Marengo, &

The first volume was published by Charles-Joseph Panckoucke (1737–98), 'le véritable chef de la race', who in 1782 had begun the publication of the *Encyclo-pédie méthodique*, which, when completed some 50 years later by his son Charles-Louis-Fleury Panckoucke (1780–1844), numbered over 190 volumes. The second volume of *Musique* (1818) was published 'Chez Mᵐᵉ veuve Agasse, Imprimeur-Libraire, rue des Poitevins, nᵒ. 6'.

3 See M. d'A's letter 466, pp. 117–18.

4 See FBA's L. 462 n. 8.

5 Pierre-Auguste Lajard (iv, L. 291 n. 5), now living in the Faubourg Saint-Martin (L. 443); and Antoine Bourdois (iii, L. 245 n. 10), who was not to return from France until early April (see L. 501, p. 205).

one to M. Lajard—to whom I beg to be most particularly remembered.⁷¹⁶ I will give the rest of my paper to our Boy, who is in extacy at my design. Heaven bless my best friend!

[By Alexander d'Arblay]

My dear Papa on New years day Cousins Maria and Sophy gave Me a New Map of england and Wales I would write more onnly

[Madame d'Arblay hastily concluded the letter]

the post Boy—
⌐M. de Jaucourt's⁷ Letter I sent instantly post pd to the Alien office with a demand to be forwarded immediately if they knew the address of M. Dumas.⁷¹⁸

476   Dover, 24 January [1802]

M. d'Arblay
To Madame d'Arblay
and Alexander d'Arblay

A.L. & PS. (rejected Diary MSS. 5344–[46], Berg), 24 Jan.
Double sheet 4to 3 pp. *pmks* DOVE[R] 25 JAN 1802 wafer
Addressed: Madame Darblay / Westhumble / near Dorking / Surry
Edited by FBA, p. 1, *annotated and dated*: II 1802 1802
Edited by CFBt *and the* Press.

Douvre Janvier Ce 24 après le plus triste diner
que j'aye fait de ma vie

Encore une lettre de moi, ma chere ame, car malgré que je n'aye que de facheuses idées à te communiquer, il m'est impossible de resister au besoin de causer un moment de plus avec toi. ⌐Avant hier dans la nuit, c. à. d. hier ⟨avec⟩ très grand ⟨emotion⟩ je t'ecrivis un mot à la hâte ainsi qu'à James, et j'en chargeai un courrier de Lord Cornwallis¹ imaginant qu'il

---

⁶ Of these letters, only 459, 460, and 471 can be identified with any certainty.
⁷ See L. 446 n. 14.   ⁸ Mathieu Dumas (L. 450 n. 10).
476. ¹ See L. 474 n. 2.

arriverait beaucoup plutôt que moi, et que même il partirait plutôt. Le fait est neanmoins que nous sommes à peu prés partis et arrivés ensemble. J'ai bien fait, malgré cela, de lui donner ma lettre pour James qui j'espere l'a reçue au moment où j'ecris, parce que ce courrier est parti sur le champ, c. à. d. à minuit. Si mon passeport eut été ici, comme je le demande depuis dix jours,[2] je me serais arrangé pour partir avec lui, et je jouirais actuellement du bonheur d'être prés de toi. Quelle difference! Au lieu de cela je n'eprouve que contrarieté depuis mon arrivèe. A ⟨la sortie⟩ on m'a fouillé avec une severité sans exemple. J'ignorais que les gravures payassent un droit. J'en avais beaucoup pour Norbury. D'abord il m'a été impossible de les porter moi même, ni de les confier à personne du batiment; aprés un espece de ⟨tête dure⟩ Anglais attachè à la douanne s'en est emparé, et comme il pleuvait beaucoup et que malgré toute recommandation, il en a pris très peu de soin, il en est resulté que beaucoup sont mouillées et seront probablement un peu gatées. Juge de ma surprise lorsqu'arrivé à la Douanne on m'a dit que chaque estampe payait *6 pence* de droits. Comme j'en avais beaucoup, et qu'il ne me restait point assez d'argent pour acquitter ces droits, J'ai dit que c'était une commission, et que ce qu'on me demandait doublant presque le prix de l'achat j'ignorais si celui qui m'en avait chargé trouverait bien que je fisse cette dépense. On s'est contenté de ma reponse, et les estampes, empaquetées et sous cachet, doivent être envoyées à la Douanne de Londre sous l'adresse de Mr Locke à qui on donnera avis de leur arrivée.⌐

Cette nuit j'ai ecrit dix lettres toutes relatives à mon passeport. S'il tarde à m'arriver, je ne sais en verité ce que je deviendrai. ⌐J'aurais pu, à ce qu'on me dit, m'en passer en prennant le precaution de faire viser à Paris mon ⌐ passeport français par Mr ⟨J   cablon⟩. Que n'ai je saisi cela plutôt! J'ai⌐ beau chercher à me distraire, Je suis d'une tristesse mortelle, de ce retard, et mon imagination que j'ai beau vouloir occuper ailleurs n'enfante que des monstres. Je te vois malade et hors d'etat de m'ecrire Conçois si tu peus l'etat où je dois être! En verité je sens que je ne pourrais y tenir

---

[2] In spite of requests that the family attend to a passport that would allow him to travel inland, d'Arblay was delayed at Dover. Of the eleven letters on the subject written on 24 Jan. 1802, only L. 476 is known.

longtems. Hate toi de m'en tirer si tu le peus. *In my last terrible trial*, je me disais à Paris, je paye actuellement tout le bonheur dont j'ai joui avec elle depuis dix ans! En verité l'epreuve dont je ne fais que sortir a été assez severe, et je ne devais pas m'attendre à voir son tourment se prolonger ici.

Ne va pas croire, ô mon amie que mon courage m'abandonne, et que je me laisse aller, sans combattre, à l'impression facheuse que me fait eprouver l'espece de combinaison de maux aux quels je suis depuis quelque tems en proie. Ce matin je ne pouvais dormir. j'etais ecrasé de fatigue presqu'autant que d'inquiètudes et j'etais incapable de prendre aucun repos. J'ai pris Petrarque[3] et après avoir lu le premier Sonnet, j'ai cherché à me distraire un moment par ce qui suit.

> L'Amour est il un bien? l'Amour est il un mal?
> On le met en Enfer, aux Cieux, à l'Hopital!
> Ah! ce dernier gîte, peut être,
> Convient le mieux à ce souverain maître!
> Ses plus cruels tourmens ont tous quelque douceur,
> A ses plus doux plaisirs se mêle quelque peine,
> Et les rigueurs d'une inhumaine
> Loin d'amortir ses feux redoublent cette ardeur
> Contre la quelle envain la Raison se déchaine
> Et qu'aurait changée en tiedeur
> une faveur un peu soudaine.
> Jamais trompè, l'Espoir devient trompeur, |
> Et l'Amour baille à la fadeur
> D'un facile triomphe: une constante gêne
> Lui semble preferable au plaisir sans douleur.
> Mais comment plaindre le malheur
> D'un esclave adorant sa chaine?
> Comment envier un bonheur
> Dont les plus vifs chagrins sont la suite certaine!
> Ou le delire, ou la langueur,
> Choisissez, Vous qu'Amour entraine.

Que l'amour peint dans ces vers est different de la tendresse! de ce sentiment que toi seule m'as fait connaître, ô mon amie — appuyer sur un contraste si frappant me semblerait un blas-

---

[3] M. d'A's poem is certainly not a translation of Petrarch's first sonnet, but the awesome torments of love, the subject of M. d'A's poem, is the concern of sonnets I, II, VI, XXIX.

phême. Jamais je ne pourrais exprimer que bien imparfaite-
ment ce que je sens si bien.

˥⟨Le cocher du landaulet⟩ qui est parti à Midy s'est chargé
de mes lettres. Celle ci devra être confiée à la poste et ne te
parviendra que Mardy matin. Le ⟨cachet⟩ que je ne fais qu'en
ce moment me fait craindre que mes trois lettres n'arrivent
⟨toutes avant⟩ mon retour. Mon dieu que vais je devenir
jusqu'à une reponse?˥

My dearest Alex

Give for me to your dear Mama the tenderest kiss. I shall
very soon ask you one for myself. I hope you have improved
your French, and I bring you some very pretty things to study.
Voici la poste

477   Greenwich, 3 February 1802

Conjointly with Charles Burney
To Mrs. Broome

A.L.S. & A.L. (Berg), 3 Feb. 1802
Single sheet 4to, 2pp.   *pmk*   5 FE   .802   wafer
Addressed: Mʳˢ Broome / Brighton / Sussex
Endorsed by CBFB: Broʳ Charles & Sister d'Arblay / Feb— / 1802 / ansᵈ
March

[*By Charles Burney*]
                                  Greenwich, Febʳʸ 3, 1802
                                        one o'clock
My dear Charlotte,

Many thanks for your Shawl, which I shall find the source of
comfort on many a wintry night. — —

Clement[1] is just arrived—He is well; but thin;—& why not
thin?—There is no reason for all the world to be fat.—

477. [1] Clement Robert Francis, now about ten years old and a pupil in CB Jr.'s
school at Greenwich.

Rosette is quite well—& so is Charles,[2] who spent his Christmas with me, in Cheshire, at Mr Crewe's, where our time passed away very pleasantly.—[2]

Your former letter reached me very safely, on my return home.—The draft, I doubt not, is duly recorded, in Pall Mall.—

The d'arblays are just now, on a visit, with us:—they will only stay a few days.—[3]M^r D Arblay looks very well, after his Parisian expedition.—Remember me to Bro. Broome, & tell him my Champagne is in fine order.—

Always affect^ly your Brother
C Burney— |

[By Madame d'Arblay]

P.S. *all* send kindest love & *I* will write as well as send it—to my dear Charlotte, whose little note by Miss Baker[4] was forwarded me from Twickenham. —I was disappointed of seeing that dear & good friend, for she could not cross the downs to us, on account of the deep snow, & no track. I expected her two mornings. But all chagrin is at this moment more than lightened, removed, by the safe return of my so long absent Traveller. He went for 3 weeks, & was detained, by various business & accidents, 3 months, & many circumstances concurred to render his stay alarming & anxious. He is well, I thank God, but harrassed, & utterly disappointed in his expectations & hopes of saving something from the wreck of his family fortune. I can regret nothing at this moment, though I feel for his mortification, which has been severe. We are come to Greenwich for a little visit, & your dear Clement is not sorry it happens at this time. He is a sweet Boy, & well.

---

[2] CB Jr.'s son, Charles Parr, now sixteen. A letter to his mother 'Rosette', dated Crewe Hall, 10 Jan. 1802, and extant in the Folger Shakespeare Library, gives some idea of the exertions expected of the guests by the Lady of the Hall. The lad of sixteen, having had to fag until two in the morning getting the lines for two parts, found himself, on the drawing of the famous green curtain, 'all cover'd with Mrs Crewe's Jewels seated on my *Throne as King John*; we had the first scene, . . . & the famous scene between *King John & Hurbert*, after which we had Chrononhotonthologos; & I assure you, what with the trouble of Learning nearly 200 Lines, the dressing, speaking them, the battle, which I had in Chrononhotonthologos, the fright, & the *tout ensemble*, I hardly ever was more tired in my life.' Having had to turn poet as well as actor, CPB composed the verses normally solicited for the White Album (see also i, L. 24 n. 62), and urged, conjecturally by his father, he took copies of many of the verses in the Album, copies now in the Osborn Collection.

[3] It was while visiting CB Jr. at Greenwich that d'Arblay received the letters (see L. 478) conveying acceptance of his services at San Domingo.

[4] Sarah Baker (i, L. 10 n. 6), who lived in Richmond.

I hope my dear Charlotte Jun[r] & Marianne[5] are flourishing, & little Ralph, who all agree in admiring. Have you yet a nurse for him to satisfy you? Pray give my kindest love to my dear Charlottina, & comp[ts] to Mr. Broome. M. d'A. joins—

adieu my dearest Charlotte.—

478   [West Humble], 11 February 1802

To Margaret Planta

A.L. draft (Diary MSS. vi. 5348–50, Berg), 11 Feb. 1802
Double sheet 4to   3 pp.
Edited by FBA, p. 1 (5348), *annotated:* ⁙ × [*with the heading:*] Letter written for Her Majesty but addressed to Miss Planta. on M. d'A's fixed departure for the West Indies. [*expanded later by the words:*] orders of Napoleon, for S[t] Domingo
p. 3 (5350), *lower margin, dated:* Camilla Cottage, / West Hamble, 11. Feb[y] 1802.
Edited also by the Press.

11th Feb[y] 1802.

A most unexpected—&, to ME, severe event, draws from me now an account I had hoped to have reserved for a far happier communication—but which I must beg you to endeavour to seek some leisure moment for making known, with the utmost humility, to my most gracious Royal Mistress, whose true benevolence always finds room for some little interest in the concerns of Her Majesty's humble, but ever grateful & devoted servant.

Upon the total failure of every effort M. d'Arblay could make to recover any part of his natural inheritance, he was advised by his friends to apply to the French Government for half pay, upon the claims of his former military services. He drew up a memoir,[1] openly stating his attachment & loyalty to his late King, & appealing for this justice, after undeserved proscription. His RIGHT was admitted; but he was informed it

[5] Charlotte and Marianne Francis, aged 16 and 12 respectively, and Ralph Broome, Jr., aged about six months (i, pp. lxxii–lxxiii).
478. [1] This initial 'memoir' the editors have not been able to identify.

could only be made good by his re-entering the army; & a proposal to that effect was sent him by Berthier, the Minister at War.

The disturbance of his mind at an offer which so many existing circumstances forbade his foreseeing, was indiscribable. He had purposed, faithfully returning to his Hermitage, with his fellow-Hermit, for the remainder of his life; & nothing upon Earth could ever induce him to bear Arms against the Country which had given ⌐ him asylum, & birth to his wife & Child;— & yet, a military spirit of Honour, born & bred in him, made it repugnant to all his feelings to demand even retribution from the Government of his own Country, & refuse to serve it.— Finally, therefore, he resolved to accept the offer Conditionally—to accompany the expedition to St. Domingo, for the restoration of order in the French Colonies, & then, restored thus to his rank in the army, claim his *retraite*. This he declared to the Minister at War,[2] annexing a further clause of receiving his instructions from the Government.[3]

The Minister's answer to this was That these conditions were impossible.

Relieved rather than resigned—though dejected to find himself thus every way thrown out of *every* promise of prosperity, M. d'Arblay hastened back to his Cottage,[4] to the inexpressible satisfaction of the Recluse he had left there—Short, however, has been its duration!—a pacquet has just followed him, containing a Letter from Berthier[5] to tell him that his appoint-

---

[2] M. d'A learned of this proposal in a letter from Lafayette (see L. 465, where this letter is copied).

[3] See L. 468, pp. 121–2.

[4] M. d'A had landed at Dover on 24 Jan. 1802.

[5] Berthier's letter to M. d'A (on official letterhead), dated 27 January and signed Alex Berthier, is extant in the Berg Collection, as is a copy in the hand of FBA. An unsigned draft, also on official letterhead, is included in M. d'A's dossier (Vincennes). The original reads as follows:

'Je vous préviens, Citoyen, que d'après votre demande vous êtes autorisé à vous rendre par Brest à Saint Domingue; il vous sera délivré à cet effet une route avec l'indemnité attribuée à votre grade.

'A votre arrivée dans la Colonie vous serez admis au traitement de réforme pour en être payé à dater du premier Vendémiaire dernier, jusqu'au moment ou le Général Leclerc vous mettre en activité.

'Je l'informe de cette disposition et je l'invite de la part du Gouvernement a utiliser vos talents et votre zéle; vous trouverez cy joint une copie de la lettre que je lui écris à ce sujet.

Je vous salue
Alex Berthier.'

ment was made out according to his own demands! & enclosing another Letter to the Commander in Chief, Le clerc,[6] with the orders of Government for employing him, delivered in terms the most distinguished of his professional character. — —
All hesitation, therefore, now, necessarily ends; & nothing remains for M. d'Arblay but acquiescence & dispatch,—while his best consolation is in the assurance he has universally received ⏐ that this expedition has the good wishes & sanction of England.—And, to avert any misconception, or misrepresentation, he has, this Day, delivered to M. Otto a Letter addressed immediately to the first Consul,[7] acknowledging the flattering manner in which he has been called forth, but, decidedly & clearly repeating, what he had already declared to the War minister, that though he would faithfully fulfil the engagement into which he was entering, it was his inalterable resolution NEVER to take up arms against the British Government.

I presume to hope this little detail may, at some convenient moment, meet Her Majesty's Eyes—with every expression of my profoundest devotion.

I am &c

My own plans, during his absence are yet undetermined.—
I am, at present, wholly consigned to aiding his preparations—

[6] Almost identical with the above letter is an official copy (Berg), as well as a copy by FBA (Berg), of Berthier's letter to General Leclerc informing him that d'Arblay was to be employed at San Domingo . 'Cet officier possedant des talents distinguées, je vous préviens, Citoyen Général, que le Gouvernement desire que vous utilisiez son zéle et ses connaisances', Berthier concluded. An unsigned draft on official letterhead is in M. d'A's dossier at Vincennes.

[7] A copy in the hand of M. d'A of his letter of 10 February to the First Consul is extant in the Berg Collection:

'General

La Generosité et la grandeur etant inseparables, ce qui pourrait me perdre avec un autre va être ma saufe-garde avec vous. Admirateur sincere du bien que vous avez dejà fait, Animé par l'espoir de celui qui vous reste à faire, je veux et j'espere me rendre digne de la maniere flatteuse dont vous venez de me traiter. Je pars, et vous pouvez comtez sur ma reconnaisance; mais ce serait vous en donner une preuve indigne de vous que de me rendre coupable d'ingratitude envers un autre. Enthousiaste de la liberté, je fus encore plus ami de l'ordre, et restai jusqu'au dernier moment un des serviteurs les plus fideles, et j'ose le dire, les plus energiques, d'un Monarque dont plus qu'un autre j'ai connu la patriotisme et les vertus. Forcé de fuir, rien n'eut pu me faire manquer au serment de ne jamais porter les armes contre ma patrie; determiné de même à ne jamais m'armer contre la patrie de mon epouse, contre le pays qui pendant 9 ans nous a nourris; je vous jure sur tout la reste fidelité et devouement.

Salut et respect
Alexandre Darblay.'

to me, I own, a most melancholy task,—but which I have the consolation to find gives pleasure to my Father & Friends, glad to have him, for a while, upon such conditions, quit his spade & his Cabbages.

479   Greenwich,—15–19 February 1802

To M. d'Arblay

A.J.L. (rejected Diary MSS. 5356–[59], Berg), 15–19 Feb. 1802
Double sheet 4to 4 pp. pp. 1 & 4 retraced *pmks* FOREIGN OFF[ICE] T.P.P.P. / Gree[nw]ich seal & wafer
Addressed: France / À / A Darblay / Chef de Brigade— / hotel Marengo, nº 1185 / Rue Miromenil / à Paris. / où / a Brest, / post restante
Edited by FBA, p. 1 (5356), *annotated and dated and date* 1802 *retraced*: 1802
(2) Written upon the 2ᵈ return of General d'Arblay to France.
Edited also by the Press.

Greenwich, Febʸ 18. 1802

Ah my amico!—in what manner must I begin writing so as to satisfy both You & myself?—to give *You* pleasure, I must talk only of your Expedition—of voyages, St. Domingo, Battles & victories—to soothe *myself*—I can speak only of the blest epoch of your return—of PEACE, of retirement, of our Boy & our Cottage. — — But let me begin my promised journal, as a prelude to the severer promise I will hold sacred.—

Febʸ 15—From my window—between every prayer for your safety, & our re-union, with which I curbed my Sorrow, I looked at the chaise,—& saw Mrs. O Kelly¹—& fancied I distinguished animated features, & a character of that sort of

479. ¹ The French gentleman of Irish extraction (L. 480, p. 153) and his wife, who is to reappear at Minehead in the summer of 1820, the editors have not been able to identify.
    The father, whom d'Arblay knew formerly in the army, may have been Jean Charles O'Kelly (b. 1732) of Canac, Ireland, cadet in the Dillon regiment (1746), ensign in the Lowendal regiment (1748), lieutenant en 2ᵉ (20 Oct. 1756), lieutenant en 1ᵉʳ (1 July 1759), which regiment, incorporated with the former Anholst regiment in 1760, was then called the 62nd Infantry. In this regiment O'Kelly was promoted to capitaine (1776), capitaine de grenadiers (1778), major (1789), Lt.-Col. (1792), and he appears in the Army Records (Vincennes) for the last time (1793–4) when his promotion to colonel was under discussion.

gaiety which springs from a good, as well as light heart. This consoled me for you.—I know the power of an amiable companion over worn spirits, & harrassed nerves—& I know well what you must feel for *ME*, whatever be the spirit with which you look forward to your own ameliorated prospects.—When the Chaise drove off, & I saw the last of the waved hand & hat —I won't speak of that moment!—⌐yet it was certainly heightened by my own over anxiety, at the approach of night, that you should be ⟨induced⟩ to set off without your best Friends, and⌐ in an instant, however, I was forced to set myself aside, & give the comfort I could not take: our Alex in almost a storm of sorrow, sobbing, stamping, his whole little expressive face full of despair, flew from his aunt, ⌐& Mrs. Bicknell⌐,[2] & rushed into my room, casting himself into my Arms in such an agony of tears, that it seemed nearly convulsive. Ah! then I saw how rightly you had determined in keeping us together! his frame is not yet so strong as his sensibility, & it was very long ere the fondest carresses & endearments could sooth him into my composure. Dear little, lovely, tender soul! how gratified am I to find his volatile spirits flow not from insensibility of heart, but mere gaiety of nature, & that he merits his dear Father by thus, with all his might, adoring him!—I made him— though with difficulty, go down to Tea—He returned very indignant, saying *a Lady had laughed*! & when he asked what at? she had l answered at his *dismal Face*.! — — I assured him this was only to enliven him, & he was then reconciled. At night, I had a most kind Letter from Miss Cambridge[3] — she will find me apartments at Richmond, & Miss Baker[3] begs me to make use of her house while I suit myself, & they desire their best & kindest remembrances to you, & a thousand thanks for fixing upon their neighbourhood. This was all that broke into that sad Evening—dim Eyes & severe head-ache obstructed all attempt at employment—I had agreed, even with *You*, to allow those first few Hours to Nature—but my Boy took so large a share of my attention as to keep me tolerably in order. The poor little Soul could not close his Eyes—in vain I bid him try to sleep, or at least be silent—he tossed & rolled about

[2] 'Rosette', CB Jr.'s wife, and Sabrina Bicknell (i, L. 7 n. 18), his housekeeper.
[3] Charlotte Cambridge (i, L. 1 n. 6) of Twickenham Meadows and Sarah Baker (i, L. 10 n. 6) of Richmond.

his little restless person, & called out continually 'My Pap! My Pap!—'

Feby 16. To Day brought me a few lines from Dartford[4]— what a painful pleasure to be again, so soon, living upon Post days & post Gifts!—⌐and not one word of yourself! yet I was much delighted by your account of your companions, & I trust they will take upon themselves compelling you to a LITTLE personal care. I have just discovered you have left behind here 4 of your blue bordered mouchoirs.⌐ I had also a Letter highly interesting from Miss Planta[5]—our *Great Friend* directed her to write, & express her concern at all failures, & kind hopes of better days — This has been deeply consolatory, & will make my Richmond residence, I think, truly desirable. You have instinctively, as well as intentionally, hit upon the very spot where all promises best, for what can more enforce my own promise of exertion than such a vicinity? where sadness would be deemed weakness, & must be repressed with extremest care— yet where affection is allowed, & approved, & need never be disguised? ⌐Besides, the skilful Mr. Dundas,[6] should our Boy be ill—that will be a real blessing, & for measles & whooping Cough, I shall now almost wish them while I can thus devote myself to him entirely.⌐ |

Feb. 17th I had again a few lines from the hand most dear to me—⌐but I think I have missed some others, since you speak of being *reviving a time*, though you had never mentioned embark- ing, or arriving at Dover—Besides, I expected a copy of the Letter I wished to possess—perhaps that very copy has secured its miscarriage. How grievous should I never receive it, when so many other things may be in it relative to me. The Flannel advice I am very glad you have had in time, & I hope the blue worsted will get to you. I shall be anxious to know. I must⌐ now acknowledge that our dearest Boy has been ill—& his illness has made me well!—it has operated like a Fire in a theatre upon a lame, or old person: All the 16th he looked pale, & wanted appetite—& I had a nervous head ache that threatened

---

[4] This note is missing, as is a second, received by FBA on 17 February.

[5] The letter dictated by Queen Charlotte to Margaret Planta (L. 429 n. 4) is missing, but FBA was apparently encouraged by its friendly tone to expect that when settled at Richmond she might be received at Kew.

[6] Sir David Dundas (1749–1826), sergeant surgeon to the King (1791–1826), who, according to Walpole (xi, 373), lived at Richmond Green. See iii, L. 219 n. 4.

hard just such a [sei]zure as I had suffered at Norbury Park—
I went to [be]d scarcely alive, — but found him burning hot, &
was instantly cured!—I was like your driving on the anchor in
your passage to France, & its sending off your sea-sickness.[7]
He had a dreadful Cough, & tightness upon his Chest—I gave
him James's powders,—2 grains,—it lessened the inflamatory
symptoms,—I repeated the dose,—they gave way further, —
last night he had a 3ᵈ doze, & he is now at this instant nearly as
well as ever! amazing & delicious is the power of that medicine
where it agrees. An apothecary was continually in the house,[8]
but I never called upon him. I have studied his constitution
from his birth, & have never failed, I thank God, to treat it well.
He has now the most certain signs of true convalescence, for
he interrupts me every other minute for some biscuit—Orange
—toasted bread, tamarinds—pudding—or whatever he can
demand. This has retarded, however, my return home, &
determines me upon going straight to Norbury Park, that I may
be sure to have every indulgence bodily for my Boy, as well
as mental for myself, till we are both more robust. We shall go
by Chelsea—to see my dear Father is all I shall attempt, till
I have parted with my maids, & quitted our dear Cottage. |

Feby 19th I have a few lines from my Father highly gratifying:[9]
he exhorts me to Courage, & says every one who thinks rightly
himself, will think you have done right. This is very healing to
many a wound.—

⌐My sister Burney writes most kindly anxious enquiries about
you, & says kind Bood is expected in about 10 days, by Viller's[10]
information—I am heartily glad for Maria, who is quite
revived by Mr. Sandford[11] having himself declared, he thinks
the climate of France may give her a new constitution, for
strength & vigor. This is extremely comforting to her mother
& all her family, especially poor affectionate Blue.[12] Sweet
Amine⌐ has written me 3 Letters of tenderest sympathy[9]—all

⁷ See M. d'A's L. 441, pp. 37–8.
⁸ In attendance, doubtless, on some of the pupils in Charles Burney's school at
Greenwich.
⁹ CB's letter is missing, as are those of Amelia Angerstein and William Locke.
¹⁰ Possibly the Hon. John Charles Villiers (1757–1838), later (1824) 3rd Earl
of Clarendon. His wife Maria Eleanor (c. 1759–1844), daughter of Admiral John
Forbes (1714–96), kept a diary of their continental tour of 1802–3 (see Greatheed,
p. 8).
¹¹ William Sandford (Intro. i, p. lxxv), a surgeon, who had married Rebecca
Burney (1758–1835), Maria's aunt. ¹² See L. 464 n. 5.

like herself, of honeyed gentleness & sweetness—& when I proposed going to Norbury, instead of West Hamble, I received my answer from the Chief himself, with his own venerated hand, joined to his beloved Partner's, to press our arrival. I shall be only at Camilla Cottage as much as necessity demands for arranging Books, & packing. Alex continues enamoured of the hundred Boys—.

⌐I shall direct this & post direct & write again by Mr. Otto[13] next week, in hopes of conveyance that may find you secured where once I concluded you gone! Heaven save & bless & keep you, mon ami—⌐ ⌐

Pray mark yʳ Letters.

480   [Greenwich, 16 February 1802]

To Doctor Burney

A.L. (rejected Diary MSS. 5352–[55], Berg), *n.d.*
Double Sheet 8vo   4 pp.   *pmks*   17 FE 1802   17 FE 1802   wafer
Addressed: Dʳ Burney / Chelsea College—
Endorsed by CB: Fanny d'A.
Edited by FBA, p. 1 (5352), *annotated and dated*: ⁑ 17. Feb. 1802 (I)   M. d'Arblay returned to France for Sᵗ Domingo.   Westhamble to be left for Richmond
Edited also by CFBt *and the* Press.

Tuesday

M. d'Arblay is gone,[1] my dearest Father!—breathe after him your benediction, I beseech!—

He was grieved at heart he could not get to Chelsea—but his difficulties about his passport, & his pursuit of Tradespeople for his preparations, with necessary applications for Maps, Books, Instruments, Weapons — — alas how dire a Catalogue of impidiments!—never once could he dine in Beaumont Street,[2] nor spend in it one hour, but in Bed time—

---

[13] The French Commissioner in London (L. 429 n. 1).

480. [1] M. d'A had set off for Dover on Monday 15 February accompanied by the O'Kellys (see L. 479 n. 1).

[2] The home of EBB, with whom the d'Arblays stayed for the period 25/26 Jan.–*c*. 3 Feb. (see L. 477 and L. 483, p. 157).

He set off yesterday for Dover in a chaise, with a French Gentⁿ of Irish extraction, M. O'Kelly,[1] whose Father he had formerly known in the army.

I must go home on Friday—to prepare for parting with my house—can my dearest Father receive me, & my shadow, with my Hostess, on Thursday?[3]—If this ¦ should not arrive in time for an answer, we shall take our chance. I mean to beg a Bed, with my dear Fanny,[4] that I may have a little discourse with you at Night, & in the Morning before I set out. I have too much to say to attempt writing—yet a quiet half Hour May tell it all.

M. d'A. fixed upon my letting our Cottage as soon as we can. And then Alex & I are to go to apartments at Richmond. I thought first of *Town*, as close to Esther, & nearer to my dear Father, as well as to Charles—but our alex could not bear the confinement. His health, growth, & improvement are my first cares—& must prove my first solace. I shall devote myself ¦ to him. Richmond has good air, & is an *attainable* distance. I shall be also much at Norbury Park, & this can leave my Maid on board Wages. I have many friends at Richmond, & M. d'A. has made me solemnly promise to mix with them, & not suffer the lone pleasures of solitude & melancholy to seize me, lest they undermine my spirits & health in his long—long absence. Miss Baker offers me her house at Richmond—while I suit myself—& Miss Cambridge will be as a sister to Me, should Alex or myself be ill. Poor aunt Beckey[5] will be delighted, & my Cottage, I trust, will pay my Apartments & all extra-expences.

To you, dearest Sir, we can come at the time most convenient to yourself. Therefore, all together, M. d'Arblay fixed up[on] this plan as the best he could form for me. ¦ He desired his tenderest respects to you, dearest Sir, & says you will easily believe & conceive what has been his harrass when it compelled him to forego e[ven] an attempt to see you again—

Adieu, dearest Sir, till Thursday—I cannot boast being quite well, but hope soon to be better.

I say nothing of the Royal Family, because my dear Father will be foremost to feel my hopes that this Richm^d Residence will lead to their gracious protection & presence.[6]

---

[3] With 'Rosette', CB Jr.'s wife, on Thursday 18 February.
[4] With SBP's daughter Fanny Phillips, who since 1800 had been living with her grandfather at Chelsea Hospital.
[5] CB's sister Rebecca, now 77 years of age.   [6] See L. 479 n. 5.

To Doctor Burney

A.L. (Berg), *n.d.*
Single sheet 8vo   2 pp.   *pmks*   T.P.P. Greenwich   18 FE 1802   wafer
Addressed: Dr. Burney, / Chelsea College, / Middlesex
Edited by FBA, p. 1, *annotated and dated*: ✳ 18. Feb. 1802   (2)   preparations for leaving West Hamble

My dearest Sir—

My poor little Boy is still too ill for removal, & I have no hope before *Saturday*[1]—when, if you have not a Note, I shall flatter myself with embracing you, & sleeping under your roof. If I can *quite* conquer the feverette, the *Cough* will be *benefitted* by change of air, as I shall take him only, at present, to Mr. Lock's, where he will have every possible indulgence of care & warmth.

I am eager to arrange my poor Cottage—where I am all this time keeping two servants for no purpose, ⌜& with Fires, &c, expenses, ruining us.⌝ Many thanks for your kind lines, dearest Sir—they are of true comfort, coming from *you*.[2] I do my very best, indeed—but Nature will not be wholly subdued in the first shock of disappointed happiness, be Reason so much its foe. ⌜Charles is much ⌐ obliged by hearing from Molly of your kind deed. He is in a bustle but writes to let us know about *The Bond* which is settled to eight May. I entreat you to let William, to whom already it has been delivered, ask for my receipt from Jas. Mathias's clerk at Whitehall?[3]—& that you will fill up the date of the Morning you can send him—⌝

adieu, ever dearest [sir]

I have sweet gracious lines from Her Majesty's order—direct

---

481. [1] Saturday 20 February. The visit had been planned for the 18th (L. 480). It was finally on Sunday the 21st (see L. 483, p. 157) that CB Jr. 'carried' his sister and nephew to Chelsea.

[2] CB's 'lines' of this date to FBA are missing.

[3] At one time it was James, then Charlotte, sometimes Esther, who used to call upon Thomas James Mathias (iii, L. 157 n. 6), Treasurer to the Queen's Household, or upon his deputy, for the 'receipt' or claim that would entitle FBA to the quarterly payments of her annual pension of £100. She is now relying on CB and his servant for the transaction.

M. d'Arblay
To Madame d'Arblay
and Alexander d'Arblay

A.L. & A.L.S. (Berg), 19 Feb. 1802
Single sheet 4to   1 p.   *pmks*   22 FEB 1802   22 FE .802   T.P.P. ⟨F⟩E
22   wafer
Addressed: Madame D'arblay / Dᴿ C. Burney's Academy / Greenwich
Kent.
Readdressed: W. Lock's Esq / Norbury Park.—Surry.—
[*in hand of* CB, Jr.:] J Sansom¹ is paid.—
Edited by FBA, p. 1, *top margin, dated and annotated*: 1802 Nᵒ 12/1 Written
upon a New Separation dreadful to me—which called my honoured Husband
to join the French army at St. Domingo, after he had returned to England,
in the belief his conditions of military service had been unacceptable.

Calais February 19ᵗʰ 1802

Here I am, my dearest friend, after a long and tedious
passage. ⌐I am in the greatest hurry and busy this post.¬ I have
so many things to do, that I don't know by which I must
begin. My books have been very luckily taken out of the ship
⌐where they were and many of french ⟨hoam⟩. Very fortunately Mᴿ Grandsirc² has ⟨surrendered⟩ and here they are
perfectly sound & safe.¬ I shall take those I want, and shall
direct the others to Bood,³ who will keep & enjoy them till my
return. ⌐⟨Calais fini write to me⟩ directed *to Cᵗⁿ d'Hermand
Chef de Bureau des Consulats chez le Ministre des [aff]aires etrangeres*⁴
puis mets la lettre sous le couvert de *Monᴿ Otto, Ministre [des
relations exterieures]* de la Republique française à Londre.⁵ Tu ferais
bien / comme tu ⟨sais⟩ fort [bien faire] / d'y joindre [un] mot
[supplementaire] en Anglais qu'il parle et ecrit parfaitement.¬

Pardon, mon ange si je te quitte, mais en verité je suis
obligé de courrir pour [mes] effets. Je n'ai pas besoin de te dire

---

482. ¹ James Sansom (iv, L. 292 n. 3), indigent relative of CB's first wife (*née*
Sleepe).
    ² See L. 469 n. 19.
    ³ For the name 'Bood', FBA later supplied the explanatory superscript /M.
Bourdois/. He was now in Paris.
    ⁴ See L. 450 n. 6.   ⁵ See L. 429 n. 1.

que je ne cesserai point pour cela d'être avec toi—non jamais, jamais! tu es toujours ma seule, mon unique pensée. Mille et mille choses tendres à nos parens et amis.

[*To Alexander d'Arblay*]

I hope my dear Alex will never forget that I have deposited in the hands of his best friend all my fatherly authority; keeping only all my fatherly love, in hope that he will remember he promised me to be obedient to his dear mother. To do what she advises him to do is for him the true and only good road to happiness, and will make him beloved by every body.

A revoir, mes tendres amis,—

tout à vous jusqu'á mon dernier soupir.

A. D'Arblay.

⌐P.S. Le Capt repart aujourdhui même.¬

483   [West Humble, 23?] February [1802]

To M. d'Arblay

A.J.L. (Berg), 21–22 Feb., relating events 19–22 February [1802]
Originally a double sheet 4to, of which FBA later discarded the second leaf   2 pp.
Edited by FBA, p. 1, *annotated and dated*: 1802 (13/2)

Feb^y

Till I write from Richmond, always Direct to Norbury Park. read at leisure—il n'y est rien qui presse. —

I sent off to my best Friend a diary, from the cruel 15th to the *19th*¹—which I devoted to our Boy & writing to his loved —too—too dear Father! who not for a moment will quit my thoughts.—but I will not write of them; I will proceed journalising, that you may know all we do.

20th Feby Alex was well enough to descend, & we spent the afternoon with Rosette—& pups of Charles's, Ser^t & Junr & Mrs. Bicknel,² who was all feeling & attention. I have had two more Letters from sweet Amene, melting with kindness & tenderness. Dear lovely soul, how well she knows how to appreciate my loss, & therefore to understand my sufferings—

483. ¹ L. 479.   ² See L. 479 n. 2.

I forced myself to write to her, that her soft mind might have
its inquietudes somewhat appeased. My dear Esther, too,
wrote most affectionately & anxiously—& all express their
concern very kindly.[3]

21ˢᵗ Sunday.—Charles carried us this morning to Chelsea,
where my dear Father received me with the utmost goodness:
& said all that was most consoling of the conduct of my best
beloved, speaking in terms of approbation dear to all my
feelings. He made me promise a long visit as soon as possible,
& was cordiality itself. Fanny looked very pretty—The little
rogue has had her expected offering[4]—& rejected it!—I always
saw her heart was not engaged; the pleased smiles & demeanour
were but the effects of gratified conquest. Yet she declares it is
more the fear of her Father & Grand Father, & all the family's
disapprobation, than any dislike, for, on the contrary, she
prefers him to any other she knows, & esteems him much: but
she thinks him *too old*, & very cold: yet he has written her
a Letter that, for delicacy & Love, can hardly, in such a situation, be surpassed. Prudence is so small an ingredient in her
composition, & all that is winning & amiable make so large
a share of it, that I am convinced she must be really & truly
indifferent, to all but the pleasure of victory, or she could never
thus command herself: especially unbiassed, for she never consulted il Padre, nor *any one*, & never has shewn the Letter, but
to *ME*, a fortnight after answering it. | ⌐She has promised him
to shew it to no one, don't therefore, mention it, except to me,
& not even to Bood, as his pride deserves that soothing, for his
Letter is really affecting in its humility, & its undoubted truth.
I could scarcely have helped pleading for him, myself, had I seen
it before the reply, his total freedom from all vice or evil considered—She declares she means never to marry—Poor Thing!
This had passed just before our residence in B[eaumont] street,
&, at best, the Amant has philosophy enough to support the
blow without betraying himself to be beaten.—All the rest of
my time are given to *France* & *St. Domingo.*⌐

3 Amelia Angerstein's letters are missing, as are those of EBB.
4 Fanny Phillips, to whom EBB's son, the Revd. Richard Allen Burney (1773–
1836), had made a proposal of marriage (see iv, L. 407, p. 478). Fanny, now about
twenty, was to marry on 13 July 1807 Charles Chamier Raper (c. 1777–1845);
and Richard, aged 29, Elizabeth Williams (*fl.* 1811–32), though not until 10 Oct.
1811.

22ᵈ Febʸ We breakfasted with my Father & Fanny, ⌐Tuesday he lent us his carriage to Epsom. He seems to like the Richmond scheme very well, as within reach of *all parties*.⌐ A few dear lines, *No. 3*, came from Dover⁵—We went immediately, by appointment, to Norbury Park. I had not spirits to return straight to our poor Cottage! I thought it better it should not be *at Night*. Day is so alive—so occupied—so watched. Night so meditative—so *morne!*—With open arms & hearts our incomparable friends received us. They have given me what was Mr. William'[s] room down stairs: & made me take possession of Drawers, lock & Key, to be *there* my *home*—& the Cottage only for my visits. My beloved will, I know, like to hear this. O if he saw how I try to do all & every thing I believe he would most like!— it would very much sooth, for he would see it is just what best sustains me. I was, however, extremely shaken upon re-entering the house — which I had only left to meet YOU at your own!— I was forced to beg to dine with my Boy—though the party in the house was small, & entirely kind: but my breath was quite asthmatic with nervous depression. A little indulgence— occasionally—is salutary, not enfeebling; & when I had put my alex to Bed, I had recruited my spirits into sufficient force to shew myself; & I went to the Drawing room to Tea. Mr. William—who, whenever you are absent, seems to feel a tender compassion for me that augments his kind interest in my welfare, came foremost to shake hands with me;—

[*the second leaf is missing*]

484

M. d'Arblay
To Madame d'Arblay

[Hotel Marengo],
2 March 1802

A.L. (Berg), 2 March 1802
Originally a double sheet 4to, of which FBA later discarded the second leaf. 2 pp.
Edited by FBA, p. 1, *top margin, annotated and year date encircled*: N° 14 ⌐(6) (2) ⌐

⁵ This note is missing.

Paris ce 2 Mars. 1802

Je suis ici occupé du matin au soir, ma chere bonne amie, et n'ai pas une minute à moi. Mon rhume, que je n'ai pas eu le tems de soigner, s'est lassé du peu de cas que je paraissais faire de lui, et a pris le parti de me quitter. Dieu veuille que toi et ton petit vous vous portiez aussi bien que moi. ⌐Bood qui me mandait qu'il ne s'amusait guere à Joigny y est encore, et n'en partira que le 4 pour arriver ici le 5. Probablement j'y serai encore pour l'embrasser. Je ne sais si tu as su la nouvelle de son arrivée *dans 10 jours*. J'ai reçu une lettre de lui, et il n'en est pas question. Cette lettre est datée du 2⟨8⟩ fevrier. Il me semble au contraire qu'il sera obligé de rester ici au moins une quinzaine. au reste, le vrai est qu'il ne me dit pas un mot de ses projets.⌐

Ah! ma bonne amie! quel bon medecin tu es pour ce cher Alex! Ce n'est point la seule santé que je t'aye laissée à soigner — et mon coeur te crie: Medecin! gueris toi toi-même![1] ˡ

Comme j'aime nos amis: comme je suis sensible aux marques nouvelles d'interêst, d'attachement qu'ils te prodiguent. Je ne puis surtout exprimer à quel point je suis touché de la conduite *so steady* of *our friend*![2] Ce qu'elle t'a fait dire par Mˡˡᵉ P[lanta] surpasse tout ce que j'osais me promettre de ce caractere tout à fait *rare*.

Il y a, au moment où je t'ecris une foule de masqués dans les rues. Jamais je n'en ai tant vus, et ce qui est vraiment inconcevable c'est que cette foule prodigieuse n'occasionne pas le moindre desordre. Quelques masques sont vraiment tres plaisans. Tout à l'heure une *mock-dispute* entre un pretendu cocher et une pretendu nourrice qui jettait les hauts cris et l'accusait d'avoir voulu ecraser son enfant poupée, etait reellement trés comique. Les propos poissards des interlocuteurs n'etaient que gais, et les temoins de cette scene riaient aux larmes.

La magnificence de quelques costumes prouve qu'il y a quelque parties de gens au dessus du commun. ˡ

[*the second leaf is missing*]

484. ¹ This is a reply to FBA's letter of 15–19 Feb. (L. 479).
² For the phrase '*our friend*', FBA later supplied the superscript (2) and, on the top margin, the explanatory note: '(2) Queen Charlotte—who honoured with her generous approbation M. d'Arblay's prepared expedition to Sᵗ Dominique.'

[Hotel Marengo],
                                                        2 March 1802
M. d'Arblay
To Madame d'Arblay

A.L. (Berg), 11 Ventose an 10 (2 March 1802).
Double sheet 4to   4 pp.   wafer
Addressed: Madame Darblay / West Humble / near Dorking / Surry
Edited by FBA, p. 1, *annotated*: ⌜(2)⌝ ⌜(7)⌝ N° 15

                    Paris ce 11 Ventose an 10 (2 Mars 1802)
Lis, ma chere amie les copies que je t'envoye de deux lettres
que je viens de recevoir;¹ Ces copies sont sur une feuille à
part, afin que tu puisses les garder et les consulter si par la
suitte tu as besoin d'y avoir recours.
    Tel est, ma chere amie, le resultat de ma lettre au premier
Consul,¹ de cette lettre qu'un Ministre de la Republique, et
plusieurs de ses plus chauds partisans disaient *faire autant
d'honneur à celui à qui elle etait adressée qu'à celui qui l'avait ecrite*.!!
Ce Ministre, ainsi que Lally,² O Kelly,³ et tant d'autres,
supposaient le premier Consul instruit de ma position, et du
dessein tant de fois manifesté par moi, de bouche et par ecrit,

485. ¹ Letters from Berthier, ministre de la Guerre, and from the comte Dutaillis
(L. 446 n. 7), apprising d'Arblay that his military services, under the reservations
he had imposed in his letter of 10 Feb. 1802 to Bonaparte, had been rejected. These
letters M. d'A copied as part of his narrative of these events (Berg), printed in full
below, Appendix, p. 462. Berthier wrote as follows:
    'J'ai recu, Citoyen, votre lettre datée de Londres du 20 pluviôse [9 Feb.] et
celle envoyée pour le Premier Consul.
    'D'après la declaration que vous faites de ne jamais servir contre la patrie
de votre femme qui peut encore être armée Contre la Republique, Je vous pre-
viens que j'ai annullé l'ordre qui vous autorisoit a passer à St. Domingue pour
y etre employé. Vous voudrez bien Considerer les lettres que vous avez reçues
de moi comme non avenues.
                                                        Je vous salue
                                                        Alex Berthier.'
    Thus was concluded all hope or possibility of military service in France. The
comte Dutaillis could only confirm the decision that had been taken:
    'Je vous fais passer, mon cher Darblay, la lettre que le Ministre de la Guerre
vous adresse. Il a suivi les intentions du 1ᵉʳ Consul et ne peut faire autrement.
Il regrette ainsi que moi que votre position politique enchaine vos talens et
votre bonne volonté . . .'.
    ² Lally-Tolendal (L. 425 n. 6). Perhaps a slip of the pen for Dutaillis (L. 446
n. 7).   ³ L. 479 n. 1.

160

au Gal Berthier, *de ne servir que durant l'expedition de St Domingue, où je n'allais que pour payer le prix qu'on mettait à ma retraite.*

Il m'est à present bien demontré que Bonaparte voulait, en me mettant à même d'obtenir un commandement dans les Colonies, me fournir l'occasion de reparer les pertes que j'ai essuyées, pertes dont je parlais dans le memoire que j'avais remis / pour lui / à Lauriston,[4] en m'excusant en quelque sorte de chercher à tirer parti de services qui *etaient la seule proprieté qu'on m'eut laissée.* La connaissance qu'on eut du lui donner de mes sentimens, et de mes projets, pouvait seule arrêter un jugement que comme Chef de la Republique il a du rendre.|

A present, ma chere amie, Je dois te dire à quel point ce jugement me rend malheureux. Au moment où il etait porté, je souscrivais à Londre à la condition d'être au moins *un an* avant de retourner en Angleterre:[5] sans cela, je n'aurais point eu mon passeport pour France. Si on me l'eut refusé, J'avais chargé J. Angerstein,[6] qui s'est montré mon veritable ami, d'en demander un pour l'Amerique, de sorte que c'eut été à St Domingue même que, dans ce cas, j'aurais appris la deffense de m'y rendre, et l'ordre de m'en faire partir; car on avait, m'a t'on dit, ecrit à Brest d'empêcher mon embarquement. Il faut convenir que j'ai une bien singuliere destinée. Dans l'ignorance où le Gouvernment etait de mes projets et de mes veritables sentimens, Il me jugeait ici avec justice, incapable de rester au service de mon Pays, tandis qu'à Londre j'avais été jusqu'à dire que pour partir, et pouvoir le servir, je m'exposerais plutot à être envoyé à Botany bay.

⟵———⟶

Tu me diras, peut être, qu'il n'est pas impossible, et qu'il serait peut être même facile, de faire lever l'espece d'interdit lancé sur moi en Angleterre. Je le crois, mais ne veus point le tenter. Je te prie donc de n'y point penser: mais de t'occuper des moyens de venir me rejoindre le plutôt que tu le pourras. J'ai bien besoin de te voir, et d'epancher dans ton sein le chagrin

---

[4] L. 425 n. 5.

[5] D'Arblay's passport to France was granted on the condition that he was not to return to England within a year. Unable to bear such a separation, FBA planned a visit to Paris of at least ten months.

[6] Amelia Locke's husband, John Angerstein (L. 425 n. 4).

qui me mine. En attendant, je te jure de faire mon possible pour l'empêcher de prendre le dessus; mais tout me devient à charge; et je sens que je le deviendrai bientôt à tout le monde. C'en est donc fait, et je dois renoncer à jamais à l'espoir de contribuer en rien à cette aisance que je m'etais flatté pouvoir nous assurer! Le tems de ma viellesse arrive, et des besoins de toute espece accourent avec | elle. Au lieu de me procurer, comme je l'avais cru, une ressource pour y satisfaire, j'aurai diminué, et de beaucoup, notre bien être, par des depenses qui deviennent inutiles. Que va devenir ce plan que j'avais formé de nous partager entre mon pays et le tien! Ah, mon amie! J'ai l'ame, le coeur et l'esprit bien malades! Quant au reste je n'ai guères le tems d'y penser. Je dois pourtant te dire, pour repondre au reproche que tu me fais, de n'en point parler, que mon rhume va beaucoup mieux, qu'il a perdu [son] caractere inquietant, et que je prendrai grand soin de ma santé: [comme] l'existence m'est toujours bien chere du moment que je songe à toi, et certes il n'est pas au pouvoir des hommes de m'arracher une si douce pensée. Quelqu'acharnement que le sort semble mettre à me poursuivre, quelque raffinement qu'il emploie dans les epreuves qu'il me fait subir, il est de toute verité que près de toi il n'est aucune destinée que j'envie.

⌐Acquite moi envers nos parens et amis.⌐

J'imagine que tu pourras venir avec Bood et sa femme. Il est encore à Joigny, et consequement je ne l'ai point vu: mais j'ai dans l'idée qu'une lettre de lui est allée me chercher hier à la Grange chez M. de L. F. d'où je suis revenu hier soir. je te remercie du N° I et j'attens avec la plus vive impatience ceux qui la suivront. Adresse moi desormais tes lettres | *au C^{en} Darblay | chez le C^{en} Bazille* rue de l'Etape *à Joigny*

Departement D'yonne

Je compte partir dans quelques jours pour m'y rendre. |

⌐Je te prie, ma chere amie, de faire remettre à M^{de} Anne Carter[7] la lettre que je t'envoye. Elle est de M^{de} Charles

---

[7] Of Cornhill? The parish records of St. Michael's and St. Peter's, Cornhill (now in the library of the Guildhall, London) show the burial on 1 June 1828 of a Sophia Carter of Warnford Court, 29 Throgmorten Street, aged 50. They contain, however, no trace of Anne, formerly English governess to Lafayette's daughter Anastasie-Louise-Pauline (1777–1863), the wife (since 1798) of Jules-*Charles*-César de Fay (1775–1846), comte de Latour-Maubourg, brother of César (L. 446 n. 12).

Maubourg, fille de M de La Fay. Mrs Anne Carter a été sa Gouvernante. J'imagine qu'il ne sera pas difficile de la trouver, car il n'y a pas beaucoup de Corn St. à Londre où je n'ai jamais su qu'il y en est.

P.S. J'espere que tu n'as encore rien ecrite à Richmond, et que tu ecriras pour qu'on discontinue les recherches que tes excellentes amies avaient la bonté de faire.⊓ Je m'attens bien à être blamé là comme ici. Les *malheureux* et principal^t les *Maladroits*, ont peu d'amis et encore moins d'approbateurs. Qu'il est commode de juger après l'evenement. Aussi personne ici ne s'en gêne, et je ne rencontre pas le plus mince personnage, qu'il ne me faille entendre ses regrets de ce que je ne l'ai pas consulté; et cependant malgré que je sois desolé du resultat de ma demarche je ne puis la voir d'un autre oeil.

⌐Mon camarade de voyage[8] que j'ai vu hier matin et qui m'a remis une lettre de ⟨James⟩ qui n'a pu faire ma commission, n'a pas été beaucoup plus heureux. A la prefecture il a été pris pour un autre, arreté, et gardé en secret. Tu peus te figurer la situation de sa femme qui n'entend ni ne parle le Français. Elle l'a vu assujettir, et ne savait à qui et commen demander ⟨de ses nouvelles⟩. Heureusement James n'a pas eu le tems de faire faire des ⟨tentatives⟩ serieuses. C'est la seule chose heureuse qu j'aye ⟨trouvé⟩ depuis que je suis arrivé ici. Fais [lui mes] complimens et remercimens.⊓ |

[xxxxx 2½ *lines of marginal writing*]

486   [West Humble, 3 March 1802]

To Esther (Burney) Burney

A.L. (Berg), *n.d.*
Double sheet 4to   3 pp.   *pmks*   T.P.P./U.   3 MR 1802   wafer
Addressed: Mrs. Burney / Beaumont Street, / Devonshire Place,
Edited by FBA, p. 1, dated (*probably from the pmk*): 3 Mar. 1802

I had not intended answering your Letter, my dearest Esther, till I could tell you I had heard from Paris—but the business you now open demands an immediate reply—

[8] O'Kelly (n. 3).

My Cottage is—alas!—undoubtedly to be let,—&, as yet, is quite unengaged, & has been seen by no one. Mrs. Bishopp's friend[1] shall therefore certainly have the refusal. The terms I cannot now send, as they are not fixed. Mr. Lock, by whose kind & wise & always right counsel I act in every thing, advises me to have the house looked at by some skilful & fair appraiser, by whose opinion the rent will be settled. I have been, as yet, unable to arrange even this—but your Letter has accelerated what must be done, & to-morrow, if fine, Mr. Lock will speak himself to a very honest man, who lives at Dorking & I shall admit him to make the examination & decision. We have never finished fitting up the house,—either in papering or furnishing; but if the lady's family is small, there will be room sufficient; if otherwise, the deficiencies may be easily supplied from Dorking or Leatherhead: & the appraiser will understand what deduction should be allowed. By all I have heard of Mrs. Bishopp, I should think myself fortunate to let my dear—dear little dwelling—which I quit with the heaviest of hearts—to a lady of her acquaintance. I have been so averse to any total stranger, or chance inhabitant, that I have had no bill put up, nor information sent to any neighbouring | public houses, or places. our own Bed, & the Maids', are the only two, except mere *Camp Beds* for *summer repose*, to our kind & easily satisfied friends, which have been put up. As I shall take my Books to Richmond, we think that room will make a very pretty & delightfully pleasant Bed room, should this lady—or who-ever succeeds us,—live, as all around us do, on the Ground floor. But that will depend upon what her family is, & what her intentions of receiving friends. you may mention there are only 2 rooms for large Beds, & 3 for dressing rooms, or tent or camp Beds. Down stairs is a tolerable sized drawing room, & two small parlours—kitchen, & small scullery. This is the whole house. The beauty of its situation is its great recommendation, & its newness, & tightness, & healthy & dry position. The poor Garden is compleatly out of repair—but will pay for its

---

486. [1] The 'friend' is not identified, but Elizabeth Rebecca Bisshopp *née* Swain (*c.* 1755–1826) was the wife of Hugh Bisshopp (*c.* 1755–1824) of Dorking, the occupier at this time of Sand Place (iv, L. 399 n. 1). His mother was Susannah *née* Hedges (1724–92), who had married on 8 Jan. 1750/1 Cecil Bisshopp (bur. 10 Sept. 1779 in Bath Abbey), and EBB's friend and patron the Hon. Mrs. Bateman *née* Hedges (1727–1802) was his aunt.

labourers by its products. The orchard is but 5 or 6 years old—but begins to bear plenty of apples—tolerably of Cherries, & a few green Gages, &, last year, one Pear!—with Nuts, filberds, & walnuts in great abundance. The paths in the wood & Copse belonging to it, if a little attended to, are really beautiful in the summer & autumn. We can only let it by the week, nominally,—but alas—I know a year may be depended upon!—perhaps a second summer.—But of all this more, if the terms induce the Lady to desire it. As soon as they are settled, I will write again. Miss Cambridge thinks I can obtain nothing under 2 G^s a week! at Richmond—! she is seeing for me another way —still in her neighbourhood. Do you know *Sion row*?[2] My house will be ready for L^y Day.[3] Always direct to me *here*, my dearest sister[.] I am only there for packing, &c—dear Maria is better, to my great satisf[action, b]ut I have not seen her, or Blue[4] — They cannot come to me, nor can I get to t[hem.] Alex is still an Invalide. Sophy has | been w[ith] me, for a kind morning, but *morne* & full of perplexity & bustle. I am in hourly hope of a few lines from Paris—or Brest—Heaven bless you, my dear soul—Mrs. Locke sends you her kindest Love—I have been so nervous, & my Boy so unwell, I have not once dined out of my own room since I came. But we intend to do better things!—I ought to be excited by your question of my *heroism*! They are easily contented *here*, &, indeed, I exert to my very uttermost to keep myself up with participators who suffer seriously themselves when I sink—*one* more Letter—& I shall exert still more—but while the least *possible* doubt remains, my poor spirits refuse to be calm—they are buoyed I know not how high, or depressed nearly to disease.

I have much to say upon the other subject of your first Letter — but not here, nor *now*,—I am quite of your mind as to *patience* about M. B[ourdois]'s lengthened stay—I cannot bend to it—but Maria is recovering, & I trust all will end well. Sophy tells me Richard talks of setting out alone,[5] & grows eager for departing.—

[2] Sion Row was described in 1926 by Francis Henry Skrine as 'a delightful group of early Georgian residences in Twickenham', in which (at No. 2) Laetitia Hawkins (1760–1835) and her brother Henry (1762–1841) lived from 1793 until her death. See his *Gossip about Dr. Johnson and Others: being chapters from the Memoirs of Miss Laetitia Matilda Hawkins* (1926), frontispiece.

[3] 25 March.   [4] Maria's maiden aunt Elizabeth Warren Burney (1755–1832).

[5] Without his aunt (*supra*), who was later to follow him to Rimpton.

Adieu—adieu—don't fear but I *will* be *heroical,* — when once I have heard something positive,—& no hope *can* force itself in the way of my philosophy, & undermine my best struggles for firmness by ideas—

—the post—

487   Sand Place, 5 March 1802

To Doctor Burney

A.L.S. (Berg), 5 Mar. 1802
Double sheet 4to   4 pp.   *pmks*   DARKING ⟨6⟩ MAR 1802   6 MR
1802   wafer
Addressed: Dr. Burney, / Chelsea College, / Middlesex—
Edited by FBA, p. 1, *annotated*: ⁂· (3)   Doubts & wonder at hearing M. d'Arblay is at *Paris*, not at Brest.

5. March—1802.
I have purposed waiting for a 2d. Letter from M. d'Arblay before I wrote again to my dearest Father;[1] but as I think he may in some measure have partaken of my uneasiness in not hearing from him since the 19th Feby I will not stay till I again see his hand writing, to let my dearest Father hear all I have heard myself, which is, through a Letter from Mrs. Huber,[2] that he is safe in *Paris,* & had been there Eight days when Mrs. Huber had this news. Why I have not received any Letter from him, I cannot imagine. That he has written I feel sure, though, had not this intelligence, by this accident, reached me, I should have concluded him now at Brest, if not set sail. What, also, can detain him at Paris is equally sur-

487. [1] L. 482.
   [2] Barthélemy Huber (1748–1837), originally of Vevay, Switzerland, having come to England in 1769, had married in 1780 Lydia *née* Strutt (1759–1813). An astute banker, with continental banking interests, and formerly a director of La Compagnie des Indes, he was acutely aware of the hazards of war to trading and banking interests and to assist the cause of peace he was to attach himself in 1803 to Lord Whitworth's embassy in Paris (see further L. 546 n. 2).
   A very religious man, as may be seen from his will (P.C.C. Norwich 565, pr. 1837), a friend of Hannah More, and the translator (1817) of *Coelebs* into French, Mr. Huber will presently be seen (Ll. 510 and 511) as a mentor, closely allied to the mentors (real and fictional) of his time.

prising to me. He thought he should merely see the War
Minister, receive his immediate instructions as to his route, &c,
make his uniform, & set off post for Brest. I am bewildered with
conjecture—sometimes ˡ flattering myself the information from
the Colonies is of so satisfactory a nature, that no more troops
or officers will be sent—at others, surmizing that *the Letter*[3]
was ill received, or ill understood, & the intended command
therefore withheld—In short, my brain knows no rest for variety
of suggestion. Mean while, applications are made about the
house—but I can listen to none while in this suspence; I have
displaced all, with *most admired disorder*,[4] but now stop short from
packing or preparation. I reside at Norbury Park, except while
rummaging; & I am come, at this moment, for a day or two
to Sand Place, to see poor Maria, who is now recovering, ⌐but
who has had a lingering & disheartening nervous illness. My
very best hopes for her cure from the change of climate she
will soon try.

With respect to my recommended residence—Miss Cambridge has now found me out Lodgings in Sion Row, Twickenham, which promise to suit me precisely; ˡ they are at the
house of a worthy couple, of her particular acquaintance, &
whom she esteems & loves—& they are the cleanest, & most
reasonable, & largest, of any she has met with. These I was
upon the point of accepting when this letter from Mrs. Huber
makes Me wait & hold back—˥

In answer to my making known to Her Majesty my intentions
of residing at Richmond, I have received the most gracious
command to wait upon Her Majesty, thence, when she is at
Kew;[5] & a similar benign message from my sweet Princesses.
This has given me the utmost satisfaction—&, should the
removal take place, will be amongst my very first comforts:
but other thoughts & hopes just now occupy Me. ⌐Maria
hopes to see M. Bourdois shortly—If so, he will, I should
suppose, have been at Paris, & I hope seen M. d'Arblay.˥
'Tis truly extraordinary my having no Letters, for posts,

---

[3] Though FBA had not yet received M. d'A's letter of 2 March (L. 485), she had
well foreseen the result of his letter to Napoleon (see L. 478 n. 7), and at this place
in the manuscript she later placed the superscript (*a*), and at the bottom of the
page the explanation: '(a), a Letter from M. d'Arblay to decline bearing arms,
against the English, but to accept All other orders from the Premier Consul,
Buonaparte.'

[4] Lady Macbeth, iii. 4.   [5] See L. 479, p. 150.

mails, news papers, Couriers are arriving daily. Adieu, most dear Sir,—I earnestly hope your Cough is ¹ conquered, & am ever & ever most dutifully & affectionately

Your F. d'Arblay.

ᵖ⟨Alex is all⟩ well again though still requiring much care. I again return to Norbury Park to-morrow, where is my only constant direction, tell it, AT LEAST to *Fanny*—to whom my best love.ᵖ

488   [Hotel Marengo],
                                          8 March 1802

M. d'Arblay
To Madame d'Arblay

A.L. (Diary MSS. vi. 5360–[63], Berg), 8 Mar. 1802
Double sheet small 4to   4 pp.   *pmk*   16 ⟨M⟩R .802   wafer
Addressed: England / Madame Darblay / Norbury-Park / near Dorking /
Surry
    Edited by FBA, p. 1 (5360), *annotated*: Nº 17   2   (1)
    Edited also by CFBt *and the* Press.

Triplicata   Paris ce 17 Ventose an 10.
                                              (Mars 8 1802)

ᵖUne nouvelle que j'apprens à l'instant même, à la quelle pourtant personne ici ne croit, mais qui vraie ou non ne t'allarmera pas moins sur mon compte, si, comme on le dit ici, elle vient d'Angleterre, me faitᵖ t'ecrire par *Triplicata* ma position actuelle, c.à.d. le parti que le Gouvernement a cru devoir prendre de ne plus m'employer, et l'ordre que j'ai reçu de regarder comme non avenues les lettres que m'avait ecrites le Ministre de la Guerre. La cause qu'il assigne à cette disgrace, à la quelle je n'etais rien moins que preparé, est *ma declaration de ne point servir contre la patrie de ma femme, qui peut encore être armée contre la Republique.*[1]

⌐Tu devines peut être que la nouvelle dont je parle est l'assassinat de Toussaint par les Negres,[2] ce qui prouverait mon idée que malgré *ma declaration de ne point servir contre la patrie de ma femme &c.* (declaration qui suivant quelques personnes equivaut à un refus de servir) il y aurait eu encore assez à faire pour meriter la retraite que je consentais à aller servir à St Domingue. Donc | mon destin veut que je me trompe, et faire que tout soit dejà surestimé comme ⟨on s'est flatté⟩. Toi qui me connais tu sais si ce voeu est bien dur.⌐ Pardon, ma bonne amie, je t'avoue que j'ai été depuis huit jours d'une melancholie à inquieter mes amis. Tu en seras peu surprise, quand tu reflechiras à tous les sacrifices aux quels je m'etais resigné, à toutes les depenses à present inutiles qu'il m'a fallu faire, aux caquets qu'il m'a fallu supporter, enfin à l'esperance à jamais detruite d'un meilleur avenir dans le quel j'aurais été pour quelquechose, mais plus que tout cela à l'impossibilité de voler prés de toi, et à la necessité de ne te faire part de ma position actuelle que lorsque j'aurais une presque certitude qu'elle ne pouvait changer. A present ma bonne amie, je te promets de m'occuper uniquement du bonheur que nous avons encore devant nous. Tu sais que lorsque j'ai une fois pris mon parti, je sais être ferme. Hé bien je t'assure que ma plus grande souffrance est venue de l'incertitude où j'etais forcement plongé. Comme il ne m'en reste plus, je veux m'arrêter sur l'idée si douce de te revoir bientôt. Dejà, moi qui lorsqu'il a été question de mon depart m'etais persuadé, ⌐que⌐ que je jouirais à St Domingue de la meilleure santé, vû mon âge | ma sobrieté et le soin que je comptois prendre de moi, sans pour cela faire moins qu'aucun autre relativement à mon service, je cherche dejà à me persuader que vû mon temperament billeux, et mon desir, que dis-je? mon besoin de faire plus qu'un autre, j'aurais fort bien pu succomber à l'influence presque pestilentielle d'un Climat que je commençais à regarder comme infiniment sain et agreable! ⌐J'ai eu en outre aujourdhui un autre motif de consolation: c'est qu'on m'a assuré que Bonaparte ne m'en voulait point, et certes il a bien raison car si jamais il etait dans le cas

488. [1] Cf. M. d'A's letter to Bonaparte (L. 478 n. 8).
[2] A false report (see L. 465 n. 6 and L. 489 n. 1).

de l'eprouver, je lui souhaite d'avoir prés de lui beaucoup de personnes qui le defendent aussi loyalement que je le ferais.ᵀ

Dans mon accès de melancholie — qui en honneur se dissipe depuis que j'ai cru pouvoir t'en dire la cause, j'ai été d'une telle sauvagerie que je m'etais mis dans l'esprit — et encore plus dans la tête qu'ainsi que le bouc d'Israel je portais partout la marque de la reprobation. En consequence je fuyais tout le monde, et n'en etais pas plus h⟨eureux⟩ car, ne pouvant causer librement avec toi, et ne t'ecrivant q⟨ue⟩ balivernes, je passais à faire du mauvais sang en pure perte, un tems, qu'il m'eut été si doux d'employer aux epanchemens accoutumés de ma tendresse et de ma confiance pour toi. Sans cesse j'avais devant les yeux le Sieur Lullin³ de l'Alien office, et la promesse que j'ai ᶦ été contraint de faire, pour obtenir mon passeport, d'être au moins *un an* avant de retourner en Angleterre. L'insolence de ce Lullin me fait encore bouillir le sang. Quelques personnes en font cependant l'eloge. En ce cas l'exception dont il m'a honnoré est flatteuse! Comme en tout etat de cause, il m'est impossible de t'aller trouver, que d'ailleurs tu devais toujours venir au Printems, j'espere que tu voudras bien consentir à me venir joindre avec notre cher petit. Prends donc tes arrangemens en consequence. Tache de louer la maison pour un an, et si tu as un logement à Richmond, cherche à le ceder. As tu remercié de ma part cette chere Mᵉˡˡᵉ Cambridge et Mᵉˡˡᵉ Baker?⁴ Adieu, ma chere amie, à revoir bientôt toi et notre cher — bien cher Alex! Mes tendres respects à nos excellens amis, ainsi qu'à nos bon Parens.

ᵀComme je ne puis t'aller chercher, j'espere que tu voudras bien venir avec Bood, qui au reste n'est point encore de retour de Joigny, où il a fait beaucoup de folies tout le Carnaval. On l'attend dans peu de jours. J'embrasse la femme de Bood ᶦ

Le Ministre⁵ qui ⟨renseigne⟩ Mʳ de N est toujours parfait pʳ ⟨moi⟩; Mᵈᵉ Charles M.⁶ [xxxxx ½ *line*] à Paris. Elle compte passer une partie du Printems et presque tout l'Eté chez M de La F. son père. J'espere que le [xxxxx 2 *lines*]ᵀ

---

³ Charles Lullin de Châteauvieux (1777–1858) of Switzerland. Apparently employed for some time with the Foreign Office, London, he became in 1815–16 a Senior Clerk in the Alien Office.
⁴ See L. 479 n. 3.
⁵ Possibly Dumas (L. 450 n. 10).
⁶ Anastasie (see L. 485 n. 7), Lafayette's daughter.

M. d'Arblay
To Madame d'Arblay

A.L.S. (Diary MSS. vi. 5368–[71], Berg), 10 Mar. 1802
Double sheet small 4to 4 pp. *pmks* FOREIGN OFFICE / 19 MR
1802 19 MR .802 wafer
Addressed: Angleterre / Madame d'Arblay / Westhumble / near Dorking /
Surry
Edited by FBA, p. 1 (5368), *top margin, annotated:* ⌜19⌝ Nº 18 (1)
Buonaparte sur Cecilia—
Edited also by CFBt *and the* Press.

Ce 21 Ventose an 10
10 Mars 1802.

Il me semble ma bonne amie qu'il y a un siecle que je n'ai
eu de tes nouvelles; et tu peus juger avec quelle impatience j'en
attens. l'assassinat pretendu du moins de Toussaint,[1] en me
donnant les plus vives inquietudes sur les allarmes que cette
nouvelle n'aura pas manqué de te causer, m'a beaucoup calmé
sur le contr'ordre que j'ai reçu; et je te jure qu'actuellement je
suis presque reconcilié sur mon desappointement. Comme je
t'ai ecrit par quatre voies differentes je ne te repeterai point ici
ce que je t'ai mandé à ce sujet.

⌜As tu reçu mes lettres à tems pour ecrire à Mᵉˡˡᵉ Cambridge
de mes [xxxxx ½ *line*] A. Bourdois, qui sort de chez moi, n'est
arrivé qu'hier soir assez tard. Nous n'avons pas eu le tems de
causer bien à fond sur mes affaires et jamais les ⟨actes⟩ n'ont
été autant en ⟨ ⟩ avec les siennes. Il lui faut m'a t'il ditᴨ
au moins 15 jours ici avant de pouvoir partir. Moi qui voudrais

489. ¹ Whatever the progress of the revolution in San Domingo, propagandists
could be expected to produce favourable (even if false) reports of the success of the
expeditionary force that Napoleon had sent under the leadership of his brother-in-
law General Leclerc for the quelling of the blacks and the restoration of slavery
in the islands.

In fact, in February and March, Toussaint (L. 465 n. 6) and his rebel forces
were strong in the mountains, while Leclerc, with forces depleted by fever and war,
pleaded for reinforcements. It was not until 8 May that Toussaint was persuaded
to surrender voluntarily, and not until June that he was arrested and taken to
France. In July he was hurried across France to a place of captivity, Fort-de-Joux
in the Jura mountains where, exposed to cold, half-starved, and subjected to
indignities, he was to die on 7 Apr. 1803.

bien t'y voir bientôt je trouve cela bien long. J'espere, mon amie, que tu n'as aucune objection contre ce besoin de mon coeur. Quand nous serons reunis, nous causerons ensemble sur la maniere dont nous passerons l'année. Je n'ai encore sur cela aucun plan de fixé, et t'attendrai pour prendre une determination. Tu as sans doute fait part à Norbury des lettres que je t'ai envoyées. Je ǀ desire que les copies des deux que je t'ai fait passer soient communiqueès to our generous FRIEND.

T'ai-je mandé que j'avais envoyé copie de ces mêmes lettres à Mr de L. F.?[2] je les accompagnais de quelques reflexions à peu près semblables à celles que je t'ai ecrites et voici comme je finissais[3]

Resume de toute cette affaire

'Je sollicitais ma reforme. Le Gouvernement m'a fait dire que *cette question etait ajournée mais que je pouvais être employé aux Colonies, et gagner ainsi ma retraite.* J'ecrivis que s'il s'agissait *d'aller à St Domingue travailler à y remettre l'ordre, j'acceptais avec reconnaissance, mais que partout ailleurs où il n'y aurait aucun danger à courrir je demandais la permission de refuser.* Dans l'entrevue que j'eus avec le Ministre, je lui dis qu'arrivé dans la Colonie, j'assurerais trés positivement ceux qu'on aurait mis à mes ordres, comme je l'en assurais lui même, que *mon intention etait uniquement d'acheter ma retraite le prix que le Gouvernemt y avait mis, et non de prendre une place à la quelle tant d'autres avaient tant de droits.* J'ajoutai que je le priais de se rappeller que *je demandais à me retirer aussitôt l'expedition achevée.* La lacune apparente que presenterait l'etat de mes services ayant quelques jours aprés offert au Ministre une difficulté qu'il jugea insurmontable, je retirai, non *ma demande* mais mon acceptation, et fus joindre ma femme, aprés avoir *ecrit que si le Ministre pouvait faire lever par le 1er Consul cette difficulté, qui seule s'opposait à MA RETRAITE AUSSITÔT L'EXPEDITION ACHEVÉE, j'etais prêt à me rendre à St Domingue.* Les ordres sur les quels je suis parti, sur les quels j'ai fait plus de cent louis de depenses devenues absolument inutiles, me parurent ne devoir laisser aucun doute à cet egard.

Après ces preliminaires indispensables, ma lettre au 1er Consul porte, je crois, un caractere tout different. Elle n'etait que l'expression du besoin imperieux de cette franchise

---

[2] See L. 485 n. 1.
[3] This letter of 3 Mar. 1802 is in the Berg Collection.

dont j'ai été souvent, mais jamais aussi douloureusement, la victime. Il y a sans doute eu trop de simplicité à penser que le Chef d'une grande nation, et son Ministre, pouvaient, l'un entendre, et l'autre se rappeller de si minces details. Du moins cette explication me lavera j'espere du reproche d'absurdité: car c'en serait une bien grande, bien meprisable, que *d'accepter* du service sous la condition qu'on ne servira pas.

Quant au danger de me confier un commandement dans les circonstances actuelles, ma vie entiere est ma reponse.

Ce que j'attens actuellement, de vous, mon General, c'est de faire connaître la verité au 1er Consul, et de detruire la mauvaise impression que cette affaire ne manquerait pas de laisser. Du reste si les Français accueillis par Toussaint à St Domingue, en sont paisibles possesseurs, je n'ai rien à y faire: mais apres avoir depensé 220 louis pour solliciter ma reforme, je¹ me borne à rester aux mêmes droits que ceux de mes camarades, qui ont attendu tranquillement que le Chef de la Republique puisse suivre le penchant qu'il a manifesté de leur accorder une indemnité, dont certes personne n'a plus besoin que moi.'

A. D'a

M. de L.F. vint sur le champ à Paris et demanda un rendez vous à Bonaparte qui le lui accorda sur le champ. En l'abordant M. de L.F. lui dit: Je viens vous parler d'un de mes amis et compagnons, de D'a- - - - -. 'Je connais cette affaire'; dit le premier Consul d'un ton qui marquait plus de bienveillance que je n'osais l'esperer, ou de [fermeté] qu'on ne me l'avait fait craindre.

'Je vous assure' me dit le lendemain M. de L.F. 'que vous avez près du 1er [Consul] de bons amis qui lui avaient dejà parlé de votre affaire. Il m'a paru, dés le premier instant, plutôt disposé en votre faveur, que fâché contre vous. Il a écouté avec attention et bonté tout ce que j'ai eu à dire, a rendu justice à votre loyauté, et sur ce que je lui ai parlé de la crainte qu'on vous avait inspirée, relativement à l'impression fâcheuse qui pouvait lui rester sur cette affaire, m'a repondu positivement *que cela ne nuirait en aucune maniere à vos droits acquis, et qu'il ne considererait dans cette demarche que le mari de Cecilia.*'

J'espere que tu ne seras pas trés mecontente de la maniere dont finit cette affaire, qui m'a donnè beaucoup de chagrin.

Je dois même pouvoir t'ajouter en confidence que je ne suis pas, peut-être, fort eloigné d'avoir ma retraite.

Viens donc me trouver, ma bonne amie. Comment se porte Maria? pourras tu t'arranger pour venir avec elle? où bien prefères tu venir à Douvre avec Alex, sous la garde d'un de tes frères, pour t'y embarquer et arriver à Calais où j'irais t'attendre. Cet arrangement serait bien plus selon mon coeur, mais outre que je voudrais bien que tu eusses un homme dans le passage, cela serait bien plus cher. Ne manque pas surtout de prendre un passeport de Monsieur Otto[4] et de te munir non seulement de nos actes de mariage, mais de celui de naissance de notre cher petit, *le tout bien legalisé* par la signature non seulement du *juge de paix mais d'un notaire public.*

Je te quitte, ma bonne amie, pour ecrire un mot à mon oncle. la poste me presse, et il est indispensable que je lui reponde. Voici ce qu'il me dit au sujet de ta lettre que | je lui ai envoyée.

'Il parait, mon cher D'ar. . . . que tu as tout exageré à ta femme excepté les impulsions de mon coeur! Elle le navre par ses expressions, et tu dois savoir, d'après ce que je t'ai dit qu'elles etaient genantes et laborieuses pour moi. Ni l'un ni l'autre ne m'ecrivez ni ne me parlez ainsi: car je ne puis ni ne sais y repondre que par le silence!'

Dans un autre endroit de sa lettre, ce cher Oncle dit:

'Bo. a fait à tout le monde une peinture charmante de ta femme. Je commence à croire qu'il faudra la sequestrer pour la soustraire au fracas et au caquetage souvent babillard de nos femmes. Enfin, nous la recevrons de notre mieux et avec bien du plaisir.'

⌐J'embrasse Alex et toi de toute mon ame et de toutes mes forces. Mille choses tendres à nos excellens amis et parens.⌐

à revoir — à revoir

⸔See L. 429 n. 1.

Conjointly with Alexander d'Arblay
To M. d'Arblay

A.L. & PS. (Diary MSS. vi. 5364-[67], Berg), 14 Mar. 1802
Double sheet 4to   4 pp.   red wafer
Addressed: France / Au C^n D'Hermand[1] / Chef du Bureau des Consulats /
Chez le Ministre des Relations / étrangerès, / À PARIS— / Pour le C^n /
Darblay—
Edited by FBA, p. 1 (5364), *annotated and date 1802 retraced*: ⊞ 1802   ⟨N⟩°
15/2
Edited also by CFBt *and the* Press.

West Hamble, 14. March 1802

O my dearest Friend!—can the intelligence I have most
desired come to me in a form that forbids my joy at it? What
tumultuous sensations your Letter of the *8th* has raised![2] Alas!
that to relinquish this purpose should to You be as great
unhappiness as to ME was its suggestion!—I know not how to
enter upon the subject—how to express a single feeling—I fear
to seem ungrateful to Providence—or to you, ungenerous—
I will only, therefore, say, that as all your Motives have been
the most strictly honourable, it is not possible they should not,
ultimately, have justice done them by ALL.

What *I* feel for your disappointment I need not tell you,
when you find it has power to shake to its foundation what would
else be the purest satisfaction of my soul.—Let us—let us hope
fairer days will ensue—& do not let the courage which was so
prompt to support you to St. D[omingo]—fail you in remaining
at Paris—

What you say of the *year's probation* I knew not before—
would you have me make any enquiry if it be irreversible? I
should think not, & am most ready—& eager to *try* by every
means in my power, if you will authorize me. — If not — — to
follow you, whithersoever you will, is much less my Duty than
my Delight! You have only to dictate *whither*, & *how*, & every

490. [1] See L. 450 n. 6.
    [2] M. d'A's letter of 10 March (L. 489) had arrived before his letter of the 8th
(L. 488).

doubt, every fear, every difficulty, will give way ⏐ to my eager desire to bring your little Boy to you—would I not have left even *HIM*—to have followed You & your fate even to St Domingo? 'Tis well, however, you did not listen to me, for that poor little susceptible soul could not, as yet, lose us both at once, & be preserved himself. He has lived so singularly alone with us, & for us, that he does not dream of any possible existence, in which we should be both separated from him. Maria re-counted to me, the other day, a touching proof of this, that passed when he was in Clarges Street: Molly,[3] I think, having pleaded she had a right to direct him, because she was *oldest*, he answered 'You're oldest, are you? — 'Why then you'll die first.' 'And should not *you*, said Sophy,[4] like to die, Alex?' 'Not before Mama.' he replied,—& when she laughed, he added 'And not *after* Mama!—' She laughed again—but not when he concluded with his full meaning—'but I should like to die just when Mama begins to be deaded.' Dear little fellow! — & who shall disbelieve his tenderness when your departure so instantly brought on a fever that demanded James's powders 4 times? — — But of him—our retreat—our Books—our scribbling—our Garden—our *unique* mode of life—I must not talk to you now, now, that your mind, thoughts, views & wishes are all distorted from themes of peace, domestic life, & literary pursuits — — yet Time, I hope, Reflection, your natural philosophy of accommodating yourself to ⏐ your fate, & your kindness for those who are wholly devoted to you, will bring you back to the love of those Scenes, modes, & sentiments which for upwards of Eight years have sufficed for our mutual happi-ness.—

Maria, in extreme amazement, has still no Letter—& is again unwell. Is Bood sure he can have another passport to *return*, when he comes to fetch her?—Most unfortunately your Letter for their ⟨Property⟩ was too late for any of her regula-tions. I had been negociating for apartments at Twickenham, opposite Richmond, with Miss Cambridge & Miss Baker, ever since you went—& on Friday, upon your Letter of the 2d

---

[3] CB's maid, Mary More (ii, L. 68 n. 30).
[4] EBB's daughter.

March⁵ concluding your going quite fixed because now un-
conditional, I wrote to close with the engagement.—& this
very morning, I have two Letters, full of delight at our approaching neighbourhood, telling me she had found me the
best of hostesses—one of the worthiest women in the world, who
showed so great a desire for having Alex & me, for her Lodgers,
that she would take us at half the price she could let her apartments for to any others, & that the rooms were all aired, &
everything settled & I need carry into it nothing, but linnen,
as she would find me a stove, Glasses, Crockery, plates, kettle,
knives, forks, spoons, &c, while poor Miss C[ambridge] herself
writes in tears, she says, of joy, that I should be so near her, &
that *you* should have wished it,—& *blesses* you for your confidence
in her warm friendship— | it is quite impossible to read of such
affection & zeal & goodness with dry Eyes. I am confounded
how to *dis-enchant* her—yet so generous & disinterested she is,
that, however disappointed, she will be sure to rejoice for *ME*
in our re-union—for *you*, my dearest friend! — — ah, who can
rejoice?—your mind was all made up to the return of its professional pursuits, & I am frightened out of all my own satisfaction by my dread of the weight of this chagrin upon your
Spirits.—what you *can* do to avert depression, that cruel under-
miner of every faculty that makes life worth sustaining, I
beseech you to call forth. Think how *I* have worked for fortitude since *Feby 15th*⁶—alas, vainly I have tried what MOST
I wished—my poor pen!—but now—'*ocupe toi pour realiser
l'esperance*'—⁷those words will operate like Magic, I trust, &
I will not close my Eyes this Night till I have committed to
paper some opening to a new Essay—Be *good*, then, & don't let
me be as unhappy *this* way as I have been the other! direct
always to me, Norbury Park—Dorking. Heaven bless—bless
you!

Alex is quite well—

[*By Alexander d'Arblay*]

Mon cher Papa comme je ame la copie Mon cher Papa
comm⟨e je⟩ vous ame —

---

⁵ L. 484.   ⁶ The date of M. d'A's departure for France.
⁷ See pp. 161–2.

[*By Madame d'Arblay*]

He means to [say] I love the *Copy mama* gives me to ⟨write
Co⟩*mme je vous aime, Mon* cher *Papa!* — ⏐

The Lady[8] I have mentioned to you is in full treaty about
the house, & I hope will like it. It has been a wearisome
experience.

491   Norbury Park, 17 March 1802

To Doctor Burney

A.L.S. (Berg), 17 Mar. 1802
Double sheet 4to   4 pp.   *pmks* DARKING   18 MR 1802   18 MAR
1802   wafer
Addressed: Dr. Burney, / Chelsea College, / Middlesex.
Endorsed by CB: Tied up, unex- / amined, Apr. / 13th 1802 / 1802
Edited by FBA, p. 1, *annotated*: ⁑ (4)   Fearful Suspense relative to St.
Domingo expedition.   M. d'A. at Paris.

March 17. 1802

Another Letter has at length reached me, my dearest Father,
of the most interesting nature[1]—& which if I dared build upon
no future disappointment or draw back would make Me the
most grateful of Mortals—M. d'Arblay does not go to St.
Domingo!—Such, at least, is his present belief—but he has
written a very long Letter, with full details, which I have never
received, & which will explain his situation fully—alas—I have
been so long in a state of anxiety & discomfort, my mind dare
not yield at once to a joy like this—& till I have seen the details,
& know what to infer from them, I feel rather shook afresh all
over, than relieved. I *imagine* his positive assertion *never to bear
arms against Great Britain* must be the cause—but I know
nothing positively—& he writes in ⏐ such agitation of mind,

---

⁸ See L. 486, p. 164.
491. ¹ This was probably L. 488. It was apparently L. 485 that had not yet
arrived.

& deep depression of spirits, that I am unable to rejoice, though I am full of hope I ultimately *may* rejoice—but the heavy expenses he has incurred weigh him down—& at the alien office he was made to solemnly promise *Not to return hither for a Year—at least,*[2]—In this case, he seems to plan that the Child & I should go over to him, with M. Bourdois & Maria.— Indeed, at all events, if he does *not* go to that pestilential climate, St. Domingo, he meant we should pass the summer in France—But when I receive the promised Letter of detail, I can better understand & judge what must ensue. I have now only to wait with what patience I may—& try to keep Hope from mounting to Expectation. I had just taken my lodging— at *Twickenham*, Richmond proving too dear; & at [|] Twickenham Miss Cambridge had recommended me to a friend of hers, who would just have suited me, in all ways. This I must *untake* as well & handsomely as I can. My Cottage he charges me to still try to let *for a year*—it *was* to have been for *2 summers*, as he purposed—if he went to St. Domingo,—& returned— spending the *next* summer in France, to appease his good Uncle for the disappointment of our not going *this*.

I am sure I shall have your good & kind wishes, my dearest Padre, that this may not be a new illusion!—I *hope*, not *fear*, Buonaparte is unequal to being served by one who dares declare aloud he will never swerve from his own sense of right & principle—but this must be as yet kept to very confidential communication—should any thing get to the news papers of the affair, the consequence might be dreadful,—for all our papers Are translated & read by the 1er Consul. |

The sweet Amelia Angerstein writes word that my dearest Father was at Mr. Angerstein's,[3] looking, as usual, all animation, & in charming spirits, & full of entertainment—& that our dear Fanny P[illips] was in her best looks—

Heaven bless that dearest Father, & long long preserve his animation!—My Alex is well—Mr. & Mrs. Lock, from whose house I now write, desire their best & kindest Compliments to you, & their love to Fanny—who, I hear, was *well approved* by the very worthy Mr. Vansittart,[4] one of the Treasury—so

---

[2] Cf. L. 488, p. 170.
[3] Amelia *née* Locke, wife of John Angerstein, lived in Cumberland Place (L. 425 n. 4); his father John Julius (1735–1823), at 100 Pall Mall.
[4] Nicholas Vansittart (L. 425 n. 1), Secretary to the Treasury.

let her hold up her head—he is not only *rich*, but singularly good, charitable, & honourable. adieu, most dear Sir—*pray for me!* Your ever dutiful & affectionate

F. d'Arblay.

492   West Humble, 18 March 1802

To M. d'Arblay

A.L.S. (rejected Diary MSS. 5372–[75], Berg), 18 Mar. 1802
Double sheet 4to   4 pp.   wafer
Addressed: Au Citoyen D'Hermand, / Chef du Bureau des Consulats / Chez le Ministre des Relations / etrangeres. / Pour M. Darblay—À Paris
Docketed: France
Edited by FBA, p. 1, *annotated and date* 1802 *retraced*: 1802   Nº 16. / 2
Edited also by CFBt *and the* Press, *see* Textual Notes.

West Hamble—Mars 18th 1802

O mon ami! never did I so wish for Wings as at this moment! —I have just received the account of your disappointment[1]— & your sorrow & misery damp all my natural feelings—which, suffered to be uncontrolled, would give you at least *reflected* joy that might console you—I am all at a loss how to write—& nearly how to think!—If you *pine*, if your spirits sink, your strength will be over, & ill health & sadness will undermine all our comfort, & be as pestilential as the most pernicious Climate on Earth!—Would to God I were at least with you!— I am grieved to have even proposed taking off the interdiction here, now I have read your thoughts upon it, lest I should have distressed you—but the last Letter came first, & I had understood you only designed adhering to your Year, from *NECESSITY*: if it be, on the contrary, from your *judgement* of what is *right*, *I will* not one moment offer any pro or con to your *deliberation*. *I will* surely, on this occasion, accompany the Boods,[2] — only premising, I must positively pay my

492. [1] FBA had at length received M. d'A's letter of 2 Mar. 1802 (L. 485).
    [2] Antoine Bourdois and his wife Maria (*née* Burney), who were to set out for Paris on 10 Apr. 1802 (see L. 501, p. 205).

thirds of the whole expence of the Journey & voyage. You, now, can tell what that is—I have very serious reasons for refusing *to be taken by them*: the Poorer we are, my dearest Friend, the more oeconomical we must be in ourselves, but the prouder with others. I shall think nothing dear that can convey me to YOU, except what would degrade my own notions of what is due to your wife—i.e. a decorum which is instantly wanting, where PECUNIARY obligations are submitted to, even passively. Trust my foresight in this, mon Ami, & *believe* me, when we can talk it over, our opinions will be one. Mean while, for a little guide to my purse, endeavour to recollect enough of your expences with the good O'Kelleys[3] to give me some hint of what my thirds ought to be. *PRAY DON'T FORGET THIS.*

Now that I more compleatly understand your situation, I shall exert every means in my power to dispose of our dear Cottage for a year. It will, however, be very difficult to make any ⌐ one take it through the *Winter*, to relinquish it in the spring. But I must try what I can. I am now, perforce, in the hands of an appraiser, Morris,[4] to put it in some order. ⌐I cannot consent to have our dear Charles's beautiful Carpet to common use—I have therefore bespoke an ordinary Scotch one, to cover the best Parlour, & I doubt not but I must be at much expense in other articles to make the House let to any advantage. But I shall first wait an answer from the friend of Mrs. Bishopp,[5] before I proceed with the orders. I have now the Chimney piece in hand, it is impossible to even shew the best room in its present state. Ockely[6] is to compleat it, for our absence, by a moulding, which is to be painted in two Greens. The marble is now taken down, & Bliss[7] is to try if he [can] join it, apparently, by screws into the brick work. I have also given the Blinds you bought in London to Morris, to cut & mend them, & put new tassels, &c, & fit & put them up in the Parlour where some were much wanted, & new ones would come very

---

[3] M. d'A had shared a chaise with the O'Kellys in his travels from Greenwich to Dover (see L. 479, p. 148; and L. 485, p. 160).

[4] Apparently George Morris (*fl.* 1802–32) of Dorking, the 'upholsterer' who in an advertisement in *The Times* (7 Apr. 1802) was to offer Camilla Cottage for rent. See L. 496 n. 10.   [5] See L. 486 n. 1.

[6] Probably Samuel Ockley *or* 'Oclee' (1749–1809), the carpenter employed in the construction of Camilla Cottage in 1796–7 (iii, L. 122 n. 7).

[7] Possibly Benjamin Bliss (*fl.* 1792–1802) of Dorking, whose marriage (18 Aug. 1792) to Mary Gilliam (*c.* 1762–1814) is recorded in the parish records, as is also the baptism of their son Joseph (4 Jan. 1796).

high. Morris is the young man who prepared the rooms: Wilkinson,[8] his master, had left off Business in Dorking, & he is now principal himself, & very intelligent & reasonable. I have given him the ci-divant Bedside carpet (of Bookham) to sew together, & bind, for the little spare room. Do these details of my *furniture debuts* fatigue or interest you?⌐ I hope to turn, by application, into a tolerably good Upholsterer. Ah, my dearest —beloved friend! what would I not attempt to smooth the passage to our re-union?—

How kind is Mͤ D'Henin![9] I am quite charmed with her goodness. ⌐Speak for me to her, I beg—for it is in Truth I ought to thank her, & you know—too well!—my incapacity — — yet⌐ I hope—since we are to be a year in France, we are to have some place of *our own*? There is nothing I dread so much as the loss, & | nothing I covet so earnestly as the possession of our mutual, our happy, our inappreciable independence.— surtout, now that I shall so much want TIME AT *my own free & unaccounted for disposal.* — weigh that, my own beloved, & be cautious of any arrangements that may interfere with the unshackled leisure so necessary for our well doing. You, also, will, I have no doubt, enter upon some work to demand our old fashion & system of a scribbling Table in common. And I will no longer be *sauvage* to you if you wish me not, as to what progress I may make.—I think of nothing with satisfaction but how to soften to you a blow which—did not *YOU* so feel it, would be to *me* the first of blessings!—

It is barbarous to me that I dare not give way to [wh]at I want to write, lest I should wound where I most wish to heal!—

our dear Alex is quite well—I must not yet hint to him our plan, it would make him so wild with joy. My dear Father is

8 Possibly James Wilkinson, whose wife Hester was buried in Dorking on 12 Aug. 1802. London Directories of these years show a firm of Wilkinsons, up-holsterers.

9 M. d'A's remarks on the kindness of the princesse d'Hénin are lost, either in obliterations or in missing letters, but in a letter (Barrett, Eg. 3698, ff. 210–11b), dated Richmond 26 [Mar.] 1802, to FBA, the comte de Lally-Tolendal mentions a letter he has just received from the princesse expressing her pleasure in the prospect of meeting 'cette chère Cécilia' in Paris. On her departure for Le Bouilh, she goes on to say, 'je lui laisserai mon petit appartement qui sera à souhait pour le Mari & pr la femme'.

earnest with us to spend some time at Chelsea[10]—he knows nothing yet of your abortive voyage—I must now write it all around, especially to our ever steady Great *Friend*, who, I have reason to believe will be really disappointed in my not going into her neighbourhood.[11] Miss Cambridge has taken her own disappointment with so good a grace you would be quite enchanted could you see her Letters: yet she had built upon me for a Comforter in the declining health of her excellent Father, who seems suddenly falling into superannuation![12] This is a heavy calamity to his family, & more lamentable than Death.—

The good Miss Baker has written me twenty Letters,[13] of her joy in my approach, with her favourite little Alexander; but she, also, is so generous & disinterested in her nature, that all her regret will be sunk in *my* satisfaction, when your revived spirits permit me to be natural.— ⌐ ⌐Poor Maria is still by no means well, though not worse—still it is amazing how Bood— kind Bood, can enter into so many expedients to swell up his time, while she is in this state, as he means to return to France & quickly, there to abide! she has now, alas, hardly any *Letters*, after receiving them 3 times a week. But this will have a fair explanation, I doubt not, though it is mischievous en attendant. Sophy is yet with her.⌐

our own precious, bosom friends, of Norbury, seem now to think & breathe only for *us*, such is their interest, in my spirits & happiness, in our Boy's health, in your Letters & accounts, & in our house-letting, Grounds, & affairs. I have, indeed, so much now, continually, to consult them about, that I see them nearly as much for use as for consolation. Their sweetness & sympathy surpasses all description — & their AMELIA is truly but another part of THEMSELVES. *Their* joy in the late accounts has no scruple, & is truly exhilarating to see. They confess a dread of the CLIMATE, & of rash eagerness, so great, as to have been truly miserable to them.

⌐You bid me first, write to Joigny,—not by M. d'Hermand,[14] pray, in every Letter be explicit as to my direction how to

[10] CB's invitation is not extant.   [11] Queen Charlotte. See L. 479 n. 5.

[12] FBA's old friend Richard Owen Cambridge (i, L. 11 n. 2), wit and author, now 84 years of age, was to die in September of this year.

[13] Sarah Baker (i, L. 10 n. 6). These letters have not survived.

[14] See address (*supra*) and L. 450 n. 6.

address you. I conceive that M. D'Hermand has a delightful nature—I have taken a sort of partiality to his *ideas*, from his kind consideration for me in his triform billet, that reached me but to add to his kind former intercourse by Letter.—ᵖ mon ami! mon ami!—revive!—to revive wholly la plus reconnoissante des femmes! — — et la plus tendre—

Your F. d'A.

— — The Letter written upon your arrival at Paris is just now forwarded to me from Charles!! I have now in all received —3 while you were in England. 1 from Calais & from Paris, *3 Ventose*; *2 Mars*; *16 Ventose*; *17 Ventose*; *Duplicata, 17 Ventose, Triplicata*¹⁵ Thanks! Thanks! Thanks! — These last came all to[gether] & have made me a new creature—Poor Mᵉ O Kelly!¹⁶ how shocked I have felt for her!—I hope she is now again happy!

493

To Doctor Burney

[West Humble],
22 March 1802

A.L.S. (Berg), 22 Mar. 1802
Double sheet 4to   4 pp.   *pmks*   DARKING   2⟨ ⟩ MR 1802   23 MAR 1802   wafer
Addressed: Dr. Burney, / Chelsea College, / Middlesex—
Edited by FBA, p. 1, *annotated*: ✲· (5)   The expedition to Sᵗ Domingo annulled by Buonaparté.   Preparation for joining him at Paris with Alex.

22ᵈ March. 1802.

How is my life changed, my dearest Father, from a tranquility & quiet sameness that were almost unexampled, to perpetual anxiety & eventful expectations!—I feel, now, no security in any plan,—yet I have, now, Letters that *seem* definitive—& that, all things considered, I earnestly pray may prove so!—M. d'Arblay's commission for St Domingo has been

---

¹⁵ Of these seven letters, written since M. d'A's departure on 15 February, only five, Ll. 482 (19 Feb.), 484 (2 Mar.), 485 (2 Mar.), 488 (8 Mar.), and 489 (10 Mar.) are known to the editors.
¹⁶ See L. 485, p. 163.

annulled.—& the War Minister has written to him again, to desire, *puisque* he will not *servir contre la patrie de sa femme, qui peut encore s'armée contre la republique,* that he will ⌜ever⌝ regard his appointment & former Letters as *non avenues.*[1]

My dear—tormented—fate-persecuted M. d'Arblay is in deepest dismay & perturbation by this arrêt—for though he had neither wished for nor solicited this employment, yet, once having made his mind up to it as a professional duty, & a duty to his own future establishment—he had grown fond of it, & worked up his military spirit to its original tone—& if in this point he feels the change—what does he not experience from the cruel, useless expense into which he has been plunged!— 220 guineas he │ sunk here & by his journey to Paris—However, if his own mind & spirits will but recover, I shall bless God with my whole soul in gratefullest joy that here the mischief ends!—Nevertheless, he holds it incumbent upon him to remain upon the spot, lest he should seem again to hasten off, glad to depart, the moment the first difficulty occurred. A year, he says, he must now stay in France, & he desires that Alex & I will join him there immediately, that he may settle with me where & how to spend it, at Joigny, Paris,—or where. — — — But afterwards, he writes word that kind Bood is coming over very soon, & he will wait for our accompanying him & Maria, ⌜if they start speedily. Otherwise we must find a way, as he is absolutely without settlement or plan, &c till we arrive. I shall certainly far prefer going with Maria & Bood, but not *fear* going without them, as it is but one day to Dover, & after passing the sea, (which I shall fear with or without them)—the road from Calais to Paris must be as easily travelled as from │ hence to Bath—Yet—⌝ the whole scheme has a something tremendous in it!—But he!—what does he not merit from me? —the sacrifice he makes to me & my feelings robs him not only of present profit, but of all future rank & resource in his own Country—& in This he has none, & no chance! — — My gratitude to him passes all expression, for wretched indeed

---

493. [1] Having received on 18 March M. d'A's informative letter (L. 485) of 2 Mar. 1802 (with its critically definitive enclosures, i.e., copies of letters from Berthier and Dutaillis), FBA proceeded to convey the contents to her father, to her sister Esther (L. 494), and to her brothers Charles (L. 496) and James (L. 497), supplying in the first three instances quotations from Berthier's letter or that of the comte Dutaillis (see L. 485 n. 1 and Appendix).

would a contrary conduct have made me.—I long to shew you, my dearest Padre, the Letters, or copies he has sent me— they are truly interesting & curious. I shall bring them all with me, when I come to Chelsea, to pay a debt you delight me by claiming—& where I hope to be, under your dear roof, & in your loved society, to the moment of my departure.—I have much to do here, & must not stir till something is arranged, I have now Carpenters, upholsterers, gardeners, &c — — about, preparing the poor Cottage & grounds for giving us a right to demand a good Tenant.—⌐but what most heavily weighs upon me, is a Letter from Le Clerc, which I have just read, from St. Domingo, dated 9th, in which he complains of *5 artillery officers* having failed I him![2] I tremble lest this should tempt Buonaparte to pass by the declared condition, & accept Mr d'Arblay upon his own terms—as Berthier had already done!—God forbid! but I languish for another letter, of the date of these dispatches being received. *My* last date is *March 10th*[3] but these dispatches did not arrive till the *5th*— Bood is at Paris—but has not fixed his day for his return. M. d'A is hastening him with his utmost might.⌐ My Heart is truly heavy in going—from you & those I leave,—yet *this* is so much better than St. Domingo—that fatal, pestilential Climate! —that I feel it the far best thing which, in the present state of affairs, can happen.

⌐I write all this also to the Queen who (& the Princesses) deign to expect seeing me from Richmond![4] Miss Cambridge had after all, taken my lodgings!⌐ Thanks for your kind lines, my dearest Father, ⌐should anything new occur, I will write it instantly—but I fear I may not have rest!—My poor Mate & my[self] want it grievously—these last 3 months have [so]rely tried us. Alex is well—believe me, most dear Sir, your most truly affectionate

& dutiful F. d'Arblay.

My love to dear Fanny⌐

---

[2] FBA had evidently seen in *The Times* (20 Mar. 1802) a translation of General Leclerc's letter, dated Headquarters at Le Cap, 9 February (printed in *Le Moniteur Universel*, 15 Mar.). In this letter, the General complained bitterly, as he had in a series of letters (see C. L. R. James, op. cit., p. 304 and *passim*) of the lack of reinforcements, naming specifically a général de brigade, three chefs de brigade, and a chef de bataillon who had failed to appear. 'Are not the officers of engineers, like the other military men of the army, to march where honour directs?'

[3] This is L. 489.   [4] See L. 479 n. 5.

To Esther (Burney) Burney

A.L.S. (rejected Diary MSS. 5376–[79], Berg), 22 Mar. 1802
Double sheet 4to   4 pp.   *pmks*   DARKING   23 MAR 180⟨2⟩   wafer
Addressed: Mrs. Burney, / Beaumont Street, / Devonshire Place / London
Endorsed by EBB: 1802   answ^d 1802
Edited by ?FBA, CFBt, *and the* Press.

West Hamble, March 22^d 1802

I know well how my dearest Esther will feel for the mingled sensations—yet Joy which predominates over them all—when I tell her M. d'Arblay writes me word his *commission has been annulled,* in consequence of his own positive declaration, that though he would re-enter the army to fight against all *other* of his Country's Foes, he would *never bear arms against England.* They will listen, they say, to no *conditions* in the service, & therefore he must take his chance against *all* nations, or *renonçer à Jamais au service de France.*[1]

The generous sacrifice thus made to me, of interest, profit, honour*s*, (not *Honour*, dieu Merci!) I feel more strongly than any language can express—& shall think my whole life well spent in manifesting my gratitude; for, God knows, had he acted otherwise, I think I must have *buried myself alive,* had a new war broken out, & *he* commanded an expedition against This Country!—

Yet many are *my* drawbacks in *his* to comfort, & far enough has this transaction removed him from the tranquility he enjoyed before his first journey to Paris: the fatigue,—hopes—fears—struggles he has suffered—the disappointment of his renovated views to Fame & Fortune—& the enormous, now wholly useless expences ǀ he has [i]ncurred, which, so far from ultimately *adding,* as he had believed, to our income, now diminish it considerably, have chagrined him so as nearly to put him in a state of despondence. He is now, however, somewhat rising from it—& if once I see him recovered in spirits, God knows how little I shall ever think of our losses, & how

494. ¹ See L. 493 n. 1.

NOTHINGLY they are — even at this moment, compared with
the ease & peace which now result from them: for indeed, my
dearest Esther, the expedition was every way frightful to me—
not only for the *contention*, with a ferocious set of irritated, &
probably ill used africans, but the risks of the stormy Voyage,
& the far greater risks of the pestilential climate—for such, to
bilious constitutions, it generally proves—Yet—I dare not feel
even now secure—as he waits upon the spot, to see if they will
change, & determines there to abide for a year!—he desires
alex & ME to go over to him—in company with Maria & Bood,
if they go speedily; if not, to find some other means, that we
may hasten to him, as he will form no plan, no scheme, &
enter into no agreements, &c, till we meet, & can consult
together how we shall best spend the ¦ year—at Paris, Joigny,
or *where*, & *how*. I need not tell you how this consideration will
hasten my motions. Yet I own I am very cowardly in the scheme,
—& love not quitting my dear Father—*you*—& my other dear
Friends & Family for so long a time—but say not this to Maria!
—&, indeed, draw back as this is to my happiness, I yet would,
& eagerly, follow HIM to the furthest corner of the Earth, if so
only I could live with him. But after such hopes of living with
HIM, & yet in the bosom of my other friends, & native land —
this change will needs be grievous!

I had a note from Mrs. Bishopp[2] just now about the Cottage,
which her friend declines. She thinks it, I doubt not, too dear;
but the price was fixed by an Appraiser,[3] who told me he would
take upon himself the responsibility of its fairness. I shall now
put the affair into his hands as much as possible. I have been
doing, & am still doing, much to finish the furniture, & am
setting about putting the garden, also, into order. Mr. Lock
advises this; & though it will cost a good deal of money at the
instant, he is persuaded it will well pay it. How happy I am in
the COUNSEL of such a friend! whom I revere as much as I love!
I cannot MORE. M. Bourdois was but just returned to Paris
from Joigny *March 11th*,[4] when Maria ¦ last heard from him.
God send the business may be finished at St. Domingo before
the signing the Definitive Treaty![5] — I dread else, lest, when all

---

[2] See L. 486 n. 1.   [3] Probably George Morris (L. 492 n. 4).
[4] See also L. 489.
[5] The Peace of Amiens, establishing peace between France and Britain, was
signed on 25 Mar. 1802.

war & talk of it with this Country is over, M. d'Arblay may be still called upon to serve in the French Colonies!—*Five Artillery Superior Officers* are at this Moment demanded from the first Consul by the Commander in Chief at St. Domingo! — —6 —I may too easily be alarmed—but who, after What has twice happenned to me within 2 Months, upon a subject so close to my *vitals*, can wonder I shall be ill at rest till St. Domingo is subdued?—My dear Friends at Norbury Park desire their kind Love to you—I am but little there just now, yet see or hear from them Daily. I have a very tender Letter from Charlotte, who seems to write from your house,7 but dates not: if so, my kindest love & thanks to her, & tell her my present hopes, but that it is impossible for me to get to Brighton —though I will write soon—as I also shall immediately to our Brothers. I hope Mr. B[urney] & Amelia are well?8 & that you have good news of Richard & Blue?9 I could mix no subject with that of this Letter—but do not *feel* or *think* less on others— on all that concern my ever dear Esther, whose true & faithful & affectionate I am ever

F. d'A.

Maria is again better, yet never est[ablishe]d—I have much hope from the change of climate.

495   West Humble, 23 March 1802

To M. d'Arblay

A.L. (Berg), 23 Mar. 1802
Originally a double sheet 4to, of which the second leaf is missing and the left margin of the first leaf damaged   2 pp.
Edited by FBA, p. 1 *annotated and date* 1802 *retraced*: Nº 17/2

6 See L. 493 n. 2.
7 This letter is missing.
8 The polite letter of the time 'named' each member of the family likely to be present at the delivery of the letter. Thus, EBB's husband, Charles Rousseau Burney, and her daughter Amelia (i, p. lxix).
9 The Revd. Richard Allen Burney and his maiden aunt, Elizabeth Warren Burney (see L. 464 n. 5), now at Rimpton, Somersetshire

West Hamble, 23ᵈ Mars. 1802

Why cannot I fly to you instantly, my better Half—my
almost Whole?—I have just received yours of Mars. 17.¹—
& my whole Heart—whole soul yearn to answer it in person.
Your desire to hasten us penetrates me with the tenderest
feelings—& to hope we may brace again your shattered nerves
is my dearest consolation—The *'NOTHING'* which seems to
shock you, mon ami—do you not yet understand? alas, it was
far worse than nothing,—it was the deep disappointment of
a Hope I had involuntarily conceived from hearing, through
Mᵉ Huber,² you had been a week in Paris—I then flattered
myself the Expedition to St. Domingo had succeeded at once,
& that no other troops or officers would be sent,—&, consequently, that the separation so dreadful to me would not take
place: Thus much my Hopes & Imagination had suggested,
when I received a Letter which, by naming only common
[ma]tters, I concluded was written to keep me at peace simply
about your [hea]lth, & shew me all else went on as you had
expected, & therefore was [not] worth mentioning. Upon this—
I relinquished all my Castle-building, [bla]med myself for
erecting such airy structures,—& engaged my Lodgings
[*tear*]n! — — but what of regret, *now*, can I admit? though my
[fea]r so long uppermost, & my mind so lacerated by wretched-
ness, [*tear*] within seems still sore!— Ah mon ami! mon bien
aimé — Mon Ame! — que ne puis-je vous re-trouver tout de
suite? —I am unwilling to wait for any one. ⌐I have, besides,
received *no proposition* to join the party near us, & I feel that as
at least uncordial.—I shall want no carriage to travel to *you!*—¬
I knew not the spirit I could muster, till we were parted!—⌐I
only wish, if possible, to dispose first of our Cottage. I think, if
that were done,¬ I should run every risk to be again under
your protection. I am glad you are not gone to Joigny; ⌐we
should alter our plans before that journey, that we may give
no disappointment on our arrival by false expectations.¬ We
cannot be on a *visit* for a year, I should think, even at your
dear uncle's, though, ⎮ more & more I love the thoughts of
seeing him, & his Lines, which you copied,³ brought tears of
gratitude into my Eyes.—Do you think *other* lines did not also?
—Yes, that phrase, ⌐the¬ qu'il *ne considerait dans cette demarche*

495. ¹ This letter is missing.   ² See L. 487 n. 2.   ³ See L. 489, p. 174.

que[4]—&c surprised me, I own, into a flood of tears—for I had feared being regarded de mauvaise oeil tout à fait —& an expression so good humoured was so truly unexpected, that you would almost have imagined, for a while, it had pained me, from a too strong contrary effect.—you tell me no more of how M. de Narbonne has borne the *vaccination?* we all honour his courage, here, & doubt not its success.

The poor Alphonse![5] How shocked I have been at his early fate & for his poor unhappy Mother, though I never had seen her, & his poor Father!—Yet how I rejoice the benevolence of my best beloved h[as] spared the latter any self-regret at implacability!—What a pleasur[e] to you must that give! ⌐I will not fail to have enquiry made about the annual Register, nor to bring it, if it be to be found. I am glad you regain no worse Backers than those you name [*large tear*] is so exorbitant, & especially as there are some I [*large tear*] -bly being for myself. What can I do as to *old Letters, Papers, & MSS.?* I am undone if I may not carry a cargo with me. All your commissions shall be what I shall first pack up. Where am I to be when I arrive? I am hardly to undertake to set off to morrow! — —

I mean to pack the Books, one on another, in the deep Closet of the first little Parlour, & the upholsterer says he can put me a hook into the Door, & cover it with the same paper as the rest, so as to leave an appearance of no door at all. And there are quite closets enough in the house for one to be dispensed with by those not used to them *all.* I think one, well fixed, will hold all, & it is very⌐

I beg you in every fresh Letter to mention how you would have me direct.

[*the second leaf is missing*]

4 Bonaparte's comment, as reported to M. d'A by Lafayette and cited by M. d'A (L. 489, p. 173).

5 Alphonse-Louis-Nicolas de La Châtre (1779–1802), vicomte de Nançay, whom FBA had met at Juniper Hall and Norbury Park in 1793. He had died in San Domingo on 10 Feb. 1802 while serving as an aide-de-camp to Donatien-Marie-Joseph de Vimeur de Rochambeau (1755–1813).

His mother, Marie-Charlotte-Louise-Aglaé-Perrette *née* Bontemps (1762–1848), was now the wife of Arnail-François de Jaucourt (L. 446 n. 14), who as an *émigré* had been her companion at Juniper Hall (see Intro. ii). His father, Claude-Louis (1745–1824), comte de La Châtre, had served as colonel of the first *émigré* corps recruited in England (ii, L. 60 n. 3). Though acquainted with Alphonse's parents through SBP's Journals of 1792–3, FB had never met them.

To Charles Burney

A.L. (John Comyn, grangerized *Diary*, vi. 122), 24 Mar. 1802
Double sheet 4to   4 pp.   *pmks*   DARKING   ⟨ ⟩02   wafer mended
Addressed: Dr. Charles Burney, F. R. S. / Greenwich, / Kent.
Markings: arithmetic on address page.

24. March. 1802
West Hamble—

My dear Carlos,
A long & torturing suspense is at length—for *ME*, happily
terminated[1]—M. d'Arblay does not go to St. Domingo!—
Sing Te deum with Me, my dearest Charles. Indeed I know
not how I could have supported the eternal terrors, of various
kinds, that would have preyed, in succession, upon my mind.
See, too, by the reception of Le Clerc,[2] how false was the idea
that nothing was to be done, & the troops would be met, open-
armed, by Toussaint!

You know the Letter to B[onaparte][3]—the *conditions* are
deemed inadmissable. Buonaparte had meant to call M. D'a
back to the army, for the restoration of his rank, & the openning
to Fame & Fortune—but he had meant it *unconditionally.*—M.
d'Arblay is steady—& therefore The appointment is annulled.
It has been done, however, with civility, & even regret that
*his talents & his good will to his Country should be chained up by his
peculiar position.*—This is the expression of the aid de Camp of
the War Minister,[4] in enclosing the order of non-service from
Government. Buonaparte, also, has done justice to his Letter,
in so much as to say, to a Friend[5] sent to him by M. d'Arblay to

496. [1] In the receipt on 18 March of M. d'A's long letter of the 2nd (L. 485).
Cf. L. 493 n. 1.
  [2] The arrival of General Leclerc on 2 Feb. 1802 off the harbour of Le Cap and
the reception accorded him had been reported in *The Times* of 18, 19, 20, 22, 23
March. In spite of the opposition offered, the disembarkation was effected, and the
blacks, retreating to the mountains, set fire to the town. See also C. L. R. James,
op. cit.
  [3] M. d'A's letter to Bonaparte (see L. 478 n. 7; and Appendix I, Item 14).
  [4] The comte Dutaillis (L. 485 n. 1).
  [5] The 'Friend' was Lafayette, but, considering his reputation in England, FBA
apparently thought it politic to suppress his name. Even in France, the association
with Lafayette would not have advanced M. d'A's cause.

clear up the affair, that he understood his motives, & could
allow for them, without resentment or ill will: on the contrary,
he saw a frank & loyal Character—but could not employ
him.— |

But for the deep mortification this has caused M. d'A. & his
deep distress at the unavailing expence by which he has considerably *diminished* the poor income he hoped to have aug-
mented—*I* should be happier than I have been these two
years—but it is impossible to read his dejected Letters, &
suffer my own feelings to suffice for my satisfaction. However,
I hope when we meet, & he knows what I am spared, & I have
owned how ill I could have supported what seemed awaiting
me, I trust all will take a more chearful turn.

Many things conspire to determine him to pass a year, at
best, *now* in France— & he cannot, from peculiar impediments,[6]
too long to write, yet *insurmountable*, come over for Alex & me;
he desires us, therefore, to hasten to him. If M. Bourdois comes
quickly, & *returns* quickly, we are to go with him & Maria—[7]
if not,—by some other means: & he desires me, en attendant,
to consult with you, not only as a dear & kind — kind friend, but
as one, he says, who will most readily comprehend the necessity
of our re-union, for our mutual consolation after such anguish;
& indeed, for our affairs. |

What I wish you to help me in is — —

1st to let some one enquire after that conveyance you mentioned
to me that took passengers, for a given Sum, from London to
Paris. Does it exist? pray sift that out.[8]

2dly If *not*, whether you think, if Alex & I go to Dover, your
Friend Mr. Fector[9] could put us under the care of some

[6] Among which impediments was the English passport that would not admit
of a return from France within a year (L. 485, p. 161).

[7] In L. 485, p. 162, and L. 489, p. 174, M. d'A had suggested that Fanny should
travel with Antoine Bourdois and his wife. But see L. 495, p. 190.

[8] With an eye to 'demand', that is, to the thousands of English travellers who
were waiting only for the Peace to be signed to set out for France, one bookseller
at least, R. Phillips, 71 St. Paul's Churchyard, as Charles was likely to know,
had got out *A Practical Guide during a Journey from London to Paris . . . illustrated with
Maps and Useful Tables* (1802), which, to be sold 'by all the booksellers in London,
Brighton, and Dover', offered a section (pp. 20–2) on 'Modes of Travelling'. One
could travel 'By private Conveyances' (that is, by post), 'By the Diligence from
Calais', or 'By the Diligence all the Way'. It was this last diligence, setting out
from the White Bear, Piccadilly and costing £4. 13s. for each passenger, that FBA
was to take.

[9] John Minet Fector (c. 1754–1821), a wealthy banker of Old Dock, Strand
Street, Dover, High Sheriff of Kent, and owner of Kersney Abbey on the London

honest *man*, whom he could trust for our Guardian, with a proper consideration; to take care of us to Calais? For at Calais M. d'Arblay, in that case, would meet us. But he is totally against our crossing the strait without a male protector.

Should you not be able to procure me this information, my dearest Charles, write if only an *O*! to keep me from suspense, as I am so situated that I must then find some other means as quickly as possible.

I am going to have my Cottage advertised,[10] It has been kept back as yet, from wavering hopes of a return!—My lodgings were actually taken by Miss Cambridge at Twickenham! What a life of change & anxiety & uncertainty I have lived these last 3 Months! — adio, my dear F.R.S.[11] —My kind love to Rosette & Carlino, & best coms. to Mrs. Bick[nell]— |

pray enquire to Mr. Paynes[12] for two odd volumes of annual Registers—one, for 1759—the other 1782.

I am desired to take them with me for a lady, Me de Luynes[13] ci-divant Duchesse

poor Maria is still very far from well—

Alex is well.

road. Famous for his lavish hospitality, he had entertained, according to his obituary (*GM* xci[1]. 573), four of the 'greatest reigning monarchs in Europe', including Alexander I, Louis XVIII, and the Prince Regent.

For his truly 'Old English entertainment', of which, among the Burneys, Charles was most likely to have known, see the accounts of the barons of beef (2,514 lbs.), the barrels of ale, the processions, flags, ensigns, banners, and bands marking the celebrations of a reception given on 27 Oct. 1820, in *A Short Historical Sketch of the Town of Dover* . . . (Dover, 1828), pp. 207 ff.

[10] The advertisement for Camilla Cottage duly appeared in *The Times* (7 Apr. 1802): 'SURRY. — To be LET / and entered on imme / diately, a small Modern COUNTRY RESIDENCE, fitted / up in the cottage stile, with 5 acres of garden, orchard, pleasure, / and meadow land, in a rural and healthy situation, between / the Town of Dorking, and the beautiful Vale of Mickleham, in the / centre of many romantic and extensive prospects, 22 miles from / London, and a quarter of a mile from an Inn on the London Road, / where horses, &c. may stand at livery, there being no coach-house / or stables on the Premises; for the term of 12 or 18 months. Ad / dress G. Morris, Upholsterer and Auctioneer, Dorking, Surry.'

[11] Charles was elected in this year a Fellow of the Royal Society.

[12] Thomas Payne (1752–1831), the younger, bookseller, Castle Street, next the Mewsgate.

[13] See L. 469 n. 8.

West Humble, 26–28 March 1802

To James Burney

A.L.S. (PML, Autog. Cor. bound), 26–28 Mar. 1802
Double sheet large 4to   3 pp. trimmed   *pmks*   DARKING   31 MAR
1802   wafer
Addressed: Capt. Burney, / N° 72 / Margaret Street / Cavendish Square /
London

West Hamble, March 26. 1802

I know well with what satisfaction you will hear—for my
sake, my dear James, that M. d'Arblay does not go to S^t
Domingo. I am so excessively hurried by incessant employment
relative to my house, that I have no time to enter into particulars,—except to satisfy what might else become uneasy to
your curiosity & interest.—namely, that it appears the Ministers
had never made known to the first Consul the conditions of
M. d'Arblay's acceptance of service—his own Letter was his
first information—& it was followed by the annulling his
appointment. — — Not, however, in wrath—he has done
justice to the feelings & motives of M. d'A. but declared he
must be served *unconditionally*—or to that effect—but I will try
to get time for reading you the history. I shall go to Chelsea
as soon as my house business is arranged, & thence I will see
you as speedily as I can, & shew you copies of all the Letters
that have passed.[1] I, mean while, am as happy as it is possible
to be while M. d'Arblay is otherwise! but he is painfully
oppressed by this whole business, & mortified by the result, &
afflicted at the useless expences which again diminish our poor
Income, by the very acts which he thought would augment it!
He desires me ⌐ to go over to him, with Alex, in company with
M. Bourdois & Maria, if they go *soon*; if not, he will find us some
other companions. Do you know whether any conveyance is
set up, as before the War, for carrying passengers from London
to Paris, at a fixed expence?[2] Poor Maria is so indifferent, that

---

497. [1] Comparison with Ll. 493, 494, anf 496 to CB, EBB, and CB Jr. respectively,
illustrates how the content can be modified or varied according to the recipient
and the expected reaction. In no letter, however, does FBA mention much less
stress, the interdict of a year on d'Arblay's return to England, a condition imposed
by the Foreign Office in granting his passport to France (see Appendix, p. 460).
[2] The same query FBA had put to CB Jr. (see L. 496, p. 193).

I fear she will not be able to travel so soon as we ought to go —
for you may believe how I long to see & thank one to whom I
OWE such sacrifices.

If Sophy cannot stay till M. Bourdois arrives, Maria builds
upon seeing Sally,³—& has some hopes of you—I have heard
from M. d'Arblay almost daily, of late—he is harrassed &
unwell, & I am & shall be ill at ease till I join him. Particular
reasons determine to remain a year, now, in France, the chief
part of which we shall spend at Joigny, at his good Uncle's.
That the *fie for shames*⁴ did not get to him, is the only piece of
good fortune, he says, that has happenned to him since he left
England.

God bless you, my dear Brother—My kind love to Sally—
Alex is riotously well.

ever truly yours, F. d'A.

My Cottage is to be advertised this week, or next.⁵ |

March 28.

I open my Letter to add a few words—as it missed Friday's
post,⁶ & yesterday there was none—

I have just received a Letter from M. d'Arblay to tell me
he has applied to M. de Lally, his old friend, & school fellow,
to take charge of Alex & me to Paris, with a little Mlle de
Chavagnac, a Child under the care of Mrs. Locke.⁷

This will be an admirable opportunity. I have so much to do
here, & am so anxious to get the house parted with ere I set off,
that I know not when I can get away, but I shall write you a
note the day after my arrival at Chelsea. We shall go to France
as soon as Mr de Lally receives his next Letters. I am hurried
inexpressibly.

My love to all you or Sarah meet with of our kin—Have you
ever been able to ask for my Letters to poor Kitty Cooke?⁸
I should be truly glad to recover them. |

³ Sarah Harriet Burney (1772–1844), about Maria's age, was still living with
her half-brother JB (see iv, L. 297, pp. 214–17; and *passim*).
⁴ An allusion lost with M. d'A's missing letters.
⁵ See L. 496 n. 10.   ⁶ Friday 26 March.
⁷ M. d'A's letter to FBA asking her to travel with the comte de Lally-Tolendal
is missing. See further L. 498 and n. 2; also L. 437 n. 3.
⁸ Papilian Catherine Cooke (*c.* 1731–97), who, with her aunt Sarah Hamilton
(*c.* 1705–97), ran a boarding-house at Chessington Hall, the favourite retreat for
many years of CB and his family (*ED*, i. lxi–lxii, 322–7; *HFB*, p. 121; i, L. 22 n. 4).
FB's letters to 'Kitty', one of her earliest friends, have not been recovered.

To M. d'Arblay

A.L.S. (rejected Diary MSS. 5380–[83], Berg), 28 Mar. 1802
Double sheet 4to   4 pp.   page 2 has six lines of crosswriting   wafer
Addressed: au Cⁿ D'arblay, / Rue de Miromenil, / Hotel Marengo, / À
Paris
Edited by FBA, p. 1 (5380), annotated: N° 18 / 1 17: / 3 and the date March
28ᵗʰ 1802 retraced and 1802 framed
Edited also by CFBt and the Press.

March 28ᵗʰ 1802

Amelia—the sweet lovely Amelia is safe — & blessed with
a little Girl![1] —This delicious news arrived with another
scarcely second to it, that M. de Lally, in the kindest manner,[2]
yields to your proposition. What a Breakfast this gave us at
Norbury Park! ⌐this Morning.⌐ I am indeed happier than any
thing now can make me till we meet. ⌐ But that will not be so
soon as you had planned—& far—far later than I could wish—
but yet as quickly as I really believe I could be ready.—so much
remains to be done, from my constant uncertainty, till within
these few days, whether some new change might not render all
positive expectations abortive—Mardi the 13ᵗʰ is the Day!
M. de Lally has paid nothing, I eagerly hope, till these present
are setting out.⌐

I will do my utmost to observe all your commissions, except
the requiring ⌐Charles⌐ to advance such a sum for 3 months.

___

498. ¹ Amelia Angerstein's daughter Caroline was born in Great Cumberland
Street on 25 Mar. 1802 (see GM lxxii. 372).
    ² This is the letter, dated Richmond 26 Mar. 1802 (see L. 492 n. 9), in which
the comte de Lally-Tolendal, after mentioning the request that he had just
received from d'Arblay ('qui, grace à Dieu, ne va plus à St. Domingue'), goes on to
explain that his return to France will be delayed for a fortnight or more. 'C'est
mercredi seulement que je livre ma maison à celui qui l'achette avec les meubles . . .
J'ai ensuite des affaires de la dernière importance à terminer . . . Mais il me semble
que vous partez pour un an et j'espère que les amis qui vont vous regretter con-
juront un peu avec moi, pour vous retenir quelques jours de plus.'
He looks forward to seeing his daughter and his friends, yet his 'Départ d'Angleterre sera triste. Je quitte avec une profonde douleur ce beau et bon pays, les
hommes qui l'habitent, leur loix qui le gouvernent, Ma douce et Noble indépen-
dance et le voisinage du sanctuaire de Norbury'. 'Il me sera bien doux d'être votre
Chevalier', he concludes, 'et le Tuteur de voyage de vos deux jolis Enfans. Mais
je tremble que vous ne puissiez m'attendre.'

That I really cannot do! forgive me, my dearest of friends,—
I have no courage of that sort—& never shall gain it, as my
judgement revolts from such sort of obligations as much as my
pride & my inclination. ⌐ ⌐Whether I shall be allowed to
receive ANY of my pension when abroad, I am not sure—
certainly not without first signing, at the *given date* of every
first quarter, how can I ask another to run this risk?—as to
Coutts, you can draw upon him through his Banker in Paris,
but I will enquire who that is, & how it is to be drawn.⌐ I
grieve sincerely not to comply, but indeed it would be a pain
so severe, & so totally against all my professions, opinions, &
conduct, that I know not how to set about it. I pray you let us
do the best we can with our own simple & actual income! I see
nothing but mortification, coldness, changed manners, from
all who assist in money matters. The *ease* of equality is lost; one
side *fears* being assuming, & the other seeming humbled &
neither, in ALL I have seen, are, thenceforth, perfectly natural
& free. Do not be angry, my beloved — indeed what I say is from
long & strong observation — & what I feel is insurmountable,
to any thing but a direct command, ⌐ which I trust you will not,
where you know it would be so hard to me, issue. Let US wait
the 3 months—& then enjoy, as well as possess, our right.

What a delightful *voisinage* you place me in!—& M. de Lally
has written me the sweetest Letter![2]—& will undertake,
he says, ⟨M⟩es *jolis Enfans* I will surely try to see our steady
& exalted Great Friend, & her lovely daughters.[3]—Miss
Cam[bridge] & Miss Baker demand a Day here before I go.—
My Father—deeply disappointed in my departure, though
rejoiced in your *non* departure demands a MONTH—I shall not,
however, I cannot take *one Hour* from the time M. de Lally
will himself be ready. My impatience is almost trembling—&
my hurries are very *head-aching* between times, but *light hearting*
always, yet so shaken have I been, I am always cold & terrified
as I open your Letters, though I *receive* them with a glow of
rapture.—Ah, mon ami, dieu nous preserve from further
struggles!—I think, indeed, I should sink under any more: or,
at ⟨least⟩, banishing all the joy of life, HOPE, seek, & fall into
a calm apathy, that might compose my mind, by annihilating
my feelings. ⌐My indispensable friends are in the ⌐ utmost

3 The Queen and the Princesses.

delight that I go only with a protector—& though sad in parting with Adrienne,[4] rejoice it is with Alex & me she quits them. The chere petite is enchantée & desesperée tout à tour. I am obliged to purchase several articles for the poor house—new— but, which I am told are indispensable for residence—& Haynes[5] is to work up 3G^s in the larder! & we shall not be able to clear *in course* of the first half year, but it was necessary— The court yard MUST be paved from Gate to Gate, & from the kitchen, to the tool house—& Gravel laid around the house, &c, & a new Bed for the Book room, as *only ourselves* could do with one large Bed. No one, else, will come—However, we shall enjoy the improvements afterwards. *Mr. Sharpe,*[6] an acquaintance of my Father's, rode hither to see the place this Morning. I fear it will not be completed before I go. I have written to *White.*[7] How can I get Letters for Mr. Jackson?[8] I never see any one, & I except Monday for business ⟨visits to⟩ France. I am while *here* upset every instant, but I make my draft note immediately. I know some of his family. Mrs. Damer & Miss Berry[9] are going soon. I must now write to my Father, Brothers, sisters, &c—

Also M. de Lally—they will all be reviving—go or stay— I am raving I go so late!—Poor Maria is much the same— I don't think it possible to extract the quittance before I go. Every business is much *charged* for in the monnies. I shall enquire all I can whether I may have quittance sent me abroad—[n]

---

[4] Adrienne de Chavagnac, now aged 6, whom the Lockes were now returning to her father (see L. 437 n. 3).

[5] The Dorking registers of these years show families by the name of Haines; e.g. Robert, whose son Charles was born on 30 June 1803.

[6] Richard Sharp (1759–1835), merchant, man of affairs, M.P. (1806–12), known as 'Conversation Sharp'. His clubbable talents earned him the friendship of men like Dr. Johnson and Burke. A resident of Mickleham, Sharp had at one time complained of the 'ugly house built by D'Arblay just near them', a complaint provoking Sheridan's facetious suggestion that it be packed off 'out of the country under the Alien Act'. See Thomas Moore, *Memoirs*, iv, 312.

[7] Possibly John White (*fl.* 1801–17), 'upholsterer' and auctioneer of Storey's Gate, Westminster, with whom FBA seems to have stored sundry chattels (see ix, Ll. 950, 1052).

[8] Francis James Jackson (L. 470 n. 3), Minister Plenipotentiary to France.

[9] Anne Seymour Conway (1749–1828), the sculptress, daughter of Field Marshal Henry Seymour Conway (1721–95). She had married in 1767 John Damer (1744–76), eldest son of Joseph Damer (1717/18–98), cr. Viscount Milton of Milton Abbey and Earl of Dorchester (18 May 1792). See Walpole, xi and xii *passim*; also *DNB*.

The Hon. Mrs. Damer (see also i, L. 3 n. 113) and Mary Berry (iv, L. 389 n. 5) had set out for France on 8 March. See Berry, ii. 123.

[Marginal writing]

⌐Speak for me to all you have interested in my favour— chiefly & most gratefully to Mᵉ d'Henin,[10] whose generous & delicate kindness delights all at Norbury as much as myself.

Thanks for my chaise directions which I shall read to M. de Lally—

Don't fear Alex, he is of an Age to regard a future in French, *in France*, with excitement, positively.

Mrs. Lock went immediately to Town, & she continues there. Mr. Lock has a cold, & is forced to stay—Augusta nurse to him. I now go to Tea & supper & dress & when quiet after— much packing.⌐

[Cross-writing]

We are delighted at the non departure—particularly William & Amelia—who both feared the Climate would be fatal — O mon ami what will be ever hard to me, when I think of that escape! They all think it would have killed *ME* here & *YOU* there! & Mrs. Lock says she had even *not loved* you for going!— & *Mr.* Lock's spirits were such as to cruelly hurt him. Heaven preserve him with a deep pang I shall leave him.

499   [West Humble, ?*post* 28 March 1802]

To M. d'Arblay

A.L., fragment (pasted to L. 498), *n.d.*

A cutting (3·2 × 7·1″) from an unidentified letter, the remainder of which is unlocated.

The letter was evidently edited in the original by FBA, who obliterated part of it. Later the above cutting was excised presumably by CFBt who used it as a substitution for the lines obliterated by FBA on the first page (5380) of L. 598.

[top of page cut away]

I have this moment received our certificate of my greatest earthly happiness[1]—& that which all my hopes & feelings fix

---

[10] See L. 492 n. 9.

499. [1] A certificate of the marriage of Frances and 'Alex: Gabl: Pieuchard D'arblay', which took place on 28 July 1793 at the Church of St. Michael, Mickle-

for my view of that to which I humbly—but fervantly look forward.—And with it, the note from the pious Mr. Andrews,[1] so singularly kind & flattering, of his regret in my departure, & his earnest desire of my resuming my pen, for reasons which he deigns (can I use any other word for a Clergyman of his character) to think serious, that I am truly penetrated by his good opinion, & feel it a Spur of that sort which most pleasantly urges me on. How glad I am to receive it just when all my wishes go to that point!—my best beloved! your exhortation upon that subject is always present to me, but Time, at this moment, is never mine. Secure it me when we meet! I promise to use it as *you* LIKE, & no longer continue my own *farouche* method.

[*remainder of page cut away*]

[*The verso of the cutting concerns Maria and her plans to join her husband Antoine Bourdois in Paris*]

ᴨpreparations, so heavy, to her, to make in so short a time. She nearly fainted from hurry & distress on coming into the house, & between her desire to comply with a wish of Bood's, & her dread of her inability, she was so much agitated as to seriously alarm me. What is she to do about the Books, the images, & the papers, the plate? the servants, the house, & her immense quantity of linen? &c She is so unfit for undertaking what would undo even ME — so much stronger than herself—ᴨ

[*remainder of page cut away*]

[*Cross writing, the ends of the lines being cut away*]

  I proposed Maria to take Adri[enne] [for fear]
of crowding M. de Lally, Maria th
overpower her: & that she ought to
she finds ⟨necessary⟩. This in
at Dover, & thence they together
Alex is
Speak
but the

ham. A facsimile of the entry in the registers is printed in *Juniper Hall*, p. 166. The Revd. Gerrard Andrewes (L. 432 n. 3) was at this time the rector.

To Doctor Burney

A.L.S. (Diary MSS. vi. 5384–[87], Berg), 30 Mar. 1802
Double sheet small 4to   4 pp.   *pmks*   DARKING   MR   1802   red
wafer
Addressed: Dr. Burney, / Chelsea College, / Middlesex —
Edited by FBA, p. 1 (5384), *annotated*: ⁙ (6)   Preparations for going to
France   M. de Lally
Edited also by CFBt *and the* Press.

March 30. 1802.

Now, indeed, my dearest Father, I am in an excess of hurry
not to be exceeded by even any of your's — — I have a Letter
from M. d'Arblay to tell me he has written to M. le Comte
de Lally Tolendahl,[1] to beg him to be my Chevalier, & conduct me & his little Boy to him: & M. de Lally sets out the
13th of April!—M. Bourdois has so much still to do in Paris,
preparatively to fetching Maria, that he cannot fix his day, &
Maria wishes him to make some stay here when he arrives. He,
also, desires not to hasten back immediately. To wait his time
is therefore, impossible, the unsettled state of M. d'Arblay, &
many circumstances belonging to it, considered. He has already
taken us an Apartment, to date from the *5th of April*,[2] in Paris,
where he has reasons for remaining some time, before we go
to his good Uncle, at Joigny. Just as I ¦ received this instruction,
Charles wrote to offer to conduct us to Dover, & see us safe on
board. I am truly sensible of his kindness, but hope he will
rather come & peep at us at Whitsuntide when he can stay
a few weeks,—than at Easter when he could not even cross the
Water—I could not, out of our own family, have a guide &
companion I should prefer to M. de Lally, who is one of the
most amiable men breathing, & of the highest principles, &
most entertaining; & who was a school fellow, at the College
d'Harcourt,[3] with M. d'Arblay. All you say is but too true, but
I must turn to the best side I can! I am trying to fit our Cottage

500. [1] M. d'A's letter to the comte de Lally-Tolendal and the letter (possibly
that of 17 March, referred to in L. 495) to FBA suggesting that he should escort her
to Paris are missing.   [2] Hôtel Marengo, 1185, rue de Miroménil.
    [3] The Collège d'Harcourt, founded in 1280 and enlarged in 1682, had in 1790
five hundred students. Closed in 1793, it was rebuilt in 1814 and in 1820 resumed
its functions under the name Collège Saint-Louis.

for a good Tenant. M. Lock advises me to spend a rather considerable sum upon it, for that purpose, as he says no one else will take it, & the whole advantage of possessing it will be lost. I have, to day, agreed with a Bricklayer to pave a path through our Court Yard, & a Gardener is sewing peas, beans, &c, & weeding, & an upholsterer is finishing to furnish the rooms. | Every body in this neighbourhood says this will well answer. A Gentleman yesterday sent to beg to see the house & grounds, on the score of being an acquaintance of *your's*; I complied, of course. He said he was Mr. Sharp,[4] & seemed a pleasant & sensible man. I know not if it will suit him but however, alterations & improvements added, I have no fear of letting it. The beauty of the situation is very uncommon, & though slight, it is new, tight, healthy, & modern. I am to take the little sweet Child with me you saw here one day, M[lle] de Chavagnac,[5] whose Father, le Comte de Chavagnac, has desired her restoration! My kind Mrs. Lock is almost in affliction in parting with her, though glad of an opportunity of sending her with friends the poor thing knows & loves. I fear, I have so very much to do here, that I shall have a very, very short enjoyment of my beloved Father at Chelsea, but I shall get there as soon as possible, & stay there to my last moment. M. de Lally offers to fetch me hence, but I shall entreat it may be from Chelsea. I have a thousand things, & very curious ones, to tell you, but I | must defer them for *vive voix*. I am grieved I cannot write to our dear Fanny & pray, with my kindest love, tell her so. I am really bewildered & almost trembling with *hurry*, & with *what I am going to undertake*! yet through all, I bless God every moment of my life that M. d'Arblay went not to that pestilential Climate! bilious as he is, naturally, every body that knows St. Domingo, now owns that he had *hardly a chance* for safety, independant of tempests in the Voyage, & massacres in the mountains. May I but be able to console him for all he has sacrificed to my peace & happiness, & no privation will be severe, so that at our stated period, Michaelmas twelvemonth, we return to my Country, & to my dearest— dearest Father, whom Heaven bless & preserve,

prays his dutiful, affectionate & grateful
& devoted Daughter F. d'A.

[4] Richard Sharp (L. 498 n. 6).   [5] Adrienne de Chavagnac (L. 437 n. 3).

I do ALL — ALL I can to keep up my courage—or, rather, to *make up* & when I feel faultering—I think of St. Domingo!— Mrs. Damer & Miss Berry[6] are gone to Paris. I am quite solaced to hear of *women* going *thither*. If you should happen to know *Mr. Jackson*,[7] or any of his friends, it would be of great import for me, dearest Sir, if you could possibly promise me a Letter to him, I should feel more *English*, & better protected— |

P.S. I will write again when I can fix my day—which I fear will be late in next week.

501   West Humble, 4 April 1802

Conjointly with Alexander d'Arblay
To M. d'Arblay

A.L. & A.N. (Barrett, Eg. 3693, f. 238-b, with P-tab, f. 237), 4 Apr. 1802. Originally a double sheet 4to, of which the second leaf (i.e. the address cover) is torn away and missing   2 pp.
Edited by FBA, p. 1, annotated and year 1802 circled: N° 8   N° 18/2
Edited also by CFBt.

West Hamble, April 4. 1802

I have just received (N° 12) my beloved Friend[1]—& I can hardly allow myself time for writing even to you, now, so supremely busy I am in preparing to fly to you. —ᴦadjust to a little delay as yet. as I ⟨conclude⟩ I have so much to do as nearly to demand night as well as day—ᴨ Tuesday week!— from the moment I set out, I shall feel already with you— I shall get to town as soon as possible—to Chelsea I mean, ᴦto arrange with Mr. Coutts & M[athias].[2] I leave orders for him, to deposit it, for I have no carriage & shall be very helpless—

---

[6] See L. 498 n. 9.   [7] See L. 498 n. 8.
501. [1] This letter is missing.
[2] Thomas Coutts, the well-known banker, and Thomas James Mathias (iii, L. 157 n. 6), the Treasurer to the Queen's Household. FBA hoped to make arrangements with respect to the quarterly payments of her pension of £100.

but⟍ my chief anxiety is to see our generous Friend³—I go to
Mr. Locke every other Evening to Tea, & return early next
morning, by which Means I see him daily—alas—alas!—so
thin! so weak he is!—he cannot now stir out from an obstinate
Cold, & he grows daily more delicate! Amelia is delightfully
well, & her sweet Mother is with her. ⌐I have got Letters for
Mr. Narbonne—but fear he will be run away ere I arrive.⌐⁴ I
have 1000:0000 things to say—but perhaps *in a fortnight* I may
speak them!— mon ami! —what joy is bounding in my poor
heart in a prospect such as this of an end to so much grief!—
your eagerness makes me long, sometimes, to leave *all* unfinished, instead of *half*, & set off; but I will not delay M. de
Lally one minute—all that is incomplete on Mardi week, shall
be left so—but what I *can* effect in the mean time, shall surely
be done. Alex is quite well, & ¹ shall take my pen—or a better—
to his dear Father—& scribble at will—⌐I have no time for
line drawing—⌐⁵ How rejoiced I was to see Bood I can hardly
tell you—his arrival was positively *necessary* to Maria, & I hope
will recover her. ⌐They set out on *Saturday*,⁶ & will go post—
therefore you will see them first, unless wind & waves detain
them, & then we shall all sail together. Pray thank M. de
Chav[agnac] for a very polite Letter.⁷ I will take the same care
of the dear little Adrienne as of Alex—though not with the
same feeling!—⌐ I repose so little, & am now so tired, I believe
I shall require a month's rest, ere I quit my new Apartment.
I am delighted at the Servante you mention—how kind of you
to secure me one who can work, & at her needle—Thanks,
thanks, thanks!—

Mr. Locke's tenderest remembrances—

⌐Bood approves my repository for the Books, which I have
just shown him—He & Maria & Sophy ⟨called⟩ here this
minute—

I hope to write in my next that I shall write here no more.⌐
Heaven bless my Heart's first best friend!—

---

³ Queen Charlotte.
⁴ FBA may have heard of the comte de Narbonne's intended trip to Trieste,
where his mother, wife, and daughter were staying. He was not to leave for Trieste,
however, until June 1803 (Dard, p. 143).
⁵ That is, guide lines to assist Alex's efforts in calligraphy.
⁶ Bourdois had now acquired an apartment at 4, rue de Choiseul, and the
couple were to set out by post for Paris on Saturday 10 April.
⁷ The letter from Louis-Vigile, comte de Chavagnac (iii, L. 201 n. 5), is missing.

[By *Alexander*]

Mon cher Papa how happy I Shall be to see you but do not think we are on the road for Mama has not got her things with her. ⌐Maria (Bood) goes on Saturday and I saw her to day¬ *dear* Papa how I long to see you dearest Papa. ⌐this is sunday¬

502   [43 Beaumont Street,
pre 11 April 1802]

To Charles Burney

A.L.S. (The Hyde Collection), *n.d.*
Double sheet 8vo   1 p.   *pmks*   T.P.P. / High St. M.bne   12 AP 1802
12 AP 1802   wafer
Addressed: Dr. Charles Burney, / Greenwich, / Kent
Docketed in pencil: 470
Dated in pencil: 1802
Docketed in pencil, p. 1; 4 / ..10

My dearest Charles—you will come I trust to embrace me on *Sunday*[1]—& if possible let me know *when,* as I am engaged & have business more than it is easy to imagine.—I go on Tuesday Morn[2]—& have not one moment sure—but will *make* it so for the time you can fix—I hope to see also dear Rosette & carlini— but let me know—& don't let me miss a farewell—

I have all my affairs with Bankers—Mathias[3]—passports— commissions—& leave takings, to do—& have *hardly any head left on my poor shoulders*—but much of Heart beneath them— where warmly I keep you a place forever—witness

F d'Ay.

Kindest Comp[ts] to Mrs. Bicknel[4]
I have brought Martin[5] the last offering of poor West Humble —some ancient Walnuts & Hedge nuts—

502. [1] On 11 April. FBA had evidently come to London on the 8th or 9th and, as the postmarks of her letters indicate, she was staying with her sister Esther in Beaumont Street.
[2] FBA meant to leave for France on Tuesday 13 Apr.
[3] Treasurer of the Queen's Household (L. 501 n. 2).
[4] The housekeeper at CB Jr.'s establishment (i, L. 7 n. 18).
[5] JB's son, Martin Charles Burney, now about 14 years old, and attending CB Jr.'s school at Greenwich.

RECOLLECTIONS

502a [*c.* 12 April 1802]

An exercise in French (Berg), being an account of an evening spent at
Mrs. Crewe's villa at Hampstead before FBA's departure for France.
Written at Passy in the spring of 1805 in a cahier in a brown mottled
paper cover, 15 pp. (*c.* 7·3 × 4·3″)
Corrections, supplied at the bottom of the pages by M. d'A., have not
been incorporated in FBA's text.

3ᵐᵉ sem. Avril

Comme je n'ai rien à cet instant à vous conter de nouveau,
puisque je vous ai tout dit de vive voix, et comme il faut conter,
puisque c'est tout juste ce qu'il y a de plus difficile à faire, je
vais vous parler de ma dernière visite, c'est à dire de ma rentree
dans le beau monde, chez Mᵉ Crewe,[1] deux ou trois jours
avant mon départ de Londres. C'étoit avec mon cher Pere &
Fanny P[hillips][1] que je me rendis à cette assemblee, où Mᵉ
Crewe m'avoit invitée quand elle avoit appris que je fus chez
mon Pere. Mᵉ Crewe nous reçu le mieux du monde, et, comme
à son ordinaire, avec le meilleur ton. Elle m'a fait approcher
du feu, & me plaça sur un sofa la plus commode pour une
frilleuse. Mon Pere se plaça lui meme près du piano, où étoit à
chanter et à jouer Mˡˡᵉ Crewe,[2] & Fanny P. resta pres de moi.
Puisque tout de suite, Mᵉ Crewe me presenta M. Crewe son
mari,[3] que je n'avois jamais vu, et qui est fort peu vu par ses
amis, puisque il se donne presque tout à fait à la politique, et
aux amis de celui qu'il adore en ce ⎮ genre, M. Fox.[4] Il m'étoit
extremmement poli, et presque plus que poli, car il avoit un
air qui annonçoit quelque chose d'amitié. Il s'assit à mon
côté, et nous causâmes assez gaiment ensemble. Après quoi, il
me quitta, mais pour retourner bien vite, avec une dame dont

502a. [1] Among the guests invited by Mrs. Crewe (i, L. 1 n. 10) were her old
friends CB, FBA, and Fanny Phillips, now twenty years old and living with her
grandfather.
[2] Elizabeth Emma Crewe, aged 21.
[3] For John Crewe, M.P., see L. 584 n. 8.
[4] Charles James Fox (see also L. 584 n. 8), with whom Crewe 'had long been on
intimate terms' (Namier).

j'ai tout de suite reconnoit les traits, quoiqu'elle étoit viellie de beaucoup d'années — comme moi! — depuis que nous nous sommes vues; c'étoit sa soeur, Madame Hincheliffe, ⁵ qui avoit, dans sa jeunesse, épousé son precepteur, Dr. Hincheliffe,⁵ un homme de beaucoup de merite, et qui étoit devenu, par cette alliance, quand ce fut reconnoit par la famille, Eveque de Peterborough. C'étoit un homme d'infiniment d'esprit, et dans la société tout ce qu'il y avoit de plus instruit, gai, piquant, et spirituel. Il étoit mort pendant le longue tems que nous nous sommes perdus de vue, quoique je croye que c'étoit que dernière-ment, car son habit avoit encore quelque chose de deuil. Quand M. Crewe me la ⎪ nomma, il disoit 'Ma soeur'; — mais ce n'étoit pas necessaire, car elle étoit très peu changée: mais elle me dit — 'Je n'ai pas oser vous addresser après une si longue absence, sans être nommée.' Et alors elle s'asseya à mon côté, et nous entràmes dans une conversation très interressante, sur le tems passé, et les évenemens et les amis que nous avions sus ensemble. C'étoit avec Mᵉ Thrale⁵ que j'avois fait connoissance avec elle, à Brighthelmstone, dans la première visite que j'y ai faite. Dans cette semaine que nous y avons resté nous avons passé toutes les soirées regulierement en société commune, à trois maisons, tour à tour; c.à.d. chez M. l'Eveque, chez le colonel Holroyd,⁶ qui avoit le commande du regiment alors cantoné à Brighton, et qui, depuis ce tems, a eu le titre de Lord Sheffield, pris d'une terre et chateau magnifique qu'il posseda près de Brighton, — ou chez M. Thrale. Ce furent des soirées charmantes, où tout le monde étoit à leur aise, et ou il n'y avoit rien à désirer, sinon des heures plus longues. Je ne pouvois que toucher legerement sur tout cela avec ⎪ Madᵉ Hincheliffe, puisque son mari faisoit en grande partie le charme de cette société. Il n'y avoit rien de plus brillant et en même tems de plus solide que lui. Mᵉ Thrale étoit aussi brillante, il est vrai,

⁵ John Crewe's sister Elizabeth (*c.* 1744–1826), who had married on 16 May 1767 John Hinchliffe (1731–94), Bishop of Peterborough (1769), famous in his day as a 'speaker and preacher' (*DNB*). His association with the Crewes began through his assistant-mastership at Westminster School (of which he was later headmaster) and he held the Mastership of Trinity College, Cambridge (1768–88). For his friendship with Mrs. Thrale, see *DL*, i. 372 and *passim*; and for his lasting loyalty to her, Clifford, pp. 196, 198, 293 and *passim*.

⁶ John Holroyd (*c.* 1735–1821), later Baker-Holroyd, colonel of the Light Dragoons (22nd of Sussex) in 1779, who in 1781 had been made an Irish baron (Baron Sheffield of Dunamore, co. Meath), cr. Earl of Sheffield (1816). See *DL*, i. 464–5; iv. 371.

mais pour solide, tout à fait le contraire, car c'étoit par des saillies qui n'avoient que le ⟨charme⟩ de la vivacité et de l'esprit en passant; pendant que tout ce qui étoit dit par l'Eveque Hincheliffe n'avoit pas seulement cet eclat du moment et de circonstance, mais aussi toujours quelque chose de reflechi, ou à donner bien à reflechir. Un troisième de cette société, dans ce tems, avoir tout autant d'esprit, mais d'un tout autre tournure, c'étoit M. Murphy,[7] auteur fameux, et ami des sa jeunesse à M. Thrale.[8] Il n'avoit pas les mêmes saillies vives, gaies, spirituelles & promptes qu'avoient l'Eveque ou Mᵉ Thrale, mais il avoit le don de conter à merveille, d'une maniere tout à fait dramatique, pleine de gaieté, de satire sans aigreur, et d'ironie avec bon humeur et du bon ton. Jamais il ne se fachoit, jamais il ne donnoit | lieu aux autres de se facher. Il avoit singulierment l'air d'un françois, et la galanterie, et la politesse, et les attentions minutieuses et flatteuses. Il n'étoit pas beau, mais il étoit supérieurement bien fait, svelte, et agréable. Il étoit toujours elegamment mise, et un admirateur décidé de l'elegance et de la grace dans tout autre. Enfin, il étoit tout autant aimable que célébre. Quel dommage qu'un pareil homme étoit perdu pour la société des femmes, qu'il étoit né pour adorer, et desquelles il étoit fait pour être adoré, et pour la vie domestique qu'il étoit formé de rendre heureuse, et pour les premiers circles dans le monde, où il n'avoit qu'à paroître pour briller avec éclat, par l'effet d'une malheureuse passion qui lui avoit presque oté la raison par sa violence, et la

---

[7] Arthur Murphy (1727–1805), actor and dramatist. For the parts of his career touched on by FBA in her reminiscences, see *DNB* and Howard Hunter Dunbar, *The Dramatic Career of Arthur Murphy* (1946), p. 142 and *passim*. The 'jeune actrice ... belle comme un ange' was Ann Elliot (1743–69). In the year of her death she vilified by an erroneous account purportedly 'Written by a Gentleman Intimately acquainted with her' and wrongly attributed to Murphy, namely, *Genuine Memoirs of the Life and Adventures of the Celebrated Miss Ann Elliot* (1769).

The Citizen, in which Ann Elliot took the part of Maria when it was first played in 1763, was adapted in some respect, as FBA says, from *La Fausse Agnès* (1759) by Philippe Destouches (1680–1754). *Know Your own Mind*, based on *l'Irrésolu* (1713), was first produced in 1777; *The Way to Keep him*, in 1760; and *The Grecian Daughter*, Murphy's best-known tragedy, in 1772. His translation was published in 4 vols (1793).

FB, who in private theatricals at Barborne Lodge in 1777 had acted in *The Way to Keep him*, had doubtless seen most of Murphy's plays, as well as James Townley's farce, *High Life below Stairs* (1759), which she wrongly attributes to Murphy. See *ED*, ii. 164–79; *DL*, i. 91, 103, 202; and *passim*. Murphy was first among those who encouraged FB herself to try her hand at comedy (*DL*, i. 203–4).

[8] For Murphy's friendship with Henry Thrale (c. 1729–81) and the wealth of Thrale's father, see Clifford, pp. 34–5.

vie par son desespoir! Je ne sais pas l'histoire du commence-
ment de sa carière, mais il étoit surement | celui d'un Gentil-
homme, puisque il avoit reçu un education des plus erudite,
et puisque il est un des hommes les plus savans de son tems:
et il étoit le camarade favori et intime toujours de M. Thrale,
qui, quoique d'une naissance assez basse, avoit un pere tres
riche, et fut élévé avec la noblesse. Ses manières encore, si bien
formées, si engageants, étoient des garantis les plus sures d'un
homme bien élévé: mais il étoit fou de la théatre et de Garrick,
et son premier coup d'essai dans le monde fut celui d'un
acteur. Il n'avoit pas réussi et ne voulant pas être autre que
très distingué, il quitta vite la theatre; mais un oncle dont il
étoit l'heritier, et qui étoit un baronet d'Ireland,[9] fut si enragé
de son essai, qu'il le desherita. Il se donna alors à écrire pour
le théatre, et il avoit un succès le plus flatteur possible. Un de
ses pièces, Comment il faut le garder, est toujours jouée encore
| toutes les fois où il y a des acteurs qui meritent de jouer les
roles celebres et distingués qui en composent la dramatis
personae. D'un tout autre genre, la tragedie de la *Grecian
Daughter* a joué de la même faveur publique; et la petite piece
de High Life below stairs a eu toutes les mêmes avantages.
All in the Wrong, Know your own mind, (pris de l'Irresolu de
Destouches,) et d'autres pieces, ont aussi été reçues à merveille.
Mais une petite piece tout autant celebrée, composée dans ce
tems où le public étoit à ses pieds, lui a perdu à jamais, et par
son succés même, le répos et le bonheur de sa vie. Il y avoit
dans ce tems une jeune actrice qui reunissoit en elle tout
d'attraits qu'elle étoit l'idole du theatre, elle avoit de la beauté,
de la jeunesse, de l'esprit, de gaieté, de jugement, de finesse,
l'air spirituel, et de la grace en chaque mouvement. Elle fesoit
le délice de tout le monde, et on ne parla que d'elle. | Elle
étoit autant celebre comme courtisanne que comme actrice, et
recherchée autant par les grands et les libertins, que par les
acteurs et les auteurs dramatiques. Elle étoit d'une extravagance
innouie, mais tant comblée de biens, de bijoux, d'argent, et
de cadeaux magnifiques, qu'elle étoit enormement riche même
au commencement de sa carière, egalement brilliant et désor-
donnée. Dans cette plenitude de ses succés et heights de ses

[9] Jeffrey French (d. 1754) of Cloonyquin, co. Roscommon, barrister-at-law,
Argyle Buildings, London, M.P. (1741–7, 1754).

charmes, M. Murphy lui composa le role de Maria dans le Citoyen, dont l'idée est prise d'une comedie de Destouches, Je crois, La Fausse Agnès.[7] C'étoit ecrite exprès pour elle, et elle la joua avec une perfection si étonnante, que rien ne pourra la remplacer, rien autre n'étoit joué, ni gouté, et le public, ravi, enchanté, demanda toujours la même piece, toujours la même sorcière, Mlle Elliot. Ah! sorcière en effet pour le pauvre auteur! De lui devoir tant d'honneurs pendant qu'elle lui avoit ravi le coeur — | c'étoit trop! il commença par l'admirer, il finit par l'adorer: il n'avoit pas autre idée qu'elle, il quitta la société, ses amis, ses camarades, ses études, et ses plaisirs; il n'y avoit qu'un seul objet — c'étoit Mlle Elliot! Et, ce qui est plus surprenant, il prît sur elle le même ascendant qu'elle avoit prise sur lui: elle ne voudroit jouer que les rôles qu'il lui composa, elle detestoit tout autre amant aussi bien que tout autre auteur; les grands, les riches, les puissans, tous lui devenoient insuppor-tables, et, au milieu des succés les plus rapides, des conquêtes les plus brillantes, et de la renommée la plus extraordinaire, elle quitta le Theatre, la ville, ses amans et ses richesses, pour s'abandonner en entière à l'homme | qui lui avoit vraiment gagné le coeur, et qui, fou de joie et ivre de plaisir, se retira de même et ne voudroit plus entendre parler ni de ses amis, ni de fortune, ni de poursuite quelconque, pour oublier en entier tout le monde que Mlle Elliot. Ceci ne dura pas longue tems: dans leur retraite elle prît un rhume, qui, peu soigné, produisoit une consomption, et dans très peu, elle mourut dans ses bras — encore dans sa première jeunesse, et belle comme un ange. Un fin si triste, si inattendu, au sein de la volupté, le plongea dans un desespoir qui n'a point de nom, et qui ne fut qu'aggravé par la preuve qu'elle lui donna de sa tendresse en mourante en lui laissant tout son bien. Ce n'étoit pas alors beaucoup, puisque elle avoit cessé de gagner pour quelque tems, et con-tinué de depenser; mais, c'étoit le tout, et le testament étoit fait dans | ses derrières heures. Il étoit long tems comme un homme qui avoit perdu la raison; et il a toujours resté comme quelqu'un pour qui le bonheur étoit enseveli. Enfin, il se donna à des études, et il commença à traduire Tacite. Cela l'avoit forcé de revoir le monde, du moins les savans, et peu à peu ses amis l'on de tems en tems attiré chez eux: mais rarement, et difficilement, quoique, une fois avec eux, sa gaité naturelle sembloit toujours prête à revivre, et les charmes et les agrèmens de sa société à se renouveller. Cette episode m'a bien eloignée de mon sujet; revenons, donc, à l'assemblée chez Mᵉ Crewe. Madᵉ Hincheliffe a resté, causant sur ces personnages, et surtout sur Mᵉ Thrale, et son extraordinaire marriage, et sur les demoiselles Thrales,[10] et leurs caractères et leur conduite, assez long tems, et bien agréablement car elle est de nature gaie et gentille tout à fait — |

Mon Dieu! je n'ai pas encore fini mon histoire de la dernière assemblée où j'ai assisté la bas! et je l'ai commencé il y a un siècle! Pendant cette conversation qui m'a fortement interessée avec Mᵉ Hincheliffe, une autre dame m'a approchée avec un certain air de plaisir, de curiosité, d'empressement, qui m'a forcé de la remarquer; elle étoit accompagnée par Mᵉ Crewe, qui avoit l'air de m'avoir nommé comme quelqu'une que cette dame avoit fort envi de voir. 'Madᵉ d'Arblay,' disoit Mᵉ. Crewe, — quand cette dame, avec grand vivacité, et même beaucoup d'emotion, la pria de ne pas me la nommer; 'Je veux savoir, s'ecrioit-elle, 'si Mᵉ d'Arblay me reconnoîtra.' Effectivement, allors, par l'aide de la voix à mille et mille minauderies, j'ai cru me rappeller qui c'étoit — | Lady Corke, une dame que j'avois connue il y a bien des années comme Mlle Monckton.[11] Et meme alors il y avoit quelques soupçons repandus contre elle d'une nature très desavantageuses, et qui m'avoient fait eluder soigneusement de me lier avec elle, quoique elle a fait de son mieux pour m'engager d'être de ses intimes amies. Mais depuis ce tems ces soupçons sont plutot realisés qu'aggravés, et on l'accuse des torts les plus graves contre la première femme de Lord Corke,[11] qu'elle a succedé, et qu'on dit qu'elle a voulu perdre de toute maniere. La jeune

---

[10] Of Henry Thrale's surviving daughters, Hester Maria, Susanna Arabella, Sophia, and Cecilia, now aged 38, 32, 31, and 25 respectively (see Clifford, Appendix A), only Cecilia had married before this time (vi, L. 594 nn. 8, 9).

[11] The Hon. Mary Monckton (1748–1840), the daughter of John Monckton (1695–1751), Viscount Galway. A leader of fashion, living in Charles Street, Berkeley Square, she was one of the London hostesses who in 1782 shared in the lionizing of the authoress of *Cecilia* (see *DL*, ii. 123–4; and *passim*). FB had described her in 1782 as 'between thirty and forty, very short, very fat, but handsome; splendidly and fantastically dressed, rouged not unbecomingly, . . . [with] an easy levity in her air, manner, voice, and discourse'. In 1786 the Hon. Miss Monckton had become the second wife of Edmund Boyle (1742–98), 7th Earl of Cork (1764), a man 'devoted to the most wretched voluptuousness', whose marriage to Anne Courtenay (*c.* 1742–85) had been dissolved in 1782. See Sir Herbert Croft, *The Abbey of Kilkhampton* (1780).

Lady Templetown[12] m'avoit tant parlé à ce sujet, et avec tant d'horreur de cette dernière Lady Corke, que je me suis trouvée très peu disposée à renouveller avec elle une connoisance faite il y a si long tems, et dejà rompue, et jamais, même dans le commencement, à mon gré, puisque j'étois parvenue contre elle des le commencement: mais plus je me suis reculée, plus je l'ai vue d'avancer, de sorte qu'il ne m'étoit pas possible ׀ dans le tems de l'eviter. J'étois peinée de la rencontrer, mais bien resolue de ne pas renouveller aucune liaison avec elle, à present que je sais mieux comment l'apprecier que dans le tems ou sa conduite été plus equivoque. Je me suis bien gardée, donc, d'avoir l'air de la reconnoître, & quand elle m'a demandé avec instance si je ne pouvais pas la remettre, je n'ai fait autre reponse que de me reculer, avec une reverence froide mais honnête. Elle m'a toujours poursuivie, avec empressement, mais toute troublée, disant 'Comment, donc, vous ne me remettez pas? du tout? du tout? du tout?' Mad[e] Crewe, alors, me chucheté à l'oreille 'Lady Corke!' mais je n'avois pas l'air de l'entendre, et, enfin, Lady Corke s'est nommée elle même, tout en me demandant quand elle pouvoit me revoir, & où on pouvait me retrouver. Je lui repondis froidement que je n'étoit que ׀ pour 24 heures à Londres; et quand elle m'a pressé pour passer une soirée chez elle le jeudi, je lui repondis que je serois alors en France. Me trouvant tant sec et deplaisant, elle m'a enfin quitté, à ma grande joie. Bientot après, une autre dame m'approchât, se rejouissant très poliment de me revoir, et ajoutant 'Vous ne me reconnoissez pas?' C'étoit bien vrai, je n'avois pas même l'idée qui elle étoit, et je cherchois vainement mais vraiment à la remettre. Elle attendoit quelque tems, avec un air tant soit peu chagrin, ou du moins peiné de se trouver changé jusqu'à être meconnoissable, et après une minute de silence, elle prononça 'Lady Pembrooke.'[13] J'étois encore plus fachée de n'avoir pas pu la remettre, quand je

---

[12] Lady Mary *née* Montagu (iv, L. 292 n. 22).

[13] Probably Elizabeth *née* Spencer (1737–1831), dowager Lady Pembroke, the widow of Henry Herbert (1734–94), 10th Earl of Pembroke. She was the daughter of Charles Spencer (1706–58), 3rd Duke of Marlborough, and sister of Lady Diana (1734–1808), the Di Beauclerk often mentioned by Walpole, who had married as her second husband Topham Beauclerk (1739–80). FB had first met the sisters in the Public Rooms at Brighton in 1779 (*DL*, i. 283) and Lady Pembroke often appears in FB's Court Journals (*DL*, iv *passim*) as Lady of the Bedchamber, to which honour she was appointed on 4 Jan. 1783, holding the post until the Queen's death in 1818 (R.H.I.).

trouvai que c'étoit cette femme respectable à tant de titres, surtout

[*This is the last page of the Exercise Book. The account was probably continued in a fifth book, which is missing.*]

503   Dover, [15] April 1802

To Charles Burney

A.L. (Osborn), *misdated* 14 Apr. 1802
Single sheet 4to 1 p. *pmks* DOVER 17 APR 1802 17 AP 1802 wafer
Addressed: Dr. Charles Burney, / Greenwich, / Kent

April 14. 1802

My dearest Charles
The very night I saw you, I received from George Lock[1] a Letter directed to me at Norbury Park from M. d'A telling me he was quite worn out by the continual delay, & desiring me to come to him by the first Paris Diligence in which a Female had taken a place. I went the next Day for my passports —I obtained them on Wednesday[2]—& on enquiry found a Lady had secured a place for herself & femme de Chambre for *to Day*—I could not hesitate in securing 3 others—for Adrienne de Chavignac,[3] Alex, & me — — as I see it would be highly inconvenient—perhaps improper,—that M. d'A. should leave Paris at this moment to meet me at Calais—yet could I not for my life find a single moment to write this to you though last night I never an instant went to Bed, or even lay down. Accept now my warmest thanks—& fail not to lead on your kind propensity to the summer Holydays, when we may all three delight in embracing you. I thought the present scheme so selfish, I could not endure to profit from your kindness,[4] unless I had vainly tried all other methods of safety. We are

503. [1] George Locke (L. 472 n. 2) had evidently brought to FBA in London a letter, now missing, that had been first delivered at Norbury Park.
   [2] On Wednesday 14 April.   [3] See L. 437 n. 3.
   [4] Charles's offer to take his sister and her party by coach to Dover and put them on the boat.

now come to Dover, whence we Expect to sail to-morrow. I beg my love to Rosette, & Carlos, & best Compts to Mrs. Bicknl. I am going to put my two Children to roost, & hope to get a little Sleep to-night myself. Ever & ever yours, dear Generous Charles

504   Dover, [15] April [1802]

To M. d'Arblay

A.L. (Barrett, Eg. 3693, f. 239–b), *n.d.*
Single sheet 4to 1 p. *pmks* CALAIS 29 wafer
Addressed: M. Darblay, / Rue Miromenil, / Hotel Marengo, / à Paris. Delivrée sur le champ.
Edited by FBA, p. 1, *annotated and dated*: 1802 (Nº 19) [*and later in blacker ink*:] Dover 16th April.
Edited also by CFBt.

J'arrivè, *mon ami*! mon Cher — Cher ami! frightened — harrassed — embarrassed — but eager, happy, & with a whole soul beating with trueest tenderness, *J'arrive* pour ne jamais vous quitter, j'èspere, encore pour la vie! Amen!

Dover, Thursday Night, April 14.[1]

This, as you enjoin, is ready to put to the post at Calais when we Land—

If I could be fetched by a safe Messenger to you from the Inn —near the palais Royale[2]—I should *rather* be received by you— after this eventful separation—in our apartment alone—but you must do as you think best—whatever may be my preference of an uninterrupted meeting, *all* must be solacing & delightful— adrienne & alex are quite well—

Est-ce — bien vrai?! —

Voyez what your Letter & injunction & eagerness has made me enterprise!—I cross the sea to-morrow[3]—an element I so dread—with 2 Children, & not a soul that knows me, or to whom I am known!—

504. [1] On Thursday 15 April, according to the Perpetual Calendar.
[2] The stagecoach from Calais stopped in the rue Notre-Dame-des-Victoires (see L. 510, p. 243). At No. 11 was the Hôtel des Messageries, which later became the Imperial headquarters for messages to all parts of the world. The lower part of the building was probably the 'station' itself, and the upper floors an actual hotel.
[3] On Friday 16 April.

505   Journal for 15 April 1802

To Doctor Burney

A.J.L. (Diary MSS. vi, not numbered, but between the foliations 5387
and 5668, Berg), written at the Hotel Marengo, 1185 rue de Miroménil,
Paris, *post* 21 April 1802, but concluded and posted in early May.
Double sheet 4to   greenish 4 pp.   *pmks* P. P. Paris FOREIGN OFFICE
FOREIGN OFFICE / 14 MA 1802
   Addressed: ANGLETERRE / Dr. Burney, / Chelsea College, / Middlesex,
/ near *London*.
   Endorsed by CB: 1st letter. journey / to Dover / Apr. N° / 3
   Edited by FBA *who annotated* p. 1: ⁕ New Numbers (1) Journey to
Dover.
   *Conjecturally most of this Journal was copied by M. d'A into the 'Paris Letter
Book' (burned in 1919, see i, Intro., p. xxiii), where together with Ll. 506 and 507
he formed a composite account of FBA's Journey to Paris. A copy of this account was
made for CFBt and corrected by her (Diary MSS. viii. 5400–52 plus 5454–6,
Berg), 28½ pp., dated 15–18 April 1802. This copy was abridged and edited by
Colburn and his staff.*
   *Extracts, in typescript, also taken from the 'Letter Book' are in the National Portrait
Gallery (grangerized DL, v. 493–503) and it is these that were printed by Brimley
Johnson in* Fanny Burney and the Burneys *(1926), pp. 19–32.*

April, 1802, Paris.
   I seize, at length, upon the largest Paper I can procure, to
begin to my beloved Father some account of our Journey—&, if
I am able, I mean to keep him a brief Journal of my proceedings
during this destined year, or 18 months, of separation;—secure
of his kindest interest in all that I may have to relate, & certain
he will be anxious to know how I go on in a strange land.—Tis
my only way, now, of communicating with him, & I must draw
from it one of my dearest Worldly comforts, the hopes of seeing
his loved hand with some return.
   Thursday, April 15. Good little faithful Molly, & Beckey,[1]
will let you know they sat up till 4 o'clock in the morning to
help, as well as see me off; I could not endure to wake my dear

505. [1] FBA's departure from Chelsea Hospital was aided, as she says, by CB's
servants Mary More (ii, L. 68 n. 30) and her sister Rebecca More (*fl.* 1798–1819),

PLATE I

The Paris Diligence, 1803

From a drawing by Sir John Carr as an illustration for his book The Stranger in France (1803), published by J. Johnson of St. Paul's Churchyard

Fanny Phillips,[2] though I had made for the purpose of persuading her to go to rest, a sort of tacit agreement to embrace her again before my departure—she is one amongst those I very anxiously leave, &, with all my true willingness to follow my Mate, my Heart was full, & heavy, & my spirits only supported by excess of business, which allowed no time for rumination. William & John[3] conducted my little Boy & me in excellent time to the Inn in Piccadilly,[4] where we met my kind Mrs. Lock & dear little Adrienne de Chavagnac.[5] The parting, there, was brief & hurried, & I set off on my grand expedition, with my two dear young Charges, exactly at five o'Clock. My companions—or rather fellow-travellers,—for that Englishism of reserve for which I am so noted even in the Circles in which I am known, was not very likely to be metamorphosed into *companionabilityness* in a Diligence with those whose names were as unknown to me as their faces. As I stayed to converse with my dear Mrs. Lock to the last moment, my friend the Book keeper came to me eagerly, crying 'vîte! vîte, madame! prenez vôtre place dans la Diligence—! car, voici un monsieur Anglois, qui surement va *prendre* la meilleure![6]—'&, *en | effet*, ce monsieur Anglois did not disappoint her expectations—or much raise mine; for he not only took the best place, but contrived still to ameliorate it by the little scruple with which he made every other worse, through the unbridled expansion in which he indulged his dear person by jutting out his Elbows

who is mentioned in CB's will (P.C.C. Bridport, dated 12 Jan. 1807) as 'my Cook who has served me with probity and diligence 13 years'.

2 SBP's daughter.

3 William's promotion from 'boy-man' or footman to coachman is amusingly described by CB in a letter (Osborn) to FBA, 19 Oct. 1799. John was to remain with CB until 1812 or later.

4 The White Bear, Piccadilly, from which, according to *A Practical Guide* . . . (1803), diligences 'belonging to the old National Establishment, rue Notre Dame des Victoires, at Paris, set out every day at half past four o'clock in the morning for Paris, by way of Dover and Calais'.

John Carr (p. 30) provides an informative drawing of the Paris Diligence of 1803, showing the lugubrious cloth-covered basket slung at the back, the coachman's box, and a box on the roof for luggage and outside passengers. See Plate I.

5 Adrienne de Chavagnac (see L. 510, p. 244; and L. 511, pp. 250–1).

6 The English, having been denied Paris for a decade, could not now wait to return. According to Laquiante, p. 318, 'on ne peut faire un pas dans les rues sans rencontrer des familles de bourgeois anglais, composées d'individus de toute taille, corpulents, hauts en couleur, de tournure comique, de mise singulière, se dandinant comme des canards ou enracinés devant les curiosités de la ville. Le flegme et le sans-gêne de ces bourgeois, conscients de leur *respectability*, forment un contraste vivant avec la mobilité française.

'Pour cinq guinées, tous frais accessoires comptés, un de ces braves boutiquiers

against his next, & his knees & feet against his opposite Neighbour. He seemed prepared to look upon all around him with a sort of sulky haughtiness, soon announcing himself as a Military commander of distinction, who had long served at Gibraltar, & various places, who had travelled thence through France, & from France to Italy; who was a native of Scotland, & of proud, though unnamed genealogy,⁷ & was now going to Paris, purposely to behold the First Consul, to whom he meant to claim an introduction through Mr. Jackson.⁸ His burnt complection, scotch accent, large, bony Face & Figure, & high & distant demeanour, made me easily conceive, & believe him a Highland Chief. I never heard his name, but I think him a Gentleman BORN, though not gently bred.—The next to mention is a Madame Raymond, or Grammont,⁷ for I heard not distinctly which, who seemed very much a Gentlewoman, & who was returning to France, too uncertain of the state of her affairs to know whether she might rest there or not. She had a femme de chambre who travelled in the Basket,⁴ & who waited upon her very assiduously where-ever we stopt, for refreshments, or changing Horses. She refused, the whole way to Dover, to quit the Carriage, having a little basket of provisions, of which she partook with her Maid, when the rest alighted at the Inns. I thought this an excess of penury, to avoid the eating Bills, & longed to have made her partake of our fare without that draw-back: but though I tried various means to bring this about, I could never succeed; she was polite, but firm, in ˡ all her refusals: & had only one defect to prevent my taking much interest in her: this was, not merely an avoidance, but a horrour of being touched by either of my Children, who, poor little Souls, restless & fatigued by the confinement they endured, tried to fling themselves upon every passenger in turn, [&] though by every one they were turned back to their sole prop, they were by no one repulsed with such hasty displeasure as by this old lady, who seemed as fearful of having the peticoat of her Gown, which was stiff,

---

est transporté comfortablement; la journée à Paris, y compris une soirée au théâtre, lui revient à une guinée, et il n'a rien à débourser pour visiter les musées et les monuments.' An impression, somewhat similar, 'La Famille Anglaise à Paris', is shown in J. B. Priestley, *The Prince of Pleasure* . . . (1969), p. 116.

⁷ The passengers on the coach, the editors have not been able to identify.

⁸ The Minister Plenipotentiary to Paris (L. 470 n. 3).

round, & bulging as if lined with Parchmont, deranged, as if she had been attired in a Hoop for Court. This strict formality put apart, she was far the first person of the set, her language, manners, & deportment, all announ⟨cin⟩g her superiority to the rest.—The Third personage was a Mad⁰ Blaizeau, who seemed an exceeding good sort of Woman, gay, voluble, good-humoured, & merry. All we had of amusement sprung from her sallies; which were uttered less from a desire of pleasing others, her very natural character having none of the high polish bestowed by the Graces, than from a jovial spirit of enjoyment by which they produced pleasure to herself. She soon & frankly acquainted us she had left France to be a Governess to some young ladies, before the Revolution,—& under the patronage, as I think, of the Duke of Dorset:⁹ She had *been courted*, she told us, by an English Gentleman Farmer; but he would not change his religion for her, nor She for him; & so, when every thing was bought for her wedding, they broke off the connexion; & she afterwards married a frenchman. She had seen a Portrait set richly in Diamonds of the King, prepared for a present to the First consul, & described its superb ornaments & magnificence in a way to leave no doubt of the fact. She meant to ⁱ stop at St. Denys,¹⁰ to enquire if her Mother yet lived, having received no intelligence from, or of her, these last 10 eventful years!—The 4ᵗʰ & last I have to name is a young Irishman, immensely tall, very awkward, & excessively bashful; with Eyes that dared look at nobody, yet leered at every body, & manners utterly unformed, a face marking eager curiosity, & a figure the most gawky. He was going to France to study the language, &, I presume, the

---

⁹ It was probably for some of the illegitimate children of John Frederick Sackville (1745–99), Duke of Dorset (1769), Ambassador-extraordinary and Minister Plenipotentiary to France (1783–9), that a governess was needed, as it was only on 4 Jan. 1790 that he married the daughter and co-heiress of Sir Charles Cope (d. 14 June 1781), namely Arabella Diana (1769–1825), whose dowry amounted to £140,000.

In 1801 she had married secondly Charles Whitworth (L. 525 n. 13) but retained the title Duchess of Dorset to the perplexity of the Parisians, who, seeing her in the carriage and equipage of her first husband, assumed she was the mistress of her second. Not only did the French were struck. 'It is a singular circumstance', commented Maria Edgeworth on 21 Nov. 1802 (*Life*, i. 108), 'that Lord Whitworth, the new Ambassador, has brought to Paris the same horses, and the same wife, and lives in the same house as the last Ambassador did eleven years ago . . .'.

¹⁰ Faubourg Saint-Denis, about 5½ miles north of the centre of Paris, was on the route the diligence from Calais was to take.

Graces, for he could not have more work for the one than for the other; but he was civil, good-natured, inoffensive, &, I believe, pretty well informed. In a few months he will perhaps be quite new modelled; for he is still at that pliant age when accident—new scenes, or new connexions, may change or mould the whole character. My two little ones, both tired for once, & myself, bring up the rear.—Every Creature but Alex & myself slept the first two Hours; Alex, delighted with the novelty of all he saw, lost every sleepy sensation, & myself though tired with a whole night's watching, had Adrienne in my arms, & gave repose of which I could not partake.

This long written Letter, my beloved Father, having waited a fortnight for a promised opportunity, now goes, by Post—& I entreat to hear from you by the same means, if M. de Lally still delays coming.[11] My poor Alex has been very ill indeed— but thank Heaven is recovered—I have just got my dear Fanny's MOST welcome Letter, & we [are] so rejoiced to receive it as I ca[nnot des]cribe—'Tis my only one from England![12] Maria is much b[etter.] Heaven bless [my] beloved Father—My Mate's kindest Respects

Pray direct to Me, *Rue miromenil, n° 1205—Paris*—[13]we shall have left our Hotel in about a Week, which is no: 1185.

[11] A passport (P.R.O. F.O. 610/1) was granted to the comte de Lally-Tolendal for this crossing on 19 June 1802. He was not to arrive, however, until November (see L. 536 n. 6) and, debarred from Paris by Napoleon, remained in Bordeaux or its vicinity until the Restoration.

[12] Fanny Phillips's letter is missing, though CB mentions it in his letter (Osborn) of 20 May: 'I waited with impatience for your journal, and, en attendant, made F.P. let you know that we were all alive, and some of us *merry*—particularly Beaumont Streetites after the good Mrs. Bateman's very liberal & unexpected bequest.'

[13] This is the comte de Narbonne's address.

To Doctor Burney

A.L. (PML, Autog. Cor. bound), 17 Apr. 1802
Double sheet 4to   3 pp.   wafer
Addressed by mistake to JB: Captⁿ Burney / Margaret Street
Annotated by ?*PML librarian,* p. 1: This letter is listed as '*Sarah Burney* to her
father.'

Calais April 17th 1802.

Here we are, my dear Father.—after such sufferings! O!—
half dead I am arrived with fatigue and sickness—but so glad
to be arrived.—I am almost well already—The Children
thank Heaven are now well, but my poor Alex has suffered
as severely though not as long, as myself. Adrienne has been
well all the way, and gay as a little Lark—A person comes to
me this minute to call me to the Custom House, but added
I might be dispensed with for personal attendance, if I would
give my keys, I did so—& he then said he hoped I had *Rien de
New.* Yes, plusieurs choses, I said, but all for my SELF.—O!—
they will all be taken! What! if made, and not for sale? ALL!
—ALL!—O!— | terrible!—and what am I to do, Monsieur.
'MAIS Madame—il faut payer geneurse-ment—& then perhaps — — I commissioned him to pay for me what he deemed
necessary—& thus I am left.—My dear Fanny[1] will be much
interested in this business—which I will conclude from Paris[2]—
but must now finish unfinished. Adieu, dearest Sir—these few
lines will put you at ease as to our SAFETY—& as soon as I have
slept in Paris, I will write again—The Fees which were
demanded *sans cesse* at Dover, & are now demanded here, are
beyond measure surprizing—& I am afraid to refuse any thing,
or any body—How happy I shall be when under better
guidance! I entreat my dear Fanny to write of our safety to
my sisters & Brothers—& to Miss Cambridge—and to poor
dear Aunt Beckey,[3] with my particular concern at my utter
inability to go to her before I sailed—

---

506. [1] Fanny Phillips.   [2] In Journal-Letter 508.
   [3] CB's sister Rebecca (d. 21 May 1809), whom FBA was not to see again.

Journal for 17 April 1802

To Mrs. Locke

L. excerpt, copy in hand of CFBt (Diary MSS. viii. 5412, Berg), *n.d.*
Written at 1185, rue de Miroménil, Paris, *post* 21 April 1802, and conjecturally copied by M. d'A into the 'Paris Letter Book', see L. 505, above.

... as soon as the *Red Trunk* of poor Adrienne was taken & the examiner unlocked it, the poor little thing burst into a flood of tears & threw herself upon me quite in despair. I instantly explained to the old gentleman who was opening it, that it contained all the childs gifts: & her fright lest they should be seized. Upon which with a good humour I wish you could have seen, he exclaimed — — 'O poor little dear, Pray comfort her! I will touch nothing that can make her uneasy' & he immediately locked the little trunk, without having put a finger within it: & gave the Key into her own hand. I wish, too, you could have seen how her face brightened, & the conscious smile which exulted in her little triumph. Indeed she was the best little Traveller imaginable—never ill, never sick, & sleeping when tired without difficulty. But with a comical incipient coquetry, always preferring the offered services of the *Gentlemen*, to that of any poor fair sex, whenever any choice was in her power. She will be a true little french demoiselle, for all Norbury, & for all *La bonne*:[1] a spirit of coquetry is in her nature, & her arch—smile & meaning eyes will not repress the adoration for which she will have, I fear, but too much taste.

507. [1] Mme Monbrun, the French governess at Norbury Park (iii, L. 222 n. 23).

JOURNEY TO PARIS

508   Journal for 15–19 April 1802

To Doctor Burney

A.J.L.S. continued (Diary MSS. vi, not numbered but between the foliations 5287 and 5668, Berg), written at 1185, rue de Miroménil, Paris, in early May 1802, with a PS. dated 10 June 1802

Five double sheets 4to, numbered at the tops of double sheets: 2, 3, (4), (5), (6)   20 pp.   wafer

Addressed p. 12: *Dr Burney [with the instructions:]* My dearest Padre—This / at your leisure, / il n'y est rien qui presse.

Carried to England with L. 521 by Mr. Street.[1]

Addressed p. 20: Dr. Burney, / Chelsea College, / Middlesex.

Endorsed by CB, p. 20: sheets 5 & 6

Edited by FBA *who annotated and postdated the tops of the numbered double sheets:*

p. 1, *numbered* 2: ※ 1802 Voyage. Alex. Adrienne.

p. 5, *numbered* 3: ※ 1802 Voyage—Calais—

p. 9, *numbered* (4): ※ ※ ※ + Calais Journey—

p. 13, *numbered* (5): ※ ※ ※ Highlander Blaiseaux Journey to Calais to Paris

p. 17, *numbered* (6): ※ × Journey: Calais to Paris ⟨Raymond⟩ & Highlander

Conjecturally M. d'A copied this Journal letter into the Paris Letter Book as part of his composite account of FBA's Journey to Paris. Subsequent copying is described in L. 505 above.

508. [1] After her arrival in Paris, FBA kept a register of the letters she sent to England with memoranda of their contents and the means by which they were sent, which Register, a Notebook bound in blue boards (6·4×4·1″), containing some 52 pages, is extant in the Berg Collection. Arranged confusedly, as the spaces delegated to fixed correspondents (for instance, members of her family) proved insufficient, the Register nevertheless provides information as to the dates on which the letters of the years 1802–15 were sent, the carriers, etc., and records letters now missing.

She records, for instance, that it was a Mr. Street (see also L. 522 n. 1), a friend of JB, who carried a packet of family letters to France in June 1802 and who, returning on 11 June, took letters to SHB, EBB, JB, and Charlotte Cambridge (none of which are extant), the Journal to Mrs. Locke (mentioned in L. 522), and presumably L. 521 and J.L. 508 to CB. He may have been the Charles Street, who, listed by Lewis, p. 282, in List I, 'Officer Prisoners of War', was killed in an attempt to escape on 21 July 1811.

Information from the Register, where relevant, is included in the bibliographical notes at the head of the letters.

April. Paris.

My dearest Father,

When I began my journal, I meant to give you the full detail of my journey; but the unspeakable hurries & fatigue which prevented my writing the first week, & the illness of my poor Boy, which has wholly occupied me the second, makes it impossible for me now to go back with the alacrity which would accord with my opening & my intentions: I will devote, however, every moment I can spare to that part of my adventures, & then usher you with me into this great Capital of the GREAT NATION! —— ! —

To the *15. April* once more. We Breakfasted at Rochester, almost famished; but had not a moment for seeing the City, except as we passed through it, & Brumpton, & Chatham, all appearing as one Town.—The Country was always beautiful, & the Children were always gay & happy. At Canterbury, while the Horses were changed, my little ones & I went to the Cathedral, but dared merely seize sufficient time to view the outside & enter the principal Isle.—I was glad even of that much, as its antique grandeur gave me a pleasure which I always love to cherish in the view of fine old Cathedrals— those most permanent monuments of what our Ancestors thought reverence to God, as manifested in munificence to the place dedicated to his worship. The road thence to Dover is so extremely pleasant, that it kept my fatigue in such good order, as to make it set sleep at defiance. Nor could Alex once close his Eyes, though Adrienne took several short Naps, which extremely refreshed her. At Dover we had a kind of Dinner Supper in one, & my little Boy & Girl & I retired immediately after it, took some Tea in our Chamber, & went to rest.

Friday, 16. April—As we were not to sail till 12, I had hoped to have seen the Castle,[2] & Shakespeare's Cliff,[3] but most unfortunately it rained all the morning, & we were confined to

---

[2] Walmer Castle, about seven miles north of Dover, had been built by Henry VIII for coastal defence, but had become (and remained until 1903) the official residence of the Lord Warden of the Cinque Ports. CB had written long letters to FBA about his visit there with Mrs. Crewe in 1799, on the occasion of the embarkation of the 'Secret Expedition' to the Helder. See iv, L. 328 n. 7; CB's letters of 9 and 15 Sept. 1799 (printed in Scholes, ii. 297–302); and his letter (Osborn) to the Revd. Thomas Twining, 1 Oct. 1799.

[3] Shakespeare's Cliff (or the Hay Cliff) CB had visited with Canning and Miss Crewe on 1 Sept. 1799.

the Inn, except for the interlude of the Custom House, where, however, the examination was so slight, & made with such civility, that we had no other trouble with it than a wet walk— & a few shillings. Our passports also were examined & ratified as readily: ˡ We then went to the Port, &, the Sea being perfectly smooth, were lifted from the quay to the Deck of our Vessel, with as little difficulty as we could have descended from a common Chair to the ground. The rain had now ceased, & my purpose was to remain on Deck during the whole passage, as, by that means, I escaped sickness, when I went, in the Commissioner's yatcht, to the Isle of White, with Mʳ Mrs. & Miss Thrale.⁴ We had seats brought us, & I placed my Children before me. Alex was delighted with the grandeur & manliness of the idea of being at Sea, & astonished to find it a matter of so little apparent danger or toil: Adrienne was playful & happy, & the first quarter of an Hour, during which we were steering from the Port, all was pleasant & agreeable, the whole party remaining on Deck, & expecting to arrive to a 3 o'Clock Dinner at Calais. We were joined by some other parties from the Inn, one consisting of a lady & her Daughter; another of a Dutchman & his English Wife; & a third of 3 young Bucks, who were crossing the strait for a frolic, wholly undetermined whether to go only to Calais,—or to Dunkirk, or to Bologn, or to Paris; or to *return sharp* in the Vessel which was to be again at Dover as quick as possible. Scarcely, however, were we out of the Harbour, when my poor Alex was taken sick; the steward of the Vessel carried him down to the Cabbin, while I rose to accompany him; but before I could move a step, the contagion of his example so suddenly prevailed, that I was compelled to take a side view of the Vessel, not to shock all the party by a front view of my poor self. Here I was stopt, & restopt, in spite of every effort to follow my poor ˡ Boy, a considerable time; &, at last, was compelled to commit myself in silence to the same steward, hopeless of reaching him by any more active means, & only by signs able to summon Adrienne to be of our party: but the little Girl, still perfectly well, was so

---

⁴ The visit occurred in mid-June 1780 (the month of the Gordon riots), when FB accompanied the Thrales in their flight (10–18 June) from Bath, via Salisbury, Wilton, Southampton, and Portsmouth to Brighton (18 June). In a letter (Berg) to CB, dated Portsmouth, 14 June, FB mentions the plans of the party for a jaunt next day to Spithead—and thence to the Isle of Wight.

much amused, & so much courted by all, that my signal was not obeyed, & I was forced to be drawn on alone. I threw myself on the first Hammock, & could with difficulty pronounce whether I suffered most in body or in mind; for I was unable to utter a single word, from a sickness without a moment's intermission, that tore me to pieces, while I was quite wretched to join my poor Boy, who was unfortunately on a Hammock in the next Cabbin; & still more miserable for Adrienne, lest any accident should befal her while with only strangers on the Deck. I really think I was two Hours in this terrible situation, before I could utter a phrase of sufficient length to pray the steward to bring me the two Children. My poor Alex was then placed on the other end of my Hammock, & as much relieved as myself by the approximation, though neither of us were above a few minutes at a time allowed any respite: but Adrienne, still well, positively refused to leave the Deck, where she eat & sung & chatted with all around: & my helplessness to obtain her, caused me an incessant inquietude. Unused to consider me as a person who had any authority over her, & delighted to find herself the play thing of the Party, she was too young to have any compunction for my uneasiness, &, as I never could pronounce more than 3 words without a stoppage to my eloquence as little inviting to the beholder, as to the speaker, I could never frame a message of sufficient [|] energy to counterbalance the little Gipsey's delight in her amusement & her liberty.

When, at length, I heard some one say it was 3 o'clock; I was endued with sudden power to exclaim, 'I hope, then, we are in sight of Calais?'—but what was my check, when I was answered 'of Calais? You are hardly out of the Port of Dover!' & I was then told a dead calm had completely stopt our course.—In this suffering state Alex & I passed the day; Adrienne was tempted to come down to us at about 5 o'clock, &, when once I could speak to her, I found voice & breath to assure her she would be drowned, inevitably, if she left us any more, & her innocent credulity then detained her; this relieved me from almost the most painful solicitude I ever experienced. The Daughter of the lady I have mentioned came down also, &, as both were quite well, they danced & sung together, clambered up & down the Hammocks, & told each other little stories. Adrienne, young as she is, became the confident of the other, though ten years old; & heard from her that she was carried over to her papa, who was in France, by her mama, who was very unkind to her, & meant to leave her, because her papa hated her Mama, & they could not live together: she regretted nothing but school, where she had friends, & where alone she was happy! Poor little Girl!—At Night, the calm continuing, no further attempt was made at sailing, & the whole party came down to the Cabbins. When the Hammocks were filled, the rest laid on the floor, getting what they could reach for Mattrasses & pillows: & now it was that our 3 Bucks became diverting; for they ranted out such unmeaning rattle, of their unmeaning excursion, that it was just bad enough to ⎰ be good enough for laughable folly. Any thing ridiculous in a higher style would have failed, if requiring attention or combination to give it effect. Adrienne now submitted to lie down, in the same Hammock with her new friend, & fell fast asleep, & enjoyed the most perfect repose all night. Alex & myself had no such rest, a few intervals of suffering were all we could obtain, & those of that unquiet sort that belonged to the most perfect stillness, & were broken by the smallest motion, or even speech. Towards morning, however, the poor little Boy grew better, & from about 6 o'clock had no further return of sickness. At 9, my own abated, & as I heard we were at length in sight of Calais, I ventured to rise, & crawl, with my Children, to the Deck: &, as there was now sufficient Air for the Vessel to get on, I presently recovered in some measure, & though never quite easy, found myself able to keep above, & saw my Alex entirely revive, though still pale as death from his so wretched a day & night. A dutch vessel made up to us, with offers to tow us to shore; but we all refused, except our Bucks, who were enchanted at a sort of new enterprise, & skipt on board with the smart vulgar agility of a City apprentice skipping on a Form to look around him, at Sadler's Wells, or Vauxhall. The calm which caused our slow passage, & our sickness, was now favourable, for it took us into the Port of Calais so close & even with the quay, that we scarcely accepted even an hand, to aid us from the vessel to the land. Many, however, were the hands that were offered us; the quay was lined with crowds of people, men, women, Children, & certain amphibious females, who might have passed for either sex, or any thing else in the world, except what they really were, European Women!— Their Man's Hats, man's Jackets, & man's shoes, their burnt skins ¹ & most savage looking peticoats, hardly reaching—nay, not reaching their knees, would have made me instantly believe any account I could have heard of their being just imported from the wilds of America. The vessel also was presently filled with men, who, though dirty & mean, were so civil & gentle that they could not displease, & who entered it so softly & quietly, that, neither hearing nor seeing them approach, it seemed as if they had availed themselves of some secret trap doors through which they had mounted, to fill the ship, without sound or bustle, in a single moment. When we were quitting it, however, this tranquility as abruptly disappeared; for in an instant they rushed round me, one demanding to carry Alex, another, Adrienne, another seizing my Ecritoire, another my arm—& some one, I fear, my Parasol, since I have never been able to find it since. However, not to be scandalous, I am by no means sure it was not left at the Inn. We were informed we must not leave the ship till Monsieur le Commissaire arrived,⁵ to carry us to—I think—the Municipality of Calais, to shew our Passports. Monsieur le Commissaire, in white, with some red trapping, soon arrived, civilly hastening himself quite out of breath, to save us from waiting. We then mounted the quay, & I followed the rest of the passengers, who all followed the Commissary, accompanied by two men carrying the two Children, & two more carrying one my Ecritoire & the other insisting on conducting myself. The quantity of people that surrounded & walked with us, surprised me, & their decency, their silence, their quietness, astonished me. To fear them was impossible, even in entering France with all the

⁵ The name of this officer was given by Mary Berry (ii. 193) as M. Mengaud. Appointed in August 1801 as commissaire général de police from Ostend to Dieppe was an officer, by name Mengaud, on whom there is a large dossier ('L'Affaire Mengaud') in the Archives Nationales. An unpleasant character, bad-tempered and offensive, he was detested by the Mayor and the Chief of Police at Calais and by the administrative official at Boulogne, where he was later posted. Though in favour with the central government for his ruthlessness in searches for smuggled goods, his detection of false passports, and his rigorous enforcement of official decrees, the local antagonisms he provoked made his postings untenable. He was in Paris in 1806 and last heard of in Strassburg in 1807, deeply in debt.

formed fears hanging upon its recent, though past, horrours. But when we came to the Municipality, I was, I own, extremely ill at ᴵ ease, when, upon our Governante's desiring me to give the Commissary my Passport, as the rest of the Passengers had done, & my answering it was in my Ecritoire, she exclaimed 'Vîte, vîte, cherchez la, ou vous serez arretéz!'—You may believe I was quick enough!—or at least tried to be so, for my fingers presently trembled, & I could hardly put in the Key. My gentle Carrier gave up his charge without resistance, however, & I parted from it no more. It was still very formidable to me, from a thousand starting recollections, to mount a sort of Tower, where were seated two civil officers, who examined our Passports. They wrote in them—I never examined what—& I was desired to go into a round Closet on one side the room. I took my two Children, for my protectors, & a formal, but civil old Gentleman asked me if I brought any thing contrary to the Laws of the republic? Another adding it was the room where an oath was taken to that effect. I did not chuse to give a very categorical answer to this demand, all my new peticoats jumping in the Mouth of my Conscience, which answered, inwardly, it would rather I should lose them all than give a plump negative: I merely therefore replied, That I brought nothing for sale. This, to my equal surprise & pleasure, satisfied them; they took hold of my Ecritoire; I told them it only contained Letters,—& they returned it unexamined. I told them the simple truth in both my answers; but was much gratified by their so readily believing it. They bowed, & we returned to the other passengers, & were conducted by the same Commissary, & all our first companions of the shore, to some other municipal association, as I suppose, for I understood nothing that passed, though the tremor I experienced in all these ceremonies, & my many previous fears, joined ᴵ to total ignorance of continental travelling, & constant solicitude about the Children, from the impossibility of always having a hand for each, kept me in a state of apprehension not very favourable to observation at the time, or to memory afterwards. Nevertheless, & though all these impediments, the novelty of the scene, & of the persons surrounding me, afforded me, in the intervals of my Cowardice, much entertainment.—In the Hall, to which we now passed our Passports were taken, & deposited—& we had new ones drawn up & given us in their stead. On quitting this place, we were accosted by a new crowd, all, however, gentle, though not silent, as our first friends, who recommended various Hotels to us,—one begging we would go to Grandsire,[6] another to Duroc,[7] another to Meurrice[8]—& this last prevailed with the Gouvernante, whom I regularly followed, not from preference, but from the singular horror my otherwise worthy & wellbred old lady manifested, when her full round Coats risked, from being touched, the danger of being modernized into the Flimzy falling drapery of the present day. At Meurrice's our Goods were entered, & we heard they would be examined at the Custom House in the afternoon. We Breakfasted, & the crowd of fees which were claimed, from the Captain, steward, sailors, carriers, & Heaven knows who besides, of demanders incessant, are inconceivable. I gave whatever they asked, from ignorance of what was due; & from fear of offending those of whose extent—& yet less of whose use of power I could form no judgement. I was the only one in this predicament, the rest refusing or disputing every claim. They all, but us, now went out to walk; but I stayed to write to my dearest Father, to Mrs. Lock, & to my expecting Mate. We were all 3 too much awake by the new scene to try for any repose, & the Hotel windows sufficed for our amusement l till Dinner. For this we

6 Or, the Hôtel Kingston (L. 469 n. 19).

7 Joseph Ducrocq, the proprietor since 1802 (at the latest) of the Hôtel du Lion d'Argent, which in previous years had been run by the Grandsires (see L. 469 n. 19). Situated in the rue Neuve (now the rue de l'Amiral Coubet), this hotel was reconstructed after its partial ruin by a fire of 1764, after which its original owner Dessein built in the rue Royale his far-famed hotel, the largest, it was said, in Europe, and called by one traveller 'a town within a town'.

As may be seen in a copy of a poster (in French and English) that a librarian at Calais (M. Lucien Saint) was kind enough to send us, Ducrocq, like his predecessors in the business, catered especially to the English trade: 'Buys. Sells. and Lett. CARRIAGES of all sorts. to any part of the Kingdom. / Joseph Ducrocq, having Furnished this Hotel entirely in the English Style, and considerably enlarged it respectfully informs the Nobility & Gentry resorting to CALAIS, that they may depend on the best Accomodations. A choice assortment of Wines of the best quality . . .'. It was here that Fuseli and Farington and their party stopped on their way to Paris in August of this year (see L. 526 n. 24).

8 The Hôtel Meurice was established in 1750 in the rue de Guise by a 'maître de poste', an Englishman named Meurice who a few years later established another hotel of the same name on the rue St. Honoré in Paris, a forerunner of the famous Hôtel Meurice on the rue de Rivoli today. Renowned for its cuisine and its wines, the Meurice at Calais attracted a distinguished clientele, including, it is said, the Duke of Brunswick, the Duke of Gloucester, Napolèon III, and Princess Victoria. Sometimes designated from these circumstances 'l'Auberge des Rois', it was bombarded and destroyed in 1940 but, rebuilt, still enjoys its reputation for excellent food and wines.

were all assembled about one o'clock, & I have rarely seen a better, & never a better served Dinner than was now presented us, for half a crow[n] a Head! but imagine, my dearest sir, how my repast was seasoned, when I tell you that, as soon as it began, a band of Music came to the Windows, & struck up God Save the King. I can never tell you what a pleased emotion was excited in my breast by this sound, on a shore so lately hostile, & on which I have so many so heart felt motives for wishing peace & amity perpetual!—Even what you cannot like *ME* feel, you can *FOR* me, I am sure, conceive.—This over, we ventured out of the Hotel, to look at the Street. We were to stay all the Day, but I had not courage to think of *walking in France* with only my Children; nor inclination to join my party beyond the limits of our contract. The Day was fine, the street was clean, two or three people, who passed us, made way for the Children, as they skipt out of my hands, & I saw such an unexpected appearance of quiet order & civility, that, almost without knowing it, we strolled from the Gate, & presently found ourselves in the Market place,[9] which was compleatly full of Sellers & Buyers, & Booths, looking like a large English Fair. The delighted Children could not bear to retreat, & all was so tranquil, that my own great, though nameless fears, wore away, & we soon entered into the very midst of Things: & as I saw no shadow of danger, upon making the experiment, I grew much amused from the sight. The queer gawdy jackets, always of a different colour from the peticoats, of the Women, & their immense wing Caps, which seemed made to double over their Noses, but which all [|] flew back so as to discover their Ears, in which I regularly saw large, & generally drop gold Earings, were quite as diverting to myself as to Alex & Adrienne. Many of them, also, had Gold necklaces, Chains, & Crosses; but Earings *ALL*: even the maids who were scrubbing or sweeping; ragged wretches who were carrying burthens on their heads or shoulders; old women selling fruit or other eatables; Gipsey-looking Creatures with Children tied to their backs,—*all* wore these long, broad, large, shining Gold Earings!

[9] Edmund John Eyre (p. 39), taking the whole morning of 10 July 1803 for a walk about Calais, found the market-place 'a large handsome square, surrounded by lofty houses. The Hôtel de Ville, or Town-hall erected on one side of it, has so noble an appearance without, that curiosity is excited to examine the interior, which does not, however, repay the labour . . .'.

Beggars, however, we saw not—no, not one, all the time we stayed, or sauntered; &, with respect to civility & gentleness, the poorest & most ordinary persons we met, or passed, might be compared with the best dressed & best looking walkers in the streets of our metropolis, & still to the disadvantage of the latter. I cannot say how much this surprised me, as I had conceived an horrific idea of the populace of this Country, imagining them all transformed into bloody monsters.— Another astonishment I experienced equally pleasing, though not equally important to my ease; I saw innumerable pretty women, & lovely Children, almost all of them extremely fair. I had been taught to expect nothing but mahoghany complexions & hideous features, instantly on crossing the Strait of Dover!—when this, however, was mentioned, in our party, afterwards, the High-lander haughtily exclaimed: 'But Calais was in the hands of the English so many years,[10] that the English race there is not yet extinct!' The perfect security in which I now saw we might wander about, induced us to Walk over the whole town, & even extend our excursion to the Ramparts surrounding it. It is, now, a very clean & pretty Town, & so orderly, that I there was no more tumult, or even noise, in the market place, where the people were so close together as to form a continued crowd, than in the by streets leading to the Country, where scarcely a passenger was to be seen. This is certainly a remark which I believe could never be made in England.

When we returned to the Hotel, I found all my fellow travellers had been to the Custom House! I had quite forgotten, or rather neglected to enquire the Hour for this formality, & was beginning to alarm myself, lest I was out of rule, when a young man, Commissary, I heard, of the Hotel, came to me, & asked if I had any thing contraband to the Laws of the Republic? I answered as I had done before;— 'Mais, Madame — avez vous quelques Chose de neuf? — "Oui, Monsieur." — "Quelque Jupons?" — "Beaucoup, Monsieur." Quelque bas de Coton?" — "Plusiers, Monsieur." "Eh bien, Madame — tout ça sera saisi!" — "Mon Dieu, Monsieur! quand ce n'est

10 For over 200 years, between the reigns of Edward III and Mary I of England —1347–1558.

pas de tout pour Vendre! seulement pour porter?" — "C'est egal, Madame. tout ça sera saisi." — "Eh — mon dieu, que faut-il donc faire? — " "Il faut, Madame — payer genereusement; &, si vous êtes bien sûr qu'il n'y est rien a vendre — alors — peut-être — " ' I entreated him to take charge himself as to what was *right*, & GENEROUS,—& he undertook to go through the ceremony for me, without my appearing. I was so much frightened, & so happy not to be called upon personally, that I thought myself very cheaply off in his after demand, of a Guinea & a half. I had two & a half to pay afterwards for additional luggage.

We found reigning through Calais a general joy & satisfaction at the restoration of *Dimanche*,[11] & abolition of *Decade*. I had a good deal of conversation ǀ with the Maid of the Inn, a tall, fair, extremely pretty woman; & she talked much upon this subject, & the delight it occasioned, & the obligation all France was under to the premier Consul for restoring Religion & Worship.[11]

Sunday, April 18th We set off at 5 O'clock in the Morning; I had just time to get my Children ready, but had not dared risk undressing myself. You may believe, therefore, I was not much refreshed; & the poor things were unwilling enough to rise; but Alex, once awaked, could sleep no more, & Adrienne, more happy as a Traveller, reposed upon my lap till she had finished her night's requisite rest. There was not, indeed, much lost by those who spared their Eyes in this part of the journey! The Country, broad, flat, or barrenly Steep, without Trees, without verdure, without buildings, & scarcely inhabited, exhibited a change from the fertile fields, & beautiful woods & Gardens, & civilization of Kent, so sudden & unpleasant, that I only lamented the fatigue of my position, which regularly impeded my making use of this chasm of pleasure or observation for repose. This part of France must certainly be the least

---

[11] On 16 July 1801 a Concordat was signed suppressing the Civil Constitution of the Clergy (1790), as well as other revolutionary Church laws, and declaring Catholicism to be the religion of the majority of Frenchmen (Lefebvre, p. 131). It was not until 8 Apr. 1802, however, that the Concordat was made law by the French legislature, and on Easter Sunday 18 April., the very day on which FBA was taking notes on the subject, it was solemnly promulgated. For the impressive ceremony at Notre-Dame, see Madelin, iv. 163–5, and for a lively account by an eye-witness, Wilmot, pp. 59–60.

frequented, for we rarely met a single Carriage, & the villages, few & distant, seemed to have ⏐ no intercourse with each other. *Dimanche*, indeed, might occasion this stillness, for we saw, at almost all the villages, neat & clean peasants going to, or coming from Mass, & seeming elated & happy indiscribably by the public permission of divine worship on its originally appointed Day.

⟶

At Boulogne we dined—& here, most unexpectedly, we were joined at Table by a tall well made young woman, not handsome, but of a rather striking countenance, & singularly ceremonious in reverences & gestures, & sententious & self-complacent in discourse, as well as fashionable, though not indecent, in attire: & she travelled in the Basket! though she begged leave to join the inside Company at Table. There was something so civil in her manners, it was impossible not to be civil in return, yet so little *as usual*, it was equally impossible not to draw back from any acquaintance. I ought, however, by no means to omit mentioning how much I was struck with the change in Mad^e de Raymond, who joined us this morning from another Hotel. Her Hoop peticoat was no more visible, & what remained was as lank, or more so, than her neighbour's; & her distancing the Children was not only at an end, but she prevented me from renewing any of my cautions to them of not incommoding her! &, when we were together a few moments before we were joined by the rest, she told me, with a significant smile, not to tutor the Children about her any more, as she had only avoided them, from having something of consequence to take care of, which was now removed. I then saw she meant some English Lace, or Muslin, which she had carried in a peticoat, &, since the Custom house examination was over, had now packed in her trunk—Poor lady! I fear this little merchandize was all her hope of succour on her arrival! She is amongst the emigrants who have twice or thrice returned, but not yet been able to rest in their own Country. ⏐

When we returned to the Coach, Mad^e Raymond informed us that she had learnt, from her femme de Chambre, that the lady who now joined us at Meals was an Actress. This was not very surprising to me, from her appearance, though I felt a little awkward in her junction, without knowing something of her Character. However, it was amongst the chances I was forced to run. But our merry-hearted Gouvernante now conceived a plan to make this Dame undertake to form, & to teach French to, the young Irishman, who declared, half frightened, half amused, he had rather put himself under the protection of Mad^e Raymond: but the High-land Chief entered into the project, &, from this time, whenever the Coach stopt, whether for our refreshment, or simply for that of our Horses, the Gentleman & lady were brought to a conference by the lively Gouvernante, encouraged by the Highlander, & listened to with some, though more dignified amusement, by Mad^e Raymond, who, seeing my shyness of this Farce, whispered me That, in France, Actresses, where they had talents, were always well received, if they behaved with propriety. I told her I was amongst the last not to do them justice; & where they had Character as well as talents, I should be proud to be the first to do them honour: This might be the case here, but I always prefer holding back to drawing back; & therefore I was constantly silent, & absorbed by the Children. The approbation of the Highlander So stimulated the Gouvernante, that her spirits now were above her discretion, & she knew no bounds to her laughing scheme, which I soon saw brought the Actress rather more into the front ground than shewed her to advantage; Mad^e Raymond luckily perceived it too, &, by a grave though mild interference, checked the progress of the essay; as much, I really believe, to the relief of the poor ┊ young Irishman, as to mine. The Highlander, who would have kept up the sport, & the Gouvernante, were now such friends, that they sung, chatted, told stories in broken French & broken English, alternately, & were alive to each other's pleasanteries with mutual joy in lightening the tediousness of the night journey; the Highlander glad to be diverted out of his haughty sulleness, & the Gouvernante delighted with all & every opportunity of making mirth.

This lasted till, tired all around, one by one, all the party dropt asleep—except myself, & my two charges were too miserably accommodated, except by leaning wholly upon me, to obtain any repose: of course, I could get none. An Hour or two passed now in dark & silence, my sole amusement arising from the poor Irishman's head, which dropt down on Mad. Raymond's shoulder, from its tall & thin height above it, twenty times in a quarter of an hour, & which she repulsed, with a dignity that would have been anger, had not her own sleepiness been so potent, she could only awake for the single instant requisite to push the unfortunate Pate away from her: but about 4 o'Clock in the Morning, the Highland Chief, suddenly awaking, let down the window: the Gouvernante, who was fast asleep, being roused by a sharp blast of air, lost her good humour by the cold, & pulled it up. The Highlander, motioning her to be quiet, resumed his first sullen pride, & let it down: 'What for you do that?' cried she, 'I won't suffer no such thing to get my nose full of cold at such time of night.' He, however, roughly insisted; but the Gouvernante, not chusing to submit, exclaimed: 'What for you think only of yourself? Nobody will let no Gentleman do such thing!' & she held the Glass up with her hand. The Highlander ¹ seemed indignant beyond words; but looked as if he should have felt no small solace to his wounded pride, had it been possible for him to make some manual exertions with his broad hand upon her broad plump Cheeks. He forbore, however; but spoke to her no more; & though, when she had taken another nap, & awoke to the sun beams which succeeded to the nightly blast, she was as gay & chatty as before, & told her stories, & sung her Songs,—all were cast away; the Highlander neither heard her nor saw her; he spoke only with the young Irishman, whom he had not before heeded, & shewed every mark of respect he could devize to Mad. de Raymond, by way of manifesting her superiority to the poor Gouvernante: who was by no means unmoved at the change, & so angry, that she could only look at him with disgust. Two spirits of such fiery materials, both offended, were not likely to remain long without striking again at each other; &, in a few Hours, upon some new change from hot to cold, the Highlander put down the Glass, & the Gouvernante pulled it up. This was repeated with the pristine vivacity of the original struggle, till the Gouvernante, natural as well as violent, called out 'What for you think conquer a lady, you rude Man?' 'A lady?' repeated he, 'what do you mean by a lady? you are a mere poor low bred woman, & never till now sat at the same table with such

a man as me!—' 'Did not I? who told you so, Mr.? You are
nothing but for a Brute to talk so? I have been at the same Table
with you many times enough!' 'Yes,' cried he, 'to stand behind
the Chair, when I have been seated upon it!' | 'How dare you
say such thing?' cried she, 'I will shew you what a lady I am
the next Town I come to! You may speak so to your English,
if they will let you, English as you are, for a Brute to speak so to
me! I will have you to the Municipality!'

He had just got his head out to call to the Conductor, when
this word, municipality, checked him; he drew back, & applied
to Mad. Raymond, who gravely told him he was in the wrong,
but consented to let him change places with her, to be on the
side where the Glass was down by general consent. He accepted
the offer, making her many compliments upon her being A
Gentlewoman, & protesting he would no longer sit opposite so
low a Creature. The Gouvernante again declared she would
take him to the Municipality at Amiens; & from that time No
one spoke till we arrived there, except the dear Children.

Arrived at Amiens, where we were to Dine, Mad. Raymond,
after a previous conference with our enraged but really good
hearted Gouvernante, called me to assist at the discussion;
I would fain have retreated, for every possible reason; but
could not get excused: what, however, was my consternation,
when she told me she must send for the Conductor, & make
him come before us in a body, while we declared the offence
offered to Mad^e Blaiseaux, that justice must be done, that we
must all join to vindicate the right to have one Glass up while
the other was down; & to let the mistaken Gentleman know
That, in public Machines, the Majority always prevailed, &
therefore, since by this ⟨deed⟩ he had offended a lady, we must
desire, in a body, that the Conductor would insist upon his
relinquishing his place, & proceeding in some other con-
veyance. |

I can hardly tell you my consternation at this proposal. To
make my entrance into France run the risk of being announced
by a dispute so likely to end by our all being called before the
Municipality of Amiens—& thence, perhaps, sent with some
Guard to Paris!—English, too, myself, to appear against
a Member of our United Kingdom—but my fright luckily
made me eloquent enough to save me from this exposition;

I represented so urgently my hopes the Culprit was already alarmed, which indeed, in defiance of his rage, I had observed to be the case, & that the victory was sufficient, if he were forced to offend no more, that the good humoured Gouvernante gave way, & it was agreed we should let him have one more trial before we proceeded to extremities. This foolish affair swallowed up all the time in which I might have strolled a little about the Town of Amiens; & when we returned to the Carriage, the Highlander, getting in first, & sitting forward, said to Mad. Raymond, who followed him 'Mettez vous là, Madame — ' pointing to the Seat opposite him. 'Pardonnez-moi, Monsieur?' answered she; & composedly, Added, that she begged him to alight a moment, & speak with the Conductor, who had been prepared to give him a little counsel. This effectually quieted him, & he left the Glass to the discretion of his triumphant *vis-à-vis*, but the painful care with which they each determined never to look at the other, was ridiculous to behold, though it must have been very difficult to sustain. But, at Chantilly, at about 5 O'clock in the following morning, this Highland Chief descended, to make some enquiries concerning that famous place,—& then, sending for his baggage into the Inn, appeared no more: how ǀ deeply regretted by our Gouvernante I leave you, dearest Sir, to imagine.

What most, in the course of this journey, struck me, was the satisfaction of all the Country people, with whom I could converse,[12] at the restoration of the *Dimanche*, & the boasts they now ventured to make of having never kept the *Decade*, except during the dreadful reign of Robbespierre, when not to oppose any of his severest decrees was insufficient for safety—it was essential even to existence to observe them with every parade of warmest approvance! The horrible histories I heard from every one of that period, of wanton, as well as political cruelty, I must have judged exaggerated, either through the mists of Fear, or the heats of resentment, but that, though the details

---

[12] By aptitude of ear and memory, long training and practice, it was FBA's mode to listen, particularly to the speech of the people, whereas Mary Berry tended to use her eyes. Travelling along a similar route a few weeks earlier, therefore, Mary Berry noted the 'melancholy and ruinous appearance' of 'the poor churches, all of which, even in the little villages, have their windows broken, the tops of their spires knocked off, and with most of them their roofs falling to pieces; at the same time I believe they are almost all used. Those belonging to abbeys . . . are, for the most part, actually pulled down . . .' (Berry, ii. 126).

had innumerable modifications, there was but one voice for the excess of barbarity. Where-ever the Coach stopt, to change, or only feed the Horses, my Children & I alighted, & walked on, to stretch our limbs, or entered some Cottage, or some shop, for som⟨e⟩ refreshment; without which management, I know not how the poor little Souls could have endured continued confinement for 2 Days & 2 Nights, after so fatiguing a passage. Indeed the change of posture was equally necessary to myself— perhaps more; for so crampt I sometimes felt myself I could hardly descend from the Coach.—At a little Hamlet near Claremont, where we stopt some time, two good old women told us This was the happiest Day ('twas Sunday) of their lives; that they had ALL lost le bon Dieu for these last 10 years, but that Buonaparte had now found him!—In another Cottage, we were told the villagers had kept their own Curé all this time concealed, & I though privately & with fright, had therefore saved their Souls through the whole of the bad times. And in another, some poor Creatures said They were now content with their destiny, be it what it might, for they should be happy, at least, in the World to come; but that, while denied going to Mass, they had all their sufferings aggravated by knowing they must lose their Souls, hereafter, besides all they had to endure here!—O my dearest Father! that there can have existed wretches of such diabolical wickedness as to have snatched, torn from the toiling Indigent every ray even of future Hope!— Various of these little conversations extremely touched me; nor was I unmoved, though not by such painful emotion, in the sight of the Sunday Night Dance, in a little village through which we passed, where there seemed two or 3 hundred peasants engaged in that pastime, all clean & gaily dressed, yet all so decent & well behaved, that but for the poor old Fidlers we might have drove on, & not have perceived the rustic Ball.

Here ends the account of my Journey,—& if it has amused my dearest Father, it will be a true delight to me to have scribbled it; my next Letter brings me to the Capital—and —— to the only person who can console me for my always lamented absence from Himself—witness Fr. D'arblay

June 10. I eagerly [seize an] offered opportunity[1] to send this to my dearest Father,

Paris, 21 April 1802

To Doctor Burney

A.L. unfinished (Barrett, Eg. 3690, ff. 108–9b, with P-tab, f. 107), 21
Apr. 1802
    Double sheet 4to 2 pp. *pmks* T.P.Po[st] / ⟨   ⟩ / 28 AP 1802
red seal
    Addressed: Dr Burney, / Chelsea College, / Middlesex—
    Carried to London and posted by Barthélémy Huber[1]
    Endorsed by CB: (Apr. 21) M^rs D — from Paris / N° 2
    Edited by FBA, p. 1, *annotated*: ⚬∴ ⟨   ⟩st   (8)   A new Number^g begins
Paris   N.B After this letter a new numbering begins of the same year
Arrival at Paris—all gay & happy in delicious re-union
    Edited also by CFBt.

Paris 21st April 1802.

An opportunity has just presented itself by which I can send
a Letter to my dearest Father—who I know will be gla[d—]
since I have left him—to see the date, & hear of my safe arrival—
though I have not power now to add more—for such has been
my fatigue that I can still hardly use either hands or Eyes.
I am but just up—& this must be got ready immediately for
M. Huber[1]—but I will try, in a Day or two, to begin a regular
history of my voyage & journey,[2] which I hope will not tire
you quite as much to read as it did me to perform: & then it
shall wait for the first opportunity to be forwarded.

⌐I enclose a few lines, which I entreat my dearest Father
to direct for me to *Miss Planta*.⌐ I have not yet been able to
deliver my Letters[3]—nor even shew my passport—but when
I am a little rested, it will be my first business. Alex is recovered,
but much thinned by his sickness & fatigues. Adrienne is
perfectly well—& I have delivered her to her delighted Father
& Grand Mother, who came instantly to claim her on the
news of our arrival.[4]

⌐I entreat my dear Fanny to put up my black veil, which I
unfortunately left behind me, & carry it, when you can be so

509. [1] Barthélemy Huber (L. 487 n. 2).   [2] This was Journal Letter 508.
[3] Letters sent by Mrs. Harcourt (see L. 513 n. 1).
[4] The delivery of Adrienne de Chavagnac to her family is described in the
Journal Letters 510 (p. 244) and 511 (pp. 250–1).

good as to let her have a coach, to Mrs. Huber, & solicit her kind counsel whether M. de Lally may bring it,[5] if sealed up in a Letter or parcel directed to me. As it is not new, though good, I should think there would be no danger & ⌐ M. de Lally I am sure will undertake the commission, though he cannot pay copious duty,¬ *Moyennant payer genereusement.* I brought all secure here: but as I had nothing for sale, & nothing unmade, though new, I was perhaps too soon frightened by my counselling assistant. I thank God M. Darblay is quite well, & he has procured me a most pleasant & airy apartment. I have a thousand little things to tell—none important, except as your kindness to the teller may give them weight.

My dear Fanny must again speak for me to my dear sister, &c &c as to my safe arrival in Paris—for I have not another Moment but to recommend myself to the kind remembrance of my dearest—dearest Father.—
Rue Miromenil,
Nº 1185. à Paris.

I shall so build upon Letters by M. de Lally that if he comes without them I believe I shall behave very ill—So save my credit in a strange Land, dearest Sir!

I find M. Darblay quite well—& he has prepared every thing that can make me comfortable. I know not when I shall be able to go abroad, but I am never in any haste to quit my home. Maria has been with me twice already, & looks much better, & is in spirits upon her own opinion of recovery by this change of Climate.

We find the people here all enchanted by the restoration of the *Dimanche.* In our journey on that Day we passed innumerable flocks of clean tidy country people, going to or coming from Church. This has been a very popular Act. ⌐I have not had time for an intended half to ⟨Esther⟩.¬[6]

[*Except for the address, the second leaf is blank*]

5 M. de Lally was not to leave England until November 1802.
6 Esther Burney.

PARIS JOURNAL

510   *for* 20–21 April 1802

To Doctor Burney

A.J.L. continued (Diary MSS. vi. 5458–[61], Berg), written at 1185, rue de Miroménil, but concluded in Monceaux on 29 [Prarial, *an error for* 18] June 1802
Double sheet 4to, numbered 7 [*as the 7th ds. sent to CB from Paris in 1802*]
4 pp. *pmks* T. P. P. / High St. Mbne 28 JU 1802
Addressed: ENGLAND / Dr. Burney, / Chelsea College, / Middlesex
Carried to London by Anthony Merry
Endorsed by CB: (Apr. 20) sheet 7
Edited by FBA, *who annotated* p. 1 (5458): Happy arrival, M. d'Arblay M^d d'Henin.
Edited also by the Press.
Conjecturally portions of this letter must have been copied by M. d'A into the 'Paris Letter Book' in combination with passages from L. 511 to form a composite account of the events of 20–1 April. This account was later copied for CFBt, who corrected and edited it (Diary MSS. viii. 5456 and 5468, the intervening 8pp. unfoliated, Berg). A typescript copy, also made from the Letter Book, is now in the National Portrait Gallery (grangerized DL, v. p. 504) and it is this latter that is printed by Brimley Johnson, in Fanny Burney and the Burneys (1926), pp. 32–9.

Paris, April. 1802.

At length, My dearest Padre, I come to our safe arrival here on *Tuesday, April 20ᵗʰ*, which we entered with perfect quietness, & found as quiet as ourselves. The Carriages, indeed, from some peculiarity in their construction, make triple the noise of those in London,—a noise so stunning as to nearly deafen me; but the people move so gently, make way for one-another so civilly, & look so peaceably, that, in streets without Carriages, you may walk through Crowds as tranquilly & unmolested as through so many flocks of sheep. I was forcibly, however, struck with the immense superiority of London in the appearance of the Streets: their narrowness here, & the surprising height of the Houses, gives them the air of what, in England, we should merely denominate Lanes: while the breadth of ours, & our noble foot pavement, give a facility of intercourse to the passengers, & a healthy & pleasant airyness to the Inhabitants, as much more agreeable as I should suppose it to be more salubrious. Against this, however, for constant residence, our Coal fires & smoke must be balanced—& then, perhaps, with respect both to health & pleasure, the scales may become even.

When we drove to the Hotel where we were to alight [Rue Notre Dame des Victoires],[1] the first object I saw was M. D'arblay, awaiting us: it was between 10 & 11 o'clock, & there he had stationed himself from 7!—It was not what I wished so publicly to meet him, after so painful & eventful an absence; but it might not have been, perhaps, what I should have expected, had he stayed quietly at home till we could have joined him there. To the kind heart of my dearest Father—which but too feelingly knows the perfection of conjugal partnership—I need not enter upon the solace of this moment to all its preceding conflicts.—Even my little Alex—seized with speechless fondness to his Father's breast, I felt his loquacious & ardent spirit softened by joy into silent tenderness.—I took a brief leave of my fellow-travellers, who, by their congratulations, shewed they discovered by my looks the happiness which not a word, I am sure, betrayed, & M. D'arblay ordered a Fiacre, which conveyed us to Rue Miromenil, where, in Hotel Marengo,[2] he had prepared for our reception. We have a very pretty apartment, consisting of a sallon, a sal à manger, nôtre Chambre, a dressing room within it which we make Alex's Bed room, a little dark closet for a fille de Chambre, & an anti Room which separates all this from our little kitchen; & the whole has been papered, with new linen Beds, & much new furniture, put up entirely to prevail with M. D'arblay to fix his little family for the present where he had all the winter, in a single room, fixed himself. We are up 3 pair of stairs, to be sure—but *The nearer the Gods*, you know! & we see the Gardens of the ci-divant Hotel Beauvau[3] from our windows, & have the

510. [1] See L. 504 n. 2.

[2] The Hôtel Marengo, at 1185, rue de Miroménil, must have been on the west side of the street (L. 520, p. 322), perhaps closer to the rue Verte (now rue de Penthièvre) than to the rue du Faubourg Saint-Honoré.

Eighteenth-century houses in Paris were usually of four to six stories. ' "Les marchands occupent les boutiques (peu de maisons en sont dépourvues) . . . les gens riches le premier, les gens aisés le second, les salariés le troisième, les ouvriers le quatrième, les pauvres les étages supérieurs", et, comme il n'y a pas encore d'escaliers de service, ces locataires de fortune si diverses, se rencontrent dans le grand escalier' (Madelin, xi. 74).

[3] The Hôtel Beauvau, built by the architect Nicolas le Camus de Mézières (1721–89) for the maréchal Charles-Just de Beauvau (1720–93), faced a large courtyard with an entrance opening on Place Beauvau, at the intersection of the

fields open at one end of the street, & are close to les Champs elisés from the other. The situation is all that I can wish, entirely out of the violent bustle & close air of Paris. M. D'arblay had been most kindly assisted in preparing for me by Mad^e cidivant Princesse d'Henin d'Alsace, whom I had known particularly in England,—& as my dear Fanny can well relate, who has a claim to my respect & affection from having inspired both in one whose feeling & judgement in the characters she appreciated were nearly unerring!⁴—This truly amiable lady— who has been a daily comfort, resource, & pleasure to me, came almost instantly to welcome me to Paris,—amply supplying me immediately with Tea, sugar, Urn, Tea-pot, &c, *à l'anglaise.*—M. de Narbonne came also; he lives just opposite us,⁵ &, as far as I can gather, in the most retired private life. I was much affected by many recollections at his sight—& so he seemed himself. He was extremely pleased with his little Godson, cordially embracing & blessing him. Soon after came the cidivant Comte de Chavagnac,⁶ for his pretty little Daughter, my dearest Mrs. Lock's Adrienne, with the child's Grand Mother, ci-divant ⌐Marq^{se} de Montecler, a very respectable old lady, & a young lady, who seemed about 12 years old, but who I found was MARRIED!—& Adrienne's young Brother.⁶ They received her with great joy, but so much grave solemnity, that the poor Child seemed quite in consternation at the change from happy Norbury Park! but she revived in playing with her Brother, & their great kindness will soon, I hope, reconcile her to the change of scene—& persons!

rue de Faubourg Saint-Honoré and the rue de Miroménil, and the avenue de Marigny (Hillairet, ii, 506, 508–9). There were large gardens extending to the north from the back of the hotel, a fine view of which FBA may have enjoyed from apartment on the third floor.

⁴ Susanna Phillips. Fanny Phillips would remember her mother's association with the princesse d'Hénin (L. 446 n. 23) and the friendship that developed between the two women when, in the winter of 1795–6, they were engaged in carrying aid to destitute *émigrés*.   ⁵ At 1205, rue de Miroménil.

⁶ Louis-Vigile, comte de Chavagnac (iii *passim*), whose wife, Agathe-Françoise *née* de Montecler (iii, L. 201 n. 5) had died in 1798. Their son Henri, *styled* comte de Chavagnac, was born in the summer of 1794 in Brussels. The children were thus 7 and 8 years old respectively. Their maternal grandmother was Hyacinthe-Jeanne-Marie de Montecler (1750–1805), who had married in 1768 her cousin René-François-Georges-Marie de Montecler (1739–1810), comte, *later* marquis de Montecler.

The young married lady must have been their twenty-year-old daughter Eugénie-Henriette de Montecler (1782–1863), who had married in this year Gaspard de Montecler (1773–1848).

Mr. Bourdois & Maria came quickly looking in high spirits, & very happy. They are in a house as yet all unfinished, & unfurnished,[7] but as TIME, only, is wanting, not MONEY for its completion, their condition is not very deplorable. Some other persons called also,[8]—& I had a young Maiden brought me, who had already been hired for my *femme de Chambre* — & *femme de Cuisine* — & *Bonne* for Alex,—&c &c—with la Portiere of the House for all drudgery, *moyennant payez genereusement.* This young Maiden, Pauline,[9] is remarkably pretty, of a very well made figure, *douce* in voice & manner, a good milliner, a tolerable manteau-maker, & really fitted to be only *femme de Chambre*; but she undertakes the rest, *moyennant* that same *payer genereusement*, which, for us, is extremely cheap, as her various talents make her constantly useful & comfortable, & She is extremely pleasing in her manners.

April 21st I spent the whole Morning in Bed, while at least a score of M. D'arblay's friends came to enquire after me. But when Bood & Maria were of the number, I arose: not, however, much refreshed, for I had been too much fatigued for sleep. My little Adrienne also came to see me, & her good Father & Grandmother; & I was struck to see how serious the poor little Girl was grown,—not, however, from any apprehensions of her future welfare & happiness, for she could have had no heart to be gay at once upon having such an adopting Mother as Mrs. Lock,—such a House as Norbury Park. Mr. Huber[10] called also, &, after the terrific account he had given to Mrs Huber, communicated no small comfort to me, by saying That, many as were the licentious & profligate here, I there was no City in Europe where Foreigners were more completely at liberty to chuse their own society, & their own plans, than the visitors of Paris: & that those who thought they must needs follow the stream, were entirely mistaken. 'And, Ma'am,' he added, 'however many people, & things, you may see here to shock

---

[7] The apartment that Bourdois acquired at 4, rue de Choiseul is described in L. 520, p. 322.
[8] The caller, whose name FBA here diplomatically omits, was Mme de Laval (see L. 511 n. 6).
[9] Pauline was later to marry the comte de Narbonne's valet 'Augustin' (ii, L. 68 n. 46) and to give birth to a son at Tronchoy in 1805, having by that time taken service with Maria Bourdois, with whom she remained until 1806. See the letters of Maria Bourdois to her family (*Catalogue*).
[10] Barthélemy Huber (L. 487 n. 2).

you, you will find many persons of real worth ready to receive you, & to do you every service in their power.' He then particularly instanced Madame de Tessé,[11] an old lady, ci divant first Dame d'honneur to the Queen—whose wishes, he said, to know me, were stimulated, *en outre* other civil reasons, by her long esteem & personal regard for M. D'arblay. Madame D'Henin he also named as particularly amiable & benevolent: & he gave me a hint—in very flattering terms, that I required nothing but care to pretty much chuse for myself.

We closed this Day by a visit in the Evening, from M. Bazille Junr the son of M. D'arblay's so much beloved Uncle.[12] He seems a very amiable young Man, & is remarkably handsome—*FOR.*—our Alex has a strong family resemblance to him! *N'est-ce pas tout dire?* That excellent Uncle has written us the kindest, most cordial invitation to Joigny, where he would have us fix our residence: but M. D'arblay thinks it essential to remain in Paris till it is pretty generally abandonned for the Summer.

June 29. I seize an opportunity of enclosing to my dearest Father this old Journal, with a new *Bulletin* in the Letter I send by M. Merry[13]—We are in a Country Lodging,[14] for our poor Alex, who is getting better daily, & we are well ourselves, but I live wholly shut up with my Boy, from terror of another relapse, till he is quite restored. I long for more frequent news My

---

[11] Adrienne-Catherine de Noailles (1741–1814), formerly dame d'honneur to Marie-Antoinette, had married in 1755 René-Mans de Froulay (1736–1814), comte de Tessé. Sister of the duc d'Ayen (1739–1824), aunt therefore to Mme de Lafayette, she emerged in revolutionary times as one of the most resourceful (with her dairies and farms) and one of the most energetic and generously helpful members of the Noailles family. Her friendship for d'Arblay is attested by five extant letters (Berg) from [1802–5] to 22 June [1813]. See L. 526, pp. 342–3; and *Catalogue*.

[12] Probably the eldest son of Jean-Baptiste-Gabriel Bazille (1731–1817), namely Jean-Baptiste-Gabriel-Edme (1767–1804). See Genealogical Table, iii, facing p. 1.

[13] Anthony Merry (c. 1756–14 June 1835) of Dedham, Essex, to whose memory a mural tablet may be seen in the beautiful church of St. Mary's there. An able diplomat (Rose, i. 312), he had been sent to Madrid (1789–90), to Copenhagen (1799–1800), and to the congress at Amiens (1801–2), as Secretary to the Embassy, having recently (18 Apr. 1802) presented his credentials to Bonaparte as Minister Plenipotentiary *ad interim* to France. Childless, he seems to have had, according to his will (P.C.C. *Glocester* 440), an array of snuff-boxes (of agate and precious jewels) to dispose of. Reputedly austere, he had provoked Bonaparte's ironic quip '*Mons. Toujours Rire!*' See the Revd. Canon A. R. Johnston, R.D., *The Parish Church of St. Mary* (1967); and for his marriage on 21 Jan. 1803, *AR* xlv, 'Chronicle', 475.

[14] At Monceau (see Ll. 520 and 525).

dearest Father—& entreat to have it *per post*, if *les occasions* are so rare. always direct to Rue Miromenil, whence our Letters follow us safely. Heaven bless my most dear Padre M. D'arblays kindest love

PARIS JOURNAL

511   *for* 20–21 April 1802

To Mrs. Locke

J.L., copy in an unknown hand (Diary MSS. viii. 5462–[71], with two unfoliated sheets, Berg) presumably from the original A.J.L. lent to CFBt by the Lockes. The original would seem to have been composed in two or three sections at 1185, rue de Miroménil, Paris, in May 1802, with an explanatory conclusion[1] added (probably on the address fold) of the first double sheet. Dated 1st ⟨June⟩, the first part was probably sent on that date by post.

Three double sheets (9·3 × 7·6″) and a double sheet (8·9 × 7·3″), the first much mutilated by CFBt, the second bearing paste-overs, as see Textual Notes 13 pp.

Edited by CFBt and the Press.

Conjecturally portions of this letter must have been copied by M. d'A into the 'Paris Letter Book' in combination with passages from L. 510 to form a composite account of the events of 20–1 April 1802. Two copies were made of this account, as described in L. 509 above.

Paris 1802

I go on with the Day of our Arrival (*April 20.*[2] from its peculiar interest to my beloved Fredy My first intention was to put the two Children & myself to Bed! but Alex and I forgot all fatigue & lost all sleepiness, from the happy feelings we experienced;

511. [1] 'This and two more sheets were intended for an opportunity which has failed. I entreat to hear from you, my dearest friend—all I write for opportunities I leave open enough for directing by post if disappointed. Heaven bless you. at this moment we are all three nearly well but my dear Alex has again frightened me Mille & mille bien tendres complimens a tous nos excellens amis de la part de leur devoire. I long for full bulletins of your precious health and eyes & my beloved oracle & Amine, & all.'
[2] Arrival at rue Notre-Dame-des-Victoires, Paris, 'between 10 & 11 o'clock' on Tuesday 20 Apr. 1802.

& Adrienne had been so well, & reposed so frequently, she was in perfect health. Scarsely had we looked around us, when Mad*e* D'Henin,[3] whose apartments are nearly opposite, arrived to welcome me to Paris. She had already prepared me Tea & Sugar, for my refreshment, an urn & Teapot, to make it with, & 3 pots of *Groseille* for little Alex, with small articles innumerable of immediate use & comfort. She recieved me with the greatest kindness, was charmed to see Adrienne so much improved, & talked of my dearest friend, & all hers, with a warmth of regard & respect & affection very delightful to my ears & my heart—but alas—with what a pang, a sadness, did I see her!—we had not met since my ever & for ever irremediable loss—& the knowledge she had of it—& the value that angel set upon her & her friendship—all rushed into my mind, & I was so much overpowered as, I fear, to distress her—But this place, my dearest friend,—this scene—this country—this society—all of which she [our Susanna] ⌐ would so have delighted to have joined—whether personally or by my accounts —O my beloved friend—what a constant—a gnawing—an endless drawback to all perfect enjoyment—is that fatal separation!—[4]

Feelingly, and prudently, she hastened away advising me to take some rest—But she had only descended the stairs, when Augustin[5] mounted them, to bring me the compliments of Madame de Laval,[6] who desired to know how I did after my

[3] For the dwelling of the princesse d'Hénin, see L. 513, p. 265 and n. 15.

[4] The death of Susanna Phillips (*née* Burney) on 6 Jan. 1800, which marked the end, as FBA had said before, of any 'perfect Happiness on Earth'. See iv, L. 354, p. 382; L. 393, p. 453; L. 414, p. 492; L. 421, p. 508.

[5] Augustin, valet de chambre of the comte de Narbonne until the latter's death. The Countess Potocka speaks of Narbonne as being 'Gouverné par son valet de chambre, véritable valet de comédie qui le menait en flattant son goût pour le luxe' (Solovieff, p. 222 n.)

[6] FBA's embarrassment arose from her knowledge of the 'particular' friendship between the comte de Narbonne and Mme de Laval (cf. iii, p. 152) and the 'ménage singulier' in which the comte, with his valet Augustin, occupied the first floor, and Mme de Laval, with her servants, the second (L. 469 n. 6).

Mme de Cazenove d'Arlens, who, like FBA, had much experience of Mme de Laval's kindness, describes her appearance one day when, 'un grand chapeau de paille sur le nez, une petite cane à la main, elle vient toute seule à pied du faubourg Saint-Honoré, sachant que j'étais trop enrhumée pour courir ce matin.' Her lively conversation touched on many subjects— 'société, mariage, religion, et sur tous les sujets elle est également piquante'. On that occasion, some talk of a Paris marriage gave rise to her observations on the fifty 'demoiselles à marier dans cette première société: peu de fortune, beaucoup de luxe, plus de couvents et, dans un certain cercle d'amies, on est difficile, dénigrante: on jette un ridicule sur

journey. I sent my thanks, & that I was tolerably well, but meant to take a week's rest before I should feel recovered. My dear Friend will not think this quite so elegant as it was sincere: but here comes another alas! certain reports against this lady, with respect to her *amitié* for an old & admired friend of ours, had made me anxious to defer the acquaintance, till I could know better with what degree of intimacy or coldness to begin it. I soon found, however, my precaution rather too late; she had already formed the project of a free connexion, had sent, also, *des-confitures*, for Alex, & persuaded Mr D'arblay to let her choose me a Cap & a Hat, from her own ˡ milliner. This was embarrassing, especially as I had not time to speak upon the subject before there came another message that she would inquire herself how I did, if it would not be indiscreet. M. D'arblay said it would be impossible to refuse—& up stairs she took the trouble to mount. She is still even *pretty*, nay, almost *more*, except for very bad teeth; her complexion is fair, & smooth, her eyes very fine & all her features very good; her dress was a very elegant dishabille, though not in first repair, & she has a look that, had I not been prejudiced against her, would have struck me as mingling benevolence of character with spirit of disposition. But I held back involuntarily, from thinking the best, lest I should again have to crush, as with Made de S[taël], an intimacy, too hastily and unhappily formed. Her civilities were unspeakable; her offers of services had the solicitude of begging them, & her whole mind seemed at work to oblige, & to engage me. She would not, however, she said, so soon have forced her way, but that, understanding how much I was fatigued, she concluded I should be invisible for some days, & she could not command her forbearance so long a time. She seemed, indeed, so ardent, & so kind, I was truly disturbed by my incertitude, what to think of her, which, joined to my entire disuse of speaking french, ˡ made the visit extremely—to be sincere—oppressive to me. I made, however, no engagement, anxious first to discuss the subject; but not a moment now was to be allowed for it, as I seized the instant of her retreat to look for the small pacquet of dear Adrienne, &

l'homme qui ne danse pas à ravir, qui n'est pas la perfection de la mode, de la grâce. On s'exalte sur ses défauts, on refuse: on devient laide, vieille, aigre, et voilà, ma chère, ce que nous commencons à voir à Paris. — ' (p. 106).

prepare her for her friends: I had not, however, taken out the first pin (all sewings being demolished at the Custom House when Augustin returned, with the compliments of M. de Narbonne, and a request to know if I was too tired to receive him before I took my projected long repose. There was again no denying—but O what bitter pangs of bitterest recollection—& retrospection—accompanied this interview.[7] It was long before I could speak to him—even a word—and he was pale, M. D'arblay says as death, and trembling all the time—but I hardly discerned any part of his face—& though in introducing to him his little God-son I a little recovered, I believe it was nearly an equal relief to us both when M. D'arblay said I ought now to take a little rest — — For rest, however, I had as little time as, at that moment, power; my poor Adrienne's pacquet was still unpinned, when Made de Montecler was announced.[8] She was recieved of course, instantly; she was accompanied by M. de Chavagnac, M. Louis, his little Son, & a young Lady, who was not named but seemed a relation, & appeared about 12 years of age. Poor Adrienne now changed colour—She came to me, & clung to me, was pale and trembling; but nevertheless, though this first emotion conquered her, & I saw her ready to burst into tears, & longing to cry *O take me back to my Mamma* I *Locke*! She subdued it with a presence of mind, & power over her feelings that announce uncommon fortitude & sense in so young a creature, for when her Papa opened his arms, & fondly called her, she instantly went to him, & affectionately embraced him. Made de Montecler called her next; Made de Montecler bears a character of highest respectability, & I think it very fortunate for the future welfare of my Fredy's dear little protegee, that she will be in such worthy hands: but for the present—Made de M[ontecler] has an air so naturally austere & cold, though studiously kind to the child, that the contrast from the *other* mamma was irresistably felt, & the poor thing's head droopt, her eyes filled with tears, wisely, however dispersed, even untouched, as

---

[7] The recollection of the days at Mickleham in 1793, when d'Arblay and the comte de Narbonne dined regularly at the home of Mrs. Phillips (see her letters, *Catalogue*) and probably a good deal of unwritten history of the years 1793–4, when the unconscionable roué, lingering in the Surrey environs, was intimately received in the Phillips home.

[8] For the Chavagnac and Montecler families, see L. 510 n. 6.

slowly and reluctantly, she obeyed the call. The young Lady then took her hand, &, courtsying, made her a compliment on her arrival with the ceremony she would have done to a woman of forty. To this Adrienne only hung her head. I never knew who she was, but while I thought, from her youth and stiffness, she had been allowed one day in a year from some strict school discipline, judge my surprise, to find from, Madᵉ de Montecler's ceremonials with her, when they were departing, & from the word *Madame* that she was already a married woman! — — The fourth call for our Adrienne was by no means the [most] melancholy—it was from her young Brother &, presently getting into a corner with him, she ᴵ caressed him very fondly, & they soon chatted & laughed together as if they had never been parted. What, now, was her joy, that all her cakes, &c, which you had intended for her journey, were fortunately packed up, by the conductors, so that we could never get at them! Untouched, she had the pleasure of carrying them all home, & the thought of making a feast with her Brother, soon lightened all her rising sorrows. Every one was anxious to make her happy. And M. Louis⁸ admired her beauty with the fondest paternal partiality. He & Madᵉ de M[ontecler] were extremely gratified by your kind letters, & poor little Adrienne told me *she would write to Mamma Locke* every day. They brought some-one with them to take the baggage. I explained why she was not dressed, & they went altogether. ᴵ

When poor little Adrienne was gone—whom I must long pity, be the worth & the kindness of her friends what they may, Mʳ Bourdois, and Maria arrived, both looking gay and happy— & then came the worthy Ferdinand,⁹ full of warmest enquiries after all Norbury Park, & very tenderly touched by the sight of Alex, & all the recollections to which that, & my view, gave rise. He is, indeed, I believe, a really good creature. I had next to receive the Maid whom M. D'arblay had engaged for me, as 'femme de chambre, to coiffer, dress, work &c, & as *cuisiniere*, & *valet de chambre*—& Housemaid—& Bonne for Alex. Not a few occupations, you will allow. She is fit, however, only for one, a *femme de chambre*, for she is very clever in milinarying &

---

⁹ Félix Ferdinand (iii, L. 245 n. 3), Narbonne's secretary, had accompanied the group of *émigrés* to Juniper Hall, Mickleham, in 1793 (ii, L. 46, p. 13; see also iii, *passim*).

Mantua makings versed in all the modes, fond of them in the extreme & very young, very *gentil*, & remarkably pretty—It was so late, & I was so much fatigued, notwithstanding the lightening to all mortal evil in the re-union my own beloved friends beyond almost all others know how to appreciate for me, that I did not rise the next day till 3 o'clock—nor yet repose in bed, for company was arriving all the morning, & my Alex, wild with pleasure, in again being with his Papa, & in enjoyment of hearing drums & seeing soldiers, scampered backwards & forwards, from room to room, with such un-appeasable spirits, that though I saved my voice from any exertions of receptions, my mind was employed upon ⎪ every Guest. The two only visitors I admitted *à la francaise* to my Bedside were Maria Bourdois & little Adrienne: the former came to sit with me, & the latter was brought by Madᵉ de Montecler & her Father. I am sorry I could not see them, as they live at an immense distance¹⁰—but I have no intention to adopt the french mode of Bedside visiting; which is not wider from my custom than from my inclination. Adrienne looked very serious, but smiled with her best smile when she pointed to her bosom, saying 'Look!' and shewed me a miniature of her Papa, which had just been given her by her Grandmother. She brought me her letter for my dearest of Friends, & but reluctantly, poor little thing, obeyed the call that drew her away. Time only can make her new abode happy to her, after the perfect one she has left, & lost. I will always at all times see as much as I can of her, & I only regret she is so far from me, that it is almost a mornings work to walk to her, by her own & her family's account.—My embarrassment relative to the lady I have mentioned in my last,¹¹ was now already, at a height; as she sent a note to M. D'arblay, to ask him if he would *be amiable enough* to bring Alex & me to dine with her the next day, when her dinner would consist of a *pot au feu* & M. de N[arbonne] adding that, if he said no, he would deserve to be banished to the wilds—Fortunately, for the present moment,

---

¹⁰ Forced in 1798, as the mother of an *émigré*, to give up the family residence at 100, rue du Cherche-Midi, Mme de Montecler (L. 510 n. 6) settled on family property on the rue Garancière, on the Left Bank near the Jardins de Luxembourg. She bought back her *hôtel*, but resold it in 1804.

¹¹ Mme de Laval, described in the first sheet of this Journal, which had been sent earlier (see p. 249).

M. D'ar had engaged his cousin, the young Bazille,[12] to dinner with us: this sufficed for an immediate excuse but, I had hardly been risen ten minutes, when I had a visit that much confounded me upon this subject; it was from a Gentleman,[13] with whom I am but slightly acquainted | but who seems to have taken a singular interest in my proceedings, & whose wife is professedly amongst my most ardent—what shall I say? supporters: or Puffers?—or Enthusiasts?—This Gentleman began a discourse upon Paris, which could not but engage my deepest attention. I had already in England, been informed that he reckoned it the *seat of corruption,* & lamented his own passing even a week in it upon business as a real evil: I expected, therefore, from him every thing that was discouraging & depressing upon my own arrival and prospects; to my great contentment, however, he took another turn; he spoke generally, but briefly, of the want of principle & purity, & then hastened to add 'But *you,* Ma'am, will find here many persons of high worth, & amiable manners, eager to recieve you, & well meriting a social intercourse with you: You have only to choose!' & then with an emphatic seriousness, he said much was expected of discrimination from those who had no local ties already formed, but that to mingle with all, was as little necessary as it was right: That Paris, was, perhaps, the most free city now in Europe, for strangers, as they had the most complete independence in their power | with respect to every connection they might form. All this, as you will believe, was calculated to give me the greatest satisfaction: but it was mixt with Another subject extremely destressing to me: no one was *named,* but hints & cautions, were given me, relative to the lady I have already wrote about so fully, that seemed to call upon me, almost authoritatively, to be on my guard against intimacy,— if not acquaintance—with her!—The [*blank*] of grief & difficulty & difficulty this would cause him when I wished to spare *any* made the intimations on this head very melancholy to me; & I received them in silence, from utter uncertainty what measures I might be yet able to take, & mortification at having begun at all a commerce I now so earnestly wished to shun! This

---

[12] Probably Jean-Baptiste-Gabriel-Edmé Bazille (L. 510 n. 12).
[13] Barthélemy Huber (487 n. 2), whose moral warnings about Mme de Laval, FBA had diplomatically omitted in her L. 510 to her father. Mme de Tessé and Mme d'Hénin, on the other hand, could be safely mentioned.

Gentleman, who was going to England, where he resides, mentioned one Lady, however, in particular, with high praise, whom M D'arblay has long considered with admiration & esteem, Madame de Tessé; & comforted me, also, by Kind words upon this truly and beneficient character of Madame D'Henin: but he left me upon the whole, extremely disconcerted, for the feelings of my own *best,* ⎮ & for his, *nearly,* dearest Friend: &, indeed, when he came home, & I opened upon the subject, I found I gave him almost as much amazement, as consternation; he had considered the connexion from the Lady's time of life, as necessarily innocent, &, as such, held it an abomination to attack the few possible comforts in the power of his ruined friend; by calumniating an intercourse from which he derived the only remaining consolation of his life, that of reposing his griefs, and discussing his affairs with a person in whom he could place entire confidence, & from whom he might expect a faithful & rational regard. I was quite afflicted to break into this persuasion by relating the rumours that had reached, & tormented me,—and truly pained to be forced, to disturb the opinions which soothed his own probity & delicacy. As well as friendship, for one so dear to him: yet with such warnings given me, ought I to run a risk a *second* time, where the first still subsisted in mischevous consequences? No, & he felt that himself,—felt it so forcibly as to agree immediately to a suspension of all intimacy, though the change from What he intended, & from what he knew was even ardently expected, was forced to be so abrupt, that his consent made really wretched —& the more, from his finding it impossible to believe ⎮ the report was otherwise than scandalous. I know how my dear Friends will regret I had such pain to inflict—but, not to dwell longer on the ungrateful detail, I will now only give you the result, which was a compromise; for as he could not affirm an innocence thus controverted, neither could I oppose to his fond belief any conviction of guilt, we settled, therefore, that I should decline accompanying her to any Public place, or going to any of her parties; but that I should return her visit by a morning call, & behave to her with all the civility I could make compatible with the restraint & coldness hanging upon my doubts.

As I feel that this subject—for the sake of both the Gentlemen concerned, will be peculiarly interesting to my beloved Friends, I have given it full length & breadth: but I earnestly entreat that no part of it may in any way transpire.

5 1 2   1185, rue de Miroménil
                               Paris, 21 April 1802

To Margaret Planta

A.L.S. (Berg), 21 Apr. 1802
Double sheet 4to   greenish   4 pp.
Annotated and dated, p. 1: To Miss Planta. 1802
Edited by FBA, p. 1, *annotated*: ⁜ [p. 4:] This Letter was never sent à son adresse as Mr. Huber, who was to carry it, missed it—I forget *how*.

                                    Paris 21ˢᵗ April, 1802.
My dear friend,
     As I have just received a message that a Gentleman, M. Huber,[1] is going back to England to-morrow, by whom I may write to my Father, I seize the opportunity of enclosing you a few lines, which I shall beg him to direct & forward.
     We arrived yesterday about Noon—M. Darblay was eagerly awaiting us. He has taken me a little apartment in Rue Miromenil which, though up two pair of stairs,[2] is really very pretty, & just new papered & furnished. The view from the windows is very pleasant, open to the Country, & airy & healthy. I have a good sized (*for me*) little neat Drawing room, a small ante-room which we make our Dining Parlour, a tidy Bed Chamber, & a closet within it for Alexander. This, with a kitchen & a bit of a bed-room for my Maid, all on the same floor, compose my habitation. M. Darblay had taken the utmost pains to prepare every thing clean & neat that could make me comfortable, knowing that to be what I least expected, yet most desired. He had made a female friend hire me a femme de chambre, who is to make me *fit to be seen*, by various manoeuvres,

512. ¹ (see L. 487 n. 2).
     ² Elsewhere the apartment is described as 'up 3 pair of stairs' (cf. L. 510, p. 243 and n. 2).

which I don't rightly understand, but which are to metamor-
phose me from a rustic Hermit into a figure that may appear in
this celebrated capital without causing convulsions or fainting
fits to its Inhabitants. How this is to be brought about; I don't
yet know, but if by such means as I have seen represented, or
heard described, I foresee my young Abigail will find me too
refractory for a convert. Mean while, the very idea of such an
attempt amuses me doubly from recollecting how much Miss
Rose[3] diverted herself with the thought of seeing me return
in the light Parisienne Drapery so much talked of, & in vogue.[4]
However, I am at present so extremely fatigued, I can make
no | experiments. I had fully meant to wait upon M[lle] de
Mortemar[5] to Day, but I woke with so violent a head ache—
&, indeed, an *every* ache, for I feel bruised all over,—that I am
utterly unable to go abroad, & only rose at five o'clock. My
voyage was cruelly long, from a dead calm, which kept the
vessel motionless for 8 Hours, just after we had sailed from the
Port of Dover. We were a whole Day, & a whole Night at sea,
& I was sick nearly without intermission all the time, & quite
terrified for my poor Alexander who was so ill, & so pale &
exhausted, I thought he would have been demolished. Adrienne,
my other little charge, was, on the contrary, perfectly well, &
gay as a Lark. M. Darblay sent instantly to inform her Father

---

[3] Princess Augusta. FBA supplies the code names to be used for the Royal
Family in L. 528, p. 361.
[4] *The Times* itself, to speak of no more likely journals on the subject, kept the
public well informed on the high points of Paris fashion, and not always with
approval. A letter, allegedly from Paris, printed on 26 December 1801, speaks of
the 'licentiousness' of fashionable dress, the 'naked display of charms', and the
'libertinism it provokes in the other sex'. 'The arms, to the very shoulder, and the
whole of the bosom are *en nature*, and the rest of the person is distinctly visible
through the woven wind that plays about it.'
The sixteen-year-old Charlotte Francis, returning with her mother to England
in 1802, found her beautiful Empire dress somewhat inconvenient in the sea winds
of Ramsgate. 'The wind was so intolerable that we dared not walk about . . . lest
our light french clothing should give way & no shade be left to our complete
perfections . . . I am sorry to say I must have all my gowns altered again & what is
worse give up my favourite practise of holding my tail à la greque, together with
my repenters & my anneaux, for these . . . excited the risible attention of all the
beggar boys and girls in Ramsgate. how different is the behaviour of these nasty
english to that of the polite & enlightened french beggars!' Even to Charlotte
Broome, the most John Bullish of CB's children, the English ladies looked over-
heavy, 'as if they had two or three heads of Hair on their foreheads, & half a dozen
sleeves on each arm, & 5 petticoats . . . .' See A.L.S. (Barrett, Eg. 3693, ff. 84–5),
[23 Oct. 1802].
[5] See L. 513, pp. 261–3 and nn. 2, 3, where FBA describes her meeting with
Mlle de Mortemart and Mme de Beauvau and her family.

& Grand mother of her arrival. They came hither directly. The poor little child, who had never seen her Father since she could remember, nor Me de Montecler at all, nor her little Brother, who accompanied them, nor a young lady, just married, of about 12 years old!—who is a Relation,[6] & was of their party, was quite confounded by their first appearance, but soon reconciled to accompany them, by their fond carresses & endearments. They have all been here again this morning, to see me; but I was inevitably invisible, except to little Adrienne, who came to my Bedside, & brought me a Letter she had written for her *mama Lock*, whose Name she cannot hear without bursting into tears, from tender gratitude & regret. I doubt not, however, she will soon be happy, as her Relations are good & respectable, & delighted to have her restored to her family.

I cannot express to you with what emotion I heard, while Dining, at Calais,[7] a band of music, that came to the windows of the Hotel, strike up God save the King. The surprise & pleasure were of the best kind I ever experienced. As we were forced to remain some time in I that Town, we walked about it, to refresh ourselves after the long confinement, & the dress of the females amused the Children inexpressibly; all the women, without exception, wore large long Gold Earings, though under immensely wide winged french night Caps, which seemed intended to cover the cheeks, but were always flying wide open, to display this ornament. The Girls who were scrubbing the floors at the Inn, women with large baskets on their heads, young creatures draggled, dirty, & sweeping the streets, old ones, wrinkled, bent double, & carrying Babies at their backs,— all still had these huge shewy dropping Earings, & many of them Gold necklaces round their throats. I observed, also, with some surprise, that most of them were fair, & that the youthful were commonly very handsome: in mentioning this to an English Gentleman here, he *modestly* accounted for it, by saying Calais was so long in the possession of the English, that our race must still subsist in it.—

Pardon this Paper & vile writing; I am forced to scribble on as fast as possible, not to lose so good an opportunity. I hope

---

[6] Eugénie-Henriette de Montecler (L. 510 n. 6).
[7] On 18 Apr. 1802 (cf. L. 508, p. 231).

you received a few words I sent from Dover.[8] I had no time to tell you a quarter of that Fable, but could not forbear what I mentioned, as my only means ever to obtain any satisfactory information of a Tree I hold in such natural reverence as the Oak,[3] or a Plant of which I have always found the perfume so delicious as the Magnolia,[3] as well as of the bloom of the other sweet Flowers I enumerated.

I found the people quite enchanted throughout the whole Country from Calais to Paris, by the restoration of The Dimanche.[9] One poor old woman, where we changed Horses, at Claremont, said that le bon Dieu had been lost for Ten years—but Bonaparte had now found him: & another further on, told us, They could bear all their sufferings & hardships nows, [1] for they might now hear mass, & their souls would be saved.

Adieu, my dear friend—You will endeavour to speak for me where you know I most fervantly covet not to be forgotten—& believe me ever

Your affectionate friend & serv^t
F. Darblay.

Rue Miromenil
N° 1185. Paris.

[8] This note is missing.   [9] Cf. L. 508, p. 234.

PARIS JOURNAL

513   *for* 22–24 April 1802

To Doctor Burney

A.J.L. continued (Diary MSS. vi, not foliated, but between the foliations 5387 and 5668, Berg), written at 1185, rue de Miroménil, probably at the end of April 1802, but only sent, through Anthony Merry, the British Minister, on 23 July.

Originally (?) three double sheets 4to, of which the first leaf of the first double sheet was cut away, numbered by sheets [(8)], (9), (10) 8 pp.

Addressed, p. 2: *England* / Dr. Burney, / Chelsea College, / Middlesex.

Endorsed, p. 2, *by* CB: (Sheet 8) Apr. 22ᵈ / (Nº 1)

Addressed, p. 6: Dr. Burney, / Chelsea College, / Middlesex—

Endorsed, p. 6, *by* CB: Apr. Sheet 9 / (No. 2.)

Addressed, p. 10: Dr. Burney, / Chelsea College, / Middlesex *with an explanation*: Read all this entirely at leisure— / pray forgive this horrid envellope which accident thus smeared after the 1ˢᵗ leaf was written.—

Endorsed, p. 10, *by* CB: Sheet 10 / Apr. 24

Edited by FBA *who annotated the top of each sheet (single or double)*: p. 1: *numbered* (8) × ⋇.

[*The first phrase of the opening sentence was added later as an editorial link, probably taken from the missing first leaf*:] For Madame cidivant Psˢᵉ de Beauvau, & Mˡˡᵉ de Mortemart, I had Letters from

p. 3, numbered (9): × ⋇ Beauvaus.   Mortemart.   Mᵉ de Staël   M. de Narbonne.   Chevalier. D'Henin.   Mᵐᵉ de Poix.

p. 8, numbered (10): ⋇ ⋇ × de Beauvaus,   d'Henin—de Stael,   de Tessé

It seems probable that FBA's Journal Letters to CB (Ll. 513, 514, 517, and 518), recounting the events of 22 April—5 May 1802, were copied by M. d'A into the 'Paris Letter Book', for typescript excerpts are preserved (grangerized DL, vi. 4, NPG, printed in FB & the Burneys, pp. 46–62). A copy was also made (conjecturally from the Letter Book) for CFBt who corrected and edited it (Diary MSS. viii. 5468–5572, Berg), 54 pp. This copy was also edited and abridged by Colburn and his staff.

Curiously, no copy contains material that might have come from the missing first leaf, suggesting that it was cut away and destroyed at the time of writing.

[*pages 1 and 2 were cut away*]

259

[For Madame cidivant PS^se de Beauvau,[2] & Mlle de Mortemart,[3] I had Letters from] Mrs. Harcourt,[1] & a message from a young lady, of the name of Elizabeth:[4] M. D'arblay mentioned this to Mad. D'Henin, who is aunt to Mad^e de Beauvau,[5] ⟨&⟩ who, from her, I imagine, received the information: for this Day ⌐of which I write, when I was conversing with Mad.

513. [1] In a letter (Comyn) dated 11 Apr. 1802 Mary (Lockhart) Harcourt *née* Danby (*c.* 1750–1833), wife of General William Harcourt (1742/3–1830), had requested FBA to 'carry a little parcel . . . to Madle. de Mortemart', suggesting also that FBA call on the sisters, granddaughters of Henri-François d'Harcourt (1726–1804), comte de Lillebonne, duc d'Harcourt (1785).

William, 3rd Earl Harcourt and Henri-François, duc d'Harcourt, were direct descendants of Anchetil, Sire d'Harcourt, in Normandy, whose son had served William, Duke of Normandy, at the Conquest. The French and English branches became friendly when Simon Harcourt (1714–77), 1st Earl Harcourt (1 Dec. 1749), was sent in the years 1768–9 as English Ambassador to France.

In 1792 the English Harcourts, General William and his brother George Simon (1736–1809), 2nd Earl Harcourt (see iv, L. 255 n. 10), had provided an asylum and an annual income for their French relatives, first at Sunning Hill and, later, at Staines, where some of them resided for nearly ten years. 'The poor old Duke', Mrs. Harcourt had related in her 'Anecdotes', *Harcourt Papers*, v. 355–6, 'seems quite broken hearted; he has lost his spirits and activity; but is calm, reasonable, and resigned, and does not flatter himself with the hope of better days during his life. He suffers most for the sake of the two next generations of his family, who are the objects of his affection, and are indeed worthy of being so. I never saw three more charming girls than his grand-daughters; they are very pretty and very amiable; the eldest, the Princesse de Croy, has two lively little boys; the second, the Princesse de Craon, is with child; Victorine is still unmarried, and likely, in these times, to remain so.' See, however, n. 3.

[2] It was the 2nd and 3rd of these granddaughters whom FBA was to meet, namely, Nathalie-Henriette-Victurnienne (1774–1854) and Catherine-Victurnienne-*Victorine* (1776–1809), daughters of Victurnien-Jean-Baptiste-Marie de Rochechouart (1752–1812), styled prince de Tonnay-Charente, duc de Mortemart (1771), and his first wife Anne-Gabrielle d'Harcourt de Lillebonne (1750–78). Nathalie had married in 1792 Marc-Étienne-Gabriel de Beauvau (1773–1849), prince de Beauvau-Craon (1793). In the winter of 1792–3 the young couple emigrated to England, where their three eldest children were born, François-Victurnien-*Charles*-Just (1793–1864), Edmond-Henri-Étienne-Victurnien (1795–1861), and Nathalie-Irène-Marie-Victurnienne (*c.* 1798–1852). The youngest child Henriette-*Gabrielle*-Appoline was born in Paris *c.* November 1801.

The duc de Mortemart, emigrating also to England and taking service with the British army, helped in the autumn of 1794 to raise one of the corps of *émigrés*, the 'White Cockade'. This corps, after spending most of 1796 in the Channel Islands, was sent to Portugal in 1797, remaining there until after the Peace of Amiens. It was disbanded in August 1802.

[3] Catherine-Victurnienne *or* 'Victorine' de Rochechouart de Mortemart (1776–1809), sister of Nathalie (*supra*). She was to marry on 19 Jan. 1807 Adrien-François-Emmanuel de Crussol d'Uzès (1778–1837), colonel de cavalerie, député du Gard (1824–30), pair de France, duc de Crussol (1830). See vi, L. 604 n. 6. For further meetings with Mlle de Mortemart, see L. 515, pp. 285–7 and L. 517, pp. 304–5.

[4] Princess Elizabeth.

[5] Actually the prince d'Hénin (1744–94) and the prince de Beauvau (1773–1849) were cousins, the difference in age perhaps confusing FBA as to the relationship.

de Cadignan[6] I was much surprised—Letter & Message both undelivered,—by a visit from the Ci divant Prince de Beauvau, Madame his Wife, & Mad[lle] de Mortemar, her sister; all brought by Mad[e] d'Henin. If gratified in the first instance by a politeness of attention so little my due, & so completely beyond my expectations, how was my pleasure in it enhanced when I found they all three spoke English with the utmost ease & fluency! & how pleased, also at the pleasure I was able to give them, in reward of their civility;—for Mrs. Harcourt's Letter was received with the warmest delight by Mad[lle] de Mortemar, & the message from the young lady, (Elizabeth) with the profoundest gratitude. I was quite sorry I had not brought Mrs. Harcourt's note to myself, in which she mentions Mad[e] de Beauvau, who would have been very grateful for the manner in which she is named. ⌐If I have left it loose in my dear F[anny] P[hillips]'s room, I beg my dearest Father, you will let me know &, should accident offer some way of sending for it.¬ M. de Beauvau is extremely tall, rather large, & though not handsome, has a very pleasing smile, when to smile seems good to him! but he seems very reserved, & distant, & rather taciturn. His wife, who looks not yet twenty, & is not many years more, though she was married so early as to have a son near 9 years old! is quite beautiful; fair, with a high, yet soft tinted Colour, lively blue Eyes, an acquiline nose, & mouth & teeth extremely pretty, she has a look of modesty, goodness,

6 Catherine *née* Hunter (1773–1860), the youngest daughter of William Hunter (1729–77), M.D. (Edinburgh), of Newport, Rhode Island, and his wife Deborah *née* Malbone (d. 15 Oct. 1813) of Newport. In 1785 the widow had taken her eldest daughter Eliza (b. 20 July 1762) to England in the vain hope of a cure for her eyesight and, with two other daughters, was to remain abroad for the remainder of her life.

Eliza, becoming completely blind, was to die in Paris in 1849; Anne (1766–1859) married Jean-Louis-Théodore de Palézieux-Falconnet (*fl.* 1760–1825), a Swiss banker; Catherine married, presumably in England, the *émigré* Anne-*Charles*-Guy-Gérard Dupleix (1767–1804), comte de Cadignan, Lt.-Col. in the 4e régiment de chasseurs and aide-de-camp to Lafayette (1791). Arrested in that year, he escaped, and emigrating to England, married and settled with his wife apparently at Wallington, Surrey, for a time at least, where d'Arblay (along with FBA) once visited them. Their son Charles Frederick Lewis was baptized at St. Mary's, Lambeth, on 12 Aug. 1797 (see parish register). The comte was removed from the proscription lists in April 1800, but by then badly afflicted with paralysis, he returned only with great difficulty to France, where he died in 1804; and his 2nd son Samuel was to die there in 1805.

For this family history, see Archives (Vincennes); J. H. Beers, *Representative Men and Old Families of Rhode Island* (?3 vols., 1908), i. 229–30; and the notes supplied by Miss G. Rutherford to *Memoirs of the duc de Lauzun*, trans. C. K. Scott Moncrieff (1928), p. 249.

& dignity, joined to an ⏽ air, a manner, & a voice, of the most interesting softness. You would be in love with her, my dear Daddy, immediately. I felt myself quite charmed with her. She has four Children—& yet you would think she was but just brought forth from some Convent, in which she had received an examplary education, to be disposed of in marriage. Nevertheless, there is not the least look of *mauvaise honte* —no embarrassing because embarrassed timidity; on the contrary, though every thing she said had a tone that shewed the most unaffected diffidence of her own merits, there is an ease as well as grace in her deportment to others, evidently resulting from a consciousness of what is due to her situation in life, which she feels without vanity, & sustains without pride, because the humility of her character saves her from annexing to it any idea of self. Indeed she is a sweet Creature, & I am the more tempted to admire & to like her, from the novelty to my expectations of beholding, in France, so much loveliness of Youth & beauty in a faithfully attached Wife, & tenderly affectionate Mother. At this very moment she nurses herself her youngest Child, who is about 6 months old, [Gabriella.] ⏽

Mademoiselle de Mortemart, her sister, has more spirit in her countenance, but less beauty; she appears to be lively & clever, yet full of sensibility. She has spent 10 years in England, which, as she is not yet 25, makes so much the greatest part of her conscious Life, that she always, she says, thinks it her real country. She has been returned but two or three Months, & came over in the same pacquet with M. D'arblay,[7] though they then did not know each other. She loves England with such enthusiasm, that she talks of it with a rapture that presently fills her Eyes with Tears in bitter regret at having left it; & her heart's first wish, she assured me, was to return thither as soon as possible. Mrs. Harcourt had been a Mother to her, she told me, & her reception every where had been as if born her Daughter. She hinted not that her own birth had yet higher claims as to all *ceremonial* of respect; but though her sense & judgment silence her on this subject, there is something in her look & manner that always announce she does not forget

---

[7] The name of Mlle de Mortemart was not included in the list of passengers ('Ship News from Dover', *The Times*, 18 Feb. 1802), where, however, d'Arblay's name appeared. The sailing was delayed, and passengers may have been transferred at the last minute.

what she was born to think her due. They are two charming Creatures, & if Mad. de Beauvau, from superior beauty, & winning softness of voice & manner, is more immediately engaging, it is very possible that Md^{lle} de Mortemart, from the animation of her character, & the quick feeling displayed in her very fine Eyes, may be equally or even more attractive where she fixes her own desire to please. They made me a long & extremely pleasant visit, assuring me that they came the very moment they heard of my arrival. I have the more reason to be obliged to them, as I am informed it is not the custom of the French Ladies to visit any strangers, till they are waited upon first.—This, however, was not more agreeable to me, than another overture of intercourse which followed was painful & perplexing: A lady whom M. D'arblay called upon soon after,[8] told him she had had a visit from Mad. de St^{aël} who, having heard I was come to Paris, mentioned her expectation of soon receiving my visit: the lady—a little in the confidence of our notions upon that subject—said she doubted my going much abroad, & understood I meant to live in a very retired manner. That was nothing Mad. de St^{aël} answered, with regard to her, as she had been so much acquainted with me in England; the lady again expressed her doubt of my calling myself into notice by any voluntary action. She then said 'Croyez vous qu'elle me reçevra avec amitié? Si cela est, Je vais la voir, quoique ce ne soit pas d'usage des dames en France. — ' A hesitation of our friend to this demand changed the tone of its condescendsion into scornful resentment, & she added 'Sinon — à la bonne heure! — qu est que c'est que Mad^e D'arblay pour moi! — ' Here the matter rested—&, here, though sorry to offend, we yet concluded it best to let her own pique end the difficulty.

M. Bazille junior, son of M. D'arblay's beloved uncle, was admitted to our little dinner to Day;[9] We have resolved never to attempt giving Dinners, from the beginning, lest soon we should be without them, excepting only to the Sons of M. Bazille, when in Paris; & M. de Lajard,[10] who, having partaken of our

---

[8] Again, in letters to CB, the name of Mme de Laval was withheld.

[9] Cf. L. 511, p. 253, where the visit of Jean-Baptiste-Gabriel-Edmé Bazille had served as an excuse to avoid dining with Mme de Laval.

[10] Pierre-Auguste Lajard (iv, L. 291 n. 5), with whom d'Arblay had stayed on his arrival in Paris. For his brothers César and Daniel, see L. 458 n. 1; and iv, L. 292 n. 8.

Hermit fare at West Hamble, we judged sufficiently initiated in the secret of bad living to be continued a member of our Table. Young Bazille was going the following Day to Joigny,— where we are all expected with the kindest impatience, though M. Bazille, l'aîné, with the best grace possible yields to the desire of his Nephew to keep me in Paris while the season is yet favourable for my seeing it.

April 22ᵈ The good & respectable M. Lajard this morning breakfasted with us. I was rejoiced to see him, & felt myself received by a sincere & worthy friend. Having lost every thing during his exile, he has been soliciting, ever since his return, for his *retraite*, & is living, meanwhile, in the most penurious manner, from delicacy to the friends by whom he is aided, though by them—a Mother & two Brothers—he is loved with the utmost tenderness.—Just as he went, arrived M. Chevalier;[11] —do you remember him in England? He enquired after you, & after Charles, with warm expressions of gratitude; to you he owed, he said, the kind proposition of translating Baretti's dialogues[12] for Miss Thrale, & to Charles much kindness & service. You are of his party, I well know, in support of *Troy*,— both of you!—Heavens! undermine the ⎮ very existence of belief so classic! What is to become of every allusion in every Poet? Who is to understand a single Simile in an ancient author? 'Tis almost teaching one to read without an Alphabet. —His visit was presently succeeded by one from M. de Narbonne —whom I amused—amazed, at least, not a little, when, in return to innumerable offers of service & kindness, in procuring me Tickets—admissions—or accompanying me to public places, or celebrated people, I answered I required nothing at present but repose, for I lived so much in the World, I must rest before I could undertake any thing new. And this, ridiculous as it sounds to those accustomed to the life of a Capital, is, with

[11] Jean-Baptiste Le Chevalier (1752–1836), classical scholar and traveller. His theory that Homeric Troy was situated away from the coast (see iii, L. 130 n. 2) caused considerable controversy in England involving, among others, FB's old friend Jacob Bryant (1715–1804). A brief and clear summary of eighteenth-century theories concerning Troy is found in M. L. Clarke, *Greek Studies in England 1700–1830* (Cambridge, 1945), pp. 182–5.

[12] Giuseppi Baretti's *Easy Phraseology, for the Use of Young Ladies, who Intend to Learn the Colloquial Part of the Italian Language* (1775), known popularly as Baretti's *Dialogues*, and written for Miss Hetty Thrale (i, L. 11 n. 4), at that time 11 years old (*DL*, ii. 206, 398). No translation by Le Chevalier or Koliades (his pseudonym) has been located.

me, so long a real Hermit for retirement, a simple matter of fact.

After him, came our Bood & Maria, with M. Bourdois *l'ainé*, who is a physician of much eminence,[13] & a perfectly well-bred & much admired man. I was very happy to find that Maria likes him extremely, as much of her life will be spent in his society.

Madᵉ D'Henin had made us promise to dine with her, to meet only M. Malhouët;[14] but M. Malhouët had an indisposition, & we found her alone. She is so friendly & amiable, that I am always pleased in her society, & so inexpressibly kind to me, that I apply to her upon every difficulty. She lives nearly opposite us, in apartments which she has made elegant by the fitting up, & which her friends had ornamented by various presents at once useful & decorative, before her return from England. It is up two pair of stairs—Her sole lodging,—& she resigns herself to it with as much modest chearfulness of content, as if she had never been Mistress of any more spacious residence.[15]—In the evening we were joined by Madame la cidivant Princesse de Poix,[16] who for 30 years past has been

---

[13] Edmé-Joachim Bourdois (see iv, L. 381 n. 1), who had been chief medical officer of the army of Italy in 1798 and was, in private practice in Paris, to attract a fashionable clientele.   [14] See L. 450 n. 17.

[15] FBA was probably thinking of the princesse d'Hénin's girlhood, which was spent with her mother Mme de Monconseil in 'le château que remplaça le pavillon actuel de Bagatelle' (Welvert) and of the brilliant fêtes there. After her marriage to the prince d'Hénin, then capitaine des gardes du comte d'Artois, she lived with her husband for a brief time in a house in the rue de Varenne, owned by her mother. Later she seems to have rented a series of houses in the rue Sainte-Anne, in the rue de Verneuil, and once again in the rue de Varenne.

On her return from emigration, the princesse had bought or rented 'un petit hôtel' (once owned by Chateaubriand) at the corner of the rue de Miroménil and the rue Verte (today known as the rue de Penthièvre).

[16] Anne-Louise-Marie de Beauvau (1750–1834), who had married in 1767 Philippe-Louis-Marc-Antoine de Noailles, prince de Poix (L. 526 n. 2). Only daughter of Charles-Just de Beauvau (1720–93), prince de Beauvau-Craon, maréchal de France (1783), by his first wife, Marie-Sophie-Charlotte *née* de la Tour d'Auvergne (1729–63), she was 'contrefaite, boîteuse, impotente une grande partie de l'année; mais ses souffrances n'altéraient ni les charmes de son visage, ni ceux de son esprit, ni même sa gaieté' (see Welvert, p. 20, where the intimate friendship that existed for many years between the princesse de Poix and the princesse d'Hénin is also described).

The prince and princesse de Poix had two sons, Charles-Arthur-Tristan-Jean-Languedoc de Noailles (1771–1834), *styled* duc de Mouchy, lieutenant-général (1816), pair de France (1819); and Antonin-Claude-Dominique 'Juste' de Noailles (1777–1846), comte de Noailles, who was to become a chamberlain to Napoleon, comte de l'Empire (1810), and was to succeed to his brother's titles in 1834.

Remaining in Paris during the revolutionary years, the princesse had taken care of the comte de Lally-Tolendal's daughter Élisabeth (iii, L. 215 n. 10).

the confidential & intimate friend of Mad. D'Henin. You may recollect, my dearest Sir, a Letter written by M. le ci-divant Prince de Poix to M. D'arblay upon our marriage;[17] that Gentleman is husband to Mad^e de Poix, who is of [the] highest estimation in this Country, for her virtues & her wit & accomplishments. As she is quite—by some accident—lame, & has dreadful Health, she was literally incapable of emigration; but great as ⎮ were her sufferings & danger in remaining, during the dread reign of Terror, when hardly a relation or a friend survived but by flight, in the result it has left her so much of her own fortune as to enable her to receive her husband, when erased from the fatal list, to pay his debts, which were enormous, to save him from his Creditors, & to live with him in a style the nearest to elegant of any I have yet seen, though far—far removed from what they had been born & bred to before the revolution. Mad^e de Poix looks near sixty, but has still fine bright piercing Eyes, & the most pleasing remains of beauty; her manner is vivacious, striking & highly agreeable; her speech has a rapidity that does not seem the mere effect of female volubility & love of prate, but of quick ideas, which demand immediate vent, because others are crowding upon them, which insist upon making way. Her civility was of the most distinguished & elegant sort, & though, as I could only speak my miserable french, I could not be at my ease with her, I liked her too much to form my usual wish of retreat. She soon slipt the discourse into Cecilia; but with an adroitness of turning every way but towards me, that prevented its being oppressive—I was not, I own, much surprised to find, by what I observed in her, that the character with which she seemed the most deeply impressed was that of Mrs Delville.[18] I was sorry when she went, which was very soon, as she was engaged; & as she declared this visit was not to Mad^e D'Henin, but merely to begin an acquaintance which her lameness alone had prevented her opening by mounting my stair case at Hotel Marengo. I really hope for the honour of seeing her often. ⎮

This morning Mad^e d'henin was so kind as to accompany us in making our visit to Mad^e de Beauvau, her niece, & Mad^lle

---

[17] The letter (Barrett, Eg. 3700A, f. 197) is dated 5 Aug. 1793. It is a polite congratulatory note to d'Arblay on his marriage.
[18] The aristocratic mother of the hero of *Cecilia* (1782).

de Mortemart. We found them at home, with M. de Beauvau, & they indulged me with the sight of their Children, who are the most flourishing & healthy possible, & dressed & brought up with English plainness & simplicity. The two eldest, who are Boys, & will soon look like the Brothers of their beautiful young Mother, speak English pretty well, the 3ᵈ who is a little Girl, about 5 Years old, *looks* english only, for she is wholly without that early formed womanhood of which I have heard so much in France. The youngest, who is still in arms, & nursed by her Mother, we did not see. When I praised the healthy, blooming looks of those who appeared, Madˡˡᵉ de Mortemart said, with a meaning smile, 'They were all 3 born in *England,* you know!' She delights to be taken for English herself, & thinks nothing excellent but what will bear comparison with that Country. I was quite charmed with the domestic *menage,* & apparent domestic happiness of this house— & could not refrain, like Mˡˡᵉ de Mortemart, continually exclaiming 'How English is all this!—' for they appear to live a completely happy as well as virtuous family life. The visit was very pleasant, & Madᵉ d'henin made a party for us all to meet again the next day,[19] & go to the Opera Buffa. Madᵉ d'Henin then took us to leave cards at Madᵉ de Tessé's,[20] & at Madᵉ de Poix. With the last I was most ready to do it, as it became a devoir after the meeting of the preceding Evening, & as I was so much pleased with her: but I should have thought it a liberty to begin myself an acquaintance with Madᵉ de Tessé, her age, former rank, high talents, & remaining distinction in all the society she yet associates with considered; but that I was assured where French ladies desire to make an acquaintance, it was the settled etiquette for strangers, foreigners, to wait upon them. | They were both out, &, to my no small surprise, I found upon returning home, a card left for me of Madame de Stael Holstein, Neckar.[21]—This was a renewal of a perplexity I had thought ended, & a renewal that caused me a good deal of uneasiness, from the fear that a determination of intercourse

---

[19] Since the Opéra Bouffe, or the Théâtre Favart, as it was called, was dark on the 23rd and 24th of April (see *Journal de Paris*, 25 Apr. 1802, p. 1316), Mme d'Hénin must have had to postpone her theatre party until Sunday the 25th, on which evening *Le Nozze di Dorina* (see L. 514, p. 271) was performed.

[20] For FBA's meeting with Mme de Tessé, see L. 526, pp. 342–3.

[21] For FB's former acquaintance with Mme de Staël, see ii *passim*.

was formed, that resolved to resist all offence from the most manifest coldness. We concluded, however, still to try its chilling influence, & that my card only should be returned, & that not for 3 days. The courage, however, which this required, was by no means of a pleasant sort, for as I could declare no reasons, I seemed not only forgetful of the intimacy so unfortunately begun in England. but insulting to the civility so eagerly offered me here. How truly sorry I am to find her now in Paris! for nothing is so painful as repressing kindness, & nothing seems so odious as returning condescendsion by contempt.—Upon our entrance into the Hotel, we met M. de Lajard, who came to introduce one of his Brothers to me, & to offer us places in a Loge at the Theatre Rue Feydou.[22] We went late, & arrived in the middle of an opera of which I know not the name, but which was quite in the heroics, though the airs were mixt with speeches, not recitative. All my pleasure, I confess, was from the after piece, in which the heroics were omitted. It is called La Maison à vendre, & two very agreeable singers, & charming actors, Martin & Elvieu, delighted the whole audience, & would have had me amongst their strongest admirers, if I were capable of fully following them in the words, which make so much the chief charm of their performance: but I have not yet acquired the use of listening with such profit to the sense conveyed by lengthened tones in the French language.

I forgot to mention that while we were at the Opera Buffon, Italien, M. Charles de Poix announced to us that Paesiello[23] was just arrived in Paris. |

[22] On Saturday 24 April when Lajard and his party attended the Opéra-Comique National, rue Feydeau, they would have heard the opera *Ariodant* by Etienne Méhul (1763–1817), which FBA did not recognize, and *Maison à Vendre*, an afterpiece in one act by Nicolas Dalayrac (1753–1809). Jean-Blaise Martin (1768–1837) was a comedian renowned more for singing than for acting; and Pierre-Jean-Baptiste-François Elleviou (1769–1842), a celebrated actor and composer, was at this time one of the directors of the combined Opéra Bouffe and Théâtre Feydeau.

[23] Giovanni Paisiello or Paesiello (1740–1816), an Italian composer, who at St. Petersburg (1776–85) had enjoyed the patronage of Catherine the Great and later, at Naples, that of Ferdinand IV. Invited to Paris by Bonaparte, who offered him the directorship of the Opéra, the Conservatoire, and the 'Musique de la Chapelle', he accepted only the latter, remaining in Paris until August 1804. He arrived to take up his appointment on 25 Apr. 1802.

PARIS JOURNAL

5I4   *for* 24–25 April, 1802

To Doctor Burney

A.J.L. continued (Diary MSS. vi, not foliated but between the foliations 5387 and 5568, Berg), written at 1185, rue de Miroménil, probably in late Apr. or May 1802, and carried to England by Mr. Payne[1] on 28 Aug. Two double sheets 4to, numbered by 4tos (11) (12.)   8 pp.

The first double sheet was
Addressed, p. 4: Dr. Burney, / Chelsea College, / Middlesex.
Endorsed by CB: Sheet 11 / April 25. — / N° 1
Annotated by FBA, p. 1: ⊞ ⊹ × Miss Berry. ch. de Poix.   Mme
d'Henin. Mme de Tessé.
The second double sheet was
Addressed, p. 4: Dr. Burney, / Chelsea College, / Middlesex.
Endorsed by CB: Sheet 12. / N° 2
Annotated by FBA, p. 5: ⊞ × Mad^e de Tesse   Mad^e de Poix.   Mlle de
Mortemart.   Mme de STAËL

The copies made of this journal are described in the headnote to L. 513.

Paris. April.

In our way home, which was through the Boulvards, we turned into Rue Choiseul, to call on Bood & Maria[2]—but they were preparing for Bed—little expecting such dissipation on *MY* part as a visit after the Play! I have heard much of the visit of Mrs. Damer & Miss Berry to Paris,[3] & their difficulty to get

514. [1] Possibly James Payne (d. 1809), bibliophile and bookseller (*GM* lxxix[1], 389), younger brother of Thomas Payne (1752–1831), bookseller, who had succeeded his father 'honest Tom Payne' at the Mews-Gate, removing in 1806 to Pall Mall. 'Justly esteemed', according to Lawrence (ii. 221–7), 'as one of the best Bibliographers in Europe', James Payne, visiting Paris in the interval of peace and detained from day to day by French librarians seeking his advice, was caught there at the outbreak of war, arrested, and in spite of the protests of his French friends, interned at Verdun. Seized in the course of a few months by an 'apoplectic fit', he was permitted only after long delay (not until June 1806) to try the waters at Plombières and in April 1807, the sulphur springs at Barrèges. On 15 September of that year he was allowed to reside under surveillance at Versailles (Hauterive, iii. 552) and finally to live in Paris, where he died in March 1809.
[2] On Saturday, 24 April, on the way home from the Opéra-Comique National (see L. 513 n. 22). Antoine Bourdois and Maria lived at 4, rue de Choiseul (see L. 517, p. 297).
[3] Mary Berry (iv, L. 389 n. 5) and the Hon. Mrs. Damer (L. 498 n. 9) had been presented to Letizia Bonaparte (Madame Mère) on 1 Apr. 1802 and to Bonaparte himself on 8 April (see Berry, ii. 168, 185–9).

introduced to the first Consul. A lady here told us she had been called upon by Miss Berry, who had complained with much energy upon this subject, saying 'we have been every where— seen every thing—heard everybody—beheld such sights! listened to such discourse! joined such society!—& all to obtain his notice—& all in vain!—Don't you think it very extra- ordinary that he should not, himself, desire to see Mrs Damer'? — 'Madame,' replied the lady, 'perhaps if you had done but half this, the First Consul might have desired to see you both!—' 'But you don't imagine,' answered she, laughing, 'we came over from England to see you *cidivants*? We can see such as you at home!'

She was gone before our arrival; &, as I understand, succeeded, at last, in obtaining an introduction. They were both, Mrs. D[amer] & Miss B[erry], I am told, very gay & agreeable, as well as enterprizing, & extremely *bien repandues*. The *Lady*, or ci-divant was Mme la Princesse d'Henin.

April 25. Yesterday M. d'arblay waited upon Mr. Merry,[4] with my Letters, from Lord Pelham,[5] &c, & a Note from me, & his own, (M. d'Arblay's) Card! and & this Morning Mr. Merry very politely came to our apartment; taking the trouble to mount our heights: but I was a good deal indisposed, &, to my great mortification, obliged to decline seeing him; & M. D'arblay was abroad. He left me an extremely obliging message, desiring me at any time to make use of him, if he could be of the least service to me. Had I seen him, I might have turned this extensive, but vague compliment into some- thing rather more limitted, but more useful, in soliciting his permission to send him a few Letters for England. |

I was not much better in the Evening, but the party for the Opera buffa, being formed by Mad^e D'Henin on my account, my going was indispensable. She had borrowed the loge of M. de Choiseul,[6] which, being entailed upon the family *à perpetuité*, has, in a most extraordinary manner, continued unalienated through the whole course of massacres & proscrip-

4 Minister Plenipotentiary *ad interim* (L. 510 n. 13).
5 Thomas Pelham (L. 437 nn. 2, 10), Home Secretary.
6 Claude-Antoine-Clériadus-Gabriel de Choiseul (1760–1838), duc de Choiseul-Stainville (1785), who having assisted Louis XVI in his attempt to escape (1791), later fought with the armée de Condé, was twice captured and once condemned to death by the Directory, but escaping, fled the country. Allowed to return in 1801, he remained in private life until the fall of the Empire.

tions, to the present day, when the right owner possesses it. It is the largest & best box, except that which is opposite to it, in the Theatre. M. & Mad. de Beauvau, Ma^{lle} de Mortemart, & M. Malhouët, with our two noble selves, made the party invited; but M. Malhouët failing, M. de Guignes,[7] formerly ambassador in England, took his place. Do you remember him, my dear Padre, at one of your Concerts? & *ses Gens?*—Do you think I could help recollecting his haste? M. Charles de Poix, eldest son of M. de Poix, finished our party. He is lively & intelligent, has been much in England, & speaks our language extremely well. When I remarked this to him, he answered, with great vivacity, 'When there are but two Nations in the World, surely they ought reciprocally to know each other's language!' 'It is not for us,' cried I, 'to whom you allow this participation, to dispute the point, but 'tis modest, you must confess, to set Austrians, Russians, Prussians, & all the rest of mankind, down for nothing!' The opera was *Le Nozze di Dorina*,[8] by Sarte, & extremely pretty: though I wished it had been as new to M. de Charles de Poix as to myself, for then he would not have divided my attention, by singing every note with every performer. In truth, I was so far from recovered from the fatigue of my journey, that I was fatigued to a drowsiness the most distressing by the end of the second act—which, being but too obvious, Mad. D'Henin & M. D'arblay took me away before I risked a downright Nap by waiting for the third! | The next day, however, *April 26.* my menaced illness yielded to a very serious alarm for my Alex, who had looked pale & unwell ever since our arrival, but whose spirits had always deceived our expectations for his health; a fever, however, now took place of our hopes, & but for my faith in my experienced success with James's powders,[9] I should have been terrified beyond expression. I gave him 3

---

[7] Adrien-Louis de Bonnières (1735–1806), comte, *later* duc de Guignes (1776). Sent as French ambassador to England in the days (1775) when he 'was looked upon . . . as one of the handsomest of men, as well as one of the most gallant' (*Memoirs*, ii. 64–5), he had attended one of Dr. Burney's musicales in St. Martin's Street (*ED*, ii. 114), and the Burneys never forgot the 'pomposity of his exit', when 'upon quitting the music room with an abrupt *French leave*' and failing to find 'half a dozen of our lackeys waiting to anticipate his orders . . . he indignantly . . . called out aloud: "*Mes gens! où sont mes gens? Que sont ils donc devenu? Mes gens! Je dis!*"' which phrases remained in the private vocabulary of the Burneys ever after.

[8] *Le Nozze de Dorina* (1782) by Giuseppe Sarti (1729–1802).

[9] For the ingredients of this universal cure, see, i, L. 7 n. 2.

grains—& the quickness with which the fever subsided was exactly proportioned to the rapidity with which it had broke out. But though he was so well before the Evening that all rational fear was passed, you will easily believe how little I felt disposed to quit him: yet I had an appointment for meeting Mad^e de Beauvau & Mlle de Mortemart at Mad. D'Henin's which it was difficult to relinquish, as it had [been] made immediately for me, & on my arrival: however, M. D'arblay went over to endeavour to effect what I so much wished: Mad. d'Henin unluckily dined out, & he could not see her: & soon after, her femme de chambre came, & with an earnestness that amazed me, entreated I would not disappoint her lady, who was still out, but who, she knew, had appointed Mad^e de Tessé[10] & Mad. de Poix, as well as the other 2 ladies, purposely to meet me. The affectionate creature so interested herself in her lady's feelings, even upon such a trivial affair, that her Eyes were full of tears while she pleaded for them; & when, upon M. D'arblay's representing I could be called in a moment, should my Alex be again worse, I thought it incumbent upon me to consent to go, the good creature brightened up, & smiled, & courtsied, & *thanked* me, as warmly & gratefully as if I had presented her with 5 Guinies. How rare is a character of an attachment of this sort, minutely entering into the happiness, as well as interest, of a Master or Mistress, to be found in our Country! You, however, my dear Sir, I really believe possess one in our good little Molly—& I could name one, or two, others—but not more! |

This Assembly at Mad. d'Henin's was one of the most select & agreeable at which I was ever present,—assembly, however, I ought not to call a meeting within the number of Twenty. We went very late, as I could spare but an hour from my little Boy, whom I left in a sweet & refreshing sleep. I was immediately presented to Mad^e de Tessé, who received me with every display of the most flattering distinction. She seems between 60 & 70, is upright, & of a stiff & formal deportment,

[10] The daughter of Louis (1713–93), duc de Noailles, Mme de Tessé (see Intro., pp. xliv–xlv) was in fact 61 years old. Her husband, René-Mans de Froulay (1736–1814), comte de Tessé, appointed at the age of 16 a colonel in the Grenadiers of France, was made as well equerry to Marie Leszczynska. With early connections with the Court, great wealth, and intellectual pretensions, she united, it was widely agreed, 'imposing firmness of character', with 'une sagesse positive, un jugement sain'. See L. 526, pp. 342–3.

her speech is slow & & her words are delivered with an air of precision that appears the result of weighing every one she utters: & the whole of her manner is ceremoniously affable, & therefore depressingly discouraging. When I have said all this, from the first shock of observation, I must tell you the far more pleasant result of what I have heard than of what I have seen; M. D'arblay says she has high principles, elevated sentiments, & talents for conversation equal, though not of a similar nature, to those of Mad. de Staël. She is sister to the *cidivant* Duc D'Auyent,[11] & was a Lady of the first rank with the *cidivant* Court. She had a very large fortune, & appointments of the first dignity & profit joined, M. de Tessé being Master of the Horse to the Queen. All, however, has been lost, in the revolution, except what enables them to live in modest comfort. Neither this account nor my own remarks, put me much, you will believe, at my ease in this interview, especially as I saw, on her own part, expectations excited I was horribly sure to disappoint. ⟨Such⟩ French ladies so much consider Courage as a mark of being *bien elevé*, that they think the want of it mere *mauvais ton.* |

Such being my embarrassed, & almost frightened situation in this opening intercourse, you will not marvel, my dearest Father, that I was relieved very agreeably by the entrance of the Beauvaus & Mlle de Mortemart, & by being placed between the two charming sisters by Mad. d'Henin. The '*How d'y'do?*' of Mlle de Mortemart transported me immediately to England, & we began an English that with mutual eagerness & openness—in which Mlle de Mortemart told me, with a hearty laugh, she had been informed, at the time of my marriage, that M. D'arblay could speak no English, & I could speak no French!—a natural enough exaggeration of our habit of each speaking our own language. M. de Crillon,[12] a Gentleman who, by continuing here during the variations of Seasons,

FBA, who was in future to profit from her competence and kindness, copied a portrait of her in verse in a Commonplace Book (greenish, marbled covers, 6×3·9″, Berg).
[11] Mme de Tessé's brother, Jean-Louis-Paul-François (1739–1824), duc d'Ayen (1766), who, having been made a colonel in the régiment de Noailles at the age of 14, served with distinction in the Seven Years War. A wit, a facile versifier, a favourite at Court and a friend also of writers and scientists, he was elected in 1777 to the Académie de Science. He had emigrated and, though allowed to return, did not appear in public life until the Restoration.
[12] François-Félix-Dorothée des Balbes de Berton (1748–1820), comte de Crillon,

has retained a considerable portion of his property, & who now, with his son, is preparing to visit England, Ireland, & Scotland, for a summer's excursion, came to converse with Mlle de Mortemart upon his route, &c; & she expatiated upon the pleasure she had derived from English society, English customs, & English places, people & things, with a joy & delight in the subject truly animating. Madame de Poix, after this, invited me to a little conference, forcing me to take a *fauteuil,* while she seated herself on a *Chaise de paille* close to me! Yet though this excess of condescendsion from a person of her rank & peculiar situation confounded me, her manners soon put me at my ease, in some measure,—or, rather, though I attained not ease, succeeded in giving me pleasure; for her vivacity is of such quick & ready conception, that her penetrating Eyes not only aid her to express her own meaning, but to seize that of others: & therefore, while the grave, nay, respectful attention of Mad. de Tessé not to lose a word I uttered, made me regularly forget every idea I meant to convey, the rapidity with which Mad. de Poix conceived every half pronounced phrase, always helped me on to something further, by appearing to comprehend, though unsaid, all that should have preceded. We were separated by her being summoned to a Card Table,—& I did not love Cards the better for taking her away. M: Mounier[13] also was there, but some engagement made him depart as soon as we had been named to each other. His Daughter[14] & a

marquis (1806). His military career had culminated with the rank of lieutenant-général in the Armée du nord (1792). He emigrated in that year to Spain, but, returning under the Directory and having obtained a pension, he was made under the Empire conseiller général de l'Oise and, after the Restoration, pair de France (1815) and duc de Crillon (1817).

Of his two sons Marie-Gérard-Louis-Félix-Dorothée-Rodrigue de Berton (1782–1870) and Louis-Marie-Félix-Prosper de Berton (1784–1869), it was probably the younger who planned to visit England.

13 Jean-Joseph Mounier (1758–1806), writer, avocat (1779), juge royal (1783), and député aux États généraux (1789). He emigrated first to Switzerland, then to Germany, where in Weimar he conducted a school for emigrant and German children. Erased from the proscription lists, he returned to France early in 1801 and, currently prefect of Ille-et-Vilaine, he was to become in 1804–5 a member of the Légion d'honneur and conseiller d'État. He was the author of, among other works, *Considérations sur les gouvernements* (1789), *Recherches sur les causes qui ont empêché les Français de devenir libres* (1792), and *De l'influence attribuée aux philosophes, aux francs-maçons et aux illuminés sur la révolution de la France* (1801).

14 Victorine Mounier (b. 1783), the eldest of the three children of J.-J. Mounier and Philippine *née* Borel de Champvillon (1763–95). Upon the death of her father in 1806 she received by imperial decree an annuity of 600 francs. Though known to the youthful Stendhal only through his friendship with her brother, she was,

son[15] remained; of the latter I saw little or nothing, but Mlle du Mounier fixed herself upon me without mercy, paying me compliments incessant with such full smiles as to fatigue my poor muscles in keeping up a decent return. The rest of the names that I heard were M. de Noailles,[16] de Damas,[17] De Mun,[18] de Guignes — 7

M[e] D'Henin had provided a very elegant little light supper, of creams, biscuits, Cakes & various confectionaries, all arranged with Taste & effect, at which the ladies alone sat down, & the men helped themselves as they could while waiting upon them. It was very pleasant—& Mad. d'Henin placed me between herself & Mlle de Mortemart, with whom, as I speak English, I am always quite at home: but I was uneasy for my poor Alex, & therefore stole away as soon as possible: not, however, till Mad. de Tessé made a party for us the on following Thursday at her House; nor till I had held a private discourse with Mlle de Mortemart upon my embarrassment as to Mad[e] de St—[19] from the terrible character she held in England— which embarrassment was not much lightened, by her telling me that it was not held more fair in France!—yet that every where the real evil is highly exaggerated by report, envy, & party spirit, all allow. She gives, however, great assemblies, at which all Paris *assist*, &, though not solicited, or esteemed, by

between 1802 and 1805, his 'fantôme idéal' and, according to some critics, the prototype of Mathilde in *Le Rouge et le Noir*.

[15] Claude-Philippe-Edouard (1784–1843), baron Mounier (1809), an articulate administrator who published a number of statements on the issues of his time. His appointments were to include auditeur au conseil d'État (1806), secrétaire du cabinet et intendant des bâtiments de la couronne (1813), membre du conseil d'État (1815), pair de France (1819), and directeur général de l'administration départementale et de la police (1820).

[16] Probably 'Juste' de Noailles, the younger son of the prince de Poix (L. 513 n. 16).

[17] Probably Joseph-François-Louis-*Charles*-César Damas d'Antigny (1756–1829), duc de Damas (1825), a brother of Mme de Simiane (1761–1835). A colonel in the Monsieur Dragoons, he was arrested at Varennes in 1791, but, escaping, joined the Armée des princes. Imprisoned for a time at Dunkirk, he again joined the princes, serving in 1795 as aide-de-camp to the comte d'Artois and in 1796 as maréchal de camp with the Armée de Condé. Emigrating then to England, he remained there until, apparently with the amnesties of the 1800s, he returned to Paris. He was not to resume army service until the Restoration, when he was made 'Capitaine-Lt. puis Lt. Gén. des Chevaux légers'. Like d'Arblay, he was to follow Louis XVIII to Ghent, becoming (1815–17) gouverneur de la 1er division militaire and in 1824 1er gentilhomme de la chambre.

[18] Jean-Antoine-Claude-*Adrien* de Mun (1773–1843), comte (1809), pair de France (1815), marquis-pair héréditaire (1817). He served for a time as chamberlain to Napoleon.

[19] See ii, Ll. 52–4. She was to depart for Coppet *c.* 5 May.

her early friends & acquaintances, she is admired & pitied, & received by them—I would she were going to Copet! —— On our return, I found my dear little Boy still asleep—but very feverish; & so thin & weak, that I grew much alarmed; & his Father still more, & when we found, in the morning, no amendment, M. D'arblay went in search of M. Bourdois, the physician, &, missing him, brought home M. Coët,[20] a physician who had been recommended to me by Mad. de Beauvau. The operation of James's powders not being yet decidedly over, he ⏐ wisely forbore giving any new medicine, & only ordered cooling drinks: In the morning he was abundantly better, & M. Bourdois & M. Coët both allowed nothing more was required but care & gentle dozes of Bark: & both also granted, that the timely administration of James's powders had, in all probability, saved him a putrid Fever!—I omit the journal of this Week, which was devoted to my dear Boy; only mentioning, that M. & Mad. de Tessé called upon us the next day, —& kindly accepted my apologies for the intended Dinner at their house;—Mad. de Poix came also, &, lame as she is, insisted on mounting our high Stairs, & yet was so tenderly considerate to my inquietude, she would not let me be called from my Alex, but stayed & conversed a few minutes with M. D'arblay, in our *sallon*, & then quietly descended.

Mad^e de Grandmaison,[21] also, a very favourite friend of M. D'arblay, came to visit me, & M. D'arblay urged me to admit her to the sick room, from an opinion she could help my nursery. She is a very handsome woman, & thought very clever & agreeable; but I was too much disturbed either to enjoy or judge her. What, however, most surprised, & perplexed me at this period, was the following truly extraordinary Note from Mad. de St[aël].[22]

Je voudrais vous temoigner mon empressement, Madame, et je crains d'être indiscrette. J'espere que vous aurez la

[20] Probably Charles-Louis Couad (*fl.* 1802–6), an officier de santé, of 1188, rue de Miroménil. Described in the *Almanach du Commerce de Paris* ... (1806) as 'médecin du prince Joseph', he published in that year his *Dissertation sur quelques points relatifs à la dysenterie*.

[21] Marie-Pierre Sonnerat (1759–1848) of Lyons, who had married (1) Pierre Descombes (d. *pre* 1788), avocat en parlement; and (2) in 1788 Alexandre-Paul Millin de Grandmaison (1739–1811). She was to marry (3) in 1818 Alexandre-Paul-Augustin-Félix-Élisabeth Barrin (1757–1828), comte de la Gallissonière.

[22] The original of this note [of 25 Apr. 1802] is extant in the Pierpont Morgan Library.

bonté de me faire dire quand vous serez assez remise des fatigues de vôtre voyage pour que je puisse avoir l'honneur de vous voir, sans vous importuner. Neckar Stael de Holstein.

How it is possible, when even the common civility of a Card for her Card is unreturned, that she can have brought herself thus to descend from her proud heights to solicit a renewal of an acquaintance broken so abruptly in England, & so palpably shunned in France? Is it that the regard she appeared to conceive for me in England was not only sincere, but constant? if so, I must very much indeed regret a waste of kindness her character & conduct make it impossible for me to repay; even though, on this spot, I am assured all her misdemeanours are aggravated, nay, caricatured, by report, & that she [|] exerts her utmost influence, & calls forth her best talents, upon every occasion which presents itself for serving those who have been her friends, & that, notwithstanding circumstances, & disunion, either in politics or morals, may have made them become her enemies. Her generosity is cited as truly singular upon this head, & I have heard histories of her returning, personally, good for evil, that would do honour to any character living. What a strangely complex mixture, my dearest Father, is that mixture which forms human Nature!—What good, or rather grand qualities may unite with almost every species of frailty! After much deliberation & discussion, my French Master composed for me the following reply.

^{Made} D'ar. ne peut qu'être infiniment flattée de l'extreme bonté de Mad^e la Comtesse de St — Elle aura très certaine-ment l'honneur de se presenter chez Mad. de St. aussitôt que possible. —

Cooler than this it was not easy to write, & the *ne peut qu'être* is a *tournure* that is far enough from flattering. I hope, however, it will prepare her for the frozen kind of intercourse which alone can have place between us. You know, my dearest Father, the WHY I am not at liberty to seem softened—though not to BE so is a liberty my Heart refuses to reject, after such condescendsion from such Genius. [|]

'FEMALE WORTHIES' Part I

515   April–May 1802

To Mrs. Locke

J.L. (Diary MSS. viii, not numbered, Berg), copied in an unknown hand from the original A.J.L. lent to CFBt by the Locke family.
The original journal was probably written in Paris or Monceaux in May–June 1802. The first double sheet, No. 6, was carried by Anthony Merry on 23 July; nos. 7 & 8 were sent with James Payne on 28 August 1802.
Three double sheets 4to, *numbered* No. 6, 7, N° 8 12 pp.
Corrected but not edited by CFBt.

Extracts from this letter were copied by M. d'A into the 'Paris Letter Book' as 'Notes or rather margins' to the A.J.L. to Margaret Planta, 27 Apr. 1802, recopied as part of that letter, for CFBt, and at a much later date, again recopied in typescript, see L. 516 below, and Textual Notes.

As I think there is no one my beloved friends will feel more interest to hear about, After M. De N[arbonne] than the Lady they know so particularly in England,[1] I shall now give them the whole narration of all that I should recount to them were we to meet.

M. D'[Arblay] was informed, by a friend,[2] that, as soon as she heard of my arrival, she expected I should wait upon her: but finding I did not, she applied again to that friend, &, hearing, probably, of the visits I had received from divers ladies, said 'Croyez vous que Mᵉ D'Arbly me reçévra avec Amitié? Adding, if you think she will, I will go to her, notwithstanding it is not the Custom of *les dames francoises* to make the first visit.—Our Friend (a lady) hesitated, rather *discouragingly*:—She perceived it, &, firing with proud—yet most natural resentment, said 'Eh bien, donc! soit!—qu'est ce que c'est pour *Moi que Mᵉ D'arblay!*' Here it dropt, and I was well content a first indignation should suffice for my acquittal of expectation—my whole mind being strongly bent, as you will know, against

515. [1] For the history of Mme de Staël, see Herold and Intro., v, pp. xxxvii–xxxviii.
   [2] Mme de Laval. Cf. L. 511, p. 252.

278

renewing an acquaintance which had already cost me so much
pain & difficulty.[3]

In a few days, however, her anger subsided; for among the
fine qualities which try to balance th[eir] opponents must always
be reckoned a complete freedom from malice or vengeance.
She spoke again to that Friend, & said that, as she found other
Ladies had *begun first*, she would not hold out, but either call or
send her carte. Our Friend councelled the latter; her advice
was taken, &, during my little Boy's first illness, came a Carte
M^e d S^t & — H: *ne N*[ecker] —I was too much disturbed at
that time to think upon the subject, but when he grew better,
I wanted a Carte in return,—but feared it might too grossly
repulse an acquaintance, unhappily, already made, in my own
country: while we loitered in hesitation, however, from fear
of going too far—imagine my surprise, to recieve the billet I
shall here copy:

À Me D. Je voudrois vous témoigner mon empressement,
Madame, et je crains d'etre indiscrette; j'espore que vous
aurez la bonté de me faire dire quand ⏐ vous serez assez
remîse de fatigues de votre voyage pour que je puisse avoir
l'honneur de vous voir sans vous importuner N — S^t de
H. —[4]

This excess of concession,—after avoidance so markcd, &
coldness so undisguised, was inexpressibly painful to me. this
I am sure you will concieve, from the same recollections which
made it so,. I will copy you the answer which M. D'arblay drew
up for me:

M^e d'ar ne peut qu'être infiniment flattré de l'extreme bonté
de Me. la comtesse de — st   Elle aura certainement l'honneur
de se presenter chez M. de St — aussitôt que possible. —

You will feel the courage it required thus to decline all appointment, as well as the more than coldness of the *ne peut qu'être* but
you will feel, also, my increased dread of the interview, from

[3] FBA expected a battery of reproaches similar to those she had provoked by
her failure to visit Juniper Hall in 1793. See FBA's meeting with Mme de Staël
at the Lockes' in Portland Place on 5 May 1793 (ii, L. 68, p. 105 and *passim*).
[4] See L. 514 n. 22.

such unequivocal demonstration how much it was desired. We all concluded that so supercilious an answer to so humble a note, would awaken all the fierté of the high spirit to which it was addressed, & terminate the affair; & our friend thought *the ne peut quêtre* quite too repulsive, & almost impertinent: however it did not prove so!—for you will be surprised to hear, that, in a few days afterwards, she came in person. Fortunately, on account of a hint she had enabled our friend to give us of her intention, we had been upon our guard, & the Portiere had previous orders to say my child was still unwell, & I was not visible: a message was sent up to desire to see M' D'ar: but he was *in dishabille*, & —— not chusing to indulge every body with that view as he does his friends of Norbury Park,—he only returned an excuse—Upon the consultation which ensued after this grand stroke, it was decreed that to return the visit was indispensable: though it was also resolved that she should only be on the list for the day on I was to make my first general round for payment of all such debts. Before this day, however, arrived, Our friend received a note from this—I doubt ⌐ not, *unhappy* persecutrix—with all her talents, all her consciousness of them, all her good qualities, & all her bad ones, *unhappy!* persecutrix, announcing that she was quitting Paris.[5] We thought, nevertheless, it would be right to leave our names,— or rather, wrong *not* to leave them: & on a morning which I had filled from 11 to 5 by incessant calls, I finished My Career at the door of her grand Hotêl:—Paint to yourselves, my dearest friends, what were my feelings, & how great was my consternation, when, as we were preparing, without enquiry, to give our *Cartes* to the *Portiere*, we heard the Lady was still in Paris, and *at Home!* How sick I turned! the reproaches I expected—my inability to speak one word that might clear them—the intimacy formed with a dear departed Angel in ignorance of all that has since been so repulsive—all crowded upon me, & like a culprit for terror lest the whole should end in unavoidable reconciliation, I had just given my hand to M. D'ar who was nearly as much disturbed as myself, to descend from our [voiture] when a person came out to say that Madame, though still in Paris, was just gone out, unknown to the Portiere. We escaped as fast

[5] According to the timetable offered by FBA's letters, Mme de Staël was not to set out for Coppet until 5 May.

as possible—I heard afterwards that the next morning she left Paris. Thus ends, in nothing thank Heaven, a little history that menaced me so much pain, embarrassment, unjust judgments from others, & cruel feelings in myself. I thought you would like it all thus concentrated, my dearest Friends, as I have not been able to let you know, from time to time, how the matter proceeded.—You will I am sure, more than any one, concieve, how irksome to myself has been the seemingly, ungrateful, Nay, insolent part I have appeared to act, towards one whom I all the world admires, & whom we have All—once—been so disposed to love—But I need not write those comments you can so well make. She left Paris to join—I know not for what reason, her husband[6]—& immediately upon their reunion, their meeting I should say, he was so obliging, according to report— as to reward her conjugal attention by sudden liberty—or rather, by the open property of that blessing. People here are extremely witty upon this subject: & I, amongst the rest, find some benefit from it, as it is conjectured the widowhood will be passed out of France. Will she venture again into a state of so much thraldom? But now I have said so much upon two acquaintances, I have thus laboriously sought to shirk let me console my beloved friends, & myself by an account of those I wish to cultivate—My next letter shall tell them of Me de Poix,[7] or M' de Tessé,[8] or Me de Mauboug[9] or Me de Maisonneuve,[10]

[6] Eric Magnus, baron de Staël-Holstein, was to die at a roadside inn on 8 May 1802 (Herold, pp. 185–8).
[7] See L. 513 n. 16.
[8] See L. 514 n. 10; and Intro., v, pp. xliv–xlv.   [9] See (L. 446 n. 12).
[10] With César's sister, Marie-Françoise-Élisabeth de Fay de Latour-Maubourg (1770–1850) FBA was to form a close and lasting friendship, though she was long in learning about the missing husband, namely, Bidault de Maisonneuve (*fl.* 1770– 1800), soldier and diplomat, whom Marie-Françoise had married in 1791 and from whom she had obtained a divorce in 1800.
As a young officer, Maisonneuve had served as a volunteer in the Imperial Army of Russia, participating in the war against the Turks. Sent next to the Court of Poland, as attaché to the Polish king, he soon became chamberlain and was for fifteen years minister for the Order of Malta in Warsaw. Coming up through military grades as well, he eventually attained the rank of Major General (Polish Army), which brevet he had converted in 1791 to the French equivalent of maréchal de camp. Appointed Minister Plenipotentiary to the Court of the Duke of Württemburg in February 1792, he wrote the Manifesto of the duc de Rohan against the Republic, which was published both in Berne and Leyden.
He seems to have aided Admiral Hood at Toulon in 1793 and later to have joined the army of the Emigrants, but his career in revolutionary times is obscure, ending as far as his French dossier is concerned, with a petition of 1799 claiming the Croix de Saint-Louis as the honour normally conferred with the rank of maréchal de camp, a petition refused on 2 Mar. 1800. The researchers and editors

or M de Beauveau,[11] or Me de Cardignan,[12] or Me de Montagu,[13] or M^{dle} de Mortmart[14] & M^e D'Henine is included in All. And the Family La Fayette[15] must have a volume to themselves ǀ

I shall begin My list of female Worthies according to the order in which I met with them. Immediately upon being informed of my arrival Me de Cadignan hastened to me. You have heard me already heard me speak of her, & of my pleasure in the thought of finding her here. She is of English Parentage, though born in America, & married to M. de Cadignan, one M. de la Fayettes etat Major, who, with Messrs de Norneuf,[16] *Piccard*,[17] Boinville,[18] la Columb,[19] &c, came into England during their Exile. I forget if you know of his unfortunate story? But as he & his wife are two of the Most interesting characters I can mention, I will risk its repetition, briefly, should you already be acquainted with it. M. de Cad[ignan][20] was one of the gayest & handsomest & richest of that Etat Major; he bore the loss of his very large fortune with unbroken spirits: he married a very pretty young woman, who had been sedulously educated in every principle of female worth, & who had a very small fortune, but which, joined to that of her Mother, & sister, was sufficient, with oeconomy, for elegance as well as comfort. M. De Cad[ignan] entered into some scheme of Commerce—I am ignorant of the particulars of this part of

have not been able to trace him further. Their son Frédéric-Gérard-Benoni-César *called* 'Maxime' was born in Passy on 28 Apr. 1797.

¹¹ Marc-Étienne-Gabriel de Beauvau (L. 513 n. 2). ¹² See L. 513 n. 6.

¹³ Mme de Lafayette's sister, Ann-Paul-Dominique 'Pauline' de Noailles (1766–1839), who had married in 1783 Joachim de Montagu-Beaune (1764–1834). From the rank of cadet gentilhomme in the Lyonnais Regiment (1778) he had by 1792 been promoted to colonel of the régiment de Noailles, owned by his father-in-law. Emigrating, he became maréchal général des logis in the army of the duc de Bourbon and had returned to France only in 1802.

¹⁴ Catherine-Victurnienne 'Victorine' de Mortemart (L. 513 n. 3).

¹⁵ For the members of Lafayette's family, see Intro., v, pp. xlii–xliv.

¹⁶ Norneuf is CFBt's erroneous transcription for Romeuf. Of the brothers Romeuf, Jacques-*Alexandre* (1772–1845) and Jean-*Louis* (1766–1812), both of whom were in the National Guard in 1789, it is probably Louis who is meant here. Fleeing with Lafayette, the younger was imprisoned by the Austrians (19 Aug.), but the elder, Louis, was locked up with Lafayette at Olmütz. Released in 1797, he resumed military service (see Six), becoming in 1805 état-major général of the Grande Armée under Mathieu Dumas and was later (1808) with the Armée du Rhin. Created chevalier de l'ordre de Saint-Henri de Saxe (1808), baron de l'Empire (1809), he was to die at Borodino (7 Sept. 1812).

¹⁷ CFBt's error in transcribing Sicard. See Charles Sicard (L. 425 nn. 8, 9).

¹⁸ See L. 425 n. 8 and n. 21 below. ¹⁹ See L. 425 n. 8.

²⁰ For Catherine Hunter, her daughters, and her son-in-law, see L. 513 n. 6.

his history; I only know the result: he broke: & the shock caused him a stroke of apoplexy which, for 3 days rendered him utterly insensible, & nearly lifeless. He has never, alas! recovered,—though his senses are restored, & his spirits, at times, re animated: but his mouth is still distorted, & he can only move upon crutches. It is now I must talk to you of his wife: young, pretty, & naturally not only gay, but extremely fond of fashion, Dress & shew—She has devoted her whole existence to nursing, Day & night, her infirm & helpless husband, & taking sole & tender charge of their two little Children & to studying all his rights, claims, & affairs, so as to act for him not merely as his housekeeper, & steward, but as his Lawyer. To a conduct thus Exemplary she joins pleasing & unaffected manners, the utmost ⏐ fondness for her two very fine little Boys, & an attention as tender to the happiness of her poor husband as to his interest & welfare. From the time of her marriage with so intimate a Friend as M. D'arblay,—She—as well as Mᵉ de Boinville—²¹ has desired to make acquaintance with his wife: but my dearest friend knows how little I have covetted adding to my list of creditors—such alas! being the proper name of almost all who visit me—& therefore I had always declined a meeting; till, when Cadignans were preparing to re-enter France, they were so urgent with M. Darblay, that he fixed a day for their coming to West-humble without consulting me. They came; I found M. Cadignan a frank, gay, natural character, interesting from his sufferings, which he bears with astonishing Courage, & attached to M D'arblay with a warm friendship for his person, & an open Admiration & respect for his military talents & reputation, in a manner that could not but be

²¹ Harriet *née* Collins (*c.* 1773–1 Mar. 1847) was the elder daughter of 'a retired West Indies planter' John Collins (d. *pre* 7 Feb. 1813) of 44 Berners Street, London, and the sister of Cornelia (d. 2 Sept. 1816), the wife of John Frank Newton (1767–1837). Harriet had married in 1794 Jean-Baptiste Chastel de Boinville (L. 425 n. 8). Cornelia Boinville (b. 1795), who in 1812 married Thomas Turner (*fl.* 1803–16), was their daughter. See L. 425 n. 8; Cameron, iii. 253–8, 275–8 *passim*; also iv *passim*.

In the French Exercise Books of 1803–4 (Berg) FBA wrote somewhat disapprovingly of Mme de Boinville, on whose position 'Je ne puis pas me taire . . . ni m'empêcher de la plaindre de tout mon coeur Bien que son pere — sa soeur, une patrie ont suffis autre fois à son bonheur, du moins à ses vues, cela ne se peut plus: ayant tant aimé un mari qui sembloit l'adoré, le perdre comme ça de vue, de societé, et même sans qu'il y soit aucun terme fixe pour leur re-union — je ne conçois rien de plus mclancholique. Ses pensées ne peuvent pas être plus consolantes sur le passée que pour l'avenir. Tout doit lui être presque egalement triste.'

283

winning to me. M^e Dé Cadignan I have already described. They made us engage to spend a day with them at Wellington, whither we went, & I liked each of them still better for further acquaintance: since this period they have resided here, & poor M' de Cadignan has had several relapses, & is now utterly hopeless of being restored to health though he is still but 30 years of age. The conduct of his wife has excited, in this country an ardent admiration that is every where spread, & to hear her named & to here her praised is always the same thing. She is an evident proof that to act well, with consistency, in our proper post, is to ensure approbation from all sorts & descriptions of persons & of nations. I have frequently told her this ¦ to console her in her misfortunes, & to encourage her in her difficulties. She has the comfort—amidst her disasters—of a first Cousin here, M^e — — — to whom she is very much attached; & of having made herself an intimate friend of Me Pinkney,[22] the beautiful daughter of M. La Tour Maubourg—a young Lady whom I have not yet seen, but whom M. D'arblay tells me is somewhat in the style of a certain *Amene*.[23] Do you think I intend to hate her? She has a friend, also, in M^{de} de Maison neuve, sister to M. La Tour Maubourg, & a lady of the first eminence for every virtue. As her heart is extremely affectionate, These are circumstances considerably to lessen the weight of her calamities: for, besides all that I have related, she has the whole conduct upon her mind & her cares of three Lawsuits in which poor M. De Cadignan is involved with rapacious relations, who have seized his property in his exile, & since his radiation, refuse him even what was unsold, except as he can recover it by force of litigation. I have dwelt upon her thus long, from a wish to interest my beloved friends for a person who seems so worthy of their kind wishes & to let them know I have such a country woman settled here, who has put English wives in fashion, & who is warmly, eagerly disposed to attach herself to one to whom they so tenderly desire all good.

To go on in the order in which my acquaintance were made, I shall next proceed to a fair & lovely picture upon which my

---

[22] Eléonore-Marie-Florimonde de Fay (1779–1831), daughter of César de Latour-Maubourg (L. 446 n. 12). She had married Daniel Huger Horry (1769–1828), author of *Pensées et sentiments* (1805), who at the time of his marriage changed his name to Charles Lucas Pinckney-Horry (Pinckney being his mother's maiden name).   [23] Amelia Angerstein *née* Locke. See L. 472 n. 2.

dearest Friends will love to look, & wish to dwell. You know my Fredy, I had a pacquet from Mrs Harcourt for Mlle de Mortmart, daughter to the ci devant Duc,[24] & that I had a message of singular sweetness for the same Lady from the Lady Elizabeth,[25] who spoke to me of her in warmest terms, & at whose injunction Mrs Harcourt wrote by me. I had a note, also, Mrs H. before my departure, desiring very much I should become acquainted not merely with Mlle de Mortemart, but with her sister, M^e la ci devant Princesse de Beauveau. while I was still too much tired with my journey for delivering my letter, I heard from M. D'arblay that M^{de} de ǀ Henin was preparing a select assembly purposely for introducing me to her particular friends, & amongst them, Mentioned *her niece* Me de Beauveau. M. D'arblay then mentioned my commissions, which M^e D'Henin immediately communicated to the Ladies Concerned, in consequence of which intelligence, they determined, without waiting for my visit & credentials, to come & see me themselves—though it was as Me de H. said, the Custem *les Dames françoises*; & Mad^e de Cadignan was still with me, in our first interview here, when, to my great amazement, M. & Mad^e de Beauveau, & Mlle de Mortemart mounted to our *Salloon*, conducted by the kind M^{de} D'Henin, who, from morning till night seems to study what will do me most honour, or procure me most comfort ǀ

My dearest Friends will easily believe how gratefully I recieved the surprise of being thus saved an awkward introduction of my self with my recommendatory letters. M. de Beauveau[26] has a serious countenance, but without much mark, & his dress & air, are both very English, & in the style of a common English young man of fashion, not of elegance: his wife— Ah my dearest Fredy—not so his wife—she, too, has an English air—but it is of elegance, & *not* of fashion, 'tis a look of sweetness with dignity, not pretention,—'tis a beauty of so chaste a character, as far as features & countenance & complexion can combine to give an idea of mental though bodily perfection, that my imagination flattered itself with seeing something like my own beloved Fredy in the early years of her marriage. Do you think, then, I did not feel myself drawn—attracted— almost bewitched by her? Mlle de Mortemart, had by no

[24] See L. 513 n. 1.   [25] Princess Elizabeth.

means as much beauty, nor as much grace, but she has extremely fine speaking eyes, a look that is *spirituelle*, great native gaiety & quickness, & a feeling as strong, perhaps, or stronger than her sister's, but not so well curbed for herself nor so soothing for others. Warm, energetic, enthusiastic, for all she loves, she seems prone to an indifference bordering upon disdain for all else: while Mᵈᵉ de Beauveau has an air, a voice, & a manner, of such fascinating softness, as to inspire whomever she addresses with an opinion—a hope, at least, of her personal kindness.— If their appearance & deportment thus pleased me, you will easily imagine my added gratification upon their addressing me in my own language: I am so little able to say *what* I mean *as* I mean in French, that I am perpetually entangled in difficulties when I attempt a phrase of more than 5 or 6 words: & the moment any embarrassment begins, my very ideas become obscure from the horrible provocation of searching ǀ in vain for words that may explain them.—Yet every body assures me I speak so well, that I am not without hopes they fill up all the chasms formed by my ignorance how to fill them up myself, with so high an opinion of my untold meaning, as to make it pass for something excellent beyond expression.

Every way, therefore, happy in the acquaintance of these charming sisters, we returned their visit almost immediately, Mᵉ de 'Henin accompanying us. We were admitted & Mᵈᵉ de Beauvau indulged me with a sight of 3 of her 4 children—& again My Fancy resembled he[r] to my Fredy, when I saw her eldest Boy 9 years old![26]—while she, who hardly looks 20, & is but 26, will soon like my Fredy seem to have a Brother in her Child. They are 3 very fine Children, Though not one of them inherits their Mother's beauty. *There*, when I think of William[27] & [Elizabeth], I drop my comparison. When I admired them, however, for their very healthy, flourishing, & blooming looks, Mˡˡᵉ de Mortemart exclaimed—'Ah, they were born in England!—' Mˡˡᵉ de Mortemart has spent 10 Years in England —where she lived from the age of 15 to the last 2 months: & she is so passionately fond of that nation, that tears of mingled

[26] For Marc-Étienne-Gabriel de Beauvau (still only about 29 years of age) and his family, see L. 513 n. 2.
[27] William Locke II (L. 472 n. 2), whose handsome appearance is often noted in SBP's Mickleham Journals (Berg). He had married the beauty Elizabeth Catherine Jennings. See *Locks of Norbury*, pp. 224–6.

pleasure & regret glisten in her eyes whenever it is the subject of discourse. She lived almost wholly with the Harcourt family while there, to which she is nearly related, & she loves Mrs Harcourt, in particular, as a most affectionate daughter loves a Mother. I had much conversation with her upon the Lady Elizabeth, & others of that revered House. The Beauvaus seem to like a life of perfect domestic comfort, with the extremest simplicity & Elegant œconomy. Their youngest child, a little Daughter, 6 months old is now nursed entirely by her lovely Mother, who entirely nursed the 3 elder. What encouragement I to maternal duties, to see the bright natural colour of her beautiful cheeks eclipsing all the rouge of art that seeks to supply its place!—M^e d'Henin had the Choisiul loge at the Opera lent her for the following day, with 8 tickets at her disposal. She kindly made a party[28] for us with the Beauvaus & Mlle de Mortemart, adding M. Charles de Poix, son of the *ci-divant* Prince—& meaning to add M. Malhouit;[29] but that Gentleman was indisposed, & M. le duc de Guignes,[30] formerly ambassador for England, took his place. The opera, called le Nozze di dozina the Music by Sorte, is very pretty, but had no singer that much charmed, or at all affected me; & the whole was so very long, that, unused to public places, & still not recovered from my travelling fatigues, I was—I must blush & own—tired to the most terrible sleepiness before the end of the 2nd Act—& that, though I sat between my charming Me de Beauvau & my kind M^{de} D'Henin, with M. de Poix,[31] an agreeable, vivacious tonnish, yet pleasing and intelligent *Elegant* behind us. obliging by singing every air with every singer, & announcing all that was coming with arbitrary decision upon the merits or defects we were to expect. He told us, however, that Paisiello[32] was that night arrived in Paris. I heartily wish I may happen to meet with him. M. Cha[rles] de Poix had been long in England & speaks our language very well. When I mentioned that, upon his making me some compliment when I was introduced to him, he gaily answered, 'O when there are only two nations in the world, it is but fair they should each speak the language of the other!'

[28] The night at the Opéra is described in L. 513, pp. 267–8.
[29] See L. 450 n. 17. [30] See L. 514 n. 7.
[31] Charles, the elder son of the prince de Poix (see L. 513 n. 16).
[32] See L. 513 n. 23.

Alas, poor Austria! Russia! Prussia! Spain Portugal &c to what are ye all dwindled in this French & English Century!—

The assembly projected on my arrival by our dear Me de Henin took place the next day. I will not now, | needlessly, afflict my dearest Friends with the detail preceding it of my Poor Alex's first seizure. It had made me renounce going—but, as he was much better that night, & I was allowed to wait till ten o'clock before I even adorned my gracious person, & he was then asleep, I found it impossible to resist the earnestness of M^e^ D Henin, who having invited her friends purposely to do Me honour & introduce me to them, declared flatteringly, she had not the courage to recieve them without me!!—But she lives only opposite our Hôtel, & I could be called in a moment. At half after 10, therefore, we presented ourselves, my hopes, at that moment, all happily alive to the belief my Poor Boy's illness was ending in the tranquil Sleep in which I left him Here we met again the attractive Me de Beauvau & her sister—& her husband, who at least I love for loving *her* as I heard him, at the opera, the preceding Evening, once call her, when whispering some observation, *ma bonne Aimë,* & another time, *ma belle aimé*

516 *Events of* 15–27 April 1802

To Miss Planta

A.J.L., copy in an unknown hand (Diary MSS. viii. 5388–98, Berg). The original was written at 1185, rue de Miroménil, Paris, on or about 27 Apr. 1802. It was sent to Miss Planta (i.e. the Queen and Princesses) through the British Minister Anthony Merry. This copy was presumably made from the 'Paris Letter Book' wherein M. d'A had appended extracts from L. 515 and FBA wrote, perhaps at a later date, the explanatory note:

> The notes or rather Margins were copied by my partial Partner willing to keep my first sentiments of his country and countrymen, from parts of my Letters to my beloved Friend *Frederica Lock*

Originally 5 double sheets 4to, numbered 1, 2, 3—, 4, 5, this copy was cut and pasted, eliminating passages from L. 515, as see Textual Notes 11 pp. *Edited by* CFBt *and the* Press.

At a later date typescript extracts were taken from the Letter Book (*grangerized* DL, vi. 2–3, *NPG*); *printed* in FB & the Burneys, pp. 39–46).

Paris. 27th April 1802

A week have I been here, my dear Miss Planta, so astonishingly engaged, so indispensably occupied, or so suffering from fatigue, that I have not been able till now to take up my pen except to satisfy my dear Father of our safe arrival.¹ To give you some idea of these *engagements, occupations, & fatigues,* I must begin with the last. We were a whole long languid day, a whole restless painful night, upon the sea, my little Alex sick as death, suffering, if possible, yet more than myself, though I had not a moment of ease & comfort. My little Adrienne de Chavagnac was perfectly well all the time, singing and skipping about the Cabin & amusing everyone by her innocent enjoyment of the novelty of the scene. At Calais we spent a day, & half a night to refit, & pray try to imagine my pleased emotion & surprise, when as soon as we were seated to dinner at the Hotel, a Band of Musicians came to the window, with french horns & other instruments & struck up *'God Save the King'.* So unexpected a sound in a foreign Country & a country *so* lately hostile affected me with uncommon pleasure. I had heard so much of the plainness and mahogany ˡ skins I should view when I had crossed the strait of Dover, that I was amazed at the number of pretty woman & of lovely children I saw in Calais, most of them very fair. Mentioning this circumstance afterwards to an english gentleman, he hastily replied 'Dont you recollect the reason? Calais was so long in possession of the English that the Race is not yet extinct'. You will acknowledge this was modest, whether true or not. Two days and two nights, we then travelled to reach Paris, Adrienne leaning upon my arms, & Alex nestling against my knees—Need I enter into further detail to give you a notion of my *fatigue?* Indeed I am not yet recovered from it, though I will confess to you I forgot it all for some hours after my arrival, from the reception my exertions met with from the person for whom I made them.

Secondly, as to my *occupations*—my little apartment to arrange, my trunks & baggage to unpack & place, my poor Adrienne to deliver to her friends, my Alex to nurse from a threatening malady;—letters to deliver, necessaries to buy; a femme de chambre to engage; & most important of all! my own sumptuous

516. ¹ Sent to the Queen through Margaret Planta (L. 429 n. 4), this Journal, a rewrite of Ll. 508, 510, and 511, introduces no new matter.

wardrobe to refit, & my own poor exterior to reorganize! I see you smile, methinks, at this hint, but what smiles ᐧ would brighten the countenance of a certain young lady called Miss Rose,[2] who amused herself by anticipation, when I had last the honour of seeing her, with the changes I might have to undergo, could she have heard the exclamations which followed the examination of my attire!—*This* wont do!—*That* you can never wear! *This* you can never be seen in! *That* would make you stared at as a curiosity!—THREE petticoats! No one wears more than one!—STAYS? every body has left off even corsets!— Shift sleeves? not a soul now wears even a chemise! &c &c.— In short I found all that I possessed seemed so hideously old fashioned, or so comically rustic, that as soon as it was decreed I must make my appearance in the *grande monde* hopeless of success in exhibiting myself in the *costume francais*, I gave over the attempt, & ventured to come forth as a Gothic *anglaise*, who had never heard of, or never heeded, the reigning metamorphoses.

Now, Thirdly, as to my *engagements*:—when should I finish should I tell of all that have been made or proposed even in the short space of a single week? The civilities I have met with, contrary to all my expectations, have not more amazed me for myself, than gratified me for M. D'arbly who is ᐧ keenly alive to the kind, I might say distinguished reception I have been favoured with by those to whom my arrival is known. I must pass by however, all other to speak of one introduction in which I was most peculiarly interested—that to Melle de Mortemar whom I have already seen four times,[3] & always with added pleasure: A certain honey suckle[4] message with which I was honoured for her, has caused her so much delight, that I believe she can never see me without a pleased sensation from its recollection. I find her lively, agreeable, interesting, & intelligent: & her beautiful sister, M^de de Beauveau, seems a composition of grace & virtue. Their lives, by all I have observed, or gathered, are exemplary for discretion, right conduct, & domestic seclusion. Most fortunately for me, Mad^e

---

[2] Princess Augusta (see the code, v, p. 361).
[3] See L. 513, p. 261 and p. 267 (when she called on Fanny and vice versa); L. 514, p. 271 (at the Opéra Bouffe); and L. 515, p. 287 (at Mme d'Hénin's).
[4] According to the key (L. 512 n. 3), Princess Mary, although here obviously Princess Elizabeth.

[d'Henin d'Alsace,] whom I had known in England, and who had assisted M. d'Arblay in all his preparations for making me comfortable upon my arrival, had already settled a meeting for me with these Ladies before I came, & while I was recruiting to enable myself to wait upon them with my letter, & my *Honeyed* message, they were so good as to come to me themselves arm in arm with [M. le Prince de Beauvau,]⁵ ⎸ whom M: D'a had know[n] intimately when a child, though they have hardly I believe met since. I can scarcely tell you with what sensibility & delight the Honeyed words & the letter of Mrs Harcourt were recieved by Melle de Mortemar. I was only sorry I had not a similar pleasure to bestow upon her charming sister, whose beauty & whose gentle manners rival each other in attraction. As two other ladies who had called upon me were in the room, our conversation upon what I most coveted to talk, the Oak, the Magnolia, & the fair flowers of England, was brief though expressive & heartfelt: but not so, as to Mrs Harcourt; they both spoke of her with fondest admiration & friendship, and seemed quite solaced to meet with one who had been personally known to her—to the General to Lord & Lady Harcourt;⁶ & could enter upon a subject that enabled them to give vent to their affection & gratitude for that noble family in general and Mrs Harcourt in particular.

We returned their visit as speedily as possible, Made[d'Henin] having the goodness to conduct us. I have the pleasure to find they live very near us, & that the walk between our habitation is, at this season, clear and pleasant. ⎸ They were so kind as to let me see all their children, except a little one of eight months old, who was sleeping. M. de Beauveau fetched us the others himself, & seems as fond a Parent, & as good a husband as any our own dear Isle, so famed for parental & conjugal characters, can boast. You will believe, my dear Miss P[lanta] I name him not as *singular* for those domestic qualities, though born in France! The children are healthy, blooming, & well behaved, though none of them have half the beauty of their mother. I forgot to mention how much I was charmed & surprised by both sisters, as well as by M. de Beauveau, in being addressed by them in English: I am still so very, very, little accustomed

---

⁵ L. 513 n. 2.
⁶ Elizabeth *née* Vernon (1746–1826), wife of the 2nd Earl (L. 513 n. 1).

to speaking French, that the attempt embarrasses even my thoughts.

A party was now formed for our all meeting again, by M^de d'Henin who wished to take me to the Italian opera [Buffa],[7] & who had the *Loge* with eight tickets, of M. de [Choiseul], for a day or two after. There accordingly we all met, the 8 tickets being disposed of by M^de d'Henin to M^r et M^de de Beauveau, Melle de Mortemar, Mr Charles de [Poix], Mr Malhouët & ourselves: but Mr Malhouët failing, M. de Guignes, formerly ambassador in England, took his place.[8] The music l was by Sarte, & very pretty, but the *altogether*, was so very long, that, little used as I now am to public places, I was so oppressively tired, that being unable to disguise my weariness, &, in defiance of all my efforts to be pleased, on the very point of falling asleep, M^e D'H[enin] et M^r D'A[rblay] had the charity at the end of the second act, to convey me away.[7] I must however observe, that I saw, with much satisfaction, a general decency of *costume* at this Theatre that was wholly unexpected: neither in *les loges*, nor on the stage, was there any thing that could shock the most scrupulous spectator: the exceptions being so very few as to be rather objects of mingled pity & curiosity, than of horror & disgust with which I was prepared to behold them. Entre nous, nevertheless, it is but right to notice, in this favourable account, that I am horribly near sighted!

Again I met these two charming Sisters at a very select & elegant assembly & *petit Soupé*, chez M^de D'Henin, consisting of M^r et M^de de Tessé, Ma^de la [Princesse de Poix], Mr Charles de [Poix], son fils, Mr de Guignes, Mr de Crillon & his son, who are preparing to visit England; M^r et Melle Mounier, Mr de Noailles, Mr Adrian de Maun, Mr de Montagu, Mr de Damas, Mr de Beauveau, & a very few others whose names I forget though the ceremonial of introduction passed with almost all, for it is impossible for me to give any idea of l the politeness, & kindness that are shewn me. *I dare not even attempt it.*—My own ease & delight, however, was chiefly with the two sisters, & I had now an opportunity to converse at full length with Melle de Mortemar, upon the trees, plants, & flowers, she had seen in England, & which she spoke of with a warm admiration that came close to my heart. We sat together at supper & talked of

---

[7] Cf. L. 514, pp. 270–1.　　　　[8] For this group, see L. 514, pp. 273–5.

nothing else. That exquisite plant the Magnolia, which she seems to have had good opportunity of seeing, & which, though not a native of our soil, has taken root in its very heart; she agreed with me in thinking possessed the highest & most elegant perfume possible; she indeed was chiefly listener here, my own opportunities of seeing & studying the virtues & sweetness of that plant having far exceeded hers: & I may say the same also of our Rose, which has a flavour always so peculiarly delicious to me, that it is difficult for any one to keep pace with me it its commendation. Our Honey-suckle, however, & our Lily, she disputed with me which should praise most, thinking them the loveliest flowers she had ever smelt. You will easily believe with how much pleasure I joined in her panegyric, but the glowing carnation, & my dear, dear beautiful Violet, she permitted me to describe entirely in my own way being, compared with myself, almost a stranger to their odour.[9] I Need I tell you how delightful to me was a conversation such as this? or, how animated I became when she talked of our noble Oak, acknowledging no such Tree grew in any other country!— Melle de Mortemar could discourse upon England as long, & with just, or near as much eagerness as myself. She regards it, she says, completely as her native land, having spent in it the last important 10 years of her life, & its customs, manners & inhabitants, were all highly esteemed by her—She never, she said, suffered so much as in quitting it; especially as the last four days she spent in it were passed in waiting for a passage at Dover! 'to have left', she said 'every thing dear to me, & then to be detained from coming on, in a place were I had no interest, no pleasure! for, once fixed that I must leave England, my next wish was to arrive in Paris'. She & Mr D.ar[blay] then recollected that they had crossed the sea together, though without knowing each other's names: but the burthen of every stanza was Mrs Harcourt, whom she almost adores. She had just written to that lady by Mr Jackson.[10]

My letters for Mr Merry[11]—one of which was from Lord Pelham[12] M. D'arblay carried to that gentleman a few days after my arrival. He was out, but so polite as to call here the next

[9] This passage CFBt, as editor, attempted to improve by emending 'smelt' to 'approached' and 'odour' to 'qualities'.
[10] See L. 470 n. 3.   [11] L. 510 n. 13.
[12] The Home Secretary (L. 437 nn. 2, 10).

morning. I could not see him, having laid down, in a fit of almost insufferable fatigue; & unluckily he mounted our high stairs in vain: he left tickets for us both, & for me an especial message, with an offer his most obliging of his services, & as desire I would not scruple to employ him, | if anything occurred in which he could be of use to me. I shall avail myself of this civility by enclosing this to him, & requesting he will forward it with his next despatches. I have been 3 days writing it, by odd minutes, from the illness of my dearest Boy, who has been seized with a fever that has almost terrified us to death,—& forced us to see two physicians, though till now, I have never once had recourse to any since I married. I attribute it to the fatigue of our journey, joined to a change of water, to wine, diet & hours, & his too violent sensations of joy in seeing his Father—who in return, overpowered by pleasure, took him about till his eager spirits, & excess of animation, were heated & inflamed into Fever. I write still by his bedside having positively renounced every sort of engagement till I see him well: but he is so much recovered, that I have every reason to hope his re establishment will be as rapid as the attack. One of his Physicians, M. Bourdois: is an old Friend of Mr D'arbly's the other, M. Coët[13] was recommended to me by Made de Beauveau. Both assure me all danger is over; but are of opinion he has narrowly escaped a putrid disorder!— O my dear Miss P[lanta] how thankful am I for such an escape!—

Your favourite Hero[14] is excessively popular at this moment from three successive grand events, all occurring within the short time of my arrival—The Ratification | of the Treaty of Peace[15]—the Restoration of Sunday, & Catholic Worship,—&

---

[13] L. 514 n. 20.

[14] In her later capacity as editor FBA supplied the note: 'This was an appellation agreed upon previously for Buonaparte as a Flattering one, & therefore safe one, in case of a letters' seizure or miscarriage.'

[15] The Peace of Amiens was signed on 25 Mar. 1802; the *dimanche* was restored, officially and in open practice, on Easter Sunday 18 April; and on 26 Apr. 1802 'a *senatus consultum*, prepared a fortnight earlier at an extraordinary meeting of the *Conseil d'État*, proclaimed a "general amnesty". In fact about a thousand persons who had compromised themselves in the most extreme way remained under proscription; but all *émigrés* were to be allowed back on the condition that they return to France before 23 September 1802 and swear the oath of allegiance to the constitution of the Consulate' (Lefebvre, p. 136). The government reserved the right of surveillance and the power to impose further restrictions, for instance, the obligation to live as much as 20 leagues from one's former residence (Forneron, ii. 373–4).

the amnesty of the Emigrants. At the opera Buffa, the *loge* in
which I sat was exactly opposite to that of the First Consul;
but he & his family are all at [La Mal-maison.][16]
Shall I never have done! Yes, Yes,—Adieu!
My dear Miss P[lanta] & believe me ever
Your affectionate Friend & Servant
F. D'a[rblay]
M. de Ay entreats you to accept his best compliments.
Rue Miromenil
N° 1185
Paris

PARIS JOURNAL

517   *for* 3–5 May, 1802

To Doctor Burney

A.J.L. continued (Diary MSS. vi, not foliated but between the foliations
5387 and 5668, Berg), conjecturally written during the summer of 1802.
Three double sheets 4to, numbered by 4tos   (13),   (14),   15   12 pp.
wafers

The 1st double sheet 4to was
Addressed, p. 4: Dr. Burney,
Carried to England by Mrs. Broome *c.* 20 Oct. 1802.
Endorsed by CB, p. 4: 13
Annotated by FBA, p. 1: ⌗ × Monceau. Maria. Beaufremont. Chastel.
La Jacquemeniere Adrienne

The 2nd double sheet 4to was
Addressed, p. 4: Dr. Burney—
Carried by James Greene,[1] 24 Nov. 1802
Annotated by FBA, p. 1: ⌗ × Mme de La Fayette. de Beauvaus. Gen.
Suchet   M^e d'Henin

The 3rd double sheet 4to was
Addressed, p. 4: England. / Dr. Burney, / Chelsea College, / London.
Carried by James Greene, 20 Jan. 1803
Endorsed by CB, p. 4: 15
Annotated by FBA, p. 4: ⁖ × Hulin Lauriston — Thuilleries.
*M. d'A apparently copied this A.J.L. in the 'Paris Letter Book' as part of a running
account of the events of 22 Apr.–5 May 1802. Subsequent copying is described in*
L. 513, *above.*

16 FBA was to see something of Joséphine's château *c.* 24 July 1802 (see L. 529,
p. 365).
517. 1 Among the English visitors to Paris in the years 1802–3 was James Greene

May 3ᵈ I pass now to the Week following my poor Boy's illness: which we began by carrying him, on this May 3ᵈ to *Monsso*,[2] in Mad. de Poix' chariot, which Mad. D'Henin borrowed. The morning was delightful, & the little excursion did infinite good to the poor Alex. Mad. D'Henin took us to a place called *La folie de Chartres*,[3] ci-divant belonging to the duc d'oreleans, & now a public Garden. It is now in a state of ruin, compared with what it formerly boasted of grandeur, the River cut through it being nearly dried up, from neglect of the Fountains, the house turned into cake rooms, &c, common

(1760–1814) of Turton Tower, Lancashire, who in 1782 had come into the possession of the considerable hereditaments described by James C. Scholes, *Notes on Turton Tower* (1880). Moving to Monmouthshire in the early 1780s, he acquired the Priory at Abergavenny and later, a large estate at Llansantffraed, seeming to live in later years, however, at Raglan or Monmouth. It was by virtue of his acquaintance with the Waddingtons of Llanover that he was willing to make the acquaintance of the d'Arblays at Passy and to carry their letters to England on the occasions when, as it was to prove, he was summoned by writs of Court to return.

Deserted by or in any case separated from his wife, a wealthy man about town, and socially enterprising, he had made friends in Paris with Lady Elizabeth Foster, became an intimate friend of the flamboyant Junot, commandant, and later (1806) gouverneur de Paris; and, a good raconteur and a pleasant companion, he appears intermittently in the Journal of Bertie Greatheed (see L. 549 n. 2), which Journal also includes sketches (portraits) of him by young Bertie, the artist. The elder Bertie found him 'indefatigable in procuring us pleasure' and on one occasion thought it most 'kindly done of Green to ask d'Arblay that he might meet Junot. . . . In la Fayette's day this d'Arblay now existing on a couple of hundreds a year was Camp Marshall at Longwi where Junot now Commandant of Paris was a common grenedier. Would I had the whole conversation of that day' (p. 75).

² While in Monceau the d'Arblays lived, as FBA relates in L. 543, with Mme de Tremouilles (see L. 543 n. 8).

³ Situated in the outlying district of the parish of Clichy-la-Garenne, the Parc Monceau originally comprised the hunting grounds of the ducs d'Orléans. In 1778 Philippe Égalité (1747–93) built there a 'maison de plaisance' that came to be known as 'la Folie de Chartres'. There was nothing spectacular about the château, but the surrounding gardens, designed by the painter-engraver Louis Carrogis, *dit* Carmontel (1717–1806), were crowded with adornments—a naumachia, an obelisk, a temple, Chinese pagodas, Dutch windmills, kiosks, islands, cascades, and fountains.

In 1783 the duke, attracted by the new 'English landscape gardens' lately introduced into France, employed Thomas Blaikie (1750–1838), the Scottish gardener who had designed the gardens at Bagatelle, to make an English garden at Monceau. Blaikie described the 'confused Landskipe' he found there: 'Monuments of all sorts, Countrys and ages . . . Chinesse & Gothick buildings, Egyptian Pyramides joined to Italian vineyards . . . the whole was a Small confusion of many things joined together without any great natural Plan, the walks Serpenting and turning without reason which is the fault of most of those gardens done without taste or reason.' By improvements made 'in following the nature of the Ground and drawing perspectifs upon the different objects already placed', he wrought a great effect, he said, 'upon those Gardins and upon the Mind of the Duke'. See *Diary of a Scotch Gardener at the French Court at the end of the Eighteenth Century*, ed. Francis Birrell (1931), pp. 178–89. For views of the garden as first made, see Sir William Chambers, *Détail des nouveaux jardins à la mode* (1776–88).

Benches placed in the most open part of the Garden, & the Bridges half broken. Nevertheless, with all this, M. D'ar[blay] & I, with our West Hamble rusticity, thought it probably more beautiful, though less habitable, than in its pristine state; for the Grass wildly growing was verdant & refreshing, the uncut Lilacs were lavish of sweets, & Nature all around seemed luxuriantly to revel over the ruins of Art.

As I wished much to see the Parade, or Review, which was to take place on the 5ᵗʰ & is only once a Month,[4] we were forced to devote the preceding Day to visits, as it was pronounced, in our counsel of etiquette, that I could not appear in a place were I might be seen by those who had shewn me the civility of beginning an acquaintance, till I had acknowledged my debt to them.

May 4ᵗʰ was, therefore, a very full Day indeed; & began deliciously; for we first went to Maria, — & there, as soon as I had embraced the dear Girl, cordially, & not without wet Eyes congratulating her upon her happy, & almost superb establishment, in Rue Choiseul, I heard she had just received Letters from her dear Parents, informing her of the legacy of good Mrs. Bateman to little Amelia.[5] I have seldom received more delightful intelligence. I felt all the joy of her fond Father & Mother, & the mental relief to so great a portion of their cares. How kindly has prosperity, of late, [shone] upon them through the same medium that caused their solicitudes & difficulties, their children!—I wanted Maria to accompany us in our next visit, which was to her Brother & sister ǀ in Law, M. & Mᵉ Bourdois;[6] but there was some impediment of pavement that made the street impassable for a Carriage, & she is not strong enough to undertake a long walk. I was glad, afterwards, she was spared the trouble, as we found no one at home. The fine Weather had drawn out also Mesdames de

---

[4] This was the Parade and Audience celebrating the establishment of the Consulate (L. 449 n. 7).

[5] The Hon. Mrs. William Bateman (L. 486 n. 1; and i, L. 11 n. 9) had bequeathed to her 'god Daughter Amelia Maria Burney [Maria's sister, aged 10] one thousand pounds . . . to and for her use and benefit absolutely' (P.C.C. Kenyon 256, pr. 22 Apr. 1802).

[6] The physician Edmé-Joachim Bourdois de la Motte and his wife (since 23 Jan. 1789) Marie-Geneviève *née* d'Hermand de Cléry, sister of Louis-Joseph d'Hermand de Cléry, the diplomat. See also L. 450 n. 6.

The d'Hermand family lived on the rue Verneuil, where Dr. Bourdois was also living at the time.

Poix & de Tessé, de Duras,[7] de Luynes[8] & de Montagu,[9]—
which 3 latter I have never seen, & therefore will pass by, to
mention to my dear Father those of whom I can give some
sketch from having obtained admission. And first,—we were
let in to a cidivant Mad[e] la Princesse de Beaufremont—a lady
of *Franche Comté*,[10] & of the neighbourhood of Joigny, who had
been excessively urgent with M. D'arblay for my introduction
to her,—but who, I fear, will find her desire subside, now, in
sickened rather than satisfied curiosity,—as, being a good deal
fatigued with so many presentations, & some what indisposed,
I never felt more forcibly my want of ease in the French language
than during this visit—in so much, that I could not twice open
my mouth. She has still fine prominent & lustrous Eyes, though
her person is immense, & her youth is passed; she has a pleasing
voice, & high bred manner, & I wonder, now, why I was so
dumb-founded in her presence; but I had heard so much of her
wish for the acquaintance, that it frightened me. M. D'arblay,
however, made amends for my silence, as he had so much to
enquire, or communicate, relative to Joigny & its vicinity, that
the conversation never flagged, though I only appeared to
assist at it in character of Audience. Her Daughter, Madame
de Listenois,[11] a tall thin & elegant young lady, was one the
interlocutors, & seemed lively & sensible; but an accident
happened | on my entrance that was truly comic; Mad[e] de
Listenois, after I had been saluted in the usual way by her

7 Probably the duchesse de Duras, Louise-Henriette-Charlotte-*Philippine née*
de Noailles (L. 440 n. 3).
8 The duchesse de Luynes (L. 469 n. 8).
9 'Pauline', of the Noailles family (L. 515 n. 13).
10 Louise-Françoise-Bénigne-Octavie-Marie-Jacqueline-Laurence de Bauffremont (1750–1803), chanoinesse de Remiremont (1754), dame de la Croix-Étoilée
and dame grand'croix de Saint-Jean-de-Jérusalem (1766), who had married in
1762 her uncle Joseph de Bauffremont (1714–81), *styled* chevalier de Bauffremont
(1757), marquis de Mirabeau, comte de Cézy, prince de Bauffremont-Listenois et
du Saint Empire (1762). For two centuries at least, the Bauffremonts owned properties in Franche-Comté that, having been controlled by the Austrian and the
Spanish Habsburgs for two hundred years, was conquered for France in 1674 and,
according to the peace of Nijmegen, annexed to France in 1678.
An ancestor, Claude de Bauffremont (*fl.* 1528), had been governor of Franche-
Comté in the 16th century. The heir was prince Alexandre-Emmanuel-Louis de
Bauffremont (1773–1833), marquis de Listenois, Mirebeau, Marnay, comte de
l'Empire (1810), pair de France (1815), at this time Lieut.-Col. in the service of
Spain (1796–1803). Cézy was about two miles from Joigny.
11 Hortense-Geneviève-Marie-Anne (1782–1848), princesse de Bauffremont.
She was to marry in 1804 Joseph de Narbonne-Lara (1767–1825), vicomte de
Saint-Girons, and secondly in 1834 Pierre-Jules, comte Ferrari de Romans
(d. 1864).

mother, approached me with an eagerness that seemed so determined to be affectionate, that, judging by her youth & her manner that she really meant to embrace me, as soon as she jutted forward, with vivacious smiles & sparkling Eyes, her Cheek, I met it with my lips,—but it was withdrawn before they touched it; yet the other side was presented with a precipitancy of expressive pleasure that again deceived me, & again my lips did their office,—so that twice in the same moment I literally kissed the air.—This served me, however, for a lesson, during the rest of my first visits, against a similar simplicity of credulity.

We next were admitted by Mad^e de Chastel,[12] wife to the eldest Brother of M. de Boinville. She is a french American by birth, & fair, fresh & of elegant, but entirely decent appearance. She surprised me a little, by apologising for not having come to see me immediately, in saying she should certainly have done it, but that she was informed there were *tant de curieuses* qui l'avoient fait, that she would not risk being included in their number!—

We then went to see the Lady of General d'Hennesel,[13] who is an ancient Camarade de Guerre of M. D'arblay, & was an intimate friend of his eldest & favourite Brother in their mutual youth. The General was at home, with his Wife, who appears a perfectly good sort of woman, strongly attached to her husband, whose immensely tall person is striking, & whose attentively polite manners speak the early *ci-divant* military education. They had 3 Children[14] in the room with them, whom they appear to love with great fondness; & indeed their whole *menage* seems that of complete domestic comfort.

[12] Catherine-Françoise (b. *c.* 1763), the wife of Nicolas-Charles Chastel (1749–1822), seigneur de Moyenpal. See further vi, L. 565 n. 7.
[13] Anne-Eulalie Roussel (d. 25 Oct. 1858), who had married in 1796, as his second wife, Charles-Nicolas d'Hennezel (1747–1833), chevalier d'Hennezel et de l'Empire (1810), baron d'Hennezel de Valerois (1818). An artillery officer, educated at the École de Metz (1763), he had come up through the ranks, having been named Lt.-Col. (1791), sous-directeur d'artillerie à Metz (1792), and chef de brigade d'artillerie (1793). Suspected in 1794, he was deprived of his rank, but re-instated in 1795, he attained the rank of général de brigade d'artillerie (1797) and, with various commands (see Six), was to retire on 20 Dec. 1803.
In his long career in the artillery he could easily have met d'Arblay and his brother Jean-Pierre Bazille Piochard d'Arblay (1750–78).
[14] The three children of the Roussel-d'Hennezel marriage mentioned at this time would have been Gabriel-Thélesphore-Babylas (1793–1807), Sosthène-Romaric (1796–1855), who was to become the next baron d'Hennezel; and Eulalie-Algine (1801–35).

We were received, also, by Mad^lle La Jacminiere,[15] Daughter
to an old friend & Townsman [& Cousin] of M. D'arblay, a
very worthy, upright Man, who is now of the *Tribunat*—which,
if composed of many such, must be truly respectable:—but —
— well,—Mlle La Jacminiere has just the air of a modest,
quiet, silent, shy young English woman. We did not see her
Father. ˈ

Last, we went to Mad^e de Montecler,[16] to see my dear
Adrienne, as I wished to make that my longest visit. M^e de
Montecler, seeing us from the window, brought down her
little Grand Child to the Gate to receive me: she is extremely
stiff & formal, but perfectly good. I believe her amongst the
cidivants the most to be pitied, because suffering most, in lost
dignity & consequence, from the new order of things. Monsieur
de Chavagnac, also, is truly sad & serious, & I should tremble
for the happiness of my poor little Adrienne, but that there is
a brother in law, M. Rozelay,[17] who resides with them, & who
is naturally gay, & very pleasing, & who is fond of the Child,
& plays with her, & is almost adored by her in return already.
I was sorry not to carry my Alex there, but he has been too ill
for such a course as we took in the middle & the heats of Paris.
Indeed, though we were nearly as much in Fiacres as on foot,
I was so thoroughly tired when I returned from all these visits,
which took us up in time from Eleven O'clock till five, that I
could not sit up even to Dinner—& my feet were blistered,
with the walk & the heat, so as to make me unable to bear not
only shoes, but any covering whatever, & I was forced to rest
them upon a Bed, for the remainder of the Day—to my no
small distress before the Evening was closed— ˈ

In a close Cap,—my feet, in their native undrapered state,
hidden by a long large wrapping Morning Gown, your
Daughter, my dearest Sir, lay reclined on a Bed,—when,
rather late in the Evening, I was told Mad^e D'Henin was in the
Sallon. I was going to send in my excuses, while I rose to get

15 Adelaïde-Louise Thérèse (*c.* 1773–1842), daughter of Louis-Charles Gillet de la
Jacqueminière (L. 448 n. 10). She was to marry in June 1809 Denys-Victor Huard
de la Marre (*c.* 1783–*post* 1842), a notary (1811–27) in Paris.

16 Hyacinthe-Jeanne-Marie de Montecler (L. 510 n. 6) and her grandchild
Adrienne de Chavagnac (L. 437 n. 3).

17 Michel-Robert-Gabriel (1761–1840), marquis de Rasilly, had married in
1792 a sister of M. de Chavagnac's wife, namely, Jeanne-Baptiste-Aglaé de Montecler (1771–1815).

ready for waiting upon her, but Alex: flung open the door, &, seeing where I was, & how fatigued, insisted upon my keeping still, & came to my Bed side, & sat, in friendly converse, listening to the history of my morning's excursion, till a ring at the Bell of our anteroom made me desire to have nobody admitted. Alex again, however, frisking about, & preventing Pauline, my little femme de chambre, from hearing me, occasioned her to come to me & name Madame La fayette![18]

You may easily believe this name, & my present situation, put me into no small commotion; I was beseeching Mad^e D'Henin to go to the Sallon, with my apologies, when Alex, whose illness, though it has diminished his strength & his flesh, has left his spirits as wild, & his motion as perpetual as ever, called out to proclaim where I was—&, while Madame La fayette was gently moving on, flung the Bed room door wide open, saying 'Mama is here!' Madame La fayette, concluding, I suppose, that I received *du monde* in the french manner, immediately presented herself at the door—where I had now no resource but to entreat Mad. D'Henin, who is her intimate friend, to receive her—for I was wholly powerless, with my *unsandled* feet, to rise.

Mad^e D'Henin now brought her to my Bed side—where nothing could have been more awkward, more embarrassing,

---

[18] Adrienne de Noailles (1759–1807) was the daughter of Jean-[Louis]-Paul-François de Noailles (1739–1824), duc d'Ayen (1766), duc de Noailles, marquis de Maintenon. His sister Adrienne-Catherine (1741–1814), who became in 1755 Mme de Tessé, was therefore Adrienne's aunt.

Married at the age of fourteen (11 Apr. 1774) to Lafayette (1757–1834), Adrienne bore three daughters, Henriette (1775–7), Anastasie (1777–1863), and Virginie (1782–1849), and a son George Washington (1779–1849), whose marriage (6 June 1802) to Françoise-*Emilie* (1780–1860), daughter of Antoine-Louis-*Claude* Destutt (1754–1836), marquis de Tracy, comte de Tracy et de l'Empire (1808), was in negotiation at this time. See also L. 526 n. 11.

Revered for her domestic devotion, active zeal, and the heroic self-sacrifice with which, when freed from the series of prisons in which she herself had been incarcerated (1793–5), she determined to share her husband's confinement in the nauseating prison of Olmütz (24 Oct. 1795–19 Sept. 1797), she has attracted the attention of biographers including André Maurois, whose *Adrienne, ou la vie de Madame de La Fayette* (1960) was translated into English by Gerard Hopkins the following year. Both editions provide descriptions and plates of La Grange, a château with farms and woodlands, once forming part of the vast Noailles possessions, about thirty miles from Paris. The road leading to La Grange, the château itself, and the manner of life there, is described by Lady Morgan, ii. 298–312; and among the striking plaudits that her life and conduct inspired are the reflections of Lady Jerningham, *The Jerningham Letters (1780–1843)*, ed. Egerton Castle (2 vols., 1896), i. 303–4.

or more distressing than my situation, but that the real reverence
I had conceived for her character & her virtues, made the sight
of so singular a person, | her condescendsion in the visit, & her
goodness, though lame, in mounting up 3 pair of stairs, gave
me a sensation of pleasure that, by animating my spirits,
endowed me with a courage that overcame all difficulties, both
of language & position, & enabled me to express my gratitude
for her kindness, & my respect for her person, with something
far nearer both to fluency & clearness, than any thing in
speech I have yet attempted; my mind instantly presented her
to me torn from her beloved family, & thrown into the death-
impending prison of Robbespierre—& then, saved, by his
timely destruction, from the Scaffold, & then using her hard
recovered liberty only by voluntarily sacrificing it to be immured
with her husband in the dungeon of Olmutz.—Various as may
be the opinions of the politics of M. La fayette, all Europe,
I believe, concur in admiration of the character & conduct of
his virtuous & heroick Wife. Indeed nothing, since my arrival,
has so sensibly gratified me, from *WITHOUT*, as this visit.

Madame de La fayette is Daughter of the *cidivant* Duc
d'Ayen, &, consequently, Niece of Mad^e de Tessé, the Duc's
Sister. She was married to M. de La fayette when he was only
17 years of age. By some Cold, or mismanadegement, & total
want of exercise, in the Prison of Olmutz, some humour has
fallen into one of her ancles, that, though it does not make her
absolutely lame, causes walking to be so painful & difficult to
her, that she moves as little as possible, & is always obliged
to have a stool for her feet. She now resides, with M. de
Lafayette & their three Children, entirely in the Country, at
a Chateau which has descended to her since the revolutionary
horrors, & therefore has not been confiscated, called La
Grange. They never come to Paris but upon business of
positive necessity. She had arrived only this morning, on a
visit to her Aunt, Mad. de Tessé, to make some preparations
for the | approaching marriage of her only son. Her youngest
Daughter, Mlle de La Fayette, accompanied her. She is
a blooming young Creature, of English fairness—as we English
chuse to say!—with a bright native colour, & beautiful light
Hair; otherwise, with but indifferent features, & not handsome:
but her air, though modest even in the extreme that borders

upon bashfulness, is distinguished, & speaks her to be both sensible & well brought up. Mad^e de Lafayette, also, is by no means handsome, but has Eyes so expressive, so large, & so speaking, that it is not easy to criticize her other features, for it is almost impossible to look at them. Her manner is calm & mild, yet noble; she is respected, even by surrounding Infidels, for her constant piety, which, in the true character of true religion, is strict only for herself, lenient & chearful for all others. I do not say this from what I could see in the Hour she was so good as to pass with me—but from all I have heard, & much I have observed since.—I regretted extremely that M. D'arblay was not within, as Mad. de La fayette is, most deservedly, one of the Beings he reveres; & as he has the happiness to be enlisted amongst those who are honoured with her regard.

She warmly invited me to La Grange, & pressed me to name an early Day for passing some time there; I proposed that it might be after the marriage had taken place, as till then all foreign people or subjects might be obtrusive—She paused a moment, & then said Après — — c'est vrai, —we could then more completely enjoy Mad^e D'arblay's society, for we now must have continual interruptions, surrounded as we are by workmen, Goods, & preparations—so that there will be a nail to hammer between almost every word;—& yet, as we are going to Auverne after the Ceremony—it will be so long before a meeting may be arranged, that I believe the less time lost the better!' I knew M. D'arblay desired this acquaintance for me too earnestly to offer any opposition; & I was too much charmed with its opening to make any myself; ˡ it was therefore determined we should go the following week.

May 5. Again a full Day, my dearest Father; M. D'arblay had procured us 3 Tickets for entering the Apartments at the Thuilleries to see the Parade, [from] General Hu[llin],[19] now

¹⁹ Pierre-Augustin (1758–1841), comte Hulin, sometimes dubbed 'l'illustre blanchisseur', by reason of his retreat in 1789 from the army to a laundry establishment. He states in his dossier (Archives Nationales) that from 14 July to 15 Oct. 1789 he had commanded the 'Corps des Volontaires Nationaux de la Bastille' with the rank of capitaine and that during 1790 he had served as 'capitaine de la 8ᵉ compagnie de chasseurs de la Garde Nationale Parisienne soldée'. This must have been the period when he was captain under d'Arblay, for he was next assigned to an infantry brigade.
On 5 Feb. 1802 he had been appointed 'Adjudant Supérieur Chef de Brigade

high in actual rank & service, but who had been, formerly, [a Captain under] M. d'Arblay. our 3d. Ticket was for Mad. D'Henin, who had never been to this sight,—nor, indeed, more than twice to any spectacle since her return to France, till my arrival—but she is so indiscribably obliging & good as to accept, or seek, every thing that can amuse, of which I can profit. We Breakfasted with her early,—& were appointed to join the party of M. de Beavau[20] who had a General in his carriage, through whose aid & instructions we hoped to escape all difficulties. Accordingly, the coach on which they went was desired to stop at Mad. D'H[enin]'s door,[21] so as to let us get into our Fiacre, & follow it strait. This was done; & our precursor stopt at the Gate leading to the Garden of the Thuilleries. The de Beauvaus, Mlle de Mortemar,[22] & their attending General alighted, & we followed their example, & joined them—which was no sooner done, than the General, viewing M. D'arblay, suddenly drew back from conducting Mad. de Beauvau, & flew to embrace him—They had been ancient camarades, but had not met since the Revolution, General [*Songis*][23] having never, I believe, emigrated. They embraced cordially,—& he then returned to his beautiful charge, Mad. de Beauvau, M. D'arblay had the arm of M^e D'Henin, someone I know not ⌐ of Mlle de Mortemar; & M. de Beauvau fell to my own share. His reserve & mine put together, did not produce much brilliancy of repartee in our way to the Palace—The crowd was great, but civil & well dressed, & we

de l'État Major du Palais', and he was presumably serving in this capacity when d'Arblay saw him at the Tuileries on 5 May. In September 1802 he was made 'commandant des grenadiers à pied de la garde des consuls', but, as he records, he had never enjoyed the favour of Lafayette and his friends.

[20] See L. 513 n. 2.

[21] At the corner of the rue de Miroménil and the rue Verte (today the rue de Penthièvre). See L. 513 n. 15.

[22] L. 513 n. 3.

[23] 'Souchet' was later corrected by FBA to Songis. Probably Charles-Louis-Didier Songis (1752–1840), général d'artillerie who, having joined the régiment de Metz in 1774, was sent, temporarily, to the Forges de Champagne in 1790. Employed in May 1792 in the Armée du centre as 'sous-directeur' of the 'Parc d'Artillerie', he was promoted by Dumouriez to the rank of Lt.-Col. (Sept. 1792), fought in the battles of Valmy and Jemappes and at the siege of Maestricht. With successive commands in the artillery of the Armée du nord, he was made 'général de division, commandant l'artillerie à Lille' (19 Aug. 1794), but leaving the Armée du nord, he continued service as 'inspecteur des ateliers d'armes' in Lille. In 1795 he was named a 'commandant' at Brussels, and with various commands (see Six), he retired finally on 4 June 1801 and was at this time 'conservateur des eaux et forêts' at Caen (Vincennes).

met no impediment till we came to the great entrance.—Alas—
I had sad recollections of sad readings in mounting the steps!—
We had great difficulty, notwithstanding our Tickets, in making
our way; I mean Mad. d'Henin & ourselves; for Mad. Beauvau
& M¹¹ᵉ de Mortemart, having a power in the existing military
to aid them, were admitted & helped by all the attendants, &
so forwarded, that we wholly lost sight of them, till we arrived,
long after, in the apartment destined for the exhibition. This,
however, was so crowded, that every place at the Windows,
for seeing the Parade, was taken, & the row formed opposite,
to see the First Consul as he passes through the room to take
Horse, was so thick & threefold filled, that not a possibility
existed of even a passing peep. General [Songis],²³ however,
found means to obtain admission for his two ladies into the
next apartment—but could not extend his powers to our service.
Mad. D'Henin would now have retired, but as the whole
scene was new, & curious to me, I prevailed with her to stay,
that I might view a little of the *costume* of the Company;
though I was sorry I had detained her, when I saw her per-
turbed spirits from the recollections which, I am sure, crowded
upon her on re-entering this palace—& that her sorrows were
only subdued by her personal indignation, which was unconscious, but yet very prominent, to find herself included in the
mass of the Crowd, in being refused all place & distinction
where, heretofore, she was amongst the first for every sort of
courtesie. Nothing of this, however, was said! If you may believe
my pity for her was equally un-uttered.—We seated ourselves,
now, hopeless of any other amusement than seeing the uniforms
of the passing officers, & the light drapery of the stationary
ladies; which, by the way, is not by any means so notorious nor
so common as has been represented; on the contrary ¹ there
are far more who are decent enough to attract no attention,
than who are fashionable enough to call for it.—During this
interval, M. D'arblay found means, by a Ticket lent him by
M. de Narbonne, to enter the next apartment, & there to state
our distress, not in vain, to General Hulin¹⁹ for presently he
returned, accompanied by this officer, who is, I fancy, 7 feet
high, & was dressed in one of the most shewy uniforms I ever
saw, & introduced me to him. He expressed his pleasure in
seeing the Wife of his old Camarade, &, taking my hand,

caused all the Crowd to make way; & conducted me into the Apartment adjoining to that where the first Consul receives the Ambassadors, with a flourish of manner so fully displaying power as well as courtesie, that I felt as if in the hand of one of the 7 champions, who meant to mow down all before him, should any impious elf dare dispute his right to give me liberty, or to shew me honour. Accordingly, he gave me the best place in the Apartment, which was sacred to General officers, & as many ladies as could be placed in two rows only at the Windows. M. D'arblay, under the sanction of his big friend, followed with Me. D'Henin; & we had the pleasure of finding Me de Beauvau & Mlle de Mortmart at the same windows.

The scene, now, with regard to all that was present, was splendidly gay, & highly animating. The room was full, but not crowded, with officers of rank, in sumptuous rather than rich Uniforms, & exhibiting a martial air that became their attire, which, however, generally speaking, was too gorgeous to be noble. Our window was that next to the Consular apartment, close to the steps ascending to it, by which means we saw all the forms of the various exits & entrances, | & had opportunity to examine every dress & every Countenance that passed & re-passed. This was highly amusing, I might almost say historic, where the past history & the present office were known. Sundry footmen of the first Consul, in very fine liveries, were attending, to bring Chairs, or arrange them, for who ever required them; various peace officers, superbly be-gilt, paraded occasionally up & down the Chamber, to keep the ladies to their windows, & the Gentlemen to their ranks, so as to preserve the passage, or lane, through which the First Consul was to walk, clear & open; & several gentlemen-like looking men, whom in former times I should have supposed pages of the back stairs, dressed in black, with Gold chains hanging round their necks, & medallions pending from them, seemed to have the charge of the door leading immediately to the First Consul. But what was most prominent in commanding notice, was the array of the aid de Camps of Buonaparte, which was so almost furiously striking, that all other vestments, even the most gaudy, appeared suddenly under a gloomy cloud when contrasted with its brightness. We were long viewing them, before we could discover what they were to represent, my 3 lady companions being as new to this scene as myself: but, afterwards, M. D'arblay, starting forward to speak to one of them, brought him, across the lane, to me, & said, 'General Lauriston.'[24] His kind & faithful friendship to M. D'arblay, so tenderly manifested upon his splendid embassy to England, made me see him with great pleasure. It was, of course, but for a moment, as he was amongst those who had the most business upon his hands. General d'Hennesel, also, came to me for a few minutes, & 3 or 4 others, whom M. D'arblay named, but whom I have forgotten. Indeed I was amazed ǀ at the number of old friends by whom he was recognized, & touched—far more than I can express, to see him—in his old Coat & complete undress, accosted by his fine (former) Brethren, in all their new & beautiful array, with a respect & affection that, resulting from first impulse, proved their judgement, or rather knowledge of his merits, more forcibly than any professions, however warm, could have done. He was, indeed, after the aids de Camps, the most striking figure in the Apartment from contrasting as much with the general herd by being the plainest & worst dressed, as they did by being the most eminently the gayest & most shewy. General Lauriston is a very handsome man, & of a very pleasing & amiable countenance; & his manly air carried off the finery of his trappings, so as to make them appear almost to advantage. While this variety of attire, of carriage, & of physionomy amused us in Facing the passage prepared for the first Consul, we were occupied, whenever we turned round, by seeing, from the Window, the Garden of the Thuilleries filling with troops,—this, however, my dear Father will not wonder to hear was a sight more pleasurable to those who surrounded me, than to myself, who, never loving War, can take no joy in its appendages.— ǀ

[24] Jacques-Alexandre-Bernard Law, comte de Lauriston (L. 425 n. 5).

PARIS JOURNAL

518 *for* 5–6 May, 1802

To Doctor Burney

A.J.L., continued (Diary MSS. vi, not foliated, but between the foliations 5387–5668, Berg), written at Paris or Monceaux, during the summer and autumn of 1802.

Four double sheets 4to, numbered by 4tos (16), (17), 18, (19) 13 pp. wafer

The 1st double sheet 4to was
Addressed, p. 4: Dr. Burney, / Chelsea College, / Middlesex—
Carried to England by James Green on Jany 20 1803[1]
Endorsed by CB: Journal N° 16, / to May 1802
Annotated by FBA, p. 1: ⁑ + Grand Review at the Thuilleries

The 2nd double sheet 4to was
Carried by Mrs. Barthélémy Huber[2] on 16 June 1803
Annotated by FBA, p. 1: ⁑ × Grand Review continued.

The 3rd double sheet 4to was
Addressed, p. 4: Dr. Burney, / Chelsea College, / Middlesex.
Carried by Dugald Stewart,[3] Secretary to the British Ambassador, 9 Oct. 1806
Endorsed by CB: N° 18.
Annotated by FBA, p. 1: ⁂ × Review finished. d'Henin. de Beauvau. de Mortemart. The Petition.

518. [1] See L. 532 n. 1. In manuscript (p. 4 of the 1st double sheet, carried by Greene) FBA had inserted the comment: 'My dearest Padre must be Sly!—he will perceive—as well as that it is not by *all opportunities* I can send *SUCH* stuff as this!'

[2] Accompanying Lydia Huber *née* Strutt (L. 487 n. 2) to Paris was her niece and god-daughter, Lydia Strutt (born *c.* 1793), the daughter of the Revd. Samuel Strutt (*c.* 1773–1837), rector of Tichborne, Hampshire. In leaving bequests to the three surviving children of his brother-in-law, Barthélémy Huber prayed God 'to bless them and endow them with the same Christian spirit as their blessed Sister Lydia Huber Strutt was blessed with for the edification, the happiness and example of those who had the happiness to be acquainted with her' (see will P.C.C. Norwich, pr. 21 July 1837).

Evidently it was this niece and adopted daughter Lydia who called for the 2nd sheet of the Journal, for FBA notes on the 3rd double sheet: 'N° 17. was taken by Miss Hub[er] & I hope arrived safely, though I have never heard of it.'

[3] Dugald Stewart (1753–1828), Professor of Moral Philosophy at Edinburgh (1785–1820), who in pre-revolutionary years had formed acquaintances among the learned men in France (see *DNB*). Probably an acquaintance of CB Jr., if not of CB, he was to pay friendly calls on the d'Arblays in 1806. For a list of the letters he carried to England in that year, see entries for 25 Sept. and 8 Oct. in FBA's Notebook, vi.

308

This Journal for 1802 was continued (but not completed) on the 1st page of the 4th double sheet.
Carried by Dugald Stewart (*supra*) on 9 Oct. 1806
Annotated by FBA: ⚕ × Mme de Maisonneuve. & 4 years concentrated—from 1802—to 1806

On page 2 of the 4th double sheet (*supra*) FBA began her Journal for 5 October 1806 (see L. 575).

Most of the Journal for 1802 (I shall go on, . . . made their bows.—) *was copied by M. d'A in the 'Paris Letter Book' as part of a continuous account of the events of 22 Apr.—5 May 1802. Subsequent recopying is described in L. 513, above.*

The account of 6 May was also copied into the 'Paris Letter Book' at some time before 5 Oct. 1806. A copy (Diary MSS. viii. 5606–8, Berg), 3 pp., was made for CFBt, evidently from the Letter Book, and was edited by the Press. A typescript copy is preserved (grangerized DL, 25th or Supp. Vol., pp. 111–13, NPG; printed in FB & the Burneys, pp. 62–4).

I shall go on, my dearest Padre, with the grand Review, for though I keep hints of Notes every day for you, no subject has offered since that I think stands an equal chance of amusing your curiosity.

In the first row of females at the window where we stood were three ladies who, by my speaking English with Mlle de Mortemart, & Mad^e de Beauvau, discovered my Country, &, as I have since heard, gathered my name: & here I blush a little to own how unlike was the result to what one of This nation might have experienced from a similar discovery in England—for the moment it was buzzed 'C'est une Etrangére — c'est une anglaise'—everyone tried to place—to oblige—to assist me—& yet no one looked curious, or stared — — ah, my dear Padre—do you not a little fear, in a contrasted situation, *NO* one would have tried to place, oblige, or assist—yet every one would have looked curious, & stared?—Well, there are virtues, as well as defects, of all classes,—& John Bull can fight so good a Battle for his share of the former, that he need not be utterly cast down in acknowledging, now & then, a few of the latter.—The best view from the Window, to see the marching forward of the troops, being now bestowed upon me, —which I vainly offered to the ladies of my own party, to whom the whole of the sight was as new as to myself,—the 3 Unknown ladies began conversing with me, &, after a little general talk with them all, one of them, with sudden importance of manner, & a tone slow, but energetic, said 'Avez vous vûe, Madame, le premier Consul?' — 'Pas encore, Madame.' — 'C'est, sans doute, ce que vous souhaitez le plus, Madame?' — 'Oui, — Madame.' — 'Eh bien, Madame, — Voulez vous le voir parfaitment bien, et tout à fait à vôtre aise?' — 'Je le desire, Madame, beaucoup.' She then told me to keep my Eyes constantly upon her, not an instant to lose sight of her movements, & to suffer no head, in the press that would ensue when the First Consul appeared, to intervene between us: 'Faites ⏐ comme cela, Madame, continued she, et vous le verrez bien, bien,—car—added she, very solemnly, & putting her hand to her breast, 'Moi — Je vais lui parler! — ' I was very much surprised, indeed, & could only conclude I was speaking to a wife, sister, or cousin, at least, of one of the other consuls, or of some favourite Minister. 'Et lui, Madame — She said, il me repondra; vous l'entendrez parler, Madame! oui, vous l'entendrez! car il est bon! bon! — bon homme tout à fait! et affable! — O affable! — oui, vous l'entendrez parler!' I thanked her very much; but it was difficult to express as much satisfaction as she displayed herself. You may suppose, however, how curious I felt, for such a conversation, & how scrupulously I followed her injunctions of watching her motions.

A lady on my other side now demanded my attention also. She looked infinitely good humoured, & told me she came regularly every month to the great Review, that she might always bring some friend who wanted to see it. I found by this she was a person of some power—some influence, at least; & not entirely averse to having it known. She was remarkably short, & thick, & sallow, with little sunk Eyes, a concise Nose, & a mouth that her constant smiles seemed literally extending from Ear to Ear. She had yellow flowers in her hair, & yet a kind of Mob Cap under her Chin. She was extremely civil to me, but as my other friend had promised me so singular a regale, I had not much voluntary time to spare for her; this, however, appeared to be no impediment to that she was so obliging as to determine to bestow upon me, & she talked on, satisfied with my acquiescence to her civility, till a sort of bustle just before us making me look a little sharp, she cried 'Vous le voyez, Madame!' 'Qui? exclaimed I, le premier Consul?' —

'Mais non! — pas encore, — mais — Ce — ce Monsieur, là!'
I looked at her, to see whom I was to remark, & her Eyes led
me to a Tall, large, heavy figure, with a broad gold laced Hat,
who was clearing the lane, ⌐ which some of the Company had
infringed, with a stentoric voice, & an air & manner of such
authority as a chief constable might exert in an English riot.
'Oui, — Madame, I answered, not conceiving why I was to
look at him; Je le vois, ce Monsieur — il est — bien grand!'
'Oui, Madame, replied she, with a yet widened smile, & a look
of lively satisfaction; — il est bien grand! — vous le voyez
bien?' — 'Mais — oui, et — et — il est très bien mis. — '
'Oui, surement! — vous êtes sûre que vous le voyez?' 'Bien sur,
Madame — mais — — il a un air d'autorité, il me semble. —'
'Oui, Madame — et — — bientôt — il ira dans l'autre aparte-
ment. — il verra — le premier Consul! — — ' 'O, — fort bien,
cried I, quite at a loss what she meant to make me understand,
— till, at last, fixing first him, & then me, she expressively
said 'Madame, — C'est mon Mari!' The Grin now ⟨she⟩
distended to the very utmost limits of the stretched lips, & the
complacency of her countenance, forcibly said 'What do you
think of me, now?' *MY* Countenance, however, was far more
clever than my head, if it made her any answer. But, in the
plenitude of her own admiration of a Gentleman who seemed
privileged to speak roughly, & push violently, who-ever, by
a single inch, passed a given barrier, she imagined, I believe,
that to be known to belong to him, entitled her to be considered
as sharing his prowess—though I am sure she could not have
wrestled with a Child,—& even as participating in the merits
of his height & breadth,—though he could easily have put her
in his pocket.

Not perceiving, as I imagine, all the delight of felicitation in
my Countenance that she expected, her own fell, & took, by a
disappointed pause, ⌐ all the length of which its circular form
would admit from its breadth; it recovered, however, in another
minute, its full merry rotundity by conjecturing, as I have
reason to think, that the niggardness of my admiration was
occasioned by my doubt of her assertion; for, looking at me
with an expression that demanded my attention, she poked
her face under the arm of a Tall Grenadier stationed to guard
our window, &, trying to catch the Eye of the object of her

devotion, she called out, in an accent of tenderness, 'Ma Mie! ma Mie!' The surprise she required was now gratified in full, though what she concluded to be excited by the Honour of her happiness, was simply the effect of so carressing an address from so diminitive a little Creature to so Gigantic a big one. Three or four times the soft sound was repeated ere it reached the destined Ear, through the Hub-bub created by his own loud & rough manner of calling to order; but when, at last, caught by the gentle appellation, he looked down upon her, 'twas with an Eye brow so scowling, a mouth so pouting, & an air that so rudely said *What the D - - - l do you want*, that I was almost afraid he would have taken her between his finger & thumb, & have given her a shake: however, he only grumbled out 'Qu'est-ce, donc?' A little at a loss wha to say, ⌐ she gently stammered 'ma Mie — le — le premier Consul — ne [vient]-il pas?' 'Oui, oui!' was blustered in reply, with a ⟨tone⟩ that completed the phrase by *you fool, you!* though the voice left it unfinished. Not disconcerted, even yet, though rather abashed, she turned to me, with a pleased grin, that shewed her proud of his noble ferociousness, & said 'C'est mon Mari, Madame!' as if still fearful I was not fully convinced of the grandeur of her connexion. — *Ma mie* having now cleared the passage by ranging all the Company in two direct lines, the officers of highest rank were assembled, & went, in a sort of procession, into the inner apartment, to an Audience with the First Consul. During the time this lasted, some relaxation of discipline ensued, & the Gentlemen from the opposite row came peeping at the Windows [to chat] with the ladies: but, as soon as the Generals descended the steps they had mounted, their short conference being over, *Ma mie* again appeared, &, to the inexpressible gratification of his loving little Mate, again hustled every one to his post—& the Flags, next, as I think, were carried, in procession, to the inner Apartment; & soon after brought back; —& then again *Ma Mie*, ⟨& then⟩ The Prince of orange,[4]—who passed us, to enter the Audience Chamber, with a look so

---

[4] William, 6th prince of Orange (1772–1844) and statdholder, was to assume the title of 'William I, Sovereign Prince of the Netherlands' only on 2 Dec., 1813, while his position as king of the United Netherlands was to be confirmed only by the Vienna settlement of 1814–16. He might well look depressed, for at this time the French occupied his country and by the Treaty of Amiens the Dutch had seemed to lose their hope of help from Britain. For his distressing situation at this time, see Rose, 'The Peace of Amiens', i. 306–28.

serious, an air so depressed, that I have not been at all surprised to hear he was, that very night, taken very ill!—The last object for whom the way was cleared, was the 2ᵈ Consul, Cambaceres,⁵ who advanced with a stately & solemn pace, slow, regular, & consequential: dressed richly in Scarlet & Gold, & never looking to the right or the left, but wearing a Mein of fixed gravity & importance—He is short & rather square, — — He had several persons in his suite, ⏐ who I think—but am not sure, were counsellors of state.

At length, the two human hedges were finally formed, the door of the Audience Chamber was thrown wide open with a commanding crash, a vivacious officer-Centinel—or I know not what, nimbly descended the three steps into our Apartment, &, placing himself at the side of the door, with one hand spread as high as possible above his head, & the other extended horizontally, called out, in a loud & authoritative voice, 'Le Premier Consul!' You will easily believe nothing more was necessary to obtain attention; not a soul either spoke or stirred as he & his suite passed along; which was, so quickly, that had I not been placed so near the door, & had not all about me facilitated my standing foremost & least crowd-obstructed, I could hardly have seen him: as it was, I had a view so near, though so brief, of his face, as to be very much struck by it: it is of a deeply impressive cast, pale even to sallowness, while not only in the Eye, but in every feature, Care, Thought, Melancholy, & Meditation are strongly marked, with so much of character, nay, Genius, & so penetrating a seriousness—or rather sadness, as powerfully to sink into an observer's mind:—yet, though the Busts & Medallions I have seen are, in general, such good resemblances, that I think I should have known him untold, he has by no means the look to be expected from Bonaparte,— but rather that of a profoundly studious & contemplative Man, who, 'o'er Books consumes'—not only the 'midnight oil,' but his own daily strength, & 'wastes the puny body to decay' by

⁵ Jean-Jacques-Régis de Cambacérès (1753–1824), duc de Parma (1808), Second Consul (since Dec. 1799), 'le chef de l'administration judiciare' under the Consulate and the Empire, who had helped to draft the Civil Code. 'Ce fut un véritable homme d'État' (Godechot, p. 482), 'maintes fois l'inspirateur de Bonaparte', and he was to be instrumental (2 Aug. 1802) in ensuring Napoleon the Consulship for Life.

abstruse speculations, & theoretic plans, or, rather, visions, ingenious, but not practicable. But ┃ the look however, of the Commander who heads his own army, who fights his own Battles, who conquers every difficulty by personal exertion, who executes all he plans, who performs even all he suggests— whose ambition is of the most enterprizing, & whose bravery of the most daring cast — —This, which is the look to be expected from his situation, & the exploits which have led to it, the spectator watches for in vain. The plainness, also, of his dress, so conspicuously contrasted by the finery of all around him, conspires forcibly with his countenance, which seems 'Sicklied o'er with the pale hue of Thought,'[6] to give him far more the air of a Student than of a Warrior.

The intense attention with which I fixed him, in this short, but complete view, made me entirely forget the lady who had promised me to hold him in conference; when he was passed, however, she told me it was upon his return she should address him, as he was too much hurried to be talked with at the moment of going to the Parade. I was glad to find my chance not over, & infinitely curious to know what was to follow.—The Review I shall attempt no description of; I have no knowledge of the subject, & no fondness for its object: it was far more superb than any thing I had ever beheld—but while—with all the 'Pomp & circumstance of War—'[6] it animated all others— it only saddened me!—& all of past reflection—& all of future dread—made the whole of the grandeur of the martial scene, & all the delusive seduction of the martial music, fill my Eyes frequently with Tears—but not regale my poor Muscles with one single Smile! Buonaparte, mounting a beautiful & spirited white Horse, was closely encircled by his glittering Aid-de-Camps, & accompanied by his Generals, ┃ rode round the ranks, holding his bridle indifferently in either hand, & seeming utterly careless of the prancing, rearing, or other freaks of his horse; in so much as to strike some with a notion he is a bad Horse-man; but I am the last to be a *Judge* upon this subject, but as a *Remarker*, he only appeared to me a Man who knew so well he could manage his Animal when he pleased, that he

6 FBA here invokes John Gay, *Fables*, intro., Series 1; John Dryden, *Absalom and Achitophel*, pt. 1; Shakespeare, *Hamlet*, iii, i; and *Othello*, iii, iii.

did not deem it worth his while to keep constantly in order what he knew—if urged or provoked,—he could subdue in a moment. Precisely opposite to the Window at which I was placed, the Chief Consul stationed himself, after making his round, & there he presented some swords of Honour—spreading out one Arm, with an air & mein which, during that action, & from my distance & inability to examine his countenance, changed, to my view, his look from that of Scholastic severity, to one that was military & commanding.

Just as the Consular band—with their brazen Drums, as well as Trumpets, marched facing the First Consul, the Sun broke suddenly out from the clouds which had obscured it all the morning—& the effect was so abrupt, & so dazzling, that I could not help observing it to my friend, the Wife of *Ma Mie*,—who, eyeing me with great surprise, not unmixt with the compassion of contempt, 'said 'Est-ce que vous ne savez pas cela, Madame? Dès que le premier Consul vient à la Parade, le soleil vient aussi! — il a beau pleuvoir tout le matin; — c'est egal, il n'a qu'a paroître, et tout de suite il fait beau!' !!! — I apologised for my ignorance, but doubt whether it was forgiven.

The Review over, the Chief Consul returned to the Palace; the lines were again formed, & he re-entered our Apartment, with his suite;—as soon as he approached our window, I observed My first acquaintance I start a little forward; I was now all attention to her performance of her promise; &, just as he reached us, she stretched out her hand, to present him — — a Petition!—The ænigma of the conference was now solved, & I laughed at my own wasted expectation. *Parler lui*, however, the lady certainly did; so far she kept her word; for when he had taken the scrole, & was passing on, she rushed out of the line, & planting herself immediately before him, so as to prevent his walking on, screamed out—for the voice was shrill with eager impetuosity to be heard, & terror of failure, 'C'est pour mon fils! — Vous me l'avez promis! —' —The First Consul, stopt thus, spoke,—but not loud enough for me to hear his voice, while his Aid de-Camp, & the attending Generals, surrounding him more closely, all in a breath, almost, rapidly said to the lady 'Vôtre Nom, Madame, Vôtre nom!' trying to disengage the Consul from her importunity;—in which they succeeded, but not with much ease, as she seemed to purpose to cling to him till she got his personal answer. He faintly smiled, as he passed on, but looked harrassed & worn; while she, turning to me, with an exulting Face & voice, exclaimed 'Je l'aurai! Je l'aurai! —' meaning what she had petitioned for, —'Car — tous ces Generaux m'ont demandés mon nom!'

Could any inference be clearer?—The moment the Chief Consul had ascended the steps leading to the inner Apartment, the Gentleman in Black with Gold Chains gave a general hint that all the Company must depart, as the Ambassadors & the Ministers were now summoned to their Monthly public Audience with the Chief Consul. The crowd, however, was so great, & Made D'Henin was so much incommoded, & half ill, I fear, by internal suffering,[7] that M. D'arblay procured a pass for us by a private door, down to a Terrace leading to a quiet exit from the Gallery to the Garden. Arrived at this Terrace, we missed M. de Beauvau, who had been unable to keep near us during the Review, or to find us after it. M. D'arblay desired us to remain upon the Terrace while he sought him. We had it entirely to ourselves, except for two foreign officers, in gay, but not splended Regimentals, who offered us their services, & Ps d'Henin, extremely fatigued, accepted an arm of one of them, while Me de Beauvau, tired also, held by another. We had all stood the whole time. Mlle de Mortemar & I walked up & down the Terrace, talking over the past Scene; but Me D'Henin seated herself on the steps; &, presently, the direction of her Eye shewed she was speaking of me, to the officer attending her, who, hastily quitting her, & coming up to me, said in English—'I understand, Ma'am, — — you are English?' 'Yes, Sir',—I answered, surprised; '& I fancy, by your accent, you have learnt my language in my own Country?—' 'True, Ma'am replied he, smiling, 'I learnt it there—for I was born there!' 'And you have entered, said Me de Beauvau, into the Austrian service?' 'No, Ma'am,—into the Prussian,—I have been engaged in the Prussian service 24 years.—' Then, turning to me, while he looked at Me de Beauvau, 'That lady, he added, is English too,

---

[7] For the desolating history of Mme d'Hénin's earlier life, her husband, his mistress, and his death by the guillotine, see the French Exercise of which FBA made this the theme (Notebook iv, pp. [28–32], Berg).

I am sure!' 'No,' I cried, she is not! but I know why you think her so!'—'And why, Ma'am?' cried he; 'And why?' repeated Me de Beauvau, eagerly. 'I must not tell *YOU*; I answered, I but I will tell my Country man—' He leant down his head, very curious, & I added 'Whenever an English man sees a female beautiful, fair, & modest—he concludes, nay, takes it for granted, she must come from his own Country!'—M. D'arblay now joined us, & these Gentlemen, having no pretence for remaining, made their bows.

We all walked home,—a walk very delightful, through the Gardens of the Thuillerie, & les Champs elises, which lead immediately to our Street, Rue Miromenil—one of the prettiest in Paris.

I hope this account will afford my dearest Father some amusement, I fear it is the best subject, for writing, I shall have to offer him.

The good M. de Lajard[8] came to our little dinner, &, as Bood was engaged, we made Maria also partake of it. We never mean to extend further our convivial feasts! ⌐I was glad to have Maria dine with M. Lajard, with whom I wish her an increased acquaintance, though that I most wish for her is an intimacy with Me. de Greffay,[9] our countrywoman, who is as sociable in manner as she is meritorious in conduct, & who is nearly of her own age, &, like herself, a fixed resident in France though [also], like herself, happy in a promise & a prospect of frequent returns to England—⌐

May 6th Mad. D'Henin, having borrowed the Carriage of M^e De Poix, carried us this morning to Passy, a very pretty Village about 3 miles from Paris, to pay a visit to Mad^e de Maisonneuve,[10] a great favourite of M. D'arblay's & a lady of singular estimation for her perfect private character. She is sister to M. La Tour Maubourg, but young enough, I believe,

[8] See L. 513 n. 10.

[9] Possibly Jeanne-Pauline-Louise *née* Randon de Pully (1776–1859), who had married in London on 14 Oct. 1793 Louis Greffulhe (1741–1810) and was to marry secondly in 1821 Pierre-Raymond-Hector (1765–1848), comte d'Aubusson de la Feuillade. Royalist in sympathy, the Greffulhes had lived in England for some time.

[10] Marie-Françoise-Élisabeth *née* de Fay de Latour-Maubourg (1770–1850), sister of César de Latour-Maubourg (L. 446 n. 12). Having divorced her husband Gérard-Joseph Bidault de Maisonneuve (L. 515 n. 10), she lived in reduced circumstances at 18, rue Basse, in Passy, up two or three flights of 'crooked, ladder like stairs', as FBA explained at a later time [*c.* 27 Feb. 1819] to the Duchess

to be his Daughter. She is *nearly* beautiful—*certainly* beyond pretty; particularly in her profile, which is in a very noble style: dignity & modesty I divide the expression of her fine & serious Countenance, the first announcing all that is reported of her unblemished character, the second seeming to indicate a purity that rendered its preservation perfectly natural to her. She devotes her virtuous life to giving the rudiments of his education to an only little Son,[10] in this retirement, where her Brother & his family also spend much of their time, but whence she never departs for any spectacle, or amusement, though so near their first attraction. Her Husband is still I believe, in emigration. She received us with a gentleness which, though nearly timid, was perfectly graceful. M. D'arb[lay]'s admiration of her is not bestowed on an Ingrate, for she has long been anxious he should fix himself & his little family at Passy, during our French residence, & she had been sedulously employing herself in seeking us an habitation. She had one immediately to propose, which we all went to examine; but it smelt of fresh paint, & would not do. We were led, next, to an interesting—melancholy sight,—that of a small Villa belonging, before the revolution, to Me D'Henin: a place constructed, while hers, for elegant retirement from her more magnificent Mansions, & where she most loved to receive the favourite Friends of her youth, Me de Biron,[11] Me de Poix,[12] & Me de

of Gloucester. 'She lived with an oeconomy hardly credible; for she had not above 80 a year, yet was always well, though simply dressed; kept one young Maid for every thing, the Child included,—& educated that Child in the best manner, made his external appearance accord with his real, not fortuitous rank in life; while her own pleasing deportment & high character were so universally admired, that she was never seen but with distinction & pleasure wherever she could be induced to quit her Cell. Her disposition however, was of so quiet a cast, that she mixt with no society but of her family & its circle. To ME—what a bond of union, was such a propensity to retirement—rare even here, but in France almost *unique*. What obligations did I not owe to her! She came to me daily, . . . if I was sick, she Nursed me; if I was embarrassed or perplexed . . . with regard to customs, habits, & expectations, she relieved & enlightened me; . . . if I wished to see any places, any Curiosity, any Spectacle, she procured me Tickets or admission if I required retired exercise, she engaged the owners of great Chateaux to send me Keys of their Gardens, . . . if I wanted to make purchases, she accompanied me to the best *boutiques* If I had any difficulty about my Alexander, she considered it as an affair of her own Maxime, & found means to remedy it accordingly.'

[11] The late Amélie de Boufflers (1751–94), who had married in 1766 Armand-Louis de Gontaut (1747–93), comte de Biron, duc de Lauzun (1767), duc de Biron (1788), commandant en chef de l'Armée du Rhin (1792), d'Italie (1792–3). Arrested on 16 July 1793, he was tried, condemned, and guillotined (31 Dec. 1793).

[12] See L. 513 n. 16.

Bouillon,[13] with whom she had been connected in strictest friendship above 30 years—The intercourse formed while they were all
in their teens. The dreadful fate of the 1st of these ladies made
the sight of the room which, in early days, Me de H[enin] had
appropriated for her, & fitted up to her taste, saddening
indeed!—The second lady still, happily, lives, & delights all
who know her by worth mingled with talents; the 3d—after
they had all been separated 9 years, returned from her Exile
to meet the, then, two remaining of the Quartetto, mesdames
de Poix & d'Henin—&, almost immediately after, expired in
their arms. My kind Padre's interest in them will not be
diminished by hearing they read Cecilia together, as I think,
Three times. While we were examining the windows, & hearing
some incident of every room, some people from the house
came & offered poor Me d'H. to enter it: but this she hastily
declined—unable to bear! she had resolution enough, however,
to walk over the grounds, which had been laid out by her own
orders, & are extremely pretty, — — for France: for I must confess I have seen nothing here, as yet, to bear comparison with
what is really beautiful, in the disposition of grounds, in
England. The time, however, may come, when I travel further,
& see more.

   After spending with the amiable & deserving Me de Maisonneuve the whole morning, Mad. d'Henin took us back through
le Bois de Boulogne, that my Alex—indulged by all who wish
to indulge us—might have the longer airing. The mischief done
in this very pretty Bois, during the times of turbulence, in
slashing & hacking Trees, was such as greatly to shock M.
D'ar[blay] who had not seen it since its almost desolation, &
declared I could scarcely form a notion of what it had been!—
Me d'H[enin] had made us promise to dine with her, |

13 The late Maria-Hedwig-Éleanor Christine von Hesse-Rheinfels-Rothenburg
(c. 1748–1801), who had married in 1764 Jacques-Léopold-Charles-Godefroy de
La Tour d'Auvergne (1746–1802), 7th duc de Bouillon.

[1185, rue de Miroménil],
10 May 1802

To Mrs. Locke

L., excerpt in an unknown hand, the beginning only (Diary MSS. viii, not numbered, Berg), 10 May 1802
Double sheet 4to 1 p.

Paris, May 10. 1802.

How many are the Letters, my dearest—dearest Friends—
that mentally I have written you during this period of silence
But my first week was Completely filled with receiving nearly
incessant visits, & a weakness from excess of fatigue which
compelled me to lie down every little spare moment: my
second in a Most alarming illness of my poor Alex & my third—
the present, in recruiting him & myself from its effects, which
are great feebleness in both—& again, in *du monde*! *du monde*!—
But henceforth, should we have no relapse, I hope to prepare
my beloved Friends a sheet at least every week for post or
opportunity, as Circumstance may direct. And let me hope my
own dearest Friend, you will do all in your power to give me,
in return the fond & dear comfort of as nearly as possible a
similar arrangement. Let us always, mutually have a letter
upon the stocks, & then, I trust, we shall no more be so long
again without shaking pens. The sight of your dear hand
yesterday was a true—true joy to me, & redoubles my anxiety
to get you a claim for renewing it. I not only could not write
while my poor Boy was ill—& all of possible time I have since
been able to squeeze from *him*, from engagements

[1185, rue de Miroménil],
24 May, 1802

To Esther (Burney) Burney

A.L.S. (Berg), 24 May 1802
Double sheet 4to 4 pp. wafer
Addressed: England. / Mrs. Burney, / Beaumont Street, / Devonshire Place, /
London—
Sent by Anthony Merry, 23 July 1802
Endorsed by EBB: 1802 / Answered—1802

Paris, May 24ᵗʰ 1802.

I can never tell you, my dearest Esther, the exquisite pleasure
with which I received the intelligence of dear little Amelia's
legacy.¹ I bless the spirit of good Mrs. Bateman, whom I always
esteemed as a worthy & amiable woman, & whose memory I
shall always respect for a generosity so timely, so kind, & so
fully proving her sense of my dear Esther's desert, & her feeling
for her cares & difficulties—for though Amelia is the receiver,
it is her Mother that, to *her*, is the Donor. How delightful to
think that dear Child, so young, & of so tender health, already
secured from all fear of helpless dependance, happen what may,
as to her neglect of talents, or inability of strength to assert
them! If, on the contrary, with this capital aid before her, she
can be urged to assist herself, she may early be mistress of an
independance that may make all her life happy. Or perhaps,
without any other effort than obtaining the science in which
she has an hereditary right to shine as an accomplishment, she
may worthily & happily connect herself with some good Partner, who, though not mercenary, might have held it imprudent
to chuse her only upon his own Materials for taking her in
charge. |

In short, I make myself quite happy now, both for her & for
you, whether she remains single, or prefers a partnership in
life; &, in some degree, whether she improves to excellence, or
stops short at *tolerability*. What a weight of care is removed from
my dearest Esther & Mr. Burney by this seasonable provision!

520. ¹ A legacy of £1,000 bequeathed to Amelia by the Hon. Mrs. William
Bateman (See L. 517 n. 5).

Through their Children, at length, they are blessed, after the struggles of so many years in parental solicitude to preserve them! God be praised! I am so seriously penetrated with this 3ᵈ blessing² upon your race, that it has been truly my uppermost thought since I heard it. I am vexed that the opportunity by which I write this happens at a period when I cannot make better use of it,—but some Relations of M. D'arblay are arrived at Paris,³ purposely to see his wife,—& they dine with us, on our little Dinner, daily—so that I have no time for a longer Letter than will speak my joy & congratulations— which are so buoyant, they require scarcely a moment to fill a folio. Indeed, since my arrival in Paris, I have lived a life of so little privacy, except for *rest* from fatigue, that I never wrote so few letters in my life,—except to our ǀ dear Father, I have, indeed, not written at all—save one poor sheet to my Mrs. Lock⁴—but I build upon our Padre's communicating whatever he thinks may interest or amuse you—& I could but repeat my accounts, had I time to write more fully. I saw Maria on Saturday Evening,⁵ when she called here, looking remarkably well. She is charmingly placed, near the Boulvards, & has a sumptuous establishment, of a whole floor of an Hotel. It is not yet finished, but the furnishing—where œconomy [is] not an object, is in itself a very great pleasure & gratification. I do not think her, therefore, a subject of much compassion, from the present disjointed state of her mansion. For ourselves, we have a very comfortable Apartment, in a very pretty & genteel new street, up 3 pair of stairs, indeed! but all the more pleasant, once mounted, for its height,—as we overlook, by that means, & by a short House opposite, a beautiful Garden, of the ci divant Hotel Beauvais, which is full of Lilacs & sweet shrubs, & delightful & airy at once. And at once end of our street we have the Country, open to the village of Monsso,⁶

² The first blessing was the marriage of EBB's eldest (and dowerless) daughter (now called Maria) to Lambert-*Antoine* Bourdois (iv, L. 381 and *passim*); the second, the appointment of her son Richard Allen to the living at Rimpton (L. 462 n. 8); the third, Amelia's legacy (*supra*).
³ It later appears (see vi, L. 575), that it was Marie-Edmée-Euphémie, the wife of M. d'A's uncle Gabriel Bazille, and Mme Meignen, his daughter (see Genealogical Table, iii, p. 1), who had come to Paris to meet Mme d'Arblay.
⁴ This is L. 519. Journal-letters like 508, 511, 512, and 516, though recounting events that occurred at this time, were often composed much later.
⁵ On the evening of 22 May.
⁶ Monceau, to which the d'Arblays were to move by 10 June.

which we can walk to in a quarter of an Hour, & of which we scent the air all day long; & at the other end, we have literally only to cross rue Ste Honoré to be at once in the Elysian ˡ Fields. our Apartment consists of a *sallon*, extremely well furnished, & of a very good size,—as big as our dear Father's first parlour at Chelsea;⁷ a *salle à manger* which is just as big as our Dining parlour at West Hamble; a Bed room about double the size of *yours* in that same cottage; a dressing room within it, which serves for Alex,—a dark closet for the maid,—& a sort of ante room which separates the whole from a little tiny Kitchen. But all is comfortably & pleasantly fitted up: & the people are so civil, & the house is so quiet, we find no difference from being in an Hotel Garnie, or a private Hotel—except the *price*, which is terrible—but we are too uncertain, even from day to Day, of our stay at Paris to make a change wise, till we return from Joigny. If you are so kind as to write, I think, till we are again fixed, it may be best to direct for us at Mr. Bourdois' Rue Choiseul, &c—though all Letters sent hither will be taken care of—so *n'importe* which—M. D'arblay sends you his kindest & warmest congratulations. I am charmed by your forbearance in not telling Amelia—

adieu, my dear soul—Remember me by every opportunity—most kindly to Mr. B[urney] Sophy—Amelia—James. Charles. Sally—, Charlotte, Fanny, & Richard, & to dear Aunt Beckey—whom I rouge to think of—yet ho[w] IMPOSSIBLE to me to get 4 Hours even for Richmond!—Dear soul, beg her forgiveness—& her love—My Alex has been ver[y] ill—but is well—adieu, adieu, dearest Esther—ever & aye

Yours FD.

⁷ In the apartments on the ground floor of Chelsea Hospital, which CB had occupied from 1788 to 1798 (see iv, L. 269 n. 1). See also Captain C. G. T. Dean, 'Dr. Burney's Connection with the Royal Hospital, Chelsea', *Transactions of the London and Middlesex Archaeological Society*, N.S. viii, pt. iii (1944).

To Doctor Burney

A.L. (Berg),   10 June 1802
Originally a double sheet 4to, of which FBA later discarded the second
leaf   2 pp.
Edited by FBA, p. 1, *annotated*: ⋕ 20

June 10th 1802.

My beloved Father—a thousand thanks for your most
welcome Letter—which I greedily devoured.—⌐I am truly
rejoiced if my journal amuses you; I seize eagerly an offered
opportunity to send you a fresh cargo, though not of fresh
date—⌐but ⟨pained⟩ to offer nothing more satisfactory of my
poor Alex & his repeated relapses. This makes me offer no
apology for lengthening my Journey, as I fear my after events
will be yet less striking, for I have been, nearly these last 3
weeks, wholly devoted to my Boy, who has so woefully
frightened me, by this 3^d relapse, & thus⌐ we have run out
from Paris, to sleep in purer Air, & where he can have the
liberty of constantly living in Gardens or Fields. He now is so
recovered, that, had he not twice revived so before, I should
think all inquietude might cease: as it is, I am fixed never to
quit even a moment, till I see him restored in full to his best
state.—⌐All engagements, therefore, ceasing, I can only guide
you to my details by having recourse to my original *notes*,
kept entirely for my dearest Padre, & from them I will prepare
him such food as I can promise never missing an opportunity, |
by always preparing my pacquets for the common post, where
opportunities will not offer within decent intervals.⌐

You do not tell me of your health? ⌐but Esther says you to

521.   1 This is the letter (Osborn) of 20 May 1802 in which CB acknowledges FBA's
account of her travels as far as Dover. Finding the narrative 'curious & well
drawn up', he advises her: 'Make memorandums of all you hear and see, that is
curious and national & when you return to *Cam.—Cott.* you may draw it out into
one of the most agreeable books that you or any one else has ever written—
remember this is a *hint*. That I hope you will take.'

be well.⁋ I am a little envious of this *Cyclopedia*,[2] now I do not see its progress, to find it so swallows up ALL your time! — ! — ⌐I am certainly deeply concerned at the hints you give of a certain dear person,[3] whom I had already been very uncertain & very anxious about. alas! alas! how grievous that with such attractions of amiability, there should be such drawbacks—such subjects for acclaim as well as blame! — — I shall long to hear what, however, I know not how to hope, that a 2ᵈ Lʸ Beverley is found for F.B.[4] I have seldom been more disappointed by that return, having always flattered myself something permanent would spring from Lʸ B.'s partiality, & F.B.'s real & even enthusiastic gratitude & affection. I was delighted with dear Mrs. Boscawen's speech upon the subject, so full of *sel* as well as goodness.⁋[5] You don't name Mrs. Crewe—yet I must beg you to name *ME* to her, when you meet—& tell her, the flattering picture she drew of my possible reception & treatment here, which I should have thought, had she been less kind, & less good, not merely a *badinage*, but a *mockery*, has been, to my utter astonishment, so verified, that not a day passes without my receiving some testimony, of politeness, hospitality, or kindness, as little expected as deserved, from all of the circle to which I have been yet presented.[6] It is a small one, indeed—but I fear I have little to gain by enlarging it! ⌐I am very glad you did visit at Bulstrode & liked Mr. G. Upton.[7]

[2] Rees's *Cyclopaedia*, to which, since July 1801, CB had been contributing articles on music (see Lonsdale, p. 408 ff.; Scholes, ii. 184–201; *Memoirs*, iii. 302–3; and iv, L. 419 n. 3). In his letter of 20 May (*supra*), CB had complained of the enormous '*Cyclopaedia* jobb' that was swallowing up all his time and thoughts. 'I have been an A B Cidarian long—& now am become so for life . . . I have finished but two letters of the alphabet in 10 Months.'

[3] Almost certainly CB's radiantly attractive Irish granddaughter, Fanny Phillips, whose conquest of her cousin the Revd. R. A. Burney is mentioned in FBA's L. 483. Like her father Molesworth Phillips, she seemed to be extravagant, running up bills that CB Jr. was later good enough to pay.

[4] EBB's daughter Fanny Burney (1776–1828) had been employed since 1795 as governess to the daughters of Algernon Percy (iii, L. 142 n. 3), cr. Earl of Beverley (1790), who had married in 1775 Isabella Susannah Burrell (1750–1812). Their youngest surviving daughter, Emily Charlotte (1786–1877), was now sixteen years of age.

[5] Mrs. Boscawen's remarks are lost with the second leaf of CB's letter.

[6] Further evidence of the homage offered in France to the authoress of *Evelina* and *Cecilia* is provided by Mrs. Broome in a letter of 10 Oct. 1802 (Barrett, Eg. 3693, ff. 78–96).

[7] In his letter to FBA of 20 May 1802, Dr. Burney speaks highly of Greville Upton (i, L. 16 n. 13; iv, L. 332 n. 9), whom he encountered at the Duke of Portland's. He is 'a charming young man, & an excellent Musician, whom I like extremely'.

Bood says he has written to-day about your Musical enquiries at full length.[8] When *occasions* don't offer decently often, pray write by post, always directly to Paris, Miroménil, 1185, our late Hotel, where our Letters will be safe & forwarded with care—¶

[*the second leaf is missing*]

M. d'arblay sends his tender Respects—God grant your kind wishes about the Peace may be realized! ! — —[9]

522   Monceaux, 11 June 1802

To Mrs. Locke

L. copy (Diary MSS. viii, not numbered, Berg), taken in an unknown hand from the original lent to CFBt by the Locke family. 11 June 1802. The original was probably mailed to England with the last part of J.L. No. 511, *post* 10 June 1802. The copy has such mistakes as the spelling Cisafpine.

Double sheet 4to   4 pp.   numbered 5

June 11. 1802   Rue Cisafpine, or Monceaux

I sent my most beloved friends a pacquet yesterday by means of a Gentleman[1] who had brought me one last week from my Captain Brother, & who means to set out on his return this very day. I number my sheets, that you may always know if any are missing, and I should be glad if my dearest friend would number her's also. My plan, & hope, of writing every week, I have found impracticable, but I will always keep a

---

[8] 'But will neither M. darblay nor the Bride [Maria Bourdois] procure me the intelligence I want concerning the future progress of the musical department of the new Fr. Encyclopaedie methodique?' CB had asked (loc. cit.), and not for the first time. See also L. 459 n. 7; L. 475 n. 2.

[9] CB had commented (loc. cit.) on the two-day debate (3–4 Nov. 1801) on the Peace of Amiens (see *AR* xliv (1802), 20–41; and *Parl. Hist.*, xxxvi (1801–3), 29–157): 'The attack . . . though carried on with great violence by men of great ability & weight, has been defeated, & the makers of it have been supported by a great Majority; I therefore hope now, that the two Nations will heartily shake hands, & not only be quiet themselves, but keep the rest of the world quiet.'

522. [1] Possibly Charles Street (L. 508 n. 1).

sheet, at least, ready for any occasion, &, when none offers, send it off *if possible*, without future failure, once a fortnight. I keep for my dear Father a regular sort of Journal, which seems to give him a satisfaction that so lightens his distaste of my distant sojourn, in a *strange land*, that I hold it my bounden duty to let that take place of all things else with regard to writing; my own best of perfect Friends will be foremost to encourage this, even though the effect is that of cruelly diminishing all time for herself, himself, them*SELFS*, (& Amine) My situation now is peculiar; much of soothing is necessary to make it endured cheerfully where to find it murmured at would make me wretched;[2] the mode I have adopted appears to have answered this important purpose, & therefore I call rather for your help, than fear your opposition, in its execution. Could I lengthen the hours so as to ¦ keep a double Journal, what a pleasure to me would they bring! as it is, I must select all such subjects, & personages, as I believe you most desire to read about, &, though I give regular daily occurrences, be minute, in the manner I think you like, in chosen details. At this present period, I have, indeed, none to give, for my dearest Boy, after repeated recoveries & relapses has finally driven us from Paris to a Country Lodging,[3] where I never quit him, night or day, & where I have the blessing to find that pure air, with constant, though gentle exercise, & the most scrupulous regularity in hours & diet, with asse's milk, are restoring him to health & strength, & will soon I trust, again cover his poor, little staring bones with as much flesh as encircled them when we quitted England: the day I was frightened out of Paris he looked *a live Skeleton!*—God be praised, he has a far better appearance! his spirits have never failed him they have rather, indeed, contributed to exhaust him.—You would have been much amused had you witnessed the surprise & the indignation which mingled themselves with his pleasure in hearing of Mr William's *son*:[4] for he instantly, & resentfully, recollected, that Mr William had declined, by assertions of ignorance, to assist his own researches upon that always darling topic, as to

[2] FBA here confesses that to have her sojourn in Paris 'endured cheerfully' by her father was her first concern and effort.
[3] At 286, rue Cisalpine, Monceau.
[4] William Locke III (1802–32). See *Locks of Norbury*, pp. 348–51; and Samuel Woods, *Mickleham Records* (1900), p. 57.

the parsley bed; however, he composed his wrath, by resolving to write himself his remonstrances.

I thank you for your bulletin, my dearest friend; but how melancholy that the cold & confinement of my most loved Mr Locke should have endured so long!—Here, also, the weather has been so unpleasant,—to me, at least, & ungenial, that I have by no means found the enjoyment I expected from the change of climate. In truth, till I got out of Paris, I experienced none; & now, it is in the purity, not in the warmth of the air. I May the airings have continued uninterruptedly! Tell that dearest and best of charioteers,[5] his kind present has been of the utmost service from time to time, in the course of my poor Boy's illnesses; the saline draughts have been truly refreshing to him, when well enough to leave off the James' Powders, and now that my mind is again at ease, & I have only some langour from so much solicitude, I am going a second time, to drink his precious health in them myself, My Boy, also, shall take the Bark again, when we have done with a worm medicine still in operation. A frightful Cough which had seized him in Paris, gave way immediately to asse's Milk.

I must not tell you how vexed, how disappointed I have been about the weening my youngest Amine[6]—I must think only of the flourishing consequences which you are yourself consoled by. But that sweet interesting little Cissy! I earnestly hope you may be able to give me, in your Next, a better account of that little dear love — —

I am far more grieved than surprised that Braissant[7] can no longer defer his Swiss expedition; but I had never understood any doubt as to his return before Winter! I shall grieve—grieve, grieve indeed, if he does not! be his successor worthy as he may. Pray tell that excellent Braissant we shall be as glad to see him as he passes through Paris as it is possible to be glad when he comes from Mr Locke! He was to have sent me a letter for his Brother; if he has any you can be so good as to forward,

---

[5] William Locke I, who, in his daily airing in his phaeton, had so often called for FBA and Alex.

[6] Evidently a reply to Mrs. Locke's intelligence that her daughter Amelia Angerstein had been forced to wean her younger child Caroline (b. 25 Mar. 1802; see L. 498 n. 1). 'Cissy' was Charles Locke's 2nd daughter Georgina Cecilia (iv, L. 271 n. 32), now 4 years of age.

[7] L[ouis] Braissant (*fl.* 1787–1802) was Mr. Locke's personal servant (ii, L. 68 n. 50).

M. D'ar. will take the utmost care to deliver it; or most willingly, make any enquiry he wishes, if he will send a direction & a message.

I am extremely amazed the poor cottage is not let![8] 1000 thanks for your most kind attention in respect to locking up our scattered *generalities*, which I had not a moment to finish; I hope my dearest Friend has taken to her charge the | two deal boxes?[9] they contain—O what of past treasures! ever, ever prized!—& once—& so long the whole joy of my absences from Those dearest & sweetest! Should Any accident happen to me My Fredy will consign them to my other—My best half— if he should never claim them, she will keep—or make them over to my Amelia, till My Boy is of age. I trust he will then deserve to know at full length what angel Friends his Mother has been blessed with, & to see the Heart-whole confidence she placed in them.—You have never told me if your eyes are quite well? mine have suffered from the too long stretch of watchfulness in the journey, in so much that they are weakened very Painfully, & water in all strong light. Yet I am wonderfully well, altogether.—Why is Frederick leaves Mr Harvey?[10] Who is the Clergyman in Kent? & when is he to begin his grand career? 'Tis an important time for him, & very interesting. I beg you to give him our best wishes for his happiness and prosperity—I have had but three letters from you in all! You will ask how I have merited more? But that's a sort of consideration I *make it a rule* never to discuss. My dear M^{de} de Henin encreases in my regard continually, & she enchants me by adopting all your Spoiling methods, of writing & coming, & never expecting, kindly as she welcomes, any returns. She is, indeed, past all expression, *good*, & *useful* to me, & makes me the object of her constant attention for every thing that can either serve or please me. It is well I did not wait for M. de Lally, he seems to cling to England.[11] How is your Lady

---

[8] Camilla Cottage (see Ll. 486, 496–7, 500). See also L. 536 n. 4.
[9] The boxes contained chiefly, then, voluminous Journal-Letters exchanged by FB and SBP in the 1780s and 1790s.
[10] Possibly George Harvey (*fl.* 1799–1833), who, according to Clayton's *Court Guide* (1799), ran a school in the High Street, Hampstead. Shortly after this he seems to have moved his school to 36 Tufton Street, Westminster, where, according to the rate books (deposited in the Westminster Library) it was continued until 1833, when the site was occupied by a nursery school.
[11] Lally-Tolendal was not to leave England until November 1802. See L. 536 n. 6.

11 June 1802

Templetown?[12] And how are her fair daughters? Shall you venture at any excursion this year?

523   Paris, 15 June 1802

M. d'Arblay
To Madame d'Arblay

A. Notes (Berg), 25 Prairial an 10
Three double sheets 8vo, folded together and stitched to form a cahier of 12 pp, the 1st (or cover page) being left blank. At some time a segment was cut from the first leaf of the third (or centre) sheet, and this segment bearing the concluding paragraphs of M. d'A's text, is missing 5 pp.
Edited by FBA, p. 1 annotated and misdated: ⊞ ⌐N° 13⌐ (28) 1805
Entitled by FBA, p. 1: Penetrating and Admirable / Reflections — or rather / Representations / relative to our decision of / Residence / in England or in France / during the adolescence of / our Alexander.—

Je vous prie, ma chere amie, de lire ceci avec attention, de le garder, et de n'y reponde qu'après y avoir murement reflechi.
Paris ce 25 Prairial an 10.
Notre conversation d'hier soir m'a tout naturellement conduit à faire les reflexions les plus serieuses. Voici leur resultat.
La plus grande felicité dont une creature humaine soit susceptible, je vous la dois.
Les plus grands sacrifices qu'un être delicat puisse s'imposer, je vous les offre.
Avant de les accepter, avant de decider de notre avenir, vous desirez surement les connaitre ces sacrifices?
Pour cela je vais vous soumettre le plan au quel, sauf les changemens que vous y apporterez, j'avais cru pouvoir et devoir m'attacher.
Ce plan que jusqu'à ce jour je n'avais consideré qu'en masse, l'examen le plus minutieux me le fait regarder comme le seul raisonnable: mais à moins que je n'obtienne de votre coeur et de votre raison, non pas une soumission qui ne peut me suffire,

[12] Lady Templetown (iii, L. 216 n. 16), one of Mrs. Locke's earliest friends, FBA had often met at Norbury Park. For her most recent meeting with members of the Upton family, see L. 464 n. 9.

mais une approbation sans la quelle je ne saurois être heureux, je suis prêt à y renoncer pour en embrasser un qui vous convienne. |

Il est très vrai qu'à l'epoque la plus flatteuse comme la plus fortunée de ma vie entiere, lorsque vous daignâtes unir votre sort au mien, je vous dis que mon intention etait de me fixer en Angleterre: Il l'est de même que votre reponse fut que vous me suivriez au bout du monde, determinée ajoutâtes vous à porter mon *Havresac.*

Depuis, vous m'avez relevé de cette espece de serment: moi, je ne vous ai point rendu, je ne vous rendrai jamais votre promesse: mais mon unique etude sera d'empêcher que vous n'en trouviez l'execution difficile et peu agreable.

De votre côté, en r'ouvrant mon coeur à l'espoir de finir mes jours dans ma patrie, vous avez surement pris l'engagement tacite de faciliter l'execution de ce nouveau plan; vous êtes du moins interdit tout moyen tendant à rendre cette execution impossible?

Vos amis en Angleterre sont les miens; et certes c'est de toute mon âme que je desire être près d'eux: mais d'après mon plan j'y serai plus que jamais; mais, je l'avoue, depuis qu'en me rendant ma parole, vous m'avez permis d'elever ma pensée vers ma patrie, je me suis tellement penetré de l'idée d'y vivre | de nouveau, qu'en pensant au sort dont j'y puis jouir encore, et à la consideration qu'on ne peut m'y refuser, ce serait avec le plus profond chagrin que je me reverrais soumis à l'espece de servage dans le quel vos loix retiennent les etrangers. Ceux que des affaires attirent en Angleterre, ceux que de grands interêts y fixent, et qu'une fortune suffisante y soutient, sont en raison de cette même fortune bien moins sensibles à cette distinction humiliante qui pese bien moins sur eux: mais ce qu'on peut alleguer en leur faveur ne m'est nullement applicable.

J'estime et j'honnore votre nation; mon admiration pour son Gouvernement est sincere, et mon respect pour son chef est sans bornes; mais, rentré de son aveu et du vôtre dans mes droits comme français j'ai à coeur d'en remplir les devoirs. Voyons donc à les accorder avec d'autres interêts non moins chers. |

J'ai pensé à partager notre existence entre ma patrie et la vôtre aussi longtems que nos forces et nos moyens, d'accord avec nos gouts, pourront permettre ce partage.

331

Ici je dois vous faire remarquer que le desir que j'en temoigne
à M. Locke dans ma lettre ne peut être pour lui un sujet
d'etonnement. L'anecdote suivante vous tirera j'espere de
l'erreur où vous êtes sur ce sujet.

Dans mon dernier voyage, il etoit question à Norbury de
mes demarches infructueuses relativement à ma reforme
(espece de half-pay, qui laisse celui à qui on l'accorde, dans
une demi activité.)

'J'aurais beaucoup mieux fait' dis-je à la famille rassemblée
'd'aller tout de suite dans mon departement; je crois pouvoir
me flatter qu'il ne m'eut pas été difficile de me faire porter
sur la liste nationale d'où sont tirés les membres du Gouvernement. Peut être alors, mes amis seraient parvenus à me faire
elire membre de la Legislature place qui me conviendrait
d'autant mieux que n'exigeant que 4 mois de residence à Paris
j'en pourrais passer 2 dans mon departement auprès de mon
oncle et 6 en Angleterre.' |

Rien assurement n'etait plus clair que ce language qui ne
doit pas non plus vous paroitre neuf.

Cette vie errante a sans doute ses inconveniens, mais comme
ceux d'un plan contraire me paraissent encore plus grands,
eviter ceux ci, et rendre ceux là plus supportables, est ce me
semble ce qui doit nous occuper.

[½ *page cut away*]

524   [Monceaux],
                                      25 June–17 July 1802
To Mrs. Broome

A.L.S. (rejected Diary MSS. 5574–7, Berg), 25 June–17 July 1802
Double sheet 4to   4 pp.   wafer
Addressed: England. / Mrs. Broome.
Sent by Anthony Merry[3], 23 July 1802
Endorsed by CBFB: Sister d'arblay / June 1802 / ans^d aug^t—
Edited by CFBt.

                                      Paris, June 25. 1802
Ah my dearest Charlotte if you can forgive me, it is more
than I know how to forgive myself for not immediately answering

your very kind Letter,[1] which I received at West Hamble, & which gratified & touched me at once by the affectionate concern it expressed for my then most painful situation. At that time, I meant but to wait till my suspence was over, in order to write you its result, as well as my thanks for your tender sympathy; but that suspence only ended to raise new, though different perplexities & commotions, & our uncertainty was succeeded by such excess of embarrassment & hurry; that how the whole was not terminated by a dangerous illness is my continual surprise; for the bustle of the last few weeks before I left England, in arranging my house for hire, & my Boy & self for departing, with the nameless difficulties of how to make the voyage, with whom to leave the house, how to settle about Taxes—servants, packages,—&c &c,—& the fatigues of the voyage itself, tried me so severely, that, though I have escaped, wonderfully, an immediate malady, I have scarcely yet recovered from the general languor & weakness following such strained exertions.

Still, however, in the midst of all, your Letter never was forgotten, for your kind concern was expressed with a warmth to fix it on ' my memory; but though every Day, both then, & since, I have truly intended to write, every Day has ended with the intention left in the lurch for the next—& the execution reserved for the present moment.

Since my arrival in this Country, my life, till very lately, has been completely spent between receiving visits & nursing my poor Boy, who had an ardent fever before we had been in Paris a week, from which he soon recovered, but he has had two relapses since, so that I have hardly enjoyed any time free from the fearful state of convalescence, even for the best. M. D'arblay has so very many friends in this Country—which perhaps you will hear without much wonder,—that I scarcely knew what it was to spend an Hour without a visitor, from Breakfast to Supper, inclusive; till the 3ᵈ illness of my Alex, which fairly drove us to a country Lodging, where we now live tolerably retired. These visitors are, in general, so lively, so pleasant, & so kind, that I should have no sort of fault to find with them, if I could only double my life, so as to have, at once, My Day to myself, for my several occupations, & my Day for

524. [1] CBFB's letter is missing.

them, for social amusement. But as my Days are not on the encrease, but on the wane,—my time seems seized so as to leave none to my own disposal. You know how little that suits my taste, & real love for retirement, be the seizers amiable as they may. And yet, if I could but, as I have said, *live double*, I should not here, as yet, repine, for almost every ¹ visitor has some particularity to recommend him—'tis an old friend, or a Brother in misfortune, or a near relation—or a person eminent in late transactions, either of state or in the military—or the wife, mother, or sister of one of these. This gives an interest to their sight very superior to what we can feel from visits in general, & makes them so curious that, if they pressed not so rapidly one upon another, they must needs be acceptable, because exhilarating with new ideas, or penetrating from recollections of former ones.

We have not yet been able to make our long projected tour to Joigny, to the Uncle of M. D'arblay, the poor Child's illnesse[s,] M. D'arblay's unsettled claims & affairs detaining us till now in this neighbourhood; but we mean to make that Journey next Monday,² & shall probably remain there some time. I doubt not being happy in a family who so well know how to love & appreciate Him who is Master of mine.

July 17ᵗʰ This was written for the conveyance of a friend of our Brother Charles, Mr. Banks,³ who promised to take any pacquet I could have to send: but M. D'arblay's affairs suddenly took us to Joigny, &, upon our return, we have missed him. I shall now try to frank it by another opportunity³ which I expect to offer itself next week—but if that fails I shall be forced to wait for another, as I know not your address, & must therefore enclose it to our Padre or sister Burney: a Letter I have just received from Miss Cambridge⁴ informs me you were leaving Bath, but whether for London or Brighton, she knows not. I have many accounts of the great improvement of my dear Charlotte the younger, which give me infinite pleasure.

² On Monday 28 June. The fortnight's visit to Joigny had apparently taken place between 27 or 28 June and 10 July. The d'Arblays had returned to Paris, at any rate, in time for the Fête de Paris (14 July).
³ Probably the Revd. John Cleaver Banks (i, L. 24 n. 76). The letter was eventually taken by Anthony Merry (L. 510 n. 13).
⁴ The letter is missing but Ralph Broome and his family had moved in ?1803 to Bath, where he was to die on 24 Feb. 1805. Ralph Jr., the only child of the Broome–Francis marriage, was not yet a year old.

Pray give my kindest Love to that dear & good Girl, who has it sincerely &, to your Marianne, & Clement, & a kiss to my little unknown Ralpho[4]—Is Mr. Broome recovered at all by the Bath waters? suppose he were to try the air of France? How I should rejoice to see my dearest Charlotte.[5] |

Our visit to Joigny has been productive of every pleasure that can accrue from the sight of a most worthy, amiable, & affectionate family, warmly attached to M. D'ar[blay] & determined to love & esteem all that belong to him. Alex was nearly idolized amongst them, though the idleness of his life there, & the excess of indulgence with which every one sought to make him but too happy, have not much contributed to render him sage or placid. He is, in truth, more wild & merry than ever. You will be pleased, I know, to hear that M. Bazille,[6] the excellent & beloved uncle of M. d'ar[blay] has something both in his appearance & manner that remind me of our dear & ever regretted Mr. Crisp.[7] I need not, after saying that, speak of his understanding, his Gentlemanly deportment, or his disposition to arch pleasantry. Me Bazille is one of the most amiable & exemplary women I have ever known, & all the family are agreeable, deserving, & affectionate. We have spent only a fortnight there at present, as M. D'ar[blay] is called back by business—but we are to return to them for a longer period. They wish us to spend all the winter with them: but that is not possible. Tell me all you can of yourself & of yours, my dearest Charlotte, when you are so kind as to write, & direct for me at M. A. Bourdois, N° 4. Rue de Choiseul, Faubourg St. Honoré, for Maria will take care to forward my Letters, à *Paris*. wherever I may be. At present, we are for a Month, at Monçeaux, near Paris, but in sweeter air.

> Heaven bless my dear & ever kind C⟨harlo⟩tte,
> prays her truly affectionate sister,
> F. D'Arblay—

[5] A little later this year, Mrs. Broome and her daughter Charlotte Francis were to make a visit of two months to FBA at Paris and Joigny (their passports were issued on 13 Aug. 1802 and they were back in London by 23 October).

[6] Jean-Baptiste-*Gabriel* Bazille (*c*. 1731–1817) and his wife Marie-Edmée-Euphémie *née* de la Mare (1745–1803).

[7] Samuel or 'Daddy' Crisp of Chessington (*c*. 1707–83), whose friendship for CB's children had notably included 'Charlottenburg', as he called CAB (see his letters to her, *Catalogue*).

Monceaux, 16 July 1802

To Doctor Burney

A.L.S. (rejected Diary MSS. 5578–80, Berg), 16 July 1802
Double sheet small 4to 3 pp. 2 wafers
Addressed: Dr. Burney, / Chelsea College, / Middlesex. / Angleterre.
Taken to England with L. 513, *by* Anthony Merry *on* 23 July 1802
Endorsed by CB: (July 16) 1802 N⁰ 4
Edited by FBA, p. 1, *annotated*: ⚬· ⚬· 21 M. Bazile. Joigny. Mrs. Crewe

> Rue Cisalpine, N⁰ 286
> à Monçeaux,—Paris.
> *July 16. 1802.*

It is almost in despair, my dearest Sir that I again try to melt
your flinty silence by another pacquet. It is old—but I have
nothing new; discouraged by receiving no replies, I have left
off journalizing since about the end of my first month's arrival
in this Country. My sole hope of solace to this disappointment
rests in M. de Lally, who may perhaps have Letters for me that
you may have believed I have already had the comfort of
receiving. He is still, however, not arrived, but still, as for
nearly 3 Months past, he is daily expected.[1] Wait not for him,
however, I earnestly beseech, but give me the delight &
consolation of again seeing your hand, my dearest Father—for
indeed it is a sight for which I languish. We have been to
Joigny, & I am charmed with the excellent uncle of my
Partner, & the truly amiable aunt:[2] but I am dispirited from
entering into any further details. From the wont of a[ny
ap]prehensions, however, I am relieved, that I of fearing for
your health: a Letter from Fanny P[hillips][3] happily sets
aside that inquietude—be generous, dearest Padre, generous
& kind, & don't let that *vile encyclopedie orkbornize*[4] me out of all
my best expectations in absence. How is Mrs. Crewe?[5] how is

---

525. [1] The comte de Lally-Tolendal was to arrive in November (see L. 536 n. 6).
[2] See the Genealogical Table, vi.
[3] The letter is missing.
[4] Cf. L. 521 nn. 2, 8. Mr. Orkborne was the pedant in FBA's *Camilla*.
[5] A jaunt with Mrs. Crewe and her family to Crewe Hall, Cheshire, or elsewhere, had regularly formed part of CB's summer plans.

Mr. Twining?[6] What are this Summer's plans? Is Mr. Coxe well enough to claim his share?[7] I ask this question in trembling. Do you go again to Bulstrode?[8] Has Lady Bruce[9] any chance of you? In short, *HOW—what—& where*, I long to know, about every thing that concerns you. I have had no recent news, neither, from Norbury Park. I suspect—& hope—M. de Lally is the cause of all my lamentations. M. D'arblay is well, but joins in my impatience. He can gather nothing in answer to your musical enquiries:[10] but Bood says he has written to you upon that subject at full length. Alex is, just now, in very good health: but it seems a critical season to him, & I am perpetually in some alarm. I enclose *3 Letters*, which have waited for opportunity, & which will shew you into what charming society I was admitted instantly on my arrival.—Whenever you have any doubts about our direction, from our wanderings, pray remember Boods will always be safe for us. use it, dearest Sir, & give comfort & pleasure to your ever & ever most affectionate & dutiful Daughter

Fr. D'arblay |

The Fête of the 14th which had excited universal curiosity & expectation, ended in nothing but a Grand Parade, & a small illumination.[11]

[6] The Revd. Thomas Twining of Colchester (iii, L. 133 n. 7), the friend who in former years had helped with CB's *History of Music*, CB usually met in London or Twickenham. The friends were to meet for the last time in Isleworth in July 1803 (Lonsdale, p. 418).

[7] In August of this year CB was to make his annual visit to Richard Cox (i, L. 32 n. 1), the banker, at Quarley, Hants. This was a last visit, for his friend, declining rapidly, had but one more year to live (Lonsdale, p. 416).

[8] For the circumstances of CB's first visit to Bulstrode (1793) and the boon to his health and spirits of regular summer visits there, see Lonsdale, p. 366 and *passim*. In 1802 CB was to spend two weeks of September at Bulstrode.

[9] Henrietta Maria (*post* 1768–1831), daughter of Noel Hill (1745–89), cr. Baron Berwick of Attingham (1784). In 1793 she had married Charles Brudenell-Bruce (1773–1856), *styled* Lord Bruce, 2nd Earl of Ailesbury (1814), marquis (1821), whose seat was at Savernake, Wiltshire.
Credited by her protégée Harriet Wainwright (iv, L. 418 n. 2) as 'the first amateur singer in England' and much respected as a critic, she was well known to the Burneys, appearing in CB's 'Memoirs' and also in his will (P.C.C. Bridport 202, made 12 Jan. 1807, pr. 30 Apr. 1814): 'To Lady Bruce, with whose constant regard and partiality I have been honoured ever since her days of adolescence, I bequeath the most beautiful book that the Parma press can boast, in point of typography and embellishments from antique gems, of which only 25 Copies were printed before the plates were destroyed. This rare and most elegant work was presented to me by my Friend, Pachierotti. . . .' (Scholes, ii, 265–6).

[10] See L. 459 n. 7; L. 475 n. 2; L. 521 n. 8.

[11] FBA's disappointment in the Fête of the 14th was by no means reflected in the newspapers. *Le Publiciste* (15 July), for instance, reported that 'la grande parade

337

This pacquet goes by Mr. Merry[12]—it is the last I expect to send by his Means. I shall extremely rejoice if you can manage to procure me licence to write to you by the new ambassador[13] when he arrives.

'FEMALE WORTHIES' Part II

526   Journal for May–July 1802

To Mrs. Locke

J.L. copy (Diary MSS. viii. 5622–[37], Berg), in an unknown hand, copied probably from the original letters lent by the Locke family to CFBt. The originals were presumably written during July and August of 1802, at 286, rue Cisalpine, Monceaux, on four double sheets 4to numbered 9. 10. 11. and 12. Sheet no. 9 (Me de Poix & Cottage business.) was posted *c.* 31 Oct., 1802. Sheet 10 (Me de Tessé — Me de Beaufremont.) was sent by James Green in Dec., 1802. Sheet no. 11 (Mlle de Listinois. M^e de La Fayette.) by James Green on 25 March 1803. Sheet no . 12 was not sent until 12 Oct. 1806,[1] through Dugald Stewart. Each sheet would seem to have had messages added at the time of sending.[1]

Four double sheets 4to 16 pp. numbered 9., 10, (11), 12.

Corrected by CFBt and edited by the Press.

Mistakes made in copying names are here corrected by the present editors.

. . . a été extrêmement brillante, tant par le nombre, la tenue, la diversité des troupes de toutes armes qui ont été appelées, que par le concours des militaires étrangers qui y ont paru dans l'uniforme de leurs corps & de leur nation. . . . Un concert au palais du gouvernement, des danses, des jeux, & une illumination générale, terminent joyeusement & avec éclat cette journée mémorable.'

For the distribution of flags to the soldiers, the homage of the prefect of the Seine, and the presentation to the First Consul of 'un cheval de race française, dont les meilleurs ciseleurs de la capitale avaient embelli le harnois', see *Le Moniteur* (15 July).

¹² Anthony Merry (L. 510 n. 13) was to present his recall on 10 Sept. 1802 and to leave Paris shortly after that date.

¹³ Charles Whitworth (1752–1825), Baron Whitworth of Newport Pratt (1800), Viscount Whitworth of Adbaston (1813), Earl Whitworth (1815). Having cut short a distinguished military career for the diplomatic service (see *DNB* for his missions to Poland, St. Petersburg, and Denmark), he was to be appointed envoy-extraordinary and Minister Plenipotentiary to France (10 Sept. 1802), to arrive in Paris on 16 November and to present his credentials to Bonaparte on 7 December.

526. ¹ On the third sheet of this Journal FBA later affixed the comment: 'This sheet was nearly written for my dearest friend in 1802!—but found no conveyance till 1806.'

I now my dearest Friends, come to another, & a very, very first rate worthy of this Country, Me de Poix—² *ci-devant princesse*—At a private dinner, with only ourselves, at M^e d'Henin's, soon after my arrival, this Lady by her own appointment, came in, for our first interview. She is cruelly lame, from some fall, or accident, in her early life, but she has Eyes still of Fire—& strong remains of great beauty, with a vivacity, a quickness, a rapidity of speech, a redundancy of ideas, and an animation of feeling, that make her, altogether, uncommonly striking & interesting, joining a fear of her wit & repartee with an admiration of her virtues, & a desire for her regard. Her life has been spent in the strictest morality, though encircled with every gaiety, & open to every temptation. Married in the bloom of seventeen to a Boy of fifteen, from whom she was separated after the ceremony for two years, that he might finish his education, she began life with that purity of heart which enabled her to continue it with a conduct unsullied, in the midst of every danger which the general admiration for her beauty & talents, or her own unavoidable contempt of a booby husband, could excite. A belief even romantic—at least in the World's estimation—of conjugal happiness, embittered all her early years with the most cruel resentment of her own destiny, when she found herself sacrificed, by mere family combinations, to a being so ill suited to her taste: & so incapable of fulfilling her ideas of a life's Partner: Such as he was, however, he soon concieved for her I violent a passion, & the heart which she had not power to bestow upon him in turn, she virtuously resolved to keep for ever to herself—a resolution which, with such examples, such temptation, such disappointed feelings, & such early liberty, she has preserved free from the taint of even transitory rumour. My own dearest Friends will not wonder such a character should forcibly strike me, nor that I should see with peculiar pleasure a marked disposition on her part to take a fancy to me if possible—She made me sundry compliments but all with a finesse that took off from their embarrassment: indeed, from the velocity of her speech, she had commonly run into another subject, before I was well

² The princesse de Poix, Anne-Louise-Marie *née* de Beauvau (L. 513 n. 16), who, in order to preserve life and possessions through the Revolution, went through the ruse of a divorce from her husband Philippe-Louis-Marc-Antoine de Noailles (1752–1819), prince de Poix. See also ii, L. 112 n. 1.

aware that what she uttered of a flattering sort was personal. My difficulty of expressing myself was never so little distressing to me as with this Lady, for such is the quickness of her conception, & so penetrating is the examination of her eye, that half a phrase, or two or 3 words, sufficed to let her seize, & finish & answer my meaning. I am afraid I should never to study to do better were I to live with her, from finding how easily she can comprehend me when I do so ill.

The Day after this meeting—notwithstanding Mᵉ d'Henin herself urged her earnestly, in my name, not to risk such an exertion, She came to our Hôtel, and, hearing we were above, with my then sick Alex, she mounted the 3 pair of stairs— though she resides on a Ground floor to avoid that exercise, Unfortunately, I could not then see her, my Boy, at that time, requiring me wholly: but M. D'Arblay recieved her, & endeavoured to express what he was sure I should feel from such a mark of her kindness.

At the assembly at Mᵉ D'Henin's I rejoiced again to see her; I was placed, when she arrived, between the two fair sister's,[3] but Mᵉ D'Henin came to tell me that she desired a little conference with me before she sat down to a Card Table. I hastened to her with pleasure—when, popping herself down upon a little Straw ⁱ chair Close to the door, she made me take a *fauteuil* opposite her! 'Tis in vain I resist these species of so undue civility—I gain nothing by opposition, though I am always utterly confounded in being conquered. As Mᵉ de Poix reads English with Ease, & I was told could speak it also, I now entreated to be allowed to address her in that language. She complied with pleasure, but when she attempted to answer me, she coloured so violently, that I soon found that we had only changed places, & that the embarrassment of which I got rid went no farther than my companion. Both languages, however, were soon spared our alternate ill usage, for the card-table was ready, & Mᵉ de Poix could no longer be dispensed with. I was sorry to see her sit down to Cards, though it enabled me to return to unrestrained English conversation.

It is hardly possible my dearest Friends, to give you an idea of the attentions which as *une Anglaise*, I here meet with. If one sofa, or fauteuil, is better than another, I must be seated upon it; if we are changing apartments, no one must depart till I have led the way; if we are at dinner, supper, or regale, I must begin before anyone else will eat or drink!!! Of course, this must subside when I cease to be *une Etrangere*, by longer residence, though I am at present I am often so disconcerted by it as to be utterly ashamed. At this very assembly, when we were called to supper, Mᵉ d'Henin herself forced me to go first: I felt more ashamed for Mᵉ de Beauvau, who had lived 4 years in England, than for the rest, &, seizing her apart, endeavoured to apologize for my requiescence 'I have found I cried, all resistance useless, or I should not have become so compliant, But I blush more before you, & Mˡˡᵉ de Mortemart, than before any others, for, as you have lived so long in England, You must be as conscious as myself how little honours of this sort are returned, there, to foreigners: you can best, therefore, conceive the shame of one who has no right to place any where, to take it thus of those who have a right to it every where!— |

The fair Sisters,[3] however, would not allow a word of this; Mˡˡᵉ de Mortemart began a warm panegyric of England in every thing, & Mᵉ de Beauvau—to console—or confuse me— I know not which—yet more,—with an archness in her sweet smile enquired who was the female that in any country ought to take place of me?—I ought not to write this—but yet, I wish, to let the Friends in whose tenderness I most confide see the treatment I meet with in this strange land. |

I am now—July 17. so discomfitted by recieving not a line from my naughty Fredy,[4] that I have hardly any spirit left for continuing any narration: & yet, as I hope to send off a pacquet by a conveyance that I expect for tomorrow, I cannot bear not to prepare a little confabulation for any future opportunity, that I might grieve to *miss*. For while I say *naughty*, I know she is good—, good, sweet, indulgent, & tender,—& I think therefore of this long silence with dread lest her dear Eyes are again

---

[3] The princesses de Beauvau and her sister Victorine de Mortemart (L. 513 nn. 2, 3).

[4] This statement FBA softened later by the insertion (p. 8): 'Forgive the opening of this antique Letter, my beloved Friend—written when I was in a fermentation of anxiety.'

Suffering—but I will get another Sheet ready, in hope the whole anxiety arises simply from the delays of M. de Lally. To proceed, therefore with my female french worthies, in the order I have met with them—My next is one by name well known to my dearest friends, M^{de} de Tessé.⁵ I had much curiosity to see her, & should have had much more, had I not learned it was a feeling reciprocated: & nothing so completely damps me as such intelligence. My first meeting with her was at the select little assembly at M^e d'Henin's. She was there before me, seated upon a sofa upon the upper end of the room. Her appearance is extremely stiff, her air high & her manners are formal: her dress is entirely in the old style, with friezed toupee, well curled in rows towards the ears, & plastered with powdered pomatum. Her silk gown has a long waist, & half long ruffles, & her long winged cap projects over her toupee, at the sides & has bows of ribbon or lace mounting pyramidically to its summit. Her face, which wears no traces of past, nor possession of present beauty, is long, her nose & chin are picked, her mouth is small & pursed, but her smile, which is very rare, seems to well know its own value: it Changes her countenance at once from lofty coldness to an expression of benignity & graciousness, & makes words, which of themselves denote ǀ Satire or severity, merely give an impression or archness & penetration—You will not, I am sure, my dearest Friend, wonder that, with all that I had heard from M. D'arblay of her understanding & intellectual powers, An appearance such as this should be formidable to me. A favourite with her himself, & accustomed, to her figure & manner, he sees her without adverting to their stately or antique singularity, & does himself as well as her, the justice to consider only her worth & superior parts. Me de Henin, taking my hand at the door of the apartment to present me to her immediately, was stopt in her purpose by the instant approach of Me de Tessé herself to recieve me on my entrance. I saw in her a fixed determination—as in all this distinguished set—to do me honour: but I saw through the kindness & the flattery of this predecision expectations that annihilated all my faculties, what she said I cannot tell, except that her compliments were high, & marked by her best smile: but I was so much confounded, that not only I could not

---

⁵ One of d'Arblay's fondest friends (see L. 514 n. 10 and *passim*).

suggest one phrase I had courage to utter—I could not even, such was my confusion, comprehend more than the general tenour of a word that I heard: & though I felt sincerely obliged & gratified, by a condescension I was aware to be not common —it was far more from the delight I knew it gave to M. D'arblay, than from any Enjoyment I was capable of taking in it my self. But the worst is what followed, which I know will make you smile, though it will a little vex you, because it vexes me to this minute: As soon as the harangue was over, that complimented my arrival, & all that was known, or rather imagined of me, that preceded it, Mᵉ de Tessé, in returning to her Sofa, made place for me not only next, but above her—yet, recieving at the same moment, a soft address from my beautiful & bewitching Mᵉ de Beauveau, & an English '*How d'ye do?*' from Mˡˡᵉ de Mortemart, I was allured, by the ease as well as pleasure of their intercourse, into immediately joining them— nor was I conscious how ungrateful I must have appeared ǀ till I saw, upon looking round, the grave & changed look of Mᵈᵉ de Tessé. But though I then wished myself back, I preserved my new place because I could not think of a syllable of apology I could say in french.—You have hardly an idea what a check it is to my *declamatory powers* that if I think of speaking, I cannot utter a word! All my eloquence hangs upon being surprised into an harangue, before I consider in what language I am delivering it. Fortunately for me, as I then thought, she had already engaged me to dine with her the Thursday following when I hoped to recover my lost credit: but my poor Alex's illness intervening we were obliged to send an excuse. She had invited us to meet the Cousin of M. D'arblay, M. de la Brulerie,⁶ that my dearest Fredy may remember reading about, in a note I shewed her from Mᵉ Bourdois, wife of the Physician, where she says M. de la Brulerie, *Evêque métropolitain futur*, who lived in *Prison* Street, Hôtel de *Feu*, or some such goodly harmonizing names. During my confinement with my boy Mᵉ de Tessé called twice, & sent daily; I returned the call when he recovered:

---

⁶ Probably of the family Piochard de la Bruslerie de Villeinblois and, like another member of that family, François-Louis-Emmanuel (1705–55) of Joigny, prêtre regulier des Théatins, M. d'A's cousin seems also to have belonged to that order (the house in Paris, Port Royal). He may have been the superior who, confessor to Cardinal Caprara in these years, took an active part in negotiations leading to the Concordat of 1801.

but we met no more, till one memorable evening of which anon. Here, therefore, for the present she must rest, & I must introduce to my dear Friends Mad^e la cidivant Princesse de Beaufremont;[7] a lady who now resides in a small Villa she has preserved from destruction near Joigny. She was one of those who suffered the most severely in the Revolution, though from no possible provocation beyond her high rank, and magnificent possessions. She had a Chateau in Franche comté, nearly as large & superb as that of Versailles,— which a party of Brigands burnt to the ground, with all its pictures, goods, & valuables! Yet this, even this, she might have wiped from regret, in seeing her usage was general as it was abominable;—but she had a daughter,[7] just grown up, beautiful as an angel, who taken by surprise in the night, when these barbarians, these fiends, set the house in flames, rose from her bed, escaped with no other covering than what she slept in—but escaped only from the fire, not from destruction—the terror & the cold united threw her into a rapid decline, which, in a month or two, terminated her existence. Me de Beaufremont, it is said has never recovered this cruellest of losses. She is ⌐ however, very cheerful, at present, & has a kind of high bred serenity of manner, extremely engaging, with a peculiarly engaging tone of voice, & pronunciation. She has remarkably large, soft, fine eyes, & is still handsome, in defiance of a corpulency that, had she less of ease & elegance in her deportment, would be the greatest disadvantage. She has the appearance of being very amiable & very sensible. She spends her winters in Paris, & her Summers at Sezy, near Joigny, & I shall be glad of what opportunities may offer for seeing her at both. She has still a daughter, Madame de Listenois,[7] who seems about 17 years of age, & is tall, thin, handsome, well made, & strikingly graceful, with quick parts, & uncommon readiness at real conversation—but she has by no means the softly pleasing manners of her Mother, whose civility to all around her is of so attentive, nay almost humble a sort, that is seems to me as if the horrors of the Revolution, joined to a disposition naturally

Of the three daughters of the prince and princesse de Bauffremont-Listenois (see L. 517 n. 10), it was Hélène-*Adélaïde*-Marie-Charlotte (b. 1770) who died in the manner described at Scey-sur-Saône on 18 Nov. 1789 (see also L. 536, pp. 400–3). The daughter 'about 17' would have been Hortense (L. 517 n. 11), who was to marry in 1804 Joseph-Augustin de Narbonne-Lara (1767–1825).

gentle, had made her shrink from having her birth or former situation remembered. No allusions to them, no species of reference to other times escape her, & what she then was is only pointed out by her high tone of superior politeness. She has a Son, also, who I believe, sought refuge in Spain, during the reign of Terror here. I have not seen him: but I must give you a little trail of my English rusticity upon my presentation to the young Mad^e de Listenois. which I hope will draw a smile from my dearest Mr Locke |

August 20. I now go on, preparing, with all the comfort of having had good & dear news from my most beloved Friends

When first I was presented to *des Dames françoises*, upon their giving me a cheek, I kissed it, & drew back, satisfied to the full with such a mark of affection upon first sight: but as they regularly held forward the other cheek, I was fain to salute it also, not uninformed of the custom, but always taken unawares in its practice;—till at length, I recieved so many bobs of the face, in return for my kisses, that I began to—grow upon my guard, & only give bob for bob. Even this however I found, in the progress of my initiation into the minutiae of this affectionate ceremony, was more than was perfectly correct, the intention being only that the two mouths of the two meeting persons should advance merely to retreat, & that then each party should present the right cheek, for the sole purpose of drawing it hastily away, that each may present the left, which, with the same rapidity, approaches only to retire. My education upon this point being tolerably complete before my visit to Mad^e de Beaufremont, I acquitted myself with scrupulous exactness, both in apparent desire, & real avoidance of *embrassade*: but when, as the mother quitted me, the Daughter, Mad^e de Listenois, took her place, the excess of eagerness with which she seemed almost dancing into my arms, the pleasure dimpling round her lips, & the lively rapture of her eye, made me conclude her youth yet unformed to the vague ceremony I have described, or her character too ardent for its insipidity: unwilling, therefore, to check what seemed genuine, though enthusiastic partiality, my lips were once more prompt to what seemed their bidden office,—but their execution, though

345

immediate, & in a certain degree, cordial, was of none effect—
they encountered nothing—the presented cheek having darted,
rather ⏐ than slipt away; yet, as another cheek, with the same
apparent vehemence of affection, was jutted into its place, I
was again not proof against an air, look, & manner of such determined devotion & again my lips manifested my pleased
acknowledgement of her extraordinary kindness, the other
cheek, however, as rapid in its motions as its sister, was snatched
away ere touched, & twice within the same half moment,
I tenderly kissed the air. The Nymph, meanwhile, whose Airy
Form & flying motions were truly Nymph-like, was seated
in an instant, utterly unconscious,—I trust!—of my *bourgeoise*
disappointment. From this time, however, you may easily,
my dear Friends, believe, a similar plebeianism cannot disgrace me

I must now pass by sundry pleasing, but not striking acquaintances, to arrive at a Lady with whom, as you know, I most
wished to connect myself before I left England. I had been
exactly a fortnight in Paris, & my Alex was first recovered
from his first Fever, when M D'arblay procured me a ticket from
General Hulain,[8] to see the Parade & Buonaparte from the
Thulleries—but as I had a chance, there, of being seen by
various parties who had called upon me, we thought of my
Fredy's conscience, & I brought myself to a resolution of
making returning visits to my whole circle of claimants the
preceding day; This we did partly on foot, & partly in a Fiacre:
& we were out upon the duty from eleven in the morning till
half past 5 in the afternoon. I came back so utterly demolished
by fatigue both of body lungs, & brains, that I was forced to
lie down immediately and my feet were so blistered that I was
compelled to free them from all covering & restraint, & simply
coll ⏐ them in a cambric handkerchief. In this manner, *un-
bedizened*, & wrapt in a loose morning Gown, M' D'arblay was
so kind as to order the dining Table to my Bedside, where we
took our frugal repast; he was then obliged to go out upon some
affairs; but my fatigue was so great, & my feet were so sore, I
was fain to keep my recumbent posture, & consign myself to
chatting with my Alex, till at about 7 o'clock M^e D'Henin was
announced. Though always happy to recieve her, I was almost

[8] Général Hulin (L. 517 n. 19).

disabled from moving—but while calling upon Pauline—have I told you of Pauline?[9]—to aid me, Alex ran into our *Drawing room*, & having told Mᵉ D'Henin *Mamma was on the Bed*, she came peeping at the door, & desired I might not be disturbed— I was in no situation to rise abruptly & Alex, opening the door wide, danced to me with her message, & to her with '*Mama a pas ses souliers sur sa pied*—The result was a prohibition to my stirring, & a *fauteuil* by my Bedside & the shame of a moment was succeeded by a confidental & pleasant conversation of nearly 3 hours—at which time we heard *du Monde* pass through the little Salle á Manger to the drawing-room. —I called to Alex to caution Pauline from letting any one enter— but the little rebel, opening the doors all, went forward, saying '*Mama est sur sa lit*'—&, flying back said to me. 'O Mama its Madame La Fayette!'[10]

I was surprised, embarrassed, & gratified all equally—She was the person I most wished to know from the high character that from all quarters had reached me of her in England, while here I find her looked up to as a saint, from her exemplary piety, & perilous conjugal devotion; & certainly her goodness in thus mounting my lofty habitation did not lessen my pleasure in the prospect of obtaining my desire: but my immediate *unsandled*—to say no more—position, kept me a Prisoner, unabled to advance a step to recieve her, & forced, therefore, to hear Pauline tell her I was not '*visible*'—but Alex, again flinging wide open the door as she was refusing, she saw, & courtsied to Mᵉ D'Henin, who rose & hastened to embrace her,—& I was now obliged to call out my apologies,—while Mᵉ D'Henin conducted her to my Bedside. It is not easy to imagine a situation more ludicrous; I was so well as to have no claim to such indulgence, yet litterally unable to put a foot to the ground—I could only as I called out, recieve Mᵉ de La Fayette upon my Knees:—a homage, however, so due to her many & tried virtues, that I could hardly be angry or concerned accident should thus prostrate me before her. You wont imagine this latter part of my phrase uttered aloud! yet I should be willing the first part should have made it understood. M' de la Fayette

---

[9] The maid (L. 510 n. 9).
[10] Cf. the account of Mme de Lafayette's visit to FBA (L. 517, pp. 300–3); see also L. 517 n. 18. Born on 2 Nov. 1759, she was now 43.

is not above 40—but as she walks rather lamely, from some cold
or humour that fell upon one of her legs during her confinement at Olmutz, she seems older. She has very fine soft dove-
like eyes that are full of expression. & that seem to give—
like those of my Fredy,—her whole soul in a look, when they
fasten upon those she loves—I did not see this on the Evening
I am describing—But I have frequently been struck with it
since— |

I can bring forward, however, no other resemblance, her
face has no other beauty:—but the promise of her eyes, as I
afterwards found, did not disappoint me: very often, mentally,
has she brought the same beloved Friend to my thoughts:—
though just in the reverse order, as to time, to the recollections
& ideas excited by the younger & lovelier Mᵉ de Beauveau—
She came, she told me, to put in her claim for a long given
promise of M' D'arblay's that we should spend a few days at
la Grange, her country—& indeed her only residence, for she
never comes to Paris but on a visit to her Aunt, Mᵉ de Tessé.
As she was preparing for the Marriage of her son, M George
La Fayette¹¹ with Mˡˡᵉ de Tracy, I would have postponed our
visit to a more disengaged period: but she would not hear of
any procrastination—she took my hand, held it between both
her own, & *fixed* me, with looks of such determined, & pre-
determined partiality, that there was no resisting her urgency:
& urgency from the gentle is so flattering, so gratifying, so
winning, that I consented to her own time most willingly.
The following week was fixed, & Mᵉ la F insisted upon taking
the whole trouble of managing our method of travelling &c.
Her youngest daughter, Mˡˡᵉ de la Fayette,¹² who was with
her, is a most blooming young creature, with the finest white
Skin the most rose-budding cheeks, & the softest light &
curling hair I have seen in France. Her eyes, too, are pleasing,
but her other features are plain; her countenance is ingennuous,
modest, & full of sense; she is about 19, yet looks hardly 15,
from her beautiful youthful glow, & from a diffidence of manner

---

¹¹ George Washington de Lafayette's first sight of Emilie Destutt de Tracy (see
L. 517 n. 18), the love affair, courtship, and marriage provided FBA with a charming theme for an extended 'histoire' in French. See her Exercise Book IV (Berg),
pp. 39–43.

¹² See Intro., pp. xlii–xliii; L. 541; and Lady Morgan's account of her visit there
in 1816, ii. 298–312. Virginie de Lafayette was born on 18 Sept. 1782.

& demeanour approaching to bashfulness. She has nothing in common with any other French young Lady I have seen: She has neither the grace, carriage, nor the courage; but what she may have fail'd acquiring of obvious accomplishments is amply recompensed by her mental information, & thc gentleness & sweetness ⏐ of her manners & disposition. She was almost as anxious as her Mother for our visit, & not only for our visit but for our settling in their neighbourhood, a place called *Segrais*[13] being then upon sale, which is within a mile of La grange, & which they both thought might just suit us. Ah my dearest Friends—I need not tell you how, here, I drew back!

The next Female Worthy I have to introduce to my dearest Friends is Made de Maisonneuve,[14] with whom I made acquaintance the following day but one, from the always active kindness of Mde D'Henin, who, knowing M. D'arblay had promised I should wait upon her, borrowed Me de Poix' carriage to convey us all to Passy, where she lives. She is sister of M. la Tour Maubourg, & a first rate favourite with M' D'arblay: So would she be, if appearances may be trusted, with my own Fredy & Amelia, for she is modest even to timidity, yet striking for a native dignity of person & manner, which seems the result of a right & highly principled mind, & which, therefore, no diffidence can injure. Like Mde de La Fayette, she bears the Character, in Paris, of being *Dévote*, which means, she is not only mentally pious, but observcs all her religious duties with an awful reverence that shews them to be dictated by the most serious belief. She is very handsome, & her Profile, & her figure have an air of nobleness very rarely, indeed, united with a softness of speech, & a blushing humility so gentle, so retired, & so reserved as this sweet Woman's. She is the Rival of Made la Fayette, both in her desire to settle us in her neighbourhood, & her attractions for seconding her kind wish. Her husband, I believe, is still an Emigrant:[15] but I know

---

[13] Segrais, a country place within a mile of La Grange just south-east of Paris.
[14] The friendship begun at Passy in October 1802 was to end only with FBA's death in 1840.
[15] Bidault de Maisonneuve (L. 515 n. 10), about whom FBA was long curious. 'Il est sûr que le mari est un homme d'un mauvais coeur. . . . Je meurs d'en de savoir son histoire, et comment il est possible que le mari d'une telle femme peut passer d'elle et de sa société, animée que . . . elle me semble, avec un jugement sain, et un coeur tendre; et donnée d'une sensibilité . . .' (Frcnch Exercise Book I [43, 115]). His son 'Maxime' was now about 5 years of age.

not yet her history, except that it is unfortunate, & submitted to with the most pious resignation. She has a small habitation at Passy, in which she resides with a little son[15] of whom she is doatingly fond, for the sake of being near her brother | M. la Tour [M]aubourg, whom she loves & honours almost with devotion. She is in the most reduced circumstances, but treated with universal respect, & never named but with admiration.[14] We passed the whole morning with her, & accompanied her to see a Garden belonging to a small villa formerly M^de de Henin's. The Garden is extremely pretty & laid out in the English style. It was first arranged by M^e D'Henin, who planted herself various lilac walks that are truly sweet. The house she did not wish to see again—but she shewed me from the Garden, the windows of the rooms she had appropriated—jadis! to Me de Biron,[16] Me de Bouillon & Me de Poix! — — The House now belongs to a Banker of Switzerland, M. Grivel.[17] Madame de Maisonneuve exerted her utmost eloquence to induce us to reside at Passy as Mad^e La Fayette had done to fix us near La Grange. For the sake of keeping near M^de D'Henin I should prefer Passy, for with M^de D'Henin I *feel at Home*, the lovely Sisters too. Beauveau & Mortemart, with other amiable persons, will be lost to me at any greater distance. And I had not need lose what now I can preserve, & *here* preserve, of desirable society!

The next fair Lady I must introduce to my Friends is Mad^e La Tour [M]aubourg,[18] wife of M: & Mother of his 7 Children, 6 of which she had the whole care of, & fear of, during his long imprisonment! the 7th has been born since. She is a very handsome woman, with a highly dramatic face, somewhat in the style of Mrs Siddons,[19] only with an expression reversed, of *happiness*, not sorrow. The air, look, & conduct are all noble.

---

16 The late duchesse de Biron (L. 518 n. 11); the duchesse de Bouillon (L. 518 n. 13); and Mme de Poix. (L. 513, n. 16), the only surviving member of the trio of friends.

17 Almost certainly Isaac-Louis Grivel (1753–1820) of Aubonne, Vaud, associate director of the banking firm, Fulchiron & Grivel & Cie, of Paris and Lyons. His daughter Anne-Louise (1789–1842), presented for baptism at the Chapel of the Ambassador of Holland in Paris on 21 June 1789, was to marry on 23 Sept. 1811 Auguste-*Charles*-Théodore Vernes (d. 9 Dec. 1859), 'futur sous-gouverneur de la Banque de France' (1833–57).

18 Marie-Charlotte-Hippolyte (L. 446 n. 12), whose husband César de Latour-Maubourg had shared Lafayette's imprisonment at Olmütz.

19 Sarah *née* Kemble (i, L. 24 n. 9).

By remaining always here, because always nursing her youngest born, she has saved the greatest part of her own fortune, which was very considerable, & upon which, M de [M]aub[g] not having found ¹ a shilling upon his return of estate or fortune, her husband & seven children all subsist. She has not—few, indeed, have—the peculiar attractions of her sister in law, M[e] de Maisonneuve; but to a judgment that in conduct seems unerring, she joins the strongest religious principles, & a never failing equanimity of temper. Her friendships alone would suffice to do her honour, both from their choice & their steadiness, for she lives with 3 ladies with whom she was brought up, by their being educated in the same convent, with all the confidence, & all the affection of the most tender of sisters. During the whole period of public misery here, in the days of the Revolution, these 4 friends were constantly aiding each other, & they keep up still the same invariable intimacy now that more tranquil times make such species of reciprocated regard and exertions Unnecessary, their names are Mesdames de Sully (from *The* Sully)²⁰ de Tracy,²¹ & de Segur.²² M[e] de [M]aubourg's

²⁰ Gabrielle-Louise de Châtillon (1731–1824), dame du Palais de Madame la Dauphine (1753). She had married in 1749 Maximilien-Antoine-Armand de Béthune (1730–86), prince d'Henrichemont et de Boisbelle, duc de Sully, pair de France (1761); *styled* duc de Béthune. Their only surviving son was Maximilien-Gabriel-Louis (1756–1807), vicomte de Béthune, prince d'Henrichemont (1761), duc de Sully, pair de France (1786).

²¹ Émilie-Pérette-Antonie de Durfort de Civrac (1754–1824), who had married in 1799 Antoine-Louis-Claude Destutt (1754–1836), marquis de, comte de Tracy (1808), a member formerly of the Académie and in 1808, of the Institut. Sharing the liberal ideas of his friends Lafayette, César de Latour-Maubourg, and the Lameths, he voluntarily renounced on 4 Aug. 1789 his titles and privileges. Arrested and imprisoned, nevertheless, in 1793, but freed in 1794, he retired to his villa in Auteuil, disapproved the pomp and tyranny of the new regime, and devoted himself to writing, publishing among other works *Principes d'idéologie* (4 vols., 1804, 1824). See further, vi, L. 589 n. 4.
It was his daughter Émilie (1780–1860) whom George Washington de Lafayette (L. 517 n. 18) was to marry on 6 June 1802. It was probably through this connection as well as the proximity to and friendship with the Latour-Maubourgs at Passy, that the d'Arblays came to know the family at Auteuil.

²² Antoinette-Élisabeth-Marie d'Aguesseau (1756–1828), who had married in 1777 Louis-Philippe de Ségur (1753–1830), 4th marquis de Ségur (1801), comte de (1808), baron de (1824), He has described himself in his *Mémoires* (3 vols., 1824) as 'successivement colonel, officier général, voyageur, navigateur, courtisan, fils de ministre, ambassadeur, négociateur, prisonnier, cultivateur, soldat, électeur, poëte, auteur dramatique, collaborateur de journaux, publiciste, historien, député, conseiller d'État, sénateur, académicien et pair de France'.
Sent as Minister Plenipotentiary to St. Petersburg in 1784, he returned in 1789 to find revolutionary changes with which he was at first sympathetic. He did not emigrate, but, being deprived of his property, retired to write, producing *Pensées politiques* (1795) and *Histoire . . . de Guillaume II roi de Prusse* (3 vols., 1801). He was

family is, I think the handsomest I have seen in this Country, & every member of it is honourable & amiable.

One of these friends, la duchess de Sully, whom I have never seen, now scarcely admits to her sight any other human being than Mᵉ de [M]aubourg, save her own & only son; for, upon losing the duc, She has shut herself up from all mankind, & devoted herself solely to his remembrance. To visit, & walk in the Gardens which he loved, to inhabit the Chateau which he inhabited, & preserve about her whatever had last been seen or touched by him, is now, with reading, & her son, all her existence. Madame de Segur is in a situation exactly the reverse, just as public as that of Mᵉ de Sully is retired; for her husband is made grand Maitre des ceremonies to the Emperor with her also, Mᵉ de [M]aubourg preserves the same connexion, equally faithful to the severity & retirement of the one, as dignified & steady with the splendour & luxuries of the other.

The third Madᵉ de Tracy

[Here the text of the Journal ends]

[In November 1802, when Madame d'Arblay was preparing the first sheet for the post, she added several paragraphs to it]

I send off now, Nov. 1ˢᵗ a sheet written months ago, I meant to be conveyed by my sister Charlotte[23] but an accident prevented its setting off—I have just recieved the letter from my sister Burney which mentions the offer of letting our Cottage for a year—& M' D'. Ar. says 'tis impossible to hesitate at it, for the sake of the security for the ensuing winter & spring, *&c &c* though our plan of return is unaltered for the next summer or autumn—perhaps even sooner—but we shall do as I have already told my dearest Friends—We are quite solaced by the news, after our disappointment upon this subject. but M. D'Ar supplicates from Mʳ Locke—dearest—dearest—Mʳ Locke—

elected a member of the Institut in 1803 and in the same year became conseiller d'État.

By 1806, when FBA had found an opportunity to send her journal, she could report Ségur's emergence under Napoleon as grand-maître des cérémonies (1804). He found later honours as comte de l'Empire, grand aigle de la Légion d'honneur, grand officier civil de la couronne, and, then, sénateur (5 Apr. 1813). His title pair de France (1814) was lost at the Second Restoration but restored in 1819.

23 CBFB and her daughter CFBt had set out from Paris *c.*15 October and arrived in London on the 22nd.

a sketch of the emplacement of the new servants' Hall. He is
now making the plan according to his own ideas—
 M. Fuseli²⁴ has never sent me a line—How shall I find him
& make my claims. I have not had a word since the short,
but dear lines intended for Charlotte's convoy I long— we
both long to hear that the fair has been
 pray, my beloved Friend give me some particulars. And my
sweet Amelia & her loves? & the new little William?²⁵ I hear
all are well through my sister Burny But I am *Non compos*
with—or against M Fuseli
 M d'Arblay's kindest tenderest devoirs, adieu—dearest of
Friends   Kindest loves to all

527   [Monceaux, 20 July 1802]

To Esther (Burney) Burney

A.L.S. (Berg), *n.d.*
Double sheet 4to 4 pp. wafer
Addressed: England. / Mrs. Burney, / Beaumont Street, / Devonshire
Place, / London.
Sent by Anthony Merry, 23 July 1802
Docketed: S. 817 1802
Endorsed by EBB: only half / answered / August 5ᵗʰ 1802 / 1802 fully
answered August 18ᵗʰ
Dated, p. 1: July 1802

I shall give you, at least, the pleasure I have experienced
myself, when I tell you that Bood's sister, Madᵉ de Veremont,¹
is disposed to most affectionately love her, & is a woman so

²⁴ Henry Fuseli (1741–1825), the painter, who was often a guest at Norbury
Park. A party including the surgeon James Carrick-Moore (iii, L. 222 n. 25),
Joseph Farington (1747–1821), Fuseli, and the young artist John James Hall
(*fl.* 1791–1841) had recently arrived in Paris to see, among other sights, the treasures
of art that Bonaparte 'had torn by violence from Italy, Germany, and Holland'.
See Farington, *Diary*, ii. 1–61; and John Knowles, *The Life and Writings of Henry
Fuseli, Esq. M.A. R.A., Keeper and Professor of Painting to the Royal Academy in London;
member of the first class of the Academy of St. Luke at Rome* (3 vols., 1831), i. 253–9.
²⁵ William Locke III, aged one month (L. 522 n. 4).
527. ¹ Edmée-Flore Bourdois (b. 1759), the widow of Goudot de Vermond
(d. 1785), an officer in the infantry. See iv, L. 381 n. 1.

much loved herself, in Joigny, where she was born & has always lived, that she is the general favourite of all classes in the whole town. She is sensible without any pretensions, & gay without either satire or coquetry. she is, indeed, rather *too* gay, for she laughs with the unbounded & loud merriment of a wild school Girl of 13 years of age. A natural character, however, is so delightful to me, & so rare, that I took a fancy to her, & think I could very easily & with much satisfaction love her. She is extremely clever about business, & has the spirit, activity & address of a Man in its execution. She has farming concerns at Joigny, & oversees them all herself. her *bled*, her *vines*, her *foin*, she inspects always personally, & keeps her accounts with the most scrupulous exactness in her own hands. I shall be much disappointed if Maria does not love her very warmly.—With the nearest Relations now existing of M. Darblay I am myself more pleased than I can well tell you. we have spent a fortnight at Joigny,[2] & found them all awaiting us with the most enthusiastic determination to receive with open arms & open heart the choice & the offspring of their returned Exile. Their kindness has truly penetrated me: & the heads of the family, the Uncle & the Aunt, are so charming, as well as so worthy, that I could have remained with them for Months, had not the way of life which their residence in a Country Town has forced them to adopt, been utterly at War with all that, to me, makes peace & happiness & chearfulness, namely, the real domestic Life of living with my own small but all-sufficient family. I have ¦ never loved a dissipated life, which it is no virtue in me, therefore, to relinquish; but I now far less than ever can relish it, & know not how to enjoy any thing from home, except by distant intervals: & then, with that real moderation; I am so far from being a Misanthrope, or sick of the World, that I have real pleasure either in mixt society or public places. It is difficult, however, in the extreme, to be able to keep to such terms. M. D'arblay has so many friends, & an acquaintance so extensive, that the mere common decencies of established etiquettes demands, as yet, nearly all my time!— & this has been a true fatigue both to my body & my spirits.— I am now endeavouring to make an arrangement, after a fashion of my own, to put an end to these claims—at least to their

[2] This was the fortnight *c.* 26 June–*c.* 10 July.

being *fulfilled*!—I am sure I shall have a far better chance to do well by those I mix with, as well as by myself, if I succeed, for my voice is as wearied of pronouncing as my brain is wearied in searching words to pronounce. All I experienced, however, from Company, interruption, & visiting, at Paris, was so short of what I found at Joigny, that, in the comparison, I seemed completely mistress of my time: for, at Joigny, I can truly affirm I never had one hour—or even half a one, to my self. By myself, I mean to *our three selves*. M. D'arblay is related, though very distantly, to a quarter of the town, & the the other 3 quarters are his friends or acquaintance: & all of them came first to see me; next to know how I did after the journey; next were all to be waited upon in return; next ⏐ came to thank me for my visit; next to know how the air of Joigny agreed with me; next to make a little farther acquaintance; & finally to make a visit of congé. And yet, all were so civil, so pleasant, & so pleased with my Monsieur's return, that could I have lived three lives, so as to have had some respite, I could not have found fault; for it was hardly ever with the Individual intruder, but with the continuance or repetition of interruption.

July 20ᵗʰ We are going to Day to dine, for the first time, with M. Bourdois the Doctor,[3] where we are to meet Bood & Maria, who were both here yesterday, in good looks & health. The number of visiting debts I have upon my hands, notwithstanding all my complaints of dissipation, is tremendous: & now [m]y little Alex seems recovered, my excuses are all cavilled at. We shall take him with us, for he has been so often ill, I am never easy when he is out of my sight.

I want much to know, my dearest Esther, if the 1000. is left for Amelia on her coming of age,[4] or if the interest may be employed for her en attendant, in helping you with her education, &c. This, I think, ought, at least, to have been its express destination. Pray tell me. How much I shall rejoice if this little further relief is allotted to her dearest Parents! I am quite glad you think Charlotte Francis improved. Miss Cambridge gives me the same pleasure. Tell me something of my dear Fanny P[hillips]—I am not quite easy about her. She is too much her

3 Edmé-Joachim Bourdois, M.D. (L. 450 n. 6).
4 The Hon. Mrs. Bateman's legacy (L. 517 n. 5).

own directress for her youth & height of spirits, & native small-
ness of grave thoughts: yet she is *able* to think, & to judge well,
& to act exactly as she ought: but youth, spirits, & power!
O how ⌐ rarely are they combined with safety! — — As to our
plans, they depend much upon a pursuit now in existence of
M. Darblay's—but no plan, thank Heaven, breaks into our
purpose of return at the appointed period of the year or year &
half. We have no news of our poor Cottage, which, while we
inhabited it, we were for ever hearing would let at any price!
Your hints as to business quite grieve me—dearest soul!—
how can that be?—but every one is poor—& will yet seem to
be rich: there is only money, therefore, for Dress & Eating
& drinking. I am not surprised you declined Dorset[5] for this
year, but I hope you will be tempted thither the next. It is
a sweet County, & surely Richard will be awaked to real joy
in receiving you. How is his health? & how long will that
excellent Blue stay with him. I shall fear both for his health
& happiness when she quits him. You may be but too sure of
the pang I feel in any of our family going NOW to Ireland![6]—
ah—had that happened 3 years ago!—Heaven bless my
dearest Esther—prays her ever & ever affect[e].

F.B.

My Kind Love to Mr. B[urney] & Amelia. & to your Girls
when you write—& to Edward when [you] see him—& James.
& Sally.

I write myself to good [*wafer*] Aunt Beckey, & send the little
draft.

[5] The Revd. Richard Allen Burney, EBB's son, had recently been presented to
the rectory at Rimpton, Somersetshire (L. 462 n. 8).

[6] EBB's daughter Fanny (L. 521 n. 4), who was now, or shortly to be, employed
as governess to the daughters of the Right Hon. John Beresford, whose seat was at
Walworth in co. Londonderry. She was to be conducted there, or in any case soon
visited there, by her uncle James (see L. 538, a letter to JB, which had been
readdressed to him at Walworth).

Three years ago, that is, in 1799, JB or Fanny, travelling in Ireland or visiting
SBP at Belcotton, would have learned of the precarious state of her health and
perhaps have conducted her to London or Dublin in time to save her life (iv
passim).

To Miss Planta

J.L., copy (Diary MSS. viii. 5600–[5], Berg) in an unknown hand taken
from M. d'A's 'Paris Letter Book', 20 July 1802.
Double sheet and single sheet 4to   6 pp.
Corrected by CFBt, *edited by the* Press.
A typescript copy, also from the 'Paris Letter Book', is extant (grangerized
DL, 25th or supp. vol., pp. 54–9, NPG), printed in *FB & the Burneys*, pp. 64–8.
The copyist introduced errors, e.g. the spelling of the street Cisalpine.

> Rue Cysalpine à Monceau
> *Paris July 20. 1802*

My dear Miss Planta

I hope my last long letter arrived safely.[1] I had expected to
have had another to have written on the 14th the only day[2] in
which I have been any where in public since my Boy's 3d
relapse: but the Fête, though it excited a curiosity that had
been big with conjecture for some months previous to its
taking place failed in satisfying it. Nothing was done in the
famous Champ de Mars, where it was expected the *Consulat à
vie* would have been declared & proclaimed: no spectacles
were given to the people, & Paris was as tranquil, & business
was as placidly pursued as upon any other day. The parade,
however, was far more numerous than upon any former
occasion, for not only the Court of the Thulleries, but the
[Corouzel was][3] filled with troops, the preparations for which
were nothing less than trifling, since not only all common
incumbrances were removed to make place for them, but
houses were levelled to the ground, & whole hosts were employed in filling up cellars & hollows, removing rubbish &
making and making an even pavement of the whole space. The
condition in which I saw it, covered with rain & dirt, but two
days before, as we drove through it upon our return from le
Bouigogne, made me conclude it to be utterly impossible that

---

528. [1] The Journal-Letter (L. 516), which in manuscript runs to eleven 4to pages.
[2] The Fête de Paris (14 July) celebrating the fall of the Bastille on 14 July 1789.
[3] The Place du Carrousel was a vast square situated between the Louvre and
the Tuileries. It owes its name to the 'carrousel' given there by Louis XIV on
5–6 June 1662.

the parade would extend to that spot; & indeed, the celerity ¦ with which the workmen finished it continues a wonder to me.

Our imaginations not being less awake than our neighbours upon the approach of this day, we hurried from our visit to Joigny in order to be present at the interesting, or eventful scenes to which all looked forward. M D'arblay applied for places too late to obtain them any where but on a scaffolding in the Carrousel, belonging to a begun house of M. Auguste,[4] formerly a fevre to the Queen of France. The parade, however, had no difference from that which I saw in May, except in exhibiting double the number of troops, & adding the Mamelucks[5] to those of this country. These last, in their gay coloured full drapery, & large Turbans, riding the most beautiful light & spirited arabian horses, gave all that was novel to the sight, And though we had excellent places for a complete view of the whole, you will not I believe, wonder that I, who do not, you know, pique myself upon being military. should by no means have been as well entertained as at the parade of which I lately gave you an account, when, in fact, it was not the parade, but my situation for seeing various persons & Characters & ceremonies that amused me ¦

In the evening, we walked, with a large party, in the Thuileries Gardens to see the illuminations, which were very pretty though, for Paris, I am told by the knowing in these things, they were inferior to all rejoicings of that Kind hither too manifested

NB. It seems to me, however, as if every rejoicing commemoration of the various separate epochs of the revolution were enfeebling at least, if not dying away

Except upon this 14ᵗʰ I have not been in Paris these two months, & the change of air, with liberty of running about, succeed completely with my little boy, who has had no return of fever since we left the Capital [for] Monceaux, where we

4 Probably Henri Auguste (1759–1816), who by 1785 had succeeded his father Robert-Joseph Auguste (1725–1805), a metal worker and goldsmith, whose place of business was at the Place du Carrousel. In 1804 he was to fashion Bonaparte's crown.

5 Bonaparte had first encountered the Mamelukes (the Turkish warrior caste that had held Egypt in subjection since the 13th century) in his Egyptian campaign (1798). Astonished, as were his soldiers, by the brilliantly costumed riders, the beautiful Arabian horses, and the dazzling arms, he recruited several companies of them, and these, or French and Greek soldiers dressed like them, brightened the Paris streets, parades, and spectacles throughout the Consulate and Empire.

now abide, in Rue Citalpine, may on one side be reached through streets, but on the other, which alone we frequent, it is divided from the city by fields, & it has the great inducement of being near a very charming Garden, open at present to the public, abounding in pleasant walks, interspersed with Groves, lawns, seats, shade, flourishing trees, & flowering shrubs. *It was the cy devant Folie de chartres* made by the late Duc de' Orleans under the direction of an English Gardener,[6] who is now I am told, forming or improving the Gardens of La Malmaison. We can go there at any hour & in any dress, & it is so near our apartments, that it is little more trouble than to step into another room. There are still the remains of various slight, but very pretty structures ⎮ which, *jadis* ornamented this spot: temples, bridges, mounts, colonades, Ruins, &c, & mile stones with directions in English; & rooms imitating bowers, & walks similating cloisters: but the devastation which, violence, not time, has made, I *here* regard without any of those emotions of pity, or resentment, with which I view desolation from similar causes elsewhere; since to the owner of this Folie de Chartres, so much of the general destruction may be radically attributed. I did not quite so unmoved hear, but yesterday, the lamentation of M^de de Poix upon the degradation of the Hotel de Beauveau,[7] into an Hotel Garni (*Hotel du Prince de Galles.*)[7] She had spent there, she said, so much of▪her youth, so many of her happiest hours, & la Marechale de Beauveau, her Belle Mere,[8] still living, was a person of such eminent worth & virtue, that to see her driven into small hired apartments, while her sumptuous mansion was made an Inn, was a

---

[6] Cf. L. 517, p. 296. For English read Scottish. FBA is probably thinking of the gardener Thomas Blaikie (L. 517 n. 3).

[7] At the time of the Revolution, the Hôtel Beauvau (L. 510 n. 3) was confiscated by the State and though the princesse de Poix, daughter of the maréchal de Beauvau, returned to Paris after a very brief emigration, she was refused permission to resume residence there.

Subsequently, part of the building was converted to a *hôtel meublé* known as the Prince de Galles. In June 1803, Bertie Greatheed took there a 'most sumptuous apartment . . . for 350 *livres* a month', terming it the 'best in Paris' (pp. 164–5). During the next half-century, it passed through many hands before becoming (24 Nov. 1860) the headquarters of the ministère de l'Intérieur. See Hillairet, i. 506, 508–9.

[8] The stepmother of the princesse de Poix would have been Marie-Charlotte-Sylvie de Rohan-Chabot (1729–1807), who had married (1) in 1749 Jean-Baptiste-Louis de Clermont d'Amboise (1702–61), marquis de Renel, and (2) in 1764 Charles-Just de Beauvau (1720–93), prince de Beauvau-Craon. See also L. 513 n. 16; and L. 529 n. 30.

circumstance so poignantly painful, that she had not yet been able to completely resign to its shock. At the house of this truly charming lady, M^{de} de Poix, who seems now to have as many talents & virtues as formerly She had beauty & attractions, we had the pleasure of meeting the two fair Sisters⁹ I have So often mentioned to you, on the last day that one of them, the young M^{de} de Beauveau spent in Paris for this Season. She is now with her ' husband, & three youngest children at a seat still belonging to them near Strasbourg, the eldest son is left at a school at St Germaine en laye, under the protection of the Marechale de Beauveau,⁸ whom M^{de} de Poix spoke of with such praise, & such pity. We were engaged to spend a day with that Marechale under the auspices of M^{de} d'Henin, just as my poor boy made me a prisoner to his room. We are still, however, to have that honour when M^{de} de Poix has finished previous summer excursions. The same sort of captivity as *garde-malade* has kept me from again seeing Mlle de Mortemart, who, however has been so kind, before my journey to Joigny, to send Me a noble pacquet of a months English Newspapers. How greedily I devoured them! It is now 7 weeks ago & I have not seen one since. Mdle. de Mortmart has great hopes of recovering something of her fortune, which in her situation, will be of considerable importance to her happiness, & probably to her establishment. She is with her *Belle-mere*¹⁰ cy devant Duchesse, still I believe in Paris, & as soon as I am able, I shall endeavour to regale myself with waiting upon her. I wish I could tell you how Mde de Poix delighted to make me talk of our *English Garden*⁽ᵃ⁾ with our Noble tree^B of the forest¹¹ which she speaks as well as hears of with rapture. '

Indeed I am frequently astonished—& O how gratified! by the manner in which I find that Tree appreciated in this country.—while that graceful, fragrant, fascinating plant,^C which so much to our honour & happiness we have naturalized & fostered, is a matter of frequent enquiry & discussion, in a manner so deeply interesting to my feelings, that whenever the subject is started, I forget all my impediments to speaking

---

⁹ For Mme de Beauvau, her children, and her sister Mlle de Mortemart, see L. 513 nn. 2, 3.

¹⁰ Adélaïde-Pauline-Rosalie *née* Cossé de Brissac (d. 1808), the 2nd wife of the duc de Rochechouart (L. 513 n. 2).

¹¹ The code names for the English Royal family (cf. L. 512 n. 3).

french, lose my embarrassments in my eagerness, & my shame
and fears in the pleasure, the gratitude, & the love of justice
which excite me, & I believe I may faithfully say there is no
occasion upon which I express myself so nearly the same as in
my own language. The favourite flowers of that Garden, also
Madame de Poix loves to make me describe at very full length:
The Rose[D], The Lily[E], The Honey Suckle[F], The carnation[G],
& the Violet[H].

[a] Royal Family of England	[B] George the Third.
C The queen Charlotte	G Princess Sophia
D Princess Augusta	H Princess Amelia
E Princess Elizabeth	
F Princess Mary	

MADAME CAMPAN'S SCHOOL

The Closing or Prize-giving

529   [24–25 July 1802]

To Miss Planta
For Queen Charlotte and the Princesses

J.L., copy in an unknown hand (Diary MSS. viii. 5582–98, Berg), the
original of which, written probably in the late summer and autumn at
Monceaux and Joigny, was sent to England by Anthony Merry on 31 Oct.
1802. Before the Journal left France, however, M. d'A copied it into his
'Paris Letter Book', which copy FBA later added to,[1] and, in the year 1824,
edited, supplying footnotes, appending supplementary material, and the
explanatory note: 'In the fear that this account, although sent for England
through the then British Minister, Mr. Merry, should miscarry, M. d'Arblay
copied it, that it might be read to the Royal Personages for whom it was
intended, on our return to England.'

The copy (Berg) taken directly from the 'Paris Letter Book' comprises
four double sheets and a single sheet 4to, numbered by sheets, 1, 2, 3, 4, 5.

The copyist included FBA's editorial explanation:

This account was destined to my   Mrs C. n's School
Royal Mistress Queen Charlotte, & Her 5   but it was directed
lovely & ⌜single⌝ loved single daughters: to Miss Planta.

Madame Campans

This copy, emended by CFBt and prepared for publication, was rejected
by Colburn.

A second copy was taken in typescript from M. d'A's copy in the 'Paris Letter Book'
before it was burned, which typescript is extant in the National Portrait Gallery
(grangerized DL, 25th or supp. vol., pp. 64–80). This copy, printed in FB &
the Burneys, pp. 71–84, *includes FBA's editorial annotations, as above, and also*:

For the *Queen, Charlotte,* & the Princesses, directed to Miss Planta.
Account of the Institution of *Madame Campan* at St. Germain en laye.
Journey; Mdme d'Henin; mdme de Belloy; M. Malhouet; Mr. Jerning-
ham; Salle; Examination of the Pupils; the Murats; Mdme LeBrun;
Mdme. Louis Bonaparte; Valence; visit to La Marechale de Beaubeau;
M. de Lally Tolendal.

529. [1] That part of the supplementary material was added while FBA was still in
France is indicated by her Register of Letters and Journals (L. 508 n. 1), where she

The institution of Madame Campan[2] is for a limited & not only very small number of young Ladies who, under the superintendance of Mad[e] Campan are educated from childhood to, I cannot say to maturity, but to the age at which they are regarded, in this country, to be wise enough, experienced enough, & steady enough to become wives, mistresses of large household establishments, & mothers. You will not wonder they have, generally, such success in these characters, when I add that the most common period upon which they commence them, is when just reached their fourteenth year! It was here that the youngest sister of le Premier Consul. Mad[e] Murat,[3] & his daughter, now Sister, in Law, Mad[e] Louis Bounaparte,[4] were brought up: & in consequence, probably of such a patronage, the daughters of most of the principal Generals in the army are sent to this seminary.

The occasion of my going to St Germain en Laye to see it, was that I might be present at an examination of the young pupils

summarizes the topics: 'Diner chez Me Marechale de Beauvau après Me Campan. her character, sorrows, portrait, garden, hermitage, apartments. Belle mere de Me de Poix—'

The 'solemnelle distribution de prix' was reported at some length in the *Journal du département de Seine-et-Oise*, le 10 thermidor an X, pp. 490–1.

[2] Jeanne-Louise-Henriette *née* Genest (1752–1822), who, recognized by her father as an infant prodigy, was provided with such tutors as Goldoni and Marmontel. At the age of fourteen years gained her an appointment as reader to the daughters of Louis XVI. Soon winning her way at court, she became in 1770 Lady of the Bed Chamber to Marie-Antoinette, who arranged her marriage in 1774 to Pierre-Dominique-François Berthollet *dit* Campan (d. 1797). Escaping with her life in the Terror, but impoverished, she resolved in 1794 to establish a pension at Saint-Germain-en-Laye, the enrolment of which soon increased from 60 to 100 pupils, or more. With the avowed ambition to 'créer des mères', she soon attracted a fashionable clientele and was highly approved by Bonaparte, whose sister Caroline and step-daughter Hortense were placed in the school.

[3] Maria-Annunziata or 'Caroline' *née* Bonaparte (1782–1839), who had married in 1800 Joachim Murat (1767–1815), général, maréchal de l'Empire (1804), awarded the grand duchy of Berg (15 Mar. 1806) and Naples (1808). According to Constance Wright, *Daughter to Napoleon, A Biography of Hortense, Queen of Holland* (1961), the pleasure-loving Caroline was considered in the years 1798–9 the dunce of Mme. Campan's school. For FBA's impressions, see p. 368.

[4] Hortense (1783–1837), daughter of the vicomte Alexandre de Beauharnais (1760–94), a victim of the Revolution (see Constance Wright, op. cit., pp. 3–7). His widow Joséphine had become on 9 Mar. 1796 the wife of General Napoléon Bonaparte. Hortense, placed in Mme Campan's school in 1795, spent four fruitful years there, emerging on 9 November 1799 with developed skills in dancing, singing, and painting. Her mother later arranged the marriage with Napoléon's brother Louis (1778–1846), which took place on 3 Jan. 1802. Her first child, Napoléon-Charles, was to be born on 10 October.

She was sixteen when she left the school, where she had been very happy and where she had made a life-long friendship with Mme Campan. Now nineteen, married, and pregnant, she had returned for the closing.

before two members of *the Institute*,[5] previous to the distribution of the prizes adjudged to those who excel in writing, Ortography, Grammar, Geography, Music, Recitation, history & disposition of temper. Mad^e Campan wrote to Mad^e d'Henin inviting her to be at the Ceremony, & to use *her influence*, for bringing with her M. Malhouet,[6] & your very humble servant.

You may easily imagine my surprise at such a distinction, as well as my readiness to avail myself of the opportunity of viewing such an establishment

M^de d'Henin borrowed or hired, a carriage in which she took 6, after making them all *THÉ, à l'anglaise*, in her modest, but very elegant small lodging. Our | party consisted of M^de d'Henin, Mad^e du Belloy[7] (neice to the archevque de Paris)[7] M. Malhouet, M^r formerly called le Ch^er de Jerningham,[8] M^r

5 The report in the *Journal du département de Seine-et-Oise* (*supra* n. 1) mentioned the two members of the Institut present as examiners; first, that in geography, and history, Edmé Mentelle (1730–1815), professor successively in the École militaire, the École normale, and the Écoles centrales, and a member of the Institut since 1795 (one of the first 48 members). He was awarded the Légion d'honneur in 1814.

The second examiner, presumably in literature and politics, was Jean-François Champagne (1751–1813). Associated with the Collège Louis-le-Grand for fifty-five years, as student, professor, and finally director, he was elected member of the Institut in 1797 by virtue of his translations of Aristotle's *Politique* (1791) and in 1804 awarded the Légion d'honneur.

The costume of the members described by FBA (p. 366) is shown in such books as *L'Institut de France* (1907) by Boissier, Darbout *et al*. On the 25th, apparently, after the distribution of prizes, Mme Campan 'a pronouncé un discours, òu les plus touchans sentimens du coeur étaient exprimés avec la grace inséparable d'une diction pure et élégante'. A concert given by the pupils who had profited most from 'des maîtres les plus célèbres' terminated the fête on 10 August.

6 Malouet (L. 450 n. 17) published in this year his *Collection des mémoires et correspondences officielles sur l'administration des colonies* (5 vols). Appointed in 1803 commissaire de la Marine at Antwerp, he won high favour for his activity there (the building of ships and arsenals), was created baron de l'Empire (1808), officier de la Légion d'honneur (1810), and conseiller d'État (1810). Offending Napoleon by some of his counsels, he was banished in that year to dwellings 40 leagues at least from Paris, but on the return of Louis XVIII his talents were again in demand and he was made ministre de la Marine.

7 Henriette, daughter of François-Charles Picault and his wife Catherine *née* Colen, was not the niece of Jean-Baptiste de Belloy (1709–1808), archevêque de Paris (1802), cardinal (1803), comte de l'Empire (1808), but the wife or widow of his nephew Emmanuel de Belloy. On 10 Mar. 1810 she was to marry secondly Pierre-Victor Malouet (*supra*) in the presence of such illustrious persons as the king of Holland, Letizia Bonaparte, and members of the Noailles, Tessé, and Poix families.

8 Charles Jerningham (1742–1814), chevalier de Barfort, brother of Sir William (1736–1809) and of the poet Edward Jerningham (iii, L. 150 n. 19). Charles entered the French army, became colonel, and eventually (1784) maréchal de camp. Having lost his French property by his emigration to England during the Terror, he had returned in 1802 in an effort to regain it. See John Kirk, *Biographies*

Dar[blay] & his mate. We had a very pleasant little journey, by the borders of the Seine, & passed *la Malmaison*[9] which looked very small for your favourite Hero, though the grounds about it are considerable, & it is furnished & still furnishing, with plenty of cazernes for troops & stabling for Cavalry. It is well walling[10] also around. The country & views in its neighbourhood are extremely beautiful in a summit near one of the boundaries of the park is an elegant little villa, which has been given to the young Beauharnois,[11] son of Mad⁰ Bonaparte, And, on another summit, farther on & much higher is a beautiful Pavilion, built for, & erst inhabited by, the wretched & too famous M^de Dubarry.[12]

Arrived at St Germaine en Laye, we gave in our Tickets, & entered the Garden, whence we proceeded to the *Salle de [blank]*. We were so late owing to some accidents, that the ceremony of examination was begun, & the room was so full that we were all crowded to death, & with difficulty could squeeze ourselves into the worst & most uneasy places imaginable—

The apartment was pretty equally divided between the audience, seated in rows, & the pupils who were upon a sort of stage, or elevated floor parted, from the rest, not by an

of English Catholics in the Eighteenth Century, ed. John Hungerford Pollen and Edwin Burton (1909), p. 139; also, *GM* lxxxiv² (1814), 607–8.

9 Acquired by Joséphine in February 1799. Malmaison was an early seventeenth-century house or château situated about ten miles from Paris on the then lonely road leading to Saint-Germain-en-Laye. The estate was small, yielding at first farm produce, but Bonaparte spent lavish sums converting it into a miniature park and palace, building conservatories, greenhouses, and aviaries, laying out walks, and planting the famous orange groves. Naturally, it became one of the 'sights to see' and travellers like the Countess Potocka (pt. iii, chapter viii) devote pages to it; Constance Wright (op. cit.) gives glimpses of the family life there, including Napoléon's last visit to the famous gardens. See also *Country Life* cxxxv (16 Jan. 1964), 116–19.

10 For the phrase 'well walling', CFBt later supplied the editorial explanation 'the walls were then only begun'.

11 Eugène-Rose (1781–1824), prince de Beauharnais, général (see Six), son of Joséphine and brother of Hortense (n. 4). A gallant officer, he was at this time chef d'escadrons aux chasseurs à cheval de la garde and was soon to be promoted to colonel des chasseurs. In April 1801 Bonaparte had given him a small hunting lodge at Bougival on the left bank of the Seine, exactly opposite Croissy. Charmingly situated on a hill, it commanded a fine view, had a park of ten acres of its own in the English style, and was to become in the nineteenth century the haunt of many painters. See Carola Oman, *Napoleon's Viceroy: Eugène de Beauharnais* (1966), p. 133.

12 The pavilion of Louveciennes, constructed and decorated for Mme Du Barry (1743–93), mistress of Louis XV, was also situated on a height overlooking the Seine.

orchestra, but by those Gentlemen who were appointed as judges of the Prize-claimers. Two of these, placed conspicuously in the middle, & still more conspicuous, by dark coats, embroidered richly down the front, & at the pocket-holes, with large green ⏐ laurel leaves, were the two members[5] of the national Institut, of which the premier Consul is president.[13]

The young ladies were all dressed alike, very simply, & very elegantly in white muslin, with white shoes, coque-sashes, & their hair in ringlets, without any other sort of ornaments either for their heads or robes: a prohibition very wise to prevent any rivalry in the vanity of finery, so hurtful I should say to all youth, if I knew not a lovely sixfold exception,[(2)14] which has often made me reflect, how many mental errors & follies, may be spread & prevented, even in the very bosom of danger and temptation, by timely & regular attention to pointing out their evils & futility.

What had preceded our entrance I cannot tell; but the younger pupils had already passed their examination, & were all out of sight. Those who remained were from the age of 10 to 14. Amongst these, the most juvenile was M[lle] de Valence,[15] a daughter of the General, & a grand-daughter of the celebrated Mad[e] de Genlis. They—the Pupils—were at this time all seated round a large table. I think there were about twenty. They were all employed in writing, from the dictates of their judges or masters, who pronounced a phrase at a time, which they all committed to paper at once, till a very long paragraph was completed by every one. They then each delivered what they had separately written to one of the judges, who was to

[13] For General Bonaparte's election on 25 Dec. 1797 to the Institut and the brilliancy of his conversation with the learned men of all sections ('ils eussent tous voulu l'avoir dans leur *classe*'), see Madelin, ii. 216–17. On his expedition to Egypt he took in his *état-major* numbers of learned men, savants, artists and writers, as well as scientists, and he created there an Institut d'Égypte of four sections (Madelin, ii. 226–7, 250–1). In 1800 he had become 'président de la Classe des arts mécaniques'.
  When on 10 Apr. 1815 his place was declared vacant, it was decided that he could appear thenceforth in the lists as 'Protecteur de l'Institut'. See *Index Biographique des Membres et Correspondants de l'Académie des Sciences de 1666 à 1939* (1939).
[14] Here CFBt in her capacity as copyist and editor included what was probably FBA's superscript (2) and her footnote: '(2) Meaning the 5 English Princesses. i.e. Princess Royal—Augusta—Elizabeth—Mary—Sophia & Amelia—'.
[15] Rosamonde de Timbrune (1789–1860), the daughter of Jean-Baptiste-*Cyrus*-Marie-Adélaïde de Timbrune de Thiembronne (ii, L. 101 n. 5), comte de Valence (1808), général de cavalerie, and his wife Edmée-Nicole-Pulchérie *née* Brûlart de Genlis (1767–1847).

pronounce which was the most perfect in ortography, & correctness of accent ┃ and punctuation. The honour, however, was to be announced, & the prizes distributed, all together, at the end of the ceremony.

This over, the great table was removed, & the young ladies were scated on chairs, in a semy circle, so as all to be in sight of the audience, which chiefly consisted of their own relations & friends, or acquaintances. Mad^e Campan herself sat at the corner of the stage, from which a kind of box was lightly railed of in expectation of the premier Consul & his family. He has attended two or three times when the young ladies have performed Athaliah or Esther[16]

Mad^e d Henin being now discovered by Mad^e Campan, she took the opportunity of the interval between the writing and the next exhibition, to descend from the stage to the audience, & express her satisfaction; but as she spoke rather loud, at least not in a whisper, I had such a dread of being named, & marked that I entreated Mad^e de Henin not to mention me; & she could stay so short a time, & was so much hurried, that she had not a moment for any questions. Mad^e d Henin nevertheless enquired if there was any chance that the first consul would come: Me Campan answered that she had prepared him his place, but could not be sure, as he was particularly engaged: for this was just before the declaration of the Consulat à vie

I was extremely glad I had taken my precaution in time, for soon after she had returned ┃ to her seat, some one whispered hcr the name of M. Maloüet, & she immediately arose & called to him aloud, to say how she rejoiced in his presence, & begged him to come forward, & take a seat amongst the judges. M Maloüet gently declined the honour, & got to the farthest end of the Salle to avoid the repetition

Above our heads were two galleries, in which many of the most distinguished persons of the audience were seated. M^{de} D Henin had desired to have her places below, that she might have a better view, should he come, of the first Consul. In one of these galleries sat Mad^e Louis Bonaparte late Mlle Beauhariais.[3]

---

[16] Bonaparte did not appear, this date approaching that on which the Senate was to declare him First Consul for life. On less important days, he had found time to attend exercises and plays (like *Athalie* and *Esther*), in which, as FBA says, his step-daughter and sisters participated.

She is not at all handsome, but has singularly the look & countenance of a *good* character. She was educated in this Seminary & has very lately quitted it, for her marriage. She retains great fondness for Mad^e Campan, & all her fellow students, & for the place itself, frequently, when at liberty, going thither for two or three days following, & behaving, & even dressing as a *pensionaire*, & going through, as such, all her former exercises: a kind of taste & of industry, which reflect upon her much honour. She has done this even since her marriage! Next to her was a Sister of General Laclerc,[17] now at St Domingo, & then Mad^e Lauréston,[18] wife of the friend of M d'Arblay, who brought over the preliminaries of peace ! to England: & then a young lady[19] who was waiting for only 3 days to begin her fourteenth year, when she was to be married to M. Duroc,[19] an aid de Camp of the first Consul, & Governor of the Palais of the Thulleries.

The next trial of skill was in Grammar. A Book—I did not hear its title—was given to one of the young ladies, who was desired to read the first Paragraph, stopping upon every word to declare its part of speech. When she had done, she sat down, & gave the book to her next neighbour, who, in like manner, analysed the following paragraph: & so on till every one had gone through the same task. This took an immense time, & was not very lively.

M. Jerningham[8]—who is brother to Sir William, & to the poet, behaved very indiscreetly upon the fatigue he felt upon this part of the examination, whispering to me every other minute. 'Can you stand this?—' 'A'n't you half dead?'—'How would this do in England?'—and other such sneers, making the whole time, such abominable faces of weariness & contempt, that I was almost afraid to remain in his company, lest he

[17] Louise-Aimée-Julie Leclerc (1782–1868), sister of General Victor-Emmanuel Leclerc (L. 465 n. 6). She had married on 9 Nov. 1801 Louis-Nicolas Davout (1770–1823), maréchal de l'Empire (1804), duc d' Auerstädt (1808), prince d'Eckmühl (1809). Like Hortense, she had been a pupil at the school.

[18] Claude-Antoinette-Julie Le Duc (1772–1873), who had married in 1789 Jacques-Alexandre-Bernard Law, comte de Lauriston (L. 425 n. 5).

[19] Marie-de-las-Nièves-Dominique-Antoinette-Rita-Josèphe-Louise-Catherine Martinez de Hervas (1788–1871). Daughter of a Spanish banker, she was shortly to be married (9 Aug. 1802) to Géraud-Christophe Michel Duroc (1772–1813), aide-de-camp to Bonaparte (1796), premier aide-de-camp (1799), who, sent on a series of diplomatic missions (1800–1), was made on his return (20 Nov. 1801) gouverneur du palais des Tuileries and, in 1804, duc de Frioul.

should give some offence. Nor did he content himself with what he risked upon this subject; [|] for, whenever he observed any lady, amongst the audience, particularly in the height of the French costume, he turned to me & bid me look at her, with such grimaces of disgust & abhorrence, that I hardly knew whether to laugh, or to be frightened. 'What say you to that? M^{de} D'arblay? What say you to that? Good [God!] what a shocking form! Did you ever see the like? ever behold such a nasty creature?' Yet no one was *nasty*, I assure you, though his indignation at the light drapery could find no softer term. Indeed I saw more of *les elegantes* here, than I had yet beheld in France, as the room was almost filled with the rich & gay who first set afloat, or first adopt the modes of the day

After this, followed Geography, The Stage was filled with large sheets of strained paper, framed & hung up, on which various of the most skilled in this science sketched maps of every quarter of the globes, on which they drew the outlines of the terrestrial sphere, & marked the longitude & latitude While this was performing, one young lady was selected to come forward, & point [out] upon a Map, ready made, to all the countries of Europe naming their relative positions, & chief cities, for each of which another called out its latitude & longitude.

This lasted so long, that Mad^e D'Henin, tired of sitting on a form where she had no means [|] of procuring rest by leaning, insisted upon going for a while into the air to refresh herself. I was very sorry to remove, as the whole was curious, however its parts were tedious; but I could not risk staying without her, & we both went into the Garden. Here, while we were strolling, we were accosted by Mad^e Somebody whose name I cannot recollect, but who is first female assistant[20] to Mad^e Campan, & who asked if we would not go up stairs into the gallery.

Mad^e de Henin declined this, saying 'Mad^e D'arblay et moi nous nous promenons pour prendre l'air, et puis nous retournarons à la Salla' Away went M^{de} Somebody,—& in two

---

[20] Possibly Mme Rousseau, one of Mme Campan's sisters. The sisters are described in *Souvenirs* (i. 173–82) by one of their former friends at the Court of Marie-Antoinette, namely Vigée-Lebrun (n. 29). For the school, see also Violette M. Montagu, *The Celebrated Madame Campan, Lady-in-waiting to Marie-Antoinette and confidante of Napoleon* (1914).

minutes, out came Mad^e Campan herself, flying up to us, & exclaiming that she had not heard my name till that moment, & knew not that I was in her house. Much civility ensued— which I shall spare writing without much fear of reproach; but she said as we were so ill placed, we should go through the little door that led to the Box on the stage, for she had just been informed by an aid-de-camp of the first Consul, that the pressure of affairs would not permit him to come. I felt, however, little enough of my ease, upon being placed in this conspicuous *loge*, though I contrived immediately to get into a corner the least in sight. Mad^e Campan's ǀ civility having given me a serious alarm, I earnestly pleaded with Mad^e D'Henin to represent to her my desire of remaining unnamed & unnoticed,—I mean publicly. Mad^e d'Henin complied though rather reluctantly: but I soon saw that Mad^e Campan, though she did not resist, recieved the request with a species of surprise somewhat bordering upon contempt. They have here no idea of a retired disposition such as mine. They think it impossible that any public distinction, if attended with approbation, can be painful & distressing. I however should have found them so in England —think then how much more so in a country of which I know the language so indifferently! I mean with respect to speaking it.

The Geography had now given way to History, and the members of the Institut had notes presented to them, from which they were desired to examine the young students upon the building, the Monarchy, the consulships, & the Empire of Rome.

These members were almost inconceivably humane and delicate in their manner of making their enquiries, & turning them into fresh channels, when they discovered they had not been understood, or that their questions were too difficult or complicate: always beginning with a present, Mademoiselle, aurez vous complaisance de nous dire comment — — &c — & finishing with. 'A merveille, Mademoiselle, il est impossible de mieux repondre' ǀ

After this they were examined upon les belles lettres, & politics; & they each repeated some criticism from La harpe,[21] or some celebrated commentator, finishing with the recital of some poem.

[21] Probably selected extracts from *Cours de Littérature* (see L. 466 n. 4).

No one here excelled the young Mlle de Valence, who is very pretty, & has physionomy promising talents & intelligence. This was the conclusion of the examination. It was followed by the selection of the claimants, & the distribution of the prizes. The first of these, I think was for *Temper*; The prize was a rose. Mad[e] Campan said: She had taken the opinion of the whole school both Masters, Teachers, & Scholars, & they had all joined in giving the palm for sweetness of disposition to a young lady whose name I cannot recollect—of only 7 or 8 years of age. She was summoned & told her happy lot, & recieved the Rose with the most undisguised transport, jumping into the arms of Mad[e] Campan to embrace & thank her, & then begging permission to descend to the audience that she might shew her Rose to her Mama. This was readily granted, & the delighted little Girl, flew on the wings of joy to her enraptured Parent. This was a very pleasant part of the ceremony, & I thought it a happy idea that General conduct should take precedence of every accomplishment.

The other prizes, though less pretty, were more substantial, they consisted of presents of Books, chosen & delivered | by Mad[e] Campan. The Masters of the Seminary[22] decided to whom should be given those for writing, Music, French, singing, Italian singing, Orthography & Grammar. Geography, History & Recitation[23] were treated with greater dignity: the merits of the several Candidates were discussed by the two

---

[22] Among the masters listed in Montagu, op. cit., pp. 204–5, in 'Pensionnats de Jeunes Demoisclles. Institut de Mme Campan', *Annuaire de l'instruction publique, pour l'an ix* . . . (1801), pp. 374–9, and by Gabrielle Réval, *Madame Campan* (1931), pp. 163–73, were many artists pre-eminent in their fields: Jean-François Coulon (*fl.* 1787–1830), maître à danser; Mme Laval *née* Larrivée, professor of harp; Benoît Bonesi (d. *pre* 1812), the singer; Honoré-François-Marie Langle (1741–1807), the composer, who taught clavichord, singing, and composition; and Charles-Henri Plantade (1764–1839), professor at the Conservatoire. Called in also were Jean-Jacques Grasset (1769–1839), 'violiniste et ancien chef d'orchestre de l'opéra italien'; and among the 'maîtres de dessein' was Jean-Baptiste Isabey (1767–1855), painter and miniaturist who, under the patronage of Hortense, painted many of Bonaparte's soldiers and Bonaparte himself 'dans les jardins de la Malmaison'.

[23] As far as can be deduced from the copies, FBA had here entered the superscript ·⁑· and the supplementary matter: '·⁑· Mademoiselle de Valence [n. 23] recited admirably the ode of Rousseau to Fortune. I was quite astonished to hear such hardy indifference of Tyrants, & of Blood-thirsty Victors pronounced in such an assembly. It did high credit to Madame Campan that she ventured to instil such principles into her pupils: &, in truth, it reflected, though rather singularly honour upon the first Consul that she did not fear ordering them thus publicly to be declaimed.'

members of the National Institut, who frequently stood up, & declaimed aloud both upon the given subject, & the performances of the young ladies; always in a manner the most delicate for those who were selected, & the most soothing & encouraging for those who failed: & the pupils were all ranged in rows at the farthest end of the Salle, whence the successful were called by name, one at a time to recieve their rewards. The summons was always answered with a bound forward of the delighted person thus chosen, who in taking, with a courtsie, to the company, her book, threw her arms round the neck of Mad^e Campan, & gave & returned a warm embrace: then again courtsied to the company, & retired, with her trophy, to her companions. The audience always applauded, with violent clapping, every presentation. This was animating: yet rendered the examination rather too much like some theatrical representation. |

All the young ladies, however, were perfectly, & even elegantly modest, as well as graceful, in their demeanour, delivering all they had to say unaffectedly & gently, & seeming bent only upon their business, not their observers. Two of them were so much frightened, that upon rising, and attempting to answer the questions put to them, they burst into tears, & were forced to be allowed to re-seat themselves, though their manner announced, their distress was the effect of diffidence, not ignorance; & the company felt this so strongly, that none of the more successful were equally applauded

During the latter part of the examination, the *recitation*, Mad^e Murat,[24] the youngest sister of the premier Consul, came into our loge, attended by the tall handsome General her husband, General Valence, & various other officers. She is extremely handsome in the Cleopatra style, with soft, fine large, languishing eyes, a fair complexion, an attractive smile, which rarely quitted her features, & a look of great good nature & softness, & very pleasure-loving eyes—Her dress was striking for elegant & becoming luxury, in the finest open worked muslin, with a veil put over one side | of her head & hanging thence down to almost the train of her gown, all of

[24] 'I found myself governess to a nestful of princesses', Mme Campan later wrote, rather happy in the fact that she did not at the time know it. The princesses-to-be, educated 'with all the other boarders, were given a refined education which fitted them to become wives and mothers . . .' See Montagu, op. cit., p. 216.

Brussels lace. I have never seen one so superb. She was extremely good natured about the young ladies, joining with great vivacity in all the applause bestowed upon them. Made Louis Buonaparte went still farther, for she seemed to interest herself in all they did, as if she was a sister to every one of them. She bears the character of being a perfectly good young woman without any species of art, coquetry, pride or love of dissipation.

I was much surprised, just as the prizes were presenting, by seeing two ladies enter just opposite us, who were called *English*, but whose appearance was not what we should have chosen to denominate *national*. One was dressed extravagantly, in a most shewey, but not at all elegant manner. She was totally *passèe*, yet had strong remains of great former beauty, but a look extremely hardy, almost to defiance: the other was a great deal older dressed like Mʳˢ Cole in the Minor,²⁵ & having a not much better or more winning appearance. Mᵈᵉ Campan desired to know how they came in, & by what Tickets? & a message came to say that Margravine d'Anspach,²⁶ happening to pass through St Germain en laye, had heard at the Auberge, of the Seminary & Examination, & had therefore come to see it. Ma*de* Campan seemed extremely surprised |

The comments I could make upon this establishment, both in its favour & against it, must be sunk, from the enormous length of this letter, which I dare not augment. I must now only add, that the return of my sister Broome to Paris enables me to send this by her, to be delivered into the hands of Mʳ

²⁵ Mrs. Cole in Samuel Foote's farce *The Minor* was 'wrapt up in flannels all over for the rheumatic'.
²⁶ The Hon. Elizabeth Berkeley (1750–1828), daughter of Augustus (1716–55), 4th Earl of Berkeley, had married in 1767 William Craven (1738–91). Suspected of adultery with, among others, the duc de Guignes (L. 514 n. 7) and eventually turned away by her husband, she went to France, settled for a time at Versailles, and thereafter pursued the colourful life of travel and adventure delineated by herself in the autobiography edited by A. M. Broadley and Lewis Melville, *The Beautiful Lady Craven* (2 vols., 1814). After her husband's death she married her lover Christian Friedrich Karl Alexander (1736–1806), margrave of Brandenburg-Anspach and Bayreuth (1769), who at that time abdicated his margravate and settled in England. Brandenburgh House, purchased *c.* 1792, and Brandenburgh theatre on the banks of the Thames, even at this late date, afforded material for the gossip-columns, and the unheralded appearance of the Margravine d'Anspach at the innocent school-closing must have caught every eye.

Merry,[27] whom she is to see for her passport back, & that I fear I have made it tiresome, from a too great desire to make it clear & full.

[The following instalment of the Journal Madame d'Arblay added in 1824 to the copy that d'Arblay had made of the original in his 'Paris Letter Book'. It was from this Letter Book, since burned in the fire in Camilla Lacey (1919), that CFBt in turn took her copy.]

While we were in the *Loge* of Bonaparte, & before the arrival[28] of the Murats, an English Map being prepared by one of the Pupils, Mad⁰ Campan, looking full at me, begun a speech with saying That a most excellent Judge of all that belonged to that country being then present, she should demand her pointed opinion of the merits of the *Carte*—& she advanced with it to the *Loge*: but I was so intolerably averse to such a public display, that I sunk back instantly out of sight, behind Mad⁰ d'Henin, who was obliged through shrugging her shoulders with amazement & dissatisfaction, to plead for my alarm, & excuse my vanishing

But when Mad⁰ Murat—afterwards Queen of Naples,[28] & the Generals Murat, Valence, &c, entered, Mad⁰ d'Henin, unwilling either to take or give place to such a personage, retired to the back of the Loge herself; while I, curious to witness all that might pass, where I saw no risk of personal publicity, returned to my seat, & continued by the side of this destined Queen during the rest of the examination: flattering myself that, if I did wrong in Etiquette, it would only be imputed to English Barbarism. ¹ We were afterwards joined by the famous Paintress Madame de Brun[29] whose picture of the

---

[27] CBFB and her daughter had left Joigny for Paris *c.* 9 Oct. 1802, and FBA, having missed that opportunity (L. 533, p. 389), later applied in her own right to Anthony Merry (L. 510 n. 13) to carry the original Journal to the court.

[28] It was in August 1808 that the Murats were set on the throne of Naples; and not until 5 June 1806 that Louis Bonaparte and Hortense were proclaimed king and queen of Holland. These dates along with the date of the Malhouet–Bélloy marriage (10 Mar. 1810) mark the later composition of the concluding pages of this Journal, which FBA herself dates as 1824.

[29] From a later vantage-point in time, FBA could recall the career of Marie-Anne-Élisabeth Vigée (1755–1842), the well-known portraitist (see also n. 20), who was married in 1776 to Jean-Baptiste-Pierre Lebrun (1748–1813), artist, art critic, and picture dealer. Fleeing for her life to Italy in 1789, she visited Turin, Rome, Naples, Florence, and Venice, travelled on in 1793 to Vienna, and two years later to St. Petersburg (where she spent five years). Received everywhere with distinction by heads of state, who were only too happy to have their portraits

unhappy & meritorious Queen of Prussia is one of the most interesting of Portraits, & was exhibited in the Grand saloon of painting a few years afterwards

At the conclusion, the assistant of Mad^e Campan desired to shew me the whole establishment, which indeed was elegantly & usefully & completely arranged. Madame Louis Bonaparte afterwards Queen of Holland[28] met us in almost every room, running about as if still une *petite ECOLINE.* Mr Jerningham joined the Musgravine of Anspach; But, as soon as the whole ceremony was concluded, & we had completely viewed the premises & the Gardens, Mad^e d'Henin took M. D'arblay & myself to the dwelling of Madame la Marechal de Beauveau,[30] widow of the Marechal: & a widow so heart-broken, from the loss of a husband she adored, that she has renounced all society, & shut herself up in a small & insignificant House, at St Germain en laye, that she may live only upon his remembrance! To the ruin caused by the Revolution she was utterly indifferent, her own views, hopes, & cares in life having lost all object that made splendour, or even comfort worth her regret. She had been, in the time of her too happy union with M. le. Marechal,[30] one of the most highly accomplished, highly gifted women: she was now very old, and—though I hate the word for such a woman, —very ugly: but as she had consented to recieve us, at the request of la Princesse d Henin, who was her niece, she dis-playcd to us an elegance of politeness that soon I wore away the

painted, she went on in 1801 to Berlin, Dresden, and other German cities, returning to Paris only in 1802. It was at this time, she states in her *Souvenirs* . . . (3 vols., 1837), iii. 350, that she completed 'Le portrait de la reine de Prusse [Louise, 1776–1810], que j'avais faite d'après Sa Majesté, à Berlin. Grand buste.'

With the wanderlust attributed to her, and perhaps with Royalist rather than Napoleonic sympathies, she was to spend the next three years in England, where she painted, among other portraits, that of the Prince Regent. See Joanna Richardson, *George IV, A Portrait* (1966), pp. 91–2.

[30] Marie-Charlotte-Sylvie de Rohan-Chabot (1729–1807), the widow of Charles-Just de Beauvau (1720–93), prince de Beauvau-Craon (1754), maréchal de France (1783), whose salon provided a genuine glimpse of the *ancienne noblesse.* See Forneron, ii. 225–6: 'La vieille dame occupait un petit appartement dans une assez chétive maison du faubourg Saint-Honoré. Les jolis meubles, derniers restes de l'ancienne splendeur, annonçaient dès l'entrée que l'on pénétrait dans un milieu où tout était noble et gracieux: la princesse était étendue dans un fauteuil à oreilles, derrière un paravent orné de peintures galantes; elle avait devant elle, sur une table en bois de rose, une boîte à effiloquer; des statuettes de Saxe, des émaux, des bonbonnières niellées couvraient la cheminée; on apportait le café dans une petite cafetière d'or. La princesse s'éteignit doucement, comme dans un sanc-tuaire, au milieu d'amis qui revenaient de tous les pays du monde pour recueillir de ses lèvres les traditions françaises de goût et de tact.'

ill impression made by the fastidious eye; & though there was no thinking her handsome, one soon looked for, & found, something better than Beauty in the benevolence & the sense of her air & conversation. Mad^e d'Henin took me to her Bed-chamber, to shew me the Picture of the late Marechal, the only thing of value his widow had retained. This charming woman— for such she proved, in defiance of ugliness, age, & unhappiness, kept us to dinner, & to spend the day, which turned out delightful, for, once having suffered her seclusion to be broken in upon, she gave herself wholly up to affording us all the entertainment in her power, &, by degrees, she enlivened not only into spirited & informing discourse, but into the most pleasing & attractive tones & manner of growing kindness. I regretted much that she did not live in Paris, for it is evident she would have honoured me with the same social & partial goodness that made so great a part of my happiness in that Capital, through the admirable niece, la Princesse d'Hénin her *spirituelle* daughter in Law, la Princesse de Poix, & her very amiable *Petit niece* la Princesse de Beauveau. Mad^e d'Henin took us in the evening, to see a small house in the forest, which had formerly been inhabited by the Marechal, as a spot for private retirement, in fine weather, with only her husband, or a very small Party. They called it *une maison anglaise*. It was plain & simple, & beautifully situated. I took leave of her with great regret—which she appeared most condescendingly to reciprocate, saying to Madame d'Henin—that if she could permit herself to love any one again, she felt as if she should take her English Friend to her own heart — — Mad^e d'Henin was gratified. General d'Arblay's Eyes had a proud lustre in them: & to me this was a speech & a kindness to make the first feature & the first pleasure of the day.

We called afterwards, at different houses, for Madame de Belloy, for M. Malhouet (who afterwards married that Lady)[28] & for the chevalier Jerningham. And, upon our return to Paris, we had the great satisfaction to meet with M. de Lally Tolendall just arrived from England, where he had lived in Emigration many years.[31] I had long & intimately had the real

---

[31] Recalling in 1824 the events of 1802, FBA seems to have forgotten the date of Lally-Tolendal's return to Paris, which was, according to the newspapers, *c.* 27 Nov. 1802.

honour of knowing him: & my best Friend had been brought up with him at *le College d'Harcourt*, at Paris. A man of more worth & honour & Patriotism I do not think exists—for he still lives—now, in 1824, when I write this little addition to my letter of 1803:[32] & for abilities, he is generally called the Cicero of France. This title he earned by his pious eloquence in redeeming the character of his injured & sacrificed father. |

530   [Monceaux, *c.* 27 July 1802]

To Mrs. Waddington

A.L.S. (rejected Diary MSS. 5614–[17], Berg), *n.d.*
Double sheet 4to   4 pp. *pmks*   P. P. PARIS   FOREIGN OFFICE
31 AU 1802   31 AU 1802   wafer
Addressed: Mrs. Waddington / Lanover Court, / Abergavenny, Monmouthshire. / Angleterre.
Sent by post, 27 July 1802
Edited by CFBt *and the* Press.

I know not by what strange fatality it happens, loving you my ever dear Marianne, as tenderly and as faithfully as I love you, that I seem destined never to begin a Letter to you but as a Culprit—Do not, however, imagine because the blame is all mine, the fault is so also; your reproaches upon my scraps of paper, & little Letters, have made me, these last 3 or 4 Years, put by writing to you, till I could build, in some sort, upon a clear Hour or two for that purpose:—& how seldom have I so much time without expected interruption!—you can hardly imagine the little leisure a *ménage* narrow as mine allows, with a Child whom I have no right to detain from school but by being myself his constant instructress. General causes, however, though constant in their effects, I must now put aside, to give you a narration of my peculiar situation, & never ending difficulties, since last October,[1] when—I am

---

[32] This was a Journal not of 1803 but of 1802. It was sent to England, according to FBA's Register of Letters, on 31 Oct. 1802.
530. [1] This letter is missing; the last extant letter to Mrs. Waddington was that of 4 Apr. 1801 (L. 410).

pained to recollect, I last wrote to you. Inconceivable is it to myself to reflect, notwithstanding all my obstacles, that it can have been so long.—Forgive it, my dear Marianne—*if possible!* I am almost hopeless of doing better, for my epistolary spirit is flown!—try, therefore, to forgive it; & to bear with me *as I am,* confident my love & friendship for you can never a moment waver;—do not, then, be hard-hearted enough to resent I am not *what I was,* or what you *would have me* — — Letter writing is become a severe task to me; & I cannot but regret the time past, when, without the hint of a reprimand, you so kindly gave me 3 or 4 Letters for one, as a thing of course. You, certainly, are now older, & have more cares. — — but I, Marianne, am I younger? or have I fewer?—

Weigh a little all this, in your moments of sweetness & kindness, not of *exigeance* & resentment, & then read, & answer, my little history. ˡ

In October, as you know, the preliminaries of peace with France were signed & published.[2] M. D'arblay, who had resisted till that epoch every wish for returning to his own country—always dearer than all things to his heart, except his Child & its Mother,—now decided upon immediately visiting it. He meant to take with him his small family, & I began my preparations,—but when I had spent a fortnight in diligent exertions to get ready, my poor little Boy was seized with a fever, which, though not of long continuance, nor, perhaps, really dangerous, left him so much Thinner & weaker, that we were both too much alarmed to suffer him to take a voyage so near as it then was to November, especially as M. D'arblay had no intention to stay above a Month or two on the Continent. It was impossible for me, you will easily conceive, to offer to leave him in so delicate a state — — in *any*, I might, perhaps say, but that I have since found, upon another trial, the contrary,—M. D'arblay therefore now settled to make an excursion of only 3 Weeks in all, merely to see his Country, his Relations—& still surviving Friends, & then to return for the rest of the winter to our Hermitage, & make a longer visit in France early in the summer, with us all. He went[3]—& you

---

[2] The Preliminaries of Peace had been ratified in Paris on 5 Oct. 1801 and in London on the 10th (see L. 423 nn. 1, 3).

[3] M. d'A set out *c.* 26 Oct. 1801 and was at Dover again *c.* 24 Jan. 1802.

will say why not then, when alone & disengaged, write me an account of such an event? — — Never was I less capable,— never! the anxiety of my mind during his absence unfitted me for every occupation, but close attendance on my Boy. First, I feared the Voyage—he did not set out till the end of october,— the winds were then in their most direful conflicts[4]—& though we had obtained, in fact, a passport for us all from Lord Pelham, by Dover—it arrived the day after M. D'arblay had set sail, while despairing of procuring it, from Gravesend.[5]—The weather was never more boisterous—& instead of seeing him return, as he meant, & as I hoped, in 3 weeks—3 weeks had separated us nearly when he got to Calais. As every leaf that shook was to me, in that period, a storm, you may suppose my solace upon my first Letter from France[6] — — Well, *then*, you cry, why not write? — — O, that was a *solace*, it is true, but not ease! not peace!—how he might be received in Paris— after an exile so long—you have, I am sure, an imagination to fully paint | the various evils my doubts pictured to myself, if you will give it leave to dwell a while upon the subjects of uneasiness open at such a crisis. A fortnight elapsed ere I had any intelligence at all; the posts not being settled, I could only hear by chance conveyances; & nothing very explicit could be written, so that I was kept in a most restless suspence as to his situation, till—at the very moment I was expecting his return, after various unaccounted for delays, he desired Mr. Lock to come to me, & prepare me for receiving the tydings of his re-entering his profession,[7] & — — instead of returning to his Hermitage, — — setting sail for the West Indies according to his rank in the Army!—I leave you to judge my feelings— I could not trust myself to them in my now abandoned solitude, & I flew, therefore, with my Boy, to seek refuge from lonely terror & sorrow in the bosoms of my faithful & sympathising friends, with whom I kept alive my shaken existence for about 3 weeks, & whose tender consolations are engraven upon my heart, & were doubly enabled to sustain me, from my conviction of their full knowledge & appreciation of the value of that safety which I thought endangered:—January of this Year was

---

[4] See Ll. 438, 442 for the storms.   [5] See L. 437, pp. 27–9.
[6] L. 441, dated 7 Nov. 1801, which Fanny received on the 12th (see L. 443).
[7] See M. d'A's letter to William Locke of 2 Jan. 1802 (L. 471 n. 1) and Locke's reply of the 12th (L. 472 n. 4).

just closing, in these dark scenes, when one morning, at 8 o'clock, Mrs. Lock, in her Bed Gown & night Cap, came suddenly to my Apartment, breathless with a Joy that brightened every feature of her fine face, & told me Mr. Lock had that moment opened a Letter from M. D'arblay,[8] to acquaint him a new turn in his affairs had changed his measure, & he was relinquishing St. Domingo for England!—My beloved Mr. Lock, in his powdering Gown, & half shaved, followed, to congratulate & embrace me—& my sweet Amelia—then heavily carrying the lovely little Girl[9] she now nurses, threw herself out of bed, & hurried to me in her night clothes, to pour forth her soft participation in my revival in my rooms.— Augusta—Mrs. Charles—Mr. William his wife—all the house followed, in affectionate succession; &, to crown this morning's recompense of so many Weeks of suffering, a pacquet of no less than 7 Letters were delivered to me,[10] which various accidents had withheld till they arrived all together, con-firming to me, from M. D'arblay, ׀ the intelligence so much covetted. — — Yet thus relieved, & in this joy, you will cry, you did not write? — No, I could not, — I was in joy, in thankfulness, — but I had not a moment to spare, — I scarcely breakfasted at Norbury Park, before I abruptly left it, to pre-pare my deserted home for its expected Master. In a few days he arrived — & we only spent a few more together, — amongst the shortest of my life — when we left our Cottage to see my Father & Brethren — &, in less than a week, while we were at Dr. Charles's at Greenwich[11]—a Letter arrived from abroad, acquainting M. d'A[rblay] the conditions which he had exacted, but which had been refused, were now granted[12] — — & that he had only to prepare himself for his embarkation.— I will not attempt to write you one word upon this sudden reverse—all pleading against it was ineffectual—the acceptance was deemed a point of honour, & a dismal 10 Days[13] were devoted to procuring passports, making purchases of Linnen, Bedding, Weapons, &c &c—fitted for hot climates, & — — in

---

[8] This letter is missing.

[9] Caroline Angerstein, born 25 Mar. 1802; and for other member of the Locke family, see L. 472 n. 2.

[10] The packet of seven letters probably included Ll. 466 to 470.

[11] The d'Arblays arrived at Greenwich *c.* 3 Feb. 1802. M. d'A left for France on the 15th; FBA, for Chelsea, on the 21st.

[12] See L. 489.   [13] M. d'A had set out on 15 February.

the middle of February, I was again widowed—though not till
I had offered to leave even my Boy—to his Uncle Charles's
care—& go myself to St Domingo — — This crowded Sheet
shall now be packed off, & I will *try* to send you another as
soon as I hear this is received—I dare not promise—yet I think
I may—

I won't ask you to send me your free pardon till I have
communicated all I have to urge in my *excuse*—I won't say
justification, except of my faithful & ever affectionate regard—&
friendship—to which witness my hand & seal

F D'Arblay

Don't forget to pay the Inland Post, to Dover.—
Direct for me, Rue de Miromenil, Faubourg St. honoré,
Hôtel Marengo, à Paris.
We are not there, but it a safe address, whence our Letters
are forwarded. ǀ

I earnestly beg to know how you do, & your dear Children—
& never be so naughty again as to let your opinion of my
affection hang upon my punctuality—fie! fie! fie! be kinder,
my dear Marianne, & more just.

531

[Monceaux], 1 August 1802

To Charlotte Cambridge

L., typescript extracts (grangerized *DL*, 25th or Supp. vol., pp. 60–3,
NPG) taken from M. d'A's 'Paris Letter Book' and printed in *FB & the
Burneys*, pp. 68–71. The original was sent by post 20 Aug. 1802.
The text following is taken from FB & the Burneys.

August 1st, 1802.

I must now come to ourselves beginning with the little boy
you and my dear Sally[1] so kindly take to your hearts. Alas, my
dear friends, he is not yet re-established into anything like

531. [1] Sarah Baker (i, L. 10 n. 6).

permanent health! he has had another fever since I wrote last, and though it is now over, for I could not, and I would not have written while it existed—it is his 4th attack within 4 months! and the little flesh he gains upon every recovery is always shrunk away upon every relapse. How discouraging, how distressing this is, I need not say.—I cannot!—Yet he is so well between every attack, that all around me think my fears mere maternal exagerations, till a sudden seizure shews what too—too just reason I have for apprehension. The dear little soul also has spirits that deceive all but myself into a belief of his security; but I know well they make no part of his health, since neither sickness, nor fever, nor weakness rob him of them, except during the time of immediate pain. I am often told this is a critical year, his eigth,—and that when he has turned it, his constitution may radically strengthen. I am sure your kind prayers, and my kind Sally's[1] will join yours that this may be granted us. Amen! Amen!

I have told you we have been to Joigny, and as I know the kind interest you will feel upon the subject of that visit, I shall put aside other more general matters, to give you some account of it.

The Town, built upon the side of a high hill, or rather mountain, is full of scrambling, narrow, ill-built, and worse paved up and down streets. Here and there, the prospect[s], especially from the heights of the houses, are fine in the extreme; but this is the good fortune of the favoured very few. I saw nowhere a view so beautiful as from the house in which M. D'Arblay was born. It is still inhabited by a relation of the family, a distant cousin, Mdlle. Chollet,[2] an ancient virgin of the most courteous manners, with which she mixes a degree of

---

[2] Marie-Anne-Julie Chollet (1731–1821), demoiselle de Bèze. The daughter of Louis Chollet (d. 1759), sieur de Bèze, avocat au parlement, lieutenant général au Baillage, prévôt de Joigny, bailli de Villiers sur Tholin, she was well known in her day for her good works, social activity, and hospitality.
Colonel Pierre Bertiaux of Joigny, to whom the editors are deeply indebted for his identifications of the residents of Joigny appearing in the d'Arblay papers, is of the opinion that the house in which M. d'A was born must have been 'le château de Joigny, dont le Gouverneur, un Piochard de la Bruslerie, était un oncle de Piochard d'Arblay'. There, the records in the chapel seem to suggest, 'le jeune ménage Piochard-d'Arblay/Bazille a dû resider au moins quelque temps', and the Colonel is inclined to think that 'malgré la Révolution, qui à Joigny même n'a pas été sanglante, Mlle Chollet a continué à habiter le château, autorisée par le nouveau propriétaire, un Mr. Picard, qui n'avait rien d'un farouche sans-culotte'.

dignity that ensures her receiving as much good breeding as she bestows. She perfectly remembers M. D'Arblay's Father,[3] who has been dead these 40 years, and she invited me to a meeting of 20 of his cousins, that I might dine with all that remained of him, in the very room in which my mate was born. She gave us a noble repast, and a dessert fit for an Emperor's Table. We would have scolded, but she said it was *le diner de noces*, and promised *to do so no more*. We saw here many curious family portraits, but all that had had, in the old style, the family arms painted in the corner, had that part either cut out, or pasted over! This precaution had been taken in the reign of Rob. to preserve not merely the pictures but the lives of those who were so hardy as to possess them!

As Mr. D'Ar. was the only son of an only son, all the cousins are very distant, though my Alex, upon hearing this remarked, innocently exclaimed: 'Distant? how can they be my distant cousins, when they are all so near me?' It is singular that amongst the whole tribe, though there are almost countless children, not one from the principal stock, bearing the old family real name, Piochard, has a rising male. Our Alex is the last and the only one existing. Perhaps 'tis from instinct he has so prodigious a desire to be Papa to all those hundreds of children he enumerated to you and your Cornelia![4]

To have done, however, with these *distants* on the male side, let me come to the more interesting near ones on the female. M. Bazille brother to the mother of Mr. D'Ar. answered all my expectations, both in character and kindness, though he disappointed them by his feebleness and infirmities. He is a man of high and honourable sentiments and conduct, strikingly gentlemanlike in his person and his manners, and to a deep and sagacious judgment, joining a dry pleasantry extremely entertaining, which he communicates with a sort of arch gravity, that for a while, makes his listener in doubt whether he is in jest or in earnest. He doats upon his nephew,—not one of his children can be dearer to him, and his kindness to him

---

[3] M. d'A's father Pierre Piochard (*c.* 1702–7 Apr. 1761), sieur d'Arblay, an artillery officer, chevalier de Saint-Louis, is buried in the église Saint Thibault, Joigny. For the family tree, see the Genealogical Table, vi.

[4] Charlotte Cambridge (i, L. 1 n. 6) and her sister-in-law Cornelia (iv, L. 311 n. 5), the wife of the Revd. George Cambridge, had visited FBA at West Humble on Friday 25 Sept. 1801, when Alex was about seven years old.

and to *his* was so great, that he wanted us to settle with him during the whole of our stay in this Country. This, however, was impossible, as Mr. D'Ar. has still a pursuit, urged on by his friends in Paris, which he thinks right to follow up. We shall, return nevertheless to Joigny in about a fortnight to spend there the time of les *vendanges.* Mdme. Bazille, wife of this dear and worthy Gentleman, is one of the most excellent, nay, exemplary characters I have ever met with. Every thought and every hour of her life are devoted to the service of others. To see the use she is of to her husband, whom she quite adores, you would think she had not a moment for anyone else; yet to see what she does and contrives for each and all her children, would make you conclude, next, that they alone employed her. For her domestics, her house, her guests, you may almost say the same. I can hardly tell you how much I love and admire her; yet I could never make her believe either; for amongst her perfections is that of humility, which characterizes to herself every exertion and every task as a simple duty, culpable to withhold, but not laudable to fulfil.

I must now say adieu, entreating you to remember me to all your house, and singularly to our revered Mrs. Boscawen;[5] and let her know all she has the goodness to desire hearing of my affairs. My reception in this country has been the most flattering possible, as far as I have been able to see of it: and I have kept out of the way of all those whose civility could only have shocked or worried me.

532   Monceaux and Passy,
                         August—22 November 1802

To Mrs. Waddington

A.L.S. (rejected Diary MSS. 5618–21, Berg), Aug.-22 Nov. 1802
Double sheet 4to   4 pp.
Taken to England by James Greene, 23 Nov. 1802.
Edited by CFBt *and the* Press.

5 The Hon. Mrs. Boscawen, who since 1787 had resided at Rosedale, which, situated between Richmond and Kew, is now part of the Richmond Royal Hospital. See *Admiral's Widow,* p. 120; also iii *passim.*

August 1802
N° 286 Rue Cisalpine à Monceaux,
Paris

Mr. Green[1] has this moment left me—& I have been so much touched by his account of your illness, & of your real & serious concern at my silence,—& so deeply shocked by his hinting you had suspected it to spring from coldness, or changed regard,—that it has forced me from every other call & occupation to take my pen to my dear Marianne—ever & inalterably dear—to entreat her, once more, to forgive me, & to beg & supplicate her never, never again to suffer so false a notion to make her unjust to us both. Both, I say—for I must see a change—a great one, in You, ere I could FEEL one in myself. Write me word, then, that you shake hands & heart again— that you hope I shall never try you so hardly in future—but that, should my terrible disease prove incurable, you will be angry—& scold—but never turn a defect, that is the offspring of a bad habit, into a crime, the result of native inconstancy;— an Abomination of which I am so incapable, that Those whom I have once loved have always & invariably a hold upon my kindness—even where, —as twice in my connexions it has

532. [1] This visit of August, in which James Greene (L. 517 n. 1), presumably on his arrival in Paris, had given accounts of Mrs. Waddington of Llanover, may have marked his first visit to Passy and FBA's first introduction to him. By 22 November, when she had found an opportunity to complete and send her reply to GMAPW, the acquaintance had improved (see pp. 388–9) and Greene was entrusted not only with the above letter to GMAPW, but also with the 2nd and 3rd double sheets of the Journal (No. 517) and the letter of 22–23 Nov. (533), both addressed to CB.

Having been served with a writ by the Court of Chancery, Greene departed on 27 November via Dieppe and Brighton ('as being cheapest') for London, but, learning *en route* that the examination was postponed, he set off for a visit to Monmouthshire, returning to the Royal Hotel, Pall Mall, on Thursday 9 December, too late for the hearing, which was then postponed to the 11th. One suit in question was that of Edward Frere (1770–1844), the wealthy husband of Greene's eldest daughter Mary Anne (1780–1846), *v*. Greene or *v*. a son lately born to Mrs. Greene, named William Owen Brigstocke, who, if proved illegitimate, would as such be excluded from the legal inheritance of Greene's considerable properties and fortune. For his five legitimate daughters, and adulterous wife, see L. 542 n. 8.

While in the Hotel Royal he was served an additional writ, this time by the Court of the Exchequer, requiring him to appear as defendant in suits pressed by a group of small debtors, for, as Professor Edward A. and Lillian D. Bloom explain (vii, L. 751 n. 3 and L. 788 nn. 2, 3), Greene, with assets at his death amounting to £250,000, resisted paying numbers of small debts totalling a few thousand pounds. Required to appear at the Court on 24 Jan. 1803 and plead on 7 February, he must nevertheless have made a short visit to Paris between 18 Dec. 1802 and 24 Jan. 1803, for according to FBA (L. 518, p. 1) he had on 20 Jan. 1803 carried a letter for her to England. It is not until 7 March that we hear of him again (see L. 540).

unfortunately happened, I have believed them to have for-
feited any claim to it. I must drop this unpleasant subject—
I feel a sincere [|] regret that I permitted any impediment to
cause you a moment's uneasiness:—& I will now put this hasty,
but heartfelt mark of contrition apart till I hear of the arrival of
my long Epistle.

Novr 22^d My dearest Marianne's kind & soothing Letter has
not reached me till this Month,[2]—it waited, by mistake, my
return to Paris from Joigny, where we have spent our Autumn.
Cordially I thank you for renewing your ancient style, of
confidence &—I fear ⟨!⟩—ill-merited but dear & welcome
partiality. Can you, indeed, retain it with the warmth that
animates the conclusion of your Letter, in defiance of absence,
other scenes, varying life, & separating connexions? To Me all
these are nothing in the scale of remembered affection, which
always outweighs whatever vainly attempts to counterpoise it.
Keep alive the kind feeling, my dear Marianne; since you are
capable of such constancy, take at least the reward of knowing
how it knits to you forever one of your earliest friends, one the
most intimately acquainted with your affairs, & the first
entrusted with your juvenile bosom feelings. This is a species of
Friendship rarely supplied if broken, & never to be relinquished without regret. Your prayer, at the end of your Letter,[2]
for our restoration to the society of each other, was extremely
touching to me; & the more, as it satisfies my Mind you had
never, *au fond*, believed in that estrangement on my part of
which you only, I trust, accused me, to accelerate my amendment of my *real* offence,—omission.—That is heavy enough!—
Tell me I have divined you. You will give me real pleasure, in
doing me, there, but real justice. I have too much contempt of
caprice, & abhorrence of instability in attachment, to rest
quietly under their stigma from one I love. Tell me, also, &
very fully, to what it is [|] You allude in saying 'you have heard
something that you hope is 'untrue',—You ask me to unravel
the mystery, & I am wholly in the dark what it may be, or
belong to. Pray do not forget to write your intelligence, or
suggestions, more clearly, & then I will not fail to satisfy them
explicitly. I should like much you should meet with Lady Lucy

[2] The Waddington letters are missing for the reasons explained in Intro., i,
p. xxii.

Foley,[3] who is a truly charming woman, unaffected in her manners, unassuming in her character, & zealous in her friendships & attachments, with excellent good sense, & invariable good nature. I earnestly wish Capt. Foley may deserve her.

I always sincerely thank you for writing to me about your children, for I always feel you know I must love them when you do it, & that you know why. Your Fanny must be a treasure, your Emily a delight. What will your Augusta be? Poor little Thing! how I wish for better news of her![4] Yet how literally might I say, as a French officer, M. de Meulan,[5] lately did to me, when my Alex was indisposed 'Dès que j'entend que M. Alex se porte mal, je meurs d'envie d'avoir des nouvelles de sa mere. — '

We have been much pleased with Mr. Green; both M. d'Arblay & myself find him of easy intercourse, amiable in his manners, & fraught with anecdote & intelligence, that neither hang back with reserve, nor obtrude themselves with forwardness. He seems a good discriminator—which always makes a good Converser. I have only one fault to find with him—he has so rooted an aversion to a certain friend of mine, that he is never so happy as in finding opportunities to utter sarcasms against her, & in declaring he thinks her made up of every defect & abomination of which poor human nature is susceptible. I know not whether he abuses her most mentally or personally, but 'tis certainly a terrible antipathy, for it seems to occupy his heart, head, & imagination at once. |

I have no recollection of the *Grey of the Mountains*, & Lady Clarges,[6] to which you have more than once alluded.

[3] Lady Lucy Anne Fitzgerald (iii, L. 175 n. 3), sister of Lord Edward (1763–98), daughter of the dowager Duchess of Leinster (1731–1814), and sister-in-law of Charles Locke (iii, L. 177 n. 4). On 31 July 1802 Lady Lucy had married Sir Thomas Foley (1757–1833) of Ridgeway, Pembrokeshire, and as he had estates in Abermarlais, Carmarthenshire, FBA hoped that his proximity in Wales might lead to a meeting. At this time flag-captain of the *Elephant* (see *DNB*), he was promoted to the rank of rear-admiral (1808) and was commander-in-chief in the Downs when FBA landed at Dover in 1812. Vice-admiral in 1812, he was gazetted admiral in 1825.

[4] Frances and Emelia Waddington were now aged 11 and 8 respectively. Augusta was born on 21 Mar. 1802.

[5] Marie-Joseph-Théodore de Meulan (1778–1832), comte de Meulan (1818), maréchal de camp (1817), an officer in high favour with Louis Bonaparte, whom FBA met at Joigny. Meulan was to marry in 1814 Alexandrine-Louise-Élisabeth-Lancelot de Turpin-Crissé (d. 1846).

[6] Louisa Skrine (1760–1809), who had married in 1777 Sir Thomas Clarges (1751–82), 3rd Baronet (1759). She was a devotee of Pacchierotti, and part of her

Mr. Green will tell you what a mighty pretty small house M. d'A. has purchased at Passy, a village about 2 miles out of Paris.[7] We still adhere to our plan of residence in England, but M. d'A. has many incentives to make France his place of frequent abode, &, for that purpose, & others, he deems it right to establish himself as a French Citizen before our departure. Terrible have been his disappointments in all his expectations here, of a pecuniary sort—but they have not, I bless God, soured his Temper, or affected my happiness; & our home, therefore, with all its wants & privations, is such as I would change for no other. I trust I might here speak in the plural number—I should be far indeed, *else*, from the power of so speaking in the singular! — — — Pray beg your good little Fanny to send me a new Cutting by Mr. Green, who gives us hopes we may see him again in a Month. To what may be owing what you hint as to the distaste of your Children? I live here a most retired life, but purpose, this winter, to see Paris as completely as I am able. My dear Boy's frequent illnesses have hitherto prevented my making any engagements that could separate me, even a moment, from his side. I must make him *declaim* to Mr. Green, that Mr. G. may carry a flourishing account of him to Fanny & Emily. He interests himself warmly about them, since he has seen the Cuttings, especially of the skipping ropes.[8] I hear extremely good news from Norbury Park, & from Chelsea, which greatly contribute to keep me tranquil at this distance.

Adieu—How happy I shall be to hear a better account of you!—& of your poor youngest darling.—Ever, & with faithful affection,

dearest Marianne—
Yours F d'A

My Comp[ts]. to Mr W.

lively correspondence with SBP on that subject is extant (see *Catalogue*). Lady Clarges had the skills of the age in singing and playing, but no composition of hers by this or any other name has been found.

[7] See L. 536, pp. 398–9.

[8] Cuttings like these, executed, presumably by the young Waddingtons, in silhouette on white paper, are extant in the Berg Collection. See iv, L. 410 n. 2.

[54, rue Basse, Passy],
22–23 November 1802

To Doctor Burney

A.L. (Berg), 22–23 Nov. 1802
Single sheet 4to 2 pp.
Addressed: Dr. Burney, / Chelsea College, / Middlesex—
Taken to England by James Greene, 24 Nov. 1802
Docketed: 14
Edited by FBA, p. 1, *annotated*: ⊰ Passy (22) Characters of M. & Mᵉ.
Bazile
NB. This exemplary Woman died the following year—

Novʳ 22ᵈ 1802.

It is so long since I have written to, or heard from, my dearest Padre, that I will wait no longer for opportunities of private hands, but seize the only sure & always open mode of the public post. ⌐I hope you have received safely my Nᵒ 6¹ & entreat you will not fail, if you may be ⟨ill⟩, to let me know.¬ I Thank God I hear frequent accounts of my dearest Father's good looks, & chearing spirits, sweet & reviving, as of old, to all around him.² 'Tis impossible to say with what joy I always receive this essential intelligence.

The Charlottes will have told you the provoking circumstance by which I missed sending my dispatches by them, but I the less regret it, as they were couriers who could supply them so completely. Indeed my whole intended history of *les vendanges* is nullified by their presence, for one viva voce account of a scene of that sort is worth a thousand written narratives.³

533. ¹ FBA's Nᵒ 6 and Nᵒ 5 are missing. The last extant (or at least, known) letter to her father is L. 525 (16 July 1802), marked by her, Nᵒ 4.
² Cf. Maria Edgeworth's account of her father's impression of CB, whom he met at Mrs. Crewe's villa in Hampstead on 21 June 1805: 'He was charmed with old Dr. Burney, who at eighty-two was the most lively, well-bred, agreeable man in the room. Lord Stanhope . . . thought him the most wonderful man he ever met' (*Life*, i. 152).
³ Mrs. Broome and her daughter Charlotte Francis, arriving in Paris *c*. 13 August, had visited with the d'Arblays at Joigny, and returning to Paris *c*. 9 October, arrived in London on the 22nd. Mrs. Broome's 'thank-you' letter (Eg. 3693, ff. 78–9*b*), dated 'hotel de Mirango', Sunday 10 October, makes acknowledgement of the kindness of a wide range of M. d'A's relatives in Joigny.

They could paint, [in] living colours, the worth, virtues, amiability & hospitality of [the inestima]ble Uncle & Aunt of M. D'Arblay, who are indeed amongst [the best of h]uman beings, & so happily adapted to each other, that [they] unite, between them, almost every excellence. Her character, calm & gentle, corrects his, which is warm & irritible, while his unbounded generosity, & quick sensibility, are kept from excess by the quietness of her prudence, & the sanity of her judgement. She devotes herself compleatly to the care of his health, his fortune, his family, & his affairs; while, in return, it is evident to us the World would be nothing to him without her.— This is always a beautiful—but fearful sight! — — — though this last epithet might not have saddened the first, but for their present situation; we have had news of this excellent woman having been taken extremely ill since we left Joigny, & though she is now better, she is not re-established, if recovered.[4] ⌐As I am sure my dearest Father will feel interested where happiness hangs upon such worth, I shall not close my Letter till we have further intelligence. ⌐

Nov. 23ᵈ
We have had good news of dear Mʳˢ Bazile—my dearest Father—& this moment enters a gentleman Mr. Green,[5] who is so kind as to take what I have ready for England. The Lord bless my beloved Father—
he cannot wait for more — —⌐

---

⁴ Mme Bazille had less than a year to live (see vi, L. 555 n. 1).
⁵ See L. 532 n. 1.

534 [54, rue Basse], Passy,
23 November 1802

M. d'Arblay, with a PS. by
Madame d'Arblay
To Charles Burney

A.L.S. & PS. (John Comyn, grangerized *DL* (1842–6), v. 29), 23 Nov.
1802
Double sheet 4to 2 pp. *pmks* EPSOM 3 DEC 1802 3 DE 1802
wafer mended
Addressed: Dr Charle Burney / Greenwhich / Kent—
Taken to England 24 Nov. 1802 *and posted by* James Greene.

[*By M. d'Arblay*]

Passy ce 23 November 1802
My dearest Charles
In spite of my certainly *improved in Worse* blunders, I cannot
refrain my sending you a true & most fraternal love, and many
many thanks for your dear little notes & even for the long
letter you had intention to finish & we had the misfortune not
to receive. Your Mr Boissonade[1] to whom I carried the letter
very late, though not so much the time it arrived being considered, told me it was perfectly useless, because he had received
one other of fresher date. As to the manuscript, Mrs Broome,
being gone, I did not know how to forward it to you. However
I hope the bearer of this note will be able to take it, & with that
hope I remain of you and yours the sincerest friend
A. d'arblay

Though I am lame, I shall scrawl to Paris in order to fetch
the Manuscript. If I find myself totally disabled to walk, I
shall Ride for my fifteen pence go & fro M. Boissonade |

[*By Madame d'Arblay*]

Heaven bless you, dearest Charles
1000 thanks for the Books — — |

534. [1] The Greek scholar Jean-François Boissonade (1774–1857) was transcribing
for CB Jr. the *Lexicon Technologicum* of the seventh-century grammarian, Philemon,

[54, rue Basse] Passy,
                                                                    November 1802

To Charlotte Cambridge

L., typescript extracts (grangerized *DL*, 25th or supp. vol., pp. 81–6,
NPG), taken from M. d'A's 'Paris Letter Book' and printed in *FB & the
Burneys*, pp. 84–8. The original was sent to England by James Greene on
23 Nov. 1802.
A passage (the typescript copy of which was edited and printed as a footnote in
FB & the Burneys, p. 84) *evidently made part of FBA's editorial annotation of the
Letter Book (see n. 2 below).*
*Additional annotations, characteristic of FBA's editorial work, are also preserved
in the typescript and printed in* FB & the Burneys *(loc. cit.):*
    To Miss Cambridge. Passy. Death of Mr. Cambridge and character;
Joigny; Louis Buonaparte; Troops met repairing from Joigny to join the
invading army of England at Boulogne.

*Evidently FBA had added, perhaps while still in France, her further recollections
of Louis Buonaparte (printed, pp. 395–6).*
The text following is taken from FB & the Burneys.

                                                            Passy, Novr 1802.

What kindness is yours, my dear, valuable friend, to think of
me again so soon at such a period! That you should be sure of
my deep interest in this awful event,[1] and in you, and its
consequences, cannot surprise me, but that you should expand
your feelings so generously to the care of mine, so immediately
after your great personal trial, touches me extremely.[2]

the manuscript of which made part of the Bibliothèque de Coislin in the Bibliothèque Nationale. CB Jr.'s edition of this work was to appear in 1812.
    Boissonade had informed Charles in a letter of 26 October that he planned to
send the second part of his transcription by James Greene (L. 532 n. 1), the first part
having already been sent by John Cleaver Banks (L. 524 n. 3). Boissonade was living
at this time at 541, Boulevard Montmartre, about 4 miles from Passy. See CB Jr.'s
correspondence (*Catalogue*).

535. [1] The death of Richard Owen Cambridge on 17 Sept. 1802, aged 85. See
D. Altick, *Richard Owen Cambridge: Belated Augustan* (Philadelphia, 1941); and for
FBA's curious friendships with the Cambridges, see *HFB passim*.
    [2] At a later date FBA appears to have added the following footnote: 'This
alludes to the death of Miss Cambridge's father, Richard Owen Cambridge, Esq.,
author of *A History of India*, of *Martinus Scriblius the Second*, of sundry gay pieces of
poetry, and of many of the best papers in *The World*. He was a man of excellent
parts, and peculiar talents: his understanding was as deep as his fancy was playful,
and the solid worth of his character equalled the rare entertainment of his conversation. With him, and with Mrs. Delany, and with Dr. Johnson, I had the high

PLATE II

Rue de Miroménil and the Hôtel de Beauvau

A view of Passy

From a drawing by Le Veau

Who indeed, if not I, can know how to appreciate your loss. What a friend he was to me! for several years of my life I owed many, very many of my most pleasant hours to his society, which he bestowed upon me with a partial kindness, nay I may say eagerness, never to be rooted from my memory or my gratitude. . . .

. . . In the innumerable conversations with which he indulged me he opened to me, not only most of his intentions, but as far as subjects occurred, all his most private opinions, both of persons and things; interspersing his admirable discourse with anecdotes not only of his own life, but of almost all the persons with whom either design or accident had led him to mix. What a fund of delight and instruction, insensibly yet invariably mingled, did his society afford me! and with what partial sweetness did he accept from me the smallest returns! The day rarely passes, the week never, in which I do not recollect with use as well as pleasure, some notion, maxim, or counsel that dropt from his lips. I lost him from the time I left my home for the Q[ueen's] H[ouse], and it was one of the deprivations, exacted by circumstances, which I always the most lamented. . . .

. . . Heaven rest his soul!—Amen! How sweet to hope it may already have met your loved sister's.

We are fixed at Passy, a village just out of Paris,[3] for the rest of our sojourn. We have but just come to it from Joigny,[4] where we spent 6 weeks, this last time, with the dear and most excellent uncle and aunt of M. d'Arblay. Worthier or more amiable people never existed, nor can the fondest father more tenderly love a son than this uncle loves his nephew. They would fain have persuaded him to pass the winter, or rather, to *fix* at Joigny; but sundry reasons prevented his listening to the first part of the request, and I need not tell you what—or who operated against the second. You will be glad for me, I am sure, that I shall not spend the winter in Paris. Neither that nor London suits me for long residence; and my taste for the

honour to become the reigning favourite of their latter days from the time of the discovery of the authorship of Évelina and with all three, I had the infinite happiness of being treated as their bosom friend and confident to their last hours. What of pride, gratitude and joy did I not owe to them! and what, in succession, of grief at their loss!' (See *FB & the Burneys*, p. 84.)

[3] The house that the d'Arblays had acquired *c.* 5 Oct. 1802 at 54, rue Basse, Passy, FBA is to describe in full in her letter (L. 536) to Margaret Planta.

[4] 'We settled ourselves at Passy the last day or so of October.' See L. 544, p. 436.

Country is happily most compleatly participated in by my mate; while for our Boy it is truly & literally essential. We are so near, however, to this famed & gay Capital, that with the potent arm of my Knight errant, I can reach it in an Hour, upon my own dear independent terms i.e. feet.

While we were at Joigny, the youngest Brother of the Premier Consul, Colonel Louis Bonaparte,[5] whose regiment is quartered there made it a fortnight's visit, and we had the pleasure of frequently seeing him.

You will not be sorry to hear that he was extremely polite, nay flattering in his behaviour to M. d'Arblay, nor that he desired in the most gratifying manner, to have his English mate introduced to him, coming immediately himself to our residence for that purpose: and neither you nor Sally,[6] will be very angry with him, when I add that he was peculiarly kind to our little man whom he noticed and caressed with striking distinction. Alex was by no means insensible to this goodness. From the moment he heard his name, he surveyed him with a mixture of awe and curiosity very comical; and after the Colonel's first caress, he flew, jumping, to me exclaimed 'O Mama! I've a great secret to tell you! Bonaparte's Brother has kissed me!—he has indeed! But you must not tell it! for it's a great secret.'—'And why, my dear must not I tell it!'— 'Because Mama . . . for fear people should think I'm boasting.'

[5] Here the copyist, presumably following FBA's editorial work, supplied the superscript 1 and the footnote: '1 Afterwards King of Holland'.

Louis Bonaparte (1778–1846) is referred to in the Army Records (Vincennes) not as a colonel at this time, but as 'Capitaine, chef de Brigade, commandant du 5ᵉ reg't des Dragons', which regiment had been sent in May 1801 to Portugal to carry out the conquest planned by Bonaparte. By the time Louis arrived in Lisbon, a treaty of peace had been concluded with France. Quartered for a time in Portugal, the regiment had arrived in Joigny in January or February 1802. Inspected by General Ney and badly needing refitting, it was allowed to remain in Joigny until 1804 before being moved. Though fond of his men and much liked by them, Louis himself was ordered to the camp at Boulogne, where, promoted on 24 Mar. 1803 from chef to général de brigade, he was to be employed in the 2nd division of dragoons.

Generally gentle and sympathetic in his dealings with people, he was extraordinarily jealous of anyone close to Napoleon. His marriage to Hortense de Beauharnais (L. 529 n. 4), which had taken place on 3 Jan. 1802, brought his misogynic tendencies to the fore (see Ernest Jones, 'The Case of Louis Bonaparte, King of Holland', *The Journal of Abnormal Psychology*, iii, Dec. 1913–Jan. 1914, 289–301. His son Napoléon-Charles was born on 10 Oct. 1802.

[6] Here FBA had presumably supplied the superscript 2 and the footnote: '2 Miss Sarah Baker'. The conclusion ('N.B.—The following year . . . to simple threats.') she apparently added at a later date—probably in 1824 to the copy that M. d'A had made of her letter in his Paris Letter Book.

This Colonel appears to be of a truly Gentlemanly character, modest, sensible, reserved, and well bred; generally silent, speaking only to the purpose, yet entirely unassuming, decorous and gentle. He chose to be considered simply as the Commandant of his Regiment, without seeming ever to recollect or ever to know his peculiar claims of further distinction. I had much conversation with him, during his short stay at Joigny, for whereever I had the pleasure to meet with him, he constantly, either before or after his card party, took a seat by my side. I had great reason to regret his departure, for I was as much pleased with the good sense of his discourse, as surprised by the graceful simplicity of his manners, & gratified by his personal attentions. He is but 23. . . .

[It was probably in 1824 that Madame d'Arblay added the following section to the copy that M. d'Arblay had made of the first part of this letter in his Paris Letter Book]

N.B.—The following year, when we returned to make our annual visit to our dear Uncle Bazille, we were met by a troop of Horse about 10 miles from Joigny. Soon afterwards, we were accosted by one of the Officers, M. de Meulan,[7] a gaily amiable man, of our intimate acquaintance; and he informed us that the *Colonel Louis* was coming on, heading his Regiment,[8] which was just obeying orders to repair to Boulogne,[9] to join in the expedition then planned of invading England.[9] I was so totally overset, overwhelmed with grief and alarm at this

[7] Marie-Joseph-Théodore de Meulan (L. 532 n. 5).
[8] According to the Army Records, not the 5ᵉ, which was left at Joigny, but in the 2ᵉ division de dragons (Baraguev d'Hilliers). See n. 5; and Six.
[9] Bonaparte was at this time assembling a spectacular camp at Boulogne for a projected invasion of England. To comprise before September 1803 five divisions of 50,000 men each, the Camp was particularly remarkable for the elegance and the solidity of its construction. 'Chacun de ces camps, percés de rues spacieuses alignées au cordeau, resemblait plûtot à une ville qu'à une réunion de troupes.' The French soldiers, noted for their ability to make a camp a home, had planted trees, lawns, and brightly flowering gardens. Nor were formal ornaments wanting, 'des colonnes, des pyramides, des obélisques, des statues en argile et des groupes allégoriques se trouvaient placés de distance en distance'. See Albert Chatelle, *Napoléon et la Légion d'Honneur au Camp de Boulogne (1801–1805)* (1956), pp. 41 ff., for the extent of the camp and illustrations of it.
Transports (of the flat-bottomed type) were built by the thousands to convey this, the first of Napoleon's Grand Armies, to England, but anticipating the formation of the Third Coalition, which was concluded between Britain and Austria in August, Napoleon decided on 24 July 1805 to march his troops from the coast towards Germany, and further plans for the Boulogne flotilla were discouraged by the battle of Trafalgar (21 Oct. 1805).

intelligence and at the melancholy circumstances of entering the Birth place of my beloved Husband at the moment it was being evacuated for so hostile and terrific a project against my own adored country, that I could not answer nor speak to M. de Meulan, nor yet hold up my head to look at the Colonel, (for only such he still was,) when, in passing us, he bowed, M. D'Arblay told me, with marked distinction. M. de Meulan had acquainted him who we were: and, indeed, he probably knew our Uncle's Calesh, which had been sent to meet us at Senlis. He did not, M. d'Arblay informed me, appear either surprized or hurt at my avoidance of his salutation: the idea of his Brother's infallibility in arms made him naturally surmize that such a *rencontre* must give rise to the most painful alarm; and the general opinion that universal conquest was both the aim and the destiny of Buonaparte, must forcibly have explained both my depression, and my averseness to the sight of his Brother just accoutred for hostility, and heading a Regiment ordered forth to the Battles of Invasion. No one was more prone than myself to believe in the invulnerability of Great Britain; but it was not upon that spot, and at that period that the menaced attack could be viewed with composure; for upon that spot I had met with kindnesses, and formed connections, to make my Nation's enemies, there, be held amongst my dearest Friends: and at that period no news of combat ever reached my ears that did not resound with victory and Buonaparte as words so amalgamated as to have become inseperable. And, consequently, with all my proud reliance on England's ultimate success, I foresaw with horrour and affliction, the intervening ravages of war, the scenes of slaughter, the deluges of blood, the heart-rending loss of beloved individuals, which must accompany the Invasion, and precede the final evacuation of the Invaders. None of this, I thank God, happenned, for Buonaparte while assaulting, with unbounded prowess, all other Nations, limitted his vengeance on Great Britain to simple threats.

536 [54, rue Basse, Passy],
19 December 1802

To Miss Planta

L., copy (Diary MSS. viii. 5640–9, Berg), in an unknown hand from M. d'A's 'Paris Letter Book', 19 Dec. 1802. The original was sent by Lord Whitworth on 14 Jan. 1803.
Two double sheets & 1 single sheet 4to 9 pp. lettered a, b, c foliated 35–40
Corrected by CFBt, *who probably provided the heading*: Addressed to Miss Planta / for the Queen and Princesses
Edited also at the Press.
The typescript extracts, preserved (Grangerized DL, 25th or supp. vol. pp. 87–90, *NPG; printed in* FB & the Burneys, pp. 88–90), *include FBA's editorial annotations of the 1820s:*

Account of Joigny, preceded by relating the purchase of a small estate at Passy; Narratory *eloge of Louis Bonaparte*, afterwards King of Holland. His character and exemplary conduct. Mad^e de Souza, niece of M. del Campo and her reminiscence of our court. Mad^e de Baufremont, and her chateau, daughters, and story. Mad^e de Villeheurnois, and Sydney, and Spencer.

Decr 19. 1802

Rarely, indeed, my dear Miss Planta, I have received more pleasure than from your last most truly welcome letter, with assurances so unspeakably seasonable, of the flourishing state of that noble Oak¹ & delicious garden, in the prosperity of which, my whole heart & soul, are interested: Little as is the credit which I give to common report, & uncertain as are are my view or knowledge of newspaper anecdotes & assertions, there are some subjects so exquisitely tender, that we cannot rest, where a surmise is raised upon them, till we know all

536. ¹ FBA had evidently seen reports in the Paris newspapers of the discovery in London of a plan to assassinate George III and an account of the arrest of the conspirators, Colonel Edward Marcus Despard (1751–1803) and about 40 labourers and soldiers, most of whom were Irish. *Le Publiciste* of 26 Nov. 1802 carried the following report: 'L'objet des scélérats qui ont trempé dans ce complot étoit, dit-on, d'assassiner le roi mardi, pendant qu'il irait au parlement, de s'emparer ensuite de la tour & de la banque, & de renverser le gouvernement. . . . La mort de sa majesté, . . . ne devoit être que le premier acte de cette sanglante tragédie. Les conspirateurs, après l'attaque de la tour, pour s'emparer des armes qui y sont renfermées, & celle de la banque, devoient aller chercher à Buckingham-House (palais de la reine) le reste de la famille royale.'

that is to be known. My kind father, well aware of this had immediately caused a true relation to be sent me of the matter to which I allude, & most fortunately it came to my quiet retirement before any other intelligence reached me. Nevertheless my joy on the arrival of your letter,[2] was inexpressible; & none you have sent me have been so rapid in their journey; a lacquay of the English Ambassador brought it & came the instant the dispatch was recieved. I had it here at Passy, the 5th day after its date. ⎸ I thank you again & again, but Oh! how I thank God!

The small house[3] we inhabit in this village has kept us rigidly within its precincts since our return from Joigny, for we have entered it with the workmen who are making repairs which they promised should be finished in a week, but of which the superintendance, still keeps us prisoners. It would be difficult, however to find two persons who with less murmuring would submit to such confinement, were that the only evil resulting from the procrastination; but I. much apprehend these hardy mechanics, will put the philosophy of our purses into yet greater jeopardy than that of our persons. M' d'Arblay, nevertheless, finding all he formerly either possessed, or expected, lost, deems it essential to substantiate his right of claim to being a french Citizen, by making himself master of a small estate; & this, our present habitation was offered to him upon terms so seducingly reasonable, that you would rather laugh than be surprised at the purchase, were I to give you its history. The repairs however were not taken into the estimation, & I am terribly afraid they will not prove quite as risible! But they will secure us we trust, a good Tenant, when we return to West-Humble: & they keep us, *en attendant*, in healthy air, with a small dwelling, English fashion, to ourselves, affording us a beautiful prospect from the banks of the Seine. ⎸ And here let me mention that our cottage of Westhumble was let for the last four months to the Miss Rolles of Devonshire.[4]

[2] Margaret Planta's reassuring letter on the subject of the king's health, included in the official dispatches sent to Lord Whitworth (L. 525 n. 13), is missing.
[3] This is the house, acquired *c.* 5 Oct. 1802, at 54, rue Basse. See also pp. 405–6.
[4] In all probability Lucilla (*c.* 1757–1851) and her sister Ann (*c.* 1758–1842), the unmarried sisters of John Rolle (1756–1842), Baron Rolle of Stevenstone (1797). In his will (P.C.C. 568, pr. 14 July 1842), he made careful provisions not only for his ageing sisters but for such relatives as would be willing to care for them in their declining years. The certified copies of entries of death (Somerset House)

It is now, I fear, again unoccupied.

M. D'ar. always nourishes his hope of obtaining finally his so long expected *retraite*, for former services, though the decision of his demand is still *ajournée*.[5]

—Quiet, however, & litterally stationary as has been my residence at Passy, these last two months, the french newspapers, I am told, have all sent me to Bourdeaux![6]

—Permit me now to go back to Joigny for the purpose of giving some account of two very interesting acquaintance, we made there. The first was Colonel Louis Bonaparte youngest

show that Lucilla died on 24 July 1851, at the age of 94; and Ann, on 18 June 1842, aged 84.

In a letter (Archives Nationales, F7 6505, folder 955) of *post* 19 June [1803], acknowledging FBA's letter (No. 550) of 12 June [1803], Mrs. Locke reported that the 'Miss Rolles are again settled in the poor dear Cottage for 6 months certain at 2 guineas & half p^r week I am happy to find that we did exactly as you wished in agreeing to the little additions that they required—'.

5 That d'Arblay had not given up hopes of his 'retraite' (see L. 478 nn. 1, 3, 4, 5; L. 485 n. 1; and Appendix) is attested by a letter (Vincennes) to Bonaparte of 4 Mar. 1803.

Citoyen premier Consul,

Daignez accueillir avec indulgence la priere que je vous adresse de vouloir bien vous faire remettre sous les yeux la demande de ma retraite ajournée par vous il y a six mois. Après avoir perdu parens, fortune, etat, santé, par une combinaison de malheurs aussi imprevus qu'irreparables, je n'en suis pas moins fier du tître de citoyen français, de ce titre que je n'aurais jamais du perdre, mais dont vous seul me faites jouir. Le plus beau jour de ma vie, a été, Citoyen premier Consul, celui où j'ai pu manifester mon attachement à la chose publique, et mon amour pour mon Pays, en mettant, des premiers, le voeu de rendre inseparables votre destinée et celle du Gouvernement reparateur que nous vous devons. Dans la sphere retracie où les circonstances m'ont renfermé, je ne puis offrir que des voeux; mais ces voeux sont bien sinceres.

Salut, respect et devouemens
Alexandre Darblay

This letter is annotated: 'Renvoyé au Ministre de la Guerre pour en faire un rapport. Ce 1er Germinal [22 March] Le 1er Consul [*signed*] Bonaparte.'

6 Announcements of the arrival of the comte de Lally-Tolendal at Bordeaux, appearing on 27 or 28 Nov. in such newspapers as the *Journal des Défenseurs de la Patrie, Journal des Débats, Journal de Paris, Journal du Commerce*, and *Journal du Soir*, had included the erroneous statement: 'M. Tollendal est accompagné de miladi Burnet, auteur de plusieurs romans anglais très-estimés.' *Le Publiciste* (30 Nov. 1802), while praising other newspapers for the welcome accorded Lally in France, offered a correction with respect to 'miladi Burney': 'Tout le monde littéraire sait qu'il y a une *miss Burney, auteur de romans anglais généralement estimés*, & en effet dignes de l'être, comme des ouvrages pleins d'esprit, de talent & de bonne morale. Mais *miss Burney* a changé son nom en épousant le colonel *d'Arblay*, avec qui elle est venue en France il y a quelque tems.'

At the royalist centre Bordeaux (see Madelin, xiii. 33-5) Lally was associated with the comte de Latour du Pin, whose house 'était signalée par la police de Bordeaux comme un centre de royalistes . . .', and Lally, who, under the Empire, 'continuait à se faire passer pour prisonnier anglais', was soon to be found on Napoleon's proscription list.

brother but one (Jerome)[7] of the first Consul. His regiment was quartered at Joigny, where he happened to be upon our last arrival at that Town, & where the first visit he made was to M. Bazille, the worthy maternal unkle of M. D'ar He is a young man of the most serious demeanour, a grave, yet pleasing Countenance, & the most reserve[d] yet gentlest manners. His conduct in the small Town (for France) of Joigny was not merely respectable, but exemplary: he would accept no distinction in consequence of his powerful connexions, but presented himself every where with the unassuming modesty of a young man who had no Claims beyond what he might make by his own efforts & merits. he discouraged all gaming— to which the Inhabitants are extremely prone, by always[l] playing low himself; and discountenanced all parade, by never suffering his own servant to wait behind his Chair where he dined. He broke up early both from table & from play; was rigid in his attentions to his military duties; strict in the discipline of his officers as well as men; & the first to lead the way in every decency and regularity. When to this I add that his Conversation is sensible, & well bred, yet uncommonly diffident, & that but 23 summers have yet rolled over his head, so much good sense, forbearance, and propriety, in a situation so open to flattery, ambition, or vanity, obtained as they meritted, high consideration & perfect good will. I had a good deal of conversation with him, for he came to sit by me both before & after his card party where-ever I had the pleasure to meet with him; & his quiet & amiable manners, & rational style of discourse, made him a great loss to our society, when he was summoned to Paris, upon the near approach of the event which gave him a son & heir.[7] He was very kind to my little Alex, whom he never saw without embracing, & he treated M. D'ar with a marked distinction extremely gratifying to me. [l] We have never seen him since we left Joigny, nor indeed, any one else, for we are truly, as yet, shut up in our premises.

The second acquaintance to which I have alluded is a Lady Madame de Souza.[8] She soon found the road to my good will

---

[7] Of the Bonaparte brothers, Joseph (1768–1844), king of Naples (1806), of Spain (1808), was the eldest; Lucien (1775–1840), prince de Canino, the second; Louis (1778–1846), king of Holland (1806), the third brother; and Jérôme (1784–1860), king of Westphalia (1807), the youngest. For the character of Louis Bonaparte and the birth of his son, cf. L. 535, pp. 394–5 and n. 5.

& regard, for she told me that she, with another lady, had been fixed upon by M. del Campo,[8] my old Tea-visitor—for the high honour of aiding him in his reception of the first Lady of our Land & her lovely daughters, upon the Grande Fête which he gave upon the dearest & next memorable of occasions, & she spoke with such soft sensibility of pleasure & gratitude of the sweet condescension she then experienced, that she charmed & delighted me, & *we struck up an intimacy* without further delay. Our Theme was always ready, & I only regretted that I could see her but seldom, as she lived 2 or 3 miles out of Joigny, at Cesy, in the small chateau of la *cy-devant* Princesse de Beaufremont,[9] a lady with whom I had had the honour of making acquaintance in Paris. She is one of those who suffered most during the horrours of the revolution. At the dreadful period when all the rage was to burn the property & title deeds of the rich & high born; her noble chateau, one of the most considerable in France, was utterly consumed; & all her

[8] To be distinguished from Mme de Souza-Botelho *née* Filleul (1761–1836), the novelist, mother of the comte de Flahaut (1785–1870), is the Spanish Mme de Souza (*fl.* 1789–1802), niece of Bernardo, marquis del Campo (*c.* 1750–1800), Spanish envoy and later (1787) ambassador to England, whose appearances at the tea-table presided over by the Keepers of the Robes at the Court of Queen Charlotte in the years 1786–7 is mentioned by FB in *DL*, ii. 425, 427; iii. 288–9, 302, 325–7. A fête given by the Ambassador on 2 June 1789 to celebrate the recovery of George III from his illness of 1788–9 was one of the most magnificent ever given in London, and FB's invitation to it is extant in the Osborn Collection.

On the character of the Spanish Mme de Souza FBA was shortly to have the arresting information that she imparted to M. d'A is one of the 'petites histoires' included in her French Exercise Book (Berg) of 1804 5—'une histoire pour moi la plus étonnante, et qui ne manquera pas d'être de même pour vous'.

The lady, it seems, was in the grips of 'une passion criminelle' for M. de Listenois (n. 9), whom, invited or uninvited, she had accompanied or followed to France. Listenois had prevailed upon Mme de Bauffremont his mother (L. 517 n. 10) and his sister (L. 526 n. 7) to receive his Spanish guest at Cézy, and charmed by her manners and touched by her illness and mysterious sorrows, they had allowed her to remain there even after the confession that their goodness finally elicited from her. 'Elle . . . raconta que . . . elle avoit donner en entier son coeur à son fils — qu'elle ne respirer que pour lui . . . et qu'elle étoit la plus malheureuse des femmes.'

When Listenois's wife, also soliciting the protection of Mme de Bauffremont, arrived with two children at Cézy, Listenois refused to enter his home, insisting that his family be sent away in favour of his mistress. When, however, he appeared in the vicinity, his mother went forth to meet him in a vain attempt to soften his demands. Returning to dismiss the poor wife, 'elle s'echauffa, s'enrhuma, se trouva mal, . . . la fievre la saisie, et en moins d'une semaine la voilà morte! Quel fin cruel pour une si digne mere, devouée en tous à un fils ingrat et abominable!'

[9] For the family de Bauffremont, see L. 517 n. 10, and for the daughter Hortense (copied incorrectly as M^de), L. 526 n. 7. For Listenois's wife *née* Marie-Antoinette-Rosalie-Pauline de Quélen de la Vauguyon (1769–1847) and her affair with William Beckford (1760–1844), see *The Journal of William Beckford in Portugal and Spain, 1787–1788*, edited by Boyd Alexander (1954), pp. 296 ff.

papers; that no record of her genealogy might remain, were |
committed, with barbarous triumph, to the flames; yet was
this, such is her unhappy fate, the least of her misfortunes: her
eldest daughter, a beautiful young creature, upon whom she
doated, was in the chateau at this horrible period, & forced to
make her escape with such alarm & precipitance, that she
never recovered from the excess of her terror, which robbed
her of her life before she was quite seventeen years of age!
Around the small & modest *Chateau* de Cesy, in which Made de
Beauffremont & her youngest & now only daughter Mlle de
Listenois, at present reside, the grounds have been cultivated
in the English style, & the walks, now shady, now open, now
rising, now descending, with water, bridges, cascades, &
groves, & occasional fine picturesque views from the Banks of
the Yonne, are all laid out with taste, & pretty effects. We
strolled over them with a large party, till we came to a little
recess. Me de Beaufremont then took me by the arm, & we
separated from the company to enter it together,—& she
shewed me an urn surrounded with Cypress Trees & weeping
Willows, watered by a clear small running rivulet, & dedicated
to the memory of her first-born & early lost lamented daughter.
There was yet no inscription, & she was meditating where to
find one that could bear being adapted to her peculiar hard lot
Perhaps she led me to this melancholy spot, with an idea that
I might assist her researches; but I was quite of opinion with
M. D'arblay, that what should be dictated | by herself, & her
own affection, in the simplest manner, would most conduce to
soothe her design of demonstrating her maternal tenderness
& regret. Poor Lady! she seems entirely resigned to all the rest
of her deprivations, but here the wound is incurable! Yet this
subject *à part*, she is cheerful, loves society, or rather social
discourse, with a chosen few, & not only accepts with pleasure
whatever may enliven her, but exerts herself to contribute all
that is in her power to the entertainment of others. She has still
preserved enough from the wreck of her possessions to live
elegantly though not splendidly; & her table is remarkably well
served. She has a son M. de Listenois, whom I did not see; but
her remaining daughter Mdl de Listenois, is a very fine young
woman, & the best lady dancer, in a lady like manner, I have
been in the way of seeing in this Country, where the ladies in

general to my english eyes, foot it away with the graces the agility & intrepidity of opera *figurante*[*s*.] But Mad^e de Listenois, with the form & air of a nymph, & the attire which Van Dyke would have liked to paint, has a decency in her look & demeanor that speak so forcibly in her favour, that they make one forget that her steps, motions, & appearance are theatrical. & leave one only to admire them as light, graceful, & picturesque. Mad^e de Souza[8] has spent the whole summer with these Ladies. She told me she liked England, so very much, & was so happy during the 6 weeks she passed there, that she wept bitterly in quitting it. She was received, she says, at court, in the most bewitching manner: & she | delights in retracing her honours, & her sense of them. She is still so very handsome, though sickly & suffering, that I imagine she must then have been exquisitely beautiful. I am told, by a French officer who has served in Spain, M. de Moulan,[10] that when she left that country she was reckoned the most celebrated beauty of Madrid.

I had another new acquaintance at Joigny, also, in a Lady who came from Auxerre, as she was pleased to say, to see me, Mde La Villheurnois, widow of M. La Villheurnois[11] who was amongst the unhappy objects *deportés*, by the order of the directory, *à la Guyanne*. As soon as the first civilities were over, she said 'Permettez, Madame! — connaissez vous Sidney?'[12] I could not doubt who she meant, though there is no helping smiling at this drolly concise way of naming a man by his *nom de baptême*. She was extremely surprised when I answered. No; telling me she had concluded que *tout le monde en Angleterre* must

[10] See L. 532 n. 5.
[11] Charles-Honoré Berthelot de la Villeheurnois *or* Villeurnoy (*c.* 1750–99) of Toulon, formerly maître des requêtes under Louis XVI, who under the Directory had organized a conspiracy for the restoration of the Bourbons. When 'powers' signed by Louis XVIII were found in his possession (30 Jan. 1797), he was first imprisoned in the Temple and later deported to Sinnamari, French Guiana, where in a short time he died. See Louis Madelin, *La Révolution* (1914), p. 514. His wife (since 1776) Charlotte-Claude, the daughter of Pierre-Louis-Ann Drouyn de Vaudeuil (b. 1726), was living in Fontaines, near Joigny.
[12] It was apparently in the Temple prison that M. de Villeheurnois and his wife had first met Commodore Sir William Sidney Smith (1764–1840), who, having been captured (18 April 1796) while running down French privateers, was held as a prisoner of war until his escape on 8 May 1798. Communication between prisoners, social life, and visiting was allowed in the Temple, and the commodore, a handsome and dashing officer, made many conquests among the female sex. See John Barrow, *The Life and Correspondence of Admiral Sir William Sidney Smith* (2 vols., 1848), chaps. vii, viii.

know Sidney!—Yes, I said, by character certainly; but personally I had never the gratification of meeting with him. She told me she was intimately acquainted with him herself, from seeing him continually, when he was confined in the Temple, as she attended there son malheureux [epoux]; & she saw also she said, *son Valet, et son Jockey*, whom she never suspected to be disguised Emigrants, who were watching to aid his escape: *Surtout*, she added, ⟨*comme*⟩ *le Jockey avait des trous aux bas terribles* —which induced her daughter to buy him a new pair ⎮ of stockings, for charity. A Gentleman who accompanied her to Joigny, her secretary, told me he had played at Ball with Sidney, every day for six months, while he also attended upon poor Mʳ La Villheurnois.

When we parted, she begged me, as soon as I returned to England, *d'aller voir Sidney pour lui faire ses reproches de ce qu'il n'avait pas reponda à sa lettre*; though she was sure it had been delivered to him because her son had given it lui même to SPENCER,[13] when he passed through Paris on his return from Constantinople.

Shall I never have done, you will say, with Joigny?—Nay, you don't yet know what I could add! I could give you lists of the dinners with which M D'ar's return was celebrated, that might grace a Lord Mayor's feast. But Basta, Basta,

How thankful I am that the lovely, & loved violet[14] droops no longer! That was most kindly inserted—

How I delighted to hear it! Methought I smelt again all its sweetness.

You encourage me to write long letters, my dear Friend, & for that Encouragement, & all else, receive the best thanks of your sincere &

13 It must have been the son (thus far, unidentified) of Villeheurnois (*supra*) who delivered one of the above letters to Sir Sidney's brother, John Spencer Smith (1769–1845), who in the years 1796–9 (Haydn) was Minister Plenipotentiary to the Porte. In December 1798–9 the office was vested conjointly in the two brothers (Barrow, op. cit. i. 234–5). The latter was to be the hero of Acre (1799), M.P. (1802–6), Rear-Admiral of the Blue (1805), Vice-Admiral (1810), K.C.B. (1815), Admiral (1821), G.C.B. (1838).

14 FBA had herself edited this Journal, supplying at n. 12 (above) the superscript + and the identification: '+ Sir Sidney Smith.' At our n. 14 she had supplied the superscript ⁙· and the footnote: '·⁙· The Princess Amelia.'

537

[54, rue Basse], Passy
28 December 1802

To Mrs. Locke

L., copy in the hand of CFBt, probably from the original lent to her by the Locke family (Diary MSS. viii. 5650–[5], Berg), 28 Dec. 1802. The original was taken to England by a 'fr^d of M. Green, [20]? Jany 1803'.
Double sheet and single sheet 4to   6 pp.
Edited by the Press.

Passy, prés Paris

To Mrs Locke

Decr 28. 1802

With what joy I have received your two last letters my most dear Friend! — — I find it a little hard to forgive Mr Fuseli for—or rather, something *beyond* hard!—for having left at Dover what I was so languishing to possess in Paris!—¹

Our absence from that City, both then at Monsseaux,² & afterwards at Joigny, & now at Passy, makes me only by accident know what English arrive; and as visiting & gadding are not precisely what I live for, I have not had more curiosity upon that subject than I have been able to support with tolerable patience. I do all that is in my power to keep quiet, here as in England, & only to see those I already know, & *like*, or have reason to believe I shall number with such when seen & known. We always find our day too short, far! far!—little as we mix with the World;—& to reside either in Paris or in London, under the mingled heavings & flutter ' of constant company, or constant struggle to avoid it, would, I have not the smallest doubt, shorten my existence. To such a life my taste was always averse, and now my spirits are unequal.

—As to Passy—we shall not reside *longer* in France for that possession, only more comfortably. You would rejoice for me, my kindest Friends, if you knew the tranquillity of this dwelling.

537. ¹ Probably a letter given by the Lockes to their friend Henry Fuseli (L. 526 n. 24), the artist, to carry to the d'Arblays.
² The d'Arblays had spent most of June 1802 at Monceaux and about two weeks (*c.* 28 June—*c.* 10 July) at Joigny, returning to Paris in time for the fête of 14 July. A second visit to Joigny (about six weeks during the vintage) terminated at the end of October, when they settled in Passy (L. 543, p. 436).

Our Evenings are as clearly, as decidedly uninterrupted as at Westhamble. I am not, indeed, sure this will always be literally the case, as we have near Neighbours in Friends highly valued by M: d'Arblay,[3]—but, as yet, we have made known our general habits, and my particular *sauvagerie* with great success; especially as, added to those clauses, we have no apartments yet *open to company.* The manner in which we have entered this habitation is as singular as any part of our lives and adventures; for we came into it when we had really only one Room, like the Cobler, for Parlour, for Bedroom, & Hall.[4] And we have but just got another apartment, & I have got, with it, a ⏐ cold which answers all the purposes possible of seclusion, yet I am really very sensible to all the kindness I meet with; but so strongly the love with the habit of retirement, grows upon me, that I cannot even *wish* I may like these *Voisins* & *voisines* sufficiently to be drawn from it with consent. When I say this, I need not, of course, add, That my Partner is not become a more dissipated character than when you knew him—*saw* him, rather,—no, were that the case, I must adopt an altered plan myself, for Solitude, my dearest Friends, I could not endure!— I have no occasion to point out to what dread recollections & regrets I should fall a prey.[5]—But, Heaven be praised, we assimilate *here* as we did *there* — — — & can I drop anything my ever partial & most tender Friends will hear more kindly, more sympathizingly?—

And now let me thank my Amine for her Books which are a great resource to us, as I brought no English Books for want of room. Her Letter to Alex is yet unopened.[6] I kept it back

[3] The family of César de Latour-Mauberg (L. 445 n. 12) and that of his sister Mme de Maisonneuve (L. 518 n. 10).

[4]   A Cobler there was, and he liv'd in a Stall,
       which served him for Parlour, for Kitchen and Hall,
       No Coin in his Pocket, nor Care in his Pate,
       No ambition had he, nor Duns at his Gate.
       Derry down, down, down, derry down.
This is the first stanza of a popular song entitled 'The Coblers End'. It was composed (both words and music) by Richard Leveridge (c. 1670–1758) and sung to the accompaniment of a flute at the Theatre in Lincoln's Inn Fields in 1765, and probably earlier. Arranged later for harpsichord, violin, German flute, or guitar, and entitled simply 'The Cobbler', it was still sung in the 1780s, and now survives as a piece of sheet music in the British Museum.

[5] In grief for the sufferings and death of Susanna (Burney) Phillips (L. 446, p. 51; L. 451, p. 69).

[6] There is an allusion as late as 1812 to this much-prized letter written by Amelia Angerstein to AA.

for a Birth day Gift, & the Bourdois were invited to a dinner of Alex's own choice ,which—as he could ∣ not name a *Hare*, consisted of Two Tureens of Soup, Two plats of Cutlets à l'anglaise, & two plates of Fried Potatoes for the Dessert.—But my cold interfered, & the Fête is yet unsolemnized, & the seal yet unbroken!—I must tell my dear Fredy & Amine a little simple, yet how true! trait of my Alex's reasoning powers, that will amuse, at once, & touch them: I was moralizing with him, upon some occasion I have forgotten, about goodness, virtue, & such sort of old fashioned matters, when, upon some lectures mixed relative to his own conduct—& *mis*conduct, he gravely asked me if I thought some people were *always* good?—In their *intentions*, I answered, I had the happiness to know many who were, but, as we were all human, &c &c—'But, mama', cried he, with a look of disappointment, 'dont you think Mr Locke *always* good in his actions as well as his intentions?' — — 'In all I can judge, my dear Boy, YES!—& in all I cannot decide upon, *nearer*, I believe, than any other mortal.'—He paused upon this a good while & very gravely, & then, with a face comically solemn for his age & ∣ character, he said, 'I am sure if he is ever in the wrong it must be very seldom, for I never remember it in all my life.'

No more, I am sure, do I.—

You have conceived a far higher idea of our new Cottage than it merits; it is a queer, irregular, odd, house:—yet full of conveniences, and affording from one room a superb view of Paris, just far enough off to be picturesque—nay, magnificent; & from another, a sweet prospect from the banks of the Seine, of cultivated Hills, white villas, & beautiful woods & fields. It is just a place for such odd folks, for we *descend* to enter it, as it is built on the declivity of a rock. M: d'A. has greatly improved it;—but I shall enjoy his amendments more comfortably when they are *all* settled. — —7

But the poor Cottage—my dearest Friend, may we entreat some account of our debts, some *memoir*, the Taxes—Morris8— &c &c—that we may try to clear ourselves—the poorer we grow, the more exactly we must keep free from encumbrances that may end in claims to ∣ surprize & distress us.—

7 Cf. L. 532, p. 388; L. 536, p. 398.
8 George Morris (L. 492 n. 4), 'upholsterer, and auctioneer'.

Adieu my most beloved Friends—
Heaven preserve & bless you ALL!—
My kind love to la chére Bonne. Alex never forgets her
telling him he could not have a Son without a Wife—which is
the reason, he says, of his marrying; *tender*, is it not?

My dearest Friend might have spared her alarm at the idea
of our losing £3000 by the Coulons[9]—or the any body's—it
would not be very possible to be so UNLUCKY, without being
first a little more fortunate—Our money matters all, all go
ill! — —

538   [54, rue Basse, Passy
                                     pre 14 February 1803]

Conjointly with M. d'Arblay
To James Burney

A.L.S. & A.L. (PML, Autog. Cor. bound), *n.d.*
Double sheet 4to   4 pp. *pmks* F 60 / ⟨PY⟩ PORT PAYE FOREIGN
OFFICE / 14 FEB 180⟨3⟩
Addressed in hand of M. d'A: To Cap^n James Burney / of the Navy. N°
72 *Margaret Street* / *Cavendish—Square* / *London* / *England*
Re-addressed: M / The Right Honble Esq / J Beresford / Walworth / near
Derry / Ireland[1]
Docketed in pencil, p. 1: Feb. 1803.

[9] The brothers Marc and Henry-François-Grégoire Coulon, tanners of Bercy,
who had declared bankruptcy in the autumn of 1802 in an ambitious enterprise
founded in 1801. The list of Coulons' creditors (Archives nationales) include both
d'Arblays (she, for 3,000 francs and he, for 1,440), Antoine Bourdois (for 16,281
francs), and his friend the comte de Riccé (iv, 178–9).
The loss was not £3,000 but apparently £750, which, as d'Arblay explains in
a property statement of 4 July 1813 (Berg), he had placed with M. Coulon only
because 'nous avions lu sur les murs de Paris une affiche imprimée dans la quelle on
proposait comme les modeles les plus respectables des furnisseurs dont la speculation tout à fait neuve a été de faire rehabiliter a memoire de leur Pere en faisant
pour payer les dettes de sa banque route un sacrifice d'environ deux millions, au
moyen des quels peu de mois après ils en ont emporté une vingtaine aux dupes de
notre espéce. 27p% furent ensuite offerts et j'avais accepté, mais n'ai jamais rien
touché. . . .' See also vii, Appendix II.

538. [1] Conjecturally JB had accompanied his niece Frances Burney (L. 521 n. 4)
to her new post as governess to the daughters of the Rt. Hon. John Beresford (L.
527 n. 6) at the above address.

Mon cher James
Je vous remercie sincerement et de tout mon coeur de votre lettre et de la proposition qu'elle renferme.² Je vous proteste que c'est très serieusement que je vais tâcher de me mettre à même de ne pas trop gâter votre ouvrage en le faisant passer dans notre langue. Mais à propos vous avouerai-je que je ne puis me rappeller son titre. N'est-ce pas une Histoire generale des decouvertes faites par les divers Navigateurs?² Cet ouvrage de tous les tems et de tous les lieux ne peut être en de meilleures mains. Je desire que vous ayez la bonté de m'envoyer sur le champ ce qui est corrigé. Vous auriez la bonté d'en faire un paquet adressé *au Citoyen Dhermand Chef des relations commerciales*,³ avec une Seconde adresse au *Cᵉⁿ Talleyrand Ministre des relations | exterieures de la Republique française à Paris.*

Brother Charles pourrait adresser ce paquet à Douvre à quelques uns de ses amis, par exemple au Banquier chez le quel il m'avait envoyé avec une lettre de recommandation qui m'a valu un magnifique diner.⁴

Le paquet ne doit pas être plus gros qu'une brochure in 8°. Il faut autant que possible lui donner cette forme.

Deux envois faits de cette maniere le plus promptement possible suffiront.

Pour les autres, vous aurez, mon cher James moins d'embarras. Il faudra seulement porter chez Monsieur Coquebert-Monbret⁵ Commissaire general des relations Commerciales de la Republique et ami intime de l'Ambassadeur les epreuves à mesure qu'elles paraitront. Monsieur Coquebert les fera certainement passer par le premier Courrier à mon ami D'Hermand le quel me les remettra sur le champ. Ce dernier ecrit à ce sujet à Monsieur Coquebert et | le premier courrier

---

² JB's letter is missing but he seems to have suggested that M. d'A translate his forthcoming work *A Chronological History of the Discoveries in the South Sea or Pacific Ocean*, pt. I, which, according to Manwaring (p. 216), appeared in June of this year. Succeeding volumes published under the title *A Chronological History of the Voyages and Discoveries in the South Sea or Pacific Ocean* were to appear in 1806, 1813, 1816, and 1817. It was by virtue of this work and the patronage of the Duke of Clarence that JB was promoted from Captain to Rear-Admiral in 1821, the year of his death.

³ Louis-Joseph d'Hermand (L. 450 n. 6).

⁴ John Minet Fector (L. 496 n. 9).

⁵ Charles-Étienne Coquebert de Montbret (1755–1831), like JB, had an interest in the history of geography, but it was in his capacity as 'commissaire' or 'consul général' in London or as 'agent général des relations commerciales' that his aid was to be solicited at this time.

du Gouvernement sera chargé de sa lettre. Je suis à la recherche d'un dictionnaire de Marine Anglais[6] et français, car j'avoue que je ne suis pas trés versé dans les termes techniques d'un art que vous connoissez si bien. Il en existait un assez bon dont il parait que l'édition est epuisée. Si je ne puis me le procurer, je vais faire un travail qui m'en tiendra lieu.

S'il etait possible que dans la Preface vous dissiez un mot de l'approbation donnée à votre plan par Sir Joseph Banks[7] et le Major Renuel[8] cela me serait ici d'un trés grand secours. Ce dernier surtout jouit comme Geographe d'une reputation qui serait d'un grand poids auprés de l'amirauté qui interessée à cette publication en facilitera j'espere le succès. Je ne suis point inquiet de celui qu'elle aura en Angleterre. Le difficile est de ne rien lui faire perdre en la transplantant. Vîte vîte ce qui est près, je m'y mettrai sans perte de tems et soumettrai mon travail à quelque personne de l'art. S'il l'approuve je continuerai; | S'il trouve, au contraire, que dans ce qui concerne l'art de la Marine, je sois au dessous de mon sujet, je le confierai sur le champ à quelqu'un de mieux en etat de rendre justice à l'original — Sur ce, je prie Dieu mon cher James qu'il vous ait en sa sainte et digne garde. Respects et complimens, je vous prie, à nos parens et amis que nous reverrons avec bonheur.

A. d'Arblay

[By Madame d'Arblay]

The very morning your Letter arrived, my dearest James, I was lamenting having so rarely any intercourse with you;

[6] Such a dictionary had in fact been lately printed in England, e.g. J. J. Moore, *British Mariner's Vocabulary* (1801).

[7] JB had needed no such prompting to dedicate his work to Sir Joseph Banks, Bart., K.B., President of the Royal Society: 'You have visited, and are well acquainted with the scenes I am endeavouring to describe. To you my plan was first communicated, and the encouragement it received from you, determined me to the undertaking. You indulged me with the most unrestrained use of your valuable library; not merely with access, but with permission to take away, for more deliberate consideration, whatever appeared connected with my pursuit; thus rendering it, to all purposes of utility, my own. To these reasons I may justly add, that, next to his Majesty, you have been one of the greatest patronisers and promoters, in this or in any country, of Geographical Discoveries.'

[8] JB had also thanked James Rennel (i, L. 12 n. 16), the geographer, who had approved the outline of his plan; and also, among others, Alexander Dalrymple (1737–1808), the first Hydrographer to the Admiralty, for access to 'his large collection of scarce Spanish books' and for the information provided in his own translations of them. Dalrymple's work 'has, indeed, been my *Vade Mecum*'.

I was doubly therefore rejoiced at the sight of your hand; & I heartily congratulate you upon the forwardness of your literary toils, from which I have very sincerely the best expectations, upon a subject of which you are both scientifically & practically master. 2 of your Plan—Approuvers are named here, of the National Institute, Sr Joseph Banks & Major Rennel.—You say nothing of your dear young ones, neither Boy nor Girl, so I conclude them well—for we seldom forget to complain.

Adieu, my own Brother. |

Pray what is the real name of those *birds* called by seamen Mother Carey's chickens, & which they think prognosticate a storm? are they not called in French *Goëlands*?[9] I have just bought J. Moore's British Mariner's Vocabulary, 1801[6]—Is it a good one?

539

[54, rue Basse], Passy,
Passy, 5 March 1803

M. d'Arblay
with a PS by Madame d'Arblay
To James Burney

A.L.S. & PS. (PML, Autog. Cor. bound), 5 Mars 1803
Double sheet 4to 4 pp. *pmks* TPP G^t Russell St MAR⟨ ⟩1803 wafer
Addressed: Capt James Burney, / of the R^al Navy / N° 72 Margaret Street / Cavendish Square / *LONDON*
Carried to London and posted by James Greene

Passy ce 5 Mars 1803

J'ai reçu, mon cher James, votre second envoi c'est à dire les feuilles E, G, H, I, K que Mr Coquebert à qui vous les

---

[9] According to legend, Mother Carey's chickens, or stormy petrels, were the receptacles for the souls of dead seamen. To kill one might bring retribution in the form of death. Cf. Captain Marryat's *Poor Jack*, edited by R. Brimley Johnson (1929), pp. 311–12.

avez remises a fait passer à mon ami Dhermand. Mais nous
n'avons aucune nouvelles des feuilles A, B, C, D, E[1]

Je n'ai consequement aucune connaissance de votre plan
dont il faudroit neanmoins que je fusse instruit, avant de
prendre avec le Ministre de la Marine[2] quelques arrangemens
qui seuls peuvent me mettre à l'abri du danger de me donner
une peine inutile.

Les paquets remis à Mr Coquebert[3] nous arrivant par les
courriers que depêche l'Ambassadeur, ne peuvent s'egarer, et
nous sommes assurés pour l'avenir contre tout accident de
cette espece: mais je crains fort que les premieres feuilles qui
sont venues par une autre voie ne soient perdues, et que je
ne sois dans la necessité de vous les redemander. Véritablement,
quoique cela vous donne un nouvel embarras dont je suis bien
faché, il me semble que c'est | un sacrifice auquel il faut se
resoudre plutôt que plustard.

Je n'ai jamais entendu parler de ce *Fernando de Magalhanes*
que je suis actuellement à traduire d'après vous Vous en citez
une traduction française; je l'ai cherchée et ne puis la trouver.
L'aimable petite soeur veut elle bien me rendre le service de
m'en copier le titre. Me pardonnera t'elle de m'adresser à elle
pour eclaircir les difficultés qui pourront se presenter.

Je lui aurois par exemple une obligation infinie de me mander
ce que c'est que the *ambrosian Manuscript*[4]

J'ai interompu ma lettre pour lire d'un bout à l'autre les
cinq feuilles que j'ai reçues afin de demander les explications
dont j'aurais besoin. Tres heureusement, je crois qu'elles sont
inutiles: mais je dois vous avouer ma surprise en trouvant que
ce *Fernando de Magalhanes* dont Bourdois ni moi ne pouvions
trouver la relation dans aucun recueil de voyages, n'est autre

539. [1] These are the gatherings (page proofs) of JB's forthcoming *Chronological History* (L. 538 n. 2).

[2] Denis Decrès (1762–1820), who after an active career at sea (1780–1800) was appointed in October 1801 ministre de la Marine, a position that he filled brilliantly until 1814. [3] See L. 538 n. 5.

[4] The Ambrosian Manuscript, considered the most authentic record of the voyage (1519–21) of Ferdinand Magellan (c. 1480–1521), the first circumnavigator of the globe, is preserved in the Ambrosian Library at Milan. Written in Italian by Antonio Pigafetta (c. 1491–*post* 1534), a volunteer on the voyage, the MS. had been lately re-edited (1800) by Carlo Amoretti (1741–1816), who also supplied a French translation made by himself (1801). These were the works that evidently James wished to see, and this was not the first difficulty encountered by d'Arblay and Bourdois in keeping up with the bibliographical knowledge of the Burneys and their demands for books.

que le fameux MAGELLAN, decouverte que je n'ai faite qu'après être parvenu à celle qu'il fit du detroit ^l qui porte son nom. Sur ce, je prie Dieu qu'il vous ait en sa sainte et digne garde en attendant que vous m'ayez fait passer les premieres feuilles et dans l'esperance que vous voudrez bien les faire suivre exactement par leurs cadettes à mesure qu'elles verront le jour.

Pouvez vous, mon cher James, me dire à peu près quelle sera l'etendue de l'ouvrage. Son utilité ne me paraît point douteuse, et je suis convaincu que vous en retirerez en Angleterre honneur et profit. Le premier n'est pas moins assuré ici: mais notre marine est trop peu nombreuse à present pour fournir u[n] debouché considerable. Sans un arrangement fait d'avance avec le Ministre pour un certain nombre d'exemplaires il est à craindre qu'on ne retirerait point les frais dans lesquels une pareille entreprise ne peut manquer d'entrainer. Pour Dieu, ayez la bonté de m'envoyer ^l ce qui me manque et surtout l'avertissement où j'espere qu'il est question du Major Rennel qui jouit ici de la plus grande reputation. Respects et complimens à tous et chacun

Votre feal
A. D'arblay

[Madame d'Arblay added a postscript]

How provoking your first paquet missing, my dearest James— what can be become of ⌜you⌝—it?—Heaven bless you. / Love to Sarah & Martin — —

540   [54, rue Basse], Passy,
7–13 March 1803

To Mrs. Waddington

A.L. (Berg), 7 Mar. 1803
Double sheet 8vo 3 pp.
Addressed: Mrs. Waddington, / Lanover Court, / Abergavenny—

Passy, March 7th 1803

No, no, a Letter — — no! I am too dreadfully in debt all around me—but a few lines to say your last Letter is safely arrived. My dear & kind Marianne, I hasten to write, as Mr. Green[1] assures me he has means to forward them. How interesting & entertaining is that Letter! & in parts how astonishing to me—Having had no *intelligence*, I formed no *ideas* upon the principal topic at all anticipating the truth—& much has sincerely grieved me—& disappointed, too.—

Alexander has made a point of answering your lovely Emily *all his own Self*, & he told me 'do you know, Mama, I shall begin like a real Letter, with only one word at the top!'— I imagine he has remarked ¦ the *Sir*, *Madam*, Monsr or Mad^e of Letters of ceremony, & concluded the *form* was to *begin* with *one word quelconque*. He fixed upon Mr. Green for his subject both because he supposes him a great friend of your little girls, & because he is a great favourite of his own. Commend me to both your lovely companions, & kiss the sweet little one for me —& bring all hither before our departure, & I will pay good interest for every advance you make for me—

I am not yet well—but I have never been *seriously* ill.— I must wish your sister happy—& hope she will be so. The Layards[2] are esteemed in general. God bless you
my ever dear Marianne — — ¦

540. [1] Greene, having departed *pre* 24 Jan. 1803, had returned to Paris *pre* 13 Mar. 1803, for according to Lady Elizabeth Foster (see Dorothy Margaret Stuart, *Dearest Bess* (1955), pp. 108, 113), he was present, along with Junot, at the Tuileries on the occasion of Napoleon's direct attack that day on Whitworth. '*Come and dine with me once more before we fight each other*', suggested Junot. For Greene's visit to Monmouthshire and the lawsuits that had detained him in England, see L. 532 n. 1.

The surviving Waddington daughters, Frances and Emelia, were now aged 12 and 9 respectively, and the unabridged memoirs of Frances, later Lady Bunsen (see Maxwell Fraser, ed., 'The Waddingtons of Llanover', *The National Library of Wales Journal*, xi. 4 (1960), 285–329), show her mother in an attractive light, as an unusually beautiful and intelligent woman, though delicate in health and oppressed by excessive child-bearing. The 'Memoirs' throw light as well on many of the allusions in Madame d'Arblay's replies to Mrs. Waddington's letters (since returned to her). Augusta (later Lady Llanover) was less than a year old.

[2] Mrs. Waddington's sister Louisa Port (1778–1817) was to marry, much against the wishes of her family, the Revd. Brownlow Villiers Layard (1779–1861), of Huguenot descent, who in 1803 succeeded his father as Rector of Uffington, Lincs. Married on 6 Oct. 1803, she was to bear seven sons, and 'a few days after the birth of the last, she expired, without illness, of total exhaustion of vital powers, on the 3rd July 1817' (see Fraser, op. cit., p. 314).

His father, the Revd. Charles Peter Layard (1748–1803), F.R.S. (1778), D.D. (1787), Rector of Uffington (1798), became Chaplain in Ordinary to the King (1790–1800) and Dean of Bristol (1800). The family objections to the marriage

I won't pray—believe me—that you may have another CHILD! — — but only that, should it so chance — — as your Girls fulfil already all your wishes, that it may be a Boy— & prove to you, & promise to you—what my Boy now proves & now promises to me.—*So far* you will forgive me, will you not? — —

I assure you I forgive *you*, if you wish *me* one of your blessings! —and how I should have prized it! — —

Sunday ⟨Morng.—⟩ [13 March 1803]

Mr—G[reene] this moment brings a sad account of your poor little Augusta, that quite afflicts me. ǀ

541   54, rue Basse, Passy,
10 March 1803

To Miss Planta

L., copy in an unknown hand (Diary MSS. viii. 5654–[67], Berg), from M. d'A's 'Paris Letter Book', 10 Mar. 1803.
Single sheet & 3 double sheets 4to 14 pp. the double sheets lettered d, e, f
Corrected by CFBt, edited by the Press.
A typescript copy, also taken from the Letter Book (grangerized DL, vol. 25, supp. vol., pp. 91–103, NPG, and printed in FB & the Burneys, pp. 91–9), preserves Madame d'Arblay's editorial annotations:
TO MISS PLANTA, for Her Majesty, Queen Charlotte and the Princesses; the infectious La Grippe at Paris; in 1803; M. de la Harpe; Madame de Staël Holstein; M. et Made. de la Fayette; La Grange; Mme. Charles de Maubourg; George et Virginie de la Fayette and Mlle. de Tracy; Colonel Sebastiani; Alexandre; Lord Whitworth.

seemed to be that the Dean's emoluments and distinctions were attained, as they thought, through the interest of his sister Mary Anne (1743–1804), originally a governess to a sister of Brownlow Bertie (1729–1809), the 5th and last Duke of Ancaster and Kesteven, whom she succeeded in marrying. As for the nephew of the Duchess, the Revd. Brownlow Villiers Layard, to retain the rich living of Uffington, he had only to 'throw off his regimentals, & put on a black coat, & go through a short preparation at Oxford, & be ordained—if only some bishop would ordain him'.

To Miss Planta.

Passy, rue Basse N° 54.
March 10th 1803.

For her Majesty Queen Charlotte, & their R. Hnss the Princesses Augusta, Eliza, Mary, Sophia Amelia

It would be difficult to give you an idea of the eagerness with which I have received your letter, my dear Miss Planta,[1] after so long a *famine* of such intelligence as is most precious to me: but when I came to that part where you mention the encouragement you are authorized to give me for writing long letters, & the hint that I am not forgotten by those for whom my heart beats in constant remembrance, I was melted quite to tears, & could not but wish I could have dried them at the feet of those for whom they were shed—but the more I see of the rest of the world, the more attached I feel my self to their rare—rare excellence. The thanks I know not how to express, their goodness will, I am sure, supply: for while they deserve so much more gratitude than I can ever find means to offer, they expect little, & exact none. They are good because it is right to be good, & they are kind because kindness is congenial to their nature. I am sure I need not say how great is my concern in your account of the ill effect of the cold winds to the most charming of plants & flowers, nor my joy that their & our prop escaped suffering by them. Here there has been a disorder the most pernicious, which has been called *la Grippe*, & which, though appearing but as a cold, has proved so frequently fatal especially were joined or succeeding to any other complaint, that it ǀ has operated like a sort of plague, & the doors of apothecaries shops have been crowded by buyers of drugs, with as much *monde* as if they were the entrance into public places; & in the Streets of Paris, there were scarcely more cabriolets than funerals:[2] This is the account that has been brought to me;

---

541. [1] Margaret Planta's letter is missing, but, possibly, FBA's account here of Mme de Staël may be in response to some expression of curiosity about her in the English court.
[2] Cf. *AR* xlv (1803), 'Chronicle', 368: '[Feb.] 12th. The mortality by which Paris is desolated, in consequence of a catarrhal fever, which now rages there, may be said to exceed all bounds of credibility. Within the last ten days, the number of interments were officially reported to amount to 400 a day on the average, or 4000 in the whole of that term.' A report on 'la fièvre catarrhale qui règne à Paris depuis près d'un mois' was published in *Le Moniteur Universal*, 10 Feb. 1803, pp. 568–9.

for into Paris I have not once been since my residence at Passy. Early in the winter I caught a cold, which has not yet entirely left me, & it has only allowed me at intervals of convalescence, which have enabled me much wrapped up, to walk sometimes in the Bois de Boulogne, which is very near us; or upon the Banks of the Seine. The purity of the air of this house saved all who steadily remained in it from this disorder, though M D'arblay, from his occasional excursions to the Capitale, caught it, he had it so slightly, that it neither infected his family, nor lasted beyond a few days for him self. The person whom, in this recent mortality is regarded as the greatest public loss, is M. de La Harpe,[3] who was esteemed the most correct writer of the french language remaining from the Voltaire School: & he is the more to be regretted, as he had publicly renounced the irreligious doctrines of that sect.

It is so long now since I have been able to go out, or see any body, from my tedious, though | not dangerous confinement, that my only chance of getting rid of egotism in my letter, is by recollecting the names of those not yet mentioned with whom I had any intercourse before my Passy residence.

One of the first persons who was pleased to seek me upon my arrival was a lady with whom I had formed an intimate, though short lived acquaintance in England, many years ago, while I was warm with admiration of her talents, & wholly uninformed of her character.[4] As, from advice, I had latterly completely shunned her in my own country, though with infinite difficulty, from her persevering pursuit, I had hoped her pride would have made her distance me in my turn, upon my coming hither: but on the contrary, she was eager to have me acquainted that she impatiently expected to see me; & she sent me immediately a visiting ticket, with her address, &

---

[3] Jean-François de La Harpe had died on 10 February. His obsequies were celebrated on the 14th 'dans l'église métropolitaine de Notre-Dame. Une députation de l'Institut s'est rendue dans la maison où était exposé le corps, qu'elle a accompagné ensuite au cimitière de Vaugirard, où il a été inhumé. Avant qu'on déposât le corps dans le lieu de sa sépulchre, M. Fontanes, l'ami et le collègue de la Harpe, a prononcé un discours noble et touchant' (*Le Moniteur*, 15 Feb. 1803, p. 587).

[4] Fanny Burney and Mme de Staël had met, very probably, at Norbury Park soon after the arrival of the latter at Juniper Hall, Surrey, on 26 or 27 Jan. 1793 (see ii, Ll. 45, 49 *passim*), and a friendship, based on mutual admiration, had flourished until Dr. Burney relayed the fatal letter of 21 February (L. 52) from James Hutton, informing him of Mme de Staël's 'adulterous' liaison with the comte de Narbonne, who was also at Juniper Hall.

enquiries after my health.⁵ I was a good deal distressed, from a real unwillingness, to return civility by offensive rudeness; yet felt so great a repugnance to renewing an acquaintance I had so bitterly regretted ever making, that I determined at least, to leave the matter alone for a week, & then without calling, send my ticket in return. This coldness, however, was insufficient, she commissioned a Lady whom I frequently saw,⁶ to say to me, that though it was not the ⌐ custom for *les dames francoises to make* the first visit, she would put by that *etiquette*, & come to me directly 'if she were sure Madᵉ D'ar. would give her a kind reception' The unexpected humility of this message quite disconcerted me; but I had at that time an excuse only too good for declining to make any direct answer, my dear little Boy was beginning to be ill of his first fever. As soon as she heard of his recovery she wrote me the following note⁷

'Je voudrais vous temoigner mon empressement, Madame, et je crains d'être indiscrete. J'espère que vous aurez la bonté de me faire dire quand vous serez remise des fatigues de votre voyage, pour que je puisse avoir l'honneur de vous voir sans vous importuner'

I was now more disturbed than ever, being extremely unwilling to make her an enemy, yet fixed to retreat from any appearance of considering her as a friend. We consulted together & M D'a, equally anxious upon both these points, with myself, determined that, in about 15 days, I should call upon her, but without any appointment, & that, *chez nous* she should never be recieved. He wrote for me the following answer. ⌐

'Madᵉ D'ar ne peut qu'être infiniment flattée de l'extrême bonté de Madame la Baronne de St. Elle aura l'honneur de se presenter chez Mᵈᶜ de St. aussitôt que possible'

Imagine my surprise when, after evasions so palpable, at the end of about a week, upon seeing & hearing nothing more of me, she came herself in person to me in la R. de Miromenil

I had already desired, should that happen, upon my first arrival, that the *portiere* would say I was not *visible*; this however

---

⁵ See pp. 267–8, 276–81.
⁶ Undoubtedly Mme de Laval (L. 511 n. 6), whom, however, FBA did not see frequently and whose name she often found it impolitic to mention (cf. L. 513, p. 263).   ⁷ Cf. L. 514, p. 277.

did not suffice: she insisted that her name should be brought up, & begged that If I really could not recieve her, M^r D'ar would come down. I sent her word I was a mere *garde malade* to my boy, & could not see any body, & M^r D'ar having no ambition to monopolize all the *sallies* these various provocations might call forth, excused himself from descending. I can hardly tell you in what a tremour I presented myself, at last at the Gate of her Hôtel, nor my joy that she was really abroad: & the very next day she set off for her Father's house at Copet.[8] And there for my great good luck, she has continued ever since. But the business, altogether, gave me a great deal of pain. I was kept, however, the firmer, by having spoken upon my embarrassment to Melle de Mortemart,[9] who when I expressed my wish to avoid all renewal of acquaintance with her on account of the terrible character she bore in England, answered 'It cannot be worse than it is in France.' How greatly is it to be lamented that such parts & talents should be bestowed where there are no principles! & the more is it to be regretted, as she has qualities the most bewitching, of kindness, generosity, & zeal, joined to almost every intellectual attribute that can elevate a human being. Unrestrained passions, in short are her bane; for her heart is as good as her head; & she is so eminently agreeable & engaging, vivacious & clever, & possesses such a boundless fund of good humour, & such nearly matchless charms of conversation, that I can never cease regretting the ungrateful part I have seemed to act towards her, though I was impelled to it by a belief it was indispensably right.

[8] See L. 515 n. 5. FBA was not to see Mme de Staël again in Paris—Napoleon saw to that. Of all the persecutions of women in the Napoleonic era, wrote Forneron (iii. 372–80), the most persevering was that directed against Mme de Staël. The general intention of the First Consul was that 'cette dame, trop connue par son esprit d'intrigue', should not approach the capital. To Faubourg Saint-Germain she would be as good as a banner. On the news that in 1803 she was on her way from Coppet to Paris, orders were given to intercept her at Melun, but the police, missing her there, tracked her down at Mafliers and at the house she had ventured to take in Paris at 540, rue de Lille, and the story of her arrest and conviction is told at length by Herold, pp. 245–55.

An examination of her dossier will show that the police continued to be occupied with her until 1812. In 1807, on the report of her attempted return via Auxerre and Seine-et-Oise, the conquerer at Jena took time to write on the hated subject from Osterode: 'Cette femme continue son métier d'intrigante. Elle s'est approchée de Paris malgré mes ordres. Je ne veux rien souffrir de cette clique.' '*C'est une véritable peste.*' Political subversion he would not tolerate. 'Votre mère n'aurait pas été six mois à Paris', he told Auguste de Staël, 'que je serais forcé de la faire mettre à Bicêtre.' See Madelin, vii. 22–6; also Intro., pp. xxxvii–xxxviii.

[9] Cf. L. 513 n. 3.

Another lady, one of a far different description, who almost as speedily, though far more gently, was so good as to find me upon my arrival, was Mad^e de La Fayette.[10] She mounted up to our apartment; though almost lame, from the result of her long confinement in the dungeon at Olmutz, to invite me herself to spend a week at La Grange, a Chateau which has fallen to her from some relation since the general confiscation of all M. La Fayette's property: | & as she insisted that we should take our little Boy then convalescent, the temptation was too great for resistance:[11] & for the time; it quite reinstated him. La Grange is a very antique Castle, in an airy, healthy & pleasant, though not very picturesque country, only one room of which, an octogone, they have modernized.

The more than unsullied, the exemplary character of Madame de La Fayette, & which supported her blameless, & even honoured by all parties during the horrors of the Revolution, & amidst the bitterest enemies, as well as most enthusiastic friends of her husband, induced me to make this acquaintance without my usual shy reluctance; & I found in her all I could expect of real & solid virtue. She is eminently pious, & her prayers & devotion to God are followed up by the most active & meritorious discharge of her conjugal, maternal, & filial duties; for her father, cy devant Duc d'Ayen[12] still lives. She has singularly expressive eyes, but otherwise is far from handsome: her manners are pleasing, & amiable, & her mind is religiously humble | She lives with the utmost simplicity & economy, have educated their children[13] wholly themselves, keep no sort of equipage, dress in the plainest & cheapest style, & never come to Paris but upon business too important to be arranged by commission. M de La Fayette, who is extremely fond of agriculture, employs all his mornings in his Farm, or his Garden, & gives his Evenings to his Family & books. Withall the various faults charged against him in public life, his conduct in private can admit but of one description. In his own house, he is all that is reputable & amiable, fond, attentive, & instructive to his children, active & zealous for his

---

¹⁰ Cf. L. 517, pp. 301–3.
¹¹ This visit to La Grange must have been made in early May 1802.
¹² Jean-Louis-Paul-François (1739–1824), duc d'Ayen (1766), duc de Noailles (1793). See also L. 514 n. 11.
¹³ For Lafayette's family, see L. 517 n. 18.

friends, gentle & equal with his servants, & displaying, upon every occasion the tenderest gratitude to the wife, who followed him to captivity, & to whom, from that period, he became, by universal account, far more warmly & exclusively attached than he had ever been formerly: though her virtues & conduct had always been objects to him of respect & esteem. Their eldest daughter[14] is about 23 & of a sensible & I serious & estimable character. She is married to M. Charles de la Tour [M]aubourg, a young man, who having no fortune, resides with his wife & 2 little babies, at la Grange,[15] Made de la Fayette told me a most affecting anecdote of the filial devotion of Me C. de [M]aubourg when she was only 16. At that period her father was a captive at Olmutz, & Made de la Fayette was torn from her family, & imprisoned by Robespierre, She languished to follow & comfort & nurse her poor Mother, whose health was always very delicate, but knew not how to travel nor how to whom to apply for protection. She grew so very unhappy, that she determined in her sorrow, in order to fulfil what she thought her first duty, to marry their old Gardener, a working man of upwards 70, who she believed was low & poor enough to escape the Guillotine, & conduct her in safety to the prison: & she had resolved, said Made de la F., if she had done it, to have made him a very good wife, for she would not break a vow once uttered for the universe. Happily, however, the death of that monster, Robespierre prevented this desperate resolution from taking place; & her mother was permitted to return to her children, & take her Girls with her to I share the dungeon of their Father. The Son, M. George La Fayette is a perfectly modest unassuming & worthy young man. He has been married though but just 20, to Mlle de Tracy, since our arrival:[16] & as she has at present no fortune, they, also, have apartments fitted up for them in the attics of the Chateau, which the young lady is in a fair way of soon wanting to enlarge for a coming Heir.[16] Mlle Virginie de Laf[ayette] the youngest daughter is 19;

[14] Anastasie-Louise-Pauline (L. 485 n. 7), her husband Jules-*Charles*-César de Fay (1775–1846), comte de Latour-Maubourg, and their daughter Célestine-Louise-Henriette (1799–1893). Célestine's twin Adrienne had died a few days after birth, and Louise was not born until 1805. Virginie de Lafayette (L. 517 n. 18) was still unmarried.   [15] See L. 446 n. 5.
[16] George Washington du Motier, 6th marquis de Lafayette (1834), and Emilie Destutt de Tracy were married on 6 June 1802 (L. 517 n. 18). Their daughter Nathalie was born in 1803.

but has so high a bloom upon a fair complexion, that she hardly looks to be 15. She has a very good understanding, & a very distinguished air, though she stoops, &, for France, has a bad carriage; 'How should it be otherwise?' said her Mother, to whom it was remarked by a friend, 'elle a eté elevée dans les prisons!'

The family came to Paris about 6 weeks ago, to prepare for marrying M. G[eorge] La Fayette to Mlle de Tracy, when M. de L.f. during the severe frost slipt down & broke his thigh.[17] He has been extended ever since, by a wooden machine, upon his bed; & has suffered, & is suffering, at times, the utmost torture; yet whether he can ever perfectly recover the use of his limb is still doubtful. It is now forced down to its proper length by the means of screws fastened to the wooden machine, which encases it, in a manner that ┃ causes him excrutiating pain. His wife & children never quit him a moment. They are all at the house of M^de Tessé,[17] who is sister to the duc d'Ayen & Aunt to M^ade de La Fayette.

When we had finished our visit at la Grange, M^ade La Fayette et Mlle la fille accompanied us to Paris, where they had calls to see & prepare for Mlle de Tracy, whose marriage was then to take place in a few days. We were all cheerful in the route; but when we approached the capital, M^de de Laf[ayette] sunk into profound silence, & the most melancholy rumination: & as we passed through the Barriere her eyes were raised in fervent prayer. She soon after struggled to revive, but her spirits returned no more. A lady of the party gave me a hint to make no enquiry, & informed me afterwards, that, at that very Barriere, this poor lady had lost in one morning, her grandmother, her mother, the D^s d'Ayen, & her favourite Sister, La V^elle de Noailles by the Guillotine![18] She had mentioned to me herself this dreadful catastrophe, but not the spot

---

[17] The accident was reported in *Le Publiciste* (8 Feb. 1803, p. 4): 'M. de Lafayette s'est cassé la cuisse le 15, en tombant sur la glâce; il sortait de chez le ministre de la marine. Cette fracture est accompagnée de beaucoup de douleurs; mais le malade montre un grand courage. . . .' Mme de Tessé's town house was at 24, rue d'Anjou.

[18] La Barrière de Picpus, one of the 50 or more structures (gatehouses or custom-houses), usually of classical design, erected in the early nineteenth century on the principal approaches to the city.

In the spring of 1794 the three ladies of the Noailles family, Mme de Lafayette's sister Louise, her mother, and her grandmother (then aged 70 and stone deaf) had been accused of 'conspiracy', removed from the Hôtel de Noailles-Mouchy to the

on which it happened, in shedding a deluge of tears, while I was still at la Grange

I must run away from those sad subjects | And how can I do it more successfully than in reciting a speech which has been repeated to me of a certain bonny Duchess. She has a *loge* at the Opera house, in which she wished to recieve only a select party. She called therefore, to the Box-opener & said *'Ouvrier! Si vous laisses vener aucun personne dans mon boite, je vous chasse!'*

Last summer we met with a gentleman who has since made no small Noise in the world, Colonel Sebastiani.[19] My little Alex was asked by some of the company who understood English to declaim in his own language.

He chose a speech of Tom Thumb,[20] which I recollect he had once the happy fortune to recite within the fragrant scent of a sweet violet: this speech demands a sword & the little [*blank*] strutted up to the Colonel, & made him a Sign for he could not then speak french, that he must disarm. The Colonel, who could with difficulty recover it from him, said if he were so fond of warlike instruments, he would take him into his

Luxembourg, unfeelingly treated as prisoners, and guillotined on 22 July 1799 with the marks of contemptuous brutality described by André Maurois in the chapter 'La Sombre Boucherie', pp. 294–303. Their bodies were then carted to a common burial pit, containing some 1,300 headless corpses, in a bit of wasteland nearby (formerly the garden of a convent) opening off the rue de Picpus. In 1803–5 Mme de Lafayette and her sister Pauline (Mme de Montagu) were instrumental in re-establishing a religious community in the enclosure (the Ladies of the Sacred Heart and of the Perpetual Adoration, whose vows included an unbroken chain of prayer). There was also a chapel in which an annual Mass for the 1,300 martyrs was to be celebrated (Maurois, pp. 500–5). See also Intro., p. xliv.

Of the three ladies, the eldest was Catherine-Françoise-Charlotte de Cossé de Brissac (1724–94), who had married in 1737 Louis de Noailles (1713–93), duc d'Ayen (1737), maréchal de France (1775), duc de Noailles (1766). The second, Mme de Lafayette's mother, was Henriette-Anne-Louise d'Aguesseau (1737–94), who had married in 1755 Jean-Louis-Paul-François de Noailles (1739–1824), duc d'Ayen (1766), duc de Noailles (1793). Her daughter Louise (1758–94) had married in 1773 a cousin Louis-Marie (1756–1804), vicomte de Noailles.

[19] The comte Horace-François-Bastien Sébastiani de la Porta (1772–1851), a Corsican, général de brigade (29 Aug. 1803). Having been employed in a diplomatic mission to Turkey in 1801, Sébastiani was sent in August 1802 to Egypt, ostensibly on a fact-finding mission, and the publication of his report (*Le Moniteur*, 30 Jan. 1803, pp. 523–6), a document highly derogatory to the English ('Le général Stuart est un homme d'esprit médiocre . . . Six mille Français suffiraient aujourd'hui pour conquérir l'Egypte') but highly laudatory of Bonaparte and fraudulently encouraging his fondest wishes and designs, was considered by the English a deliberate provocation to war. See *AR* xlv (1803), 742–52; Whitworth's remonstrance, *Despatches*, p. 166; *CMH*, ix. 103; *The Times*, 5 Feb. 1803. See also Thompson, pp. 219–21, for the effects of the publication.

[20] This speech from Fielding's burlesque, AA would have recited on the occasion of his presentation to Princess Amelia on 10 Apr. 1800. See iv, Ll. 371, 374; and L. 466 n. 7.

regiment 'Et vous vie, avec moi' he added 'à | Constantinople? Qui en dites vous?' The child, when this was explained, very simply answered 'Yes, if Mamma'll go' The Colonel could do no less than offer to take la Mamman. What a pretty group such a trio would have made in such an expedition!

Of the same party was the good Abbê Ricard[21] who was lately a victim to *la Grippe*. He was the translator of Plutarch into french, & a writer upon Astronomy for youth, in verse and other works for juvenile instruction. He sat next la *Mamman*, & his plainness, quietness, & simplicity made her wish to see him again, which, however she never did & much regrets his loss by this fatal infection.

The note with which I sent my last letter to Lord Whitworth[22] procured me an answer not merely polite but kind, professing the most obliging readiness at any time, & on any occasion, to be of service to me. I regret excessively my distance from his chapel, though for this last winter, indeed, I must have refrained from going to it, had it been in the next street. I am | reduced to reading the morning service of a Sunday with my little Boy, who I thank Heaven, notwithstanding his sword flourishes, has the happiest propensities for attending to & comprehending religious instructions. The Duchess of Dorset,[23] I am told, has a plan, upon removing to her new Hotel, of having her seats in the chapel close to the door, so that as soon as the service is over, She may go away. She can see company, she says, afterwards in her drawing room, but she shall avoid by this retreat, what she greatly disapproves, being surrounded by discussions of Balls & Plays, immediately upon the spot where she has heard Divine Service. She has the character of being strongly attached to her husband and children, fond of domestic life, & very seriously good: Lord Whitworth is very generally approved.

We have no news yet of *la retraite*![24] But still cherish hopes, as none remains upon any other prospect!

[21] Dominique Ricard (1741–1803) had died on 28 January. His translation of Plutarch's *Œuvres Morales* (17 vols.) had appeared 1783–95. For *Les Vies des Hommes Illustres* and *La Sphère*, see L. 543 n. 7.
[22] Charles Whitworth (L. 525 n. 13). His polite note of 22 January is extant in the d'Arblay collection: 'Lord Whitworth presents his Compliments to Madame d'Arblay and begs leave to assure her that he shall at all times and on all occasions have particular pleasure in Attending to her Commands.'
[23] Arabella Diana *née* Cope. For her marriages, and the perplexity caused by her retention of the title above. See L. 505 n. 9.   [24] See L. 536 n. 5.

Adieu, my dear Miss Planta. your letter was delivered to me again in 5 days? What a pleasure! Believe me your ever obliged, & affectionate Friend & Servant. F. D. ar.
M. D.ar presents his best Complements
My Boy is now in perfect health. I thank God

542   [54, rue Basse], Passy,
                                          22–24 March, 1803

To Mrs. Waddington

A.L.S. (Berg), 22–4 Mar. 1803
Two double sheets 4to   6 pp.
Addressed: Mrs. Waddington, / Lanover Court, / Abergavenny.
Taken to England by James Greene,[1] *c.* 25 Mar. 1803

Passy—March 22ᵈ 1803.

Let me now more fully answer your last interesting Letter, my dearest Marianne—though I feel a real concern at the opportunity which now presents itself for my writing more at length. How sincerely I hope the carrier[1] of this will bring me back the best of all Answers—a verbal one!—& not one remembered—but *living & looking.*—The anxiety we just now suffer at the bare rumour of hostilities[2] is undiscribable. With attachments on both sides so just & merited to our separate friends, imagine but the horror of being forced to renounce, for so indeterminate a Time as a War between two such nations, the

---

542. [1] James Greene (L. 517 n. 1) is going to England, Bertie Greatheed noted on 17 Mar. 1803, 'for a short time. What can this be for? He will be a great loss to our society, for he has contributed much, both to our amusement and information. We sat till two, and had some solid talk political and religious'. On 26 March he again reported, Greene has left us—'a great loss indeed to our society'.
   [2] Resentments on the part of both nations were by this time breaking into print. What alarmed the British government were Bonaparte's aggressions and annexations, amongst which were the seizure of Piedmont and Elba since the signing of the treaty of Amiens (25 Mar. 1802); the dispatch of General Leclerc and a large expeditionary force to San Domingo (14 Dec. 1801) while the treaty was still in negotiation; the implications of Sébastiani's well-publicized mission to Egypt and Syria (see L. 541 n. 19); and to cap this, the threat posed in 1803 by a French expedition to India. Other irritants included Napoleon's acquisition of Louisiana from Spain (later sold to the United States); his election as president of the new Italian Republic; and his protectionist laws and embargoes on certain classes of

sight & all intercourse with one side or the other!—But let me
fly from this painful subject, &, while hope may be indulged,
not anticipate evil.

I grieve most sincerely at your continual alarms & sufferings
for your poor little precious youngest Jewel.[3]—I am truly
concerned at the swelling of your Eye-lids, & frequent complaints of that most valuable of our senses, sight. My poor
dearest Marianne! with a youth of such perfection in the
enjoyment of every species of health, who could have foreseen
you could scarcely reach maturity without nearly forfeiting
them all! If it is to your Children, treasures as they prove to
you, you must attribute so dire a change, I do not wonder
my wish turned you sick!—You have cured me, I assure you!—
& yet, who knows but that its completion might make you
well?—However, I won't wish it, I promise You. |

I wish to hear something more of Sister Louisa. Pray tell
me whether Mr. Layard's Father, the Dean, once preached at
oxenden chapel?[4] there was an admirable preacher there of that
name, whom I frequently heard, when I lived in St. Martin's
Street.—I think you have not quite forgotten there was such
a time!—What you say of your sister's abilities is indeed surprising; but what I see you wish me to write about, is Mrs.
Piozzi.[5]—Alas, my dear Mary, that, to me, is a melancholy

foreign goods. In the face of these omens, the British Government delayed in
handing over the strategic base of Malta, as required by the treaty, to the Knights
of St. John. This considered delay and the threat it offered to French expansion in
the Mediterranean regions became the crux of the French complaint against the
British, though Bonaparte's anger was fanned continuously by the crude caricatures
of himself and his family poured forth by the British press. In short, 'entre Bonaparte
et l'Angleterre, ce n'était en réalité que le conflit de deux impérialismes' (see
Lefebvre, 'La rupture de la paix d'Amiens', pp. 154–67; also Madelin, iv. 267 ff.).

   [3] Augusta Waddington (b. 21 Mar. 1802). See L. 532 n. 4.
   [4] A chapel established in 1675 on Oxendon Street, in the parish of St. James,
Westminster, by the wife of the Nonconformist Divine Richard Baxter (1651–91).
Soon driven out, he rented the chapel for fifty years to the parish of St. Martin-
in-the-Fields. Still a chapel of the 'Established Religion' when the Burneys lived
in St. Martin's Street, it was demolished in 1876 to make way for the Civil Service
stores. For the Layard family, see L. 540 n. 2.
   [5] It may have been GMAPW's request that reminded FBA to include the Thrale–
Piozzi story in the 'petites histoires' that she was undertaking at this time to write
in French as part of her systematic exercises in French, some of which still survive
in four Notebooks, 1802–6 (Berg). This story or 'statement', by far the longest and
most detailed that Mme d'Arblay ever wrote on the subject of Mrs. Thrale, her
first sight of her at St. Martin's Street, the subsequent great friendship, and the

subject, for though she was never a character approaching to any of those ideas of perfection my mind had formed—& which so few like Mrs. Delany, Mrs. Lock, & my lost Angel sister fulfilled—yet, with all her errors & exentricities about her, she had once a fond possession of my sincere & ardent friendship. — — For though she was always vain of her talents, & proud of her pedigree, she was ever the first to laugh at her own vanity, & expose & mock her own pride, even while she cherished them. She was warm-hearted, generous, sweet-tempered, & full of active zeal for her friends, & of fervent devotion in religion. She was replete with wit & pleasantry, & her powers of entertainment exceeded those of almost any woman I ever knew. But her manners were flaunting, her voice was loud, & she had no peace, & allowed none to others, but in the display of her talents. With draw backs such as these to her better parts, you will not suppose I could ever have *chosen* her for my friend,—yet, being by her chosen, she conceived for me so enthusiastic a regard, that it nearly amounted to a species of idolatry. She was never contented when I was out of her house, never happy when away from her sight. All she did that was singular, & I had better have been left undone, all she said, that was strange, & had better have been left unsaid, she suffered me to point out, & with a frankness the most extraordinary would acknowledge she had been wrong, & make, if it were in her power, reparation, either by some change of measures, or softenings of speech. Her whole conduct to me, during the whole time of our intimacy, was of a nature the most endearing that can be conceived; but her marriage annulled, at once, the connexion. She did not trust me with her design, till she had bound herself to carry it into execution. Even then, it was accident brought it forth, for she could not doubt my entire dislike of so unaccountable a choice, nor my sincerity in speaking it. It was from the abbé Gerard's synonimes[6] that

painful estrangement, will be printed in Appendix I, volume vii, where Mrs. Piozzi reappears, as it were, in the flesh. For the story in brief, see *HFB*, pp. 174–84; and Clifford *passim*.

[6] According to the 'petite histoire' (*supra*), FB, Dr. Johnson, and Mrs. Thrale had been reading Gabriel Girard (1677–1748), *La Justesse de la langue françoise, ou les différentes significations des mots qui passent pour synonymes* (1718), wherein the Abbé had made distinctions in the usage of the words 'Penser, Songer, Rêver', as follows:

'On *pense* tranquillement & avec ordre, pour connoître son objet. On *songe* avec

the discovery was made to me, & from the article Songer, penser, rêver—But though the detection, & it's avowal were subjects of true grief of heart to me in those days, when my feelings were so tenderly involved in hers & her affairs, I did not dream of relinquishing our friendship on that account: she was not my ward—far otherwise,—I had no right over her actions, & however ill advised & imprudent—& perhaps improper her decision, it yet was not criminal: I kept up, therefore, the same connexion, & felt as much of the same affection as the change of esteem into pity could sustain—but as various circumstances relative to her Children, which occurred, retarded her plan, & at times made her seem to waver in its ultimate execution, I scrupled not expressing my earnest wishes it might be given up—& O what Scenes followed!—sometimes I prevailed ¦ entirely—then she repented her compliance—then she repented her engagement—then her senses seemed to fail her—then she raved—then she was seized with a sort of stupor—then she used to fall suddenly asleep, & talk aloud — — frightful period!—I had no peace or rest, if I conciliated for restoring her tranquility, I felt as if accessory to what seemed to me a degradation of all sorts,—for Piozzi was more beneath her in understanding & in Mind than in education & birth—& if I opposed in the hope to prevent so ill-judged an alliance, the sufferings of her health or her senses menaced me with shortening or embittering her existence. Yet, during all this time, her kindness, her sweetness, her fondness never wavered, never abated — — imagine therefore, my surprise when, upon her marriage actually taking place, she suddenly wrote me a Letter of reproach for the want of cordiality in my congratulations! — — ! as if it were possible to rejoice in what I so deeply lamented! or as if a change from sincerity to hypocrisy ought not to have been as despicable to her as it

plus d'inquiétude & sans suite, pour parvenir à ce qu'on souhaite. On *rêve* d'une manière abstraite & profonde, pour s'occuper agréablement.

'Le Philosophe *pense* à l'arrangement de son systême. L'homme embarrassé d'affaires *songe* aux expédiens pour en sortir. L'amant solitaire *rêve* à ses amours — Le Plaisir de rêver est peut-être le plus doux, mais le moins utile & le moins raisonnable de tous.'

In the discussion that followed, Mrs. Thrale fell wholly silent, fled to her room in tears, later confessing to FB in a 'billet' that the cause of all this was 'une malheureuse passion'. 'C'était un aveu que j'avais deviné', wrote FBA, 'quoique Dieu sait je n'avais rien deviner du tout!' It was only later that putting '100 things together' FB hit upon the object of the passion ('si étrange'), 'Piozzi!!!! — !'

would have been detestable in me! I wrote her for my sole reply that I committed to Time & her own Recollections my answer. She then sent me some very kind words, but very short, saying she was immediately setting off for Italy. I wrote an immediate promise to forget the only *UN*Kind words that had ever dropt from her, & added all I thought most soothing: but I have never heard from her since. Whether, as she was departing, my Letter did ᴵ not reach her, or whether she deemed our friendship a fitting sacrifice to offer up to her new engagements, I know not. Certainly as to *him*, I never was his enemy; *he* was not in fault; & deserved not any blame. She was neither of an Age nor a disposition to be seduced — — though how she could so be bewitched, I have never been able to fathom. He was an itinerant musician, admirable in his profession, but without any other recommendation. And she cared not for Music! — — I have known nothing of her, except two or three accidental sights, since her marriage; I hear from all quarters how much she is altered—& your account gave me real pain.—How differently would you have described her in the days of her triumph & of Streatham! — — I never without extreme reluctance enter upon a subject which calls forth so much regret. Dr. Johnson's opinion of her in those days did her but justice. I can only attribute all I am told of her spirits & conduct, to a determination she has taken to hide her consciousness of her fall, by seeming content to let it pass that she never held herself above her present circle. Basta! — —

You will hear from Mr. Green that M. d'Ar. is in search of his *retraite*, & its history⁷—It is all now he has left to hope here, so utterly has the revolution swallowed up all his former rights & expectations.

Poor Mr. G[reene]!—the cruelty of his early loss of such a companion as you describe, almost dissolves into pity all blame of his subsequent ᴵ conduct. And yet—who but must wish where so much seems good that all were right? I wish to know if that Miss Bull⁸ were any relation of a charming Mr. Bull I

---

⁷ See L. 536 n. 5; and L. 546 n. 6.
⁸ By this time FBA had learned something of Greene's marital history, as outlined by James C. Scholes, op. cit., who had found a marriage settlement dated 9 Sept. 1777, indicating that a marriage took place or was arranged to take place between Catherine Ball and James Greene (L. 517 n. 1), then seventeen years old and heir to the Manor of Turton Tower, the capital mansion-house, and

formerly knew, who had two very accomplished Daughters.[9] They lived in Stratton Street Piccadilly, but retired to the Isle of Wight for the health of the youngest daughter, Catherine, who died 4 or 5 years ago of a consumption. We both think Mr. G[reene] uncommonly amiable; but though he *buffets with adversity*, I fear he is unhappy to the very bottom of his Soul.

What a charming & accomplished little Girl is my namesake! I return you with a thousand thanks her Book of Drawings —& Alex says he hopes she will send it us back to look at again when she has filled up the rest of the leaves. He has conceived a great respect for her.

March 24th We return with many thanks to your lovely Emily the pretty & pious stories of her Sister, which Alex knows entirely by heart. I delight to recognize in their thoughts & manner the education they receive in the most serious points from their dear Mother.

How clever are her Maps for her Age, & for being done by Memory!—Alex was wild with pleasure in seeing them. The Diary I must keep till the next safe opportunity—be sure I will take the utmost care of your ingenious & even surprising little Pupil's composition. I have not yet read it to M. d'Arblay, & cannot part with it till I have given him that pleasure.

Adieu, my dear Friend—God bless you!—ever!—

F d'A. |

numbers of messuages, farmlands, cottages, mills, and tenements in Lancashire Whether or not this marriage took place, a second settlement, dated 5 Feb. 1780, arranged for his marriage to Anne Brigstocke (1762–1810), daughter of Owen Brigstocke (1740–78) of Blaenpant, Cardiganshire.
Described by Samuel Parr on his visit to Llansantfraed in 1791 as 'beautiful, witty, sagacious, truth-speaking, warm-hearted' (see Warren Derry, *Dr. Parr . . .* (1966), p. 151), Anne Greene had five legitimate daughters, Mary Anne (1780–1845), Arabella Penelope Eliza (1781–1865), Charlotte Alice (d. Oct. 1847), Angelina Frances (*c.* 1791–1846), and Anna Sophie (bapt. 23 Sept. 1797), and subsequently two children conceived in adultery (see L. 532 n. 1). With large dowries, at least three of the legitimate daughters made wealthy marriages, and the lawsuit initiated by the eldest daughter to prove the illegitimacy of the son necessitated Greene's visit to England in 1802. See further Edward A. and Lillian D. Bloom, vii, L. 788 nn. 2, 3.

9 Confusing the names Bull and Ball, FBA's mind skipped back to a family she had known in the 1780s (see *DL*, iii. 216), namely, Catharine Susanna Bull (d. 13 Oct. 1795) and her elder sister Elizabeth (*c.* 1750–1809), daughters of Richard Bull (*c.* 1725–1805), M.P. (1756–90), of 10 Stratton Street, Piccadilly, and of Northcourt House, Shorwell, Newport, the Isle of Wight, a house he had acquired in 1795 for the health of his younger daughter. There are memorial plaques to both sisters in the church at Shorwell, and older residents remember a Chinese pagoda erected in Catharine's memory on the hill above the village.

543

To Doctor Burney

[54, rue Basse], Passy,
23 March 1803

A.L. uncompleted (Diary MSS. vi. 5668–[71], Berg), 23 Mar. 1803
Double sheet 4to   4 pp.   foliated 41, 42
Carried to London with L. 548 (*which served as the cover*) by Mr. Hodgson[1] on
15 May 1803.
Edited by FBA, p. 1 (5668), *annotated, date retraced & repeated*: ⁛ 1803
1803 (I.) Painful silence   La *Grippe* or The Influenza fatal at Paris.
M. La Harpe,   &c Passy,   Lord Whitworth.
Edited also by the Press.

Passy, March 23ᵈ

No, my dearest Padre, *bumptious!*—no![2] I deny the charge
in toto. I had not such a thought—or rather such a feel in the
World; but 'twas very *disencouraging, Tommy,*[3] to receive none
of that Coin which urged forth my merchandise!—for I had
hoped some in the narratory Letters, in which I so delight,[4] &
which nobody writes in so interesting a manner, to *MY gusto*—
& which you used to enliven my retirement with occasionally
in our *tight little* Island. However, if it must not be expected,
I will make up my mind the best I can to the good of the World,
in this public monopolizer of a Dictionary,[5] to which I should
feel, I doubt not, less grudge, if it were more in my way.

543. [1] The Revd. Edward Hodgson (1776–1853), chaplain to the English embassy
at Paris, was to leave France on 19 May 1803. For the next fifty years (1803–53)
he was to be rector of Laindon, Essex. See *GM* lxxiii[2] (1803), 785.
   [2] This rhodomontade is missing with CB's letter.
   [3] 'Tommy' was Dr. Thomas Augustine Arne (1710–1778), musician and composer, to whom in the 1740s CB was apprenticed and with whom for a time he
lived (see *DNB*, and Scholes *passim*). '. . . rather *dis*encouraging, Tommy' was the
somewhat doleful comfort that Mrs. Arne (Cecilia *née* Young, 1711–89), the singer,
offered to her husband on his being hissed. CB and the singer had become great
friends in 1744 when in that year she 'rode on a pillion' behind him from Chester
to London; and his attribution of the phrase to her occurs in his letter (Berg) of
22 July 1799, though in the printed version of it (*DL*, v. 437), *dis*encouraging has
been emended to discouraging. The expressive phrase remained in Burneyan
vocabulary (cf. iv, L. 364, p. 395).
   [4] FBA was longing for such letters as CB had formerly written about his pilgrim-
ages to Shrewsbury, Chester, and Lichfield in the year 1797 (iii, Ll. 242, 245, 248)
or about his visit to Dover in the year 1799 at the launching of the Secret Expedition to the Helder (see Scholes, ii. 297–300).
   [5] From a popular song in T. J. Dibden, *The British Raft* (1797):
         Oh! what a snug little Island,
         A right little, tight little Island!
In later years FBA here supplied the editorial note: 'N.B.—Dr. B.—was then

I have been anxious to write since I received your last kind enquiries, my dearest Padre but ⌜this opportunity I now take has been *intended* to be ready almost from the moment I wanted it, & the hope of a full Journal, escaping such a cost made me delay writing by the Post. I trust, as Maria has written to our Esther, you have had no fear or uneasiness from my not being quicker, for she has assured me she has told my amendment. Nevertheless,⌝ so tedious has been my seizure, that I have not yet got from its wraps or confinements. I feel, however, as if this were their last day, & that to-morrow ⌐ would have the honour to see me abroad. I have had no fever, & no physician, & no important malady; but cold has fastened upon Cold, so as to utterly to imprison me. *La Grippe*, however, I escaped, so has Alex, & our maid & Helpers—& M. d'Ar[blay] who caught it latterly, in his excursions to Paris, had it so slightly, that but for the fright attached to the first seizure—(which I thought would almost have demolished me at first from the terror hanging on its very name at that fatal period) I should have deemed it a mere common cold. It is now universally over, but the mischief it has done is grievously irreparable. M. de La Harpe *I* moan the most,[6]—& much regret never having seen. The abbé Ricard, who had just published about half his translation of Plutarch, I was also very sorry for: I had dined in his Company once, & he was my next neighbour; & so gentle, so quiet, so modest, so reserved, that he appeared an almost *singular* character in these times. Do you know his poem called *La Sphere*?[7] ⌜*Qui contient les élémens de la Sphere, celeste et terrestre, avec des principes d'astronomie physique; accompagné de Notes, et suivi d'une notice des poëmes Grecs, Latins, et françois qui traitent de quelque partie de l'astronomie?* He speaks highly & justly

writing for the Encyclopedia'. She meant, of course, Rees's *Cyclopaedia* (see Lonsdale, pp. 407–31), which was not completed until 1819.
   [6] Jean-François de La Harpe had died on 10 Feb. 1803 (cf. L. 541 n. 3).
   [7] Thirteen volumes of Ricard's *Les Vies des Hommes Illustres de Plutarque* (1798–1803) had appeared by 1803, the year of Ricard's death. *La Sphère, Poëme en huit chants* . . . (1796), the subtitle of which FBA has substantially correct, includes an apostrophe (Chant II) to 'Laborieux Herschel, dont les efforts heureux / D'une nouvelle sphere ont enrichi les cieux'. The section includes praise of Caroline Herschel (1750–1848), also a 'disciple d'Uranie', who, forgetting her night's repose, has shared her brother's 'pénible étude'. The biographical notes outline the achievements of the Herschels, and Ricard explains that the new planet is named '*Georgium sidus*, l'étoile de George, à l'honneur du roi d'Angleterre, à qui l'astronomie . . . et M. Herschel . . . ont les plus grandes obligations'.
   For CB's verses on astronomy, see iii, iv *passim*.

in it of your friend & favourite, Herschel, & ┃ has composed an episode sur la planete découverte par Herschel, & he has celebrated *Miss Caroline Herschel* in his notes, & spoke properly of the great & good Patron. The poem is written professedly for the instruction of young people. It is by no means comparable with one I know, yet being written by a good & learned man, & for a good purpose, it is interesting as well as instructive.⌐ I am really sorry he is gone—& by an illness so insidious—that appeared to have so little authority for the havock it made!— Madᵉ Trimouille,[8] the lady of the house at Monsseau of which we occupied a *pavillon*, sunk under it also. As did the Mother in Law[9] of Bood's Brother the Doctor. It was a disastrous & frightful time. The streets of Paris were said to be as full of Funerals as of Cabriolets. For my own part, I have not once been able to enter that Capital since I left it the end of October. But I cannot help attributing much of the mortality which prevailed in consequence of this slight disease, to the unwholesome air occasioned by the dreadful want of cleanliness in that City, which but for the air & health of the beautiful & delicious walks around it, Les Boulevards, must surely have proved pestilential. ⌐For myself, I do not think I could live & *be well* in the Metropolis of either of the Kingdoms.⌐ The air of our house at Passy is perfectly pure & sweet. ⌐My colds here have but been the ┃ effect of œconomizing our fires, by living from room to room, to make *all* habitable with the expense of only one at a time being aired in rotation. But all is now over,— I trust, & my Alex is resorted to perfect health. He is much grown & looks tall, rosy & flourishing. He is able to express every thing he wishes in french, but as we always talk English together, & he lives with me constantly, English is still the superior language.⌐

By never going to Paris, I have never, of course, seen our ambassadour or his Duchess:[10] but I had particular occasion to apply to the former upon some business; I was obliged to introduce myself to him without any Sir Clem. Cott. by

[8] Louise-Jeanne-Françoise *née* Emery (1760–1803), the wife of Jacques-Ezékiel de Tremouilles, was FBA's landlady at 286, rue Cisalpine, Monceau. She had died in February.

[9] Emmanuel-Geneviève *née* de Pourgole (d. 1803), the wife of Louis-Alexandre d'Hermand de Cléry (*fl.* 1735–80), avocat au Parlement, whose daughter Marie-Geneviève (L. 450 n. 6) had married the physician Bourdois de la Motte.

[10] Lord Whitworth and his wife, the Duchess of Dorset (see L. 505 n. 9).

a Note:[11]—his behaviour was all you could have wished; he immediately complied with the request with which I had troubled him, & wrote me one of the most polite & *best worded* answers I ever read, finishing it with an assurance he should *at all times, & upon all occasions, have particular pleasure in attending to M^e d'Ar.'s commands.* The very only thing that I regret not residing in Paris for is my inability to go to his Ex's Chapel.

I send you a News-paper, to let you see *Titles* can be *bestowed* here, as well as taken away.[12]

M. d'Ar. is now making a last effort with respect to his *retraite*,[13] which has languished in adjournment above a year. He has put it into the hands of a faithful & most amiable Friend, now in high esteem with the Premier Consul, General Lauriston, who so kindly, so touchingly renewed an ancient friendship with his former Camarade when he was on his splendid short embassy in England.[14] If through him it should fail, I shall never think of those

544   54, rue Basse, Passy,
                                      6 April–16 June 1803
To Mrs. Broome

A.L. mutilated (rejected Diary MSS. 5672–[75], Berg), 6 Apr.–16 June 1803
Double sheet 4to (9 × 7·5″), the second leaf of which was cut and pasted as described in the Textual Notes 4 pp. *pmk* FOREIGN OF[FICE] / 22 JU / 1803 wafer cut and torn
Addressed: Mrs. Broome, in the care, / of Mrs Burney / Beaumont Street, / London
Sent through Mrs. Barthélémy Huber,[1] 16 June 1803
Endorsed by CBFB: [Sis]ter d'arblay / [ans]w^d July 28th / 1803
Edited and mutilated by CFBt.

[11] A generic term derived from the office of Clement Cottrell-Dormer (1686–1758), master of the king's ceremonies (1711–58). Cf. iv, L. 321 n. 3.
[12] Possibly a facetious reference to a speech made by Miot, orateur du gouvernement, in which he explained and advocated a law regulating the conferment of both *prénoms* and surnames on citizens of the Republic. His speech to the Corps législatif was reported in detail in *Le Moniteur* for 23 Mar. 1803.
Apart from the Army, the title *Citoyen* was in universal use. A chapter in A. Laquiante, 'La Cour et le monde officiel', shows the growing concern and interest in the dress, ceremonials, and usages of the ancien régime.   [13] See L. 536 n. 5.
[14] General Lauriston (L. 425 n. 5) had by this time been sent on a diplomatic mission to Austria. See L. 546 n. 5.
544. [1] Lydia *née* Strutt (L. 487 n. 2).

April 6th 1803.
Passy—Rue basse,
No 54.
Pres Paris.

I flagelate myself—*mentally!*—doubly & trebly every day for my silence to my dearest Charlotte,[2] from my certitude of her patience in bearing it. I almost fear, sometimes, nevertheless, that with all her forbearance, she will begin to want to flagellate me less sentimentally, if I do not amend!—But I hear of you, my dear soul, often, & through various Channels, though I seldom earn hearing in a direct line; & I am sure you have frequent news of me & mine, though only through the same round about roads. I have now, however, the grace to determine to get ready for the next opportunity of conveyance that offers; on the moment when they present themselves there is rarely time for more than a word. I should send a thousand apologies to my dear Charlottina, also, but that I have firmly settled in my own mind to practice the same virtue for the next occasion by her. I send her, therefore, *sans honte*, my thanks for her 3 Letters[2]—& a little hint how generous would be a fourth, *en attendant* payment! with something of the beauties of Exmouth. I have been there, & was much struck with them myself.

I am really & truly anxious, my dearest Charlotte, to know how you found your Ralph, & if he had any remembrance of you. Probably not, at least not at first; but though in the memory of such ⁱ infants, all objects are fleeting, they have some little vague impression, that makes them soon re-trace, a something that renders those they have once loved pleasant, they know not why, to their acquaintance, till, by degrees, they work their way back to their recollections. ⌐Pray let me know how you manage about seeing him, & if you have any *other* intentions? Whether Mr. B. repents his unnatural conduct,[3]

---

[2] This is FBA's apology for her failure to reply to a joint letter (Barrett, Eg. 3693, ff. 84–5b) written by Mrs. Broome and her daughter Charlotte Francis on 23 Oct. 1802, the day following their arrival in London after a visit of about two months to France.

The letters written by Charlotte Francis (later Barrett) to her aunt from Exmouth are missing, but that Charlotte, her mother, and her half-brother Ralph were there by April 1803 is indicated by a letter (Berg) of that date, addressed by Marianne Francis to her sister Charlotte at Clift End, Exmouth.

[3] During the visit of Mrs. Broome and her daughter to France, Ralph Broome, not yet two years of age, had been left with his father, who, with his natural

& whether his repentance has any chance of being acceptable? I will not write further upon a matter of so much delicacy, in which your own unbiassed feelings can alone guide you, till I have something of the state of things, lest I should be so unhappy as to drop, in ignorance, any thing that might pain where I most wish to soothe—⁷

We settled ourselves at Passy the last day or so of October. I reserve the name of Joigny for my Charlottina. We came hither while all the Workmen were still employed, &, as they be all *villagers*, of *Passy*, not artists & artisans of Paris, they have been so slow, so stupid, so sleepy, that they kept possession of the premises two or 3 months after our entrance, only in finishing what, with more skill or more alacrity, might have been done almost in as many days. Indeed, whenever M. d'Arblay did not work at their head, I believe they made it a rule to take a Nap in community, for we never ‖ could discover what was done in his absence. We were forced, at last, to send them off while all is incomplete. Nevertheless, the position is so pretty, so retired, yet so chearful, & so pure, though so near to all sort of unsavoury odours, that I am extremely fond of the place, & would not change it for any in this Country. It just suits us, & we have it, *à l'anglaise*, to ourselves.

You have left yourself much admired at [Hotel Marengo] & Charlottina, I fancy, gave some witching drug [to the Lord] of the Mansion & the Portiere,⁴ they sang her p[raises to] me

daughter Miriam (iv, L. 257 n. 11) had spent the summer in Lympstone (see Mrs. Broome's letter of 23 October (*supra* n. 2)).

The Broome marriage, so strenuously opposed by the male members of the Burney family, was now breaking up. The 'unnatural' conduct may refer to Broome's threats to separate mother and son or perhaps to an illegitimate daughter of his own, which, as his will suggests (see L. 434 n. 2), he may have begotten about this time. Broome, however, was deteriorating mentally as well as physically and was to die a howling death at Bath on 24 Feb. 1805, attended to the last by Mrs. Broome and one or the other of her daughters. See the letters and journals of Marianne Francis (Berg) for the years 1805–6; and a letter (Berg) from CPB to his mother 'Rosette', dated 24 Jan. 1804.

'Poor Mʳ Broome is quite gone:—that is to say, he *exists*:—but he is weak & imbecile both in mind and body:—his eye glares on vacancy, and he looks at least *a five thousand* removed from the clever, lively author of Simpkin's letters.— It would be no less a mercy to himself than to others, if he would take his departure; —which he has told me frequently, that he wishes. . . . Charlotte Francis and her Mother are absolute slaves to Broome's wishes and caprice, and however we may despise Broome, or hold him, & his mind in contempt, yet they are highly praiseworthy for the attention, which they pay him.—'

⁴ Mme Soubiren. See vi, L. 595, n. 24.

so enthusiastically. We were there till we could have rooms & Bedding aired here, upon our return from Joigny. I am sure how cordially you will congratulate me, when I tell you my Alex has not had one day's illness in this house. After so many seizures in Paris, & so many drawbacks at Joigny, imagine what joy this is to me. You will not wonder [that it will] endear thi[s place to me.] M. d'Arblay has bee[n well] also; but I have been tormented with Cold up[on Cold & con]fined all the autumn & winter. It was more than 5 months after my quitting Paris for Passy, before I was able to re-enter it, even for a single visit. Last week I began returning; & I have spent 3 days in call after Call, to pay off Bills of nearly a year's standing in the summing up of Etiquette. Maria & Bood were almost the only persons I admitted ⎮ here during my confinement. They are both well, & live almost splendidly.⁵ What a happiness that our dearest Esther should see her *Eldest care* thus completely & uncommonly well bestowed, &, in every respect, prosperous! for it is impossible to view a kinder or more indulgent husband than Bood.—He studies her inclinations in everything; & she, in return, seems to have no want in the world when with him. I beg a particular account how you find our dear Richard,⁶ if you stop, as I have heard you intend to do, at Rhympton. How is he settled? Can good & kind & excellent Blue remain with him? & how is his health? his Music? his spirits? Tell me about Mr. Paxton;⁷ ⌜& about Mariann⁸ & about the dear sweet James & his.⌝⁹ [I fr]equently think over your affairs, & with earnest interest always! I wish I could bring myself to *express* it but the thousandth time *as* frequently! I always name you *both*, if I have heard of you, when I write to Joigny, where you are both always most kindly remembered. Is Marianne grown? & Clement? My kind Love to both. And tell me your *present* plan: it may alter before you can execute it often enough, from

⁵ At 4, rue de Choiseul.
⁶ The Revd. Richard Allen Burney (L. 462 n. 8), who, as a former pupil of Dussek (i, L. 4 n. 5), had developed a pianoforte style very different from that of his parents. In 1809 Richard was to ally himself with a very prominent Somerset family, but at this time his rectory was kept by his maiden aunt Elizabeth Warren Burney (L. 464 n. 5).
⁷ William Paxton (*c.* 1744–1824) of Middleton Hall, Carmarthen, Wales, M.P. for Carmarthen borough (1803–6) and for the shire (1806–7), who, a friend of Broome's, CBFB mentions in her letter of 23 October (*supra*, n. 2).
⁸ Marianne Francis, now aged thirteen.
⁹ Presumably JB and his family.

the *variable winds* which blow around you—but [a]lways let me know what *probabilities* are in view. I hope M[rs] Ahmuty is more [at e]ase about her son.[10] Is Charlottina grown again by 2[d] change of climate? Kindest Love to her—& M. d'A.'s to you both—

Alex also sends you both his Love. Adieu, my dearest Charlotte—[ever] & ever with truest affection is your

F. d'A.

Tell me very [mu]ch about your health—& write *very soon*— I deserve that, you know, completely—

June 16. I have lost all opportunities—one offer for this instant which only allows room f[or] an adieu, dearest Charlotte. We are all well at [this] date.

545   [54, rue Basse, Passy
                                                     25 April 1803]

To Madame de Cadignan

A.L.S. (The Historical Society of Pennsylvania, Philadelphia), Double sheet small 4to 1 p.
Docketed, p. 2: N° 24—
Annotated in an unknown hand, possibly by Mrs. Darby: A Note from Madame D'Arblay
Inserted in another hand: Authoress of Evelina & Cecilia
Continued in former hand: to M[de] de C. the day ⟨we⟩ all breakfasted at M[r] Burg⟨i's⟩ April 26th 1803 A Paris—
Annotated by R. ⟨Gilmor⟩: This note from Miss Burney, afterwards Madame D'arblay, the authoress of some beautiful novels, Evelina Cecilia & Camilla, was given to me by M[rs] Darby at Boston in ⟨1826?⟩—
     R. ⟨Gilmor⟩

I am really sorry & quite sorry at my utter inability to join so fair & goodly a party,—but a barbarous pain in the face has

---

[10] Ursula Ahmuty (*fl.* 1755–1803), widow of Colonel Arthur Ahmuty (d. 1794) of the East India Company, Bengal Establishment, whom Broome had apparently known in this service, and the mother of two daughters and five sons (see her husband's will P.C.C. Holman 484, pr. 6 Oct. 1794). The son, probably Thomas, the youngest, Mrs. Broome had described in her letter of 23 October (*supra* n. 2) as 'in a Consumption [and] too ill to come to Town to be enter'd at the Temple'.

forced me to try a blister behind the Ear, with which I am now, though much relieved, so completely muffled up, that I dare not yet venture abroad, even though Mr. Burgass[1] would admit me as a Masquerader, & let me come amongst the three Graces wrapt up as a Witch of Macbeth's. Pray make my Compliments & thanks to M. Burgass; whom M. d'Arblay will have the honour to *remercier* himself. But my Boy must stay to console his Mother. I hope M. de Cadignan & your dear ones are well. Adieu, my dear Grace the first,—& lament for

the poor Witch—   F.d'A.

Passy, Monday Night.

546   [54, rue Basse], Passy,
6 May 1803
To Doctor Burney

A.L. (Diary MSS. vi. 5676–9, 5680–3, Berg), 6 May
Double sheet 4to 4 pp. foliated 45, 46 *pmks* CAL[AIS] / T. P 1803
JU 1803 FOREIGN OFFICE / 1 JU 1803 red wafer
Addressed: Dr. Burney, / Chelsea College, / Middlesex
Endorsed by CB: 6, / May, 1803
Edited by FBA, p. 1 (5680), *annotated and dated*: ⁜ 1803 (2) dread of
war. Mrs. Huber. Mᵐᵉ Esmongart *Camilla* &c. Dagotty.
Edited also by CFBt *and the* Press.

Passy—May—6. 1803.

If my dearest Father has the smallest idea of the anguish of suspence & terror in which I have spent this last fortnight,[1] from

545. [1] Possibly Nicolas Bergasse (1750–1832) an avocat, a royalist, and author of *Essai sur la propriété* (1820); or, less probably, his brother Alexandre Bergasse (1747–1821), 'un partisan exalté de l'ancien régime' and author of *Réfutation des faux principes et des calomnies avancées PAR LES JACOBINS, pour décrier l'administration de nos Rois et justifier les usurpateurs de l'autorité royale et DU TRÔNE. Par un Vieux François* (1816), a work strongly royalist and antagonistic to Napoleon and his administration. Alexandre Bergasse and Lally-Tolendal were strong supporters of the political views of Jean-Joseph Mounier (L. 514 n. 13), whose biographer, L. de Lanzac de Laborie (1887) describes them as 'deux compagnons de ses grandes luttes . . . qui avec lui avaient soutenu au comité de constitution la politique modérée'. Bergasse and Lally were among those who followed the funeral cortège of Mounier (28 Jan. 1806).

546. [1] The distress of the d'Arblays in the face of the decisions that had to be taken one way or the other in the event of war between France and England is reflected

439

the daily torture of the menace of War, he will be glad, I am sure, of the respite allowed me,—if NO MORE!—from a visit I have just received from Mrs Huber, who assures me the ambassadour has postponed his setting off, & consented to send another Courier.[2]—To say how I pray for his success would indeed be needless!—I have hardly closed my Eyes many Nights past. My dearest Father will easily conceive the varying conflicts of our minds, & how mutual are our sufferings. We have every where announced our intention to embrace you next October[3]—the state of M.d'A.'s affairs make it impossible for him to indulge me sooner—but if the War takes place, the difficulties of procuring licence—passports—passage—& the ruinous length of journey in travelling through Hambro', as well as the deadly sickness of so long a voyage—all these thoughts torment me night & day, & rest will, I fear, be a stranger to my Eyes, till the conflict is terminated — —& then, whether it will bring me back rest—or added rest-robbing materials for destroying it—who can tell?—At all events, let me entreat to hear from you, my beloved Padre, as speedily as possible. Our last accounts of you were good, with regard to your recovery from the Influenza, but they mentioned that you had been attacked by it in every possible direction: God grant you may be able to confirm the assurance of your re-establishment! It is very long since I heard from you, my dearest, dearest Sir! — — I hope you received the pacquet I sent you

in Bertie Greatheed's account (p. 147) of his visit of 12 May: 'I walked to see Monsr Darbley at Passi; and found him in great uneasiness. She had retired to her room, he was in the greatest agitation. This approaching war seems quite to overset them, so linked are they to both countries that to separate from either is ruin and to hold both impossible. It was the most extraordinary first visit I ever made, and affected me much; particularly as I am not able to assist. They have a nice little dwelling with a beautiful view of Paris, one maid their only servant I believe: a fine boy was in the room. It is a sad pity these modest domestic comforts should be disturbed.'

² According to Bertie Greatheed's editors, Barthélemy Huber (L. 487 n. 2), 'one of the Commissaires de la Trésorerie . . . made strenuous efforts to prevent the rupture of peace in 1803 by acting as intermediary between Joseph Bonaparte, Talleyrand, and Lord Whitworth (*Despatches*, 214, 242, 246, 263).' His wife Lydia (L. 487 n. 2), an Englishwoman, could be presumed to be well informed, therefore, on the course of events. Talleyrand also was trying to delay the rupture of the peace and the departure of Lord Whitworth (tantamount to the English declaration of war), but passports requested by Whitworth were finally granted on 12 May and the ambassador, setting out that same evening, reached London on 20 May. See *AR* xlv (1803), 'State Papers', 725–32.

³ On her departure from England on 16 Apr. 1802 FBA had intended to return in October.

by Mr. Green?[4] I am in expectation of an opportunity for conveying this, & I will therefore *work at it* on time, for I seldom hear of *des occasions*, except in time to sign & seal.— ¹

We were buoyed up here for some days with the hope that General Lauriston was gone to England as *PLENIPO*,[5] to end the dread contest without new effusion of blood: Bood brought us that news from Paris—but Paris, like London, teems with hourly false reports, & this intelligence, unhappily, was of the number. The continued kindness, & tender respect & friendship of that gentleman for M. d'A. makes me take a warm interest in whatever belongs to him. About 10 days ago, when M. d'A. called upon him, relative to the affair so long impending of his *Retraite*,[6] he took his hand, & said '*Fais moi ton compliment.*' You are sure how heartily M. d'A. would be ready to comply— 'but what,' he demanded, 'can be new to *YOU* of honours?'— 'I have succeeded,' he answered, 'for *You*!—the first consul has signed your Memoire.—'

When such delicacy is joined to warm attachment, my dearest Father will not wonder I should be touched by it. The forms of the business, however, are not yet quite completed, but it has passed all the difficulties which could impede its conclusion. At any other time I should have announced this with far more spirit, but my heart is at present so oppressed with the still remaining fear of hostilities, that I can merely state the fact: & rejoice that— — small, very small as it proves — — M. d'A. has now SOMETHING in his native Country —where all other claims are vain, & all other expectations completely destroyed. He had been flattered with recovering for a trifle some portion, at least, of his landed property near Joigny—but those who have purchased it during his Exile, add

---

⁴ The packet sent by James Greene (L. 542 n. 1) on 26 Mar. 1803 had included L. 542 to GMAPW and apparently a letter, now lost, to CB.

⁵ Bonaparte's aide-de-camp, Lauriston (L. 425 n. 5), though sent to England on 4 Oct. 1801 (Six) with the ratifications of the Preliminaries of the Peace of Amiens, was in 1802 employed (see Six) on a mission involving the demarcation lines between Austria and Bavaria. Promoted to général de brigade (13 Sept. 1802), he was in 1803–4 placed in command of the maritime expedition preparing at Toulon for the invasion of Batavia. In 1805 he was to sail with Admiral Villeneuve in the feint calculated to lure the British fleet from the Channel.

⁶ D'Arblay's applications for his *retraite*, dated Mar.–Apr. 1803 and 2 May 1803, are extant at Vincennes, as are reports on his conduct and progress as a trainee in the artillery regiment at Toul. His service totalled 26 years, 5 months, and 13 days; and the pension claimed, and now granted, was 1,500 francs, or about £62 10s. per year. See also L. 548, p. 447 and Appendix I.

such enormous & unaccountable charges to what they paid for it at ‖ that period, that it is become, to us, wholly unattainable.[7]

I have spent but one Evening in Paris since I came to Passy, half a Year ago!—I was then tempted by Mrs Huber, who, having made me fix a day for dining with her, planned giving us a little concert, to engage our staying for an Evening party invited to meet us. Her performers, however, all faild her but one Lady & Gentleman, Me Emongart,[8] & M. Nogent.[9] The first sung some Italian airs so well as to give me very great pleasure, both from her voice & expression, which are wholly free from all national faults: the second you have perhaps heard?—*read*, or sing?—he had so bad a Cold, he could only accompany Me Esmongart in some easy duos: but those he performed in a most agreeable style. He told me he knew all my family, *a family, of genius & talents,* in England.— He has been also, I find, at Mrs Crewe's,—& he talked to me, *comically enough,* of Lady C–ke[10]—*la femme la plus singulière, he* said that he had ever *rencontré.* Me Esmongart is an enthusiast of *the first Chaleur,* for a Book I have heard you mention, Camilla;— she has it by heart, has read it in England, & has named a little Boy whom she has adopted for her Son, Edgar, because it is the character she *adores* the most of any she has ever, or any where, seen delineated. She offered to come to me at any time, receive me at any time, give me an Hour's singing , or a whole Day of music, at my own choice & my own leisure, ONLY because she had heard I knew something of that Book! she told me parties

7 For the fate of d'Arblay's landed property in Joigny, see vii, Appendix I.

8 Mme E[smongart], not otherwise identified, is described by John Carr (p. 207) as 'the first dilettante mistress of music in Paris'.

9 E. R. Nugent, a public reader, who in London in the 1790s had given performances at Le Texier's (iv, L. 415 n. 3) and elsewhere in London. Included in his well-applauded repertory of 1799 was *Le prisonnier, ou la ressemblance,* a play interspersed with songs, etc., which in Paris had had 'a run of 120 Nights'. His reading of the play on 25 Apr. 1799 was 'honoured with the presence of their Royal Highnesses the Duke and Prince William of Gloucester, and his Serene Highness the Duke of Bourbon . . . and . . . a numerous audience . . . of the first distinction'. 'His excellence in reading and singing, and . . . style . . . afford that marked specimen of fine taste and elegance which are the result of high and polished life and manners, added to a professional knowledge of the art' (*The Times,* 27 Apr. 1799). In 1796 he had given readings of Lally-Tolendal's tragedy *Le comte de Strafford* (1795).

10 Doubtless the eccentric Lady Mary Coke (1727–1811), daughter of the 2nd Duke of Argyle (1680–1743) and widow of Edward, Viscount Coke (1719–53). See Walpole, 31, 135–72, and Index (*under* Mary Campbell): also A. M. W. Stirling, *Coke of Norfolk and his Friends* (1912), pp. 316, 363 *passim.*

were continually formed by the friends of good morals, for reading that work & its predecessors, in opposition & as a counter-poison to other productions of the same species, which were regarded as dangerous *et nuisibles*. It would be difficult, if not impossible, for *me* to write you the civilities of this sort which always accompany every new interview or acquaintance; I &, as I remember, of old, hearing *your* partiality for these compositions, I cannot refrain from giving you this little intimation: which you will not, I trust, like poor Merlin,[11] take for the hint of insult! — —

At this same party I met also M. ci divant le Chev^r Pougens —[12] whom you may recollect visited us in St. Martin's street, & interested us by his intelligence & literature & blindness. He is now turned Bookseller!—& is noted for having the best & most curious editions of literary works!—How strange, & how ingenious, that he should be able to undertake a profession that seems more than ALL OTHERS to demand the sense of sight!—Between the dinner & the arrival of *du monde*, Mrs Huber took me to see Dagoty's porcelain manufacture,[13] which is just at the foot of her dwelling. It is an imitation of the Seve China, infinitely cheaper, not, of course, so exquisitely delicate, but very beautiful: M. Dagotty came to shew it us himself, & I found him intelligent, communicative, & gentleman-like. The paintings are all executed by himself. He shewed several begun, half finished, & in every state, & took us to his furnace, & explained its degrees of heat, &c. He fervantly, like all the Artists, wished for peace, though he had served 5 years in the last War.—And, indeed, we scarcely meet with a man, of any description, who has done less—so universally were all the arts of peace laid aside.—Do you know Miss Sayre?[12] she was of our dinner party: & Bood & Maria came in the Evening,

[11] Joseph Merlin (i, L. 3 n. 117).

[12] Marie-*Charles*-Joseph de Pougens (1755–1830), linguist, archaeologist, and member of the Institut, said to be the natural son of the prince de Conti. Blinded by smallpox at the age of 24 and ruined by the Revolution, he ran for a time the well-known bookshop on the rue Thomas du Louvre. See his *Mémoires et souvenirs* (1834), completed and edited by Louise B. de Saint-Léon. In Paris on 29 June 1805 Pougens was to marry Frances Julia Sayer (L. 451 n. 10) of Richmond, whose visits to FBA in Paris are recorded in the Notebooks, vi.

[13] In these years the Dagoty brothers (known by the marks P.L. and R.F.) had a factory at La Seynie Limousin and another at 2, Boulevard Poissonière, Paris. See Chavagnac and Grollier, *Histoire des manufactures françaises de porcelaine* (1906), p. 605.

both quite well. My Alex is in very perfect health, & has not once been ill since we lived at Passy; our house is in the purest air, & quite to ourselves & Alex has always been ill in Paris. The pure air of West Hamble unfitted him for ANY metropolis, I fancy.

547   Passy,
                                        30 April–13 May 1803

To Mrs. Locke

L.S. copy (Diary MSS. viii. 5676–9, Berg), taken by CFBt, probably from the original lent to her by the Locke family, 30 Apr.–13 May 1803, the original having been sent to England through Joseph Talbot,[1] secretary of the British Embassy, on 14 May.
Double sheet 4to 4 pp. foliated in pencil, 43, 44
Edited by CFBt *and the* Press.

To Mʳˢ Locke—
                                        April 30. 1803.
            Nº 54. Rue Basse — Passy — near Paris
How to write I know not—at a period so tremendous—nor yet how to be silent—My dearest, dearest Friends! if the War indeed prove inevitable, what a heart-breaking position is ours!—to explain it fully would demand folios—& yet be never so well done as You, with a little consideration, can do it for us.—Who better than Mʳ Locke and his Fredy—who so well, can comprehend, that, where ONE MUST be sacrificed, the other will be yet more to be pitied?—I will not go on—I will talk only of You, till our fate must be determined.—And M. d'A—who only in the wide world loves his paternal uncle

547. [1] James Talbot (*fl.* 1797–1803), sometimes called 'Joseph' (see Aspinall, *Later Corr. George III*, iv. 37 n). Successively secretary to British legations in Switzerland, St. Petersburg, and lately at Paris, he was to remain with that embassy 'without official character, until 24 May 1803, when he left for England'. See S. T. Bindoff *et al.*, *British Diplomatic Representatives, 1789–1852* (1934), p. 48.

better / as well / (we always except *ourselves* at Westminster—)[2] how tenderly does he join in my every feeling! & how faithfully keep unimpaired all our best & happiest sympathies! — —

May 2ᵈ Better appearances in the political horizon now somewhat recruit my spirits—which have been ¦ quite indescribably tortured rather than sunk, by the impossibility of any private arrangement for our mutual happiness in the dread event of War. God Almighty yet avert it!—And should it fall to the lot of Lauriston to confirm the Peace[3]—what a Guardian angel upon Earth I shall deem him! How I wish he could meet with you!—he is so elegant in his manners, he would immediately give you pleasure, & his countenance is so true in announcing him amiable, that you might look at him with trust as well as satisfaction.

He fills his very high & powerful post in this Country with a modesty & moderation that keep aloof from him all the jealousy, envy, and calumny that usually attend such stations. He receives M: d'A. upon exactly the same terms of intimacy, regard, and equality as formerly, & always admits him, be his engagements ever so pressing, be who will present, or be the moment he can accord him ever so short or hurried.—

M. de Lally has long been gone to Bordeaux,[4] & with whom should he travel thither but Sir John Coghill.[5] I saw that dear M. de Lally but very seldom, yet I regret his immense distance. My greatest ¦ regret is, however, for the Princesse d'Henin, who set off for Bordeaux 8 months ago & is not returned. I have had a charming & most feeling account from her of Madame La Tour du Pin, & her admirable, exemplary manner of passing her time, in the regulation of her family, the education

---

[2] This is FBA's adaptation of the ancient phrase 'Witness ourself at Westminster', which, still appearing in warrants, summonses, and formal proclamations, was used by the Queen, for instance, in the summer of 1969 in the Investiture proceedings. Cf. iii, L. 152 n. 4.

[3] Cf. L. 546 n. 5.

[4] For the comte de Lally-Tolendal and the royalist group at Bordeaux and its vicinity, see vi, L. 575 n. 2; Madelin, xiii. 33–5. In the autumn of 1802 the princesse d'Hénin placed Lally's daughter Élisabeth (iii, L. 215 n. 10), then about sixteen, with Mme de La Tour du Pin at Le Bouilh to be educated (see the *Journal* of the latter, ii. 230–2). Orthography, music, and dancing the child had learned well at Mme Campan's school, but her new mentor found her woefully deficient in other subjects. 'Mon mari se chargea de lui apprendre l'histoire, la géographie. L'enseignement de l'anglais . . . me revint, et l'instituteur de mon fils lui donna des leçons d'italien.'

[5] L. 437 n. 11.

of her children, & the exertion of almost every virtue. M^de d'Henin finishes her letter with charging me to call her to the remembrance of those friends whom she so highly venerates & whom she always flatters herself she shall yet visit again.

May 13. Ah, my dearest Friends—what a melancholy end to my hopes & my Letter! I have just heard that Lord Whitworth set off for Chantilly last night—! War therefore seems inevitable —& my grief—I, who feel myself now of Two Countries—is far greater than I can wish to express.[6] While Posts are yet open, write to me, my beloved Friend—& by Hambro' I trust we may still & regularly correspond—long as the letters may be in travelling. As our letters never treat but of our private concerns, health, & welfare, neither country can object to our intercourse. Let me not therefore lose a solace I shall more than ever require in this lengthened absence—an absence for which I ˡ was so little prepared!—& to which I am so little able to reconcile myself—I can but pray for Peace! My dearest Friends will join the prayer—made with the whole troubled soul of their devotedly—tenderly affectionate, grateful, & eternally faithful

F d'A.—

548   [54, rue Basse, Passy],
                                                     14 May 1803

Conjointly with M. d'Arblay
To Doctor Burney

A.L.S. & A.L. (Diary MSS. vi. 5690–[91], Berg),   14 May
Single sheet 4to   2 pp.   foliated 47
Addressed: Dr. Burney, / Chelsea—
Carried to London with L. 543 (*for which it served as the cover*) *by* The Revd. Edward Hodgson[1] on 15 May 1803.
Endorsed by CB: May 14th 1803
Edited by FBA, p. 1 (5690), *annotated and dated*: ⹂ ⹂ 1803   (3)   Last Letter of This Year sent by the Last Courier of the Ambassadour Lord Whitworth.
Edited also by the Press.

⁶ Cf. L. 546, pp. 440–1.   548. ¹ See L. 543 n. 1.

[*By M. d'Arblay*]

Ne me haissez point, mon bien cher Monsieur, ne me haissez point: mais envoyez nous au contraire votre benediction pour nous aider à soutenir une calamité comme celle qui nous accable en ce moment. Puisse l'interêst bien entendu de l'un comme de l'autre gouvernement leur suggerer promptement les moyens les plus propres à former une nouvelle paix plus solide et qui nous rende bientôt la possibilité d'aller voir ce que nous aimons ce que nous respectons le plus. Une rupture etait peut être l'unique moyen d'amener un accomodement durable. C'est du moins ainsi que je veux l'envisager, afin de ne point fermer la porte à l'esperance d'un mieux qui seul nous soutient et peut nous faire supporter une aussi terrible epreuve.[2] Soyez mon tres cher Monsieur notre interprète auprès de nos autres amis auxquels il nous est impossible d'ecrire en cet instant. Charles surtout voudra bien nous le pardonner —

[*By Madame d'Arblay*]

My Kindest Love to my dear Fanny—& all! all! This last!— I

May 14th 1803

My dearest—dearest Father!

The enclosed missed the opportunity for which it was written—& now—the ambassadour is gone! I am offered a place for this in a conveyance that follows him—& it is well something was ready—for I am incapable of writing now—further than of expressing my ceaseless prayers for a speedy restoration of Peace!—my deare⟨st⟩ dearest Father!—how impossible to describe my distress!—Had I any other Partner upon Earth, I could hardly support it at all—but he suffers nearly as much as myself—He has just received the *Retraite*[3]—which proves but £62:10:0 or 1500 francs, *pr. ann.*!—He expected double—! but 'tis a mark of being under Government protection, & that is so much!—you will easily, however, conceive how completely it makes it impossible for him to quit his Country during a War—I need write nothing explanatory,

---

[2] The separation was to last for ten years altogether. It was only in August 1812 that FBA was able to return to England.

[3] See L. 546 n. 6.

& I cannot—in the disordered state of my nerves from this bitter stroke, do more now than pray Heaven to bless & preserve my beloved—dearest Father—& to restore the Nations to peace—& Me to his arms!—& to assure him whatever *can* solace a period so cruel falls at least to my lot, in the truest & tenderest & sympathy of one who merits his kindest paternal blessing & affection in the same degree as it is prayed for—by his truly devoted—dutiful & affectionate Daughter

F. d'A. |

549   [54, rue Basse, Passy], 14 May 1803

Conjointly with M. d'Arblay
To Esther (Burney) Burney

A.L. & A.L. (rejected Diary MSS. 5692–[93], Berg), 14 May 1803
Single sheet 4to 2 pp. *pmks* CALAIS FOREIGN OFFICE / 1 JU 1803 wafer
Addressed: Mrs. Burney— / 43 Beaumont Street—
Docketed p. 1 (5692): Probable date 1803 *in pencil*: Probʸ 1803—outbreak of War

May 14—1803

Ah my dearest Esther—my dear—dearest Sister!—how well do I know what you will feel for us at this cruel moment!— I am so shaken by it I can hardly hold my Pen—for I had entertained hopes to this last—hopes that only hearing the ambassadour was departed could have destroyed—such *here* has seemed the unwillingness to renew hostilities—& such has been my confidence in the love of peace & wish for it in England —but the blow was struck yesterday by your good Miss Sayre¹ —who came hither with Mrs. Huber¹—& concluded I must know the fatal departure—Her concern was so great at the fearful tydings she found they had *first* communicated ⟨but⟩

549. ¹ Frances Julia Sayer (L. 451 n. 10), whom EBB would have known at Richmond, and Lydia Huber (L. 487 n. 2), calling on FBA on Friday 13 May, were apprised of the ambassador's departure on the preceding evening.

you have well described her amiable & fee[ling] character—
I am sure I should love her—for her own sake, after *yours*, & she
names you with a friendship & affection that warms my heart—
I shall write again by her, next Month, when she goes—I am
now without time—or almost strength—but to pray God to
bless my dearest Hetty—& her good Mʳ Burney—& all ⟨loves⟩
—& to Grant us speedy peace & re-union!—I am well again—
my dear Soul—so be easy—but my Eyes are wofully worn with
this new & unexpected affliction—! M. d'A.'s sincerest love—
my alex's also—Maria is well again—& Bood—but they write ⎮
My kindest Love to all to whom I cannot now write I shall send
a pacquet again I hope by Mʳˢ Greatheed²—when more able—

[By Monsieur d'Arblay]

Ma chere soeur peut se faire une idée de tout ce que nous
avons à souffrir en ce moment. What a blow! je n'ai en verité
point la force d'entrer dans aucun detail. Daignez donc tous
suppleer à ce que nous ne pouvons ecrire. Donnez nous quelquefois de vos nouvelles, et croyez que toujours vous serez
present à nos coeurs. Je n'ai pas besoin de vous dire que votre
soeur sera ici ce qu'elle etait à Westhumble — le premier ou
plutôt l'unique objet de mes pensées comme de mes soins.
Puisse la paix que je ne puis croire eloignée, me permettre de
la reporter bientôt dans vos bras. Au nom du Ciel ne me haissez
pas mais aimez qui vous aime! J'embrasse Charle Mille et
mille choses tendres to *all*!

[By Madame d'Arblay]

tenderest love to my dear aunt³

² Ann *or* 'Nancy' Greatheed (*fl.* 1759–1826) of St. George, Basseterre, who had
married on 31 July 1780 her cousin Bertie Greatheed (1759–1826) of Guy's Cliffe,
Warwick. This couple, with their son Bertie (*c.* 1781–1804), a gifted artist, were
among the English families to be detained in Paris by Napoleon's decree of 22 May.
By virtue perhaps of Mrs. Greatheed's friendship with Bonaparte's mother and
Greatheed's with Junot, the family was not imprisoned, but allowed to travel to
Germany. See Greatheed's *Journal* for 1803.
³ CB's sister, Rebecca Burney, now aged 79, whom FBA was not to see again.
See i, L. 7 n. 8.

APPENDIX

M. D'ARBLAY'S MILITARY CAREER

2 October 1801–2 May 1803

M. D'ARBLAY began his military career at the age of fourteen when, on 3 July 1768, he became a student at the École d'artillerie de Strasbourg. As the documents in this appendix cover a period of only nineteen months, from 2 Oct. 1801 to 2 May 1803, a list of the major stages leading up to this point in d'Arblay's career is given here:

lieutenant en 2ᵉ au régiment de Toul, 5 June 1769;
lieutenant en 1ᵉʳ, 9 May 1778;
capitaine par commission, 11 Nov. 1782;
capitaine en 2ᵉ (détaché aux forges de Lorraine et des Évêchés), 19 June 1785;
employé à la manufacture d'armes de Maubeuge, 1 May 1788;
major de la 2ᵉ division de la garde nationale parisienne, 1 Sept. 1789;
colonel du 103ᵉ régiment d'infanterie, 3 Aug. 1791;
chevalier de Saint-Louis, 26 Oct. 1791;
adjudant général colonel, 1 Feb. 1792;
    à l'armée du Centre, 16 May 1792.

On 22 July 1792 d'Arblay was named maréchal de camp but did not receive his commission because he deserted with Lafayette on 16 August and resigned on 1 September. With the erasure of his name from the list of *émigrés* on 21 Apr. 1800 it became possible for him to claim an official discharge with pension, and it is with this attempt that the following correspondence largely deals.

SUMMARY OF ITEMS

Item 1

Letter to Berthier from M. d'A, who asks for his army pension, a favour which had been granted to other officers in similar situations.

Item 2

Letter to Dutaillis from M. d'A, who asks Dutaillis to give his letter to Berthier.

Item 3

Letter to Talleyrand, ministre des Relations étrangères, from M. d'A, who asks him to use his influence with Berthier.

Item 4

Letter to Berthier from M. d'A, who again asks for his pension and indicates that he plans to return to France with his family as soon as the Calais route is open.

Item 5

Report by Ducharneau, Combes, and Tabarié to Berthier concerning d'Arblay's military position. It lists his military appointments and states that although M. d'A is legally not entitled to his pension, Generals Lameth and Narbonne, in the same position, had been granted theirs. Berthier's intentions are asked.

Item 6

Report from Berthier to Bonaparte concerning M. d'A's request for discharge with pension. It contains a list of d'Arblay's military appointments and indicates that the request cannot be granted because he has effectively served only 24 years. Berthier then states that d'Arblay requests his retirement pension, a favour which has been granted to others, and asks to know Bonaparte's intentions.

Item 7

Letter to M. d'A from Lafayette, who informs d'Arblay of conversations he has had with Lebrun and Berthier regarding d'Arblay's position. The decision with regard to the pension has been postponed, but it is possible that d'Arblay could be given a military post in the colonies, after which he would be granted retirement with pension.

Item 8

Letter to Berthier from M. d'A, who acknowledges the offer of a military post and accepts if it means going to San Domingo. He then requests permission to refuse if combat is not involved. He states that he has lost all his property in France and has, in fact, debts to pay. He urgently desires a rendezvous with Berthier as soon as possible.

Item 9

Letter to Berthier from M. d'A, who asserts his intention to retire as soon as he has completed his mission in San Domingo. He claims

31 years of service (25 years of active service) and acknowledges that Berthier disagrees with this. He asks that his motives be fairly represented to the First Consul and in a postscript promises to go to San Domingo immediately if Bonaparte will mention in his discharge that d'Arblay's military service was uninterrupted.

Item 10

Letter to M. d'A from Berthier, who authorizes him to go to San Domingo via Brest. M. d'A will be paid his pension, retroactive to Sept. 1801, upon arrival, until he is put into active service by General Leclerc. M. d'A is informed that Leclerc has been written to, and a copy of that letter [Item 11] is enclosed.

Item 11

Letter to Leclerc from Berthier, who informs the general of M. d'A's appointment, stating that the government has a high regard for d'Arblay and desires Leclerc to employ him according to his talents and his zeal.

Item 12

Letter to Denis Decrès, ministre de la Marine, from Berthier, who requests that d'Arblay be given passage from Brest to San Domingo according to his rank.

Item 13

Letter to Berthier from M. d'A, who states that because he had been informed that his early requests had been refused, he had returned to England. He did not receive Berthier's official reply [Item 10] until 7 Feb., after which he went immediately to the ministre de la République [in England] and requested a passport. In a footnote M. d'A explains that it was granted with the proviso that M. d'A should not return to England for at least 1 year. He concludes by stating that he is coming to Paris to buy his uniform and receive his last instructions, and asks in a postscript that the enclosed letter [Item 14] be given to Bonaparte.

Item 14

Letter to Bonaparte from M. d'A, who, having affirmed his admiration for and loyalty to the First Consul, states that he will not bear arms against England. [This one statement is to entail the complete reversal of the San Domingo affair, and puts an effective end to M. d'A's military career in Napoleonic France.]

Item 15

Note by M. d'A, reporting his arrival in Paris, the receipt of his official letters of service, and his writing to Dutaillis concerning his uniform and requesting a rendezvous with Berthier. The next day he is informed that he is no longer 'employed' by the army.

Item 16

Letter to Berthier from M. d'A, who bemoans the situation that the decision of the First Consul has forced upon him.

Item 17

Note by M. d'A, which tells of his writing to Dutaillis and, on receiving no reply, of his writing again to say that he hopes the decision is not irrevocable, and that reply should be sent to La Grange [*chez* Lafayette]. He receives, through his friend Chastel, the letters [Items 18 and 19] of Berthier and Dutaillis.

Item 18

Letter to M. d'A from Berthier, who informs him that his orders have been cancelled and that he is to disregard previous letters concerning his military appointment.

Item 19

Letter to M. d'A from Dutaillis, who informs him that Berthier is following Bonaparte's wishes and cannot do otherwise and that Berthier regrets that d'Arblay's political position precludes military employment. He states that the only possible attack on San Domingo would be by the English. To say that one would not bear arms against them was to deny the wishes of the French government.

Item 20

Letter to Lafayette from M. d'A, who encloses the letters from Berthier and Dutaillis [Items 18 and 19]. He explains, chronologically and in detail, the affair up to the date of writing [2 Mar. 1802] and includes information that has not appeared in the letters and notes. He states that after receiving Berthier's authorization [Item 10] he has spent more than 100 *louis* in preparation for his departure to San Domingo. He requests Lafayette to speak with Bonaparte in the hope that the unfavourable impression which the First Consul must have of him will be erased. He insists that after spending £220 toward his discharge and pension he has more right to it than those who have done nothing.

Item 21

Note by M. d'A, reporting the outcome of Lafayette's interview with Bonaparte. The First Consul appeared favourably disposed toward d'Arblay and when told of the latter's fears replied that the affair would have no effect on d'Arblay's rights and that 'il ne considererait dans cette demarche que le mari de Cecilia'.

⟶

This interview between Lafayette and Bonaparte took place in March 1802. The correspondence, which now ceased for almost exactly one year, resumed in March 1803 with M. d'A's letter to Bonaparte.

Item 22

Letter to Bonaparte from M. d'A, who again expresses his loyalty and admiration and asks that his case, decision upon which had been deferred by the First Consul, be again examined.

Item 23

Letter, almost certainly to Berthier, from M. d'A, who thanks him for his renewed interest in the case and requests that he remove the obstacle [his refusal to grant M. d'A more than 24 years of effective service] which is preventing the discharge and pension from being granted.

Item 24

Official Discharge Paper [Apr. 1803], which gives M. d'A 26 years, 5 months and 13 days of service, with a detailed listing of all his military positions with dates.

Item 25

Certified copy of extracts from the registers of the deliberations of the French government, decreeing (1) that d'Arblay has been granted a pension of 1,500 francs per annum, beginning 2 May 1803, and (2) that the Ministries of the Public Treasury and of War are charged to execute the terms of the decree.

⟶

Item 1

A.L.S. copy in M. d'A's hand (Berg) of his letter to Alexandre Berthier, 2 Oct. [1801]
Double sheet 4to   1 p. (copied on p. 2)
Edited by FBA, *who annotated and dated top margin*: 1801 Addressed to Alexandre Berthier Minister at War to—Napoleon Citoyen Ministre [*explaining* C.M.]
This copy along with the two following, FBA provided with the heading: Letters to Le *Ministre de la Guerre*, Berthier, Le *Ministre des Relations etrangères*, & Genl de *Tailly*, aide de camp to Berthier, in the year 1801.

A.D. au Ministre de la Guerre

C.M.

Il y a 10 mois que sur la nouvelle de ma radiation, je me mis en regle en pretant entre les mains du ministre de la Republique à la Haye. J'apprens à l'instant même, que plusieurs off^ers G^aux et autres rayés comme moi d'une liste où certes mon nom n'eut jamais dû paroître, ont un traîtement de la Republique. J'ose solliciter ce traitement que la vente totale de mes biens et de ceux de toute ma famille me rendent bien necessaire. Mes titres pour l'obtenir vous sont connus, et comme ma demande n'a rien que de juste, je me permetraî de reclamer prés de vous l'interest de votre frere à qui j'ai été assez heureux pour rendre, avant mon départ, un service qu'il n'a probablement pas oublié.

S et R A d'Arblay

Item 2

A.L.S. copy in M. d'A's hand (Berg) of his letter to général Dutaillis, [1801]
Double sheet 4to   1 p. (copied on p. 2)
Dated by FBA: 1801.

Au General du Tailly
Hotel de la Guerre
rue de Varennes
f^rg St Germain

Je vous prie, mon cher G^al, de mettre sous les yeux du M^tre de la Guerre la demande que je lui fais du traitement accordé aux off^ers precisement dans la même cas que moi. Je me flatte que vous ne refuseriez pas de rendre ce service à votre ancien camarade et ami.

A.D.

Item 3

A.L.S. copy in M. d'A's hand (Berg) of his letter to Talleyrand, [1801]
Double sheet 4to   1 p. (copied on p. 3)

Appendix

Alexandre Darblay au Ministre des Relations étrangères

Citoyen Ministre

Je viens mettre à l'epreuve l'amitié sur la quelle vous m'avez permis de compter, et vous prie d'appuyer auprès du Ministre de la Guerre ⌐et, si besoin est auprès du grand Consul⌐, la demande que je fais du traitement accordé aux officiers precisement dans le même cas que moi. Vous connoissez les raisons qui m'empêchent d'aller moi même solliciter ce traitement: mais peut être vous ignorez qu'aussitôt que j'eus connoissance de ma radiation je me mis en regle, en pretant mon serment entre les mains du Ministre de la Republique à la Haye.

Salut et Respect
A d'Arblay

Item 4

A.L.S. draft in M. d'A's hand (Berg) of his letter to Alexandre Berthier, [1801]
Single sheet 4to 2 pp.
Edited by FBA, *who annotated the draft* N° 16, *numbering the sections* 1–5, *and annotating lower margin,* p. 1: This paper must be preserved for the Grand Children, or Grand Nephews of M. d'Arblay, so long as that name is preserved. 'Tis the original sketch of the Letters of M. d'Arblay to Berthier, taken to France by M. Lauriston, and delivered by M. de Narbonne.
FBA also explained the salutation: Berthier N.B. This is the faithful copy of a Letter sent to Berthier Ministre de la Guerre, in 1801; carried over to France by General Lauriston, after his Embassy to England for making Peace. . . .

Alexandre Darblay au Ministre de la Guerre

Citoyen Ministre

J'ose reclamer de votre justice ce qu'en ont dejà obtenu les Citoyens Sicard et La Colombe mes compagnons d'armes et d'exil, c'est à dire d'être remis à mon rang pour recevoir de la Republique le traitement de reforme attaché à mon grade. Presqu'aussi honteux qu'affligé de mon inactivité bien involontaire durant la terrible crise que les exploits de nos armées viennent enfin de terminer si heureusement et si glorieusement je ne sais comment parler de mes services; et pourtant ces services du moins rendus avec zele pendant plus de vingt huit ans avant l'epoque où je quittai bien forcement la France n'ont pas été sans dangers où même sans utilité pour cette Patrie de qui je sollicite une recompense que je voudrais avoir mieux meritée.

Salut et Respect
A.J.B.P. d'Arblay

P.S. Aussitôt que le passage par Calais sera ouvert, je compte en profiter pour me rendre à Paris avec ma femme et mon fils. L'ami qui veut bien se charger de cette lettre, veut bien aussi prendre le soin de faire connaitre au gouvernement les raisons que m'ont empêché de me rendre plutôt en France, mais du moment que j'ai fus instruit de ma radiation, je me rendis à la Haye pour y preter mon serment entre les mains du Ministre de la Republique.

Item 5

Report (Vincennes), Ducharneau, Combes, and Tabarié to Alexandre Berthier, 3 Dec. 1801
Single sheet folio   1 p.
Annotated in the hand of Tabarié: d'après le refus du 1er consul de statuer sur le rapport fait en faveur du g^{al} Marcel Dumas, on propose au ministre d'ajourner cette demande. Tabarié
Annotated in an unknown hand: tout ce rapport au Consul sur le citoyen d'arblay est ⟨d'inconnus⟩.

3e Division — Etats-Majors
Rapport fait au Ministre, le 12 frimaire an dix

Le Citoyen Alexandre Gabriel Darblay, ancien adjudant Général Chef de Brigade, demande à être admis au traitement de réforme.

Il n'en est pas susceptible d'après les dispositions de l'arrêté du 8 nivose an 8, mais les Généraux Narbonne et Lameth dans le même cas que lui, l'ayant obtenu en vertu de décisions particulières du 1er Consul, on demande au Ministre s'il est dans l'intention de lui rendre compte de la demande du Citoyen Darblay.

Cet officier est entré au service en 1768 dans le Corps de l'artillerie, il a été Lieutenant au reg^t de Toul en 1769, Capitaine en 1782, Major de la Garde Nationale Parisienne soldée avec rang de Lieutenant Colonel en 1789, adjudant Général du grade de Colonel le 1er fevrier 1792, et a été employé en cette qualité a l'armée du Centre depuis le 16 mai suivant jusqu'au 1er 7bre de la même année.

Il a été membre du Comité Central de la Guerre au commencement de 179⟨2⟩.

[*signed*] Ducharneau, Combes, Tabarié

Item 6

Report (Vincennes), Alexandre Berthier to Bonaparte, 18 Dec. 1801.
Single sheet folio   1 p.
Annotated in an unknown hand: ajourné par les Consuls

There is a rough draft of this report in an unknown hand (Vincennes) on a single page 4to, written on both recto and verso.

Rapport fait au premier Consul
par le Ministre de la Guerre

Le 27 frimaire an dix

Citoyen Alexandre Gabriel Darblay ancien adjudant Général,
demande a être admis au traitement de réforme.

Cet officier est entré au service en 1768 dans le corps de l'artillerie;
il a été Lieutenant au Régiment de Toul en 1769; Capitaine en
1782; Major de la Garde Nationale Parisienne soldée avec rang de
Lieutenant Colonel en 1789; adjudant Général du grade de
Colonel le 1er février 1792 et a été employé en cette qualité a
l'armée du Centre depuis le 16 mai suivant jusqu'au 1er 7bre de la
même année, époque à laquelle il a été forcé par les circonstances
de se retirer du service.

Le Citoyen Darblay ne peut obtenir la solde de retraite parcequ'il
n'a que vingt quatre ans de service effectif, mais il demande a jouir
du traitement de réforme, faveur déjà accordée a plusieurs officiers
Généraux dans le même cas que lui; je vous prie de me faire connaitre
vos intentions à cet égard.

Item 7

A.L.S. (Berg), Lafayette to M. d'A, 26 Dec. [1801]
Double sheet 8vo   1 p.   (written on p. 1)
Edited by FBA, *who annotated the upper margin*: Nº 1   de M. de La Fayette
Nº 2 at the other side   *and lower margin*: For Nº 2   Tournez
M. d'A copied this letter in his L. 465. *See pp.* 110–11.

Item 8

A.L.S. copy in the hand of M. d'A (Berg) of his letter to Alexander
Berthier, 2 Jan. 1802
Double sheet 8vo   1 p.   (written on p. 4)
Edited by FBA, *who annotated the letter* Nº 2, *and identified the Minister of War:*
Berthier

M. d'A made another copy of this letter in his L. 465. *See p.* 112.

Item 9

A.L.S. (Vincennes), M. d'A to Alexandre Berthier, 10 Jan. 1802
Single sheet 4to   1 p.
Annotated in the hand of Berthier:
Cⁿ ⟨   ⟩
Renvoyé à la division du personnel —
autorisation au Cⁿ d'arblay de se rendre à Brest pour passer à St.

Domingue ou le g^{al} le clerc est invité à l'employer entièrement.

lettre au C^n d'Arblay pour le prevenir qu'aussitot son arrivée à St Domingue il se trouvera admis au traitement de reforme en rapelle de ce traitement depuis le 1er vendemiare an 10.

il sera donné une rente de son grade au C^n d'arblay —

on rapelle au G^{al} le Clerc les talents et les connoisances de cet officier et le desir du Gouvernement pour qu'il utilize son zéle —

A B
ce 26 nivose

There is a copy in the hand of M. d'A (Berg), who provided (1) on the left margin a copiously detailed explanatory note which, however, contains no new material and (2) on the upper margin, an editorial note.

FBA *annotated* (1): N° 3 ✳·
     (2): × N.B.
the copy itself: N° 4 ✳·

There is also a copy of the letter in M. d'A's L. 468. See pp. 121–2.

Item 10

L.S. (Berg), Alexandre Berthier to M. d'A, 27 Jan. 1802
Single sheet folio, official letterhead   1 p.
Annotated by FBA: N° 5
There is an unsigned draft of this letter in the hand of a scribe (Vincennes) on a single sheet folio, official letterhead, revised by Berthier and recopied by him on the verso.
There is also a copy in the hand of FBA (Berg) on a double sheet 8vo, the upper margin of which she annotated: 19   1802 ✳· ×

The original letter is transcribed in full in L. 478 n. 5.

Item 11

L.S. (Vincennes), Alexandre Berthier to Général Leclerc, 27 Jan. 1802
Single sheet folio, official letterhead   1 p.
There is a copy in the hand of a scribe (Berg) on a single sheet folio, official letterhead, which was sent to M. d'A, and annotated by FBA: N° 6

There is also a copy in the hand of FBA (Berg) on a double sheet 8vo, the upper margin of which she annotated: 20   1802 ✳· ×

This letter, substantially the same as Item 10, is summarized in L. 478 n. 6.

Item 12

L.S. (Vincennes), Alexandre Berthier to Denis Decrès, 27 Jan. 1802
Single sheet folio, official letterhead   1 p.

Marginal comment in the hand of Berthier: il jouira a son arrivée dans la colonie du traitement de Réforme a dater du 1ᵉʳ vendᵉʳᵉ dernier jusqu'au moment ou il sera mis en activité par le Gᵃˡ le Clerc.

Je vous prie de vouloir bien donner des ordres pour son embarquement.

This letter is substantially the same as Items 10 and 11.

Item 13

A.L.S. copy in the hand of M. d'A (Berg) of his letter to Alexandre Berthier, 10 Feb. 1802

Single sheet 4to   1 p. (copied on p. 1)

Annotated by FBA: N° 7.

Londre 20 pluviose an 10
Copie de la lettre au Ministre de la Guerre

General

Le Citoyen Gau qui avait bien voulu se charger de vous remettre ma lettre en date du 18 Nivose an 10, me donna pour reponse de votre part que ce que je demandais etait impossible. Deslors, ainsi que j'avais eu l'honneur de vous en prevenir, je quittai Paris pour venir rejoindre ma femme que je comptais mener dans ma famille aussitôt que sa santé et la belle saison le lui permettraient.[1] Les copies des deux lettres que vous m'avez fait l'honneur de m'adresser *en date du 7 pluviôse* ne parvinrent que le 17 très tard. Sur le champ, j'en fis part au Ministre de la Republique, en le priant de demander pour moi un passeport.[2] Dès qu'il sera expedié je ne perdrai pas un instant pour me rendre à ma destination.

J'avais dabord pensé que je pourrais aller directement de Calais à Brest: mais il parait que je ferai mieux de passer par Paris où je pourrais d'ailleurs prendre mes dernieres instructions, et vous presenter l'hommage sincere de ma gratitude. Je ne m'y arreterai surement que le tems necessaire pour m'y faire habiller.

Salut et respect
Alexandre D'arblay

P.S. Permettez, mon Gᵃˡ que je vous prie de lire la lettre que je joins à celle ci, et si vous l'approuvez, ayez la bonté de la faire

[1] Here M. d'A inserted, in explanation of the sentence following, the superscript (1) and the footnote: '(1) Je n'avais en effet que des copies envoyées par Chastel qui à mon arrivée à Paris me remit les originaux.'

[2] Here M. d'A inserted the superscript (2) and the explanatory footnote: '(2) Ce passeport demandé par le Minᵗʳᵉ fut accordé: mais on lui arrivaitit que je devais passer à *l'Alien office* pour le signer. Je m'y rendis et fut remis au jour suivant. Le lendemain après m'avoir fait attendre 3ʰ on me dit qu'arrivé depuis peu en Angleterre, je ne pourrais en partir qu'après la paix definitive. Je courrus chez Mr. Otto, et muni d'une lettre très forte de ce Ministre, je revins avec mon ami J. Angerstein. Enfin j'obtins mon passeport sous la condition de ne point remettre le pied en Angleterre durant l'espace d'au moins un an.'

parvenir au 1er Consul. J'espere bien que vous ne trouverez aucun inconvenient à la remettre: mais dans le cas contraire, ce sera entre vos mains que j'aurais consigné mes invariables sentiments, et je vous prie de vous en souvenir.

Item 14

A.L.S. copy in the hand of M. d'A (Berg) of his letter to Bonaparte, 10 Feb. 1802
Single sheet 4to   1 p. (copied on p. 1)
This letter is transcribed in full in L. 478 n. 7.

Item 15

Explanatory note in the hand of M. d'A (Berg), supplied at time of copying, and linking Items 14 and 16
Single sheet 4to   (written on *recto*, lower margin, and continued on *verso*) 2 pp.

There is a copy, substantially the same, of this and the two following items, in the hand of M. d'A (Berg), written on the recto of Item 19.
Annotated by FBA, *upper margin*: 1   1802   Historical   8
lower margin: T.S.V.P.

Debarqué à Calais je pris sur le champ la poste, et sans m'arreter, j'arrivai à Paris, où mon premier soin, après m'être fait donner par Chastel mes lettres de service, fut d'écrire au General du Taillis, son ami et le mien, pour savoir quel uniforme je devais faire faire: car c'etait là la seule chose qui me restât à acheter. Je le priais en même tems de me faire savoir si le Ministre de la Guerre (dont il est l'aide de camp) voudrait bien m'accorder un rendez vous avant mon depart. Le jour se passe, point de reponse. Le lendemain je cours chez du Taillis et ne le trouve point. Je vais chez Chastel, que j'avais promis de mener chez d'Hermand; il allait sortir. Avez vous vu, me dit il, du Taillis? — Non: je ne puis le joindre: mais allons toujours chez d'Hermand — un moment . . . Entrons (et il me conduit près de sa femme) Tous deux alors m'exhortent à m'armer de courage et j'apprens que je ne suis plus employé!

Il me serait impossible de rendre ici tout ce que j'eprouvai alors. Neamoins je conservai assez de force pour me montrer aussi ferme que je l'etais peu: 'Il ne faut pas, dis-je un instant après à Chastel, que parceque mes affaires prennent une si mauvaise tournure, nous negligions les vôtres, partons;' et nous fûmes chez d'Hermand à qui je le presentai.

Pendant qu'ils causaient ensemble j'écrivis [Item 16]

Item 16

A.L.S. copy in the hand of M. d'A (Berg) of his letter to Alexandre Berthier, [Feb. 1802]
Single sheet 4to   1 p. (copied on p. 2)

Au Ministre de la Guerre
General:

J'apprens avec une extrême douleur, la determination prise par le 1er Consul. Ma position est d'autant plus facheuse que je n'ai obtenu à Londre mon passeport que sous la condition expresse de ne pas rentrer, d'ici à un an au moins, en Angleterre où j'ai laissé ma femme malade avec mon fils. Recevez mon General mes remercie-mens bien sinceres de l'interest que vous avez eu la bonté de me temoigner. Le coup de foudre qui vient de me frapper bien à l'improviste, ne peut rien changer à mes sentimens, et jamais je n'oublierai ce que je dois et à mon Pays et à celui qui après l'avoir tiré des horreurs de l'anarchie, a mis fin à mon bannissement. Je m'étais vaine[ment] flatté pouvoir utilement encore servir mon pays; mais, je le repete, son chef ne m'en trouvera pas moins disposé à seconder de tous mes foibles moyens ses vues pour le bien public.

Salut et respect
Alexandre Darblay

Item 17

Explanatory note in the hand of M. d'A (Berg), supplied at time of copying, and following Item 16
Single sheet 4to   1 p. (copied on p. 2)

J'ecrivis en même tems deux mots à Du Taillis, et portai le tout à l'Hotel de la Guerre Le lendemain je passai chez Du Taillis, mais vainement. Le soir j'y fus encore et ne le trouvant point je lui ecrivis que s'il avait quelque chose à me faire dire sur un arrêt que j'esperais ne devoir pas être irrevocable, je le priais de me l'envoyer par un expres à La Grange chez M. de La Fayette. Je mis trois jours à faire cette course. Le 9 Ventose Chastal m'ecrivit:

'J'ai, mon ami à vous remettre une lettre du Ministre, et une de Du Tailly. je les ai reçues ce matin. Je pense que votre retour ne peut tarder.'

Voici ces lettres [Items 18 and 19].

Item 18

A.L.S. (Berg), Alexandre Berthier to M. d'A, 20 Feb. 1802
Single sheet folio, official letterhead, from the bottom of which a segment of 2–3 inches has been cut away   1 p.
Annotated by FBA: No 8

Appendix

There is a copy of this letter in the hand of M. d'A on the same page as Item 19, there misdated 25 Feb. 1802.
The original letter is printed in full in L. 485 n. 1.

Item 19

A.L.S. copy in the hand of M. d'A (Berg) of a letter from General Dutaillis, dated in error 25 Feb. 1802 [see Item 18]
½ Single sheet 4to   1 p. (copied on verso)
Edited by FBA, *who numbered the leaf 8, paged the upper margin 2, and annotated it*: Febʸ 20   Historical 8.

Je vous fait passer, mon cher Darblay, la lettre que le Ministre de la Guerre vous adresse. Il a suivi les intentions du 1ᵉʳ Consul et ne peut faire autrement. Il regrette ainsi que moi que votre position politique enchaine vos talents et votre bonne volonté. J'avais dit à Chastel, et je pense, que comme nos Colonies ne peuvent être attaquees que par les Anglais (abstraction faite des troubles interieurs) dire qu'on ne portera pas les armes contr'eux, ce n'est plus remplir de voeu de Gouvernement qui vous les remettait dans les mains.' &c. &c.

Du Taillis (Gᵃˡ de Brigade et Aide de Camp du Ministre)

Item 20

A.L.S. copy in the hand of M. d'A (Berg) of his letter to Lafayette, 2 Mar. 1802.
Double sheet 4to   2 pp. (copied on pp. 1–2)
Note on upper margin in the hand of M. d'A: Copie de ma lettre au Gᵃˡ La Fayette en lui envoyant la lettre du Mᵗⁱᵉ de la Guerre en date du 5 Ventose et celle du Gᵃˡ du Taillis son aide de camp en date du 11 Ventose.
Edited by FBA, *who annotated the document* Nº 10, *and identified the Minister*: M. Otto.

Paris ce 11 Ventose

'Tel est, mon Gᵃˡ, le resultat de ma lettre au 1ᵉʳ Consul, de cette lettre qu'un Ministre de la Republique et plusieurs de ses plus chauds partisans, *disaient faire autant d'honneur à celui au quel elle etait adressé, qu'à celui qui l'avait ecrite.* Mais ce Ministre ainsi que Lally et Kelly et tant d'autres, supposaient le 1ᵉʳ Consul instruit de ma petition, et du dessein, tant de fois manifesté par moi, de bouche et par ecrit, de ne servir que durant l'expedition de St Domingue *où je n'allais que pour payer le prix mis à ma retraite.*
Il m'est à present bien demontré que Bonaparte voulait, en me mettant à même d'obtenir un commandement dans les Colonies, me fournir l'occasion de reparer les pertes que j'ai essuyées, pertes dont

je parlais dans le memoire que vous aviez appostillé, et que j'avais remis pour lui à Lauriston, en m'excusant, en quelque sorte de chercher à tirer parti *de services qui etaient la seule proprieté qu'on m'eut laissé.* La connaisance qu'il eut fallu donner à Bonaparte de mes sentiments, et de mes projets pouvait seule arrêter un jugement que, comme chef de la Republique, il a du rendre. Au moment où il etait posté, je souscrivais à Londres à la condition exigée d'être au moins un an avant de retourner en Angleterre. Sans cela, je n'aurais point eu mon passeport pour France. Si on me l'eut refusé, j'avais chargé un membre du Parlement (J. Angerstein) d'en demander un pour l'Amerique, de sorte que c'eut été à St. Domingue même qu'en ce cas j'aurais appris la deffense de m'y rendre, et l'ordre d'en partir, car on avait, m'a t'on dit, ecrit à Brest d'empêcher mon embarquement.

Il faut convenir que j'ai une bien singuliere destinée. Dans l'ignorance ou le Gouvernement etait de mes projets et de mes veritables sentimens, il me jugeait ici, avec justice, incapable de rester au service de mon Pays, tandis qu'à Londres j'avais été jusqu'à dire que pour partir et le servir, je m'exposerais plutôt à être envoyé à Botany-bay.

Resumé de toute cette affaire

[*This concluding section of the letter was copied by M. d'A in his* L. 489. *See* pp. 172–3.]

Item 21

Explanatory note in the hand of M. d'A (Berg), supplied at time of copying, and following Item 20
Double sheet 4to   1 p. (copied on p. 3)
A substantially identical version is to be found in M. d'A's L. 489. *See* p. 173.

Item 22

A.L.S. (Vincennes), M. d'A to Bonaparte, 4 Mar. 1803
Single sheet folio   1 p.
Annotated on the upper margin in an unknown hand: Revoyé au Ministre de la Guerre pour en faire un rapport. Ce 1er Germinal. Le 1er Consul. [*signed*] Bonaparte
This letter is transcribed in full in L. 536 n. 5.

Item 23

A.L.S. (Vincennes), M. d'A to General [?Berthier], 6 Apr. 1803
Single page 4to   1 p.

Appendix

Annotated on the upper margin in an unknown hand: Renvoyer au C^n ⟨　　　⟩ [*signature illegible*]　　　*and in another hand*: vous prie de faire faire au 1er Consul le rapport qu'il a demandé sur sa retraite.

General,

Je vous dois et vous fais les remerciemens les plus sinceres sur la nouvelle marque d'interest que vous venez de me donner en ordonnant qu'on vous presentât promptement le rapport sur ma retraite de General de Brigade. Monsieur ⟨Goulhara⟩ que j'ai vu ce matin à ce sujet, m'a dit que le retard de ce rapport etait dû au besoin d'une decision particuliere pour y travailler. Je ne suis entré dans aucun détail avec lui, et me suis borné à dire: *qu'étant dans la même position militaire que la Gen^{al} La Fayette c.à.d. dans un cas qui nous est tout à fait particulier, je ne pouvais être soumis à la loi generale; que vous même aviez pensé que nous devions y faire exception, et qu'enfin c'etait precisement là l'objet de la demande presentée par vous au premier Consul, qui l'avait ajournée il y a six mois, et consentait actuellement à l'accorder.*

Veuillez, mon General, lever toute difficulté sur ce sujet, et compter sur la gratitude comme sur l'inviolable attachement de celui qui jamais ne l'a promis legerement.

Salut et respect
Alexandre D'arblay

Passy rue basse n° 53
Ce 17 Germinal an XI

Item 24

Document (Vincennes), official tabulation of M. d'A's military career, Apr. 1803
Single sheet folio　2 pp.

Paris, le Germinal an 11

RETRAITE

Le C^{en} Alexandre Gabriel Pieuchard Darblay Adjudant Commandant demande sa retraite: ci-joint les pièces à l'appui.

Suivent les services et campagnes de ce militaire, né le 1753

SERVICES

Eleve dans le Corps de l'artillerie le 3 juillet 1768
Lieutenant au Reg^t de Toul le 5 Juin 1769
Capitaine le 11 novembre 1782
Major de Division de la garde nationale parisienne le 1er 7bre 1789
Rang de Lieutenant Colonel du 1er 7bre 1789

Colonel du 103ᵉ Regᵗ le 3 aout 1791
Adjudant Général du grade de Colonel le 1ᵉʳ fevrier 1792
a donné sa demission le premier 7ᵇʳᵉ 1792.

CAMPAGNES

a fait la Campagne à l'armée du Centre du 16 mai 1792 au premier Septembre suivant

OBSERVATIONS	RECAPITULATIONS	TOTAL DES SERVICES		
		ANS.	MOIS.	JOURS.
	Du 3 juillet 1768 au 1ᵉʳ 7ᵇʳᵉ 1792	24	1	28
	Deux années d'étude préliminaire dans le corps de l'artillerie	2		
	Services effectifs	26	1	28
	Campagnes	—	3	15
	TOTAL GENERAL	26	5	13

Vérifié et certifié véritable d'après les registres.

Item 25

Document (Vincennes), *ampliation*, 2 May 1803.
Single sheet folio 1 p.

AMPLIATION

Extrait des registres

des

Délibérations du Gouvernement de la Republique

le 12 Floreal de l'an 11

Le Gouvernement de la République d'après le rapport du Ministre de la guerre, arrêté.

Art. 1ᵉʳ

Le Cᵉⁿ *Darblay* ex chef de Brigade, est admis à une Solde de retraite de quinze cent francs, qui courra du jour de l'arrêté.

Art. 2.

Les Ministres de la Guerre et du trésor Public, sont chargés de l'exécution du present arrêté.

Le Premier Consul Signé: Bonaparte. Par le Premier Consul le Secrétaire d'Etat Signé: ⟨Eugene⟩ B. Maret. Le Ministre de la Guerre Signé: Alex. Bcrthicr.

Pour ampliation
L'Inspecteur aux Revues Secrétaire Général.